THE ROMAN ANTIQUITIES

OF

DIONYSIUS OF HALICARNASSUS

WITH AN ENGLISH TRANSLATION BY
EARNEST CARY, Ph.D.

ON THE BASIS OF THE VERSION OF
EDWARD SPELMAN

IN SEVEN VOLUMES
VII

CAMBRIDGE, MASSACHUSETTS
HARVARD UNIVERSITY PRESS
LONDON
WILLIAM HEINEMANN LTD
MCMLXXXIV

American ISBN 0-674-99427-2
British ISBN 0 434 99388 3

First printed 1950
Reprinted 1963, 1984

Printed in Great Britain

CONTENTS

INTRODUCTION TO VOLUME VII

MSS. OF BOOK XI

The manuscripts used by Kiessling and Jacoby for Book XI are as follows :

L = Laurentianus Plut. LXX 5 (15th cent.).
V = Vaticanus 133 (15th cent.).
M = Ambrosianus A 159 sup. (15th cent.).
C = Coislinianus 150 (16th cent.).

The best of these four MSS. is L, which appears to be a faithful copy of a badly damaged original ; the scribe usually left gaps of appropriate length where he found the text illegible. Second best is V, which only occasionally shows interpolations ; yet this V is the manuscript that was designated as E for the first ten books and regarded there as virtually negligible. Much inferior, however, even to V are M and C (the same C as for earlier books), which show many unskilful attempts to correct the text, especially by way of filling lacunae ; see in particular chaps. 42 and 48-49.

All these MSS. derive from a poor archetype which, in addition to numerous shorter lacunae, had lost entire leaves at the end of Book XI, as well as earlier, and had some of the remaining leaves inserted out of place. See the note on chap. 44, 5 ; also vol. i. p. xli, n. 1, at end.

DIONYSIUS OF HALICARNASSUS

EXCERPTS FROM BOOKS XII-XX

Approximately one-half of these excerpts come from the imposing collection made by order of the Emperor Constantine Porphyrogenitus, in the tenth century, from classical and later historians. The excerpts were classified under various heads, and a few of these sections have been preserved, some in but a single manuscript. The sections containing excerpts from Dionysius and the abbreviations used in citing them are as follows :

Ursin.—Περὶ πρεσβειῶν (*De legationibus*), contained in several MSS. ; see the list on p. x. First published by Ursinus, 1582 ; critical edition by C. de Boor, Berlin, 1903.

Vales.—Περὶ ἀρετῆς καὶ κακίας (*De virtutibus et vitiis*), preserved in the Codex Peirescianus (now Turonensis 980). Published by Valesius, 1634 ; critical edition by A. G. Roos, Berlin, 1910.

Esc.—Περὶ ἐπιβουλῶν (*De insidiis*), preserved in a single manuscript in the Escurial (Scorialensis Ω I 11). Edited by Feder, 1848 and 1849, and by C. Müller in his *Frag. Hist. Graec.*, vol. ii., 1848. In numerous instances the same emendation was made independently, it would seem, by both these scholars ; such corrections are indicated by the abbreviation Edd. Critical edition by C. de Boor, Berlin, 1905.

Ath.—Περὶ πολιορκιῶν, a few chapters from Book XX, contained in an early manuscript found on Mt. Athos, but now in Paris. Edited by C. Müller at the end of vol. ii. of his *Josephus*, Paris, 1847, and later by C. Wescher in his *Poliorcétique des Grecs*, Paris, 1868.

Another important source is :

Ambr.—A collection of miscellaneous excerpts, in chronological order, contained in a Milan manuscript (Ambrosianus Q 13 sup.), of the fifteenth century ; also in a second manuscript (A 80 sup.), which is a copy of the other and therefore rarely cited. This collection was carelessly edited by Angelo Mai in 1816. The numerous emendations of Struve mentioned in the critical notes were entered by that scholar in his copy of the Frankfort edition, now preserved in Munich.

Each new collection of excerpts, once discovered and published together with a Latin translation, has been included in the subsequent editions of the *Antiquities.*

The order in which the excerpts are here printed is that of Kiessling, followed by Jacoby, and is based on that of the Ambrosian collection. In a few cases the correctness of that order is open to serious question. Stephanus of Byzantium, by citing the particular books of the *Antiquities* in which he found the various places and peoples mentioned (see at end of Books XIII, XV–XIX), enables us to assign nearly all the excerpts to their proper books ; but his references to Books XVII and XVIII are confused and leave it doubtful where the line of division came.

The present translation of the excerpts is the first to appear in English. Spelman did not translate the few that had been published in his day.

SIGLA

BOOK XI

L = Laurentianus Plut. LXX 5.
V = Vaticanus 133.
M = Ambrosianus A 159 sup.
C = Coislinianus 150.

EXCERPTS, BOOKS XII-XX

Ursin.

E = Scorialenses R III 14 and R III 21.
V = Vaticanus Graecus 1418.
R = Parisinus Graecus 2463.
B = Bruxellensis 11301-16.
M = Monacensis 267.
P = Palatinus Vaticanus Graecus 113.
O = All the MSS.
X = BMP.
Z = All the MSS. not otherwise cited.

Vales.

P = Peirescianus, now Turonensis.

Esc.

S = Scorialensis Ω I 11.
Edd. = Müller and Feder.

Ath.

A = Early MS. from Mt. Athos, now in Paris.

Ambr.

Q = Ambrosianus Q 13 sup.
A = Ambrosianus A 80 sup.

x

THE ROMAN ANTIQUITIES
OF
DIONYSIUS OF HALICARNASSUS

ΔΙΟΝΥΣΙΟΥ

ΑΛΙΚΑΡΝΑΣΕΩΣ

ΡΩΜΑΙΚΗΣ ΑΡΧΑΙΟΛΟΓΙΑΣ

ΛΟΓΟΣ ΕΝΔΕΚΑΤΟΣ

I. Ἐπὶ δὲ τῆς ὀγδοηκοστῆς καὶ τρίτης ὀλυμπιάδος, ἣν ἐνίκα[1] Κρίσων Ἱμεραῖος, ἄρχοντος
Ἀθήνησι Φιλίσκου καταλύουσι Ῥωμαῖοι τὴν τῶν
δέκα ἀρχὴν ἔτη τρία τῶν κοινῶν ἐπιμελήθεῖσαν.
ὃν δὲ τρόπον ἐπεχείρησαν ἐρριζωμένην ἤδη τὴν
δυναστείαν ἐξελεῖν, καὶ τίνων ἀνδρῶν ἡγησαμένων
τῆς ἐλευθερίας, καὶ διὰ ποίας αἰτίας καὶ προφάσεις,
ἐξ ἀρχῆς ἀναλαβὼν πειράσομαι διελθεῖν, ἀναγκαίας
ὑπολαμβάνων εἶναι καὶ καλὰς τὰς τοιαύτας μαθή-
σεις ἅπασι μὲν ὡς εἰπεῖν ἀνθρώποις, μάλιστα δ'
ὅσοι περὶ τὴν φιλόσοφον θεωρίαν καὶ περὶ τὰς
2 πολιτικὰς διατρίβουσι πράξεις. τοῖς τε γὰρ πολλοῖς οὐκ ἀπαρκεῖ τοῦτο μόνον ἐκ τῆς ἱστορίας
παραλαβεῖν, ὅτι τὸν Περσικὸν πόλεμον—ἵν' ἐπὶ
τούτου ποιήσωμαι τὸν λόγον—ἐνίκησαν Ἀθηναῖοί
τε καὶ Λακεδαιμόνιοι δυσὶ ναυμαχίαις καὶ πεζο-

For the list of MSS. containing Book XI see the Introduction to this volume.

THE ROMAN ANTIQUITIES

OF

DIONYSIUS OF HALICARNASSUS

BOOK XI

I. In the eighty-third Olympiad [1] (the one at which Criso of Himera gained the prize [2]), Philiscus being archon at Athens, the Romans abolished the decemvirate which had governed the commonwealth for three years. I shall now endeavour to relate from the beginning in what manner they attempted to do away with this domination which was already deeply rooted, who the leaders were in the cause of liberty, and what their motives and pretexts were. For I assume that such information is necessary and an excellent thing for almost everyone, but particularly for those who are employed either in philosophical speculation or in the administration of public affairs. For most people are not satisfied with learning this alone from history, that the Persian War, to take that as an example, was won by the Athenians and Lacedaemonians, who in two battles

---

[1] 447 B.C.   [2] In the short-distance foot-race.

---

[1] ἐνίκα LV : ἐνίκα στάδιον Jacoby (cf. iii. 36, n.).

μαχίᾳ μιᾷ καταγωνισάμενοι τὸν βάρβαρον τριακοσίας ἄγοντα μυριάδας αὐτοὶ σὺν τοῖς συμμάχοις
οὐ πλείους ὄντες ἔνδεκα μυριάδων, ἀλλὰ καὶ τοὺς
τόπους ἐν οἷς αἱ πράξεις ἐγένοντο βούλονται παρὰ
τῆς ἱστορίας μαθεῖν, καὶ τὰς αἰτίας ἀκοῦσαι δι᾽
ἃς τὰ θαυμαστὰ καὶ παράδοξα ἔργα ἐπετέλεσαν,
καὶ τίνες ἦσαν οἱ τῶν στρατοπέδων ἡγεμόνες τῶν
τε βαρβαρικῶν καὶ τῶν Ἑλληνικῶν ἱστορῆσαι,
καὶ μηδενὸς ὡς εἰπεῖν ἀνήκοοι γενέσθαι τῶν
3 συντελεσθέντων περὶ τοὺς ἀγῶνας. ἥδεται γὰρ
ἡ διάνοια παντὸς ἀνθρώπου χειραγωγουμένη διὰ
τῶν λόγων ἐπὶ τὰ ἔργα, καὶ μὴ μόνον ἀκούουσα
τῶν λεγομένων ἀλλὰ καὶ τὰ πραττόμενα ὁρῶσα.
οὐδέ γ᾽, ὅταν πολιτικὰς ἀκούσωσι πράξεις, ἀρ-
κοῦνται τὸ κεφάλαιον αὐτὸ καὶ τὸ πέρας τῶν
πραγμάτων μαθόντες, ὅτι συνεχώρησαν Ἀθηναῖοι Λακεδαιμονίοις τείχη τε καθελεῖν τῆς πόλεως
αὐτῶν καὶ ναῦς διατεμεῖν καὶ φρουρὰν εἰς τὴν
ἀκρόπολιν εἰσαγαγεῖν καὶ ἀντὶ τῆς πατρίου δημο-
κρατίας ὀλιγαρχίαν τῶν κοινῶν ἀποδεῖξαι κυρίαν
οὐδὲ πρὸς αὐτοὺς ἀγῶνα ἀράμενοι, ἀλλ᾽ εὐθὺς
ἀξιοῦσι καὶ τίνες ἦσαν αἱ κατασχοῦσαι τὴν πόλιν
ἀνάγκαι δι᾽ ἃς ταῦτα τὰ δεινὰ καὶ σχέτλια ὑπ-
έμεινε, καὶ τίνες οἱ πείσαντες αὐτοὺς λόγοι καὶ ὑπὸ
τίνων ῥηθέντες ἀνδρῶν, καὶ πάντα ὅσα παρηκο-
4 λούθει[1] τοῖς πράγμασι διδαχθῆναι. τοῖς δὲ πολι-
τικοῖς ἀνδράσιν, ἐν[2] οἷς ἔγωγε τίθεμαι καὶ τοὺς
φιλοσόφους ὅσοι μὴ λόγων ἀλλ᾽ ἔργων καλῶν
ἄσκησιν ἡγοῦνται τὴν φιλοσοφίαν, τὸ μὲν ἥδεσθαι
τῇ παντελεῖ θεωρίᾳ τῶν παρακολουθούντων τοῖς

---

[1] Cary : παρακολουθεῖ O, Jacoby.
[2] ἐν V : om. LM.

at sea and one on land overcame the barbarian at the head of three million troops, though their own forces together with their allies did not exceed one hundred and ten thousand ; but they wish also to learn from history of the places where those actions occurred, to hear of the causes that enabled those men to perform their wonderful and astonishing exploits, to know who were the commanders of the armies, both Greek and barbarian, and to be left ignorant of not a single incident, one may say, that happened in those engagements. For the minds of all men take delight in being conducted through words to deeds and not only in hearing what is related but also in beholding what is done. Nor, indeed, when they hear of political events, are they satisfied with learning the bare summary and outcome of the events, as, for instance, that the Athenians agreed with the Lacedaemonians to demolish the walls of their city, to break up their fleet, to introduce a garrison into their citadel, and, instead of their traditional democracy, to set up an oligarchy to govern the state, and permitted all this without so much as fighting a battle with them ; but they at once demand to be informed also of the necessity which reduced the Athenians to submit to such dire and cruel calamities, what the arguments were that persuaded them, and by what men those arguments were urged, and to be informed of all the circumstances that attended those events. Men who are engaged in the conduct of civil affairs, among whom I for my part include also those philosophers who regard philosophy as consisting in the practice of fine actions rather than of fine words, have this in common with the rest of mankind, that they take pleasure in a comprehensive survey of all

5

πράγμασι κοινὸν ὥσπερ καὶ τοῖς ἄλλοις ἀνθρώποις
ὑπάρχει· χωρὶς δὲ τῆς ἡδονῆς περιγίγνεται τὸ περὶ
τοὺς ἀναγκαίους καιροὺς μεγάλα τὰς πόλεις ἐκ
τῆς τοιαύτης ἐμπειρίας ὠφελεῖν καὶ ἄγειν αὐτὰς
5 ἑκούσας ἐπὶ τὰ συμφέροντα διὰ τοῦ λόγου. ῥᾷστα
γὰρ οἱ ἄνθρωποι τά τε ὠφελοῦντα καὶ βλάπτοντα
καταμανθάνουσιν ὅταν ἐπὶ παραδειγμάτων ταῦτα[1]
πολλῶν ὁρῶσι, καὶ τοῖς ἐπὶ ταῦτα παρακαλοῦσιν
αὐτοὺς φρόνησιν μαρτυροῦσι καὶ πολλὴν σοφίαν.
διὰ ταύτας δή μοι τὰς αἰτίας ἔδοξεν ἅπαντα
ἀκριβῶς διελθεῖν τὰ γενόμενα περὶ τὴν κατάλυσιν
τῆς ὀλιγαρχίας, ὅσα δὴ καὶ λόγου τυχεῖν ἄξια
6 ἡγοῦμαι. ποιήσομαι δὲ τὸν περὶ αὐτῶν λόγον
οὐκ ἀπὸ τῶν τελευταίων ἀρξάμενος, ἃ δοκεῖ τοῖς
πολλοῖς αἴτια γενέσθαι μόνα τῆς ἐλευθερίας, λέγω
δὲ τῶν περὶ τὴν παρθένον ἁμαρτηθέντων Ἀππίῳ
διὰ τὸν ἔρωτα (προσθήκη γὰρ αὕτη γε καὶ τελευταία τῆς ὀργῆς τῶν δημοτῶν αἰτία μυρίων ἄλλων
προηγησαμένων), ἀλλ' ἀφ' ὧν ἤρξατο πρῶτον ἡ
πόλις ὑπὸ τῆς δεκαδαρχίας[2] ὑβρίζεσθαι. ταῦτα
πρῶτον ἐρῶ καὶ διέξειμι πάσας ἐφεξῆς τὰς ἐν τῇ
τότε καταστάσει γενηθείσας παρανομίας.

II. Πρώτη μὲν οὖν ἦν[3] ἡ[4] δόξασα γενέσθαι τοῦ
κατὰ τῆς ὀλιγαρχίας μίσους πρόφασις ὅτι συν-
ύφηναν τὴν δευτέραν ἀρχὴν τῇ προτέρᾳ[5] δήμου τε
ὑπεριδόντες καὶ βουλῆς καταφρονήσαντες· ἔπειθ'

---

[1] παραδειγμάτων ταῦτὰ LV : παραδείγματα τοιαῦτα M (in marg. ταυτὰ).
[2] Kiessling : δεκαρχίας O (and so in later chapters).
[3] ἦν V : om. R.
[4] ἡ added by Reiske ; Ambrosch proposed to read ἔδοξε for δόξασα.
[5] τὴν τρίτην ἀρχὴν τῇ δευτέρᾳ Reiske.

the circumstances that accompany events. And, besides their pleasure, they have this advantage, that in difficult times they render great service to their countries as the result of the experience thus acquired and lead them as willing followers to that which is to their advantage, through the power of persuasion. For men most easily recognize the policies which either benefit or injure them when they perceive these illustrated by many examples ; and those who advise them to make use of these are credited by them with prudence and great wisdom. It is for these reasons, therefore, that I have determined to report in accurate detail all the circumstances which attended the overthrow of the oligarchy,[1] in so far as I consider them worthy of notice. I shall begin my account of them, however, not with the final incidents, which most people regard as the sole cause of the re-establishment of liberty,—I mean the wrongs committed by Appius with regard to the maiden because of his passion for her,—since these were merely an aggravation and a final cause for the resentment of the plebeians, following countless others, but I shall begin with the first insults the citizens suffered at the hands of the decemvirate. These I shall mention first, and then relate in order all the lawless. deeds committed under that régime.

II. The first ground for the hatred against the oligarchy seems to have been this, that its members had joined their second term of office immediately to their first, thus showing alike their scorn of the people and their contempt of the senate. Another

---

[1] In Book XI Dionysius regularly uses " oligarchy " as one term for " decemvirate " and " oligarchs " for " decemvirs."

ὅτι τοὺς χαριεστάτους Ῥωμαίων, οἷς οὐ κατὰ
γνώμην τὰ πραττόμενα ὑπ' αὐτῶν ἦν, οὓς μὲν
ἐξήλαυνον ἐκ τῆς πόλεως αἰτίας ἐπιφέροντες ψευδεῖς καὶ δεινάς, οὓς δὲ ἀπεκτίννυσαν, κατηγόρους
τε αὐτοῖς ὑποπέμποντες ἐκ τῶν ἰδίων ἑταίρων
καὶ τὰς δίκας ταύτας αὐτοὶ δικάζοντες· μάλιστα
δ' ὅτι τοῖς θρασυτάτοις τῶν νέων οὓς εἶχον
ἕκαστοι περὶ αὑτοὺς ἐφῆκαν ἄγειν καὶ φέρειν τὰ
2 τῶν ἐναντιουμένων τῇ πολιτείᾳ. οἱ δ' ὥσπερ
ἁλούσης πολέμῳ κατὰ κράτος τῆς πατρίδος οὐ
τὰ χρήματα μόνον ἀφῃροῦντο τοὺς νόμῳ κτησα-
μένους, ἀλλὰ καὶ εἰς τὰς γαμετὰς αὐτῶν τὰς
εὐμόρφους παρενόμουν[1] καὶ εἰς θυγατέρας ἐπιγάμους καθύβριζον καὶ πληγὰς τοῖς ἀγανακτοῦσιν
ὥσπερ ἀνδραπόδοις ἐδίδοσαν· καὶ παρεσκεύασαν,
ὅσοις ἀφόρητα εἶναι τὰ γινόμενα ἐδόκει, καταλιπόντας τὴν πατρίδα γυναιξὶν ὁμοῦ καὶ τέκνοις
εἰς τὰς πλησίον ἐξοικίζεσθαι πόλεις, ὑποδεχομένων
αὐτοὺς Λατίνων μὲν διὰ τὸ ὁμοεθνές,[2] Ἑρνίκων δὲ
διὰ τὴν ἔναγχος γενομένην[3] αὐτοῖς ὑπὸ Ῥωμαίων
ἰσοπολιτείαν. ὥσθ', ὅπερ εἰκὸς ἦν, τελευτῶντες
αὐτοὶ κατελείφθησαν οἱ φιλοτύραννοι καὶ οἷς
3 μηδεμία τῶν κοινῶν φροντὶς ἦν. οὔτε γὰρ οἵ
γε[4] πατρίκιοι διέμενον ἐν τῇ πόλει, θωπεύειν μὲν
οὐκ ἀξιοῦντες τοὺς ἡγεμόνας, ἐναντιοῦσθαι δὲ τοῖς
πραττομένοις ἀδυνατοῦντες, οὔθ'[5] οἱ καταγρα-
φέντες εἰς τὸ βουλευτικὸν συνέδριον, οὓς ἐπάναγκες
ἔδει παρεῖναι ταῖς ἀρχαῖς, ἀλλὰ καὶ τούτων οἱ
πλείους ἀνασκευασάμενοι πανοικεσίᾳ καὶ τὰς

---

[1] Cobet : παρηνόμουν O.
[2] ὁμοεθνές Post : εὐσθενὲς or ἀσθενὲς L, ἀσθενὲς R ; συγγενές Sylburg.　　　　　[3] δεδομένην Sylburg.

was their treatment of the most reputable Romans who were dissatisfied with their actions, some of whom, on the strength of false and heinous accusations, they were expelling from the city and others they were putting to death, suborning some of their own faction to accuse them and themselves trying these cases. But more than anything else was the licence they gave to the most audacious of the young men by whom each of them was always attended, to plunder and pillage the goods of those who opposed their administration. These youths, as if the country had been taken by force of arms, not only stripped the legal owners of their effects, but even violated their wives, when these were beautiful, abused such of their daughters as were marriageable, and when any showed resentment, they beat them like slaves. Thus they brought it about that those who found these proceedings intolerable left their country along with their wives and children and removed to the neighbouring cities, where they were received by the Latins on account of their affinity and by the Hernicans in acknowledgement of the right of citizenship lately granted to them by the Romans. Consequently, as was to be expected, there were in the end none left behind but the friends of tyranny and such as had no concern for the public good. For neither the patricians, who were unwilling to flatter the rulers and yet were unable to oppose their actions, remained in the city, nor did those enrolled in the senate, whose presence was absolutely necessary to the magistrates; but the greater part of these also had removed with their entire families and,

---

⁴ Kiessling : τε O.   ⁵ Reiske : οὐδ' O.

οἰκίας ἐρήμους ἀφέντες ἐν τοῖς ἀγροῖς διέτριβον.
4 τοῖς δὲ ὀλιγαρχικοῖς καθ' ἡδονὴν αἱ τῶν ἐπιφανεστάτων ἀνδρῶν ἐγίνοντο φυγαὶ πολλῶν μὲν
καὶ ἄλλων ἕνεκα, μάλιστα δὲ ὅτι τοῖς ἀκολάστοις
τῶν νέων πολὺ τὸ αὔθαδες προσεγίνετο μηδ' ὄψει
δυναμένοις ἰδεῖν οὓς ἔμελλον ἀσελγές τι[1] πράττοντες αἰσχύνεσθαι.

III. Ἐρημουμένης δὲ τοῦ κρείττονος ἔθνους[2]
τῆς πόλεως καὶ τὸ ἐλεύθερον ἅπαν ἀπολωλεκυίας
ἀφορμὴν κρατίστην ὑπολαβόντες ἔχειν οἱ[3] πολέμῳ
κρατηθέντες ὑπ' αὐτῆς τάς τε ὕβρεις ἃς ὑβρίσθησαν
ἀποτίσασθαι καὶ τὰ ἀπολωλότα ἀναλαβεῖν, ὡς
νοσούσης διὰ τὴν ὀλιγαρχίαν τῆς πόλεως καὶ οὔτε
συστῆναι οὔθ' ὁμονοῆσαι οὔτ' ἀντιλαβέσθαι τῶν
κοινῶν ἔτι δυνησομένης, παρασκευασάμενοι τὰ
πρὸς τὸν πόλεμον ἐλαύνουσιν ἐπ' αὐτὴν στρατεύ-
2 μασι μεγάλοις. καὶ κατὰ τὸν αὐτὸν χρόνον
Σαβῖνοι μὲν[4] ἐμβαλόντες εἰς τὴν ὁμοτέρμονα καὶ
πολλῆς γενόμενοι λείας ἐγκρατεῖς φόνον τε πολὺν
ἐργασάμενοι τοῦ γεωργικοῦ πλήθους ἐν Ἡρήτῳ[5]
κατεστρατοπέδευσαν (διέστηκε δ' ἀπὸ τῆς Ῥώμης
ἡ πόλις αὕτη τετταράκοντα καὶ ἑκατὸν σταδίους
3 πλησίον οὖσα Τεβέριος[6] ποταμοῦ), Αἰκανοὶ δ' εἰς
τὴν Τυσκλανῶν γῆν ἐμβαλόντες ὅμορον οὖσαν
σφίσι καὶ πολλὰ δῃώσαντες αὐτῆς ἐν Ἀλγιδῷ
πόλει τίθενται τὸν χάρακα. ὡς δ' ἤκουσαν οἱ δέκα
τὴν τῶν πολεμίων ἔφοδον, τεταραγμένοι συνεκά-

---

[1] ἀσελγές τι Kiessling : ἀσελγέσι LV.
[2] ἔθνους LV : μέρους M.
[3] ἔχειν οἱ Kiessling : ἐκεῖνοι οἱ O, Jacoby, Αἰκανοὶ Casaubon.   [4] μὲν added by Cobet.
[5] Ἡρήτῳ Sylburg : ῥηγῷ MV, ῥητῷ L.
[6] τιβέρεως O.

leaving their houses empty, were now living in the country. The oligarchical faction, however, was pleased with the flight of the most distinguished men, not only for many other reasons, but particularly because it greatly increased the arrogance of the licentious youth not to have before their eyes those persons whose presence would have made them blush whenever they committed any wanton act.

III. Rome being thus deserted [1] by her best element and having lost every vestige of her liberty, the nations which had been conquered by her thought they now had the most favourable opportunity both to avenge the insults they had received and to repair the losses they had sustained, believing that the commonwealth was sick because of the oligarchy and would no longer be able either to assemble its forces or to act in concord or to take hold of the affairs of state ; and accordingly they prepared everything that was necessary for war and marched against Rome with large armies. At one and the same time the Sabines made a raid into that part of the Roman territory that bordered on theirs and, after possessing themselves of much booty and killing large numbers of husbandmen, encamped at Eretum (this town is situated near the river Tiber at the distance of one hundred and forty stades from Rome), and the Aequians made a raid into the territory of the Tusculans that adjoined their own, and having laid waste much of it, placed their camp at the town of Algidum. When the decemvirs were informed of the attack of their enemies, they were confounded, and assembling their organized bands,

---

[1] For chaps. 3–4, 3 cf. Livy iii. 38, 2-13.

λουν τὰς ἑταιρείας καὶ μετὰ τούτων ὅ τι χρὴ
4 πράττειν ἐσκόπουν. τὸ μὲν οὖν ὑπερόριον ἀποστέλλειν στρατιὰν καὶ μὴ περιμένειν ἕως ἐπ᾽
αὐτὴν ἔλθωσι τὴν πόλιν αἱ τῶν πολεμίων δυνάμεις
ἅπασιν ἐδόκει· παρεῖχε δ᾽ αὐτοῖς πολλὴν ἀπορίαν,
πρῶτον μὲν εἰ πάντας Ῥωμαίους ἐπὶ τὰ ὅπλα
κλητέον[1] καὶ τοὺς ἀπεχθομένους τῇ πολιτείᾳ·
ἔπειθ᾽ ὁποίαν τινὰ δεήσει τὴν καταγραφὴν τῶν
στρατιωτῶν ποιήσασθαι, πότερον αὐθάδη καὶ
μισοπόνηρον οἵας ἔθος ἦν ποιεῖσθαι τοῖς τε βασιλεῦσι καὶ τοῖς ὑπάτοις, ἢ φιλάνθρωπον καὶ μέτριον.
5 ἐδόκει τ᾽ αὐτοῖς οὐδ᾽[2] ἐκεῖνο μικρᾶς εἶναι ζητήσεως
ἄξιον, τί τὸ κυρῶσον ἔσται τὴν περὶ τοῦ πολέμου
γνώμην καὶ τὴν στρατολογίαν ψηφιούμενον, πότερα
τὸ συνέδριον τῆς βουλῆς ἢ τὸ δημοτικὸν πλῆθος
ἢ τούτων μὲν οὐδέτερον, ἐπεὶ δι᾽ ὑποψίας ἦν
αὐτοῖς ἑκάτερον, αὐτοὶ δὲ σφίσιν αὐτοῖς οἱ δέκα.
τέλος δ᾽ οὖν πολλὰ βουλευσάμενοι τὴν βουλὴν
ἔγνωσαν συγκαλεῖν καὶ ποιεῖν ὅπως τόν τε πόλεμον
αὐτοῖς ἐκείνη ψηφιεῖται καὶ τὴν τοῦ στρατοῦ
6 καταγραφὴν ἐπιτρέψει ποιήσασθαι. εἰ γὰρ ὑπὸ
τοῦ συνεδρίου κυρωθείη τούτων ἑκάτερον, πρῶτον
μὲν εὐπειθεῖς ἔσεσθαι πάντας ὑπελάμβανον ἄλλως
τε καὶ τῆς δημαρχικῆς ἐξουσίας καταλελυμένης,[3]
ἣ μόνη κατὰ νόμους ἐξῆν ἐναντιοῦσθαι τοῖς ὑπὸ
τῶν δυνατῶν[4] ἐπιταττομένοις· ἔπειτ᾽ αὐτοὶ[5] δόξειν
ὑπηρετοῦντες τῇ βουλῇ καὶ τὰ κυρωθέντα ὑπ᾽
ἐκείνης πράττοντες κατὰ νόμους ἀνειληφέναι τὴν
ἐξουσίαν τοῦ πολέμου.

IV. Ταῦτα βουλευσάμενοι καὶ παρασκευάσαντες
ἐκ τῶν ἰδίων ἑταίρων καὶ συγγενῶν τοὺς ἀγορεύ-

___

[1] κλητέον Cobet : ἀκτέον O.   [2] Reiske : οὔτ᾽ O.

they consulted with them what measures they ought to take. That they ought to send an army outside their borders and not wait till the enemies' forces advanced to Rome itself was the opinion of all; but they were in great perplexity, first, whether they should call to arms all the Romans, even those who hated their administration, and second, in what sort of way they should make the levy, whether in an arbitrary and uncompromising manner, as had been the practice of both the kings and the consuls, or with indulgence and moderation. They thought that another point also deserved no small consideration, namely, who were to ratify their decisions regarding war and to vote the levy, whether the senate or the plebeians, or neither, since they were suspicious of both, but instead the decemvirs should confirm their own decisions. At last, after long consultation, they concluded to assemble the senate and prevail on that body to vote for war and to allow them to make the levy. For if both these measures were ratified by the senate, they imagined, first, that all would yield ready obedience, particularly since the tribunician power had been suppressed, which alone could legally oppose the orders of those in power; and, in the next place, that if they were subservient to the senate and carried out its orders, they would appear to have received in a legal manner their authority to begin war.

IV. After they had taken this resolution and had prepared those of their friends and relations who

---

³ καταλελυμένης L : καταλυομένης MV.
⁴ Cobet : δυναστῶν O.
⁵ εἴ τι after αὐτοὶ deleted by Kiessling.

σοντας ἐν τῷ συνεδρίῳ τὰς συμφερούσας αὐτοῖς
γνώμας καὶ τοῖς μὴ ταὐτὰ[1] προαιρουμένοις ἐναντιω-
σομένους, προῆλθον εἰς τὴν ἀγορὰν καὶ παρα-
στησάμενοι τὸν κήρυκα τοὺς βουλεύοντας[2] ἐξ
ὀνόματος καλεῖν ἐκέλευον. ὑπήκουε δ' αὐτοῖς
2 τῶν μετρίων οὐδείς. πολλάκις δὲ τοῦ κήρυκος
βοῶντος καὶ παριόντος οὐδενὸς εἰ μὴ τῶν κο-
λακευόντων τὴν ὀλιγαρχίαν, ἐν οἷς ἦν τὸ κάκιστον
τῆς πόλεως[3] μέρος, οἱ μὲν τότ' ὄντες κατὰ τὴν
ἀγορὰν ἐθαύμαζον εἰ περὶ μηδενὸς πώποτε συγκαλέσαντες τὴν βουλήν, τότε πρῶτον ἔγνωσαν ὅτι
καὶ συνέδριον ἦν τι παρὰ Ῥωμαίοις ἀγαθῶν
3 ἀνδρῶν οὓς ἔδει περὶ τῶν κοινῶν σκοπεῖν. οἱ δέκα
δὲ ταῦθ'[4] ὁρῶντες ἐπεχείρησαν μὲν ἐκ τῶν οἰκιῶν
τοὺς βουλευτὰς ἄγειν· πυθόμενοι δὲ τὰς πλείους
ἐρήμους ἀφειμένας εἰς τὴν ὑστεραίαν ἀνεβάλοντο.[5]
ἐν δὲ τῷ μεταξὺ χρόνῳ πέμποντες ἐπὶ τοὺς ἀγροὺς
ἐκεῖθεν αὐτοὺς ἐκάλουν. πληρωθέντος δὲ τοῦ
συνεδρίου προελθὼν[6] Ἄππιος, ὁ τῆς δεκαδαρχίας
ἡγεμών, ἀπήγγειλεν[7] ὅτι διχόθεν ἀπό τε Αἰκανῶν
καὶ Σαβίνων ἐπάγεται τῇ Ῥώμῃ πόλεμος· καὶ
διεξῆλθε λόγον ἐκ πολλῆς συγκείμενον ἐπιμελείας,
οὗ τέλος ἦν ψηφίσασθαι στρατοῦ καταγραφὴν καὶ
διὰ τάχους ποιῆσαι τὴν ἔξοδον, ὡς οὐ διδόντος
4 ἀναστροφὴν τοῦ καιροῦ. ταῦτα δὲ αὐτοῦ λέγοντος
ἀνίσταται Λεύκιος Οὐαλέριος[8] ἐπωνυμίαν Ποτῖτος,

----

[1] ταῦτα LV.
[2] Reiske : βουλεύσοντας O.
[3] πόλεως Reiske : ὀλιγαρχίας O, Jacoby.
[4] οἱ δέκα δὲ ταῦθ' Reiske : οἱ δὲ καὶ ταῦτ' O.
[5] Casaubon : ἀνεβάλλοντο O.
[6] προελθὼν Portus, παρελθὼν Reudler : προσελθὼν O.
[7] Kiessling : ἀπήγγελεν LV.

14

were to deliver in the senate the opinions that would further their cause and to oppose those who did not entertain the same sentiments, they went to the Forum, and bringing forward the crier, ordered him to summon the senators by name. But not one of the moderates paid heed to them. When the crier shouted repeatedly and no one appeared but the flatterers of the oligarchy, among whom was to be found the most profligate element of the city,[1] everyone who happened to be in the Forum at the time marvelled that the decemvirs, who had never assembled the senate on any account, recognized then for the first time that there was also among the Romans a council of worthy men whose duty it was to consult about the public interests. The decemvirs, observing that the senators did not answer to their names, attempted to have them brought from their houses ; but learning that the greater part of these had been left empty, they deferred the matter till the next day. In the meantime they sent into the country and summoned them from thence. When the senate-chamber was full, Appius, the chief of the decemvirate, came forward and informed them that war was being made upon Rome from two sides, by the Aequians and by the Sabines. And he delivered a very carefully prepared speech, the upshot of which was to get them to vote for the levying of an army and sending it out speedily, since the crisis admitted of no delay. While he was thus speaking, Lucius Valerius, surnamed Potitus, rose up,[2] a man who

---

[1] " City " is Reiske's emendation for " oligarchy," falsely repeated in the MSS. from the line above.
[2] For Valerius' speech *cf.* Livy iii. 39, 2.

---

[8] γαλέριος O (and so frequently below).

DIONYSIUS OF HALICARNASSUS

ἀνὴρ μέγα φρονῶν[1] ἐπὶ τοῖς προγόνοις· πατὴρ μὲν
γὰρ αὐτῷ Οὐαλέριος ἦν ὁ τὸν Σαβῖνον Ἐρδώνιον
ἐκπολιορκήσας κατέχοντα τὸ Καπιτώλιον, καὶ τὸ
μὲν φρούριον ἀνακτησάμενος, αὐτὸς δ' ἐκ τῆς
μάχης ἀποθανών· πάππος δὲ πρὸς πατρὸς Ποπλικόλας ὁ τοὺς βασιλεῖς ἐκβαλὼν καὶ τὴν ἀριστο-
5 κρατίαν καταστησάμενος. παριόντα δ' αὐτὸν ἔτι
καταμαθὼν Ἄππιος καὶ καθ' ἑαυτοῦ[2] τι λέξειν
ἐλπίσας· " Οὐχ οὗτος ὁ τόπος," εἶπεν, " ὦ
Οὐαλέριε, σός, οὐδὲ προσήκει σοι νῦν λέγειν, ἀλλ'
ὅταν οἵδε οἱ πρεσβύτεροι καὶ τιμιώτεροί σου γνώμην ἀγορεύσωσι, τότε καὶ σὺ κληθεὶς ἐρεῖς ὅ τι
σοι δοκεῖ· νῦν δὲ σιώπα καὶ κάθησο." " Ἀλλ' οὐχ
ὑπὲρ τούτων," ἔφησεν ὁ Οὐαλέριος, " ἀνέστηκα
ἐρῶν, ἀλλ' ὑπὲρ ἄλλων μειζόνων τε καὶ ἀναγκαιο-
τέρων, ὑπὲρ ὧν οἴομαι δεῖν πρῶτον ἀκοῦσαι τὴν
6 βουλήν. εἴσονται δ' ἐξ ὧν ἂν ἀκούσωσιν οὗτοι
πότερα ταῦτ' ἐστὶν ἀναγκαιότερα τοῖς κοινοῖς,
ὑπὲρ ὧν ὑμεῖς αὐτοὺς συγκεκλήκατε, ἢ τὰ ὑπ'
ἐμοῦ λεχθησόμενα. ἀλλὰ μή μ' ἀποστέρει λόγου
βουλευτὴν ὄντα καὶ Οὐαλέριον καὶ περὶ σωτηρίας
τῆς πόλεως λέγειν βουλόμενον. ἐὰν δὲ φυλάττῃς
τὴν συνήθη πρὸς ἅπαντας αὐθάδειαν, δημάρχους
μὲν ποίους ἐπικαλέσομαι; καταλέλυται γὰρ ἡ
τῶν κατισχυομένων πολιτῶν βοήθεια ὑφ' ὑμῶν.
7 καίτοι τίνος ἔλαττον τοῦτο κακόν, ὅτε Οὐαλέριος
ὢν[3] ὡς εἷς τῶν ἐλαχίστων οὐκ ἔχω τὸ ἴσον, ἀλλὰ
δημαρχικῆς ἐξουσίας δέομαι; οὐ μὴν ἀλλ' ἐπεὶ
τῆς ἀρχῆς ἐκείνης ἀπεστερήμεθα, ὑμᾶς τοὺς ἅμα

---

[1] μέγα φρονῶν Kiessling : μεγαλόφρων O.
[2] Reiske : ἑαυτὸν O.
[3] Ποτῖτος after ὢν deleted by Cobet.

thought very highly of himself because of his ancestry; for his father was that Valerius who took the Capitol by siege when it was occupied by Herdonius the Sabine and recovered the fortress, though he himself lost his life in the action, and his grandfather on his father's side was Publicola, who expelled the kings and established the aristocracy. Appius, observing him as he was still coming forward and expecting he would say something against him, said : " This is not your turn, Valerius, and it is not fitting for you to speak now. But when these senators who are older and more honoured than you have delivered their opinions, then you also will be called upon and will say what you think proper. For the present be silent and sit down." " But it is not about these matters that I have risen to speak," Valerius said. " but about others of greater moment and more urgent, of which I think the senate ought first to hear. And from what they shall hear they will know whether these matters for which you decemvirs have assembled them are more necessary to the commonwealth than those which I shall speak about. Well, then, do not refuse the floor to me, who am a senator and a Valerius and one who desires to speak in the interest of the safety of the commonwealth. But if you persist in your usual arrogance toward everybody, what tribunes shall I call upon to assist me ? For this relief to oppressed citizens has been abolished by you decemvirs. And yet what greater wrong is there than this, that I, a Valerius, like a man of the lowest rank, do not enjoy equality, but stand in need of the tribunician power ? However, since we have been deprived of that magistracy, I call for assistance upon all of you who together with this man have

τούτῳ παρειληφότας καὶ τὴν ἐκείνης ἐξουσίαν τῆς
ἀρχῆς καὶ δυναστεύοντας τῆς πόλεως ἅπαντας
καλῶ, οὐκ ἀγνοῶν[1] μὲν ὅτι διὰ κενῆς τοῦτο ποιῶ,
φανερὰν δὲ βουλόμενος πᾶσι γενέσθαι τὴν συνωμοσίαν ὑμῶν, ὅτι συγκεχύκατε τὰ τῆς πόλεως
καὶ μίαν ἅπαντες γνώμην ἔχετε· μᾶλλον δὲ σὲ
μόνον ἐπικαλοῦμαι, Κόιντε Φάβιε Οὐιβολανέ, τὸν
ταῖς τρισὶν ὑπατείαις κεκοσμημένον,[2] εἰ τὸν αὐτὸν
νοῦν ἔτι ἔχεις. ἀλλ᾽ ἀνίστασο καὶ βοήθει τοῖς
κατισχυομένοις· εἰς σὲ γὰρ ἀποβλέπει τὸ συνέδριον.''

V. Ὡς δὲ ταῦτ᾽ εἶπεν, ὁ Φάβιος ἐκάθητο ὑπ᾽
αἰσχύνης οὐδὲν ἀποκρινόμενος, Ἄππιος δὲ καὶ
οἱ λοιποὶ δέκα πάντες ἀναπηδήσαντες ἐκώλυον
αὐτὸν λέγειν. θορύβου δὲ πολλοῦ κατασχόντος
τὸ συνέδριον καὶ τῶν μὲν πλείστων ἀγανακτούντων,
τῶν δ᾽ ἐκ τῆς ἑταιρείας αὐτοὺς λέγειν ὀρθῶς
ἡγουμένων, ἀνίσταται Μάρκος Ὁράτιος[3] ὁ Βαρβᾶτος ἐπικληθεὶς ἀπόγονος Ὁρατίου[4] τοῦ συν-
υπατεύσαντος Ποπλίῳ Οὐαλερίῳ Ποπλικόλᾳ μετὰ
τὴν ἐκβολὴν τῶν βασιλέων, ἀνὴρ καὶ τὰ πολεμικὰ
δεινὸς καὶ λέγειν οὐκ ἀδύνατος, Οὐαλερίῳ δ᾽ ἐκ
παλαιοῦ φίλος· ὃς οὐκέτι κατασχὼν τὴν χολὴν
2 ἔφησε· '' Θᾶττόν μ᾽[5] ἀναγκάσετε,[6] Ἄππιε, τοὺς
χαλινοὺς διαρρῆξαι οὐκέτι μετριάζοντες, ἀλλὰ
τὸν Ταρκύνιον ἐκεῖνον ἐνδυόμενοι, οἵ γ᾽ οὐδὲ
λόγου τυχεῖν ἐᾶτε τοὺς περὶ σωτηρίας τῶν κοινῶν

---

[1] οὐκ ἀγνοῶν Cobet : καὶ οὐκ ἀγνοῶ O.
[2] τὸν ταῖς τ. ὑ. κεκοσμημένον Garrer : τὸν ἐπὶ ταῖς τ. ὑ. κοσμού-
μενον O, Jacoby ; τὸν ἐπὶ ταῖς τ. ὑ. καυχούμενον Schenkl.
[3] ὀρύγιος or ὀρούγιος O.
[4] ὡρατίου LV.   [5] με V : μὲν CM, om. L.
[6] Portus : ἀναγκασ᾽ V, ἀναγκάσεις R.

assumed the power of that magistracy also and exercise dominion over the commonwealth. I am not unaware, to be sure, that I do this in vain, but I desire to make your conspiracy manifest to all and show that you have thrown the affairs of the commonwealth into confusion and that you all have the same purpose. Rather, I call upon you alone, Quintus Fabius Vibulanus, you who have been honoured with those three consulships, in case you still preserve the same sentiments. Rise up, therefore, and relieve the oppressed ; for the eyes of the senate are fixed upon you."

V. When Valerius had spoken thus, Fabius sat still through shame and made no answer ; but Appius and all the other decemvirs, leaping up, sought to hinder Valerius from going on. Upon this, a great tumult filled the senate-chamber, the greater part of the senators expressing their resentment, while those who belonged to the decemvirs' faction justified what they said. Then Marcus Horatius, surnamed Barbatus, a descendant of that Horatius who had been consul with Publius Valerius Publicola after the expulsion of the kings, rose up, a man of great ability in warfare and not lacking in eloquence, and long a friend to Valerius. This man, unable longer to contain his resentment, said [1] : " You decemvirs will very soon force me, Appius, to break through all restraint by your want of moderation and by acting the part of the haughty Tarquin,—you who do not even grant a hearing to those who desire to speak in the interest of the safety of the common-

[1] For Horatius' speech *cf.* Livy iii. 39, 3-10.

DIONYSIUS OF HALICARNASSUS

βουλομένους[1] λέγειν. πότερον ὑμῶν ἐξελήλυθεν
ἐκ τῆς διανοίας ὅτι σώζονται μὲν οἱ Οὐαλερίων
ἀπόγονοι τῶν ἐξελασάντων τὴν τυραννίδα, λείπεται
δὲ διαδοχὴ[2] τῆς Ὁρατίων οἰκίας, οἷς πάτριόν
ἐστιν ὁμόσε χωρεῖν τοῖς καταδουλουμένοις τὴν
3 πατρίδα καὶ μετὰ τῶν ἄλλων καὶ μόνοις; ἢ
τοσαύτην κατεγνώκατε καὶ ἡμῶν καὶ τῶν ἄλλων
Ῥωμαίων ἀνανδρίαν ὥστ' ἀγαπήσειν ἐάν τις ἐᾷ
ζῆν ἡμᾶς ὁπωσδήποτε, ὑπὲρ ἐλευθερίας δὲ καὶ
παρρησίας μήτ' ἐρεῖν μήτε πράξειν[3] μηθέν; ἢ
μεθύετε τῷ μεγέθει τῆς ἐξουσίας; ὑμεῖς Οὐαλερίου λόγον ἀφελεῖσθε[4] ἢ τῶν ἄλλων τινὸς βουλευτῶν τίνες ὄντες ἢ ποίαν ἀρχὴν ἔχοντες νόμιμον;
οὐκ εἰς ἐνιαυτὸν ἀπεδείχθητε τῶν κοινῶν προ-
στάται; οὐ παρῴχηκεν ὁ τῆς ἀρχῆς ὑμῶν χρόνος;
οὐκ ἰδιῶται τῷ νόμῳ γεγόνατε; ταῦτ' εἰς τὸν
4 δῆμον βουλεύεσθε ἐξενεγκεῖν. τί γὰρ δὴ καὶ τὸ
κωλῦον ἔσται τὸν βουλόμενον ἡμῶν[5] τὴν ἐκκλησίαν
συγκαλεῖν καὶ τὴν ἐξουσίαν ὑμῶν, ἣν παρὰ τοὺς
νόμους ἔχετε, κατηγορεῖν; ἀνάδοτε τοῖς πολίταις
ψῆφον ὑπὲρ αὐτοῦ τούτου, πότερα δεῖ μένειν τὴν
δεκαδαρχίαν ὑμῶν ἢ τὰς πατρίους πάλιν ἀποδείκνυσθαι ἀρχάς· κἂν τοῦτο[6] μανεὶς ὁ δῆμος
ὑπομείνῃ,[7] πάλιν τὴν αὐτὴν κατάστασιν ἔχετε καὶ[8]
κωλύετε λέγειν ὁπόσα βούλεταί τις[9] ὑπὲρ τῆς
πατρίδος.[10] ἄξιοι γὰρ ἂν εἴημεν καὶ ταῦτα καὶ ἔτι
χείρονα τούτων πάσχειν ἐφ' ὑμῖν γενόμενοι καὶ

---

[1] βουλομένους M : βουλευομένους LV.
[2] δ' ἡ διαδοχὴ Kiessling.
[3] πράξειν Sylburg : πράσσειν O, δράσειν Reiske.
[4] Casaubon : ἀφείλεσθε O.   [5] βουλευόμενον ὑμῶν L.
[6] κἂν τοῦτο Kiessling : om. L in lacuna of 10 letters, καὶ εἰ
τοῦτο R.   [7] ὑπομείνῃ LV : ὑπομένειν C, ὑπομείνει M.

20

wealth. Has it slipped your minds that there still
survive the descendants of that Valerius who banished
the tyranny and that there are left successors of the
house of the Horatii in whom it is hereditary to
oppose, both with others and alone, those who would
enslave their country ? Or have you decided that
both we and the rest of the Romans have so mean a
spirit that we shall be content to be permitted to
enjoy life on any terms whatever and will neither
say nor do anything in favour of liberty and freedom
of speech ? Or are you intoxicated with the greatness
of your power ? Who are you men, or what legal
magistracy do you hold, that you are going to
deprive Valerius or any other senator of the privilege
of speaking ? Were you not appointed leaders of the
commonwealth for a year ? Has not the term of
your magistracy expired ? Have you not become
private citizens by law ? Plan to lay these matters
before the people. For what is going to hinder any
of us from assembling them and from challenging the
authority which you are exercising contrary to the
laws ? Permit the citizens to vote upon this very
point, whether your decemvirate shall continue or
the traditional magistracies be re-established ; and
if the people are so mad as to submit to the former
course, then enjoy once more the same régime and
prevent anyone from saying what he wishes in
defence of his country. For we should deserve to
suffer not only this but even a worse fate if we let
ourselves get into your power and sullied by a

---

8 καὶ R : om. L in lacuna of 5 letters.

9 λέγειν ὁ. β. τις L : ὁ. β. τις λέγειν R.

10 After πατρίδος L has a lacuna of 15 letters ; the other
MSS. supply καὶ εἰ δίκαια ταῦτα δόξωσιν.

21

ῥυπαίνοντες αἰσχρῷ βίῳ τὰς ἑαυτῶν τε καὶ τῶν προγόνων ἀρετάς."

VI. "Ἔτι δ' αὐτοῦ λέγοντος οἱ δέκα περιίστανται κεκραγότες καὶ τὴν δημαρχικὴν ἐπανασείοντες ἐξουσίαν καὶ ῥίψειν αὐτὸν ἀπειλοῦντες κατὰ τῆς πέτρας, εἰ μὴ σιωπήσει. ἐφ' ᾧ πάντες ἀνέκραγον ὡς καταλυομένης σφῶν τῆς ἐλευθερίας, καὶ μεστὸν ἦν ἀγανακτήσεώς τε καὶ θορύβου τὸ συνέδριον. 2 τοῖς μέντοι δέκα μετέμελεν εὐθέως τῆς τε κωλύσεως τοῦ λέγειν καὶ τῆς ἀπειλῆς, ὡς ἠρεθισμένην εἶδον ἐπὶ τῷ πράγματι τὴν βουλήν· ἔπειτα προελθὼν[1] ἐξ αὐτῶν Ἄππιος καὶ δεηθεὶς τῶν θορυβούντων βραχὺν ἐπισχεῖν[2] χρόνον, ἐπειδὴ κατέστειλε τὸ ταραττόμενον αὐτῶν· " Οὐδένα ὑμῶν," εἶπεν, " ἀποστεροῦμεν, ὦ ἄνδρες βουλευταί, λόγου, ὃς ἂν ἐν τῷ προσήκοντι καιρῷ λέγῃ, τοὺς δ' ἐπι- 3 πολάζοντας καὶ πρὶν ἢ κληθῆναι προεξανισταμένους εἴργομεν. μηδὲν οὖν ἀγανακτεῖτε· καὶ γὰρ Ὁρατίῳ καὶ Οὐαλερίῳ καὶ παντὶ ἄλλῳ γνώμην ἀγορεύειν ἐν τῷ ἑαυτοῦ τόπῳ κατὰ τὸν ἀρχαῖον ἐθισμὸν καὶ κόσμον ἀποδώσομεν, ἐάν γε περὶ ὧν βουλευσόμενοι συνεληλύθατε, περὶ τού- 4 των λέγωσι καὶ μηδὲν ἔξω· ἐὰν δὲ δημαγωγῶσιν ὑμᾶς καὶ διαστασιάζωσι τὴν πόλιν τὰ μὴ πρὸς τὸ πρᾶγμα δημηγοροῦντες, οὐδενί ποτε[3]· τὴν δ'[4] ἐξουσίαν τοῦ κωλύειν τοὺς ἀκοσμοῦντας, ὦ Μάρκε Ὁράτιε, παρὰ τοῦ δήμου λαβόντες ἔχομεν, ὅτε ἡμῖν καὶ τὴν τῶν ὑπάτων καὶ τὴν τῶν δημάρ-

---

[1] Portus : προσελθὼν O, Jacoby.
[2] ἐπισχεῖν L : ἐπισχὼν R.
[3] οὐδενί ποτε Post, οὐδέποτε Cary : οὐδὲν τότε O, Jacoby but in clauses like this Dionysius regularly places τότε first.
[4] δὲ LV : om. R.

disgraceful life both our own virtues and those of our ancestors."

VI. While he was still speaking,[1] the decemvirs surrounded him, crying out, menacing him with the tribunician power, and threatening to throw him down from the rock [2] if he would not be silent. Upon which all cried out, feeling that their liberty was being taken away ; and the senate-chamber was full of indignation and turmoil. However, the decemvirs, when they saw that the senators were exasperated at their behaviour, repented promptly both of their having refused permission to speak and of their threat. Then Appius, coming forward, asked those who were creating a disturbance to have patience a moment ; and having quieted their disorder, he said : " Not one of you, senators, do we deprive of the privilege of speaking, provided he speaks at the proper time ; but we do restrain those who are too forward and rise up before they are called upon. Be not, therefore, offended. For we shall give leave, not only to Horatius and Valerius, but also to every other senator, to deliver his opinion in his turn according to the ancient custom and decorum, provided they speak about the matters which you have assembled to consider and about no extraneous subject ; but if they endeavour to seduce you by popular harangues and to divide the commonwealth by speaking of matters that are not to the point, then to none of them ever. As for the power to restrain the disorderly, Marcus Horatius, we do possess it, having received it from the people when they voted to us both the magistracy of the consuls

---

[1] For chap. 6 *cf.* Livy iii. 40, 1.
[2] The Tarpeian Rock.

χων ἀρχὴν ἐψηφίσαντο, καὶ ὁ χρόνος αὐτῆς οὔπω
5 παρελήλυθεν, ὥσπερ σοι δοκεῖ. οὐ γὰρ εἰς ἐνιαυτὸν ἀπεδείχθημεν οὐδ' εἰς ἄλλον τινὰ χρόνον
ὡρισμένον, ἀλλ' ἕως ἂν καταστησώμεθα πᾶσαν
τὴν νομοθεσίαν. συντελέσαντες οὖν ὅσα κατὰ
νοῦν[1] ἔχομεν καὶ κυρώσαντες τοὺς λοιποὺς νόμους,
τότ' ἀποθησόμεθα τὴν ἀρχὴν καὶ λόγον τῶν πεπραγμένων τοῖς βουλομένοις ὑμῶν ὑφέξομεν. τέως
δ' οὐδὲν ἐλαττώσομεν οὔτε τῆς ὑπατικῆς ἐξουσίας
6 οὔτε[2] τῆς δημαρχικῆς. περὶ δὲ τοῦ πολέμου, τίνα
χρὴ τρόπον ὡς τάχιστα καὶ κάλλιστα τοὺς ἐχθροὺς
ἀμύνασθαι, γνώμας ἀξιῶ παριόντας ὑμᾶς λέγειν,
πρώτους[3] μέν, ὥσπερ ἐστὶ σύνηθες καὶ πρέπον
ὑμῖν, τοὺς πρεσβυτέρους, ἔπειτα τοὺς μέσους,
τελευταίους δὲ τοὺς νεωτάτους."

VII. Ταῦτ' εἰπὼν πρῶτον μὲν ἐκάλει τὸν ἑαυτοῦ
θεῖον Γάιον Κλαύδιον. ὁ δ' ἀναστὰς τοιαύτην δι-
έθετο δημηγορίαν·

" Ἐπειδή με πρῶτον γνώμην ἀποφαίνεσθαι ἀξιοῖ
Ἄππιος, ὦ βουλή, τιμῶν διὰ τὸ[4] συγγενές, ὥσπερ
αὐτῷ προσήκει, καὶ δεῖ με ἃ φρονῶ περὶ τοῦ
πολέμου τοῦ πρὸς Αἰκανοὺς καὶ Σαβίνους εἰπεῖν,
πρὶν ἀποδείξασθαι τὴν ἐμαυτοῦ διάνοιαν, ἐκεῖνο
βουλοίμην ἂν ὑμᾶς ἐξετάσαι, τίσιν ἐπαρθέντες
ἐλπίσιν Αἰκανοὶ καὶ Σαβῖνοι πόλεμον ἐπενεγκεῖν
ἐτόλμησαν ἡμῖν καὶ τὴν χώραν ἐπιόντες λεηλατεῖν,
οἳ τέως ἀγαπῶντες καὶ τοῖς θεοῖς πολλὴν χάριν
εἰδότες εἴ τις αὐτοὺς εἴα τὴν ἑαυτῶν ἔχειν ἀσφαλῶς.
ἐὰν γὰρ τοῦτο μάθητε, καὶ τὴν ἀπαλλαγὴν τοῦ
πολέμου τοῦ πρὸς αὐτοὺς ἥτις ἔσται κρατίστη

---

[1] κατὰ νοῦν O : ἐν νῷ Cobet.
[2] οὔτε ... οὔτε Cary : οὐδὲ ... οὐδὲ O, Jacoby.

and that of the tribunes ; and the term of it has not yet expired, as you think. For we were not appointed for a year or for any other definite period, but until we should have instituted the whole body of laws. When, therefore, we have completed what we propose and have got the remaining laws ratified, we shall then resign our magistracy and give an account of our actions to any of you who desire it. In the meantime we shall relax nothing either of the consular or of the tribunician power. As to the war, now, in what manner we may repulse our enemies most quickly and gloriously, I ask you to come forward and deliver your opinions—first the oldest members, as is customary and fitting for you, next those of a middle age, and last the youngest."

VII. Having said this, he proceeded to call first upon his uncle, Gaius Claudius, who, rising up, delivered a speech about as follows [1] :

" Since Appius desires me to deliver my opinion first, senators, showing me this honour because of our relationship, as becomes him, and since I must say what I think concerning the war with the Aequians and the Sabines, I should like, before declaring my own sentiments, to have you inquire what hopes have encouraged the Aequians and Sabines to venture to make war upon us and to invade and lay waste our country, nations which till now were quite satisfied and most grateful to Heaven if they were permitted to enjoy their own land in security. For if you once know what those hopes are, you will also know what means of deliverance from war with these

---

[1] For chaps. 7–15 *cf.* Livy iii. 40, 2-6.

[3] πρώτους L : πρῶτον R.
[4] διὰ τὸ O : τὸ or δὴ τὸ Reiske.

2 μαθήσεσθε. ἐκεῖνοι τοίνυν ἀκούσαντες ὅτι σεσά-
λευται καὶ νοσεῖ τὸ πάτριον ἡμῶν πολίτευμα ἐκ
πολλοῦ καὶ τοῖς προεστηκόσι τῶν κοινῶν οὔτε
ὁ δῆμος εὔνους ἐστὶν οὔτε οἱ πατρίκιοι, καὶ οὐ
μάτην ἀκούοντες[1] (τὸ γὰρ ἀληθὲς οὕτως ἔχει, τὰς
δ' αἰτίας ἐπισταμένοις ὑμῖν οὐδὲν δέομαι λέγειν)
ὑπέλαβον, εἴ τις ἔξωθεν ἡμᾶς κατάσχοι πόλεμος
ἅμα τοῖς ἐντὸς τείχους κακοῖς, καὶ δόξειε ταῖς
ἀρχαῖς δύναμιν ἐξάγειν τὴν προπολεμήσουσαν[2] τῆς
γῆς, οὔτε τοὺς πολίτας ἐπὶ τὸν στρατιωτικὸν ὅρκον
ἅπαντας ἥξειν[3] ἐκ προθυμίας ὡς πρότερον, ἀπεχθῶς
διακειμένους πρὸς τὰς ἀρχάς, οὔτε τοὺς ἡγεμόνας
ταῖς ἐκ τῶν νόμων τιμωρίαις χρήσεσθαι[4] κατὰ
τῶν μὴ παραγενομένων, δεδοικότας μή τι μεῖζον
ἐργάσωνται κακόν, τούς τε ὑπακούσαντας καὶ τὰ
ὅπλα λαβόντας ἢ καταλείψειν τὰ σημεῖα ἢ παρα-
3 μένοντας ἐθελοκακήσειν ἐν τοῖς ἀγῶσιν. ὧν οὐδὲν
ἔξω τοῦ εἰκότος ἤλπισαν· ὅταν μὲν γὰρ ὁμονοοῦσα
πόλις ἅπτηται πολέμου, καὶ τὸ αὐτὸ συμφέρον
ἅπασι φαίνηται τοῖς τ' ἄρχουσι καὶ τοῖς ἀρχο-
μένοις, μετὰ προθυμίας ἅπαντες ἐπὶ τὰ δεινὰ
χωροῦσι καὶ οὔτε πόνον οὔτε κίνδυνον οὐδένα
4 ὀκνοῦσιν· ὅταν δὲ νοσοῦσα ἐν αὐτῇ,[5] πρὶν ἢ τὰ
ἔνδον καταστήσασθαι, τοῖς ὑπαιθρίοις ὁμόσε χωρῇ
πολεμίοις,[6] καὶ παραστῇ τῷ μὲν πλήθει λογισμὸς
ὅτι οὐχ ὑπὲρ οἰκείων ἀγαθῶν κακοπαθοῦσιν ἀλλ'
ἵνα βεβαιότερον αὐτῶν ἕτεροι ἄρχωσι, τοῖς δ'
ἡγεμόσιν ὅτι πολέμιον ἔχουσιν οὐχ ἧττον τοῦ
ἀντιπάλου τὸ οἰκεῖον, νοσεῖ τὰ ὅλα καὶ πᾶσα

---

[1] ἀκούοντες O : ἀκούσαντες Reiske, Jacoby.
[2] προπολεμήσασαν LV.   [3] ἕξειν LVM.
[4] χρήσασθαι LV.   [5] αὐτῇ O.   [6] Sylburg : πολέμοις LV.

nations will be most effectual. Well, then, when they heard that our time-honoured constitution has for a long time been shaken and is diseased and that neither the populace nor the patricians are well disposed toward those who are at the head of the commonwealth—and this they heard not without reason, since it is the truth, though I have no need to state the causes to you who are well acquainted with them—they assumed that if any foreign war should come upon us in addition to these domestic evils and the magistrates should resolve to march out with an army in defence of the country, neither the citizens would all present themselves cheerfully, as before, to take the military oath, because of their hostility to the magistrates, nor would these inflict the punishments ordained by law upon those who did not present themselves, lest they should occasion some greater mischief ; and that those who did obey and take up arms would either desert the standards or, if they remained, would deliberately play the coward in battle. And none of these hopes was ill grounded ; for when a harmonious state undertakes a war and all, both rulers and ruled, look upon their interests as identical, all go to meet the perils with alacrity and decline no toil or danger ; but when a state which suffers from sickness within itself engages with its enemies outside before composing its internal disorders, and the rank and file stop to consider that they are undergoing hardships, not for their own advantage, but to strengthen the domination of others over them, and the generals reflect that their own army is no less hostile to them than

27

DIONYSIUS OF HALICARNASSUS

ἱκανὴ δύναμις τὰ τοιαῦτα στρατεύματα κατα-
γωνίσασθαι καὶ φθεῖραι.

VIII. '' Ταῦτ' ἐστίν, ὦ βουλή, τὰ Σαβίνων τε
καὶ Αἰκανῶν ἐνθυμήματα, οἷς πεπιστευκότες
ἐμβεβλήκασιν ἡμῶν εἰς τὴν γῆν. ἐὰν μὲν οὖν
ἀγανακτήσαντες τῷ καταφρονεῖσθαι πρὸς αὐτῶν
ἐπαρθέντων ὡς ἔχομεν ὀργῆς δύναμιν ἐξαγαγεῖν
ἐπ' αὐτοὺς ψηφισώμεθα, δέδοικα μὴ ταῦθ' ἡμῖν ἃ
προὔλαβον ἐκεῖνοι[1] συμβῇ, μᾶλλον δ' εὖ οἶδα συμ-
2 βησόμενα. ἐὰν δὲ τὰ πρῶτα καὶ ἀναγκαιότατα[2]
καταστησώμεθα—ταῦτα δ' ἐστὶν ἥ τ' εὐκοσμία τοῦ
πλήθους καὶ τὸ πᾶσι ταὐτὰ συμφέροντα φαίνε-
σθαι—ἐξελάσαντες μὲν ἐκ τῆς πόλεως τὴν νῦν
ἐπιχωριάζουσαν ὕβριν καὶ πλεονεξίαν, ἀποδόντες
δὲ τὸ ἀρχαῖον σχῆμα τῇ πολιτείᾳ, πτήξαντες οἱ
νῦν θρασεῖς καὶ τὰ ὅπλα ῥίψαντες ἐκ τῶν χειρῶν
ἥξουσιν ὡς ἡμᾶς οὐκ εἰς μακρὰν τάς τε βλάβας
. . . θούμενοι[3] καὶ περὶ διαλλαγῶν διαλεξόμενοι,
ὑπάρξει τε[4] ἡμῖν ὃ πάντες ἂν εὔξαιντο οἱ νοῦν[5]
ἔχοντες, χωρὶς ὅπλων διαπεπολεμηκέναι τὸν πρὸς
3 αὐτοὺς πόλεμον. ταῦτα δὴ λογισαμένους ἡμᾶς
οἴομαι δεῖν τὴν μὲν ὑπὲρ τοῦ πολέμου βουλήν,
ἐπειδὴ ταραχωδῶς ἡμῖν ἔχει τὰ ἐντὸς τείχους,
ἐᾶσαι κατὰ τὸ παρόν, ὑπὲρ ὁμονοίας δὲ καὶ κόσμου
πολιτικοῦ προθεῖναι τῷ βουλομένῳ λέγειν. οὐ
γὰρ ἐξεγένετο ἡμῖν, πρὶν εἰς τοῦτο καταστῆσαι

---

[1] ἐκείνοις LV.
[2] τἀναγκαιότατα Jacoby.
[3] . . . θούμενοι L, ὠθούμενοι R : οἰσόμενοι or λυσόμενοι Sylburg, ὠνούμενοι Portus, διορθούμενοι Reiske, ἐπανορθούμενοι
Kiessling, ἐξακούμενοι Cobet, καθαρούμενοι Post, ἀπολογιού-
μενοι Warmington. A future participle is wanted.
[4] τὰς LV.

is the foe, everything is diseased and any force is sufficient to defeat and destroy such armies.

VIII. " These, senators, are the reasonings of both the Sabines and the Aequians, and because they believed them to be valid, they have invaded our territory. So if we, showing our resentment at being scorned by them in their exalted state of mind, vote in our present wrathful state to lead out an army against them, I fear that all they anticipated may happen to us, or rather, I know full well that it will come to pass. But if we establish the conditions that are of primary importance and most necessary—and these are good order on the part of the multitude and the recognition by all citizens that their interests are identical—by banishing from the state the insolence and greed which are now the fashion and by restoring the constitution to its ancient form, these enemies who are now so bold will cower and, hurling their weapons from their hands, will soon come to us to make amends [1] for the injuries they have caused and to treat for peace, and we shall have it in our power—a thing which all men of sense would wish—to have put an end to the war without resorting to arms. In view of these considerations I believe we ought to defer the consideration of the war for the present, since our affairs within the city's walls are in a turbulent state, and, instead, give leave to everyone who so desires to speak in favour of harmony and good order among our citizens. For we never had the opportunity, until the war brought us to this pass, of deciding in

---

[1] The verb is uncertain, only the final letters being preserved in the MSS.

---

[5] νοῦν Steph. : νῦν O.

DIONYSIUS OF HALICARNASSUS

τὸν πόλεμον,[1] ὑπὸ τῆσδε τῆς ἀρχῆς κληθεῖσι[2]
περὶ τῶν ἐν τῇ πόλει πραγμάτων[3] εἴ τι μὴ καλῶς
4 εἶχε[4] τῶν γιγνομένων διαγνῶναι· πολλῆς γὰρ ἂν
ἐπιτιμήσεως ἄξιος ἦν εἴ τις ἐκείνου[5] ἀφεὶς τὸν
καιρὸν ἐν τούτῳ[6] λέγειν ὑπὲρ αὐτῶν[7] ἠξίου· οὐδ'
ἂν ἔχοι τις εἰπεῖν βεβαίως ὅτι τοῦτον ὑπερβαλό-
μενοι τὸν καιρὸν ὡς οὐκ ἐπιτήδειον ἑτέρου δυνη-
σόμεθα τυχεῖν ἐπιτηδειοτέρου. εἰ γὰρ ἐκ τῶν
γεγονότων τὰ μέλλοντα ἔσεσθαι βούλεταί τις
εἰκάζειν, πολὺς ὁ μετὰ τοῦτον ἔσται χρόνος ἐν
ᾧ περὶ οὐδενὸς τῶν κοινῶν συνελευσόμεθα βουλευσόμενοι.

IX. " Ἀξιῶ δ' ὑμᾶς, Ἄππιε, τοὺς προεστηκότας τῆς πόλεως καὶ τὸ κοινὸν ἁπάντων συμφέρον[8] οὐχὶ τὸ ὑμῖν αὐτοῖς ἰδίᾳ λυσιτελοῦν ὀφεί-
λοντας σκοπεῖν, ἐάν τι τῶν ἀληθῶν μετὰ παρρησίας
ἀλλὰ μὴ καθ' ἡδονὰς τὰς ὑμετέρας λέγω, μή μοι
διὰ τοῦτ' ἀπεχθάνεσθαι,[9] ἐνθυμουμένους ὅτι οὐκ
ἐπὶ λοιδορίᾳ καὶ προπηλακισμῷ τῆς ἀρχῆς ὑμῶν
ποιήσομαι τοὺς λόγους, ἀλλ' ἵνα δείξας ἐν οἵῳ
κλύδωνι τὰ πράγματα σαλεύει τῆς πόλεως, τὴν
σωτηρίαν καὶ ἐπανόρθωσιν αὐτῶν ἥτις ἔσται

[1] εἰς τοῦτο καταστῆσαι τὸν πόλεμον L : εἰς τοῦτο καταστήσαιντο πόλεμον V, εἰς τοῦτο καταστήσαιντο περὶ πολέμων M,
εἰς τοῦτον καταστῆναι τὸν πόλεμον Reiske.
[2] κληθεῖσι V : κληθεῖσι σκοπεῖν R.
[3] After πραγμάτων M adds οὕτως ἐχόντων καί.
[4] εἶχε V : ἔχει R.   [5] τοῦτον Reiske.
[6] ἐκείνῳ Reiske. But with his τοῦτον just above, ἑτέρῳ
would have been better ; see note on translation.
[7] αὐτῶν O : ἄλλων Sylburg, following Lapus.
[8] ἁπάντων συμφέρον (cf. chap. 9, 2 f.) Sylburg : ἀπὸ τῶν
συμφερόντων O, Jacoby.
[9] Steph. : ἀπεχθάνεσθε O, ἀπέχθεσθαι Kiessling, ἄχθεσθαι
Vassis.

30

a meeting called by this government about the business of the commonwealth, whether any of the measures being taken were unsatisfactory. For, had there been such an opportunity, great censure would be deserved by anyone who had neglected that occasion and only at this time saw fit to talk about these matters.[1] Nor could anyone say for certain that, if we let this opportunity pass as unsuitable, we shall be able to find one that is more suitable. For if one cares to judge the future by the past, it will be a long time before we meet again to consider any matter of the public business.

IX. " I ask this, Appius, of you men who are at the head of the commonwealth and are in duty bound to consult the common interest of all rather than your private advantage, that if I speak some truths with frankness instead of trying to please you, you will not be offended on that account, when you consider that I shall not make my remarks with any intent to abuse and insult your magistracy, but in order to show in how great a sea the affairs of the commonwealth are tossed and to point out what will be both their safety and their reformation. It

---

[1] This seems to be the meaning of the text given by the MSS., but the words " had there been such an opportunity " and " only " are merely implied in the Greek. Lapus, followed by Sylburg and others, not appreciating this ellipsis, and wishing to avoid a sentence inconsistent with what has just preceded, proposed to read " about other matters " in place of " about these matters." Reiske interchanged " that " and " this " occasion ; but it is difficult to see what " on that occasion " would mean following the neglect of " this " occasion. He might better have proposed " who, neglecting this occasion, should see fit on another occasion," thus paralleling the idea expressed in the next sentence.

2 φράσω. ἅπασι μὲν γὰρ ἴσως ὅσοις τῇ πατρίδι
. . . δωσιν[1] ἀναγκαῖός ἐστιν ὁ περὶ τῶν κοινῇ
συμφερόντων λόγος, μάλιστα δ' ἐμοί. πρῶτον
μὲν γὰρ ὅτι γνώμης ἄρχειν[2] ἠξίωμαι διὰ τιμήν·
αἰσχύνη δὲ καὶ μωρία πολλὴ πρῶτον ἀναστάντα
μὴ οὐχ ἃ δεῖ πρῶτον ἐπανορθώσασθαι λέγειν.
ἔπειθ' ὅτι συμβέβηκεν ὄντι θείῳ πρὸς πατρὸς
Ἀππίου τοῦ προεστηκότος τῆς δεκαδαρχίας ἥδε-
σθαί τε πάντων μάλιστα ὅταν[3] εὖ τὰ κοινὰ ὑπ'
αὐτῶν ἐπιτροπεύηται, καὶ ἀνιᾶσθαι παντὸς[4] ὅτου-
3 δήτινος μᾶλλον ὅταν μὴ καλῶς. πρὸς δὲ τούτοις
ὅτι ταύτην[5] πολιτείας διαδέδεγμαι[6] προαίρεσιν ἐκ
προγόνων τὰ κοινὰ συμφέροντα πρὸ τῶν οἰκείων
λυσιτελῶν αἱρεῖσθαι καὶ μηδένα κίνδυνον ἴδιον
ὑπολογίζεσθαι, ἣν οὐκ ἂν προδοίην ἑκὼν εἶναι[7]
καὶ οὐκ ἂν καταισχύναιμι τὰς ἐκείνων τῶν ἀνδρῶν
4 ἀρετάς. περὶ μὲν οὖν τῆς καθεστώσης πολιτείας,
ὅτι πονηρῶς ἡμῖν ἔχει καὶ δυσχεραίνουσιν ὀλίγου
δεῖν πάντες αὐτῇ, μέγιστον ὑμῖν γενέσθω τεκμήριον,[8] ὃ μόνον οὐδ' ἀγνοεῖν ἔξεστιν ὑμῖν, ὅτι
φεύγουσιν ἐκ τῆς πόλεως ὁσημέραι καταλιπόντες
τὰς πατρῴας ἑστίας οἱ χαριέστατοι τῶν δημοτικῶν,
οἱ μὲν εἰς τὰς πλησιοχώρους πόλεις ἅμα γυναιξὶ
καὶ τέκνοις μετατιθέμενοι τὰς οἰκήσεις, οἱ δ' εἰς
τοὺς πλεῖστον ἀπέχοντας τῆς πόλεως ἀγρούς· καὶ

---

[1] τῇ πατρίδι σώσειν L, τῇ πατρίδι δώσιν V, τῇ πατρίδι μέλει
τοῦ καλῶς ἔχειν R, ὅσοις σὺν τῇ πατρίδι μέλει τοῦ καλῶς
ἑαυτοὺς ἔχειν Reiske.   [2] ἄρχειν VM : ἄρξειν L.
[3] μάλιστα ὅταν Sylburg : ὅταν μάλιστα O.
[4] Sylburg : πάντως O.
[5] ταύτην (or τοιαύτην) added by Sylburg.
[6] διαδέδειγμαι LV.
[7] δέ μοι ταύτην τοῦ βίου προαίρεσιν after εἶναι deleted by
Smit and Schenkl. Reiske proposed to read ⟨προσήκει⟩ δέ

is perhaps incumbent upon all who . . .[1] for the fatherland, to speak of the matters that are for the public interest, and this is true particularly in my case. First, because I have been asked, as an honour due me, to take the lead in expressing my opinion, and it would be a shame, yes a great folly, for the man who rises up first not to mention the things that need to be reformed first. In the next place, because it has fallen to me, as the paternal uncle of Appius, the chief of the decemvirs, both to be pleased more than all others when the commonwealth is well governed by them and to be grieved above anyone else when it is not so governed. Besides these motives, I have inherited it as a political principle from my ancestors to prefer the interests of the public to my own private advantages and to take thought for no personal danger, a principle that I would not willingly betray and thus dishonour the virtues of those men. As to the present form of government, that it is in a bad state and that almost everyone is dissatisfied with it, let this be the strongest proof for you, the one thing you cannot be ignorant of, that the most respectable of the plebeians are daily abandoning their ancestral hearths and fleeing out of the city, some with their wives and children removing to the neighbouring cities and others to country districts that lie farthest from Rome.

---

[1] The better MSS. have a gap here in the text which has not been satisfactorily filled either by the readings found in the inferior MSS. or by the conjectures of modern scholars.

μοι ταύτην ⟨τηρεῖν τὴν⟩ τοῦ βίου προαίρεσιν, Kiessling ⟨φυλάξω⟩ δὴ τοιαύτην τοῦ βίου προαίρεσιν.

[2] πάντες οἱ τὰ κοινὰ διοικοῦντες after τεκμήριον deleted by Jacoby. Kiessling placed these words after ὀλίγου δεῖν.

οὐδὲ τῶν πατρικίων πολλοὶ τὰς[1] κατ' ἄστυ
ποιοῦνται διατριβὰς ὡς πρότερον, ἀλλὰ καὶ τούτων
5 οἱ πλείους τὸν βίον ἔχουσιν[2] ἐν τοῖς ἀγροῖς. καὶ
τί δεῖ περὶ τῶν ἄλλων λέγειν, ὅτε[3] καὶ τῶν βουλευτῶν ὀλίγοι μέν τινες οἱ κατὰ συγγένειαν ἢ
φιλίαν προσήκοντες ὑμῖν ὑπομένουσιν ἐντὸς τείχους, οἱ δ' ἄλλοι τὴν ἐρημίαν ποθεινοτέραν ἡγοῦνται
τῆς πατρίδος; ὅτε γοῦν ἐδέησεν ὑμῖν καλέσαι
τὴν[4] βουλήν, ἐκ τῶν ἀγρῶν καθ' ἕνα καλούμενοι
συνῆλθον, οἷς πάτριον ἦν ἅμα ταῖς ἀρχαῖς διὰ
φυλακῆς ἔχειν τὴν πατρίδα καὶ μηδενὸς ἀπολεί-
6 πεσθαι τῶν κοινῶν. ἆρ' οὖν τἀγαθὰ φεύγοντας
ὑπολαμβάνετε ἀνθρώπους καταλιπεῖν τὰς ἑαυτῶν
πατρίδας ἢ τὰ κακά; ἐγὼ μὲν γὰρ οἴομαι τὰ
κακά. καίτοι τίνος ἔλαττον οἴεσθ' εἶναι κακὸν
πόλει, καὶ ταῦτα τῇ Ῥωμαίων, ᾗ πολλῶν οἰκείων
δεῖ σωμάτων εἰ μέλλει βεβαίως καθέξειν τὴν τῶν
προσοίκων ἀρχήν, τὸ καταλείπεσθαι μὲν ὑπὸ τῶν
δημοτικῶν, ἐρημοῦσθαι δ' ὑπὸ τῶν πατρικίων,
οὔτε πολέμου κατασχόντος αὐτὴν οὔτε νόσου λοι-
μικῆς οὔτ' ἄλλης θεηλάτου συμφορᾶς οὐδεμιᾶς;

X. '' Βούλεσθε οὖν ἀκοῦσαι τίνες εἰσὶν αἱ βια-
ζόμεναι τοὺς ἀνθρώπους καταλιπεῖν αἰτίαι ἱερὰ
καὶ τάφους προγόνων καὶ ἐξερημοῦν ἐφέστια καὶ
κτήσεις πατέρων καὶ πᾶσαν ἡγεῖσθαι γῆν ἀναγ-
καιοτέραν τῆς πατρίδος; οὐ γὰρ ἄτερ αἰτίας ταῦθ'
οὕτως ἔχει. ἐγὼ δὴ φράσω πρὸς ὑμᾶς καὶ οὐκ
2 ἀποκρύψομαι. κατηγορίαι γίνονται τῆς ἀρχῆς

---

[1] τὰς placed before διατριβὰς by Cobet.
[2] ἄγουσιν (or διάγουσιν) Grasberger.
[3] Sylburg : ὅτι O.   [4] τὴν om. LV.

And even of the patricians not many continue to reside in the city as they formerly did, but the greater part of these also are living in the country. Yet why should I speak of the others when only a few even of the senators, and those such as are attached to you either by relationship or friendship, remain within the walls, while the rest regard solitude as more desirable than their native city? At any rate, when you found it necessary to assemble the senate, the members came together only when summoned from their country seats one by one— these men with whom it was a time-honoured custom to keep watch over the fatherland in conjunction with the magistrates and to shirk none of the public business. Do you imagine, then, that it is to flee from their blessings or rather from their evils that men abandon their native lands? For my part, I think it is from their evils. And yet what greater evil do you think there is for a commonwealth, particularly for that of the Romans, which needs many troops of its own nationals if it is to maintain firmly its sovereignty over its neighbours, than to be abandoned by the plebeians and deserted by the patricians, when oppressed neither by war, pestilence nor any other calamity inflicted by the hand of Heaven?

X. " Do you wish, then, to hear the reasons that are compelling these men to abandon temples and sepulchres of their ancestors, to desert hearths and possessions of their fathers, and to look upon every land as dearer to them than their own? For these things are not taking place without reason. Well, then, I will inform you and conceal nothing. Many charges are being brought against the magistracy

35

ὑμῶν, Ἄππιε, πολλαὶ καὶ παρὰ πολλῶν· εἰ μὲν
ἀληθεῖς ἢ ψευδεῖς οὐδὲν δέομαι ζητεῖν ἐν τῷ
παρόντι, γίνονται δ᾽ οὖν ὅμως. οὐδεὶς δ᾽, ὡς
εἰπεῖν,[1] ἔξω τῶν ὑμετέρων ἑταίρων οἰκείως τοῖς
παροῦσιν ἔχει πράγμασιν. οἱ μέν γ᾽ ἀγαθοὶ καὶ
ἐξ ἀγαθῶν, οἷς προσῆκεν ἱερᾶσθαί τε καὶ ἄρχειν
καὶ τὰς ἄλλας καρποῦσθαι τιμὰς ἃς οἱ πατέρες
αὐτῶν ἐκαρποῦντο, ἄχθονται τούτων ἀπελαυνό-
μενοι δι᾽ ὑμᾶς τὰς προγονικὰς ἀξιώσεις ἀπολωλε-
3 κότες. οἱ δὲ τὴν διὰ μέσου τάξιν ἔχοντες ἐν τῇ
πόλει καὶ τὴν ἀπράγμονα διώκοντες ἡσυχίαν χρημάτων τ᾽ ἀδίκους ἁρπαγὰς ἐγκαλοῦσιν ὑμῖν καὶ
προπηλακισμοὺς εἰς γαμετὰς ὀδύρονται γυναῖκας
καὶ παροινίας εἰς θυγατέρας ἐπιγάμους καὶ ἄλλας
4 ὕβρεις πολλὰς καὶ χαλεπάς. τὸ δὲ πενέστατον
τοῦ δημοτικοῦ μέρος, οὔτ᾽ ἀρχαιρεσιῶν ἔτι κύριον
γινόμενον[2] οὔτε ψηφοφοριῶν οὔτ᾽ εἰς ἐκκλησίας
καλούμενον οὔτ᾽ ἄλλης πολιτικῆς φιλανθρωπίας
μεταλαμβάνον οὐδεμιᾶς, διὰ ταῦτα πάνθ᾽ ὑμᾶς
μισεῖ καὶ τυραννίδα καλεῖ τὴν ἀρχήν.

XI. '' Πῶς οὖν ἐπανορθώσετε ταῦτα καὶ παύ-
σεσθε δι᾽ αἰτίας παρὰ τοῖς πολίταις ὄντες; τοῦτο
γὰρ ἔσθ᾽[3] ὑπόλοιπον εἰπεῖν. εἰ προβούλευμα τοῦ
συνεδρίου ποιήσαντες ἀποδοίητε τῷ δήμῳ διαγνῶναι πότερον αὐτῷ δοκεῖ πάλιν ὑπάτους τ᾽
ἀποδεικνύναι καὶ δημάρχους καὶ τὰς ἄλλας ἀρχὰς
τὰς πατρίους ἢ μένειν ἐπὶ τῆς αὐτῆς πολιτείας.
2 ἐάν τε γὰρ ἀγαπῶσι Ῥωμαῖοι πάντες ὀλιγαρχού-
μενοι καὶ μένειν ὑμᾶς ἐπὶ τῆς αὐτῆς ἐξουσίας

---

[1] οὐδεὶς δ᾽ ὡς εἰπεῖν Casaubon, οὐδ᾽ ἐστὶν εἰπεῖν Reiske : οὐδὲν
εἰπεῖν O.   [2] Reiske : γενόμενον O.
[3] ἔθ᾽ Kiessling.

of you decemvirs, Appius, and by many people. Whether they are true or false I do not care to inquire at present, but at any rate they are being brought. And not a man, I may say, outside of your own partisans is well disposed toward the present state of affairs. For the men of worth, descended from men of worth, who ought to hold the priest-hoods and the magistracies and to enjoy the other honours which were enjoyed by their fathers, are in-dignant when they are excluded from these by you and thus have lost the dignities of their ancestors. The men of middle rank in the state, who pursue a life of tranquillity free from public duties, accuse you of snatching away their property unjustly and lament the insults you offer to their wedded wives, your drunken licentiousness toward their marriageable daughters, and many other grievous abuses. And the poorest part of the populace, who have no longer the power either of choosing magistrates or of giving their votes upon other occasions, who are not summoned to assemblies and do not share in any other political courtesy, hate you upon all these accounts and call your government a tyranny.

XI. " How, then, shall you reform these matters and cease being the object of accusations among your fellow citizens ? For this remains to be discussed. You can do so if you will procure a preliminary decree of the senate and restore to the people the right of deciding whether they prefer to appoint consuls, tribunes and the other traditional magis-trates once more or to continue under the same form of government as at present. For if all the Romans are content to be governed by an oligarchy and vote that you shall continue in possession of the

37

ψηφίσωνται, κατὰ νόμον ἕξετε καὶ οὐ βίᾳ τὴν
ἀρχήν· ἐάν τε ὑπάτους πάλιν αἱρεῖσθαι βουληθῶσι
καὶ τὰς ἄλλας ἀρχὰς ὡς πρότερον, ἀποθήσεσθε
νόμῳ τὴν ἐξουσίαν καὶ οὐ δόξετε ἀκόντων ἄρχειν
τῶν ἴσων· τοῦτο μὲν γὰρ τυραννικόν, τὸ δὲ παρ'
ἑκόντων τὰς ἀρχὰς λαμβάνειν ἀριστοκρατικόν.
3 τοῦ δὲ πολιτεύματος τούτου πρῶτον οἴομαι δεῖν
ἄρξαι σὲ καὶ παῦσαι τὴν ὑπὸ σοῦ κατασταθεῖσαν
ὀλιγαρχίαν, Ἄππιε, λυσιτελῆ γέ[1] ποθ' ἡμῖν γενομένην,[2] νῦν δ' ἐπαχθῆ. ἃ δ' ἐκ τοῦ πεισθῆναί μοι
καὶ ἀποθέσθαι τὴν ἐπίφθονον ἐξουσίαν ταύτην
4 κερδανεῖς, ἄκουσον. ἐὰν μὲν ὅλον ὑμῶν τὸ ἀρχεῖον
ἐπὶ τῆς αὐτῆς γένηται προαιρέσεως, διὰ σὲ πάντες
ὑπολήψονται τὸν ἄρξαντα καὶ τούτους γεγενῆσθαι
χρηστούς· ἐὰν δ' οὗτοι φιλοχωρῶσιν ἐπὶ τῇ παρα-
νόμῳ δυναστείᾳ, σοὶ μὲν ἅπαντες εἴσονται τὴν
χάριν ὅτι μόνος ἐβουλήθης δίκαια ποιεῖν, τοὺς δὲ
μὴ θέλοντας σὺν αἰσχύνῃ καὶ μεγάλῃ βλάβῃ
5 παύσουσι τῆς ἀρχῆς. ὁμολογίας δὲ καὶ πίστεις
ἀπορρήτους εἴ τινας ἀλλήλοις δεδώκατε θεοὺς
ἐγγυητὰς ποιησάμενοι—τάχα γάρ τι καὶ τοιοῦτον
ὑμῖν πέπρακται—φυλαττομένας μὲν[3] ἀνοσίους εἶναι
νόμιζε ὡς κατὰ πολιτῶν καὶ πατρίδος, καταλυο-
μένας δ' εὐσεβεῖς. θεοὶ γὰρ ἐπὶ καλαῖς καὶ δι-
καίαις παραλαμβάνεσθαι φιλοῦσιν ὁμολογίαις, οὐκ
ἐπ' αἰσχραῖς καὶ ἀδίκοις.
XII. " Εἰ δὲ διὰ φόβον ἐχθρῶν ὀκνεῖς ἀποθέσθαι τὴν ἀρχήν, μή σοι κίνδυνοί τινες ἐξ αὐτῶν

---

[1] Reiske : τέ O.
[2] Sylburg : γενόμενον O.
[3] μὲν R : om. LV, Jacoby.

same power, you will hold your magistracy in accordance with law and not by force ; whereas, if they wish to choose consuls again and all the other magistrates as aforetime, you will resign your power in a legal manner and avoid the imputation of governing your equals without their consent. For the latter course is tyrannical, but to receive the magistracies with the consent of the governed is the mark of an aristocracy. And of this measure I think that you, Appius, ought to be the author and thus put an end to the oligarchy instituted by yourself, which was once an advantage to us but is now a grievance. Hear, now, what you will gain by following my advice and resigning this invidious power. If your whole college is actuated by the same principle, everyone will think that it is because of you who set the example that the others too have become virtuous, whereas if these others are too fond of their illegal power, all will feel grateful to you for being the only person who desired to do what was right, and they will force out of office with ignominy and great hurt those who refuse to resign it. And if you have entered into any agreements and given secret pledges to one another, invoking the gods as witnesses,—for it is possible that you may have done something even of this nature,—look upon the observance of these agreements as impious, since they were made against your fellow citizens and your country, and the breaking of them as pious. For the gods like to be called in as partners for the performance of honourable and just agreements, not of those that are shameful and unjust.

XII. " However, if it is through fear of your enemies that you hesitate to resign your magistracy,

ἐπαχθῶσι καὶ δίκας ἀναγκασθῇς ὑπέχειν τῶν
πεπραγμένων, οὐκ ὀρθῶς δέδοικας. οὐ γὰρ οὕτω
μικρόθυμος οὐδ' ἀχάριστος ἔσται ὁ Ῥωμαίων δῆμος ὥστε τῶν μὲν ἁμαρτημάτων σου μεμνῆσθαι
τῶν δ' εὐεργεσιῶν ἐπιλελῆσθαι, ἀλλ' ἀντιπαρ-
εξετάζων τὰ νῦν ἀγαθὰ τοῖς πάλαι κακοῖς ἐκεῖνα
μὲν ἡγήσεται συγγνώμης ἄξια, ταῦτα δ' ἐπαίνων.
2 ὑπάρξει δέ σοι καὶ τῶν πρὸ τῆς ὀλιγαρχίας ἔργων
πολλῶν καὶ καλῶν ὄντων ὑπομιμνήσκειν τὸν
δῆμον, καὶ τὴν ὑπὲρ ἐκείνων χάριν εἰς βοήθειαν
καὶ σωτηρίαν ἀπαιτεῖν, ἀπολογίαις τε χρῆσθαι
πρὸς τὰ κατηγορήματα πολλαῖς· τοῦτο μέν, ὡς
οὐκ αὐτὸς ἥμαρτες, ἀλλὰ τῶν ἄλλων τις ἀγνοοῦντός
σου· τοῦτο δ', ὡς οὐχ ἱκανὸς ἦσθα τὸν πράττοντα
κωλύειν ἰσότιμον ὄντα· τοῦτο δ', ὡς ἑτέρου τινὸς
ἔργου χρησίμου χάριν ἠναγκάσθης ἀβούλητόν τι
3 ὑπομεῖναι. πολὺς γὰρ ἂν εἴη ὁ[1] λόγος εἰ πάσας
ἐξαριθμεῖσθαι βουλοίμην τὰς ἀπολογίας. καὶ οἷς
μηδὲν ἀπολόγημα ὑπάρχει μήτε δίκαιον μήτ'
ἐπιεικές, ὁμολογοῦντες καὶ παραιτούμενοι πραΰ-
νουσι τὰς τῶν ἠδικημένων ὀργάς, οἱ μὲν εἰς
ἄνοιαν ἡλικίας καταφεύγοντες, οἱ δ' εἰς πονηρῶν
ἀνθρώπων ὁμιλίας, οἱ δ' εἰς μέγεθος ἀρχῆς, οἱ
δ' εἰς τὴν ἅπαντας πλανῶσαν τοὺς ἀνθρωπίνους
4 λογισμοὺς τύχην. ἐγώ σοι τῆς ἀρχῆς ἀποστάντι
ὑπισχνοῦμαι πάντων ἀμνηστίαν ὑπάρξειν τῶν
ἡμαρτημένων καὶ διαλλαγὰς πρὸς τὸν δῆμον ὡς
ἐν κακοῖς εὐπρεπεῖς.

XIII. " Ἀλλὰ δέδοικα μὴ πρόφασις μὲν οὐκ

[1] ὁ LV : om. R.

40

lest they should form some dangerous designs against you and you should be compelled to give an account of your actions, your fear is not justified. For the Roman people will be neither so mean-spirited nor so ungrateful as to remember your faults and forget your good services, but offsetting your past errors by your present merits, will look upon the former as deserving of forgiveness and the latter of praise. You will also have the opportunity of reminding the people of the many fine actions you performed before the establishment of the oligarchy, of claiming the gratitude due for these as a means to assist and save you, and of employing many lines of defence against the charges. For example, that you yourself did not commit the wrong, but one of the others without your knowledge ; or that you had no power to restrain the person who did the deed, since he was of equal authority with yourself ; or, again, that you were forced to submit to something undesirable for the sake of something else which was useful. Indeed, it would be a long story if I chose to enumerate all the lines of defence open to you. And even those who can make no defence that is either just or plausible, by acknowledging their guilt and craving pardon soften the resentment of the injured parties, some by falling back on the folly of youth, and others on their association with wicked men, some on the greatness of their power, and still others on Fortune that misleads all human calculations. I myself promise you, if you resign your magistracy, that all your faults shall be forgotten and that the people shall be reconciled to you upon such terms as in your unfortunate situation will be honourable.

XIII. " But I fear that the danger is not the real

41

ἀληθὴς ὁ κίνδυνος ᾖ τοῦ μὴ παραχωρεῖν τῆς
ἀρχῆς,—μυρίοις γοῦν[1] ὑπῆρξε τυραννίδας ἀποθε-
μένοις μηδὲν δεινὸν ὑπὸ τῶν πολιτῶν παθεῖν,—
αἱ[2] δ᾽ ἀληθεῖς ὦσιν αἰτίαι φιλοτιμία κενὴ τὴν
εἰκόνα τοῦ καλοῦ[3] διώκουσα καὶ πόθος ἡδονῶν
2 ὀλεθρίων ἃς οἱ τυραννικοὶ φέρουσι βίοι. εἰ δὲ
βούλει μὴ τὰ εἴδωλα καὶ τὰς σκιὰς[4] τῶν τιμῶν
καὶ τῶν εὐπαθειῶν[5] διώκειν, ἀλλ᾽ αὐτὰς καρποῦσθαι τὰς ἀληθεῖς τιμάς, ἀπόδος τὴν ἀριστοκρατίαν τῇ πατρίδι καὶ τιμὰς λάμβανε παρὰ τῶν
ἴσων καὶ ζήλου τύγχανε παρὰ τῶν ἐπιγιγνομένων
καὶ κλέος ἀθάνατον ἀντὶ τοῦ θνητοῦ σώματος
κατάλιπε τοῖς ἐγγόνοις. αὗται γάρ εἰσι βέβαιοι
καὶ ἀληθεῖς τιμαὶ καὶ ἀναφαίρετοι χαριέστατοί
3 τε[6] καὶ ἀμεταμέλητοι. τρέφε[7] τὴν ψυχὴν ἐπὶ τοῖς
ἀγαθοῖς τῆς πατρίδος ἡδόμενος, ὧν οὐκ ἐλαχίστη
μοῖρα δόξεις γεγονέναι δυναστείαν βαρεῖαν αὐτῆς
ἀφελόμενος. ποίησαι δὲ τούτων παραδείγματα
τοὺς προγόνους, ἐνθυμηθεὶς ὅτι τῶν ἀνδρῶν ἐκείνων
οὐδεὶς ἐπεθύμησεν ἐξουσίας δεσποτικῆς οὐδὲ[8] ταῖς
ἐπονειδίστοις τοῦ σώματος ἐδούλευσεν ἡδοναῖς.
τοιγάρτοι καὶ ζῶσιν αὐτοῖς ὑπῆρχε τιμᾶσθαι καὶ
τελευτήσασιν ὑπὸ τῶν ἐπιγινομένων[9] ἐπαινεῖσθαι.
4 μαρτυρεῖται γάρ τοι[10] παρὰ πάντων αὐτοῖς ὅτι τῆς
ἀριστοκρατίας, ἣν ἐκβαλοῦσα τοὺς βασιλεῖς ἡμῶν
ἡ πόλις κατεστήσατο, βεβαιόταται φύλακες ἐγένοντο. καὶ μηδὲν τῶν σεαυτοῦ λαμπροτάτων
λόγων τε καὶ πράξεων ἐπιλανθάνου. καλαὶ γὰρ

---

[1] οὖν LVM.   [2] αἱ Portus : ἐὰν O.
[3] τῆς δόξης after τοῦ καλοῦ deleted by Cobet ; Garrer and
Jacoby preferred to delete τοῦ καλοῦ.
[4] καὶ τὰς σκιὰς Sylburg : κατὰ σκιὰς V, καὶ τὰς σκοτίας M,
κατασκοτίας L.

ground for your not resigning your magistracy—at
all events, men without number have been able to
lay aside their tyrannies without suffering any harm
at the hands of their fellow citizens—but that the
true causes are a vain ambition, which pursues the
phantom of honour, and a yearning for those pernicious pleasures which the life led by tyrants brings
in its train. If, however, instead of pursuing the
vain images and shadows of the honours and enjoy-
ments, you wish to enjoy the real honours themselves,
then restore the aristocracy to your country, receive
honours from your equals and gain the praise of
posterity, and in exchange for your mortal body
leave an immortal renown to your descendants. For
these are lasting and real honours, which can never
be taken from you and afford the greatest pleasure
without any regrets. Nourish your soul by finding
pleasure in your country's welfare, of which you will
be regarded as the chief author by delivering her
from a grievous domination. In doing this take
your ancestors as your examples, bearing in mind
that not one of those men aimed at despotic power
or became a slave to the shameful pleasures of the
body. For these reasons it was their fortune not
only to be honoured while they lived, but after their
death to be praised by those who came after them.
For all bear witness that they were the stoutest
guardians of the aristocracy which our state established after banishing the kings. And by no means
forget your own most splendid words and deeds.

⁵ Reiske : εὐηθειῶν O, εὐκλειῶν Sylburg, εὐημεριῶν Jacoby.
⁶ χαριέστατοί τε Sylburg : χαρίεις τε O, χάριτές τε Reiske.
⁷ Reiske : στρέφε O.   ⁸ οὐδὲν LV, οὐδ' ἐν M.
⁹ ἐπιγινομένων VM : ἐπιγενομένων L.
¹⁰ γάρ τοι V : γὰρ M, γέ τοι L.

αἱ πρῶταί σου τῶν πολιτικῶν ἔργων ὑποθέσεις
ἐγένοντο καὶ μεγάλας ἐπέθρεψαν[1] ἡμῖν ἀρετῆς
ἐλπίδας, αἷς ἀκολούθως[2] καὶ τὰ λοιπὰ πράττειν
5 σ' ἅπαντες[3] ἀξιοῦμεν. ἀναχώρει δὴ πάλιν εἰς τὴν
σεαυτοῦ φύσιν, Ἄππιε τέκνον, καὶ γίνου τῇ προαιρέσει τῶν πολιτευμάτων μὴ τυραννικὸς ἀλλ'
ἀριστοκρατικός, καὶ φεῦγε τοὺς πρὸς ἡδονὴν
ὁμιλοῦντας, δι' οὓς ἐξέβης τῶν χρηστῶν ἐπιτηδευμάτων καὶ παρεπλάγχθης τῆς ὀρθῆς ὁδοῦ.
οὐ γὰρ ἔχει λόγον, ὑφ' ὧν ἂν γένηταί τις ἐξ
ἀγαθοῦ κακός, ὑπὸ τούτων πάλιν αὐτὸν[4] ἐκ πονηροῦ
γενέσθαι χρηστόν.

XIV. ''Ταῦτά σοι πολλάκις ἐβουλήθην ὑποθέσθαι[5] μόνῳ μόνος[6] εἰς λόγους παραγενόμενος καὶ
τὰ μὲν ὡς ἀγνοοῦντα διδάξαι, τὰ δ' ὡς ἁμαρτά-
νοντα νουθετῆσαι· καὶ παρεγενόμην εἰς τὴν οἰκίαν
οὐχ ἅπαξ, ἀπήλασαν δέ με οἱ σοὶ παῖδες ἐπὶ τοῖς
οἰκείοις[7] οὐ σχολὴν ἄγειν σε λέγοντες, ἀλλ' ἕτερά
τινα[8] πράττειν ἀναγκαιότερα, εἰ δή τί[9] σοι τῆς
2 πρὸς τὸ γένος εὐσεβείας ἀναγκαιότερον ἦν. τάχα
δ' οὐχ ὑπὸ σοῦ κελευσθέντες οἱ παῖδες, ἀλλ' ἐφ'[10]
ἑαυτῶν γνόντες, διέκλεισάν με τῆς εἰσόδου, καὶ
βουλοίμην οὕτως τὸ ἀληθὲς ἔχειν. τὸ πρᾶγμα δή
με ἠνάγκασε τοῦτο διαλεχθῆναι ἐν[11] τῷ συνεδρίῳ
πρὸς σὲ περὶ ὧν ἐβουλόμην, ἐπειδὴ μόνῳ πρὸς

---

[1] ἐπέθρεψαν Jacoby : ὑπέστρεψαν R, ὑπιστριψαν M, ὑπέθρεψαν Sylburg, ὑπέγραψαν Casaubon.
[2] ἀκολούθως L : ἀκόλουθον VM.
[3] ἅπαντες L : om. R.　　　　[4] αὐτὸν O : αὖ Naber.
[5] ὑποθέσθαι L : ἐκθέσθαι MV.
[6] μόνῳ μόνος L : μόνος μόνῳ R.
[7] ἐπὶ τοῖς οἰκείοις Cary, πρὸς τὸν οἰκεῖον Reiske : ἀπὸ τῶν οἰκείων O, Jacoby, ἀπὸ τῆς οἰκίας Sylburg.

For your first principles of political action were honourable and inspired in us great hopes of your virtue ; and we all ask you to act in future in conformity with those principles. Revert, then, once more to your own character, Appius, my son, and in your choice of policies do not espouse the cause of tyranny, but that of the aristocracy ; and shun the pleasure-seeking companions who were the cause of your departing from honest practices and of your straying from the straight path. For it is unreasonable to suppose that those through whose influence a man has been changed from good to bad will change him back again from an evil to a virtuous man.

XIV. " This advice I have often desired to give you, if I could have a private conversation with you, not only by way of instructing one who is ignorant, but also of reproving one who errs ; and I have gone more than once to your house. But your servants turned me away, saying that you had no leisure for private matters, but were attending to other more urgent business—if, indeed, anything could be more urgent for you than respect for your family ! Perhaps it was not by your command but of their own accord that they barred my entrance, and I could wish that this were the truth of the matter. This experience, then, has forced me to talk to you in the senate about the matters I wished to discuss with you, since I got no opportunity of doing

---

[8] ἕτερά τι LV.
[9] δή τί Reiske : δ' ἐπὶ O. ὥσπερ εἰ δή τί . . . ἦν Capps, ὡς δή τί . . . ὄν Cary.
[10] ἐφ' M : ἀφ' LV.   [11] ἐν added by Casaubon.

μόνον οὐκ ἐξεγένετο. καιρὸν δ' ἔχει πάντῃ λέγεσθαι τὰ καλὰ καὶ συμφέροντα παρ' ἀνθρώποις
3 μᾶλλον, Ἄππιε, ἢ μηδαμῆ. ἀποδεδωκὼς δή σοι[1]
τὰ τοῦ γένους ὀφειλήματα μαρτύρομαι θεούς, ὧν
ἱερὰ καὶ βωμοὺς κοιναῖς θυσίαις γεραίρομεν οἱ
τῆς Ἀππίου γενεᾶς διάδοχοι, καὶ προγόνων δαίμονας, οἷς μετὰ θεοὺς δευτέρας τιμὰς καὶ χάριτας
ἀποδίδομεν κοινάς, ὑπὲρ ἅπαντας δὲ τούτους γῆν,
ἣ κατέχει τὸν σὸν μὲν πατέρα ἐμὸν δ' ἀδελφόν,
ὅτι σοι παρέσχημαι ψυχήν τε καὶ φωνὴν τὴν
ἐμαυτοῦ τὰ κράτιστα βουλευομένην· καὶ ἐπανορθῶν
τὰς ἀγνοίας σου κατὰ δύναμιν τὴν ἐμὴν ἀξιῶ σε
μὴ κακοῖς[2] ἰᾶσθαι τὰ κακά, μηδὲ τῶν πλειόνων
ὀρεγόμενον καὶ τὰ παρόντα ἀπολέσαι, μηδ' ἵνα
τῶν ἴσων τε καὶ κρειττόνων ἄρχῃς ὑπὸ τῶν
4 ἡττόνων τε καὶ κακιόνων ἄρχεσθαι. πολλὰ καὶ
περὶ πολλῶν ἔτι σοι λέγειν βουλόμενος ὀκνῶ. εἰ
μὲν γὰρ ἐπὶ τὰ κρείττω βουλεύματα ὁ θεὸς ἄγει
σε, καὶ ταῦτα πλείω τῶν ἱκανῶν εἴρηκα, εἰ δ' ἐπὶ
τὰ χείρω, διὰ κενῆς καὶ τὰ λοιπὰ ἐρῶ. ἔχετε, ὦ
βουλὴ καὶ ὑμεῖς οἱ προεστηκότες τῆς πόλεως, τὴν
ἐμὴν γνώμην καὶ περὶ τοῦ πολέμου τῆς καταλύσεως
καὶ περὶ τῶν ἐν τῇ πόλει θορύβων τῆς ἐπανορθώ-
σεως. εἰ δέ τις ἕτερα τούτων κρείττω ἐρεῖ, τὰ
βέλτιστα νικάτω.''

XV. Τοιαῦτ' εἰπόντος Κλαυδίου καὶ πολλὴν ἐλπίδα τῷ συνεδρίῳ παρασχόντος ὡς ἀποθησομένων
τῶν δέκα τὴν ἀρχήν, Ἄππιος μὲν πρὸς ταῦτα
οὐδὲν ἠξίωσεν εἰπεῖν· ἐκ δὲ τῶν ἄλλων ὀλιγαρ-

[1] σοι Steph. : σου O (ἀποδεδωκότος δή σου M).
[2] κακοῖς Cobet : τοῖς κακοῖς O, Jacoby.

so by ourselves alone ; and things that are honourable and advantageous, Appius, may be mentioned seasonably anywhere in public rather than nowhere. Having now performed for you the duty I owe to our family, I protest by the gods, whose temples and altars we who carry on the succession of the Appian family honour with common sacrifices, and by the genii of our ancestors, to whom after the gods we pay the next honours and gratitude in common, and, above all these, by the earth, which holds your father and my brother, that I have put at your disposal both my mind and my voice to give you the best advice. And now, desiring to correct your ignorance as best I may, I ask you not to attempt to cure the evils by evils, nor, by aiming at too much, to lose even what you already have, nor again, by attempting to rule over your equals and your superiors, to be ruled yourself by those who are inferior and baser. I should like to say much more to you upon many subjects, but hesitate to do so. For if God is leading you to better resolutions, even this that I have said is more than sufficient ; but if to worse, then what I have still to say will also be said in vain. You now have my opinion, senators, and you who are at the head of the commonwealth, concerning the means both of putting an end to the war and of reforming the civil disorders. If anyone, however, shall offer better advice than this, let the best prevail."

XV. After Claudius had spoken thus and given the senate great reason to hope that the decemvirs would resign their power, Appius did not see fit to make any answer to his advice. But Marcus Cornelius, one of the other members of the oligarchy,

47

χῶν[1] προελθὼν Κορνήλιος Μάρκος· "'Ημεῖς μέν,"
ἔφησεν, "ὦ Κλαύδιε, περὶ τῶν ἰδίων συμφερόντων αὐτοὶ διαγνωσόμεθα τῆς σῆς οὐδὲν δεόμενοι
βουλῆς. καὶ γὰρ ἡλικίας ἐν τῇ φρονιμωτάτῃ
ἐσμέν, ὥστε μηδὲν τῶν διαφερόντων ἀγνοεῖν, καὶ
φίλων οὐ σπανίζομεν, οἷς, ἐάν τι δέῃ, συμβούλοις
2 χρησόμεθα. παῦσαι δὴ πρᾶγμα ποιῶν ἄωρον,
ἀνὴρ πρεσβύτερος οὐ δεομένοις συμβουλῆς γνώμας
ἀποδεικνύμενος. τῷ 'Αππίῳ δ' εἴ τι βούλει
παραινεῖν ἢ λοιδορεῖσθαι—τοῦτο γὰρ ἀληθέστερον
—ὅταν ἐξέλθῃς ἐκ τοῦ συνεδρίου, λοιδόρησῃ. νῦν
δ' ὑπὲρ τοῦ πρὸς Αἰκανοὺς καὶ Σαβίνους πολέμου,
περὶ οὗ κέκλησαι γνώμην ἀποδειξόμενος,[2] ὅ τι
σοι φαίνεται λέγε καὶ παῦσαι τὰ ἔξω τοῦ πράγμα-
3 τος φλυαρῶν." μετὰ τοῦτον ἀνίσταται πάλιν ὁ
Κλαύδιος κατηφὴς καὶ μεστοὺς ἔχων τοὺς ὀφθαλμοὺς δακρύων καί φησιν· "'Άππιος μὲν οὐδ'
ἀποκρίσεως ἄξιον ἡγεῖταί με, ὦ[3] βουλή, τὸν
ἑαυτοῦ θεῖον ἐναντίον ὑμῶν· ἀλλ' ὥσπερ τὴν
οἰκίαν τὴν ἰδίαν ἀπέκλεισέ[4] μοι, καὶ τουτὶ τὸ συνέδριον ἄβατον ὅσονπερ[5] ἐφ' ἑαυτῷ ποιεῖ. εἰ δὲ
χρὴ τὸ ἀληθὲς λέγειν, καὶ ἐκ τῆς πόλεως ἐξε-
4 λαύνομαι. οὐκέτι γὰρ ἂν[6] αὐτὸν ὀρθοῖς ὄμμασι
δυναίμην ὁρᾶν ἀνάξιον γεγονότα τῶν προγόνων
καὶ τυραννικὴν ἐζηλωκότα παρανομίαν, ἀλλ' ἀνα-
σκευασάμενος ἅπαντα τὰ ἐμὰ καὶ τοὺς ἐμοὺς εἰς
Σαβίνους ἄπειμι, πόλιν οἰκήσων 'Ρήγιλλον,[7] ἐξ
ἧς τὸ γένος ἡμῶν ἐστι, καὶ μενῶ τὸν λοιπὸν ἐκεῖ
χρόνον ἕως ἂν οὗτοι κατέχωσι τὴν καλὴν ταύτην

---

[1] Jacoby : ὀλιγαρχιῶν LMV, ὀλιγαρχικῶν Steph.
[2] ἀποδειξάμενος LVM.   [3] ὦ added by Sylburg.
[4] ἀπόκλεισον LV.

advanced and said : " We, Claudius, shall ourselves
decide about our own interests without any need of
your advice. For we are of the age best qualified
for prudence, so that we are ignorant of nothing that
concerns us, and we do not lack for friends whom
we may take as advisers if necessary. Cease, then,
doing an unseasonable thing in expressing your
opinions as an older man to those who do not need
advice. As for Appius, if you wish to give him any
admonition or abuse—for this is the truer term for
it—when you have left the senate-chamber, you may
abuse him. For the present, state what you think
about the war with the Aequians and Sabines, the
matter regarding which you have been called upon
to deliver your opinion, and cease talking idly of
things that are beside the point." After him Claudius
rose up again, with downcast countenance and with
tears in his eyes, and said : " Appius does not think
me, his uncle, worthy even of an answer, senators,
in your presence ; but, just as he shut his own house
against me, so he does everything in his power to
render the senate-chamber here inaccessible to me
likewise. And if I must speak the truth, I am even
driven out of the city. For I could no longer bear
the sight of him, now that he has become unworthy
of his ancestors and has emulated the lawlessness of
tyrants, but removing all my effects and my household to the Sabines, I shall live at Regillum,[1] the
city from which our family comes, and shall remain
there for the future as long as these men continue

[1] *Cf.* v. 40, 3 ff. and Livy iii. 58, 1.

---

[5] ὅσονπερ Sylburg : ὥσπερ O, om. Jacoby.
      [6] ἂν added by Kayser.
      [7] Sylburg : ἰνρίλιον O.

ἀρχήν. ἐπειδὰν δ' οἷα μαντεύομαι περὶ τὴν
δεκαδαρχίαν γένηται, γενήσεται δ' οὐκ εἰς μακράν,
5 τότε παρέσομαι. καὶ τὰ μὲν ὑπὲρ ἐμοῦ τοσαῦτα·
περὶ δὲ τοῦ πολέμου ταύτην ὑμῖν, ὦ βουλή,
γνώμην ἀποδείκνυμαι,[1] μηδὲν ψηφίζεσθαι περὶ μηδενὸς πράγματος ἕως[2] ἀποδειχθῶσι νέαι[3] ἀρχαί."
ταῦτ' εἰπὼν καὶ πολὺν ἐκ τοῦ συνεδρίου κινήσας
ἔπαινον ἐπὶ τῷ γενναίῳ καὶ φιλελευθέρῳ[4] τῆς
γνώμης ἐκάθισε. μετὰ δὲ τοῦτον ἀναστὰς Λεύκιος
Κοΐντιος ὁ καλούμενος[5] Κικιννᾶτος καὶ Τίτος
Κοΐντιος Καπιτωλῖνος καὶ Λεύκιος Λουκρήτιος
καὶ πάντες ἑξῆς οἱ πρωτεύοντες[6] τοῦ συνεδρίου
τῇ Κλαυδίου γνώμῃ προσετίθεντο.

XVI. Ἐφ' ᾧ διαταραχθέντες οἱ περὶ τὸν Ἄππιον
ἐβουλεύσαντο μηκέτι καθ' ἡλικίαν καὶ βουλῆς
ἀξίωσιν[7] συμβούλους καλεῖν, ἀλλὰ κατ' οἰκειότητα
καὶ τὴν πρὸς αὐτοὺς ἑταιρίαν. καὶ παρελθὼν
Μάρκος Κορνήλιος ἀνίστησι Λεύκιον Κορνήλιον
τὸν ἀδελφόν, ὃς Κοΐντῳ Φαβίῳ Οὐιβουλανῷ συν-
υπάτευσε τὸ τρίτον ὑπατεύοντι, δραστήριον ἄνδρα
καὶ πολιτικοὺς διεξελθεῖν λόγους οὐκ ἀδύνατον.
οὗτος ἀναστὰς ἔλεξε τοιάδε·

2 " Θαυμαστὸν μὲν ἦν καὶ τοῦτ', ὦ βουλή, εἰ[8]

---

[1] Sintenis : ἀποδείκνυμι O.   [2] ἕως LV : ἕως ἂν R.
[3] ἀποδειχθῶσι νέαι ἀρχαί Grasberger : ἀποδειχθῶσιν αἱ ἀρχαί O.
[4] φιλελευθερίῳ LV.   [5] κόιντος καλούμενος LV.
[6] δέκα after οἱ πρωτεύοντες deleted by Glareanus, Sylburg;
retained by Kiessling, Jacoby.
[7] βουλῆς ἀξίωσιν O : τιμῆς ἀξίωσιν Kiessling, ἀρετῆς ἀξίωσιν
Cobet. But perhaps βουλῆς should be rejected outright as an
interpolation due to the neighbouring ἐβουλεύσαντο or συμβούλους. For the omission of a genitive with ἀξίωσις in similar
phrases see x. 50, 4 ; vi. 81, 2 ; vi. 35, 1.   [8] εἰ VM : οἱ L.
50

in possession of this fine magistracy. But when the
fate I foresee shall have overtaken the decemvirate—
and it will overtake them soon—I shall then return.
So much concerning myself. As to the war, I give
you this advice, senators, to pass no vote concerning anything whatever until new magistrates are
appointed." After he had thus spoken and received
great applause from the senate for the noble spirit
and the love of liberty that his words breathed, he
sat down. And after him Lucius Quintius, surnamed
Cincinnatus, Titus Quintius Capitolinus, Lucius
Lucretius, and all the leading men [1] of the senate
rose up one after another and supported the motion
of Claudius.

XVI. Appius and his colleagues,[2] being disturbed
at this, resolved no longer to call upon others for
advice according to their age or senatorial rank,[3] but
according to their friendship and attachment to
themselves. And Marcus Cornelius, coming forward,
asked Lucius Cornelius to rise,—his brother, who had
been colleague to Quintus Fabius Vibulanus in his
third consulship, a man of action and not without
eloquence in political debates. This man, rising up,
spoke as follows :

" This also was surprising, senators, that men of

---

[1] The MSS. have " all the ten leading men," probably due
to confusion with the decemvirs.

[2] For chaps. 16–18 cf. Livy iii. 40, 8-14.

[3] It is uncertain whether the phrase βουλῆς ἀξίωσιν, given
by the MSS., should be rendered " senatorial rank " or
rather " reputation for (wise) counsel." The expression is
unusual and has been challenged by more than one editor ;
see the critical note. If we reject βουλῆς as an interpolation,
we shall have, in agreement with Dionysius' usage elsewhere,
" according to their age or rank."

ταύτην ἔχοντες ἄνθρωποι τὴν ἡλικίαν ἣν[1] ἔχουσιν
οἱ πρὸ ἐμοῦ γνώμην ἀποφηνάμενοι καὶ πρωτεύειν
ἀξιοῦντες τῶν συνέδρων, τὴν ἐκ τῶν πολιτικῶν
προσκρουσμάτων ἀπέχθειαν ἀδιάλλακτον πρὸς τοὺς
προεστηκότας τῆς πόλεως οἴονται δεῖν φυλάττειν,
οὓς ἐχρῆν[2] καὶ τοῖς νέοις παραινεῖν ἀπὸ τοῦ κρα-
τίστου ποιεῖσθαι τοὺς ὑπὲρ τῶν καλῶν ἀγῶνας,
καὶ μὴ πολεμίους ἀλλὰ φίλους ἡγεῖσθαι τοὺς περὶ
3 τῶν κοινῶν ἀγαθῶν ἀντιπάλους.   πολλῷ δ' ἔτι
τούτου θαυμασιώτερόν ἐστιν εἰ τὰς ἰδίας ἀπεχθείας
ἐπὶ τὰ κοινὰ τῆς πόλεως πράγματα μεταφέρουσι
καὶ συναπολέσθαι τοῖς ἑαυτῶν ἐχθροῖς βούλονται
μᾶλλον ἢ σωθῆναι μετὰ πάντων τῶν φίλων.
ὑπερβολὴ[3] γὰρ ἀνοίας τοῦτό γε[4] καὶ οὐ πόρρω
θεοβλαβείας ὃ[5] πεποιήκασιν οἱ πρόεδροι τῆς βου-
4 λῆς ἡμῶν.   οὗτοι γὰρ ἀγανακτοῦντες ὅτι μετιόντας αὐτοὺς τὴν τῶν δέκα ἀρχήν, ἧς αὐτοὶ
νῦν κατηγοροῦσιν, ἐνίκησαν ἐν ἀρχαιρεσίαις ἐπι-
τηδειότεροι φανέντες, ἀεὶ πολεμοῦσιν αὐτοῖς πόλεμον ἀδιάλλακτον, καὶ εἰς τοῦθ' ἥκουσιν εὐηθείας,
μᾶλλον δὲ μανίας, ὥσθ', ἵνα τούτους διαβάλλωσι
πρὸς ὑμᾶς, ὅλην ὑπομένουσιν ἀνατρέψαι τὴν πα-
5 τρίδα· οἳ γ' ὁρῶντες μὲν ἀνάστατον[6] τὴν χώραν
ἡμῶν ὑπὸ τῶν πολεμίων γενομένην, ὁρῶντες δὲ
ὅσον οὔπω καὶ ἐπὶ τὴν πόλιν αὐτοὺς ἐλεύσεσθαι
(τὸ γὰρ διὰ μέσου χωρίον οὐ πολύ) ἀντὶ τοῦ παρα-

---

[1] ἣν added by Cobet, οἵαν by Kiessling.
[2] οἴονται δεῖν φυλάττειν, οὓς ἐχρῆν Post : οὓς ἐχρῆν οἷόν τε
δεῖ (δεῖν M) φυλάττειν O ; Jacoby did not attempt to emend
this corrupt text.
[3] ὑπερβολὴ O : ὑπερβολὴν Jacoby.

the age of those who preceded me in declaring their opinions and claim to be the foremost men of the senate, think fit to maintain unrelenting their enmity,[1] derived from political clashes, toward those who are at the head of the commonwealth, when they ought to be exhorting the young men also to engage from the highest motives in competition for noble rewards, and to regard, not as enemies, but as friends, those who are their rivals in striving for the public good. And much more surprising still than this it is that they transfer their private animosities to the affairs of the commonwealth and choose rather to perish with their enemies than to be saved with all their friends. This is an excess of folly and not far from a Heaven-sent madness which the presiding officers of our senate have been guilty of. For these men, displeased because others who appeared more worthy defeated them at the election when they were candidates for the decemvirate,—a magistracy which they themselves now inveigh against,—continually wage an unrelenting war against them and have come to this pitch of folly, or rather of madness, that in order to slander these men to you they are willing to overthrow the whole country. For although they see that our land has been laid waste by our enemies and though they see that these foes will come almost immediately against Rome (the distance separating us is not great), instead of exhorting and

---

[1] This passage is badly corrupted in the MSS. The text of Post here adopted gives a satisfactory meaning and construction for the first time.

---

[4] τοῦτό γε Casaubon : τούτοις O, Jacoby.
[5] ὁ Naber : om. O, Jacoby.
[6] μὲν ἀνάστατον Sylburg : μεταιάστατον O.

καλεῖν καὶ παρορμᾶν τοὺς νέους ἐπὶ τὸν ὑπὲρ τῆς
πατρίδος ἀγῶνα καὶ αὐτοὶ πάσῃ προθυμίᾳ καὶ
σπουδῇ βοηθεῖν, ὅσῃ γοῦν ἐν τοῖς τηλικούτοις
ἐστὶν ἰσχύς, περὶ πολιτείας κόσμου νῦν ἀξιοῦσιν
ὑμᾶς σκοπεῖν καὶ νέας ἀρχὰς ἀποδεικνύναι καὶ
πάντα μᾶλλον ἢ τοὺς ἐχθροὺς κακῶς ποιεῖν· καὶ
οὐδ' αὐτὸ τοῦτο δύνανται συνιδεῖν, ὅτι γνώμας
ἀκαίρους[1] εἰσφέρουσι, μᾶλλον δ' εὐχὰς ἀδυνάτους
λέγουσιν.[2]

XVII. "Σκοπεῖτε γὰρ οὑτωσί· προβούλευμα
γενήσεται τῆς βουλῆς ὑπὲρ ἀρχαιρεσιῶν, ἔπειτ'
ἐξοίσουσιν οἱ δέκα τὰ βουλευθέντα εἰς τὸν δῆμον
ὁρίσαντες ἀγορὰν τὴν ἀπὸ ταύτης τρίτην. πῶς
γὰρ ἂν[3] ἀληθῶς[4] γένοιτο[5] τι τῶν ὑπὸ τοῦ δήμου
ψηφιζομένων κύριον, ἐὰν μὴ κατὰ νόμους γένηται;
ἔπειθ' ὅταν αἱ φυλαὶ διενέγκωσι τὴν ψῆφον, τότε
αἱ νέαι παραλήψονται[6] τὴν πόλιν ἀρχαὶ καὶ προ-
2 θήσουσιν ὑμῖν ὑπὲρ πολέμου σκοπεῖν. ἐν δὲ τοῖς
μεταξὺ τῶν ἀρχαιρεσιῶν χρόνοις τοσούτοις οὖσιν,
ἐὰν ἐπὶ τὴν πόλιν ἡμῶν ἔλθωσιν οἱ πολέμιοι καὶ
προσαγάγωσι τοῖς τείχεσι, τί ποιήσομεν, Κλαύδιε;
ἐροῦμεν αὐτοῖς νὴ Δία· ' Μείναθ' ἕως ἂν ἀπο-
δείξωμεν ἑτέρας ἀρχάς. Κλαύδιος γὰρ ἡμᾶς
ἔπεισε περὶ μηδενὸς ἄλλου πράγματος μήτε προ-

---

[1] ἀκαίρους (or ἀώρους) added by Cary, πονηρὰς by Kiessling, ἀσυμφόρους by Grasberger, Jacoby. See note on translation.
[2] λέγουσιν (as in vi. 52, 2) Reiske : ἔχουσιν O, Jacoby ;
ἀδυνάτως ἐχούσας Smit.   [3] ἂν added by Casaubon.
[4] ἄλλως Casaubon.   [5] γένηταί VM.
[6] Sylburg : παραιτοῦνται or παραιτοῦντας O.

urging the young men to fight for their country and going themselves to her relief with all alacrity and enthusiasm, so far at least as there is strength in men so aged, they ask you now to consider the form of government, to create new magistrates, and to do everything rather than injure the enemy ; and they cannot see even this itself, that they are introducing inopportune [1] motions, or rather uttering impracticable wishes.

XVII. " For consider the matter in this light. There will be a preliminary vote of the senate for the election of magistrates ; then the decemvirs will lay this resolution before the people after appointing the third market-day thereafter for its consideration. For how can anything that is voted by the people become really valid if it is not done in accordance with the laws ? Then, after the tribes have given their votes, the new magistrates will take over the administration of the commonwealth and propose to you the consideration of the war. During the interval before the election, which will be such a long one, if our enemies march up to the city and approach the walls, what are we going to do, Claudius ? We shall say to them, by heaven : ' Wait until we have appointed other magistrates. For Claudius persuaded us neither to pass a preliminary decree concerning

---

[1] The adjective modifying " motions " has been lost from the Greek text. The words hitherto proposed, " bad " (or " mischievous ") by Kiessling, and " disadvantageous " by Grasberger (the latter a particularly attractive emendation palaeographically), would seem to be ruled out by the statement of Valerius in chap. 19, 5, that no one had ventured to call the motion disadvantageous. The motions should here be characterized, then, not as inherently objectionable, but rather as out of place at the moment, " inopportune " or " ill-timed."

βουλεύειν μήτ' εἰς τὸν δῆμον ἐκφέρειν μήτε[1]
δυνάμεις καταγράφειν, ἐὰν μὴ τὰ περὶ τὰς ἀρχὰς
3 καταστήσωμεν ὡς βουλόμεθα. ἄπιτ' οὖν, καὶ
ὅταν ἀκούσητε ὑπάτους καὶ τὰς ἄλλας ἀρχὰς ἀπο-
δειχθείσας ὑπὸ τῆς πόλεως καὶ τὰ πρὸς τὸν
ἀγῶνα πάντα γεγονότα ἡμῖν εὐτρεπῆ, τόθ' ἥκετε
περὶ διαλλαγῶν ποιησόμενοι τοὺς λόγους, ἐπειδὴ
κακῶς ἤρξασθε ἡμᾶς ποιεῖν οὐδὲν προπεπονθότες
ὑφ' ἡμῶν. καὶ ὅσα ἡμᾶς ἐβλάψατε κατὰ τὰς
ἐμβολὰς εἰς χρημάτων λόγον, ἅπαντα ἐκ τοῦ
4 δικαίου διαλύσατε[2]· τὸν δὲ τῶν γεωργῶν ὄλεθρον
οὐχ ὑπολογιούμεθα ὑμῖν, οὐδ' εἴ τινα γύναια
ἐλεύθερα ὕβρεως καὶ παροινίας ἐπειράθη στρα-
τιωτικῆς οὐδ' ἄλλο τῶν ἀνηκέστων οὐδέν.' κἀκεῖνοι ταῦτα προκαλουμένων ἡμῶν μετριάσουσι καὶ
συγχωρήσαντες τῇ πόλει νέας ἀρχὰς ἀποδεῖξαι
καὶ τὰ πρὸς τὸν πόλεμον εὐτρεπῆ ποιήσασθαι,
τότε ἥξουσιν ἱκετηρίας φέροντες ἀντὶ τῶν ὅπλων
καὶ παραδιδόντες ἡμῖν[3] ἑαυτούς.

XVIII. "Ὦ πολλῆς μὲν εὐηθείας τούτων οἷς
ἐπὶ νοῦν ἔρχεται τοιαῦτα ληρεῖν, πολλῆς δ' ἀν-
αλγησίας ἡμῶν, εἰ τοιαῦτα λεγόντων αὐτῶν οὐκ
ἀγανακτοῦμεν, ἀλλ' ὑπομένομεν ἀκούειν, ὥσπερ
ὑπὲρ τῶν πολεμίων ἀλλ' οὐχ ὑπὲρ ἡμῶν αὐτῶν
2 καὶ τῆς πατρίδος βουλευόμενοι. οὐκ ἀνελοῦμεν
ἐκ μέσου τοὺς φλυάρους; οὐ ταχεῖαν ψηφιούμεθα
τῇ ὑπονοθευομένῃ[4] χώρᾳ τὴν βοήθειαν; οὐ καθ-
οπλιοῦμεν ἅπασαν τὴν ἀκμὴν τῆς πόλεως; οὐκ
ἐπὶ τὰς ἐκείνων πόλεις αὐτοὶ στρατευσόμεθα;
ἀλλ' οἴκοι μένοντες καὶ τοῖς δέκα λοιδορούμενοι
καὶ νέας ἀρχὰς καθιστάντες καὶ περὶ κόσμου

---

[1] μηδὲ Kiessling. [2] διαλύσατε LV : ληψόμεθα M.

any other matter nor to lay anything else before the people nor to enrol forces until we have settled everything relating to the magistracies as we wish. Depart, therefore, and when you hear that the consuls and the other magistrates have been appointed and that we have all the necessary preparations made for war, then come and make your pleas for peace, since you injured us first without any provocation on our part. And for whatever damage you have caused us in your raids, so far as property is concerned, pay us in full in accordance with justice ; but the slaying of our husbandmen and any insults and drunken abuse offered by your soldiers to women of free condition or any other irreparable mischief we shall not include in your account.' And they doubtless in response to this invitation of ours will show moderation, and after permitting us to choose new magistrates and to make our preparations for war, will then come with olive branches in their hands instead of arms and deliver themselves up to us !

XVIII. " Oh, the great folly of these men who can think of uttering such nonsense, and our own great stupidity if, when they say such things, we show no displeasure, but submit to hearing them, as if we were consulting in the interest of our enemies and not of ourselves and our country ! Shall we not remove these triflers from our midst ? Not vote speedy relief to the land that is being ravished ? Not arm all the youth of Rome ? Not march ourselves against the cities of our enemies ? Or shall we stay at home and, abusing the decemvirs, installing new magistrates and considering a form of government

---

³ ὑμῖν LV. ⁴ ὑπονοθευομένῃ O : προνομευομένῃ Sylburg.

πολιτικοῦ σκοποῦντες ὥσπερ ἐν εἰρήνῃ πάντ' ἐάσομεν ὑπὸ τοῖς πολεμίοις τὰ ἐν τῇ χώρᾳ γενέσθαι,
καὶ τελευτῶντες ὑπὲρ ἀνδραποδισμοῦ κινδυνεύ-
σομεν καὶ κατασκαφῆς τῆς πόλεως,[1] ἐάσαντες
3 τὸν πόλεμον τοῖς τείχεσι προσελθεῖν; οὐκ ἔστιν
ὑγιαινόντων ἀνθρώπων τὰ τοιαῦτα βουλεύματα, ὦ
πατέρες, οὐδὲ προνοίας πολιτικῆς τὰ κοινὰ συμφέροντα τῶν ἰδίων ἀπεχθειῶν ἡγουμένης ἀναγκαιότερα, ἀλλὰ φιλονεικίας ἀκαίρου καὶ δυσμενείας
ἀβούλου καὶ φθόνου κακοδαίμονος, ὃς οὐκ ἐᾷ τοὺς
ἔχοντας αὐτὸν σωφρονεῖν. ἀλλὰ τὰς μὲν τούτων
φιλονεικίας ἐάσατε χαίρειν· ἃ δὲ ψηφισάμενοι τῇ
πόλει σωτήρια καὶ ὑμῖν[2] αὐτοῖς προσήκοντα ἔσεσθε
βεβουλευμένοι καὶ τοῖς ἐχθροῖς φοβερά, ἐγὼ πει-
4 ράσομαι λέγειν. νῦν μὲν τὸν πρὸς Αἰκανοὺς καὶ
Σαβίνους πόλεμον ἐπικυρώσατε καὶ τὰς δυνάμεις
μετὰ πλείστης προθυμίας καὶ σπουδῆς καταγράφετε
τὰς ἐπ' ἀμφοτέρους ἐξελευσομένας. ὅταν δὲ τὰ
τοῦ πολέμου τέλος ἡμῖν τὸ κράτιστον λάβῃ καὶ
ἀναστρέψωσιν εἰς τὴν πόλιν αἱ δυνάμεις εἰρήνης
γενομένης, τότε καὶ περὶ τοῦ κόσμου τῆς πολιτείας
σκοπεῖτε, καὶ λόγον ἀπαιτεῖτε τοὺς δέκα περὶ
πάντων ὧν ἐπὶ τῆς ἀρχῆς ἔπραξαν καὶ νέας ἀρχὰς
ψηφοφορεῖτε καὶ δικαστήρια καθίζετε καὶ τιμᾶτε
τοὺς ἑκατέρου τούτων ἀξίους ὅταν ἐφ' ὑμῖν γένηται
ταῦτ' ἀμφότερα, μαθόντες ὅτι οὐ τοῖς πράγμασιν
οἱ καιροὶ δουλεύουσιν, ἀλλὰ τοῖς καιροῖς τὰ
πράγματα.''
5 Ταύτην ἀποδειξαμένου Κορνηλίου τὴν[3] γνώμην
οἱ μετ' ἐκεῖνον ἀνιστάμενοι χωρὶς ὀλίγων τῆς
αὐτῆς ἐγένοντο προαιρέσεως, οἱ μὲν ἀναγκαῖα καὶ

---

[1] ὡς after πόλεως deleted by Reiske.   [2] ἡμῖν LV.

as if we were at peace, let everything in the country fall into the enemy's hands, and at last run the hazard of being enslaved ourselves and seeing our city laid in ruins as the result of our having allowed the war to approach our walls ? Such counsels, fathers, are not those of men in their senses nor do they spring from the political foresight which regards the public advantages as more essential than private animosities, but rather from an unseasonable contentiousness, an ill-starred enmity, and an unfortunate envy which does not permit those who are under its influence to show sound judgement. Dismiss, however, from your minds the rivalries of these men ; but the measures which you should pass if your counsels are to prove salutary to the commonwealth, becoming to yourselves and formidable to our foes, I shall now attempt to indicate. For the present, vote your approval of the war against the Aequians and Sabines and enrol with the greatest alacrity and expedition the forces that are to set out against both. And after the war is terminated in the happiest manner for us and our forces return to the city upon the conclusion of peace, then not only consider the form of government, but also call the decemvirs to account for all their actions during their administration, vote for new magistrates and establish courts and honour with both these offices those who are worthy of them when both are in your power ; for you must know that opportunities do not wait upon events, but events upon opportunities."

When Cornelius had delivered this opinion, those who rose up after him were, with few exceptions, of the same advice, some looking upon these measures

---

³ τὴν om. L.

τῷ παρόντι καιρῷ ταῦτα προσήκοντα ὑπολαμβάνοντες εἶναι, οἱ δ' ὑποκατακλινόμενοι καὶ θεραπεύοντες τοὺς δέκα τῷ φόβῳ τῆς ἀρχῆς. ἦν γάρ
τι καὶ κατεπτηχὸς τὴν ἐξουσίαν οὐκ ἐλάχιστον
μέρος ἐκ τῶν συνέδρων.

XIX. Ὡς δ' αἱ πλείους γνῶμαι διηγορεύθησαν,
καὶ παρὰ πολὺ κρατεῖν ἐδόκουν οἱ τὸν πόλεμον
ἐπικυροῦντες τῶν ἑτέρων, τότε Λεύκιον Οὐαλέριον
ἐν τοῖς ἐσχάτοις ἐκάλουν, ὃν ἔφην εὐθὺς ἐν ἀρχαῖς
βουλόμενόν τι λέγειν κεκωλῦσθαι πρὸς αὐτῶν. ὁ
δὲ ἀναστὰς τοιούτους διεξῆλθε λόγους·

2   " Τὴν μὲν ἐπιβουλὴν τῶν δέκα ὁρᾶτε, ὦ πατέρες,
οἳ κατ' ἀρχάς τ' οὐκ ἐπέτρεψάν μοι λέγειν ὅσα
προῃρούμην πρὸς ὑμᾶς, καὶ νῦν ἐν τοῖς ὑστάτοις
ἀποδεδώκασι λόγον, ἐνθυμηθέντες, ὅπερ εἰκός,
ὅτι τῇ τε Κλαυδίου γνώμῃ προσθέμενος οὐδὲν
ὠφελήσω τὸ κοινὸν ὀλίγων αὐτῇ συνειρηκότων,
ἑτέραν τε γνώμην παρὰ τὰς εἰρημένας αὐτοῖς[1]
ἀποφηνάμενος, κἂν τὰ κράτιστα ὑποθῶμαι, διὰ
3 κενῆς ἐρραψῳδηκὼς ἔσομαι. εὐαρίθμητοι γάρ
τινές εἰσιν οἱ μετ' ἐμὲ ἀναστησόμενοι, οὓς ἐὰν
ἅπαντας ὁμογνώμονας λάβω, τί γενήσεταί μοι
πλέον οὐδὲ πολλοστὴν ἔξοντι μοῖραν τῶν Κορνηλίῳ
συναγορευόντων; οὐ μὴν ἐγὼ ταῦθ' ὑφορώμενος
ὀκνήσω τὴν ἐμαυτοῦ γνώμην εἰπεῖν. ὅταν γὰρ
ἀκούσητε πάντων, ἐφ' ὑμῖν ἔσται[2] τὰ κράτιστα
4 ἑλέσθαι. περὶ μὲν οὖν τῆς δεκαδαρχίας, ὃν τρόπον ἐπιμελεῖται τῶν κοινῶν, ὅσα Κλαύδιος ὁ

---

[1] αὐτοῖς R : αὐτῆς L.   [2] ἔσται Sylburg : ἔστι O.

---

[1] In chap. 4.

as necessary and suited to the present juncture, and others yielding to the times and paying court to the decemvirs through dread of their magistracy ; for no small part of the senators actually stood in awe of their power.

XIX. After most of the senators had delivered their opinions and those who declared for war appeared to be much more numerous than the others, the decemvirs then called upon Lucius Valerius among the last. He was the one, as I have related,[1] who had wished to say something at the very beginning of the debate but had been prevented by them. And now rising, he delivered a speech of the following tenor :

" You see, fathers, the plot of the decemvirs who not only at first would not allow me to say to you all that I had proposed, but now have assigned to me my turn to speak among the last, with this in mind, as we may reasonably assume, that, if I concur in the opinion of Claudius, I shall render no service to the commonwealth, since few have supported it, and again, if I deliver an opinion different from those they themselves have expressed, however excellent my advice may be, I shall have recited my piece in vain. For those are easily counted who are to rise up after me, and even if I shall have them all agreeing with me, what advantage will it give me when I shall not have the smallest fraction of those who side with Cornelius ? However, in spite of these misgivings I shall not hesitate to express my opinion. For when you have heard everybody, you will have it in your power to choose what is best. Concerning the decemvirs, therefore, and the manner in which they look after the commonwealth, consider that everything the

61

βέλτιστος εἶπε, καὶ ἐμοὶ νομίσατε εἰρῆσθαι, καὶ
ὅτι δεῖ νέας ἀρχὰς ἀποδειχθῆναι πρὶν ἢ τὸ περὶ
τοῦ πολέμου γενέσθαι ψήφισμα· καὶ γὰρ ταῦτα
5 εἴρηται τῷ ἀνδρὶ κατὰ τὸ βέλτιστον. ἐπεὶ δὲ
Κορνήλιος εἰς τὸ ἀδύνατον ἀπάγειν ἐπειρᾶτο τὴν
γνώμην πολλοὺς τοὺς μεταξὺ χρόνους ἀποφαίνων
ταῖς πολιτικαῖς οἰκονομίαις γενησομένους ἐν χερσὶν
ὄντος τοῦ πολέμου, καὶ χλευάζειν ἐπεχείρει πράγματα οὐκ ἐπιτήδεια χλευασμῶν, οἷς παρακρουσάμενος ὑμᾶς τοὺς πολλοὺς ᾤχετο φέρων, ἐγὼ
καὶ περὶ τοῦ μὴ ἀδύνατον εἶναι τὴν Κλαυδίου
γνώμην διαλέξομαι πρὸς ὑμᾶς· ὡς μὲν γὰρ ἀσύμ-
φορος, οὐδὲ τῶν διασυράντων αὐτὴν οὐδεὶς ἐτόλμησεν εἰπεῖν· καὶ διδάξω πῶς ἂν ἥ τε χώρα δι'
ἀσφαλείας γένοιτο καὶ δίκην δοῖεν οἱ τολμήσαντες
αὐτὴν κακῶς ποιεῖν καὶ τὴν πάτριον ἀπολάβοιμεν
ἀριστοκρατίαν, καὶ ταῦθ' ἅμα γένοιτο συναγω-
νιζομένων ἁπάντων τῶν ἐν τῇ πόλει καὶ μηδενὸς
τἀναντία πράττειν ἀξιοῦντος, σοφίαν οὐδεμίαν[1]
ἀποδεικνύμενος ὑμῖν,[2] τὰ δὲ πραχθέντα ὑφ' ὑμῶν
αὐτῶν παραδείγματα φέρων. ἔνθα γὰρ ἡ πεῖρα
διδάσκει τὸ συμφέρον, τί δεῖ στοχασμῶν ἐκεῖ;

XX. "Μέμνησθε ὅτι ἀπὸ τῶν αὐτῶν τούτων
ἐθνῶν ὥσπερ[3] νῦν δυνάμεις ἐνέβαλον, αἱ μὲν εἰς
τὴν ἡμετέραν γῆν, αἱ δ' εἰς τὴν τῶν συμμάχων
ἡμῶν, κατὰ τὸν αὐτὸν ἀμφότεραι χρόνον Γαΐου
Ναυτίου καὶ Λευκίου Μηνυκίου[4] τὴν ὑπατείαν
2 ἐχόντων, ἔνατον ἢ δέκατον ἔτος οἶμαι τουτί. τότε

---

[1] After οὐδεμίαν Reiske added ἐμήν, Cobet ἰδίαν.
[2] ὑμῖν La : ἡμῖν R.   [3] ὧνπερ Sintenis.
[4] Μηνυκίου Cary, Μινυκίου Sylburg, Jacoby : γενυκίου O.

most excellent Claudius has said has been said by
me also and that new magistrates ought to be chosen
before any decree is passed concerning the war ; for
this point also was treated by him in the best manner.
But since Cornelius endeavoured to show that his
motion is impracticable, pointing out that the intervening period devoted to matters of civil administration would be a long one, while the war is at our
doors, and since he attempted to ridicule things that
do not deserve ridicule and by that means seduced
and carried away most of you with him, I for my
part shall also talk to you about the motion of
Claudius, showing that it is not impracticable ; for
that it is disadvantageous no one even of those who
derided it has ventured to allege. And I shall show
you how our territory may be made secure, how
those who have dared to do it injury may be punished,
how we may recover our ancient aristocracy, and how
these things may all come about at the same time
with the concurrence of all the citizens and without
the least opposition. All this I shall do, not through
the display of any wisdom,[1] but by citing your own
actions as precedents for you to follow ; for where
experience teaches what is advantageous, what need
is there of conjectures ?

XX. " You recall that forces from these same
nations as at present made incursions, partly into
our territory and partly into that of our allies, both
at the same time, when Gaius Nautius and Lucius
Minucius were consuls, some eight or nine [2] years
ago I believe it was. When on that occasion you

[1] Or, following Cobet, " any special wisdom of my own."
[2] It was actually nine years earlier (456 B.C. by Dionysius'
chronology). See x. 22 f.

τοίνυν ἀποστειλάντων ὑμῶν νεότητα πολλὴν καὶ
ἀγαθὴν ἐπ' ἀμφότερα τὰ ἔθνη τῷ μὲν ἑτέρῳ τῶν
ὑπάτων εἰς δυσχωρίας ἀναγκασθέντι κατακλεῖσαι
τὸ στρατόπεδον πρᾶξαι μὲν οὐδὲν ἐξεγένετο,
πολιορκεῖσθαι δ' ἐν τῷ χάρακι καὶ κινδυνεύειν
σπάνει τῶν ἐπιτηδείων ἁλῶναι· Ναυτίῳ δ' ἀντι-
καθημένῳ Σαβίνοις[1] μάχας ἀναγκαῖον ἦν τίθεσθαι
πρὸς τοὺς αὐτοὺς συνεχεῖς καὶ μηδ'[2] οἵῳ τ' εἶναι
τοῖς κάμνουσι τῶν σφετέρων βοηθεῖν. ἦν τ' οὐκ
ἄδηλον ὅτι τῆς ἐν Αἰκανοῖς στρατιᾶς ἀναρπασθείσης
οὐδ' ἡ Σαβίνους πολεμοῦσα ἀνθέξει συνελθόντων
3 εἰς τὸ αὐτὸ τῶν πολεμίων ἀμφοτέρων. τοιούτων
δὴ κινδύνων τὴν πόλιν περιστάντων καὶ οὐδὲ τῶν
ἐντὸς τείχους ὁμονοούντων τίνα βοήθειαν εὔρασθε
ὑμεῖς, ἥπερ ὤνησεν ὁμολογουμένως πάντα τὰ πράγματα καὶ φερομένην τὴν πόλιν εἰς ἀτυχὲς πτῶμα
ὤρθωσεν; περὶ μέσας νύκτας εἰς τὸ βουλευτήριον συνελθόντες[3] ἀρχὴν ἀπεδείξατε[4] μίαν αὐτοκράτορα πολέμου καὶ[5] εἰρήνης, ἁπάσας τὰς ἄλλας
καταλύσαντες ἀρχάς, καὶ πρὶν ἡμέραν γενέσθαι
δικτάτωρ ἀπεδέδεικτο Λεύκιος Κοΐντιος ὁ βέλτι-
4 στος, οὐδ' ἐν τῇ πόλει τότ' ὤν, ἀλλ' ἐν ἀγρῷ. τὰ
μετὰ ταῦτα ἴστε δήπου τοῦ ἀνδρὸς ἔργα, ὅτι καὶ
δυνάμεις ἀξιοχρέους παρεσκευάσατο καὶ τὸ κινδυ-
νεῦον στρατόπεδον ἐρρύσατο καὶ τοὺς πολεμίους
ἐτιμωρήσατο καὶ τὸν στρατηγὸν αὐτῶν[6] αἰχμάλωτον
ἔλαβε· καὶ ταῦτα ἐν ἡμέραις τεσσαρεσκαίδεκα

---

[1] Sylburg : σαβίνων O, Jacoby.
[2] Jacoby : μήθ' O, μηθὲν Reiske.
[3] περὶ μέσας νύκτας . . . συνελθόντες placed here by Kiessling :
after ὑμεῖς (2 lines above) by O, Jacoby.
[4] ἀποδεῖξαι LMV.
[5] καὶ M : τῆς LV.   [6] αὐτῶν R : αὐτὸν LV.

had sent out numerous and brave youths against both these nations, it chanced that one of the consuls, being obliged to encamp in a difficult position, was unable to accomplish anything, but was besieged in his camp and in danger of being captured for want of provisions, while Nautius, who was encamped against the Sabines, was under the necessity of fighting battles with the same foes continually and could not even go to the aid of his fellow Romans who were in distress. And there was no doubt that if the army which was encamped among the Aequians should be destroyed, the other, that was carrying on the war against the Sabines, would not be able to hold out either when both armies of our enemies should have united. When the commonwealth was encompassed by such dangers and even the people inside the city walls were not harmonious, what relief did you yourselves hit upon—a relief which is acknowledged to have helped your whole cause and to have rectified the commonwealth when it was rushing to a miserable downfall ? Assembling in the senate-chamber about midnight, you created a single magistracy with absolute authority over both war and peace, abrogating all the other magistracies ; and before day came, the most excellent Lucius Quintius had been appointed dictator, although he was not even in the city at the time, but in the country. You know, of course, the deeds which this man performed after that, how he got ready adequate forces, rescued the army which was in danger, chastised the enemy and took their general prisoner ; and how, after accomplishing all this in only four-

μόναις ἅπαντα διαπραξάμενος καὶ εἴ τι ἄλλο[1]
σαθρὸν ἦν τῆς πολιτείας ἐπανορθωσάμενος ἀπέθετο
τὰς ῥάβδους· καὶ τὸ κωλῦον[2] οὐδὲν ἐγένετο νέαν
ἀρχὴν ἐν ἡμέρᾳ κυρωθῆναι μιᾷ βουλομένων ὑμῶν.
5 τοῦτο δὴ τὸ παράδειγμα μιμησαμένους ἡμᾶς[3]
οἴομαι δεῖν, ἐπειδὴ οὐδὲν ἄλλο ποιεῖν δυνάμεθα,
δικτάτορα ἑλέσθαι πρὶν ἐντεῦθεν ἐξελθεῖν· ἐὰν γὰρ
ὑπερβαλώμεθα τοῦτον τὸν καιρόν, οὐκέτι συν-
άξουσιν ἡμᾶς οἱ δέκα βουλευσομένους ὑπὲρ οὐδενός·
ἵνα δὲ καὶ κατὰ νόμους ἡ τοῦ δικτάτορος ἀνάρρη-
σις γένηται, τὴν μεσοβασίλειον ἀρχὴν ἑλέσθαι, τὸν
ἐπιτηδειότατον[4] ἐκλέξαντας[5] τῶν πολιτῶν· ὃ ποιεῖν
σύνηθές ἐστιν ὑμῖν ὅταν μήτε βασιλεῖς[6] ἔχητε μήτε
ὑπάτους μήτ' ἄλλην νόμιμον ἀρχὴν μηδεμίαν,
ὥσπερ νῦν οὐκ ἔχετε. τοῖς γὰρ ἀνδράσι τούτοις
παρελήλυθεν ὁ τῆς ἀρχῆς χρόνος καὶ τὰς ῥάβδους
6 αὐτῶν ὁ νόμος ἀφῄρηται. ταῦτ' ἐστὶν ἃ παραινῶ
πράττειν, ὦ πατέρες, ὑμῖν, καὶ συμφέροντα καὶ
δυνατά. ἢν δὲ Κορνήλιος εἰσηγεῖται γνώμην
κατάλυσις ὁμολογουμένη τῆς ἀριστοκρατίας ὑμῶν
ἐστιν. ἐὰν γὰρ ἅπαξ ὅπλων οἱ δέκα γένωνται
κύριοι τῇδε τῇ προφάσει τοῦ πολέμου, δέδοικα μὴ
καθ' ἡμῶν αὐτοῖς χρήσωνται. οἱ γὰρ οὐκ ἀξιοῦντες ἀποθέσθαι τὰς ῥάβδους, ἦ πού γε τὰ ὅπλα
ἀποθήσονται; λογιζόμενοι δὴ ταῦτα φυλάττεσθε
τοὺς ἀνθρώπους καὶ πᾶσαν ἀπάτην αὐτῶν προ-
βλέπετε. κρείττων γὰρ ἡ πρόνοια τῆς μεταμελείας
καὶ τὸ μὴ πιστεύειν τοῖς πονηροῖς σωφρονέστερον
τοῦ προπιστεύσαντας κατηγορεῖν.''

XXI. Ταύτην ἀποδειξαμένου τὴν γνώμην Οὐαλε-

---

[1] καὶ εἴ τι ἄλλο LV : καὶ εἴ τι καὶ ἄλλο R.

[2] κολυευ V, κολύσον R.   [3] Sylburg : ὑμᾶς O.

teen days and reforming whatever else was corrupt in
the commonwealth, he laid down the rods. Nothing
hindered you then from creating a new magistracy
in one day when you wished to do so. This example,
then, I think we ought to imitate, since there is
nothing else we can do, and choose a dictator before
we leave this chamber. For if we neglect this opportunity, the decemvirs will never assemble us again
to deliberate about anything. And in order that the
appointment of a dictator shall also be in accordance
with the laws, we should create an *interrex*, choosing
the most suitable person from among the citizens ;
for this is the customary thing for you to do when
you have neither kings, consuls nor any other legal
magistrates, which is the case at present, since these
men's term of office has expired and the law has
taken their rods from them. This is the course I advise you to take, fathers, one that is both advantageous
and practicable ; whereas the motion proposed by
Cornelius is confessedly the overthrow of your aristocracy. For if the decemvirs once get arms in their
hands under this excuse of the war, I fear they will
use them against us. For is it at all likely that those
who refuse to lay down their rods will lay down their
arms ? Taking these considerations into account,
then, beware of these men and forestall any treachery
on their part. For foresight is better than repentance,
and it is more prudent not to trust wicked men than
to accuse them after they have betrayed your trust."

XXI. This opinion of Valerius [1] pleased the

[1] *Cf.* Livy iii. 41, 1-6.

[4] Reiske : ἐπιτηδειότερον O.
[5] Kiessling : ἐκλέξαντες O.
[6] Sylburg : μεσοβασιλεῖς O.

ρίου κεχαρισμένην τοῖς πλείοσιν, ὡς ἐκ τῆς φωνῆς
αὐτῶν εἰκάσαι ῥᾴδιον ἦν,[1] καὶ τῶν μετ᾽ ἐκεῖνον
ἀνισταμένων (ἦν δ᾽ αὐτῶν[2] τὸ νέον τῆς βουλῆς
μέρος τὸ λειπόμενον) ταῦτα ἡγουμένων κράτιστα
εἶναι πλὴν ὀλίγων, ἐπειδὴ πάντες ἀπεδείξαντο τὰς
ἑαυτῶν γνώμας καὶ τέλος ἔδει τὰ βουλεύματα
λαβεῖν, Οὐαλέριος μὲν ἠξίου διαδικασίαν[3] τοὺς
δέκα προθεῖναι ταῖς γνώμαις, αὖθις ἐξ ἀρχῆς
πάντας τοὺς βουλευτὰς καλοῦντας, καὶ πολλοῖς
τῶν συνέδρων ἀναθέσθαι βουλομένοις τὰς προ-
2 τέρας ἀποφάσεις ταῦτα λέγων πιθανὸς ἦν· Κορνήλιος δ᾽, ὁ συμβουλεύων[4] τοῖς δέκα τὴν ἡγεμονίαν
ἐπιτρέψαι τοῦ πολέμου, κατὰ τὸ καρτερὸν ἀπεμάχετο, κεκρίσθαι τὸ πρᾶγμα ἤδη λέγων καὶ τέλος
ἔχειν νόμιμον ἁπάντων ἐψηφικότων, ἠξίου τε δι-
αριθμεῖν τὰς γνώμας καὶ μηδὲν ἔτι καινουργεῖν.
3 τούτων δὲ λεγομένων ὑφ᾽ ἑκατέρου[5] μετὰ πολλῆς
φιλοτιμίας τε καὶ κραυγῆς, καὶ τοῦ συνεδρίου
διαστάντος πρὸς ἑκάτερον, τῶν μὲν ἐπανορθώσασθαι
τὴν ἀκοσμίαν τοῦ πολιτεύματος βουλομένων τῷ
Οὐαλερίῳ συλλαμβανόντων, τῶν δὲ τὰ χείρω
προαιρουμένων καὶ ὅσοις κίνδυνός τις ὑπωπτεύετο
ἐκ τῆς μεταβολῆς ἔσεσθαι τῷ Κορνηλίῳ συναγορευόντων, λαβόντες ἀφορμὴν οἱ δέκα τοῦ πράττειν ὅ τι δόξειεν αὐτοῖς τὴν τοῦ συνεδρίου ταραχήν,
τῇ Κορνηλίου προστίθενται γνώμῃ. καὶ παρελθὼν
4 εἷς ἐξ αὐτῶν, Ἄππιος, ἔφη· "Περὶ τοῦ πρὸς
Αἰκανοὺς καὶ Σαβίνους πολέμου συνεκαλέσαμεν
ὑμᾶς, ὦ βουλή, διαγνωσομένους, καὶ λόγον ἀπεδώ-
καμεν ἅπασι τοῖς βουλομένοις ἀπὸ τῶν πρώτων

---

[1] ἦν Sylburg : εἴη O ; Vassis would delete ῥᾴδιον εἴη.
[2] αὐτῷ LV.

majority of the senators, as was easy to conclude from their acclamations ; and since those who rose up after him (those still remaining were the younger members of the senate) with few exceptions considered his measures the best, as soon as they all had delivered their own opinions and the discussion was due to be ended, Valerius asked the decemvirs to propose a division on the various opinions by calling upon all the senators over again from the beginning, and this request met with the approval of many of the senators who desired to retract their former opinions. But Cornelius, who advised giving the command of the war to the decemvirs, strenuously opposed this, declaring that the matter was already decided and legally ended, since all had voted ; and he demanded that the votes be counted and that no further innovation be admitted. When these proposals were urged by both men with great contention and shouting, and the senate split toward one side and the other, the party desiring to correct the disorder in the government backing Valerius, and the party which espoused the worse cause and suspected that there would be some danger from the change giving their support to Cornelius, the decemvirs, taking advantage of the dissension in the senate to do as they saw fit, sided with the opinion of Cornelius. And Appius, one of their number, coming forward, said : " It was the war with the Aequians and Sabines, senators, which we called you together to deliberate about, and we have given all of you who so desired leave to speak, calling upon each one from the fore-

---

³ ἀναδικασίαν Reiske.
⁴ συμβουλεύων Mb : συμβασιλεύων LVMa.
⁵ Kiessling : ἑκατέρων O.

ἄχρι τῶν νεωτάτων ἐν τῷ προσήκοντι καλοῦντες
ἕκαστον τόπῳ. τριῶν δ' ἀποδειξαμένων γνώμας
διαφόρους, Κλαυδίου τε καὶ Κορνηλίου καὶ Οὐαλερίου τελευταίου, διέγνωτε[1] περὶ αὐτῶν ὑμεῖς οἱ
λοιποί, καὶ παριὼν[2] ἕκαστος ἀπεφήνατο πάντων
5 ἀκουόντων ᾗ προσετίθετο γνώμῃ. ἀπάντων δὴ
γεγονότων κατὰ νόμον,[3] ἐπειδὴ τοῖς πλείοσιν ὑμῶν
Κορνήλιος ἐδόκει τὰ κράτιστα ὑποθέσθαι, τοῦτον
ἀπεφηνάμεθα νικᾶν καὶ τὴν ἀποδειχθεῖσαν ὑπὸ
τούτου γνώμην γράψαντες ἐκφέρομεν. Οὐαλέριος
δὲ καὶ οἱ μετ' αὐτοῦ συνεστῶτες[4] ὅταν αὐτοὶ
τύχωσιν ἐξουσίας ὑπατικῆς, δίκας τ' ἤδη τέλος
ἐχούσας ἀναδίκους ποιείτωσαν, ἐὰν αὐτοῖς φίλον
ᾖ, καὶ βουλεύματα διεγνωσμένα ὑπὸ πάντων ὑμῶν
6 ἄκυρα καθιστάτωσαν." ταῦτ' εἰπὼν καὶ τὸν
γραμματέα κελεύσας ἀναγνῶναι τὸ προβούλευμα,
ἐν ᾧ τὴν καταγραφὴν τοῦ στρατοῦ[5] καὶ τὴν
ἡγεμονίαν τοῦ πολέμου τοὺς δέκα παραλαβεῖν
ἐτέτακτο, διέλυσε τὸν σύλλογον.

XXII. Μετὰ τοῦθ' οἱ μὲν τῆς ὀλιγαρχικῆς
ἑταιρίας σοβαροὶ καὶ θρασεῖς περιῇεσαν ὡς δὴ
κρείττους τῶν ἑτέρων γεγονότες καὶ διαπεπραγ-
μένοι μηκέτι καταλυθῆναι σφῶν[6] τὴν δυναστείαν
ἐπειδὰν ἅπαξ ὅπλων καὶ στρατιᾶς[7] γένωνται κύριοι·
2 οἱ δὲ τὰ βέλτιστα τῷ κοινῷ φρονοῦντες, ἀνιαρῶς
διακείμενοι καὶ περιφόβως ὡς[8] οὐδενὸς τῶν
κοινῶν ἔτι γενησόμενοι κύριοι, διέστησαν[9] εἰς μέρη
πολλά, τῶν μὲν ἀγεννεστέρων τὰς φύσεις ἅπαντα
συγχωρεῖν τοῖς κρατοῦσιν ἀναγκαζομένων καὶ

[1] διέγνωτε Sylburg : διέγνω τὰς LV.
[2] παριὼν Reiske : περὶ ὧν LV.
[3] Kiessling : νόμων L, νόμους M.
[4] Cobet : ἑστῶτες O, Jacoby.

most down to the youngest in the proper order.
And three senators having given different opinions,
namely Claudius, Cornelius, and last of all Valerius,
the rest of you have come to your decision concerning them and each one has come forward and
declared in the hearing of all which opinion he
supported. Everything, therefore, having been done
according to law, since the majority of you thought
that Cornelius gave the best advice, we declare that
he prevails, and we are engrossing and publishing
the motion he made. Let Valerius and those who
are leagued with him, when they shall obtain the consular power themselves, grant a rehearing, if they like,
to causes already determined and annul resolutions
passed by you all." Having said this and ordered
the clerk to read the preliminary decree, in which it
had been ordered that the enrolling of the army and
the command of the war should be assumed by the
decemvirs, he dismissed the meeting.

XXII. After that those of the oligarchical faction
went about swaggering and insolent, as if they had
gained a victory over their adversaries and had
contrived that their power could no longer be overthrown when once they should be in control of arms
and an army. But the men who had the best interests
of the commonwealth at heart were in great distress
and consternation, imagining that they should never
again have any share in the government. These
split into many groups, those of less noble dispositions
feeling obliged to yield all to the victors and join the

---

[5] ποιεῖσθαι added after στρατοῦ by Reiske.
[6] μηκέτι καταλυθῆναι σφῶν L : μὴ σφῶν καταλυθῆναι R.
[7] καὶ στρατιᾶς L : om. R.
[8] ὡς added by Reiske.
[9] διέστησαν Kiessling : καὶ διέστησαν O, Jacoby.

κατανέμειν ἑαυτοὺς εἰς τὰς ὀλιγαρχικὰς ἑταιρίας,[1]
τῶν δ᾽ ἧττον ψοφοδεῶν ἀφισταμένων τῆς ὑπὲρ
τῶν κοινῶν φροντίδος καὶ[2] τὸν ἀπράγμονα βίον
μεθαρμοττομένων· ὅσοις δὲ πολὺ τὸ γενναῖον ἐν
τοῖς τρόποις ἦν ἰδίας ἑταιρίας κατασκευαζομένων
καὶ συμφρονούντων ἐπὶ φυλακῇ[3] τε ἀλλήλων καὶ
3 μεταστάσει[4] τῆς πολιτείας.   τούτων δὲ τῶν
ἑταιριῶν ἡγεμόνες ἦσαν οἱ πρῶτοι τολμήσαντες
ἐν τῷ συνεδρίῳ περὶ καταλύσεως τῆς δεκαδαρχίας
εἰπεῖν, Λεύκιος Οὐαλέριος καὶ Μάρκος Ὁράτιος,
φραξάμενοί τε τὰς οἰκίας ὅπλοις καὶ φυλακὴν
θεραπόντων καὶ πελατῶν καρτερὰν περὶ ἑαυτοὺς
ἔχοντες, ὡς μήτ᾽ ἐκ τοῦ[5] βιαίου παθεῖν μηθὲν μήτ᾽
4 ἐκ τοῦ δολίου.[6]   ὅσοις δ᾽ οὔτε θεραπεύειν τὴν τῶν
κρατούντων ἐξουσίαν βουλομένοις ἦν οὔτε μηδενὸς
ἐπιστρέφεσθαι τῶν κοινῶν οὐδ᾽[7] ἐν ἀπράκτῳ ζῆν
ἡσυχίᾳ καλὸν[8] ἐδόκει, πολεμεῖν τ᾽ ἀνὰ κράτος (οὐ
ῥᾴδιον γὰρ καθαιρεθῆναι δυναστείαν τηλικαύτην)
ἀνόητον[9] ἐφαίνετο εἶναι, κατέλιπον τὴν πόλιν.
ἡγεμὼν δὲ τούτων ἀνὴρ ἦν[10] ἐπιφανὴς Γάιος
Κλαύδιος, ὁ τοῦ κορυφαιοτάτου τῆς δεκαδαρχίας
Ἀππίου θεῖος, ἐμπεδῶν τὰς ὑποσχέσεις ἃς ἐπὶ
τῆς βουλῆς ἐποιήσατο πρὸς τὸν ἀδελφιδοῦν ὅτ᾽
αὐτὸν ἀποθέσθαι τὴν ἀρχὴν ἀξιῶν οὐκ ἔπεισεν.

---

[1] καὶ κατανέμειν . . . ἑταιρίας om. M.
[2] καὶ O : καὶ εἰς Cobet.   [3] φυλακῆς VL.
[4] Reiske : μεταναστάσει O.
[5] μήτ᾽ ἐκ τοῦ L : μήτε τι τοῦ VM.
[6] μήτ᾽ ἐκ τοῦ δολίου R : μήτ᾽ ἐκ τοῦ φανεροῦ δειλίαν κατα-
γνωσθῆναι M.
[7] οὐδ᾽ Jacoby : οὔτ᾽ O, καὶ Cobet.
[8] Sylburg : καλῶς O.
[9] (οὐ ῥᾴδιον γὰρ κ. δ. τηλικαύτην) ἀνόητον Post : οὐ ῥᾴδιον,
ἐπεὶ κ. δ. τηλικαύτην ἀνόητον O, Jacoby, ἀνόητον, ἐπεὶ κ. δ.

72

oligarchical bands, and such as were less timorous abandoning their concern for the public interests in exchange for a carefree life ; but those who had great nobility of character employed themselves in organizing bands of their own and planning together for their mutual defence and for a change in the form of government. The leaders of these groups were the men who had first dared to speak in the senate in favour of abolishing the decemvirate, namely Lucius Valerius and Marcus Horatius ; and they had surrounded their houses with armed men and had about their persons a strong guard of their servants and clients, so as to suffer no harm from either violence or treachery. Those persons, again, who were unwilling either to court the power of the victors or to pay no attention to any of the business of the commonwealth and to lead a quiet, carefree life, and to whom the carrying on of open warfare, since it was not easy for so great a power to be overthrown, seemed to be senseless,[1] quitted the city. At the head of these was a distinguished man, Gaius Claudius, uncle to Appius, the chief of the decemvirate, who by this step fulfilled the promises he had made to his nephew in the senate when he advised but failed to persuade him to resign his power. He was followed

---

[1] The MSS. have " and for whom the carrying on of open warfare was not easy, since for so great a power to be overthrown seemed to be senseless." In place of " senseless " Sylburg proposed to read " impossible," Reiske " endless " (an endless task). Kiessling wished to transpose " not easy " and " senseless." Post's emendation, adopted in the text, accomplishes the same result by a simpler change.

τηλικαύτην οὐ ῥᾴδιον Kiessling. In place of ἀνόητον Sylburg proposed ἀδύνατον, Reiske ἀνήνυτον.
[10] ἦν added by Sintenis.

5 ἠκολούθει δ' αὐτῷ πολὺς μὲν ἑταίρων ὄχλος, πολὺς δὲ πελατῶν. τούτου δ' ἀρξαμένου καὶ τὸ ἄλλο πολιτικὸν πλῆθος οὐκέτι λάθρα καὶ κατ' ὀλίγους, ἀλλ' ἐκ τοῦ φανεροῦ καὶ ἀθρόον[1] ἐξέλιπε τὴν πατρίδα, τέκνα καὶ γυναῖκας ἐπαγόμενον. οἱ δὲ περὶ τὸν Ἄππιον ἀγανακτοῦντες τοῖς γινομένοις ἐπεβάλοντο μὲν κωλύειν πύλας τ' ἀποκλείσαντες καὶ ἀνθρώπους τινὰς συναρπάσαντες· ἔπειτα —δέος γὰρ εἰσῆλθεν αὐτοῖς μὴ πρὸς ἀλκὴν οἱ κωλυόμενοι τράπωνται, καὶ λογισμὸς ὀρθὸς ὡς κρεῖττον εἴη σφίσιν ἐκποδὼν εἶναι τοὺς ἐχθροὺς ἢ μένοντας ἐνοχλεῖν—ἀνοίξαντες τὰς πύλας ἀφῆκαν τοὺς θέλοντας ἀπιέναι, οἰκίας δ' αὐτῶν καὶ κλήρους καὶ ὅσα ἄλλα ὑπελείπετο ἀδύνατα ὄντα ἐν φυγαῖς φέρεσθαι λειποστρατίαν ἐπενεγκόντες ἐδήμευσαν τῷ λόγῳ, τὸ δ' ἀληθὲς τοῖς ἑαυτῶν ἑταίροις ὡσανεὶ παρὰ τοῦ δήμου πριαμένοις ἐχαρίσαντο.

6 ταῦτα δὴ[2] τὰ ἐγκλήματα προστεθέντα[3] τοῖς προτέροις πολλῷ δυσμενεστέρους ἐποίησε πρὸς τὴν δεκαδαρχίαν τοὺς πατρικίους καὶ τοὺς δημοτικούς. εἰ μὲν οὖν μηδὲν ἐπεξήμαρτον ἔτι πρὸς τοῖς εἰρημένοις, δοκοῦσιν ἄν μοι πολὺν ἐπὶ τῆς αὐτῆς ἐξουσίας διαμεῖναι χρόνον· ἡ γὰρ φυλάττουσα τὴν δυναστείαν αὐτῶν στάσις ἔτι διέμενεν[4] ἐν τῇ πόλει, διὰ πολλὰς αἰτίας καὶ ἐκ[5] πολλῶν αὐξηθεῖσα χρόνων, δι' ἣν ἔχαιρον ἑκάτεροι τοῖς ἀλλήλων

7 κακοῖς· οἱ μὲν δημοτικοὶ τὸ φρόνημα τῶν πατρικίων τεταπεινωμένον ὁρῶντες καὶ τὴν βουλὴν οὐδενὸς ἔτι τῶν κοινῶν οὖσαν κυρίαν, οἱ δὲ πα-

---

[1] ἀθρόον MV : ἀθρόου L. [2] δὴ added by Portus.
[3] προστιθέντα VM. [4] διέμεινεν VM.
[5] ἐκ LV : διὰ M.

by a large crowd of his friends and likewise of his
clients. Following his lead, the multitude also of
citizens that were left, no longer privately or in small
groups, but openly and in a body, abandoned their
country, taking with them their wives and children.
Appius and his colleagues, being vexed at this,
endeavoured at first to stop them by closing the gates
and arresting some of the people. But afterwards,
becoming afraid lest those they were attempting to
stop should turn and defend themselves, and rightly
judging it to be better for themselves that their
enemies should be out of the way than that they should
remain and make trouble, they opened the gates and
permitted all who so wished to depart ; as for the
houses and estates, however, and all the other things
that they left behind because they could not carry
them away in their flight, the decemvirs nominally
confiscated these to the treasury, bringing against
their owners a charge of desertion, but in reality they
bestowed these possessions on their own followers,
pretending that the latter had purchased them from
the public. These grievances, added to the former,
greatly inflamed the hostility of the patricians and
plebeians against the decemvirs. If, now, they had
not added any fresh crime to those I have related, I
think they might have retained the same power for
a considerable time ; for the sedition which maintained that power still continued in the city and had
been increased by many causes and by the great
length of time it had lasted, and because of the sedition each of the two parties rejoiced in the other's
misfortunes, the plebeians in seeing the spirit of the
patricians humbled and the senate no longer possessing authority over any of the business of state, and

DIONYSIUS OF HALICARNASSUS

τρίκιοι τὴν ἐλευθερίαν ἀπολωλεκότα τὸν δῆμον
καὶ μηδὲ τὴν ἐλαχίστην ἔχοντα ἰσχὺν ἐξ οὗ τὴν
δημαρχικὴν ἐξουσίαν αὐτῶν οἱ δέκα ἀφείλαντο·
αὐθαδείᾳ δὲ πολλῇ πρὸς ἄμφω τὰ μέρη χρώμενοι
καὶ οὔτ' ἐπὶ στρατοπέδου μετριάζοντες οὔτ' ἐν τῇ
πόλει σωφρονοῦντες ὁμονοῆσαι πάντας ἠνάγκασαν
καὶ καταλῦσαι τὴν ἀρχὴν αὐτῶν, ὅπλων γενηθέντας
8 κυρίους διὰ τὸν πόλεμον. τὰ δ' ἁμαρτήματα αὐτῶν
τὰ τελευταῖα καὶ δι' ἃ κατελύθησαν ὑπὸ τοῦ δήμου
(τοῦτον γὰρ δὴ μάλιστα προπηλακίζοντες ἐξηγρίω-
σαν) τοιάδε ἦν.

XXIII. Ὅτε τὸ περὶ τοῦ πολέμου ψήφισμα
ἐκύρωσαν, καταγράψαντες ἐν τάχει τὰς δυνάμεις
καὶ τριχῇ νείμαντες δύο μὲν τάγματα κατέλιπον
ἐν τῇ πόλει φυλακῆς τῶν ἐντὸς τείχους ἕνεκεν·
ἡγεῖτο δὲ τῶν δύο τούτων ταγμάτων Ἄππιος
Κλαύδιος ὁ προεστηκὼς τῆς ὀλιγαρχίας καὶ σὺν
αὐτῷ Σπόριος Ὄππιος.[1] τρία δὲ ἔχοντες ἐξῆγον
ἐπὶ Σαβίνους Κόιντος Φάβιος καὶ Κόιντος Ποιτέ-
2 λιος[2] καὶ Μάνιος Ῥαβολήιος. πέντε δὲ τὰ λοιπὰ
τάγματα παραλαβόντες Μάρκος τε Κορνήλιος
καὶ Λεύκιος Μηνύκιος καὶ Μάρκος Σέργιος καὶ
Τίτος Ἀντώνιος καὶ τελευταῖος Καίσων Δουέλλιος
ἐπὶ τὸν πρὸς Αἰκανοὺς πόλεμον ἀφίκοντο· συν-
εστρατεύετο δ' αὐτοῖς Λατίνων τε καὶ ἄλλων
συμμάχων ἐπικουρικὸν οὐκ ἔλαττον τοῦ πολιτικοῦ
πλήθους. ἀλλ' οὐδὲν αὐτοῖς ἐχώρει κατὰ νοῦν τοσαύτην μὲν οἰκείαν δύναμιν ἐπαγομένοις, τοσαύτην
3 δὲ συμμαχίαν. οἱ γὰρ πολέμιοι καταφρονήσαντες αὐτῶν, ὅτι νεοσύλλεκτοι ἦσαν οἱ στρατευό-
μενοι, πλησίον ἀντεστρατοπεδεύσαντο καὶ τάς
τ' ἀγορὰς ἀγομένας ἀφῃροῦντο λοχῶντες τὰς ὁδοὺς

76

the patricians in seeing the people stripped of their
liberty and without the least strength since the
decemvirs had taken from them the tribunician
power. But the decemvirs, by treating both parties
with great arrogance and by showing neither moderation in the army nor self-restraint in the city, forced
the parties to unite and to abolish their magistracy as
soon as the war had put arms into their hands. Their
last crimes, for which they were overthrown by the
people, whom they had particularly enraged by their
abuses, were as follows.

XXIII. After they had secured the ratification of
the decree of the senate for the war,[1] they hastily
enrolled their forces and divided them into three
bodies. Two legions they left in the city to keep
guard over matters inside the walls; and Appius
Claudius, the chief of the oligarchy, together with
Spurius Oppius commanded these two. Quintus
Fabius, Quintus Poetelius and Manius Rabuleius[2]
marched out with three legions against the Sabines.
Marcus Cornelius, Lucius Minucius, Marcus Sergius,
Titus Antonius, and last, Caeso Duilius, taking over
the five remaining legions, arrived for the campaign
against the Aequians. They were accompanied by
an auxiliary force both of Latins and other allies that
was as large as the citizen army. But nothing succeeded according to their plans, even though they
were leading such large forces of both their own and
allied troops. For their foes, despising them because
their troops were new recruits, encamped over against
them, and placing ambuscades in the roads, cut off
the provisions that were being brought to them and

---

[1] For chaps. 23–24, 1 cf. Livy iii. 41, 7–42, 7.

[1] ἄππιος VM.   [2] πουτέλλιος O.

καὶ ἐπὶ προνομὰς ἐξιοῦσιν ἐπετίθεντο, καὶ εἴ ποτε
ἱππεῖς εἰς χεῖρας ἔλθοιεν ἱππεῦσι καὶ πεζοὶ πεζοῖς
καὶ φάλαγξ[1] πρὸς φάλαγγα μαχόμενοι πανταχῆ
πλέον ἔχοντες ἀπῄεσαν, ἐθελοκακούντων οὐκ ὀλίγων ἐν ταῖς συμπλοκαῖς καὶ οὔτε τοῖς ἡγεμόσι
πειθομένων οὔτε ὁμόσε χωρεῖν τοῖς πολεμίοις
4 βουλομένων. οἱ μὲν οὖν ἐπὶ Σαβίνους στρατεύσαντες ἐν τοῖς ἐλάττοσι κακοῖς σωφρονισθέντες
ἑκόντες ἔγνωσαν ἐκλιπεῖν τὸν χάρακα· καὶ περὶ
μέσας νύκτας ἀναστήσαντες τὸν στρατὸν ἀπῆγον
ἐκ τῆς πολεμίας εἰς τὴν ἑαυτῶν, φυγῇ παραπλησίαν ποιούμενοι τὴν ἀνάζευξιν, ἕως ἐπὶ πόλιν
Κρουστομερίαν, ἥ ἐστιν οὐ πρόσω τῆς Ῥώμης,
ἀφίκοντο. οἱ δ᾽ ἐν Ἀλγιδῷ[2] τῆς Αἰκανῶν χώρας
θέμενοι τὴν παρεμβολὴν πολλὰς καὶ αὐτοὶ λαμβάνοντες ὑπὸ[3] τῶν πολεμίων πληγὰς καὶ παρὰ τὰ
δεινὰ μένειν ἀξιοῦντες ὡς ἐπανορθωσόμενοι[4] τὰς
5 ἐλαττώσεις οἴκτιστα πράγματα ἔπαθον. ὠσάμενοι
γὰρ ἐπ᾽ αὐτοὺς οἱ πολέμιοι καὶ τοὺς ὑποστάντας
τοῦ χάρακος καταβαλόντες ἐπέβησαν τῶν ἐρυμάτων·
καὶ καταλαβόμενοι τὸ στρατόπεδον ὀλίγους μέν
τινας ἀμυνομένους ἀπέκτειναν, τοὺς δὲ πλείους
ἐν τῷ διωγμῷ διέφθειραν. οἱ δὲ διασωθέντες ἐκ
τῆς φυγῆς τραυματίαι τε οἱ πλείους καὶ τὰ ὅπλα
μικροῦ δεῖν πάντες ἀπολωλεκότες εἰς πόλιν
Τύσκλον ἀφικνοῦντο· σκηνὰς δ᾽ αὐτῶν καὶ ὑποζύγια καὶ χρήματα καὶ θεράποντας καὶ τὴν ἄλλην
τοῦ πολέμου παρασκευὴν οἱ πολέμιοι διήρπασαν.
6 ὡς δ᾽ ἀπηγγέλη ταῦτα τοῖς κατὰ τὴν πόλιν,
ὅσοιπερ[5] ἦσαν ἐχθροὶ τῆς ὀλιγαρχίας καὶ οἱ τέως

---

[1] καὶ φάλαγξ added by Kiessling.   [2] ἀργιδίῳ O.
[3] ὑπὸ L : παρὰ R, ἀπὸ Tegge.

attacked them when they went out for forage ; and
whenever cavalry clashed with cavalry, infantry with
infantry, and phalanx against phalanx, the Sabines
always came off superior to the Romans, not a few of
whom voluntarily played the coward in their en-
counters and not only disobeyed their officers but
refused to come to grips with the foe. Those,
accordingly, who had set out against the Sabines,
grown wise amid these minor misfortunes, resolved
to quit their entrenchments of their own accord ;
and breaking camp about midnight, they led the army
back from the enemy's territory into their own,
making their withdrawal not unlike a flight, till they
came to the city of Crustumerium, which is not far
from Rome. But those who had made their camp
at Algidum in the country of the Aequians, when
they too had received many blows at the hands of the
enemy and still resolved to stand their ground in the
midst of these dangers in hopes of retrieving their
reverses, suffered a most grievous disaster. For
the enemy, having thrust forward against them and
cleared the palisades of those who defended them,
mounted the ramparts, and possessing themselves of
the camp, killed some few while fighting but destroyed
the greater part in the pursuit. Those who escaped
from this rout, being most of them wounded and
having almost all lost their arms, came to the city of
Tusculum ; but their tents, beasts of burden, money,
slaves, and the rest of their military provisions became
the prey of the enemy. When the news of this defeat
was brought to the people in Rome, all who were
enemies of the oligarchy and those who had hitherto

---

⁴ ἐπανορθωσάμενοι LV.
⁵ ὅσοιπερ Kiessling : ὅσοι γὰρ O, ὅσοι μὲν Sylburg.

DIONYSIUS OF HALICARNASSUS

ἀποκρυπτόμενοι τὸ μῖσος φανεροὺς ἐποίουν αὑτοὺς
τότε χαίροντες ἐπὶ ταῖς κακοπραγίαις τῶν στρα-
τηγῶν· καὶ ἦν ἤδη καρτερὰ χεὶρ περὶ τὸν Ὁράτιόν
τε καὶ τὸν Οὐαλέριον, οὓς ἔφην ἡγεμόνας εἶναι
τῶν ἀριστοκρατικῶν ἑταιρειῶν.

XXIV. Οἱ δὲ περὶ τὸν Ἄππιον τοῖς μὲν ἐπὶ
στρατοπέδου συνάρχουσιν ὅπλα τε καὶ χρήματα
καὶ σῖτον καὶ τἆλλα ὧν ἐδέοντο ἐπεχορήγουν τά
τε δημόσια καὶ ἰδιωτικὰ ἐκ πολλῆς ὑπεροψίας
λαμβάνοντες, καὶ ἀντὶ τῶν ἀπολωλότων ἀνδρῶν
στρατολογήσαντες ἐξ ἁπάσης φυλῆς τοὺς ὅπλα
φέρειν δυναμένους ἀπέστειλαν, ὥστ᾽ ἐκπληρωθῆναι
τοὺς λόχους· τῶν τε κατὰ πόλιν[1] ἐπιμελῆ φυλακὴν
ἐποιοῦντο φρουραῖς τοὺς ἐπικαιροτάτους κατα-
λαμβανόμενοι τόπους, μή τι λάθωσι παρακινή-
σαντες οἱ μετὰ τοῦ Οὐαλερίου συνεστῶτες.
2 ἐπέσκηπτόν τε δι᾽ ἀπορρήτων τοῖς ἐπὶ τῶν στρατοπέδων συνάρχουσι τοὺς ἐναντιουμένους σφίσι
διαφθείρειν, τοὺς μὲν ἐπιφανεῖς ἀδήλως, ὧν δ᾽
ἐλάττων λόγος[2] ἦν καὶ[3] ἀπὸ τοῦ φανεροῦ, προφάσεις ἀεί τινας ἐπιφέροντας, ἵνα δικαίως δόξωσιν
ἀποθανεῖν. καὶ ἐγίνετο ταῦτα· οἱ μὲν γὰρ ἐπὶ
προνομὰς ἀποστελλόμενοι ὑπ᾽ αὐτῶν, οἱ δ᾽ ἀγορὰν
παραπέμψαι κομιζομένην, οἱ δ᾽ ἄλλας τινὰς ἐπι-
τελέσασθαι πολεμικὰς χρείας, ἔξω γενόμενοι τοῦ
3 χάρακος οὐδαμοῦ ἔτι ὤφθησαν· οἱ δὲ[4] ταπεινό-
τατοι, φυγῆς ἄρχειν κατηγορηθέντες ἢ τὰ ἀπόρρητα
πρὸς τοὺς πολεμίους ἐκφέρειν ἢ τάξιν μὴ φυλάττειν,
ἐν τῷ φανερῷ καταπλήξεως ἕνεκα τῶν ἄλλων
ἀπώλλυντο. ἐγίνετο δὴ[5] διχόθεν τῶν στρατιωτῶν

---

[1] πόλιν O : τὴν πόλιν Ambrosch, Jacoby.
[2] λόγος Cobet (cf. chap. 25, l. 4) : ὁ λόγος O, Jacoby.

been concealing their hatred revealed themselves now by rejoicing at the misfortunes of the generals ; and there was now a strong body of men attached to both Horatius and Valerius, who, as I said, were the leaders of the aristocratical groups.

XXIV. Appius and Spurius supplied their colleagues who were in the field with arms, money, corn and everything else they stood in need of, taking all these things with a high hand, whether public or private property ; and enrolling all the men in every tribe who were able to bear arms in order to replace those who had been lost, they sent them out so that the centuries might be filled up. They also kept strict guard over matters in the city by garrisoning the most critical positions, lest the followers of Valerius should foment some disorders without their knowledge. They also gave secret instructions to their colleagues in the army to put to death all who opposed their measures, the men of distinction secretly, and those of less account even openly, always using some specious excuses to make their death seem deserved. And these things were being done. For some, being sent out by them for forage, others to convoy provisions that were being brought in, and some to perform other military tasks, when they were once out of the camp, were nowhere seen again, while the humblest men, being accused of being the first to take flight or of carrying secret information to the enemy or of quitting their posts, were being put to death publicly in order to strike terror into the rest. Two causes, therefore, contributed to the destruction of the soldiers : the friends

---

³ καὶ LV : om. R.   ⁴ οἱ δὲ M : οὐδὲ LV.
⁵ δὴ Kiessling : δὲ O, Jacoby.

ὄλεθρος, τῶν μὲν οἰκείων τῆς ὀλιγαρχίας ἐν ταῖς
πρὸς τοὺς πολεμίους συμπλοκαῖς διαφθειρομένων,
τῶν δὲ τὴν ἀριστοκρατικὴν ποθούντων κατάστασιν
ὑπὸ τῶν στρατηγῶν ἀπολλυμένων.

XXV. Πολλὰ δὲ τοιαῦτα καὶ κατὰ τὴν πόλιν
ὑπὸ τῶν περὶ τὸν Ἄππιον ἐγίνετο. τῶν μὲν οὖν
ἄλλων καίτοι συχνῶν ἀναιρουμένων ἐλάττων τοῖς
πλήθεσι λόγος ἦν, ἑνὸς δ' ἀνδρὸς ἐπιφανεστάτου
τῶν δημοτικῶν καὶ πλείστας ἀρετὰς ἐν τοῖς κατὰ
πόλεμον ἔργοις ἀποδειξαμένου θάνατος ὠμὸς καὶ
ἀνόσιος ἐπιτελεσθεὶς ἐν θατέρῳ τῶν στρατοπέδων
ἔνθα οἱ τρεῖς ἡγεμόνες ἦσαν, ἅπαντας ἑτοίμους
2 ἐποίησε πρὸς τὴν ἀπόστασιν τοὺς ἐκεῖ. ἦν δ' ὁ
φονευθεὶς Σίκκιος, ὁ τὰς ἑκατὸν εἴκοσι μάχας
ἀγωνισάμενος καὶ ἐξ ἁπασῶν ἀριστεῖα[1] λαβών, ὃν
ἔφην ἀπολελυμένον ἤδη στρατείας διὰ τὸν χρόνον
ἑκούσιον τοῦ πρὸς Αἰκανοὺς συνάρασθαι πολέμου,
σπεῖραν ἀνδρῶν ὀκτακοσίων ἐκπεπληρωκότων ἤδη
τὰς κατὰ νόμον στρατείας εὐνοίᾳ τῇ πρὸς αὐτὸν
ἐπαγόμενον· μεθ' ὧν ἀποσταλεὶς ὑπὸ θατέρου τῶν
ὑπάτων ἐπὶ τὸ στρατόπεδον τῶν πολεμίων εἰς
πρόδηλον ὄλεθρον, ὡς πᾶσιν ἐδόκει, τοῦ τε
χάρακος ἐκράτησε καὶ τῆς ὁλοσχεροῦς νίκης
3 αἴτιος ἐγένετο τοῖς ὑπάτοις. τοῦτον δὴ[2] τὸν ἄνδρα
πολλοὺς ἐν τῇ πόλει διεξιόντα λόγους κατὰ τῶν
ἐπὶ στρατοπέδου στρατηγῶν, ὡς ἀνάνδρων τε καὶ
ἀπείρων πολέμου, ἐκποδὼν ποιῆσαι σπεύδοντες οἱ
περὶ τὸν Ἄππιον εἰς ὁμιλίας προὐκαλοῦντο φιλανθρώπους καὶ συνδιαπορεῖν σφίσιν ἠξίουν ὑπὲρ
τῶν ἐπὶ στρατοπέδου, καὶ πῶς ἂν[3] ἐπανορθωθείη

---

[1] τἀριστεῖα Kiessling.   [2] δὴ L : δὲ V, om. M.
[3] ἂν added by Kayser.

of the oligarchy were perishing in the skirmishes with the enemy, while those who longed for the aristocratic régime were being slain by the orders of the generals.

XXV. Many crimes of this nature [1] were committed in the city also by Appius and his colleague. The destruction of most of the victims, numerous as they were, was a matter of no great concern to the masses ; but the cruel and wicked death of one man, who was the most distinguished of the plebeians and had performed the most gallant exploits in war, only to be murdered now in that one of the camps where the three generals commanded, disposed everyone there to revolt. The man assassinated was that Siccius [2] who had fought the hundred and twenty battles and had received prizes for valour in all of them, a man of whom I have said that, when he was exempt from military service by reason of his age, he voluntarily engaged in the war against the Aequians at the head of a cohort of eight hundred men who had already completed the regular term of service and followed him out of affection for him ; and having been sent with these men by one of the consuls against the enemy's camp, to manifest destruction, as everyone thought, he not only made himself master of their camp, but enabled the consuls to gain the complete victory they did. This man, who kept making many speeches in the city against the generals in the field, accusing them of both cowardice and inexperience in warfare, Appius and his colleague were eager to remove out of their way, and to that end they invited him to friendly conversations and asked him to consult with them concerning affairs in camp, urging him

---

[1] For chaps. 25–27 cf. Livy iii. 43.   [2] See x. 36 ff., 43 ff.

τὰ τῶν στρατηγῶν ἁμαρτήματα λέγειν παρεκά-
λουν, καὶ τελευτῶντες ἔπεισαν ἐξελθεῖν ἐπὶ τὸν
ἐν Κρουστομερίᾳ χάρακα αὐτὸν ἐξουσίαν ἔχοντα
πρεσβευτικήν. ἔστι δὲ πάντων ἱερώτατόν τε καὶ
τιμιώτατον ὁ πρεσβευτὴς παρὰ Ῥωμαίοις ἐξουσίαν
μὲν ἄρχοντος ἔχων καὶ δύναμιν, ἀσυλίαν δὲ καὶ
4 σεβασμὸν ἱερέως. ὡς δ' ἀφίκετο, φιλοφρονου-
μένων αὐτὸν ἐκεῖ τῶν ἡγεμόνων καὶ δεομένων
συστρατηγεῖν μένοντα, καί τινας καὶ δωρεὰς τὰς
μὲν διδόντων ἤδη, τὰς δ' ὑπισχνουμένων, ἐξαπατηθεὶς ὑπ' ἀνθρώπων πονηρῶν καὶ τῇ γοητείᾳ
τῶν λόγων οὐ συνειδὼς¹ ὡς ἐξ ἐπιβουλῆς ἐγίνετο,²
στρατιωτικὸς ἀνὴρ καὶ τὸν τρόπον ἁπλοῦς, τά τ'
ἄλλα ὑπέθετο³ αὐτοῖς, ὅσα συμφέρειν ὑπελάμβανε,
καὶ πρῶτον ἁπάντων παρήνει μετάγειν τὴν παρεμβολὴν εἰς τὴν πολεμίαν ἐκ τῆς σφετέρας, τάς
τε βλάβας διεξιὼν τὰς τότε γινομένας καὶ τὰς
ὠφελείας ἐπιλογιζόμενος ὅσας ἔμελλον ἕξειν μετα-
στρατοπεδευσάμενοι.

XXVI. Οἱ δ' ἀσμένως δέχεσθαι τὰς παραινέσεις
σκηψάμενοι, " Τί οὖν," ἔφασαν, " οὐκ αὐτὸς
ἡγεμὼν γίνῃ τῆς ἀναζεύξεως τόπον ἐπιτήδειον
προκατασκεψάμενος; ἐμπειρίαν δ' ἱκανὴν ἔχεις
τῶν τόπων διὰ τὰς πολλὰς στρατείας, λόχον δέ
σοι δώσομεν ἐπιλέκτων νέων εὐζώνῳ ἐσταλμένων
ὁπλίσει· σοὶ δὲ ἵππος τε διὰ τὴν ἡλικίαν παρέστω,
2 καὶ ὁπλισμὸς ὁ τοῖς τηλικούτοις πρέπων." ὑπο-
δεξαμένου δὲ τοῦ Σικκίου καὶ ψιλοὺς αἰτήσαντος
ἑκατὸν ἐπιλέκτους οὐδένα χρόνον ἐπισχόντες ἐκ-

¹ τὴν γοητείαν . . . οὐ συνιδὼν Reiske.
² ἐγίνετο L : ἐγένετο R.

84

to tell how the mistakes of the generals might be corrected ; and at last they prevailed upon him to go out to the camp at Crustumerium invested with the authority of a legate. The position of legate is the most honourable and the most sacred of all dignities among the Romans, possessing as it does the power and authority of a magistrate and the inviolable and holy character of a priest. When he arrived at the camp and the generals there gave him a friendly greeting and asked him to remain and command in conjunction with them, also offering him some presents on the spot and promising others, Siccius, deceived by these wicked men and not conscious that the charm of their conversation was due to a plot, he being a military man and of a simple nature, not only made other recommendations, such as he thought advantageous, but, first of all, advised them to move their camp from their own territory to that of the enemy, recounting the losses they were then suffering and also estimating the advantages they would gain by shifting their camp.

XXVI. The generals, professing that they were glad to accept his advice, said : " Why, then, do you not take charge yourself of the army's removal, after first looking out a suitable position for it ? You are sufficiently acquainted with the region because of the many campaigns you have made, and we will give you a company of picked youths fitted out with light equipment ; for yourself there shall be a horse, on account of your age, and armour suitable for such an expedition." Siccius having accepted the commission and asked for a hundred picked light-

---

[3] ὑπέθετο Sylburg : ἐπείθετο LM, Jacoby.

πέμπουσιν αὐτὸν ἔτι νυκτὸς οὔσης καὶ σὺν αὐτῷ
τοὺς ἑκατὸν ἄνδρας ἐκ τῶν ἰδίων ἑταίρων τοὺς ἰτα-
μωτάτους ἐπιλεξάμενοι, οἷς ἐπέσκηψαν ἀποκτεῖναι τὸν ἄνδρα μεγάλους μισθοὺς τῆς ἀνδροφονίας
ὑποσχόμενοι. ἐπεὶ δὲ πολὺ προελθόντες ἀπὸ τοῦ
χάρακος εἰς χωρίον ἦλθον ὀχθηρὸν καὶ στενόπορον
καὶ χαλεπὸν ἵππῳ διεξελθεῖν, ὅτι μὴ βάδην ἀνιόντι,[1]
διὰ τὴν τραχύτητα τῶν ὄχθων, σύνθημα δόντες
ἀλλήλοις στῖφος ἐποίουν ὡς ἅμα χωρήσοντες[2] ἐπ᾽
αὐτὸν ἀθρόοι. θεράπων δέ τις ὑπασπιστὴς τοῦ
Σικκίου τὰ πολεμικὰ ἀγαθὸς εἰκάσας τὴν διάνοιαν
3 αὐτῶν μηνυτὴς γίνεται τῷ δεσπότῃ. κἀκεῖνος ὡς
ἔγνω κατακλειόμενον αὐτὸν εἰς δυσχωρίας, ἔνθα
οὐκ ἦν δυνατὸν ἀνὰ κράτος ἐλάσαι τὸν ἵππον,
καθάλλεταί τε καὶ στὰς ἐπὶ τὸν ὄχθον, ἵνα μὴ
κυκλωθείη πρὸς αὐτῶν, τὸν ὑπασπιστὴν μόνον
ἔχων τοὺς ἐπιόντας ὑπέμεινεν. ὁρμησάντων δὲ
ἅμα πάντων πολλῶν ὄντων[3] ἐπ᾽ αὐτὸν ἀποκτείνει
μὲν περὶ[4] πεντεκαίδεκα, τραυματίζει δὲ καὶ δι-
πλασίους. ἐδόκει δ᾽ ἂν καὶ τοὺς ἄλλους ἅπαντας
4 διαφθεῖραι μαχόμενος εἰ συνῄεσαν ὁμόσε. οἱ δ᾽
ἄρα συμφρονήσαντες ὡς ἄμαχον[5] εἴη χρῆμα καὶ
οὐκ ἂν ἕλοιεν αὐτὸν συστάδην, τῆς μὲν ἐκ χειρὸς
ἀπείχοντο μάχης, προσωτέρω δ᾽ ἀποστάντες ἔβαλ-
λον οἱ μὲν σαυνίοις, οἱ δὲ χερμάσιν, οἱ δὲ ξύλοις·
τινὲς δ᾽ αὐτῶν προσελθόντες ἐκ τῶν πλαγίων τῷ
ὄχθῳ[6] καὶ γενόμενοι κατὰ κεφαλῆς κατεκύλιον
ὑπερμεγέθεις ἄνωθεν πέτρας, ἕως ὑπὸ πλήθους τῶν

---

[1] ἀνιόντι Lb : ἀπιόντι LaMV, ἐπιόντι Sylburg.
[2] ὡς ἅμα χωρήσοντες Sintenis : ὡς χωρήσοντες Lc, Reiske,
ὡς ἀναχωρήσοντες LaMV.
[3] πάντων πολλῶν ὄντων MV : ἅμα πολλῶν L.
[4] μὲν ἅμα περὶ LV.   [5] ἄμαχον LV : ἄμαχόν τι R.

armed men, they sent him out without delay while
it was still night; and with him they sent the
hundred men, whom they had picked out as the
most daring of their own faction, with orders to kill
the man, promising them great rewards for his
murder. When they had advanced a long distance
from the camp and had come to a hilly region where
the road was narrow and difficult for a horse to
traverse at any other pace than a walk as it climbed,
by reason of the ruggedness of the hills, they gave
the signal to one another and formed in a compact
mass, with the intention of falling upon him all together in a body. But a servant of Siccius, who was
his shield-bearer and a brave warrior, guessed their
intention and informed his master of it. Siccius, seeing himself confined in a difficult position where it
was not possible to drive his horse at full speed, leaped
down, and taking his stand upon the hill in order to
avoid being surrounded by his assailants, with only
his shield-bearer to aid him, awaited their attack.
When they fell upon him all at once, many in number,
he killed some fifteen of them and wounded twice
as many; and it seemed as if he might have slain
all the others in combat if they had come to close
quarters with him. But they, concluding that he
was an invincible prodigy and that they could never
vanquish him by engaging hand to hand, gave over
that way of fighting, and withdrawing to a greater
distance, hurled javelins, stones and sticks at him;
and some of them, approaching the hill from the
flanks and getting above him, rolled down huge stones
upon him till they overwhelmed him with the multi-

---

[6] τῷ ὄχθῳ Jacoby : τῶν ὄχθων O, τοῦ ὄχθου Grasberger;
περιελθόντες . . . τὸν ὄχθον Reiske.

ἐξ ἐναντίας βαλλομένων καὶ βάρους τῶν ἄνωθεν
ἐπικαταραττομένων διέφθειραν αὐτόν. Σίκκιος
μὲν δὴ τοιαύτης καταστροφῆς ἔτυχεν.

XXVII. Οἱ δὲ διαπραξάμενοι τὸν φόνον ἧκον
ἐπὶ τὸ στρατόπεδον ἄγοντες τοὺς τραυματίας καὶ
διέσπειραν λόγον ὡς ἐπιφανεὶς αὐτοῖς πολεμίων
λόχος τόν τε Σίκκιον ἀποκτείνειε καὶ τοὺς ἄλλους
ἄνδρας οἷς πρώτοις ἐνέτυχεν, αὐτοί τε πολλὰ
τραύματα λαβόντες μόλις αὐτοὺς ἀποφύγοιεν. καὶ
ἐδόκουν ἅπασι πιστὰ λέγειν. οὐ μὴν ἔλαθέ γ'
αὐτῶν τὸ ἔργον, ἀλλὰ καίπερ ἐν ἐρημίᾳ τοῦ φόνου
γεγονότος καὶ μηδένα μηνυτὴν ἔχοντος ὑπὸ τοῦ
χρεὼν αὐτοῦ καὶ τῆς ἅπαντα ἐπισκοπούσης τὰ
θνητὰ πράγματα δίκης ἐξηλέγχθησαν τεκμηρίοις
2 ἀναμφισβητήτοις. οἱ γὰρ ἐν τῷ[1] στρατοπέδῳ
ταφῆς τε δημοσίας ἄξιον ἡγούμενοι τὸν ἄνδρα καὶ
τιμῆς[2] παρὰ τοὺς ἄλλους διαφόρου,[3] διὰ πολλὰ
μὲν καὶ ἄλλα, μάλιστα δ' ὅτι πρεσβύτης ὢν καὶ
ὑπὸ τῆς ἡλικίας πολεμικῶν ἀγώνων ἀπολυόμενος
εἰς κίνδυνον ἑκούσιον ἔδωκεν αὐτὸν[4] ὑπὲρ τοῦ
κοινῇ συμφέροντος, ψηφίζονται συνελθόντες εἰς
ἓν ἀπὸ τῶν τριῶν ταγμάτων ἐξελθεῖν ἐπὶ τὴν
ἀναίρεσιν[5] τοῦ σώματος, ἵνα μετὰ πολλῆς ἀσφαλείας τε καὶ τιμῆς ἐπὶ τὴν παρεμβολὴν παρα-
κομισθείη. συγχωρησάντων δὲ τῶν ἡγεμόνων δι'
εὐλάβειαν μή τινα παράσχοιεν αὐτοῖς ὑποψίαν περὶ
τὸ πρᾶγμα ἐπιβουλῆς καλῷ καὶ προσήκοντι ἔργῳ
3 ἐνιστάμενοι, λαβόντες τὰ ὅπλα ἐξῇσαν. ἐλθόντες δ' ἐπὶ τὸν τόπον, ὡς εἶδον οὔτε δρυμοὺς

---

[1] τῷ V : om. R.   [2] Kiessling : τιμαῖς O, Jacoby.
διαφόρου LV : διαφόροις M.   [4] αὐτὸν L : ἑαυτὸν R.
[5] ἀναίρεσιν L : ἀνεύρεσιν R.

tude of the missiles that were hurled at him from in front and the weight of the stones that crashed down upon him from above. Such was the fate of Siccius.

XXVII. Those who had accomplished his murder returned to the camp bringing their wounded with them, and spread a report that a body of the enemy, having suddenly come upon them, had killed Siccius and the other men whom they first encountered and that they themselves after receiving many wounds had escaped with great difficulty. And their report seemed credible to everyone. However, their crime did not remain concealed, but though the murder was committed in a solitude where there was no possible informant, by the agency of fate itself and that justice which oversees all human actions they were convicted on the strength of incontrovertible evidence. For the soldiers in the camp, feeling that the man deserved both a public funeral and distinctive honour above other men, not only for many other reasons, but particularly because, though he was an old man and exempted by his age from contests of war, he had voluntarily exposed himself to danger for the public good, voted to join together from the three legions and go out to recover his body,[1] in order that it might be brought to the camp in complete security and honour. And the generals consenting to this, for fear that by opposing a worthy and becoming action they might create some suspicion of a plot in regard to the incident, they took their arms and went out of the camp. When they came to the spot and

---

[1] Livy states (iii. 43, 6) that one cohort went out for the purpose.

οὔτε φάραγγας οὔτ' ἄλλο χωρίον ἔνθα ὑποκαθίζειν
ἐστὶ λόχοις[1] ἔθος, ἀλλὰ ψιλὸν καὶ περιφανῆ καὶ
στενόπορον ὄχθον, δι' ὑποψίας ἔλαβον εὐθέως
τὸ πραχθέν· ἔπειτα τοῖς νεκροῖς προσελθόντες ὡς
ἐθεάσαντο τόν τε Σίκκιον αὐτὸν ἀσκύλευτον ἐρ-
ριμμένον καὶ τοὺς ἄλλους ἅπαντας, ἐν θαύματι
ἦσαν εἰ πολέμιοι κρατήσαντες ἐχθρῶν μήτε ὅπλα
4 περιείλαντο[2] μήτ' ἐσθῆτα περιέδυσαν. διερευνώ-
μενοί τε τὰ πέριξ ἅπαντα ὡς οὔτε στίβον ἵππων
οὔτ' ἴχνος ἀνθρώπων οὐδὲν εὕρισκον ἔξω τῶν
διὰ τῆς ὁδοῦ, πρᾶγμα ἀμήχανον ὑπελάμβανον
εἶναι πολεμίους ἐπιφανῆναι τοῖς σφετέροις ἀφα-
νεῖς, ὥσπερ πτηνούς τινας ἢ διοπετεῖς. ὑπὲρ
ἅπαντα δὲ ταῦτα καὶ τὰ ἄλλα μέγιστον αὐτοῖς
ἐφάνη τεκμήριον τοῦ μὴ πρὸς ἐχθρῶν ἀλλ' ὑπὸ
φίλων τὸν ἄνδρα ἀπολωλέναι, τὸ μηδένα τῶν
5 πολεμίων εὑρεθῆναι νεκρόν. οὐ γὰρ ἀκονιτί γ'[3]
ἂν ἐδόκουν ἀποθανεῖν Σίκκιον, ἄνδρα καὶ ῥώμην
καὶ ψυχὴν ἀνυπόστατον, οὐδὲ τὸν ὑπασπιστήν,
οὐδὲ τοὺς ἄλλους τοὺς σὺν αὐτῷ πεσόντας ἄλλως
τε καὶ ἐκ χειρὸς γενομένης τῆς μάχης. ἐτεκμή-
ραντο δὲ τοῦτο ἐκ τῶν τραυμάτων. αὐτός τε[4]
γὰρ ὁ Σίκκιος πολλὰς εἶχε πληγὰς τὰς μὲν ὑπὸ
χερμάδων, τὰς δ' ὑπὸ σαυνίων, τὰς δ' ὑπὸ μαχαιρῶν,[5] καὶ ὁ ὑπασπιστής· οἱ δ' ὑπ' ἐκείνων ἀνῃρη-
μένοι πάντες μαχαιρῶν μέν, βέλους δὲ οὐδεμίαν.[6]
6 ἀγανάκτησις δὴ[7] μετὰ τοῦτ' ἐγίνετο πάντων καὶ

---

[1] λόχοις O : λόχους Grasberger, Jacoby.
[2] περιείλαντο LbVM : εἵλαντο La ; ἀφείλοντο Kiessling.
[3] τ' LVM.   [4] γε LV.
[5] μαχαιρῶν O : βελῶν Reiske.
[6] μαχαιρῶν μέν, βέλους δὲ οὐδεμίαν Cary : μαχαιρῶν ἢ χερμάδων ἢ σαυνίων, βέλους δὲ οὐδεμίαν (οὐδὲ μιᾶ LV) O, Jacoby.

saw neither woods nor ravines nor any other place
of the sort customary for the setting of ambuscades,
but a bare hill exposed on all sides and reached by a
narrow pass, they at once began to suspect what had
happened. Then, approaching the dead bodies and
seeing Siccius himself and all the rest cast aside but
not despoiled, they marvelled that the enemy, after
overcoming their foes, had stripped off neither their
arms nor their clothes. And when they examined
the whole region round about and found neither
tracks of horses nor footsteps of men besides those in
the road, they thought it impossible that enemies till
then invisible could have suddenly burst into view of
their comrades, as if they had been creatures with
wings or had fallen from heaven. But, over and above
all these and the other signs, what seemed to them
the strongest proof that the man had been slain, not
by enemies, but by friends, was that the body of no
foeman was found. For they could not conceive that
Siccius, a man irresistible by reason both of his
strength and of his valour, or his shield-bearer either,
or the others who had fallen with him would have
perished without offering a stout resistance, particularly since the contest had been waged hand to hand.
This they conjectured from their wounds ; for both
Siccius himself and his shield-bearer had many
wounds, some from stones, others from javelins, and
still others from swords, whereas those who had been
slain by them all had wounds from swords,[1] but none
from a missile weapon. Thereupon they all gave way
to resentment and cried out, making great lamenta-

---

[1] See the critical note.

μαχαιρῶν μέν, χερμάδων δὲ ἢ σαυνίων ἢ βέλους οὐδεμίαν πληγὴν
εἶχον Portus.　　　　　　[7] δὲ L.

βοὴ καὶ πολὺς ὀδυρμός[1]· ὡς δὲ κατωλοφύραντο
τὴν συμφοράν, ἀράμενοι καὶ κομίσαντες τὸν νεκρὸν
ἐπὶ τὸν χάρακα, πολλὰ τῶν στρατηγῶν κατεβόων,
καὶ μάλιστα μὲν ἠξίουν κατὰ τὸν στρατιωτικὸν
ἀποκτεῖναι νόμον τοὺς ἀνδροφόνους, εἰ δὲ μή,
δικαστήριον αὐτοῖς ἀποδοῦναι παραχρῆμα· καὶ
7 πολλοὶ ἦσαν οἱ κατηγορεῖν μέλλοντες αὐτῶν. ὡς
δ' οὐδὲν αὐτῶν εἰσήκουον ἐκεῖνοι, ἀλλὰ τούς τ'
ἄνδρας ἀπεκρύψαντο καὶ τὰς δίκας ἀνεβάλοντο[2]
φήσαντες ἐν Ῥώμῃ λόγον ἀποδώσειν τοῖς βουλομένοις αὐτῶν κατηγορεῖν, μαθόντες ὅτι τῶν
στρατηγῶν τὸ ἐπιβούλευμα ἦν, τὸν μὲν Σίκκιον
ἔθαπτον, ἐκκομιδήν τε ποιησάμενοι λαμπροτάτην
καὶ πυρὰν νήσαντες ὑπερμεγέθη καὶ τῶν ἄλλων
ἀπαρχόμενοι[3] κατὰ δύναμιν ὧν νόμος ἐπ' ἀνδράσιν
ἀγαθοῖς εἰς τὴν τελευταίαν τιμὴν φέρεσθαι· πρὸς δὲ
τὴν δεκαδαρχίαν ἠλλοτριοῦντο πάντες[4] καὶ γνώμην
εἶχον ὡς ἀποστησόμενοι. τὸ μὲν δὴ περὶ Κρουστομερίαν καὶ Φιδήνην στράτευμα διὰ τὸν Σικκίου
τοῦ πρεσβευτοῦ[5] θάνατον ἐχθρὸν τοῖς προεστηκόσι
τῶν πραγμάτων ἦν.

XXVIII. Τὸ δ' ἐν Ἀλγιδῷ τῆς Αἰκανῶν χώρας καθιδρυμένον καὶ τὸ ἐν τῇ πόλει πλῆθος ἅπαν
διὰ ταύτας ἐξεπολεμώθη[6] τὰς αἰτίας πρὸς αὐτούς.
ἀνὴρ ἐκ τῶν δημοτικῶν, Λεύκιος Οὐεργίνιος, οὐδενὸς χείρων τὰ πολεμικά, λόχου τινὸς ἡγεμονίαν
ἔχων ἐν τοῖς πέντε τάγμασιν ἐτάχθη τοῖς ἐπ'
2 Αἰκανοὺς στρατευσαμένοις. τούτῳ θυγάτηρ ἔτυχεν

---

[1] ὀδυρμός R (?) : ὁ δρόμος L.
[2] Reiske : ἀνεβάλλοντο O.
[3] Sylburg : ἐπαρχόμενοι O.
[4] Kiessling : ἅπαντες O.   [5] πρεσβυτάτου MV.
[6] ἐξεπολεμώθη Lb : ἐξεπολεμήθη LaV.

92

tion. After bewailing the calamity, they took up the body, and carrying it to the camp, indulged in loud outcries against the generals, and they demanded, preferably, that the murderers be put to death in accordance with military law, or else that a civil court be assigned to them immediately ; and many were those who were ready to be their accusers. When the generals paid no heed to them, but concealed the men and put off the trials, telling them they would give an accounting in Rome to any who wished to accuse them, the soldiers, convinced that the generals had been the authors of the plot, proceeded to bury Siccius, after arranging a most magnificent funeral procession and erecting an immense pyre, where every man according to his ability presented the first-offerings of everything that is usually employed in rendering the last honours to brave men ; but they were all becoming alienated from the decemvirs and had the intention of revolting. Thus the army that lay encamped at Crustumerium and Fidenae, because of the death of Siccius the legate, was hostile to the men who stood at the head of the government.

XXVIII. The other army,[1] which lay at Algidum in the territory of the Aequians, as well as the whole body of the people at Rome became hostile to them for the following reasons. One of the plebeians, whose name was Lucius Verginius, a man inferior to none in warfare, had the command of a century in one of the five legions which had taken the field against the Aequians. He had a daughter, called Verginia

---

[1] For chaps. 28–37 cf. Livy iii. 44–48, 6.

οὖσα καλλίστη τῶν ἐν Ῥώμῃ παρθένων τὸ πατρῷον
ὄνομα φέρουσα, ἣν ἐνεγγυήσατο Λεύκιος εἷς ἐκ
τῶν δεδημαρχηκότων υἱὸς Ἰκιλίου τοῦ πρώτου
τε καταστησαμένου τὴν δημαρχικὴν ἐξουσίαν καὶ
3 πρώτου λαβόντος. ταύτην τὴν κόρην ἐπίγαμον
οὖσαν ἤδη θεασάμενος Ἄππιος Κλαύδιος ὁ τῆς
δεκαδαρχίας ἡγεμὼν ἀναγινώσκουσαν ἐν γραμμα-
τιστοῦ (ἦν δὲ τὰ διδασκαλεῖα τότε τῶν παίδων
περὶ τὴν ἀγοράν) εὐθύς τε ὑπὸ τοῦ κάλλους τῆς
παιδὸς ἑάλω καὶ ἔτι μᾶλλον ἔξω τῶν φρενῶν
ἐγένετο πολλάκις ἀναγκαζόμενος παριέναι[1] τὸ
διδασκαλεῖον ἤδη κρατούμενος ὑπὸ τοῦ πάθους.
4 ὡς δ' οὐκ ἠδύνατο πρὸς γάμον αὐτὴν λαβεῖν
ἐκείνην τε ὁρῶν ἐγγεγυημένην ἑτέρῳ καὶ αὐτὸς
ἔχων γυναῖκα γαμετήν, καὶ ἅμα οὐδ' ἀξιῶν ἐκ
δημοτικοῦ γένους ἁρμόσασθαι γάμον δι' ὑπεροψίαν
τῆς τύχης καὶ ὡς[2] παρὰ τὸν νόμον ὃν αὐτὸς ἐν ταῖς
δώδεκα δέλτοις ἀνέγραψε, τὸ μὲν πρῶτον ἐπειράθη
διαφθεῖραι χρήμασι τὴν κόρην, καὶ προσέπεμπέ
τινας ἀεὶ πρὸς τὰς τροφοὺς αὐτῆς γυναῖκας (ἦν
γὰρ ὀρφανὴ μητρὸς ἡ παῖς) διδούς τε πολλὰ καὶ
ἔτι πλείονα τῶν διδομένων[3] ὑπισχνούμενος. παρ-
ηγγέλλετο[4] δὲ τοῖς πειρωμένοις τὰς τροφοὺς μὴ
λέγειν τίς ὁ τῆς κόρης ἐστὶν ἐρῶν, ἀλλ' ὅτι τῶν
δυναμένων τις εὖ ποιεῖν οὓς βουληθείη καὶ κακῶς.
5 ὡς δ' οὐκ ἔπειθον αὐτάς, ἀλλὰ καὶ φυλακῆς ἑώρα
τὴν κόρην κρείττονος ἢ πρότερον ἀξιουμένην,
φλεγόμενος ὑπὸ τοῦ πάθους τὴν ἰταμωτέραν ἔγνω
βαδίζειν ὁδόν. μεταπεμψάμενος δή τινα τῶν
ἑαυτοῦ πελατῶν, Μάρκον Κλαύδιον, ἄνδρα τολμη-

[1] περιέναι VM.
[2] ὡς added by Capps.

after her father, who far surpassed all the Roman maidens in beauty and was betrothed to Lucius, a former tribune and son of the Icilius who first instituted and first received the tribunician power. Appius Claudius, the chief of the decemvirs, having seen this girl, who was now marriageable, as she was reading at the schoolmaster's (the schools for the children stood at that time near the Forum), was immediately captivated by her beauty and became still more frenzied because, already mastered by his passion, he could not help passing by the school frequently. But, as he could not marry her, both because he saw that she was betrothed to another and because he himself had a lawfully-wedded wife, and furthermore because he would not deign to take a wife from a plebeian family through scorn of that station and as being contrary to the law which he himself had inscribed in the Twelve Tables, he first endeavoured to bribe the girl with money, and for that purpose was continually sending women to her governesses (for she had lost her mother), giving them many presents and promising them still more than was actually given. Those who were tempting the governesses had been instructed not to tell them the name of the man who was in love with the girl, but only that he was one of those who had it in his power to benefit or harm whom he wished. When they could not persuade the governesses and he saw that the girl was thought to require an even stronger guard than before, inflamed by his passion, he resolved to take the more audacious course. He accordingly sent for Marcus Claudius, one of his clients, a daring man and

---

[3] δεδομένων Kiessling.
[4] παρειγγέλλετο L; παρηγγέλετο VM : παρήγγελτο Kiessling.

ρὸν καὶ πρὸς πᾶσαν ὑπηρεσίαν ἕτοιμον, τό τε
πάθος αὐτῷ διηγεῖται καὶ διδάξας ὅσα ποιεῖν
αὐτὸν ἐβούλετο καὶ λέγειν, ἀποστέλλει συχνοὺς
6 τῶν ἀναιδεστάτων ἐπαγόμενον. ὁ δὲ παραγενόμενος ἐπὶ τὸ διδασκαλεῖον ἐπιλαμβάνεται τῆς
παρθένου καὶ φανερῶς ἄγειν ἐβούλετο δι᾽ ἀγορᾶς.
κραυγῆς δὲ γενομένης καὶ πολλοῦ συνδραμόντος
ὄχλου κωλυόμενος ὅποι προηγεῖτο τὴν κόρην ἄγειν
ἐπὶ τὴν ἀρχὴν παραγίνεται. ἐκάθητο δ᾽ ἐπὶ τοῦ
βήματος τηνικαῦτα μόνος Ἄππιος χρηματίζων
τε καὶ δικάζων τοῖς δεομένοις. βουλομένου δ᾽
αὐτοῦ λέγειν κραυγή τε καὶ ἀγανάκτησις ἦν ἐκ
τοῦ περιεστῶτος ὄχλου, πάντων ἀξιούντων περιμένειν ἕως ἔλθωσιν οἱ συγγενεῖς τῆς κόρης· καὶ ὁ
7 Ἄππιος οὕτως ἐκέλευσε ποιεῖν. ὡς δ᾽ ὀλίγος
ὁ μεταξὺ χρόνος ἐγεγόνει, καὶ[1] παρῆν ὁ πρὸς
μητρὸς θεῖος τῆς παρθένου Πόπλιος Νομιτώριος[2]
φίλους τε πολλοὺς ἐπαγόμενος καὶ συγγενεῖς, ἀνὴρ
ἐκ τῶν δημοτικῶν ἐμφανής, καὶ μετ᾽ οὐ πολὺ
Λεύκιος, ὁ παρὰ τοῦ πατρὸς ἐνεγγυημένος τὴν
κόρην, χεῖρα περὶ αὐτὸν ἔχων νέων δημοτικῶν
καρτεράν. ὡς δὲ τῷ βήματι προσῆλθεν ἀσθμαίνων
ἔτι καὶ μετέωρος τὸ πνεῦμα, λέγειν ἠξίου τίς ἐστιν
ὁ τολμήσας ἅψασθαι παιδὸς ἀστῆς καὶ τί βουλόμενος.

XXIX. Σιωπῆς δὲ γενομένης Μάρκος Κλαύδιος
ὁ τῆς παιδὸς ἐπιλαβόμενος τοιοῦτον διεξῆλθε
λόγον· '' Οὐδὲν οὔτε προπετὲς οὔτε βίαιον πέ-
πρακταί μοι περὶ τὴν κόρην, Ἄππιε Κλαύδιε·
κύριος δ᾽ αὐτῆς[3] ὢν κατὰ τοὺς νόμους ἄγω. ὃν
2 δὲ τρόπον ἐστὶν ἐμή,[4] μάθε. ἔστι μοι θεράπαινα

---

[1] καὶ deleted by Sylburg. [2] νομιτόριος O.

ready for any service, and acquainted him with his
passion ; then, having instructed him in what he
wished him to do and say, he sent him away accompanied by a band of the most shameless men. And
Claudius, going to the school, seized the maiden and
attempted to lead her away openly through the
Forum ; but when an outcry was raised and a
great crowd gathered, he was prevented from taking
her whither he intended, and so betook himself to
the magistracy. Seated at the time on the tribunal
was Appius alone, hearing causes and administering
justice to those who applied for it. When Claudius
wished to speak, there was an outcry and expressions
of indignation on the part of the crowd standing about
the tribunal, all demanding that he wait till the
relations of the girl should be present ; and Appius
ordered it should be so. After a short interval
Publius Numitorius, the maiden's maternal uncle, a
man of distinction among the plebeians, appeared
with many of his friends and relations ; and not long
afterwards came Lucius, to whom she had been
betrothed by her father, accompanied by a strong
body of young plebeians. As he came up to the
tribunal still panting and out of breath, he demanded
to know who it was that had dared to lay hands upon
a girl who was a Roman citizen and what his purpose
was.

XXIX. When silence had been obtained, Marcus
Claudius, who had seized the girl, spoke to this effect :
" I have done nothing either rash or violent in regard
to the girl, Appius Claudius ; but, as I am her master,
I am taking her according to the laws. Hear now by
what means she is mine. I have a female slave who

πατρικὴ πολλοὺς πάνυ δουλεύουσα χρόνους. ταύτην κύουσαν ἡ Οὐεργινίου γυνὴ συνήθη καὶ εἰσοδίαν οὖσαν ἔπεισεν, ὅταν[1] τέκῃ, δοῦναι τὸ παιδίον αὐτῇ. κἀκείνη φυλάττουσα τὰς ὑποσχέσεις γενομένης αὐτῇ ταύτης τῆς[2] θυγατρὸς πρὸς μὲν ἡμᾶς ἐσκήψατο νεκρὸν τεκεῖν, τῇ δὲ Νομιτωρίᾳ δίδωσι τὸ παιδίον· ἡ δὲ λαβοῦσα ὑποβάλλεται καὶ τρέφει παίδων οὔτ'
3 ἀρρένων οὔτε θηλειῶν οὖσα μήτηρ. πρότερον μὲν[3] οὖν ἐλάνθανέ με ταῦτα, νῦν δὲ διὰ μηνύσεως ἐπιγνοὺς καὶ μάρτυρας ἔχων πολλοὺς καὶ ἀγαθοὺς καὶ τὴν θεράπαιναν ἐξητακὼς ἐπὶ τὸν κοινὸν ἁπάντων καταφεύγω νόμον, ὃς οὐ τῶν ὑποβαλλομένων, ἀλλὰ τῶν μητέρων εἶναι τὰ ἔκγονα[4] δικαιοῖ, ἐλευθέρων μὲν[5] οὐσῶν ἐλεύθερα, δούλων δὲ δοῦλα, τοὺς αὐτοὺς ἔχοντα κυρίους οὓς ἂν καὶ αἱ μητέρες
4 αὐτῶν ἔχωσι. κατὰ τοῦτον τὸν νόμον ἀξιῶ τὴν θυγατέρα τῆς ἐμῆς θεραπαίνης ἄγειν, καὶ[6] δίκας ὑπέχειν βουλόμενος, κἂν[7] ἀντιποιῆταί τις, ἐγγυητὰς καθιστὰς[8] ἀξιοχρέους[9] ἄξειν αὐτὴν ἐπὶ τὴν δίκην· εἰ δὲ ταχεῖαν βούλεταί τις γενέσθαι τὴν[10] διάγνωσιν, ἕτοιμος ἐπὶ σοῦ λέγειν τὴν δίκην αὐτίκα μάλα, καὶ μὴ διεγγυᾶν τὸ σῶμα μηδ'[11] ἀναβολὰς τῷ πράγματι προσάγειν[12]· ὁποτέραν δ' ἂν οὗτοι βουληθῶσι τῶν αἱρέσεων, ἑλέσθωσαν."

XXX. Τοιαῦτ' εἰπόντος Κλαυδίου καὶ πολλὴν προσθέντος δέησιν ὑπὲρ τοῦ μηδὲν ἐλαττωθῆναι

---

[1] ὅταν Capps : ἐὰν O, Jacoby.
[2] τῆς added by Jacoby.
[3] μὲν Garrer : om. O, Jacoby.
[4] ἔγγονα LV.   [5] μὲν Reiske : τε O.
[6] καὶ deleted by Portus.
[7] κἂν Post : ἐὰν O, Jacoby, ἐὰν δὲ Steph.
[8] καθιστὰς Kayser : καθίστησιν O, καταστήσειν Kiessling.

belonged to my father and has served a great many
years. This slave, being with child, was persuaded
by the wife of Verginius, whom she was acquainted
with and used to visit, to give her the child when she
should bear it. And she, keeping her promise, when
this daughter was born, pretended to us that she had
given birth to a dead child, but she gave the babe to
Numitoria ; and the latter, taking the child, palmed
it off as her own and reared it, although she was the
mother of no children either male or female. Hitherto I was ignorant of all this ; but now, having learned
of it through information given me and having many
credible witnesses and having also examined the
slave, I have recourse to the law, common to all mankind, which declares it right that the offspring belong,
not to those who palm off others' children as their
own, but to their mothers, the children of freeborn
mothers being free, and those of slave mothers slaves,
having the same masters as their mothers. In virtue
of this law I claim the right to take the daughter of
my slave woman, consenting to submit to a trial and,
if anyone puts in a counter claim, offering sufficient
securities that I will produce her at the trial. But if
anyone wishes to have the decision rendered speedily,
I am ready to plead my cause before you at once,
instead of offering pledges for her person and inter-
posing delays to the action. Let these claimants
choose whichever of these alternatives they wish."

XXX. After Claudius had spoken thus and had
added an urgent plea that he might be at no disadvantage as compared with his adversaries because

---

[9] ἀξιοχρέους L : ἀξιόχρεως R (and similarly in chaps. 31,
34).   [10] τὴν added by Kiessling.
[11] Kiessling : μήτε O.   [12] Reiske : προσλέγειν O.

τῶν ἀντιδίκων ὅτι πελάτης ἦν καὶ ταπεινός, παραλαβὼν τὸν λόγον ὁ τῆς κόρης θεῖος ὀλίγα καὶ αὐτὰ
τὰ πρὸς τὸν ἄρχοντα εἰρῆσθαι προσήκοντα εἶπε·
πατέρα μὲν οὖν εἶναι[1] τῆς κόρης λέγων Οὐεργίνιον
ἐκ τῶν δημοτικῶν, ὃν ἀποδημεῖν στρατευόμενον
ὑπὲρ τῆς πόλεως· μητέρα δὲ γενέσθαι Νομιτωρίαν
τὴν ἀδελφὴν τὴν ἑαυτοῦ, σώφρονα καὶ ἀγαθὴν
γυναῖκα, ἣν οὐ πολλοῖς πρότερον ἐνιαυτοῖς ἀπο-
θανεῖν· τραφεῖσαν δὲ τὴν παρθένον, ὡς ἐλευθέρᾳ καὶ
ἀστῇ προσῆκεν, ἁρμοσθῆναι κατὰ νόμον Ἰκιλίῳ,
καὶ τέλος ἂν ἐσχηκέναι τὸν γάμον, εἰ μὴ θᾶττον ὁ
2 πρὸς Αἰκανοὺς ἀνέστη[2] πόλεμος. ἐν δὲ τοῖς μεταξὺ
χρόνοις οὐκ ἐλαττόνων ἢ πεντεκαίδεκα διεληλυ-
θότων ἐτῶν οὐδὲν τοιοῦτον ἐπιχειρήσαντα πρὸς
αὐτοὺς εἰπεῖν Κλαύδιον, ἐπειδὴ[3] γάμων ἡ παῖς
ἔσχεν ὥραν καὶ διαφέρειν δοκεῖ τὴν ὄψιν, ἐροῦντα[4]
ἥκειν ἀναίσχυντον συκοφάντημα πλάσαντα, οὐκ
ἀπὸ τῆς ἑαυτοῦ γνώμης, ἀλλὰ κατεσκευασμένον
ὑπ' ἀνδρὸς ἁπάσαις οἰομένου δεῖν ταῖς ἐπιθυμίαις
3 ἐκ παντὸς τρόπου χαρίζεσθαι. τὴν μὲν οὖν δίκην
αὐτὸν ἔφη τὸν πατέρα περὶ τῆς θυγατρὸς ἀπο-
λογήσεσθαι παραγενόμενον ἀπὸ τῆς στρατιᾶς[5]· τὴν
δὲ τοῦ σώματος ἀντιποίησιν, ἣν ἔδει γενέσθαι κατὰ
τοὺς νόμους, αὐτὸς ποιεῖσθαι θεῖος ὢν τῆς κόρης
καὶ τὰ δίκαια ὑπέχειν, οὐδὲν ἀξιῶν οὔτε ξένον
οὔτε ὃ μὴ καὶ τοῖς ἄλλοις ἀποδέδοται[6] Ῥωμαίοις
δίκαιον, εἰ καὶ μὴ πᾶσιν ἀνθρώποις, σώματος εἰς
δουλείαν ἐξ ἐλευθερίας ἀγομένου μὴ τὸν ἀφαιρού-

[1] οὖν εἶναι MV : οὖν ἦν εἶναι L.
[2] ἀνέστη Cobet, συνέστη Casaubon : ἔστη O.
[3] δὲ after ἐπειδὴ deleted by Reiske.

he was a client and of humble birth, the uncle of the
girl answered in few words and those such as were
proper to be addressed to a magistrate. He said that
the father of the girl was Verginius, a plebeian, who
was then abroad in the service of his country ; that
her mother was Numitoria, his own sister, a virtuous
and good woman, who had died not many years
before ; that the maiden herself, after being brought
up in such a manner as became a person of free condition and a citizen, had been legally betrothed to
Icilius, and that the marriage would have taken place
if the war with the Aequians had not intervened. In
the meantime, he said, no less than fifteen years
having elapsed, Claudius had never attempted to
allege anything of this sort to the girl's relations, but
now that she was of marriageable age and had a
reputation for exceptional beauty, he had come
forward with his allegation after inventing a shameless calumny, not indeed on his own initiative, but
coached by a man who thought he must by any and
every means gratify his desires. As for the trial, he
said the father himself would defend the cause of his
daughter when he returned from the campaign ; but
as for the claiming of her person, which was required
according to the laws, he himself, as the girl's uncle,
was attending to that and was submitting to trial, in
doing which he was demanding nothing either un-
precedented or not granted as a right to all other
Roman citizens, if indeed not to all men, namely, that
when a person is being haled from a condition of
freedom into slavery, it is not the man who is trying

---

⁴ ἐροῦντα Post : ἐρῶντα O, Jacoby.
⁵ Sylburg : στρατείας O.
⁶ Kiessling : ἀποδίδοται O, Jacoby.

μενον τὴν ἐλευθερίαν, ἀλλὰ τὸν φυλάττοντα κύριον
4 εἶναι μέχρι δίκης. ἔφη τε διὰ πολλὰς αἰτίας
προσήκειν τῷ Ἀππίῳ φυλάττειν τοῦτο τὸ δίκαιον·
πρῶτον μὲν ὅτι τὸν νόμον τοῦτον ἅμα τοῖς ἄλλοις
ἐν ταῖς δώδεκα δέλτοις ἀνέγραψεν· ἔπειθ' ὅτι τῆς
δεκαδαρχίας ἡγεμών· πρὸς δὲ τούτοις ὅτι μετὰ
τῆς ὑπατικῆς ἐξουσίας καὶ τὴν δημαρχίαν προσ-
ειλήφει, ἧς εἶναι κράτιστον ἔργον τοῖς ἀσθενέσι
5 καὶ ἐρήμοις τῶν πολιτῶν βοηθεῖν. ἠξίου τε τὴν
καταπεφευγυῖαν ἐπ' αὐτὸν ἐλεῆσαι παρθένον,
μητρὸς μὲν ὀρφανὴν οὖσαν ἔτι πάλαι, πατρὸς δ'
ἔρημον ἐν τῷ τότε χρόνῳ, κινδυνεύουσαν οὐ χρημάτων ἀποστερηθῆναι προγονικῶν, ἀλλὰ καὶ ἀνδρὸς
καὶ πατρίδος καί, ὃ πάντων[1] μέγιστον εἶναι δοκεῖ
τῶν ἀνθρωπίνων ἀγαθῶν, τῆς τοῦ σώματος ἐλευθερίας. ἀνακλαυσάμενος δὲ τὴν ὕβριν εἰς ἣν
ἔμελλεν ἡ παῖς παραδοθήσεσθαι καὶ πολὺν ἐκ τῶν
παρόντων κινήσας ἔλεον περὶ τοῦ χρόνου τῆς
6 δίκης ἔφη τελευτῶν· '' Ἐπειδὴ ταχεῖαν αὐτῆς
βούλεται γενέσθαι τὴν κρίσιν Κλαύδιος, ὁ μηδὲν
ἠδικῆσθαι φάμενος ἐν τοῖς πεντεκαίδεκα ἔτεσιν,
ἕτερος μὲν ἄν τις ὑπὲρ τηλικούτων ἀγωνιζόμενος
δεινὰ πάσχειν ἔλεξε[2] καὶ ἠγανάκτει κατὰ τὸ εἰκός,
ὅταν εἰρήνη γένηται καὶ πάντες ἔλθωσιν οἱ νῦν
ὄντες ἐπὶ στρατοπέδου, τότε τὴν δίκην ἀξιῶν
ἀπολογεῖσθαι, ὅτε καὶ μαρτύρων εὐπορία καὶ
φίλων καὶ δικαστῶν ἀμφοτέροις ἔσται τοῖς δικαζομένοις, πολιτικὰ καὶ μέτρια πράγματα προφέρων
7 καὶ τῇ Ῥωμαίων συνήθη πολιτείᾳ· ἡμεῖς δ','' ἔφη,
'' λόγων οὐδὲν δεόμεθα οὔτ' εἰρήνης οὔτ' ὄχλου

[1] ὃ πάντων Portus : πάντων ὁ O.
[2] ἔλεξε Casaubon : ἔδοξε O.

to deprive him of his liberty, but the man who maintains it, that has the custody of him until the trial. And he said that it behooved Appius to maintain that principle for many reasons : first, because he had inscribed this law among the others in the Twelve Tables, and, in the next place, because he was chief of the decemvirate ; and furthermore, because he had assumed not only the consular but also the tribunician power, the principal function of which was to relieve such of the citizens as were weak and destitute of help. He then asked him to show compassion for a maiden who had turned to him for refuge, having long since lost her mother and being at the moment deprived of her father and in danger of losing not only her ancestral fortune but also her husband, her country, and, what is regarded as the greatest of all human blessings, her personal liberty. And having lamented the insolence to which the girl would be delivered up and thus roused great compassion in all present, he at last spoke about the time to be appointed for the trial, saying : " Since Claudius, who during those fifteen years never complained of any injury, now wishes to have the decision in this cause rendered speedily, anyone else who was contending for a matter of so great importance as I am would say that he was grievously treated and would naturally feel indignant, demanding to offer his defence only after peace is made and all who are now in camp have returned, at a time when both parties to the suit will have an abundance of witnesses, friends and judges—a proposal which would be democratic, moderate and agreeable to the Roman constitution. But as for us," he said, " we have no need of speeches nor of peace nor of a throng of friends and

φίλων καὶ δικαστῶν οὔτ᾽ εἰς τοὺς δικασίμους[1]
χρόνους τὸ πρᾶγμα ἀναβαλλόμεθα, ἀλλὰ καὶ ἐν
πολέμῳ καὶ ἐν σπάνει φίλων καὶ οὐκ ἐν ἴσοις
δικασταῖς καὶ παραχρῆμα ὑπομένομεν ἀπολογεῖσθαι, τοσοῦτον αἰτησάμενοι παρὰ σοῦ χρόνον,
Ἄππιε, ὅσος ἱκανὸς ἔσται τῷ πατρὶ τῆς κόρης
ἀπὸ στρατοπέδου παραγενηθέντι τὰς ἰδίας ἀπο-
δύρασθαι τύχας καὶ δι᾽ ἑαυτοῦ τὴν δίκην ἀπολογή-
σασθαι.''

XXXI. Τοιαῦτα τοῦ Νομιτωρίου λέξαντος καὶ
τοῦ περιεστηκότος ὄχλου μεγάλῃ βοῇ διασημή-
ναντος ὡς δίκαια ἀξιοῖ, μικρὸν ἐπισχὼν χρόνον
Ἄππιος, '' Ἐγὼ τὸν μὲν νόμον,'' εἶπεν, '' οὐκ
ἀγνοῶ τὸν ὑπὲρ[2] τῆς διεγγυήσεως[3] τῶν εἰς δουλείαν ἀγομένων κείμενον, ὃς οὐκ ἐᾷ παρὰ τοῖς
ἀφαιρουμένοις[4] εἶναι τὸ σῶμα μέχρι δίκης, οὐδὲ
καταλύσαιμι ἂν ὃν αὐτὸς ἔγραψα ἑκών. ἐκεῖνο
μέντοι δίκαιον ἡγοῦμαι, δυεῖν ὄντων τῶν ἀντιποιουμένων, κυρίου καὶ πατρός, εἰ μὲν ἀμφότεροι
παρῆσαν, τὸν πατέρα κρατεῖν τοῦ σώματος μέχρι
2 δίκης· ἐπεὶ δ᾽ ἐκεῖνος ἄπεστι, τὸν κύριον ἀπαγαγεῖν
ἐγγυητὰς ἀξιοχρέους δόντα καταστήσειν ἐπὶ τὴν
ἀρχὴν ὅταν ὁ πατὴρ αὐτῆς παραγένηται. περὶ δὲ
τῶν ἐγγυητῶν καὶ τοῦ τιμήματος καὶ τοῦ μηδὲν
ὑμᾶς ἐλαττωθῆναι περὶ τὴν δίκην πολλὴν ποιήσομαι πρόνοιαν, ὦ Νομιτώριε. νῦν δὲ παράδος
τὴν κόρην.''

3 Τοῦτο τὸ τέλος ἐξενέγκαντος Ἀππίου πολὺς μὲν
ὀδυρμὸς ὑπὸ τῆς παρθένου καὶ τῶν περὶ αὐτὴν
γυναικῶν ἐγίνετο καὶ κοπετός, πολλὴ δὲ κραυγὴ

judges, nor are we trying to put the matter off to the times appropriate for such decisions ; but even in war, and when friends are lacking and judges are not impartial, and at once, we are ready to make our defence, asking of you only so much time, Appius, as will suffice for the father of the girl to come from camp, lament his misfortunes, and plead his cause in person."

XXXI. Numitorius having spoken to this effect and the people who stood round the tribunal having signified by a great shout that his demand was just, Appius after a short pause said : " I am not ignorant of the law concerning the bailing of those who are claimed as slaves, which does not permit their persons to be in the power of the claimants till the hearing of the cause, nor would I willingly break a law which I myself draughted. This, however, I consider to be just, that, as there are two claimants, the master and the father, if they were both present, the father should have the custody of her person till the hearing ; but since he is absent, the master should take her away, giving sufficient sureties that he will produce her before the magistrate when her father returns. I shall take great care, Numitorius, concerning the sureties and the amount of their bond and also that you defendants shall be at no disadvantage in respect of the trial. For the present, deliver up the girl."

When Appius had pronounced this sentence, there was much lamentation and beating of breasts on the part of the maiden and of the women surrounding her,

---

[1] Steph. : δεκασίμους O.
[2] τὸν ὑπὲρ R : τὸν δι' ὑπὲρ LM.
[3] Kiessling : ἐγγυήσεως O.
[4] παρὰ τοὺς ἀφαιρουμένους LM.

καὶ ἀγανάκτησις ἐκ τοῦ περιεστηκότος ὄχλου τὸ
βῆμα. ὁ δὲ μέλλων ἄγεσθαι τὴν κόρην Ἰκίλιος
4 ἐμφύεταί τε αὐτῆς καί φησιν· " Οὐκ ἐμοῦ γε
ζῶντος, Ἄππιε, ταύτην ἀπάξεταί τις. ἀλλ' εἴ
σοι δέδοκται τοὺς νόμους καταλύειν, τὰ δὲ δίκαια
συγχεῖν καὶ τὴν ἐλευθερίαν ἡμῶν ἀφαιρεῖσθαι,
μηκέτι τὴν ὀνειδιζομένην ὑμῖν ἀρνοῦ τυραννίδα,
ἀλλὰ τὸν ἐμὸν ἀποκόψας τράχηλον ταύτην τε
ἀπαγαγεῖν,[1] ὅπου σοι δοκεῖ, καὶ τὰς ἄλλας παρθένους καὶ γυναῖκας, ἵνα δὴ μάθωσιν ἤδη ποτὲ
Ῥωμαῖοι δοῦλοι γεγονότες ἀντ' ἐλευθέρων καὶ
5 μηδὲν ἔτι μεῖζον φρονῶσι τῆς τύχης. τί οὖν ἔτι
μέλλεις, ἀλλ' οὐ τοὐμὸν ἐκχεῖς αἷμα πρὸ τοῦ
βήματος ἐν τοῖς ἁπάντων ὀφθαλμοῖς; ἴσθι μέντοι
σαφῶς ὅτι ἤτοι[2] μεγάλων κακῶν ἄρξει Ῥωμαίοις
ὁ θάνατος οὑμὸς ἢ μεγάλων ἀγαθῶν.''

XXXII. Ἔτι δ' αὐτοῦ βουλομένου λέγειν οἱ μὲν
ῥαβδοῦχοι κελευσθέντες ὑπὸ τῆς ἐξουσίας ἀνεῖρ-
γον αὐτοὺς ἀπὸ τοῦ βήματος καὶ πειθαρχεῖν τοῖς
κεκριμένοις ἐκέλευον· ὁ δὲ Κλαύδιος ἐπιλαβόμενος τῆς παιδὸς ἀπάγειν ἐβούλετο τοῦ θείου καὶ
τοῦ μνηστῆρος ἀντεχομένη. ἰδόντες δὲ πένθος[3]
ἐλεεινὸν οἱ περὶ τὸ βῆμα πάντες ἀνέκραγον ἅμα
καὶ παρ' οὐδὲν ἡγησάμενοι τὴν τοῦ κρατοῦντος ἐξουσίαν ὠθοῦνται τοῖς βιαζομένοις ὁμόσε, ὥστε
δείσαντα τὴν ἐπιφορὰν αὐτῶν τὸν Κλαύδιον τήν
τε κόρην ἀφεῖναι καὶ ὑπὸ τοὺς πόδας τοῦ στρατη-
2 γοῦ καταφυγεῖν. ὁ δ' Ἄππιος κατ' ἀρχὰς μὲν
εἰς πολλὴν ταραχὴν κατέστη ἠγριωμένους ἅπαντας

---

[1] ἄπαγε Cobet ; ⟨κέλευε⟩ ἀποκόψαι . . . ἀπαγαγεῖν Sylburg.
[2] ὅτι ἤτοι Jacoby : ἤτοι ἢ LV, ὅτι ἢ M, ἤτοι Kiessling.
[3] πάθος Kiessling.

and much clamour and indignation on the part of the crowd which stood about the tribunal. But Icilius, who was intending to marry the girl, clasped her to him and said : " Not while I am alive, Appius, shall anyone take this girl away. But if you are resolved to break the laws, to confound our rights, and to take from us our liberty, deny no longer the tyranny you decemvirs are reproached with, but after you have cut off my head lead away not only this maiden whithersoever you choose, but also every other maiden and matron, in order that the Romans may now at last be convinced that they have become slaves instead of free men and may no longer show a spirit above their condition. Why, then, do you delay any longer ? Why do you not shed my blood before your tribunal in the sight of all ? But know of a certainty that my death will prove the beginning either of great woes to the Romans or of great blessings."

XXXII. While he wished to go on speaking, the lictors by order of the magistrate kept him and his friends back from the tribunal and commanded them to obey the sentence ; and Claudius laid hold on the girl as she clung to her uncle and her betrothed, and attempted to lead her away. But the people who stood round the tribunal, upon seeing her piteous grief, all cried out together, and disregarding the authority of the magistrate, crowded upon those who were endeavouring to use force with her, so that Claudius, fearing their violence, let the girl go and fled for refuge to the feet of the general.[1] Appius was at first greatly disturbed as he saw all the people

---

[1] Appius was one of the two decemvirs left as generals in the city ; see chap. 23, 1.

DIONYSIUS OF HALICARNASSUS

ὁρῶν καὶ πολὺν ἠπόρει χρόνον ὅ τι χρὴ ποιεῖν,
ἔπειτα τὸν Κλαύδιον καλέσας ἐπὶ τὸ βῆμα καὶ
μικρὰ διαλεχθεὶς πρὸς αὐτόν, ὡς ἐδόκει, τοῖς τε
περιεστῶσι διασημήνας ἡσυχίαν παρασχεῖν λέγει
3 τοιάδε· '' Ἐγὼ τὸ μὲν ἀκριβές, ὦ δημόται, περὶ
τῆς διεγγυήσεως τοῦ σώματος, ἐπειδὴ τραχυνο-
μένους ὑμᾶς πρὸς τὴν ἀπόφασιν ὁρῶ, παρίημι·
χαρίζεσθαι δ' ὑμῖν βουλόμενος πέπεικα τὸν ἐμαυτοῦ
πελάτην ἐᾶσαι μὲν τοῖς συγγενέσι τῆς παρθένου
δοῦναι τὴν διεγγύησιν ἕως ὁ πατὴρ αὐτῆς παρα-
4 γένηται. ἀπάγεσθε οὖν, ὦ Νομιτώριε, τὴν κόρην,
καὶ τὴν ἐγγύην ὁμολογεῖτε περὶ αὐτῆς εἰς τὴν
αὔριον ἡμέραν. ἀπόχρη γὰρ ὁ χρόνος ὑμῖν οὗτος
ἀπαγγεῖλαί τε Οὐεργινίῳ τήμερον καὶ τριῶν ἢ
τεττάρων ὡρῶν αὔριον[1] ἐκ τοῦ χάρακος δεῦρο
ἀγαγεῖν.'' πλείονα δ' αὐτῶν χρόνον αἰτουμένων
οὐδὲν ἔτι ἀποκρινάμενος ἀνέστη καὶ τὸν δίφρον
ἐκέλευσεν ἆραι.

XXXIII. Ὡς δ' ἀπῆλθεν ἐκ τῆς ἀγορᾶς ἀδημονῶν καὶ μαινόμενος ὑπὸ τοῦ πάθους, ἔγνω μηκέτι
μεθέσθαι[2] τῆς παρθένου τοῖς συγγενέσιν, ἀλλ' ὅταν
ἐπὶ τὴν ἐγγύην προαχθῇ, μετὰ βίας αὐτὴν ἀπάγειν,
ἑαυτῷ τε πλείονα φυλακὴν περιστησάμενος, ὡς
μηδὲν ὑπὸ τῶν ὄχλων βιασθείη, καὶ τὰ πέριξ τοῦ
βήματος ἑταίρων τε καὶ πελατῶν ὄχλῳ προκατα-
2 λαβών. ἵνα δὲ σὺν εὐσχήμονι δίκης τοῦτο πράττῃ
προφάσει, μὴ παραγενηθέντος ἐπὶ τὴν ἐγγύην τοῦ
πατρός, ἐπιστολὰς δοὺς τοῖς πιστοτάτοις ἱππεῦσιν
ἔπεμψεν ἐπὶ τὸν χάρακα[4] πρὸς Ἀντώνιον, τὸν
ἡγεμόνα τοῦ τάγματος ὑφ' οὗ[5] ἦν Οὐεργίνιος,

---

[1] αὔριον O : αὐτὸν Kiessling.
μεθέσθαι Reiske, μεθίεσθαι Sylburg : μεθεῖσθαι O.

enraged, and for a considerable time was in doubt
what he ought to do. Then, after calling Claudius
to the tribunal and conversing a little with him, as
it seemed, he made a sign for the bystanders to be
silent and said : " I am waiving the strict letter of
the law, citizens, relative to the bailing of her person,
inasmuch as I see you growing exasperated at the
sentence I have pronounced ; and desiring to gratify
you, I have prevailed upon my client to consent that
the relations of the maiden shall go bail for her till
the arrival of her father. Do you men, therefore,
take the girl away, Numitorius, and acknowledge
yourselves bound for her appearance to-morrow. For
this much time is sufficient for you both to give
Verginius notice to-day and to bring him here from
the camp in three or four hours to-morrow." When
they asked for more time, he gave no answer but rose
up and ordered his seat to be taken away.

XXXIII. As he left the Forum, sorely troubled
and maddened by his passion, he determined not to
relinquish the maiden another time to her relations,
but when she was produced by her surety, to take
her away by force, after first placing a stronger guard
about his person, in order to avoid suffering any
violence from the crowds, and occupying the neighbourhood of the tribunal ahead of time with a throng
of his partisans and clients. That he might do this
with a plausible show of justice when the father should
fail to appear as her surety, he sent his most trusted
horsemen to the camp with letters for Antonius, the
commander of the legion in which Verginius served,

---

³ δίκης τοῦτο πράττῃ Kayser : δίκη τοῦτο πράττῃ O ; δοκῇ
τοῦτο πράττειν Kiessling.
⁴ καὶ after χάρακα deleted by Sylburg.   ὑφ' ὃν O.

ἀξιῶν αὐτὸν κατέχειν τὸν ἄνδρα ἐν ἐπιμελεῖ
φυλακῇ, μὴ λάθῃ πυθόμενος τὰ περὶ τὴν θυγατέρα
3 καὶ διαδρὰς ἐκ τοῦ χάρακος. ἔφθησαν δ' αὐτὸν
οἱ τῇ κόρῃ προσήκοντες, Νομιτωρίου τε υἱὸς καὶ
ἀδελφὸς Ἰκιλίου, προαποσταλέντες ὑπὸ τῶν ἄλλων
ἀρχομένης ἔτι τῆς καταστάσεως, νεανίαι λήματος
πλήρεις ἀπὸ ῥυτῆρος καὶ μετὰ μάστιγος ἐλαθεῖσι
τοῖς ἵπποις πρότερον διανύσαντες τὴν ὁδὸν καὶ τῷ
4 Οὐεργινίῳ τὰ πεπραγμένα διασαφηνίσαντες. ὁ
δὲ τὴν μὲν ἀληθῆ πρὸς Ἀντώνιον αἰτίαν ἀποκρυ-
ψάμενος, ἀναγκαίου δέ τινος συγγενοῦς σκηψά-
μενος πεπύσθαι θάνατον, οὗ τὴν ἐκκομιδήν τε καὶ
ταφὴν αὐτὸν ἔδει ποιήσασθαι κατὰ τὸν νόμον,
ἀφίεται καὶ περὶ λύχνων ἁφὰς ἤλαυνε μετὰ τῶν
μειρακίων κατ' ἄλλας ὁδούς, διωγμὸν ἔκ τε τοῦ
στρατοπέδου καὶ ἀπὸ τῆς πόλεως δεδοικώς· ὅπερ
5 καὶ συνέβη. ὅ τε[1] γὰρ Ἀντώνιος τὰς ἐπιστολὰς
δεξάμενος περὶ πρώτην μάλιστα φυλακήν, ἴλην
ἀπέστειλεν ἱππέων ἐπ' αὐτόν, ἔκ τε τῆς πόλεως
ἕτεροι πεμφθέντες ἱππεῖς δι' ὅλης νυκτὸς ἐφρούρουν
τὴν ἀπὸ στρατοπέδου φέρουσαν ὁδόν. ὡς δὲ
ἀπήγγειλεν Ἀππίῳ τις τὸν Οὐεργίνιον ἐληλυθότα
παρὰ τὴν ὑπόληψιν, ἔξω τῶν φρενῶν γενόμενος
παρῆν μετὰ πολλοῦ στίφους ἐπὶ τὸ βῆμα καὶ
προσάγειν ἐκέλευσε τοὺς τῆς κόρης συγγενεῖς.
6 προσελθόντων δ' αὐτῶν ὁ μὲν Κλαύδιος τοὺς
αὐτοὺς πάλιν διεξελθὼν λόγους ἠξίου τὸν Ἄππιον
γενέσθαι δικαστὴν τοῦ πράγματος μηδεμίαν ἀναβολὴν ποιησάμενον, τόν τε μηνυτὴν παρεῖναι
λέγων καὶ τοὺς μάρτυρας καὶ τὴν θεράπαιναν
αὐτὴν παραδούς· ἐφ' οἷς ἅπασι πολὺς ὁ προσποιητὸς
σχετλιασμὸς ἦν εἰ μὴ τεύξεται[2] τῶν ἴσων τοῖς
110

asking him to detain the man under strict guard, lest
he learn of the situation of his daughter and steal
away from the camp unobserved. But he was forestalled by two relations of the girl, namely a son of
Numitorius and a brother of Icilius, who had been
sent ahead by the rest at the very beginning of the
affair. These, being young and full of spirit, drove
their horses with loose rein and under the whip, and
completing the journey ahead of the men sent by
Appius, informed Verginius of what had taken place.
He, going to Antonius and concealing the true reason
for his request, pretended that he had received word
of the death of a certain near relation whose funeral
and burial he was obliged by the law to perform ; and
being given a furlough, he set out about lamp-lighting
time with the youths, taking by-roads for fear of being
pursued both from the camp and from the city—the
very thing which actually happened. For Antonius,
upon receiving the letters about the first watch, sent
a troop of horse after him, while other horsemen, sent
from the city, patrolled all night long the road that
led from the camp to Rome. When Appius was
informed by somebody of the unexpected arrival of
Verginius, he lost control of himself, and going to the
tribunal with a large body of attendants, ordered the
relations of the girl to be brought. When they had
come, Claudius repeated what he had said before and
asked Appius to act as judge in the matter without
any delay, declaring that both the informant and the
witnesses were present and offering the slave woman
herself to be examined. On top of all this there was
the pretence of great indignation, if he was not to

---

¹ τε V : om. R.
² Sylburg : τεύξωνται LV.

ἄλλοις, ὡς πρότερον, ὅτι πελάτης ἦν αὐτοῦ, καὶ
παράκλησις μὴ τοῖς ἐλεεινότερα λέγουσιν ἀλλὰ
τοῖς δικαιότερα ἀξιοῦσι βοηθεῖν.[1]

XXXIV. Ὁ δὲ τῆς κόρης πατὴρ καὶ οἱ λοιποὶ
συγγενεῖς ἀπελογοῦντο περὶ τῆς ὑποβολῆς πολλὰ
καὶ δίκαια καὶ ἀληθῆ λέγοντες, ὡς οὔτ' αἰτίαν
οὐδεμίαν εἶχεν ὑποβολῆς εὔλογον ἡ Νομιτωρίου
μὲν ἀδελφή, Οὐεργινίου δὲ γυνή, παρθένος γαμη-
θεῖσα νέῳ ἀνδρὶ καὶ μετ' οὐ[2] πολλοὺς τοῦ γάμου
τεκοῦσα χρόνους· οὔτ' εἰ τὰ[3] μάλιστα ἐβούλετο
γένος ἀλλότριον εἰς τὸν ἴδιον οἶκον εἰσαγαγεῖν,
δούλης ἀλλοτρίας ἂν ἐλάμβανε[4] παιδίον μᾶλλον ἢ
οὐ γυναικὸς ἐλευθέρας κατὰ γένος ἢ φιλίαν αὐτῇ
προσηκούσης, παρ' ἧς πιστῶς τε ἅμα καὶ βεβαίως
2 ἕξει[5] τὸ ληφθέν. ἐξουσίαν τε ἔχουσαν ὁποῖον
ἐβούλετο λαβεῖν, ἄρρεν ἂν[6] ἑλέσθαι παιδίον μᾶλλον
ἢ θῆλυ. τεκοῦσαν μὲν γὰρ ἀνάγκην[7] τῶν τέκνων
δεομένην στέργειν καὶ τρέφειν ὅ τι ἂν ἡ φύσις
ἐξενέγκῃ, ὑποβαλλομένην δὲ τὸ κρεῖττον ἀντὶ τοῦ
3 χείρονος εἰκὸς εἶναι λαβεῖν. πρός τε τὸν μηνυτὴν
καὶ τοὺς μάρτυρας, οὓς ὁ Κλαύδιος ἔφη πολλοὺς
καὶ ἀξιοχρέους παρέξεσθαι, τὸν ἐκ τῶν εἰκότων
παρείχοντο λόγον, ὡς οὐκ ἄν ποτε ἡ Νομιτωρία
πρᾶγμα σιγῆς δεόμενον καὶ δι' ἑνὸς ὑπηρετηθῆναι
προσώπου δυνάμενον, φανερῶς ἔπραττε καὶ μετὰ
μαρτύρων ἐλευθέρων, ἵν' ἐκτραφεῖσαν τὴν κόρην

---

[1] μὴ . . . βοηθεῖν Kiessling : ἵνα μὴ . . . βοηθεῖν O, ἵνα μὴ
βοηθοῖ Steph.

[2] μετ' οὐ Jacoby in note : οὐ μετὰ O, Jacoby in text.

[3] τὰ L : om. R.

[4] ἂν ἐλάμβανε Reiske : ἀνελάμβανε O.

[5] ἕξειν LM.   [6] ἂν added by Kiessling.

[7] ἀνάγκην Steph.[2], Portus : ἀνάγκη O, ἀνάγκη ἦν Cobet.

obtain the same justice as other people, as he had previously, because he was a client of Appius, and also an appeal that Appius should not support those whose complaints were the more pitiful, but rather those whose claims were the more just.

XXXIV. The father of the girl and her other relations made a defence with many just and truthful arguments against the charge that she had been substituted for a still-born child, namely, that the sister of Numitorius, wife of Verginius, had had no reasonable ground for a substitution, since she, a virgin, married to a young man, had borne a child no very considerable time after her marriage ; and again, if she had desired ever so much to introduce the offspring of another woman into her own family, she would not have taken the child of someone else's slave rather than that of a free woman united to her by consanguinity or friendship, one from whom she would take it in the confidence and indeed certainty that she could keep what she had received. And when she had it in her power to take a child of whichever sex she wished, she would have chosen a male child rather than a female. For a mother, if she wants children, must of necessity be contented with and rear whatever offspring nature produces, whereas a woman who substitutes a child will in all probability choose the better sex instead of the inferior. As against the informer and the witnesses whom Claudius said he would produce in great numbers, and all of them trustworthy, they offered the argument from probability, that Numitoria would never have done openly and in conjunction with witnesses of free condition a deed that required secrecy and could have been performed for her by one person, when as a result she

113

4 ὑπὸ τῶν κυρίων τῆς μητρὸς ἀφαιρεθείη. τόν τε
χρόνον οὐ μικρὸν ἔλεγον εἶναι τεκμήριον τοῦ μηδὲν
ὑγιὲς λέγειν τὸν κατήγορον· οὔτε γὰρ ἂν τὸν μηνυτὴν οὔτε τοὺς μάρτυρας κατασχεῖν ἐν πεντεκαίδεκα
ἔτεσιν ἀπόρρητον τὴν¹ ὑποβολήν, ἀλλ' ἔτι πρότερον
5 εἰπεῖν. διαβάλλοντες² δὲ τὰς τῶν κατηγόρων
πίστεις ὡς³ οὔτ' ἀληθεῖς οὔτε πιθανάς, ἀντιπαρ-
εξετάζειν ταύταις ἠξίουν τὰς ἑαυτῶν, πολλὰς καὶ
οὐκ ἀσήμους γυναῖκας ὀνομάζοντες ἃς ἔφασαν
εἰδέναι Νομιτωρίαν ἐγκύμονα γενομένην ἐκ τοῦ
περὶ τὴν γαστέρα ὄγκου. χωρὶς δὲ τούτων τὰς
ἐπὶ τοῦ τόκου καὶ τῆς λοχείας παραγενομένας διὰ
τὸ συγγενὲς καὶ τικτόμενον τὸ παιδίον ἰδούσας
6 ἐπεδείκνυτο⁴ καὶ ἀνακρίνειν ἠξίουν. ὃ δὲ πάντων
τεκμήριον ἦν περιφανέστατον ἔκ τε τῶν ἀνδρῶν
πολλῶν καὶ γυναικῶν μαρτυρούμενον, οὐ μόνον
ἐλευθέρων ἀλλὰ καὶ δούλων, τοῦτ' ἔλεγον τελευτῶντες, ὅτι τῷ γάλακτι τῆς μητρὸς ἐτράφη τὸ
παιδίον· ἀμήχανον δ' εἶναι γάλακτος πληρωθῆναι
μαστοὺς γυναικὶ μὴ τεκούσῃ.

XXXV. Ταῦτα καὶ πολλὰ τούτοις ὅμοια παρεχο-
μένων αὐτῶν ἰσχυρὰ καὶ οὐδένα λόγον ἐναντίον
δέξασθαι δυνάμενα καὶ πολὺν ἐπὶ⁵ ταῖς συμφοραῖς
τῆς κόρης ἔλεον καταχεομένων, οἱ μὲν ἄλλοι πάντες
ὅσοι συνήκουον τῶν λόγων τῆς τε μορφῆς οἶκτον
2 ἐλάμβανον ὁπότ' εἰς τὴν παρθένον ἴδοιεν (καὶ γὰρ
ἐν ἐσθῆτι οὖσα πιναρᾷ καὶ κατηφὲς ὁρῶσα καὶ τὸ
καλὸν τῶν ὀμμάτων ἐκτήκουσα τὰς ἀπάντων
ἥρπαζεν ὄψεις, οὕτως ὑπεράνθρωπός τις ὥρα περὶ
αὐτὴν καὶ χάρις ἦν) καὶ τὸ τῆς τύχης ἀνεκλαίοντο

---

¹ τὴν added by Kiessling.
² διαβαλόντες Capps.　　　　³ ὡς added by Sylburg.

might see the girl she had reared taken away from her by the owners of the girl's mother. Also the lapse of time, they said, was no slight evidence that there was nothing sound in what the plaintiff alleged; for neither the informer nor the witnesses would have kept the substitution a secret during fifteen years, but would have told of it before this. While discrediting the plaintiff's proofs as neither true nor probable, they asked that their own proofs might be weighed against them, and named many women, and those of no mean note, who they said had known when Numitoria came with child by the size of her abdomen. Besides these they produced the women who because of their kinship had been present at her labour and delivery and had seen the child brought into the world, and asked that these be questioned. But the clearest proof of all, which was attested by both men in large numbers and women, freemen and slaves as well, they brought in at the last, stating that the child had been suckled by her mother and that it was impossible for a woman to have her breasts full of milk if she had not borne a child.

XXXV. While they were presenting these arguments and many others equally weighty and incontrovertible and were pouring forth a stream of compassion over the girl's misfortunes, all the others who heard their words felt pity for her beauty as they cast their eyes upon her,—for being dressed in squalid attire, gazing down at the ground, and dimming the lustre of her eyes with tears, she arrested the eyes of all, so superhuman a beauty and grace enveloped her, —and all bewailed the perversity of Fortune when

---

⁴ Sylburg : ἐπεδείκνυτο O.

⁵ ἐπὶ (cf. ix. 28, 5) Kiessling : ἐν O, Jacoby.

παράλογον, εἰς οἵας ὕβρεις καὶ προπηλακισμοὺς
3 ἐλεύσοιτο ἐξ οἵων ἀγαθῶν. εἰσῄει τ' αὐτοὺς λογισμὸς ὅτι τοῦ περὶ τῆς ἐλευθερίας νόμου κατα-
λυθέντος οὐδὲν ἔσται τὸ κωλῦον καὶ τὰς αὐτῶν
γυναῖκας καὶ θυγατέρας τὰ αὐτὰ ἐκείνῃ παθεῖν.
ταῦτά τε δὴ καὶ πολλὰ τούτοις ὅμοια ἐπιλογιζό-
μενοι καὶ πρὸς ἀλλήλους διαλαλοῦντες ἔκλαιον.
4 ὁ δὲ Ἄππιος, οἷα δὴ φύσιν τε οὐ φρενήρης ἀνὴρ
καὶ ὑπὸ μεγέθους ἐξουσίας διεφθαρμένος, οἰδῶν
τε τὴν ψυχὴν καὶ ζέων τὰ σπλάγχνα διὰ τὸν ἔρωτα
τῆς παιδός, οὔτε τοῖς λόγοις τῶν ἀπολογουμένων
προσεῖχεν οὔτε τοῖς δάκρυσιν αὐτῆς ἐπεκλᾶτο,[1]
τήν τε συμπάθειαν τῶν παρόντων δι' ὀργῆς ἐλάμβανεν, ὡς αὐτὸς δὴ πλείονος ὢν[2] ἄξιος ἐλέου καὶ
δεινότερα ὑπὸ τῆς δεδουλωμένης αὐτὸν εὐμορφίας
5 πεπονθώς. διὰ δὴ ταῦτα πάντα οἰστρῶν λόγον
τε ὑπέμεινεν εἰπεῖν ἀναίσχυντον, ἐξ οὗ καταφανὴς
ἐγένετο τοῖς ὑπονοοῦσιν ὅτι τὸ συκοφάντημα κατὰ
τῆς κόρης αὐτὸς ἔρραψε,[3] καὶ ἔργον ἐτόλμησε
τυραννικὸν πρᾶξαι καὶ ὠμόν.

XXXVI. Ἔτι γὰρ αὐτῶν λεγόντων ἡσυχίαν
γενέσθαι κελεύσας, ἐπειδὴ σιωπή τ' ἐγένετο καὶ
πᾶς ὁ κατὰ τὴν ἀγορὰν ὄχλος τὴν ὁρμὴν ἐλάμβανεν
ἐπιθυμίᾳ γνώσεως τῶν ὑπ' αὐτοῦ λεχθησομένων
προαχθείς, πολλάκις ἐπιστρέψας τὸ πρόσωπον τῇδε
καὶ τῇδε καὶ τὰ στίφη τῶν ἑταίρων οἷς διειλήφει
τὴν ἀγορὰν τοῖς ὄμμασι διαριθμησάμενος τοιάδ'
2 εἶπεν· " Ἐγὼ δὲ περὶ τοῦδε τοῦ πράγματος, ὦ
Οὐεργίνιε, καὶ ὑμεῖς οἱ σὺν τούτῳ παρόντες, οὐ

---

[1] ἐπεκλᾶτο LV : ἐπεκλᾶτο τῆς κόρης R.
[2] πλείονος ἦν LV.

they considered what abuses and insults she would encounter after falling from such prosperity. And they began to reason that, once the law which secured their liberty was violated, there was nothing to prevent their own wives and daughters also from suffering the same treatment as this girl. While they were making these and many like reflections and communicating them to one another, they wept. But Appius, inasmuch as he was not by nature sound of mind and now was spoiled by the greatness of his power, his soul turgid and his bowels inflamed because of his love of the girl, neither paid heed to the pleas of her defenders nor was moved by her tears, and furthermore resented the sympathy shown for her by the bystanders, as though he himself deserved greater pity and had suffered greater torments from the comeliness which had enslaved him. Goaded, therefore, by all these emotions, he not only had the effrontery to make a shameless speech, by which he made it clear to those who suspected as much that he himself had contrived the fraudulent charge against the girl, but he also dared to commit a tyrannical and cruel deed.

XXXVI. For while they were still pleading their cause, he commanded silence ; and when there was quiet and the whole crowd in the Forum began moving forward, prompted by a desire to know what he would say, he repeatedly turned his glance here and there, his eyes taking count of the bands of his partisans, who by his orders had posted themselves in different parts of the Forum, and then spoke as follows : " This is not the first time, Verginius and you who are present with him, that I have heard of this

---

³ ἔρραψε Kiessling : ἔγραψε LV, Jacoby, ἔπλασε M.

νῦν πρῶτον ἀκήκοα, ἀλλὰ παλαίτερον ἔτι πρὶν
ἢ τήνδε τὴν ἀρχὴν παραλαβεῖν. ὃν τρόπον δ᾽
ἔγνων, ἀκούσατε. ὁ πατὴρ ὁ Μάρκου Κλαυδίου
τουδὶ τελευτῶν τὸν βίον ἠξίωσέ με τὸν υἱὸν
αὐτοῦ παῖδα[1] καταλειπόμενον ἐπιτροπεῦσαι· πελά-
3 ται δ᾽ εἰσὶ τῆς οἰκίας ἡμῶν ἐκ προγόνων. ἐν δὲ
τῷ χρόνῳ τῆς ἐπιτροπείας μήνυσις ἐγένετό μοι
περὶ τῆς παιδός, ὡς ὑποβάλοιτο αὐτὴν Νομιτωρία
λαβοῦσα παρὰ τῆς Κλαυδίου δούλης, καὶ τὸ πρᾶγμα
ἐξετάσας ἔμαθον οὕτως ἔχον. ἐφάπτεσθαι μὲν οὖν
ἐνῆν αὐτὸν οὗ[2] προσῆκέ[3] μοι, βέλτιον δὲ ἡγη-
σάμην τούτῳ τὴν ἐξουσίαν καταλιπεῖν, ὁπότε
γένοιτο ἀνήρ, εἴτε βουληθείη τὴν παιδίσκην ἀπάγειν, εἴτε διαλύσασθαι πρὸς τοὺς τρέφοντας αὐτὴν
4 χρηματισθεὶς ἢ χαρισάμενος. ἐν δὲ τοῖς μεταξὺ
χρόνοις ἐγὼ μὲν εἰς τὰς πολιτικὰς πράξεις ἐγκυ-
λισθεὶς οὐδὲν ἔτι τῶν Κλαυδίου πραγμάτων εἶχον
ἐν φροντίδι. τούτῳ δ᾽, ὡς ἔοικε, τὸν ἴδιον ἐξετά-
ζοντι βίον καὶ περὶ τῆς παιδίσκης ἡ μήνυσις
ἀπεδόθη καθάπερ ἐμοὶ πρότερον, καὶ οὐδὲν ἄδικον
ἀξιοῖ τὴν ἐκ τῆς ἑαυτοῦ θεραπαίνης γεγονυῖαν
5 ἀπάγειν βουλόμενος. εἰ μὲν οὖν ἀλλήλους ἔπεισαν
αὐτοί, καλῶς ἂν εἶχεν· ἐπεὶ δ᾽ εἰς ἀμφισβήτησιν
ἦλθε τὸ πρᾶγμα, μαρτυρῶ τ᾽ αὐτῷ ταῦτα καὶ
κρίνω εἶναι τοῦτον τῆς παιδίσκης κύριον.᾽᾽

XXXVII. Ὡς δὲ ταῦτ᾽ ἤκουσαν, ὅσοι μὲν ἦσαν

---

[1] παῖδα O : om. Jacoby, νήπιον Kiessling.
[2] ἐνῆν αὐτὸν οὗ Post : ἐμαυτὸν οὐ R, ἐμαυτῷ οὐ LV, ἐμαυτοῦ
Jacoby, ὡς ἐμαυτοῦ Capps.
[3] προσῆκέ R : προσῆκει LV.

matter, but it was long ago, even before I assumed this magistracy. Hear, now, in what way it came to my knowledge. The father of Marcus Claudius here, when he was dying, asked me to be the guardian of his son, whom he was leaving a mere boy ; for the Claudii are hereditary clients of our family. During the time of my guardianship information was given me regarding this girl, to the effect that Numitoria had palmed her off as her own child after receiving her from the slave woman of Claudius ; and upon investigating the matter, I found it was so. Now I might myself have claimed what I had a right to claim,[1] but I thought it better to leave the power of choice to my ward here, when he should come to man's estate, either to take away the girl, if he thought fit, or to come to an accommodation with those who were rearing her, by taking money for her or making a present of her. Since that time, having become involved in public affairs, I have given myself no further concern about the interests of Claudius. But he, it would seem, when taking account of his estate, also received the same information concerning the girl which had previously been given to me ; and he is making no unjust demand when he wishes to take away the daughter of his own slave woman. Now if they had come to terms with one another, it would have been well ; but since the matter has been brought into litigation, I give this testimony in his favour and declare him to be the girl's master."

XXXVII. When they heard this, all who were

[1] Or, following Capps, " now it was right for me to claim her as my own."

ἀκέραιοί τε καὶ τῶν τὰ δίκαια λεγόντων παράκλητοι
τὰς χεῖρας ἄραντες εἰς τὸν οὐρανὸν ἀνέκραγον
ὀδυρμῷ καὶ ἀγανακτήσει μεμιγμένην κραυγήν, οἱ
δὲ τῆς ὀλιγαρχίας κόλακες τὴν ἐπικελεύουσάν τε
καὶ θάρσος ἐμποιῆσαι δυναμένην τοῖς κρατοῦσι
φωνήν. ἠρεθισμένης δὲ τῆς ἀγορᾶς καὶ παντο-
δαπῶν γεμούσης λόγων τε καὶ παθῶν σιωπὴν
2 γενέσθαι κελεύσας Ἄππιος ἔλεξεν· " Εἰ μὴ παύ-
σεσθε¹ διαστασιάζοντες τὴν πόλιν καὶ ἀντιστρα-
τηγοῦντες ἡμῖν οἱ ταραχώδεις, μηδαμῇ χρήσιμοι
μήτ' ἐν εἰρήνῃ μήτε κατὰ πολέμους, ὑπὸ τῆς
ἀνάγκης σωφρονισθέντες εἴξετε. μὴ τούτους οἴεσθε
τοὺς ἐπὶ τοῦ Καπιτωλίου καὶ τῆς ἄκρας φρουροὺς
ἐπὶ τοὺς ἔξωθεν πολεμίους ἡμῖν παρεσκευάσθαι²
μόνον, ὑμᾶς δὲ τοὺς ἔνδον ὑποκαθημένους καὶ
πάντα σήποντας τὰ τῆς πόλεως πράγματα ἐάσειν.
3 γνώμην δὴ λαβόντες κρείττονα ἧς ἔχετε νῦν ἄπιτε,
οἷς μή τι πρᾶγμα, καὶ πράσσετε τὰ ἑαυτῶν, εἰ
σωφρονεῖτε· σὺ δ' ἄγου τὴν παιδίσκην ἔχων,
Κλαύδιε, μηδένα δεδοικὼς δι' ἀγορᾶς· οἱ γὰρ
Ἀππίου σε προπέμψουσι δώδεκα πελέκεις."
4 Ὡς δὲ ταῦτ' εἶπεν, οἱ μὲν ἄλλοι στένοντες καὶ
τὰ μέτωπα παίοντες καὶ τὰ δάκρυα κατέχειν οὐ
δυνάμενοι παρεχώρουν ἐκ τῆς ἀγορᾶς, ὁ δὲ
Κλαύδιος ἀπῆγε τὴν παῖδα τῷ πατρὶ περιπεπλεγμένην καὶ καταφιλοῦσαν καὶ ταῖς ἡδίσταις φωναῖς
ἀνακαλοῦσαν. ἐν τοιούτοις δὴ κακοῖς Οὐεργίνιος
ὢν ἔργον εἰς νοῦν βάλλεται πατρὶ μὲν ταλαίπωρον
καὶ πικρόν, ἐλευθέρῳ δ' ἀνδρὶ καὶ μεγαλόφρονι
5 πρέπον. αἰτησάμενος γὰρ ἐξουσίαν ἀσπάσασθαι

---

¹ παύσησθε LV.

unprejudiced and ready to be advocates for those who
plead the cause of justice held up their hands to
heaven and raised an outcry of mingled lamentation
and resentment, while the flatterers of the oligarchy
uttered their rallying cry that was calculated to
inspire the men in power with confidence. While
the Forum was seething and filled with cries and
emotions of every sort, Appius, commanding silence,
said : " If you do not cease dividing the city into
factions and contending against us, you trouble-
makers, useless fellows everywhere whether in peace
or in war, you shall be brought to your senses by compulsion and so submit. Do not imagine that these
guards on the Capitol and the citadel have been made
ready by us solely against foreign foes and that we
shall be indifferent to you who sit idle inside the walls
and corrupt all the interests of the commonwealth.
Adopt, then, a better disposition than you have at
present and be off with you, all you who have no
business here, and mind your own affairs, if you are
wise. And do you, Claudius, take the girl and lead
her through the Forum without fearing anyone ; for
the twelve axes of Appius will attend you."

After he had spoken thus, the others withdrew
from the Forum, sighing, beating their foreheads, and
unable to refrain from tears ; but Claudius began to
lead away the girl as she held her father close, kissing
him and calling upon him with the most endearing
words. Finding himself in so sore a plight, Verginius
thought of a deed that was grievous and bitter indeed
to a father, yet becoming to a free man of lofty spirit.
For he asked leave to embrace his daughter for the

---

² Sylburg : παρασκευασθᾳ V (?), παρασκευάσαι R.

DIONYSIUS OF HALICARNASSUS

τὴν θυγατέρα τοὺς τελευταίους ἀσπασμοὺς ἐπ'
ἐλευθερίας[1] καὶ διαλεχθῆναι μόνῃ μόνος ὁπόσα
βούλεται πρὶν ἐκ τῆς ἀγορᾶς αὐτὴν ἀπαχθῆναι,
συγχωρήσαντος τοῦ στρατηγοῦ καὶ τῶν ἐχθρῶν
μικρὸν ἀναχωρησάντων ὑπολαβὼν αὐτὴν[2] ἐκλυο-
μένην τε καὶ καταρρέουσαν καὶ κατέχων[3] τέως
μὲν ἀνεκαλεῖτό τε καὶ κατεφίλει καὶ τὰς λιβάδας
ἐξέματτε τῶν δακρύων, ἔπειτα κατὰ μικρὸν
ὑπάγων, ὡς ἦν[4] ἐγγὺς ἐργαστηρίου μαγειρικοῦ,
μάχαιραν ἐξαρπάσας ἀπὸ τῆς τραπέζης παίει τὴν
θυγατέρα διὰ τῶν σπλάγχνων τοσοῦτον εἰπών·
6 " Ἐλευθέραν σε καὶ εὐσχήμονα, τέκνον, ἀπο-
στέλλω τοῖς κατὰ γῆς[5] προγόνοις· ζῶσα γὰρ ταῦτα
οὐκ ἐξῆν ἔχειν[6] ἀμφότερα διὰ τὸν τύραννον."
κραυγῆς δὲ γενομένης ἡμαγμένην ἔχων τὴν σφαγίδα[7] καὶ αὐτὸς[8] ἀνάμεστος αἵματος γενόμενος, ᾧ
προσέφυρεν[9] αὐτὸν ἡ σφαγὴ τῆς κόρης, ἔθει διὰ
τῆς πόλεως ἐμμανὴς ἐπὶ τὴν ἐλευθερίαν τοὺς
7 πολίτας καλῶν. διεκπαισάμενος δὲ τὰς πύλας
ἀνέβη τὸν ἵππον ὃς ἦν παρεσκευασμένος αὐτῷ καὶ
συνέτεινεν ἐπὶ τὸ στρατόπεδον, Ἰκιλίου τε καὶ
Νομιτωρίου τῶν ἀγαγόντων αὐτὸν ἐκ τοῦ χάρακος
νεανίσκων καὶ τότε συμπροπεμπόντων. ἠκολούθει
δ' αὐτοῖς καὶ ἄλλος ὄχλος δημοτῶν οὐκ ὀλίγος,
ὥστε τοὺς σύμπαντας ἀμφὶ τετρακοσίους γενέσθαι.

XXXVIII. Ὁ δὲ Ἄππιος, ὡς τὸ περὶ τὴν κόρην
ἐπέγνω πάθος, ἀναπηδᾷ τε ἀπὸ τοῦ δίφρου καὶ

---

[1] ἐπ' ἐλευθερίας Post, ἐφ' ἡσυχίας Capps : ἐπ' ἐξουσίας O,
Jacoby.
[2] αὐτὴν Portus : εἰς τὴν O, Jacoby.
[3] Reiske : κατέχουσαν O, Jacoby.
[4] ἦν om L.
[5] Sylburg : γῆν O.   [6] ἔχειν L : om. R.

last time as a free woman [1] and to say what he thought
fit to her in private before she was taken from the
Forum, and when the general [2] granted his request and
his enemies withdrew a little, he held her up and
supported her as she was fainting and sinking to the
ground, and for a time called her by name, kissed her,
and wiped away her streaming tears ; then, drawing
her away by degrees, when he came close to a butcher's
shop, he snatched up a knife from the table and
plunged it into his daughter's vitals, saying only this :
" I send you forth free and virtuous, my child, to your
ancestors beneath the earth. For if you had lived,
you could not have enjoyed these two blessings
because of the tyrant." When an outcry was raised,
holding the bloody knife in his hand and covered as
he was himself with blood, with which the slaying of
the girl had besprinkled him, he ran like a madman
through the city, calling the citizens to liberty.
Then, forcing his way out through the gates, he
mounted the horse that stood ready for him and
hastened to the camp, attended this time also by
Icilius and Numitorius, the young men who had
brought him from the camp. They were followed
by another crowd of plebeians, not small in number,
but amounting to some four hundred in all.

XXXVIII. When Appius learned of the girl's fate,[3]
he leaped up from his seat and was minded to pursue

[1] Or, following the reading proposed by Capps, " embrace
her . . . free from interference."
[2] See the note on chap. 32, 1.
[3] For chaps. 38 f. *cf.* Livy iii. 48, 7–49, 8.

---

[7] σφαγίδα Kiessling ; σφραγίδα La (in marg.) : μάχαιραν
LcMV.

[8] αὐτὸς Cobet : οὗτως O.

[9] ᾧ προσέφυρεν Casaubon : ὁ προσέφυσεν O.

διώκειν τὸν Οὐεργίνιον ἐβούλετο πολλὰ καὶ λέγων
καὶ πράττων ἄκοσμα. περιστάντων δ' αὐτὸν τῶν
φίλων καὶ μηδὲν ἐξαμαρτάνειν ἀξιούντων ἀπῄει
2 πρὸς ἅπαντας ἀγανακτῶν. ἤδη δ' αὐτῷ κατ'
οἰκίαν ὄντι προσαγγέλλουσι τῶν ἑταίρων τινὲς ὅτι
περὶ τὸ πτῶμα τῆς κόρης Ἰκίλιός τε ὁ κηδεστὴς
καὶ Νομιτώριος ὁ θεῖος σὺν τοῖς ἄλλοις ἑταίροις
τε καὶ συγγενέσιν ἑστῶτες ῥητὰ καὶ ἄρρητα κατ'
αὐτοῦ λέγουσι καὶ καλοῦσι τὸν δῆμον ἐπὶ τὴν
3 ἐλευθερίαν. ὁ δ' ὑπ' ὀργῆς ὡς εἶχε πέμπει τῶν
ῥαβδούχων τινὰς κελεύσας ἀπάγειν εἰς τὸ δεσμωτήριον τοὺς κεκραγότας καὶ τὸ πτῶμα μεταφέρειν
ἐκ τῆς ἀγορᾶς, ἀφρονέστατον πρᾶγμα ποιῶν καὶ
τοῖς τότε καιροῖς ἥκιστα ἁρμόττον. δέον γὰρ
ἀποθεραπεύειν τὸν ὄχλον ὀργῆς εἰληφότα δικαίαν
πρόφασιν, εἴξαντα μὲν¹ ἐν τῷ παραχρῆμα χρόνῳ,
ὕστερον δὲ² τὰ μὲν ἀπολογούμενον, τὰ δὲ παρ-
αιτούμενον, τὰ δ' ἑτέραις τισὶν εὐεργεσίαις ἀναλα-
βόντα, ἐπὶ τὸ βιαιότερον ἐνεχθεὶς εἰς ἀπόνοιαν
4 αὐτοὺς ἠνάγκασε τραπέσθαι. οὐ γὰρ ἀνέσχοντο
τῶν ἐπιβαλλομένων³ ἕλκειν τὴν νεκρὰν ἢ τοὺς
ἄνδρας εἰς τὸ δεσμωτήριον ἀπάγειν, ἀλλ' ἐμβοή-
σαντες ἑαυτοῖς σὺν ὠθισμῷ τε καὶ πληγαῖς τῶν
βιαζομένων ἐξέβαλον αὐτοὺς ἐκ τῆς ἀγορᾶς. ὥστ'
ἠναγκάσθη ἀκούσας ταῦτα⁴ Ἄππιος ἅμα συχνοῖς
ἑταίροις καὶ πελάταις εἰς τὴν ἀγορὰν πορεύεσθαι
παίειν κελεύων καὶ ἀνείργειν ἐκποδὼν τοὺς ἐν τοῖς
5 στενωποῖς. πυθόμενοι δὲ τὴν διάνοιαν αὐτοῦ τῆς
ἐξόδου Οὐαλέριός τε καὶ Ὁράτιος, οὓς ἔφην

---

¹ μὲν Portus : δ' O. ² δὲ added by Portus.
³ Sylburg : περιβαλλομένων O.
⁴ ταῦτα LV : ταῦθ' ὁ Jacoby.

Verginius, meanwhile both saying and doing many indecorous things. But when his friends stood round him and besought him to do nothing reckless, he departed full of resentment against everybody. Then, when he was already home, some of his followers informed him that Icilius, the betrothed of Verginia, and Numitorius, her uncle, together with her other friends and relations, standing round her body, were charging him with crimes speakable and unspeakable and summoning the people to liberty. In his rage he sent some of the lictors with orders to hale to prison those who had raised the clamour and to remove the body out of the Forum, thereby doing a most imprudent thing and one by no means suited to that crisis. For when he ought to have courted the multitude, who had found a just cause for resentment, by yielding to them for the moment and afterwards justifying some of his actions, seeking pardon for others, and making amends for yet others by sundry acts of kindness, he was carried away to more violent measures and forced the people to resort to desperation. For instance, they would not permit it when the lictors attempted to drag away the body or hale the men to prison, but shouting encouragement to one another, they indulged in both pushing and blows against them when they attempted to use violence and drove them out of the Forum. As a result, Appius, on hearing of this, was obliged to proceed to the Forum, accompanied by numerous partisans and clients, whom he ordered to beat and hold back out of the way the people who were in the streets. But Valerius and Horatius, who, as I have said,[1] were the chief leaders of those who

----

[1] See chap. 22, 3.

ἡγεμονικωτάτους εἶναι τῶν ἀντιποιουμένων τῆς ἐλευθερίας, πολλὴν καὶ ἀγαθὴν νεότητα περὶ αὑτοὺς ἄγοντες ἵστανται πρὸ τοῦ νεκροῦ καὶ ἐπειδὴ πλησίον αὐτῶν οἱ περὶ τὸν Ἄππιον ἐγίνοντο, πρῶτον μὲν εἰς λόγους ἐπαχθεῖς καὶ προπηλακιστὰς[1] κατὰ τῆς ἐξουσίας αὐτῶν ἐχώρουν, ἔπειτα καὶ τὰ ἔργα ὅμοια τοῖς λόγοις παρείχοντο παίοντές τε καὶ ἀνατρέποντες τοὺς ὁμόσε χωροῦντας.

XXXIX. Ὁ δ' Ἄππιος ἀδημονῶν ἐπὶ τῷ παρ' ἐλπίδα τῆς κωλύσεως[2] καὶ οὐκ ἔχων ὅ τι χρήσεται τοῖς ἀνδράσι τὴν ὀλεθριωτάτην ἔγνω βαδίζειν ὁδόν. ὡς γὰρ ἔτι τοῦ πλήθους αὐτῷ διαμένοντος οἰκείου ἀναβὰς ἐπὶ τοῦ Ἡφαίστου τὸ ἱερὸν ἐκάλει τὸν δῆμον εἰς ἐκκλησίαν καὶ κατηγορεῖν ἐπειρᾶτο τῶν ἀνδρῶν παρανομίαν τε καὶ ὕβριν, ἐξουσίᾳ δημαρχικῇ καὶ ἐλπίδι κούφῃ ἐπαιρόμενος ὅτι συναγανακτήσας ὁ δῆμος αὐτῷ παρήσει ῥῖψαι τοὺς ἄνδρας κατὰ 2 τῆς πέτρας. οἱ δὲ περὶ τὸν Οὐαλέριον ἕτερον τόπον τῆς ἀγορᾶς καταλαβόμενοι καὶ τὸ πτῶμα τῆς παρθένου θέντες ὅθεν ὑπὸ πάντων ὀφθήσεσθαι ἔμελλεν, ἑτέραν συνῆγον ἐκκλησίαν καὶ πολλὴν ἐποιοῦντο τοῦ τ' Ἀππίου καὶ τῶν ἄλλων ὀλιγαρχῶν 3 κατηγορίαν. ἔμελλέ τε, ὅπερ εἰκὸς ἦν, οὓς μὲν τὸ ἀξίωμα τῶν ἀνδρῶν, οὓς δ' ὁ τῆς κόρης ἔλεος δεινὰ καὶ πέρα δεινῶν διὰ τὸ ἀτυχὲς κάλλος παθούσης, οὓς δ' αὐτὸς ὁ τῆς ἀρχαίας καταστάσεως πόθος εἰς ταύτην τὴν ἐκκλησίαν παρακαλῶν πλείους τῶν ἑτέρων συνάξειν, ὥστ' ὀλίγους τινὰς

---

[1] προπηλακιστὰς L : προπηλακισμοὺς R.

desired to recover their liberty, having learned of his purpose in thus coming forth, came bringing with them a large and brave company of youths and took their stand before the body ; and when Appius and his followers drew near, they first proceeded to harsh and bitter taunts against the power of the decemvirs, and then, suiting their actions to their words, they struck and knocked down all who engaged with them.

XXXIX. Appius, sorely troubled by this unexpected setback and not knowing how to deal with the men, resolved to take the most pernicious course. For, feeling that the populace still remained friendly to him, he went up to the sanctuary of Vulcan, and calling an assembly of the people, he attempted to accuse those men of violation of the law and of insolent behaviour, being carried away by his tribunician power and the vain hope that the people would share his resentment and permit him to throw the men down from the cliff.[1] But Valerius and his followers took possession of another part of the Forum, and placing the body of the maiden where it would be seen by all, held another assembly of the people and made a sweeping accusation of Appius and the other oligarchs. And it was bound to happen, as one would expect, that with some being attracted thither by the rank of the men, others by their compassion for the girl who had suffered dreadful and worse than dreadful calamities because of her unfortunate beauty, and still others by their very yearning for the ancient constitution, this assembly would be better attended than the other, so that just a few were left round

[1] The Tarpeian Rock.

---

[2] Sylburg : κολάσεως O, Jacoby.

ὑπολειφθῆναι περὶ τὸν Ἄππιον, αὐτοὺς δὴ[1] τοὺς
ὀλιγαρχικούς, ἐν οἷς ἦσάν τινες οὐκέτι τῶν ὀλιγαρχῶν[2] αὐτῶν ἀκροώμενοι, διὰ πολλὰς προφάσεις,
ἀλλ᾽, εἰ γένοιτο ἰσχυρὰ τὰ τῶν ἐναντίων, ἄσμενοι
4 χωρήσοντες[3] ἐπ᾽ ἐκείνους. ἐρημούμενον δὴ θεωρῶν
ἑαυτὸν ὁ Ἄππιος ἠναγκάσθη μεταγνῶναι καὶ
ἀπελθεῖν ἐκ τῆς ἀγορᾶς, ὃ καὶ μάλιστ᾽ ὤνησεν
αὐτόν. ἐπιβαλλόμενος[4] γὰρ ὑπὸ τοῦ δημοτικοῦ
5 πλήθους καλὰς ἔτισεν ἂν[5] αὐτῷ τὰς δίκας. μετὰ
τοῦτ᾽ ἐξουσίας ὅσης ἐβούλοντο τυχόντες οἱ περὶ
τὸν Οὐαλέριον ἐνεφοροῦντο τῶν κατ᾽ ὀλιγαρχίας
λόγων καὶ τοὺς ἔτι ἐνδοιάζοντας ἐξεδημαγώγουν.
ἔτι δὲ μᾶλλον ἐξηλλοτρίωσαν τὸν πολιτικὸν ὄχλον
οἱ τῆς κόρης συγγενεῖς κλίνην τε κομίσαντες εἰς
τὴν ἀγορὰν καὶ τὸν ἄλλον κόσμον τὸν ἐπιτάφιον
οἷον ἐδύναντο πολυτελέστατον παρασκευάσαντες
καὶ τὴν ἐκφορὰν τοῦ σώματος διὰ τῶν ἐπιφανεστάτων τῆς πόλεως ποιησάμενοι στενωπῶν, ὅθεν
6 ὑπὸ πλείστων ὀφθήσεσθαι ἔμελλεν.[6] ἐξεπήδων γὰρ
ἐκ τῶν οἰκιῶν γυναῖκές τε καὶ παρθένοι τὸ πάθος
ἀποδυρόμεναι, αἱ μὲν ἄνθη καὶ στεφάνους βάλλουσαι
κατὰ τῆς κλίνης, αἱ δὲ τελαμῶνας ἢ μίτρας, αἱ
δὲ ἀθύρματα παρθενικά, καί πού τινες καὶ πλο-
7 κάμων ἀποκειράμεναι[7] βοστρύχους· ἄνδρες τε
συχνοὶ λαμβάνοντες ἐκ τῶν πλησίον ἐργαστηρίων
τὰ μὲν ὠνῇ, τὰ δὲ χάριτι συνεπεκόσμουν τοῖς
προσφόροις δωρήμασι τὴν ἐκκομιδήν· ὥστε περιβόητον ἀνὰ τὴν πόλιν γενέσθαι τὸ κῆδος, καὶ

[1] δὴ M : om. R(?).
[2] τῶν ὀλιγαρχῶν Cary : τῆς ὀλιγαρχικῆς O, Jacoby, τῆς
ὀλιγαρχίας Reiske. Unless we have the oligarchs (*i.e.* the
decemvirs) mentioned, there is nothing to show who are
meant by αὐτῶν and ἐκείνους.

Appius, consisting solely of the oligarchical faction ;
and among those there were some who for many
reasons no longer paid heed to the oligarchs themselves, but, if the cause of their opponents should
become strong, would gladly turn against the others.
Appius, accordingly, seeing himself being deserted,
was obliged to change his mind and leave the Forum,
a course which proved of the greatest advantage to
him ; for if he had been set upon by the plebeian
crowd, he would have paid a fitting penalty to them.
After that Valerius and his followers, having all the
authority they wished, indulged themselves in anti-
oligarchic speeches and by their harangues won over
those who still hesitated.   The dissatisfaction of the
citizens at large was still further increased by the relations of the girl, who brought her bier into the Forum,
prepared all the funeral trappings on the most costly
scale they could, and then bore the body in procession
through the principal streets of the city, where it
would be seen by the largest number of people.   In
fact the matrons and maidens ran out of their houses
lamenting her fate, some throwing flowers and gar-
lands upon the bier, some their girdles or fillets, others
their childhood toys, and others perhaps even locks of
their hair that they had cut off ; and many of the
men, either purchasing ornaments in the neighbouring shops or receiving them as a favour, contributed
to the funeral pomp by the appropriate gifts.   Hence
the funeral was much talked about throughout the

<hr/>

³ Cary : χωρήσειν O, Jacoby.
⁴ βαλλόμενος Reiske.
⁵ ἄν added by Sylburg.
⁶ Kiessling : ἔμελλον O, Jacoby.
⁷ ἀποράμεναι L : ἀποκράμενοι V.

προθυμίαν ἅπαντας καταλαβεῖν τῆς τῶν ὀλιγάρχων[1]
καταλύσεως. ἀλλ' οἱ φρονοῦντες τὰ τῆς ὀλιγαρχίας
ὅπλα ἔχοντες μέγα παρεῖχον αὐτοῖς δέος, οἵ τε
περὶ τὸν Οὐαλέριον οὐκ ἠξίουν αἵματι πολιτικῷ
τὸ νεῖκος διαιρεῖν.

XL. Τὰ μὲν δὴ κατὰ πόλιν ἐν τοιαύταις ἦν
ταραχαῖς. Οὐεργίνιος δ', ὃν ἔφην αὐτόχειρα
γενέσθαι τῆς ἑαυτοῦ θυγατρός, ἀπὸ ῥυτῆρος
ἐλαύνων τὸν ἵππον ἀφικνεῖται περὶ λύχνων ἁφὰς
ἐπὶ τὸν πρὸς Ἀλγιδῷ χάρακα, τοιοῦτος οἷος ἐκ
τῆς πόλεως ἐξέδραμεν, αἵματι πεφυρμένος ἅπας
καὶ τὴν μαγειρικὴν σφαγίδα[2] διὰ χειρὸς ἔχων.
2 ἰδόντες δ' αὐτὸν οἱ πρὸ τοῦ στρατοπέδου τὰς
φυλακὰς φυλάττοντες ἐν ἀπόρῳ τ' ἦσαν ὅ τι
πέπονθεν εἰκάσαι, καὶ παρηκολούθουν ὡς ἀκου-
σόμενοι μέγα πρᾶγμα καὶ δεινόν. ὁ δὲ τέως μὲν
ἐπορεύετο κλαίων καὶ διασημαίνων τοῖς ὁμόσε
χωροῦσιν ἀκολουθεῖν· ἐξέτρεχον δ' ἐκ τῶν σκηνῶν
ἃς διεπορεύετο μεταξὺ δειπνοῦντες ἅπαντες ἀθρόοι
φανοὺς ἔχοντες καὶ λαμπάδας, ἀγωνίας πλήρεις
καὶ θορύβου[3] περιχεόμενοί τε[4] περὶ αὐτὸν ἠκολού-
3 θουν. ἐπεὶ δ' εἰς τὸν ἀναπεπταμένον τοῦ στρατοπέδου τόπον ἦλθεν, ἐπὶ μετεώρου τινὸς στάς,[5]
ὥσθ' ὑπὸ πάντων ὁρᾶσθαι, διηγεῖτο τὰς κατα-
λαβούσας αὐτὸν συμφοράς, μάρτυρας τῶν λόγων
παρεχόμενος τοὺς σὺν αὐτῷ παρόντας ἐκ τῆς
πόλεως.

Ὡς δὲ κατέμαθεν ὀλοφυρομένους τε πολλοὺς
καὶ δακρύοντας, εἰς ἱκεσίας καὶ δεήσεις αὐτῶν

---

[1] ὀλιγάρχων Sylburg : ὀλιγαρχιῶν O, ὀλιγαρχικῶν Kiessling,
Jacoby.   [2] σφαγίδα La : μάχαιραν Lb (in marg.) VM.
[3] θορύβου La : θορύβῳ Lb, θορύβων VM.

entire city, and all were seized with an eager desire
for the overthrow of the oligarchs. But those who
favoured the cause of the oligarchy, being armed,
kept them in great fear, and Valerius and his followers
did not care to decide the quarrel by shedding the
blood of their fellow citizens.

XL. Affairs in the city, then, were in this state of
turmoil.[1] In the meantime Verginius, who, as I have
related, had slain his daughter with his own hand,
rode with loose rein and at lamp-lighting time came
to the camp at Algidum, still in the same condition in
which he had rushed out of the city, all covered with
blood and holding the butcher's knife in his hand.
When those who were keeping guard before the camp
saw him, they could not imagine what had happened
to him, and they followed along in the expectation
of hearing of some great and dreadful occurrence.
Verginius for the time continued on his way, weeping
and making signs to those he met to follow him ; and
from the tents which he passed the soldiers, who were
then at supper, all ran out in a body, full of anxious
suspense and consternation, carrying torches and
lamps ; and pouring round him, they accompanied
him. But when he came to the open space in the
camp, he took his stand upon an elevated spot, so as
to be seen by all, and related the calamities that had
befallen him, offering as witnesses to the truth of his
statements those who had come with him from the
city.

When he saw many of them lamenting and shedding tears, he turned to supplications and entreaties,

―――――

[1] For chaps. 40-44, 5 *cf.* Livy iii. 50 f.

―――――

⁴ περιχεόμενοί τε Sylburg : περιεχόμενοι O, Jacoby.
⁵ τινὸς στάς L : στάς τινος R.

131

DIONYSIUS OF HALICARNASSUS

ἐτράπετο μὴ περιδεῖν μήτ' αὐτὸν ἀτιμώρητον
γενόμενον μήτε τὴν πατρίδα προπηλακιζομένην.
λέγοντι δ' αὐτῷ ταῦτα πολὺ τὸ βουλόμενον ἐξ
ἁπάντων ἀκούειν καὶ ἐπικελευόμενον λέγειν ἐγίνετο.
4 τοιγάρτοι καὶ θρασύτερον ἤδη καθήπτετο τῆς
ὀλιγαρχίας, διεξιὼν ὡς πολλῶν μὲν ἀφείλοντο τὰς
οὐσίας οἱ δέκα, πολλῶν δὲ πληγαῖς ἠκίσαντο τὰ
σώματα, παμπόλλους δὲ φυγεῖν ἠνάγκασαν ἐκ
τῆς πατρίδος οὐδὲν ἀδικήσαντας, γυναικῶν τε
ὕβρεις καὶ παρθένων ἐπιγάμων ἁρπαγὰς καὶ
παίδων ἐλευθέρων προπηλακισμοὺς καὶ τὰς ἄλλας
αὐτῶν παρανομίας τε καὶ ὠμότητας ἐκλογιζόμενος.
5 " Καὶ ταῦτ'," ἔφη, " προπηλακίζουσιν ἡμᾶς οἱ
μήτε[1] νόμῳ τὴν ἐξουσίαν ἔχοντες μήτε ψηφίσματι
βουλῆς ἢ δήμου συγχωρήματι λαβόντες (ὁ γὰρ
ἐναύσιος αὐτοῖς τῆς ἀρχῆς χρόνος, ὃν ἐχρῆν
αὐτοὺς ἄρξαντας ἑτέροις παραδοῦναι τὰ κοινά,
παρελήλυθεν), ἀλλ' ἐκ τοῦ βιαιοτάτου τῶν τρόπων,
πολλὴν δειλίαν καὶ μαλακίαν καταγνόντες ἡμῶν
6 ὥσπερ γυναικῶν. εἰσελθέτω δὴ λογισμὸς ἕκαστον
ὑμῶν ὧν τ' αὐτὸς πέπονθε καὶ ὧν οἶδεν ἑτέρους
παθόντας· καὶ εἴ τις ὑμῶν δελεαζόμενος ὑπ' αὐτῶν
ἡδοναῖς τισιν ἢ χάρισιν οὐ πεφόβηται τὴν ὀλιγαρχίαν οὐδὲ δέδοικε μὴ καὶ ἐπ' αὐτὸν ἔλθοι ποτὲ
σὺν χρόνῳ τὰ δεινά, μαθὼν ὅτι τυράννοις οὐδέν
ἐστι πιστόν, οὐδ' ἀπ' εὐνοίας αἱ τῶν κρατούντων
δίδονταί τισι χάριτες, καὶ πάντα τὰ ὅμοια τούτοις,
7 μεταγνώτω· καὶ μιᾷ διανοίᾳ χρησάμενοι πάντες
ἐλευθεροῦτε ἀπὸ τῶν τυράννων τὴν πατρίδα, ἐν
ᾗ θεῶν τε ὑμῖν[2] ἱερὰ ἵδρυται καὶ θῆκαι προγόνων
εἰσίν, οὓς ὑμεῖς τιμᾶτε μετὰ θεούς, καὶ γηραιοὶ

---

[1] Jacoby : μὴ O.   [2] ὑμῖν L : om. R.

begging them neither to permit him to go unavenged
nor to let the fatherland be foully abused. While he
was speaking thus, great eagerness was shown by
them all to hear him and great encouragement for
him to speak on. Accordingly, he now assailed the
oligarchy with greater boldness, recounting how the
decemvirs had deprived many of their fortunes,
caused many to be scourged, forced ever so many to
flee from the country though guilty of no crime, and
enumerating their insults offered to matrons, their
seizing of marriageable maidens, their abuse of boys
of free condition, and all their other excesses and
cruelties. " And these abuses," he said, " we suffer
at the hands of men who hold their power neither by
law nor by a decree of the senate nor by the consent
of the people (for the year's term of their magistracy,
after serving which they should have handed over the
administration of affairs to others, has expired), but
by the most violent of all means, since they have ad-
judged us great cowards and weaklings, like women.
Let every one of you consider both what he has
suffered himself and what he knows others to have
suffered ; and if any one of you, lured by them with
pleasures or gratifications, does not stand in dread
of the oligarchy or fear that the calamities will even-
tually come upon him too some day, let him learn
that tyrants know no loyalty, that it is not out of
goodwill that the favours of the powerful are bestowed, and all the other truths of like purport;
then let him change his opinion. And becoming of
one mind, all of you, free from these tyrants your
country, in which stand both the temples of your
gods and the sepulchres of your ancestors, whom you
honour next to the gods, in which also are your aged

πατέρες τροφεῖα πολλὰ καὶ ἄξια τῶν πόνων ἀπαιτοῦντες, γυναῖκές τε κατὰ νόμους ἐγγυηθεῖσαι,
καὶ θυγατέρες ἐπίγαμοι φροντίδος οὐ μικρᾶς δεό-
μεναι τοῖς ἔχουσι, καὶ γοναὶ παίδων ἀρρένων, οἷς
8 ὀφείλεται δίκαια τὰ[1] φύσεως καὶ προγόνων.[2] οἰκίας
γὰρ δὴ καὶ κλήρους καὶ χρήματα σὺν πολλοῖς
κτηθέντα πόνοις ὑπὸ πατέρων καὶ ὑμῶν αὐτῶν
σιωπῶ· ὧν οὐδὲν ὑμῖν ἔξεστι βεβαίως ἔχειν ἕως
ἂν ὑπὸ τῶν δέκα τυραννῆσθε.

XLI. '' Οὔτε σωφρόνων οὔτε γενναίων ἐστὶν
ἀνθρώπων τὰ μὲν ἀλλότρια κτᾶσθαι δι' ἀνδρ-
αγαθίαν, τὰ δ' οἰκεῖα περιορᾶν ἀπολλύμενα διὰ
μαλακίαν οὐδὲ πρὸς μὲν Αἰκανοὺς καὶ Οὐολούσκους
καὶ Σαβίνους καὶ τοὺς ἄλλους[3] περιοίκους ἅπαντας
πολεμεῖν μακροὺς καὶ ἀδιαλείπτους πολέμους ὑπὲρ
ἀρχῆς καὶ δυναστείας, πρὸς δὲ τοὺς παρὰ νόμον
ἄρχοντας ὑμῶν μὴ θέλειν ἄρασθαι τὰ ὅπλα ὑπὲρ
2 ἀσφαλείας τε καὶ ἐλευθερίας. οὐκ ἀναλήψεσθε τὸ
φρόνημα τῆς πατρίδος; οὐ παραστήσεται λογισμὸς
ὑμῖν τῆς ἀρετῆς τῶν γονέων ἄξιος, οἳ διὰ μιᾶς
γυναικὸς ὕβριν ὑφ' ἑνὸς τῶν Ταρκυνίου παίδων
ὑβρισθείσης καὶ διὰ τὴν συμφορὰν ταύτην ἑαυτὴν
διαχρησαμένης[4] οὕτως ἠγανάκτησαν ἐπὶ τῷ πάθει
καὶ παρωξύνθησαν[5] καὶ κοινὴν ἁπάντων ἡγήσαντο
τὴν ὕβριν ὥστ' οὐ μόνον Ταρκύνιον ἐξέβαλον ἐκ
τῆς πόλεως, ἀλλὰ καὶ τὸ βασιλικὸν πολίτευμα
κατέλυσαν, καὶ τὸ λοιπὸν ἀπεῖπαν[6] μηδένα Ῥωμαίων ἄρχειν διὰ βίου τὴν ἀνυπεύθυνον ἀρχήν,

---

[1] τὰ added here by Post, before δίκαια by Kayser,
Jacoby.
[2] καὶ προγόνων Reiske : προγόνων O, Jacoby, om. Kayser.

fathers, who demand of you many acknowledgements such as the pains they have bestowed upon your rearing deserve, and also your lawfully betrothed wives, your marriageable daughters, who require much solicitous care on the part of their parents, and your sons, to whom are owed the rights deriving from Nature and from your forefathers. I say nothing indeed of your houses, your estates and your goods, which have been acquired with great pains both by your fathers and by yourselves, none of which things you can possess in security so long as you live under the tyranny of the decemvirs.

XLI. " It is the part neither of prudent nor of brave men to acquire the possessions of others by valour and then to allow their own to be lost through cowardice, nor, again, to wage long and incessant wars against the Aequians, the Volscians, the Sabines, and all the rest of your neighbours for the sake of sovereignty and dominion and then to be unwilling to take up arms against your unlawful rulers for the sake of both your security and your liberty. Will you not recover the proud spirit of your country ? Will you not come to a decision worthy of the virtue of your ancestors who, because one woman was outraged by one of Tarquin's sons and because of this calamity put herself to death, became so indignant at her fate and so exasperated, looking upon the outrage as one done to them all alike, that they not only banished Tarquin from the state, but even abolished the monarchy itself and forbade that anyone should thereafter rule over Romans for life with irresponsible

---

³ ἄλλους LV : om. R.   ⁴ διαχειρισαμένης MV.
     ⁵ ἠγανάκτησαν καὶ παρωξύνθησαν ἐπὶ τῷ πάθει L.
          ⁶ ἀπεῖπαν O : ἀπεῖπον Jacoby.

αὐτοί τε τοὺς μεγίστους ὀμόσαντες ὅρκους, καὶ
κατὰ τῶν ἐγγόνων ἀράς, ἐάν τι παρὰ ταῦτα ποιῶ-
3 σι, καταρασάμενοι; ἔπειτ' ἐκεῖνοι μὲν ἑνὸς οὐκ
ἤνεγκαν ἀκολάστου μειρακίου τυραννικὴν ὕβριν
εἰς ἓν σῶμα ἐλεύθερον γενομένην, ὑμεῖς δὲ πολυ-
κέφαλον τυραννίδα πάσῃ παρανομίᾳ τε καὶ ἀσελ-
γείᾳ χρωμένην καὶ ἔτι μᾶλλον χρησομένην, ἐὰν
4 νῦν ἀνάσχησθε, ὑπομενεῖτε; οὐχ ἐμοὶ μόνῳ θυγάτηρ ἐγένετο διαφέρουσα τὴν ὄψιν ἑτέρων, ἣν ἀπὸ
τοῦ φανεροῦ βιάζεσθαι καὶ προπηλακίζειν Ἄππιος
ἐπεβάλετο, ἀλλὰ καὶ ὑμῶν εἰσι πολλαὶ τοῖς μὲν
θυγατέρες, τοῖς δὲ γαμεταί, τοῖς δὲ νεανίαι παῖδες
εὐπρεπεῖς, οὓς τί κωλύσει πρὸς ἄλλου τινὸς τῶν
δέκα τυράννων ἢ πρὸς αὐτοῦ τοῦ[1] Ἀππίου ταὐτὰ
παθεῖν; εἰ μή τις ἄρα θεῶν ἐστιν ἐγγυητής, ὡς,
ἐὰν τὰς ἐμὰς ταύτας συμφορὰς ἀτιμωρήτους
ἐάσητε, οὐκ ἐφ' ὑμῶν πολλοὺς τὰ ὅμοια δεινὰ
ἥξει, ἀλλὰ μέχρι τῆς ἐμῆς θυγατρὸς ὁ τυραννικὸς
ἔρως προελθὼν στήσεται καὶ περὶ τὰ λοιπὰ σώματα
5 παίδων τε καὶ παρθένων σωφρονήσει. πολλῆς
μέντοι μωρίας καὶ σκαιότητος, σαφῶς ἴστε, τὰ
νοούμενα[2] ταῦθ' ὡς οὐκ ἔσται λέγειν. ἀόριστοι
γὰρ αἱ τῶν τυράννων ἐπιθυμίαι κατὰ τὸ εἰκός,
οἷα δὴ μήτε νόμον ἔχουσαι κωλυτὴν μήτε φόβον.
ἐμοί τε δὴ πράττοντες τιμωρίαν δικαίαν καὶ ὑμῖν
αὐτοῖς ἀσφάλειαν ἵνα μὴ ταὐτὰ πάθητε παρα-
σκευαζόμενοι διαρρήξατε ἤδη ποτὲ τοὺς χαλινούς,
ὦ σχέτλιοι· ἀναβλέψατε ὀρθοῖς ὄμμασι πρὸς τὴν
6 ἐλευθερίαν. ἐπὶ τίνι γὰρ ἑτέρᾳ προφάσει μᾶλλον
ἀγανακτήσετε ἢ ταύτῃ, ὅτε[3] τὰς τῶν πολιτῶν

---

[1] αὐτοῦ τοῦ R : αὐτοῦ τούτου L.
[2] ὑπονοούμενα Reiske, φοβούμενα Capps.

power, not only binding themselves by the most
solemn oaths, but also invoking curses upon their
descendants if in any respect they should act to
the contrary ? Then, when they refused to bear
the tyrannical outrage committed by one licentious
youth upon one person of free condition, will *you*
tolerate a many-headed tyranny that indulges in
every sort of crime and licentiousness and will indulge
still more if you now submit to it ? I am not the only
man who had a daughter superior in beauty to others
whom Appius has openly attempted to violate and
besmirch, but many of you also have daughters or
wives or comely young sons ; and what shall hinder
these from being treated in the same manner by
another of the ten tyrants or by Appius himself ?
Unless, indeed, there is some one of the gods who
will guarantee that if you permit these calamities of
mine to go unavenged the same misfortunes will not
come upon many of you, but having pursued its way
only as far as my daughter, this lust of tyrants will
stop and toward the persons of others, both youths
and maidens, will grow chaste ! Know of a certainty,
however, that it is the part of great folly and stupidity
to say that these imagined crimes will not come to
pass. For the desires of tyrants are naturally limit-
less, inasmuch as they have neither law nor fear to
check them. Therefore, by effecting for me a just
vengeance and also by procuring for yourselves
security against suffering the same mistreatment,
break now at last your bonds, O miserable men ;
look up toward liberty, your eyes fixed upon her.
What other ground for indignation greater than this
will you have, when the tyrants carry off the daughters

---

³ ὅτι Kiessling.

θυγατέρας ὡς δούλας ἀπάγουσιν οἱ τύραννοι καὶ
μετὰ μαστίγων νυμφαγωγοῦσιν; ἐν ποίῳ δὲ τὸ
ἐλεύθερον φρόνημα ἀναλήψεσθε καιρῷ τὸν νῦν
παρέντες, ἐν ᾧ τὰ ὅπλα περὶ τοῖς σώμασιν ἔχετε;"

XLII. Ἔτι δ' αὐτοῦ λέγοντος ἀνεβόησαν οἱ
πολλοὶ τιμωρήσειν ὑπισχνούμενοι καὶ τοὺς ἡγεμόνας τῶν λόχων ἐξ ὀνόματος ἐκάλουν ἀξιοῦντες
ἔργου ἔχεσθαι, καὶ ἐκ τοῦ φανεροῦ πολλοὶ παριόντες
ἐθάρρουν λέγειν εἴ τι δεινὸν ἦσαν πεπονθότες.
2 μαθόντες δὲ τὰ γενόμενα οἱ πέντε ἄνδρες οὓς ἔφην
ἡγεῖσθαι τῶν ταγμάτων, δείσαντες μή τις ἐπ'
αὐτοὺς τῶν ὄχλων ὁρμὴ γένηται, συνέδραμον εἰς
τὸ στρατήγιον πάντες[1] καὶ μετὰ τῶν φίλων ἐσκόπουν ὅπως παύσουσι[2] τὴν ταραχὴν τὰ οἰκεῖα ὅπλα
3 περιστησάμενοι. ὡς δ' ἐπύθοντο ἀπεληλυθότας
ἐπὶ τὰς σκηνὰς λήξαντά τε καὶ παυσάμενον[3] τὸν
θόρυβον, ἀγνοοῦντες ὅτι τῶν ἑκατοντάρχων τοῖς
πλείοσι δεδογμένον ἦν δι' ἀπορρήτων συνωμοσιῶν
ἀπόστασιν πράττειν καὶ συνελευθεροῦν τὴν πατρίδα,
ἔκριναν ἐπειδὰν ἡμέρα τάχιστα γένηται τὸν μὲν
ἐκταράττοντα τοὺς ὄχλους Οὐεργίνιον συλλαβόντες ἔχειν ἐν φυλακῇ, τὰς δὲ δυνάμεις ἀναστήσαντες ἐκ τοῦ χάρακος ἄγειν ἐπὶ τοὺς πολεμίους,
καὶ τὴν κρατίστην αὐτῶν τῆς χώρας ἐγκαθήμενοι
δῃοῦν, περὶ τῶν ἐν τῇ πόλει πραττομένων μηδὲν
τοὺς σφετέρους[4] ἔτι ἐῶντες[5] πολυπραγμονεῖν, τὰ
μὲν διὰ τὰς ὠφελείας, τὰ δὲ διὰ τοὺς ἐσομέ-
4 νους ὑπὲρ αὐτῶν ἑκάστοτε ἀγῶνας. ἐγίνετο δ'

[1] ἅπαντες Kiessling.
[2] Krüger : παύσωσι O.
[3] ἀπεληλυθότες . . . λήξαντες . . . παυσάμενοι C.
[4] τοὺς σφετέρους CbMb : τοῖς σφετέροις LVCaMa.
[5] συλλαβόντες . . . ἀναστήσαντες . . . ἐγκαθήμενοι . . . ἐῶντες

of citizens like slaves and with the lash lead their
brides home ?   On what occasion will you regain the
spirit of free men if you let slip the present one when
your bodies are protected by arms ? "

XLII. While he was yet speaking, most of the soldiers cried out, promising to avenge him, and called
upon the centurions by name, demanding immediate
action ;   and many, coming forward, made bold to
speak openly of any ill-treatment they had suffered.
Upon learning of what had happened, the five men,
who, as I have stated,[1] had the command of these
legions, fearing lest some attack might be made upon
them by the rabble, all ran to the general's headquarters and considered with their friends how they
might allay the tumult by surrounding themselves
with an armed guard of their own faction.   But being
informed that the soldiers had retired to their tents
and that the disturbance was abated and ended, and
being unaware that most of the centurions had
secretly conspired to revolt and to unite in freeing
their country, they resolved that as soon as it was
day they would seize Verginius, who was stirring up
the rabble, and keep him in custody, and then,
breaking camp and leading their forces against the
enemy, would settle down in the best part of their
territory and lay it waste, thus keeping their men
from meddling any longer with what was going on in
the city, partly because of the booty they would acquire and partly because of the battles that would be
waged in each instance to secure their own safety.

[1] Chap. 23, 2.

Kayser : συλλαβόντας . . . ἀναστήσαντας . . . ἐγκαθημένους
. . . ἐῶντας O (except that C has ἀναστήσοντας and L omits
ἐῶντας in a lacuna), Jacoby.

αὐτοῖς οὐδὲν τῶν ἐκ διαλογισμοῦ· οὐδὲ γὰρ[1] τὸν
Οὐεργίνιον εἴασαν οἱ λοχαγοὶ καλούμενον εἰς τὸ
στρατήγιον ἀπελθεῖν, ὑποπτεύ[οντες[2] μή τι πάθοι
δεινόν, ἀλλὰ καὶ τὸν] διαληφθέντ[α λόγον, ὡς] ἐπὶ
τοὺς πολεμίους ἀγαγεῖν τοὺς λόχους[3] ἐβούλοντο,
[κατωνείδιζον] λέγοντες· " Ὡς[4] καλῶς ἡμῶν ἐστρα-
τηγήκατε[5] καὶ πρότερον, ἵνα καὶ νῦν λαβόντες
ἐλπίδας[6] ἀκολουθῶμεν ὑμῖν, οἵτινες ὅσην οὔπω
πρότερον ἕτεροι Ῥωμαίων ἡγεμόνες ἔκ τ' αὐτῆς
ἄγοντες[7] τῆς πόλεως στρατιὰν καὶ ἀπὸ τῶν συμμάχων ἀγείραντες, οὔτε [τινὰ νίκην ἢ βλάβην
ἐποιήσατε κατὰ] τῶν ἐχθρῶν, ἀλλ' ἀνανδρίαν[8] τε
καὶ ἀπειρίαν [ἀπεδείξασθε,[9] κακῶς] στρατοπεδευσάμενοι, καὶ τὴν ἑαυτῶν χώραν ὡς[10] ὑπὸ τῶν
πολεμίων [καταδῃωθεῖσαν][11] πτωχοὺς καὶ ἀπόρους
ἡμᾶς ἐποιήσατε ἁπάντων, ὅσοις[12] κ[ρατοῦντες τοῖς
ὅπλοις τῶν ἐναντίων] ἐνικῶμεν ταῖς μάχαις, ὅτε
ὑμῶν κρείττους ἦσαν στρατηγοί· τρόπαιά τε καθ'
ἡμῶν ἀνιστᾶσι καὶ σκηνὰς καὶ ἀνδράποδα καὶ
ὅπλα καὶ χρήματα διηρπακότες ἔχουσι τὰ ἡμέτερα."
XLIII. Ὁ δὲ Οὐεργίνιος ὑπό τ' ὀργῆς καὶ ἐκ
τοῦ μηδὲν ἔτι δεδοικέναι τοὺς ἡγεμόνας αὐθα-
δέστερον αὐτῶν καθήπτετο λυμεῶνάς τε καὶ
ὀλέθρους τῆς πατρίδος ἀποκαλῶν καὶ παραινῶν

[1] γὰρ om. VM.
[2] The words enclosed in square brackets from here to the
end of the chapter are wanting in L and V, which usually
leave a lacuna ; they appear only in the inferior MSS., C
and M, and reflect the efforts of an unskilful interpolator.
[3] λόχους Kiessling : ὄχλους O.
[4] ὡς CM : ὅτι LV.
[5] ἐστρατηγήσατε Sintenis.
[6] χρηστὰς λαβόντες ἐλπίδας Kiessling.
[7] ἄγοντες deleted by Capps.

But they succeeded in none of their calculations; for
the centurions would not even permit Verginius to go
to the generals' headquarters when he was sent for,
suspect[ing [1] that he might suffer some harm ; nay,
they even heaped scorn upon the] intercept[ed report
that] the generals wished to lead the troops against
the enemy, saying : " How skilfully you have commanded us in the past, that now also we should take
hope and follow you—you who, after assembling a
greater army both from the city itself and from our
allies than any other generals in the past, have not
only failed to gain [any victory] over the enemy [or
to do them any harm,] but on the contrary [have
shown] a lack of both courage and experience by
encamping [in cowardly fashion], and also, by permitting your own territory [to be ravaged] by the enemy,
have made us beggars and destitute of all the means
by which, [when we were superior to our foes in
equipment,] we conquered them in battle when we
had better generals than you ! And now our foes
erect trophies to commemorate our defeats and are
in possession of our tents, our slaves, our arms and
our money, which they have seized as plunder."

XLIII. Verginius, moved by anger and no longer
standing in awe of the generals, now inveighed
against them with greater assurance, calling them
despoilers and plagues of their country, and exhorting

[1] See the critical note.

---

8 ἀλλὰ δι' ἀνδρίαν L, ἀλλὰ δ' ἀνδρίαν corrected from ἀλλ'
ἀνδρίαν V, ἀλλὰ δι' ἀνανδρίαν Kiessling, Jacoby.
9 ἀπεδείξατε C.   10 ὡς deleted by Capps.
11 After καταδηωθεῖσαν Reiske added διαθέντες. Sintenis
proposed καταδηωθῆναι ἐάσαντες.
12 ὅσοις M : ὅσοι κ . . . (lacuna of 16 letters) LV.

τοῖς λοχαγοῖς ἅπασιν ἀραμένους τὰ σημεῖα οἴκαδε
2 ἀπάγειν τὴν στρατιάν. ὀρρωδούντων δ᾽ ἔτι τῶν
πολλῶν τὰ ἱερὰ σημεῖα κινεῖν, ἔπειτα τοὺς ἡγεμόνας καὶ τοὺς στρατηγοὺς καταλιπεῖν οὔτε ὅσιον
οὔτ᾽ ἀσφαλὲς εἶναι παντάπασι¹ νομιζόντων (ὅ τε
γὰρ ὅρκος ὁ στρατιωτικός, ὃν ἁπάντων μάλιστα
ἐμπεδοῦσι Ῥωμαῖοι, τοῖς στρατηγοῖς ἀκολουθεῖν
κελεύει τοὺς στρατευομένους ὅποι ποτ᾽ ἂν ἄγωσιν,
ὅ τε νόμος ἀποκτείνειν ἔδωκε τοῖς ἡγεμόσιν ἐξουσίαν τοὺς ἀπειθοῦντας ἢ τὰ σημεῖα καταλιπόντας
3 ἀκρίτως), ταῦτα δὴ δι᾽ εὐλαβείας αὐτοὺς ἔχοντας
ὁρῶν Οὐεργίνιος ἐδίδασκεν ὅτι λέλυκεν αὐτῶν τὸν
ὅρκον ὁ νόμος, ἐπειδὴ νόμῳ μὲν ἀποδειχθέντα
δεῖ τὸν στρατηγὸν ἄρχειν τῶν δυνάμεων, ἡ δὲ τῶν
δέκα ἀνδρῶν ἐξουσία παράνομος ἦν ὑπερβαλοῦσα
τὸν ἐνιαύσιον χρόνον εἰς ὃν ἀπεδείχθη. τὸ δὲ τοῖς
μὴ κατὰ νόμον ἄρχουσι ποιεῖν τὸ κελευόμενον οὐκ
εὐπείθειαν εἶναι καὶ εὐσέβειαν, ἀλλ᾽ ἄνοιαν καὶ
4 μανίαν. ταῦτ᾽ ἀκούσαντες ὀρθῶς λέγεσθαι ἡγούμενοι καὶ² παρακελευόμενοί τε ἀλλήλοις καί τι
καὶ θάρσος ἐκ τοῦ δαιμονίου λαβόντες αἴρον-
ται τὰ σημεῖα καὶ προῆγον ἐκ τοῦ χάρακος.
ἔμελλον δ᾽, ὅπερ εἰκὸς ἐν ποικίλοις τ᾽ ἤθεσι καὶ οὐχ
ἅπασι τὰ κράτιστα διανοουμένοις, ἔσεσθαί τινες
οἱ μένοντες ἅμα τοῖς ὀλιγάρχαις καὶ στρατιῶται
καὶ λοχαγοί, πλὴν οὐ τοσοῦτοι³ τὸ πλῆθος, ἀλλ᾽
5 ἐλάττους παρὰ πολὺ τῶν ἑτέρων. οἱ δ᾽ ἐξελθόντες
ἐκ τοῦ στρατοπέδου δι᾽ ὅλης ἡμέρας ἐπιπορευ-
θέντες ἑσπέρας καταλαβούσης παρῆσαν εἰς τὴν

¹ παντάπασι Post : πᾶσιν L, σφισι Kayser, εἶναι νομιζόντων
τοῖς πᾶσιν V.
² ἡγούμενοι καὶ om. VM.　　　　　³ τοσοῦτο L.

142

all the centurions to take up the standards and lead
the army home. But most of them were still afraid
to remove the sacred standards, and, again, did not
think it either right or safe at all to desert their
commanders and generals. For not only does the
military oath, which the Romans observe most
strictly of all oaths, bid the soldiers follow their
generals wherever they may lead, but also the law
has given the commanders authority to put to death
without a trial all who are disobedient or desert their
standards. Verginius, accordingly, perceiving that
these scruples kept them in awe, proceeded to show
them that the law had set aside their oath, since it is
necessary that the general who commands the forces
should have been legally appointed, whereas the
power of the decemvirs was illegal, inasmuch as it
had exceeded the term of a year, for which it had
been granted. And to do the bidding of those who
were commanding illegally, he declared, was not
obedience and loyalty, but folly and madness. The
soldiers, hearing these arguments, approved of them ;
and encouraging one another and inspired also by
Heaven with a certain boldness, they took up the
standards and set out from the camp. However, as
was to be expected among men of various dispositions
and not all of them entertaining the best intentions,
there were bound to be some, both soldiers and
centurions, who remained with the oligarchs, though
they were not so numerous as the others, but far
fewer. Those who departed from the camp marched
throughout the entire day, and when evening came

πόλιν οὐδενὸς ἐξαγγείλαντος αὐτῶν τὴν ἔφοδον,
καὶ συνετάραξαν τοὺς ἔνδον οὐ μετρίως πολέμιον
οἰομένους στρατὸν εἰσεληλυθέναι· κραυγή τε καὶ
δρόμος ἄτακτος ἀνὰ τὴν πόλιν ἦν. οὐ μὴν ἐπὶ
πολύν γε διέμεινεν ἡ ταραχὴ χρόνον ὥστε κακόν
τι γενέσθαι δι' αὐτήν. διεξιόντες γὰρ τοὺς στε-
νωποὺς ἐβόων ὅτι φίλοι τ' εἰσὶ καὶ ἐπ' ἀγαθῷ
τῆς πόλεως εἰσεληλύθασι, καὶ τὰ ἔργα ὅμοια παρ-
6 είχοντο τοῖς λόγοις ἀδικοῦντες οὐδένα.[1] ἀφικόμενοι δ' εἰς τὸν καλούμενον Ἀουεντῖνον[2] (ἔστι
δὲ τῶν ἐμπεριεχομένων ἐν τῇ Ῥώμῃ λόφων οὗτος ἐπιτηδειότατος ἐνστρατοπεδεύεσθαι) περί τε τὸ
τῆς Ἀρτέμιδος ἱερὸν τίθενται τὰ ὅπλα, τῇ θ'[3]
ἑξῆς ἡμέρᾳ κρατυνάμενοι τὸν χάρακα καὶ χιλιάρχους δέκα τῶν κοινῶν ἀποδείξαντες κυρίους,
ὧν ἡγεμὼν ἦν Μάρκος Ὄππιος,[4] ἔμενον ἐφ'
ἡσυχίας.

XLIV. Ἧκον δ' αὐτοῖς ἐπίκουροι μετ' οὐ πολὺ
καὶ ἀπὸ τῆς ἐν Φιδήνῃ στρατιᾶς οἱ κράτιστοι τῶν
τριῶν ταγμάτων λοχαγοὶ πολλὴν δύναμιν ἐπαγό-
μενοι, ἀλλοτρίως μὲν ἔτι πάλαι διακείμενοι πρὸς
τοὺς ἐκεῖ στρατηγούς, ἐξ οὗ Σίκκιον τὸν πρεσβευτὴν ἀπέκτειναν, ὥσπερ ἔφην, δεδιότες δ' ἄρξαι
τῆς ἀποστάσεως πρότερον,[5] ὡς οἰκείων ὄντων
τῇ δεκαδαρχίᾳ τῶν ἐν Ἀλγιδῷ πέντε ταγμάτων,
τότε δ', ἐπειδὴ τὴν ἐκείνων ἀπόστασιν ἐπέγνωσαν,
ἀγαπητῶς τὸ συμβὰν ἀπὸ τῆς τύχης δεξάμενοι.
2 ἡγεμόνες δὲ καὶ τούτων τῶν ταγμάτων ἦσαν δέκα
χιλίαρχοι καθ' ὁδὸν ἀποδειχθέντες, ὧν ἐπιφα-

---

[1] Kiessling : οὐδὲν O.　　　　[2] λουεντῖνον O.
[3] θ' Kiessling : δ' O, Jacoby.
[4] Sylburg : ἄππιος O (and similarly in following chapters).

on, arrived in Rome, no one having announced their approach. Hence they caused the inhabitants no slight dismay, since they thought that a hostile army had entered the city ; and there was shouting and disorderly running to and fro throughout the city. Nevertheless, the confusion did not last long enough to produce any mischief. For the soldiers, passing through the streets, called out that they were friends and had come for the good of the commonwealth ; and they made their words match their deeds, as they did no harm to anyone. Then, proceeding to the hill called the Aventine, which of all the hills included in Rome is the most suitable for an encampment, they put down their arms near the temple of Diana. The following day they strengthened their camp, and having appointed ten tribunes, at the head of whom was Marcus Oppius, to take care of their common interests, they remained quiet.

XLIV. There soon came to them as reinforcements from the army at Fidenae the ablest centurions of the three legions there, bringing with them a large force. These had long been disaffected toward the generals at Fidenae, ever since those men had caused the death of Siccius the legate, as I have related,[1] but were afraid of beginning the revolt earlier, because they considered the five legions at Algidum to be attached to the decemvirate ; but at the time in question, as soon as they heard of the revolt of the others, they were glad to embrace the opportunity presented to them by Fortune. These legions also were commanded by ten tribunes, who had been appointed during their march, the most prominent of

[1] See chaps. 25–27.

⁵ πρότερον O : πρότεροι Sylburg, Jacoby.

νέστατος Σέξτος Μάλιος ἦν. ἐπεὶ δὲ συνέμιξαν
ἀλλήλοις, θέμενοι τὰ ὅπλα τοῖς εἴκοσι χιλιάρχοις
ἐπέτρεψαν ἅπαντα ὑπὲρ τοῦ κοινοῦ λέγειν τε καὶ
πράττειν. ἐκ δὲ τῶν εἴκοσι τοὺς ἐπιφανεστάτους
ἀπέδειξαν δύο προβούλους, Μάρκον Ὄππιον καὶ
Σέξτον Μάλιον· οὗτοι βουλευτήριον ἐξ ἁπάντων
καταστησάμενοι τῶν λοχαγῶν, μετ' ἐκείνων ἅπαντα
3 διετέλουν πραγματευόμενοι. ἀδήλου δ' ἔτι τοῖς
πολλοῖς τῆς διανοίας αὐτῶν οὔσης Ἄππιος μέν, οἷα
δὴ συγγινώσκων ἑαυτῷ τῆς παρούσης ταραχῆς
αἰτίῳ γεγονότι καὶ τῶν προσδοκωμένων δι' αὐτὴν
ἔσεσθαι κακῶν, οὐκέτι τῶν κοινῶν οὐδὲν ἠξίου
πράττειν, ἀλλὰ κατ' οἶκον ἔμενεν· ὁ δὲ σὺν αὐτῷ
τεταγμένος ἐπὶ τῆς πόλεως Σπόριος Ὄππιος,
διαταραχθεὶς κατ' ἀρχὰς καὶ αὐτός, ὡς αὐτίκα
μάλα τῶν ἐχθρῶν σφίσιν ἐπιθησομένων καὶ ἐπὶ
τούτῳ ἡκόντων, ἐπειδὴ κατέμαθεν οὐδὲν νεωτερί-
σαντας αὐτούς, ὑφέμενος τοῦ δέους ἐκάλει τὴν
βουλὴν εἰς τὸ συνέδριον ἐκ τῶν οἰκιῶν κατ' ἄνδρα
4 μεταπεμπόμενος. ἔτι δ' αὐτῶν συλλεγομένων
ἧκον οἱ[1] ἐκ τῆς ἐν Φιδήνῃ στρατιᾶς ἡγεμόνες
ἀγανακτοῦντες ἐπὶ τῷ καταλελεῖφθαι τοὺς χάρακας
ὑπὸ τῶν στρατιωτῶν ἀμφοτέρους, καὶ τὴν βουλὴν
πείθοντες ἀξίαν τοῦ πράγματος ὀργὴν κατ' αὐτῶν
λαβεῖν. ἐπεὶ δ' ἀγορεύειν γνώμην ἕκαστον ἔδει,
Λεύκιος μὲν Κορνήλιος ἔφη δεῖν ἀπιέναι[2] τοὺς
ταχθέντας εἰς[3] τὸν Ἀουεντῖνον αὐθημερὸν ἐπὶ τοὺς

---

[1] οἱ added by Sylburg.
[2] Sylburg : ἀπεῖναι O, Jacoby.
[3] εἰς added by Jacoby, ἐπὶ by Steph. : τοὺς κατέχοντας
τὸν Ἀ. Kiessling, τοὺς συναχθέντας εἰς τὸν Ἀ. Post.

whom was Sextus Malius.[1] After joining the others,
they put down their arms and left it to the twenty
tribunes to speak and act in all matters as repre-
sentatives of the whole group. Out of these twenty
they appointed two persons, Marcus Oppius and
Sextus Malius, who were the most prominent, to
determine policies. These established a council consisting of all the centurions and handled all matters
in conjunction with them. While their intentions
were not as yet generally known, Appius, inasmuch
as he was conscious of having been the cause of the
present disturbance and of the evils that were expected to result from it, no longer thought fit to
transact any of the public business, but stayed at
home. Spurius Oppius, however, who had been
placed in command of the city together with him,
although he too had been alarmed at first, believing
that their enemies would immediately attack them
and had indeed come for this purpose, nevertheless,
when he found that they had attempted nothing
revolutionary, relaxed from his fear and summoned
the senators from their homes to the senate-house,
sending for each one individually. While these were
still assembling, the commanders of the army at
Fidenae arrived, full of indignation that both the
camps had been abandoned by the soldiers, and they
endeavoured to persuade the senate to resent this
action as it deserved. When the senators were to
deliver their opinions one after another, Lucius
Cornelius declared that the soldiers who were posted [2]
on the Aventine must return that very day to their

[1] The name should probably be Manilius, as given by
Livy (iii. 51, 10).
[2] Or, following Kiessling's reading, " who were occupying
the Aventine."

ἑαυτῶν χάρακας καὶ τὰ κελευόμενα ὑπὸ τῶν στρατηγῶν ἐπιτελεῖν, μηδενὸς ὄντας τῶν γεγονότων
ὑποδίκους πλὴν τῶν αἰτίων τῆς ἀποστάσεως
μόνων· τούτοις δὲ προσθεῖναι δίκας τοὺς στρα-
5 τηγούς. ἐὰν δὲ μὴ ποιῶσι ταῦτα, βουλεύειν περὶ
αὐτῶν τὸ συνέδριον ὡς ἐκλελοιπότων τὴν τάξιν
ἐφ' ἣν ἐτάχθησαν ὑπὸ τῶν ἡγεμόνων καὶ περὶ τὸν
στρατιωτικὸν ἠσεβηκότων ὅρκον. Λεύκιος δὲ
Οὐαλέριος[1] . . . .

. . . .

6   Ἀλλ' ὑπὲρ τῶν Ῥωμαϊκῶν νόμων οὓς ἐν ταῖς
δώδεκα δέλτοις ἀναγεγραμμένους εὕρομεν οὔτε
μηδένα ποιήσασθαι λόγον ἥρμοττεν,[2] οὕτω σεμνῶν
ὄντων καὶ τοσαύτην ἐχόντων διαφορὰν παρὰ τὰς
Ἑλληνικὰς νομοθεσίας, οὔτε περαιτέρω τοῦ δέοντος
προβαίνειν ἐκμηκύναντας τὴν περὶ αὐτῶν ἱστορίαν.
XLV. Οἱ δὲ μετὰ τὴν κατάλυσιν τῆς δεκαδαρχίας[3] τὴν ὕπατον ἀρχὴν πρῶτοι παρὰ τοῦ δήμου
λαβόντες ἐπὶ τῆς λοχίτιδος ἐκκλησίας, ὥσπερ
ἔφην, Λεύκιος Οὐαλέριος Ποτῖτος καὶ Μάρκος
Ὁράτιος Βαρβᾶτος, αὐτοί τε δημοτικοὶ τὰς φύσεις
ὄντες καὶ παρὰ τῶν προγόνων ταύτην διαδεδεγ-
μένοι τὴν πολιτείαν, τὰς ὑποσχέσεις φυλάττοντες
ἃς ἐποιήσαντο πρὸς τοὺς δημοτικοὺς ὅτ' ἀποθέσθαι τὰ ὅπλα συνέπειθον αὐτούς, ὡς πάντα τὰ
συμφέροντα τῷ δήμῳ πολιτευσόμενοι, νόμους
ἐκύρωσαν ἐν ἐκκλησίαις λοχίτισι, δυσχεραινόντων
μὲν τῶν πατρικίων, αἰδουμένων δ' ἀντιλέγειν,

---

[1] After Οὐαλέριος all the MSS. indicate an extensive
lacuna, L (the best) adding the notation λείπει φύλλα β'.
They all give the two remaining sections of the Book—(a)
chaps. 44, 6-51, and (b) chaps. 52-63—in the reverse order.
The correct order was restored by Lapus and Sylburg.

camps and carry out the orders of their generals, though they should not be subject to trial for anything that had happened, save only the authors of the revolt, who should be punished by the generals. If, however, they did not do as commanded, the senate should deliberate concerning them as concerning men who had abandoned the post to which they had been assigned by their generals and had violated their military oath. Lucius Valerius[1] .   .

.   .   .   .

But it behooved me neither to make no mention of the Roman laws which I found written on the Twelve Tables, since they are so venerable and so far superior to the codes of the Greeks, nor to go on and extend my account of them farther than was necessary.

XLV. After the overthrow of the decemvirate[2] the first persons to receive the consular office from the people in a centuriate assembly were, as I have stated, Lucius Valerius Potitus and Marcus Horatius Barbatus, who were not only of their own nature favourable to the populace, but had also inherited that political creed from their ancestors. In fulfilment of the promises they had made to the plebeians, when they persuaded them to lay down their arms, that in their administration they would consult all the interests of the people, they secured the ratification in centuriate assemblies of various laws, most of which I need not mention, laws with which the patricians were displeased though they were ashamed

[1] For the gap in the MSS. at this point see the critical note. Lost is the account of the second withdrawal of the plebs to the Sacred Mount and of the resignation of the decemvirs, described in Livy iii. 52–54.

[2] For chap. 45 cf. Livy iii. 55.

<hr>

[2] ἥρμοττον LV.   [3] Ambrosch : δεκαρχίας O.

ἄλλους τέ τινας, οὓς ·οὐ δέομαι γράφειν,[1] καὶ τὸν
κελεύοντα τοὺς ὑπὸ τοῦ δήμου τεθέντας ἐν ταῖς
φυλετικαῖς ἐκκλησίαις νόμους ἅπασι κεῖσθαι Ῥωμαίοις ἐξ ἴσου, τὴν αὐτὴν ἔχοντας δύναμιν τοῖς
ἐν ταῖς λοχίτισιν ἐκκλησίαις τεθησομένοις. τιμω-
ρίαι δὲ προσέκειντο[2] τοῖς καταλύουσιν ἢ παραβαί-
νουσι τὸν νόμον, ἐὰν ἁλῶσι, θάνατος καὶ δήμευσις
2 τῆς οὐσίας. οὗτος ὁ νόμος ἐξέβαλε τὰς ἀμφισβητήσεις τῶν πατρικίων ἃς ἐποιοῦντο πρὸς τοὺς
δημοτικοὺς πρότερον, οὐκ ἀξιοῦντες τοῖς ὑπ'
ἐκείνων τεθεῖσι νόμοις πειθαρχεῖν οὐδ' ὅλως τὰ
ἐν ταῖς φυλετικαῖς ἐκκλησίαις ἐπικυρούμενα κοινὰ
τῆς πόλεως ἁπάσης δόγματα νομίζοντες, ἀλλ'
αὐτοῖς[3] μόνοις ἐκείνοις ἴδια[4]· ὅ τι δ' ἂν ἡ λοχῖτις
ἐκκλησία γνῷ, τοῦθ' ἡγούμενοι σφίσι τ' αὐτοῖς
3 καὶ τοῖς ἄλλοις πολίταις τετάχθαι. εἴρηται δὲ καὶ
πρότερον ὅτι ἐν μὲν ταῖς φυλετικαῖς ἐκκλησίαις
οἱ δημοτικοὶ καὶ πένητες ἐκράτουν τῶν πατρικίων,
ἐν δὲ ταῖς λοχίτισιν ἐκκλησίαις οἱ πατρίκιοι παρὰ
πολὺ τῶν ἄλλων ἐλάττους ὄντες περιῆσαν τῶν
δημοτικῶν.

XLVI. Τούτου κυρωθέντος ὑπὸ τῶν ὑπάτων
τοῦ νόμου σὺν ἄλλοις τισὶν ὥσπερ ἔφην δημοτικοῖς
εὐθὺς οἱ δήμαρχοι καιρὸν ἐπιτήδειον ἥκειν νομίζοντες ἐν ᾧ τιμωρήσονται τοὺς περὶ τὸν Ἄππιον,
εἰσαγγελίας ᾤοντο δεῖν ποιήσασθαι κατ' αὐτῶν,
οὐχ ἅμα πάντας ὑπάγοντες ὑπὸ[5] τὴν δίκην, ἵνα
μηδὲν ἀλλήλους ὠφελῶσιν, ἀλλὰ καθ' ἕνα· ῥᾷον
γὰρ οὕτως ὑπελάμβανον εὐμεταχειρίστους ἔσεσθαι.

---

[1] γράφειν LbR : λέγειν La.   [2] προέκειντο Sylburg.
[3] Reiske : αὐτὸν O, αὐτὸ Steph., Jacoby.
[4] Kiessling: ἴδιον O, Jacoby.   [5] Reiske : ἐπὶ O.

to oppose them, and particularly the one which
ordained that the laws passed by the populace in its
tribal assemblies[1] should apply to all the Romans alike,
having the same force as those which should be passed
in the centuriate assemblies. The penalties provided
for such as should abrogate or transgress this law, in
case they were convicted, were death and the confiscation of their estates. This law put an end to the
controversies previously carried on by the patricians
against the plebeians when they refused to obey the
laws enacted by the latter and would not at all regard
the measures passed in the tribal assemblies as joint
decrees of the whole state, but as merely private
matters for the plebeians only ; whereas they considered that any resolution the centuriate assembly
passed applied not only to themselves but to the rest
of the citizens as well. It has been mentioned earlier[1]
that in the tribal assemblies the plebeians and the
poor prevailed over the patricians, whereas in the
centuriate assemblies the patricians, though far less
numerous, had the upper hand over the plebeians.

XLVI. When this law,[2] together with some others
of a popular nature, as I have related, had been
ratified by the consuls, the tribunes immediately,
believing a fitting occasion had arrived for punishing
Appius and his colleagues, thought they ought to
bring charges against them, but not to put them all
on trial at the same time, in order to prevent their
helping one another in any way, but one by one ;
for they concluded that in this way they would be

---

[1] See vii. 59 ; viii. 82, 6   [2] Cf. Livy iii. 56–59.

2 σκοπούμενοι δ' ἀπὸ τίνος ἂν ἄρξαιντο ἐπιτηδειο-
τάτου, τὸν Ἄππιον πρῶτον ἔγνωσαν εὐθύνειν τῶν
τ' ἄλλων ἀδικημάτων ἕνεκα μισούμενον ὑπὸ τοῦ
δήμου καὶ τῶν νεωστὶ περὶ τὴν παρθένον γενομένων παρανομιῶν. ἑλόντες μὲν γὰρ τοῦτον
εὐπετῶς ἐδόκουν καὶ τῶν ἄλλων κρατήσειν, εἰ
δ' ἀπὸ τῶν ταπεινοτέρων ἄρξαιντο, μαλακωτέρας
ὑπελάμβανον τὰς ὀργὰς τῶν πολιτῶν πρὸς τοὺς
ἐπιφανεστάτους τελευταίους[1] κρινομένους ἔσεσθαι,
συντονωτέρας οὔσας ἐπὶ τοῖς προτέροις ἀγῶσιν,
3 ὃ πολλάκις ἤδη συνέβη. ταῦτα βουλευσάμενοι
συνέσχον τοὺς ἄνδρας, Ἀππίου δὲ Οὐεργίνιον
ἔταξαν ἄνευ κλήρου κατηγορεῖν. εἰσαγγέλλεται
δὴ μετὰ τοῦτο εἰς τὸν δῆμον Ἄππιος ὑπὸ τοῦ
Οὐεργινίου κατηγορηθεὶς ἐπὶ τῆς ἐκκλησίας καὶ
αἰτεῖται χρόνον εἰς ἀπολογίαν. ἀπαχθεὶς δ' εἰς
τὸ δεσμωτήριον, ἵνα φυλάττηται μέχρι δίκης (οὐ
γὰρ ἐδόθη διεγγύησις[2] αὐτῷ) πρὶν ἐπιστῆναι τὴν
ἀποδειχθεῖσαν[3] ἡμέραν τῆς κρίσεως ἐν τοῖς δεσμοῖς
ἀποθνήσκει, ὡς μὲν ἡ τῶν πολλῶν ὑπόληψις ἦν,
ἐξ ἐπιταγῆς τῶν δημάρχων, ὡς δ' οἱ τὴν αἰτίαν
ἀπολύσασθαι βουλόμενοι διεφήμιζον, αὐτὸς ἑαυτὸν
4 ἀναρτησάμενος βρόχῳ. μετ' ἐκεῖνον Σπόριος
Ὄππιος εἰσαχθεὶς εἰς τὸν δῆμον ὑφ' ἑτέρου τῶν
δημάρχων Ποπλίου Νομιτωρίου καὶ τυχὼν ἀπολογίας ἁπάσαις ἁλίσκεται ταῖς ψήφοις καὶ παρα-
δοθεὶς εἰς τὸ δεσμωτήριον αὐθημερὸν ἀποθνήσκει.
οἱ δὲ λοιποὶ τῶν δέκα πρὶν εἰσαγγελθῆναι φυγαῖς
αὐτοὺς ἐζημίωσαν. τὰς δ' οὐσίας τῶν ἀνῃρημέ-

---

[1] τελευταίους Reiske : καὶ τελευταίους O, Jacoby.

152

easier to manage. And considering which one of them would be the most suitable to begin with, they determined to call Appius to account first, since he was hated by the people, not only because of his other crimes, but particularly because of his recent lawless acts with regard to the maiden. For they judged that if they convicted him they would easily get the better of the others, whereas, if they should begin with those of humbler station, they imagined that the resentment of the citizens, which is always more violent in the earlier trials, would be milder toward the most eminent men if they were tried last—as had often happened before. Having resolved upon this course, they took the decemvirs into custody and appointed Verginius to be the accuser of Appius without drawing lots. Thereupon Appius was cited before the tribunal of the people to answer an accusation brought against him in their assembly by Verginius ; and he asked for time to prepare his defence. He was haled to prison to be guarded until his trial, as bail was not allowed him ; but before the day appointed for the trial came, he met his death in prison,—according to the suspicion of most people, by order of the tribunes, but according to the report of those who wished to clear them of this charge, by hanging himself. After him, Spurius Oppius was brought before the tribunal of the people by another of the tribunes, Publius Numitorius, and being allowed to make his defence, was unanimously condemned, committed to prison, and put to death the same day. The rest of the decemvirs punished themselves by voluntary exile before they were indicted. The estates both of those

---

² Götzeler : ἐγγύησις O.
³ Reiske : ἐπιδειχθεῖσαν O.

νων καὶ τῶν πεφευγότων[1] οἱ ταμίαι τῆς πόλεως
5 ἀνέλαβον εἰς τὸ δημόσιον. εἰσαγγέλλεται δὲ καὶ
Μάρκος Κλαύδιος ὁ τὴν παρθένον ἐπιβαλόμενος[2]
ὡς δούλην ἀπάγειν ὑπὸ τοῦ μνηστῆρος αὐτῆς
Ἰκιλίου· καὶ τὴν αἰτίαν εἰς τὸν ἐπιτάξαντα παρανομεῖν Ἄππιον ἀναφέρων θανάτου μὲν ἀπολύεται,
φυγῇ δ᾽ ἀιδίῳ ζημιοῦται· τῶν δ᾽ ἄλλων τῶν
ὑπηρετησάντων τι παράνομον τοῖς ὀλιγάρχαις
οὐδεὶς ἔσχεν ἀγῶνα δημόσιον, ἀλλὰ πᾶσιν ἄδεια
ἐδόθη. ὁ δὲ τοῦτο τὸ πολίτευμα εἰσηγησάμενος
ἦν Μάρκος Δοέλλιος ὁ δήμαρχος ἀχθομένων ἤδη
τῶν πολιτῶν καὶ πολεμίων γενέσθαι προσδοκώντων.[3]

XLVII. Ἐπεὶ δ᾽ αἱ κατὰ πόλιν[4] ἐπαύσαντο τα-
ραχαί, συναγαγόντες τὴν βουλὴν[5] οἱ ὕπατοι[6] δόγμα
κυροῦσιν ἐξάγειν τὸν στρατὸν ἐπὶ τοὺς πολεμίους
διὰ ταχέων. ἐπικυρώσαντος δὲ τοῦ δήμου τὰ
ψηφισθέντα ὑπὸ τῆς βουλῆς Οὐαλέριος μὲν ἅτερος
τῶν ὑπάτων τὴν ἡμίσειαν ἔχων τοῦ στρατοῦ
μοῖραν ἐξῆγεν ἐπί τ᾽ Αἰκανοὺς καὶ Οὐολούσκους·
2 συνῆλθε γὰρ ἀμφότερα τὰ ἔθνη. ἐπιστάμενος δὲ
τοὺς Αἰκανοὺς ἐκ τῶν προτέρων κατορθωμάτων
αὔχημα προσειληφότας καὶ εἰς πολλὴν καταφρόνησιν τῆς Ῥωμαίων δυνάμεως προελθόντας,[7] ἔτι

---

[1] πεφευγότων (cf. v. 13, 4) M : πο . . . (lacuna of 8
letters) L, πολιτικῶν V, ἀποφυγόντων Kiessling.

[2] ἐπιλαβόμενος MV.

[3] καὶ πολεμίων γενέσθαι προσδοκώντων O : καὶ τῶν πολεμίων
. . . γ. π. Kiessling, καὶ τῶν πολεμίων γ. π. Jacoby, καὶ τῶν
πολεμίων ἔφοδον γενήσεσθαι π. Hertlein, καὶ τῶν πολεμίων
γενέσθαι προσβαλὰς π. Capps, κἂν πολεμίων γενέσθαι λόγῳ π.
Grasberger.   [4] πόλιν R : πόλεις LV.

[5] τὴν βουλὴν om. L in lacuna.

[6] οἱ ὕπατοι added by Reiske.

who had been put to death and of those who had made their escape [1] were confiscated by the quaestors. Marcus Claudius, who had attempted to take away the maiden as his slave, was also accused by Icilius, her betrothed ; however, by putting the blame on Appius, who had ordered him to commit the crime, he escaped death, but was condemned to perpetual banishment. Of the others who had been the instruments of the decemvirs in any crime, none had a public trial, but impunity was granted to them all. This course was proposed by Marcus Duilius, the tribune, when the citizens were already showing irritation and were expecting that . . . would be . . . enemies. [2]

XLVII. After the domestic disturbances ceased, [3] the consuls assembled the senate and procured the passing of a decree that they should lead out the army in all haste against the enemy. And the people having ratified the decree of the senate, Valerius, one of the consuls, marched with one half of the army against the Aequians and the Volscians ; for these two nations had joined forces. Understanding that the Aequians had gained assurance from their former successes and had come to entertain a great contempt for the Roman forces, he wished to increase their

[1] Or, " who had fled," " who had gone into exile." The verb is uncertain.
[2] The text at the end of this sentence is very uncertain. The MSS. have " expecting to become enemies," an idea expressed more clearly by Grasberger's " expecting to be regarded in the light of enemies." More suitable to the context would seem to be the readings proposed by Hertlein and Capps, " expecting there would be an attack (assaults) from their enemies."
[3] For chaps. 47–50 cf. Livy iii. 60–63.

[7] Sylburg : παρόντας O, ἐπαρθέντας Reiske.

μᾶλλον ἐβούλετο ἐπᾶραι καὶ θρασυτέρους ποιῆσαι
δόξαν οὐκ ἀληθῆ παρασχών, ὡς ὀρρωδῶν εἰς
χεῖρας ἰέναι πρὸς αὐτούς, καὶ πάντα δεδιότως[1]
3 ἐποίει. χωρίον τε γὰρ εἰς στρατοπεδείαν ὑψηλὸν
καὶ δυσπρόσιτον ἐξελέξατο τάφρον τε βαθεῖαν
περιεβάλετο καὶ χάρακας ἤγειρεν ὑψηλούς. προκαλουμένων δὲ τῶν πολεμίων αὐτὸν εἰς μάχην
πολλάκις καὶ κακιζόντων τὴν ἀνανδρίαν ἠνείχετο
μένων ἐφ' ἡσυχίας. ἐπεὶ δ' ἔγνω τὴν κρατίστην
τῶν πολεμίων δύναμιν ἐπὶ προνομὴν τῆς Ἑρνίκων
τε καὶ Λατίνων γῆς ἐξεληλυθυῖαν, ἐν δὲ τῷ χάρακι
φυλακὴν οὔτε πολλὴν καταλειπομένην οὔτ' ἀγαθήν,
τοῦτον εἶναι νομίσας τὸν καιρὸν ἐπιτήδειον ἐξῆγε
κεκοσμημένην τὴν στρατιὰν καὶ παρέστησεν ὡς
4 εἰς μάχην. οὐδενός τ' ἀντεπιόντος ἐκείνην μὲν
τὴν ἡμέραν ἐπεῖχε, τῇ δ' ἑξῆς ἐπὶ τὴν ἀποσκευὴν[2]
αὐτῶν ἦγεν οὐ σφόδρα ὀχυρὰν οὖσαν. μαθόντες
δὲ πολιορκούμενον τὸν χάρακα οἱ προεξεληλυθότες
ἐπὶ τὰς προνομὰς ταχέως ἧκον,[3] πλὴν οὐχ ἅμα
καὶ ἐν κόσμῳ, σποράδες δὲ καὶ κατ' ὀλίγους ὡς
ἕκαστοι εἶχον ἐπιφαινόμενοι· οἵ τ' ἐκ τοῦ χάρακος
ἐπεὶ τοὺς σφετέρους προσιόντας ἐθεάσαντο, θρα-
5 σύτεροι γεγονότες ἐξῆλθον ἀθρόοι. καὶ γίνεται
μέγας ἀγὼν καὶ φόνος ἐξ ἀμφοτέρων πολύς, ἐν
ᾧ νικήσαντες οἱ Ῥωμαῖοι τούς τε συστάδην μαχομένους ἐτρέψαντο καὶ τοὺς φεύγοντας ἐπιδιώκοντες,
οὓς μὲν ἀπέκτειναν, οὓς δ' αἰχμαλώτους ἔλαβον,
τοῦ δὲ χάρακος αὐτῶν κρατήσαντες χρήματα

---

[1] Reiske : δεδιότος O, ὡς δεδιότος Capps; πάντα τὰ δεδιότος
Hertlein.
[2] ἀποσκευὴν O : παρεμβολὴν Hertlein.

156

confidence and boldness by creating the false impression that he dreaded coming to close quarters with them, and in every move he simulated timidity. For instance, he chose for his camp a lofty position difficult of access, surrounded it with a deep ditch, and erected high ramparts. And when the enemy repeatedly challenged him to battle and taunted him with cowardice, he bore it with patience and remained quiet. But upon learning that their best forces had set out to plunder the territory of the Hernicans and the Latins and that there was left in the camp a garrison that was neither large nor able, he thought this was the fitting moment, and leading out his army in regular formation, he drew it up as for battle. Then, when no one came out to meet him, he held it in check that day, but on the next day led it against their camp,[1] which was not very strong. When the enemy's detachments which had earlier gone out after forage heard that their camp was besieged, they speedily returned, though they did not put in an appearance all together and in good order, but scattered and in small parties, everyone coming up as he could ; and those in the camp, as soon as they saw their own men approaching, took courage and sallied out in a body. Upon this, a great battle ensued, with much slaughter on both sides, a battle in which the Romans, gaining the victory, put to flight those who fought in closed ranks, and pursuing those who fled, killed some and made others prisoners ; and taking possession of their camp, they seized much

[1] " Camp " seems the meaning required here, but the MSS. give " baggage."

---

[3] ταχέως ἦκον Reiske : τοῦ ἄστεος ἦκον VM, om. L in lacuna.

πολλὰ καὶ λείαν ἄφθονον περιεβάλοντο.[1] Οὐαλέριος μὲν δὴ ταῦτα διαπραξάμενος ἀδεῶς ἤδη
τὴν γῆν τῶν πολεμίων ἐπιὼν ἐδῄου.

XLVIII. Μάρκος δ' Ὁράτιος ἐπὶ τὸν κατὰ Σαβίνων πόλεμον . . .,[2] ἐπειδὴ τὰ κατὰ τὸν συνάρ-
χοντα ἔγνω, προαγαγὼν καὶ αὐτὸς ἐκ τοῦ χάρακος
τὰς δυνάμεις ἀντεπῆγε θᾶττον [ὅλῃ δυνάμει][3] πρὸς
οὐκ ἐλάττους ἀριθμὸν τοὺς Σαβίνους καὶ τὰ πολέμια [ἐμπειροτάτους· ἐνεδείξαντο γὰρ][4] φρόνημά τε
καὶ τόλμαν ἐκ τῶν προτέρων κατορθωμάτων
πολλὴν [πρὸς τοὺς ἀντιμαχομένους,[5] καὶ κοινῶς
πάντες καὶ ἰδίως ὁ τούτων προηγούμενος·][6] ἦν
γὰρ οὐ μόνον στρατηγὸς ἀγαθός, ἀλλὰ καὶ πο-
2 λεμιστὴς κατὰ χεῖρα γενναῖος· καὶ τῶν ἱππέων
μεγάλην προθυμίαν παρασχομένων νίκην ἀναιρεῖται
λαμπροτάτην, πολλοὺς μὲν ἀποκτείνας τῶν πολεμίων, πολλῷ δ' ἔτι πλειόνων αἰχμαλώτων τετυχηκώς,[7] τοῦ τε χάρακος αὐτῶν[8] ἐρήμου κρατήσας,
ἐν ᾧ τήν τ' ἀποσκευὴν τῶν πολεμίων πολλὴν εὗρε
καὶ τὴν λείαν ἅπασαν ἣν ἐκ τῆς Ῥωμαίων γῆς
ἐληίσαντο, αἰχμαλώτους τε πάνυ πολλοὺς τῶν
σφετέρων ἀνεσώσατο.[9] οὐ γὰρ ἔφθασαν ἀνασκευασάμενοι τὰς ὠφελείας οἱ Σαβῖνοι διὰ καταφρόνησιν.
3 τὰ μὲν οὖν τῶν πολεμίων χρήματα τοῖς στρατιώταις ὠφέλειαν ἐφῆκε ποιεῖσθαι προεξελόμενος ἐκ

---

[1] τοῦ δὲ χάρακος . . . περιεβάλοντο L : om. R.
[2] A participle has apparently been lost after πόλεμον.
Kiessling placed προαγαγὼν here instead of in the following
line.   [3] ὅλῃ δυνάμει om. L in lacuna.
[4] ἐμπειροτάτους· ἐνεδείξαντο γὰρ om. L : add. R.
[5] ἀντιμαχομένους V : ἀντεχομένους LbM.
[6] πρὸς τοὺς . . . προηγούμενος om. La : added by Lb (πρὸς
τοὺς . . . κοινῶς in lacuna, πάντες . . . προηγούμενος in margin).

money and vast booty. After accomplishing this, Valerius now freely overran the enemy's country and laid it waste.

XLVIII. Marcus Horatius, who had been sent out [1] to prosecute the war against the Sabines, when he learned of the exploits of his colleague, likewise marched out of camp and promptly led [all] his forces against the Sabines, who were not inferior in numbers and were [thoroughly acquainted] with the art of war. [For they displayed] spirit and great boldness [against their opponents] in consequence of their former successes, [not only all of them in common, but particularly their commander ;] [2] for he was both a good general and also a gallant fighter at close quarters. And since the cavalry displayed great zeal, he won a most brilliant victory, killing many of the enemy and [taking] far more of them prisoners, and also gaining possession of their abandoned camp, in which he found not only the baggage of the enemy in great quantity but also all the booty they had taken from the Romans' territory, and rescued a great many of his own people who had been taken prisoner. For the Sabines, in their contempt of the Romans, had not packed up and sent away their booty before the battle. The effects belonging to the enemy he allowed the soldiers to take as spoils after he had first selected such a portion of them as he intended

[1] See the critical note.
[2] The words enclosed in brackets are found only in the inferior MSS. and, in part, as later entries in L ; there is an error somewhere, since the words " he was a good general " obviously refer to the Roman commander.

---

[7] τετυχηκώς om. L in lacuna.   [8] αὐτῶν LV : αὐτοῦ M.
[9] ἀνεσώσατο L : εὗρε καὶ ἀνεσώσατο VM.

τῶν λαφύρων ὅσα τοῖς θεοῖς καθιερώσειν ἔμελλε·
τὴν δὲ λείαν τοῖς ἀφαιρεθεῖσιν ἀπέδωκε.

XLIX. Ταῦτα διαπραξάμενος ἀπῆγεν εἰς Ῥώμην
τὰς δυνάμεις, καὶ κατὰ τὸν αὐτὸν χρόνον Οὐαλέριος
ἧκεν· ἦν τ᾿ ἀμφοτέροις μέγα φρονοῦσιν ἐπὶ ταῖς
2 νίκαις[1] ἐλπὶς ἐπιφανεῖς κατάξειν θριάμβους. οὐ
μὴν ἐχώρησέ γε αὐτοῖς κατ᾿ ἐλπίδα τὸ ἔργον.
συναχθεῖσα γὰρ κατ᾿ αὐτῶν ἡ βουλὴ κατεστρατο-
πεδευκότων ἔξω τῆς πόλεως εἰς[2] τὸ καλούμενον
Ἄρειον πεδίον, καὶ τὰ πραχθέντα ὑπ᾿ ἀμφοτέρων
μαθοῦσα τὴν ἐπινίκιον οὐκ ἐπέτρεψε ποιήσασθαι
θυσίαν, πολλῶν μὲν καὶ ἄλλων ἐναντιωθέντων αὐ-
3 τοῖς ἐκ τοῦ φανεροῦ, μάλιστα δὲ Κλαυδίου Γαΐου
(θεῖος δ᾿ ἦν οὗτος, ὥσπερ ἔφην, Ἀππίῳ τῷ κατα-
στησαμένῳ τὴν ὀλιγαρχίαν καὶ νεωστὶ ὑπὸ τῶν
δημάρχων ἀναιρεθέντι) τούς τε κυρωθέντας ὑπ᾿
αὐτῶν νόμους προβαλλομένου, δι᾿ ὧν ἠλάττωσαν
τὸ τῆς βουλῆς κράτος, καὶ τἆλλα πολιτεύματα
ὅσα οὗτοι πολιτευόμενοι[3] διετέλεσαν· τελευταίαν
δὲ τὴν τῶν δέκα ἀνδρῶν, οὓς προὔδωκαν τοῖς
δημάρχοις, τῶν μὲν ἀπώλειαν, τῶν δὲ δήμευσιν,
ὡς παρὰ τοὺς ὅρκους καὶ τὰς συνθήκας, διεξιόν-
4 τος (τὰ γὰρ ἐπὶ τῶν ἱερῶν συνομολογηθέντα τοῖς
πατρικίοις πρὸς τοὺς δημοτικοὺς ἐπ᾿ ἀδείᾳ τε
πάντων γενέσθαι καὶ ἀμνηστίᾳ τῶν προτέρων)·
τόν τ᾿ Ἀππίου θάνατον οὐκ αὐτοχειρίᾳ γενέσθαι
λέγοντος, ἀλλ᾿ ἐπιβούλως ὑπὸ τῶν δημάρχων πρὸ
δίκης, ἵνα μήτε λόγου τύχῃ κρινόμενος μήτ᾿ ἐλέου,[4]

---

[1] After νίκαις L has a lacuna, VM add καὶ. Grasberger
proposed either to omit καὶ or to substitute καλὴ.
[2] εἰς added by Kiessling.

to consecrate to the gods ; but the booty he restored
to the owners.

XLIX. After accomplishing these things he led
his forces back to Rome, and Valerius arrived at
about the same time. Both of them, being greatly
elated by their victories, expected to celebrate
brilliant triumphs ; however, the matter did not turn
out according to their expectation. For the senate,
having been convened in their case while they lay
encamped outside the city in the Field of Mars, as it
was called, and being informed of the exploits of both,
would not permit them to perform the triumphal
sacrifice, since many of the senators opposed their
demand openly, and particularly Gaius Claudius,
uncle, as I have stated,[1] to Appius who had established
the oligarchy and had been put to death recently by
the tribunes. Claudius reproached them for the laws
they had got enacted by which they had weakened
the power of the senate and for the other policies they
had constantly pursued ; and, last of all, he told of
the killing of some of the decemvirs, whom they had
betrayed to the tribunes, and the confiscation of the
estates of the others, in violation, as he claimed, of
their oaths and covenants ; for he maintained that
the compact entered into by the patricians with the
plebeians had been made on the basis of a general
amnesty and impunity for what was past. He added
that Appius had not perished by his own hand, but
by the treachery of the tribunes before his trial, in
order that he might not by standing trial either

[1] In chap. 7, 1.

---

3 ὅσα οὗτοι πολιτευόμενοι VM : ὅσα του . . . πολιτευόμενοι
L, ὅσα περὶ τοῦ δήμου πολιτευόμενοι Kiessling.
4 Grasberger : ἐλέους O.

DIONYSIUS OF HALICARNASSUS

κατὰ τὸ εἰκός,[1] εἰ κατέστη γοῦν εἰς κρίσιν ἀνὴρ[2]
γένους ἀξίωμα παρεχόμενος καὶ πολλὰ τὸ κοινὸν
εὖ πεποιηκὼς[3] ὅρκους τε καὶ πίστεις ἐπιβοώ-
μενος, αἷς ἄνθρωποι[4] πιστεύοντες εἰς διαλλαγὰς
συνέρχονται,[5] τέκνα τε καὶ συγγένειαν καὶ αὐτὸ
τὸ ταπεινὸν σχῆμα καὶ ἄλλα πολλὰ [φέρων[6]] εἰς
5 οἶκτον ἐφελκόμενα τὸ πλῆθος. ταῦτα δὴ[7] πάντα
κατηγορήματα τῶν ὑπάτων [κατ' αὐτῶν ἐκχέαντος Κλαυδίου Γαΐου, καὶ αὐ]τῶν παρόντων,[8] ἔδοξεν
ἀγαπᾶν[9] αὐτοὺς εἰ μὴ δώσουσι δίκας· θριάμβων
δὲ καταγωγῆς ἤ τινων τοιούτων συγχωρήσεων[10]
οὐδὲ κατὰ μικρὸν ἀξίους εἶναι τυγχάνειν.

L. Ἀποψηφισαμένης δὲ τῆς βουλῆς τὸν θρίαμβον
ἀγανακτοῦντες οἱ περὶ τὸν Οὐαλέριον καὶ δεινὴν
ὕβριν ὑπολαμβάνοντες ὑβρίζεσθαι συνεκάλεσαν εἰς
ἐκκλησίαν τὸ πλῆθος· καὶ πολλὰ τῆς βουλῆς κατ-
ηγορήσαντες, συναγορευσάντων αὐτοῖς τῶν δημάρχων καὶ νόμον[11] εἰσηγησαμένων, παρὰ τοῦ δήμου
λαμβάνουσι τὴν καταγωγὴν τοῦ θριάμβου, πρῶτοι
Ῥωμαίων ἁπάντων τοῦτο εἰσηγησάμενοι τὸ ἔθος.
2 ἐκ δὲ τούτου πάλιν εἰς ἐγκλήματα καὶ διαφορὰς

---

[1] κατὰ τὸ εἰκός Post, ὡς εἰκός Sylburg : ὡς O, Jacoby.
Reiske and Jacoby added ἀπέφυγεν ἂν ofter ἀνὴρ, while Portus
wished to add οὐκ ἂν κατεκρίθη at the end of the sentence.
[2] Kiessling : ἀνὴρ O.
[3] πολλὰ ἃ τὸ κοινὸν ἐφαίνετο εὖ πεποιηκὼς Reiske.
[4] ἄνθρωποι Kiessling, οἱ ἄνθρωποι Steph. : ἄνθρωποι O.
[5] ἔρχονται Kayser.
[6] φέρων om. L.
[7] δὴ VM : δὲ L.
[8] ὑπάτων πολ . . . τῶν παρόντων L (lacuna of some 20
letters), ὑπάτων πολλὰ κατ' αὐτῶν ἐκχέαντος κλαυδίου γαίου
καὶ αὐτῶν παρόντων V, ὑπάτων πολλὰ φέρων εἰς οἶκτον ἐφελκόμενα τὸ πλῆθος κατ' αὐτῶν ἐκχέαντος κλαυδίου γαίου καὶ αὐτῶν
παρόντων M. The words supplied by V and M are obviously

162

get a chance to speak or obtain mercy,—as might well have been the case if the man[1] had come into court citing in his defence his illustrious lineage and the many good services he had rendered to the commonwealth, appealing too to the oaths and pledges of good faith, on which men rely when accommodating their differences, [bringing forward] his children and relations, [displaying] even the humble garb of the suppliant, and doing many other things that move the multitude to compassion. When [Claudius had poured out] all these accusations against the consuls [and all] who were present [had expressed their approval],[2] it was decided that the consuls ought to be content if they were not punished ; but that they were not in the least worthy of celebrating triumphs or of gaining any concessions of that sort.

L. The senate having rejected their request for a triumph, Valerius and his colleague were indignant, and feeling that they had been grievously affronted, they called the multitude to an assembly ; and after they had uttered many invectives against the senate and the tribunes had espoused their cause and introduced a law for the purpose, they obtained from the people the privilege of celebrating a triumph, being the first of all the Romans to introduce this custom. This gave occasion to fresh accusations and quarrels

[1] Or, to make the condition more general, "a man," the reading of the MSS.

[2] The translation follows Kiessling's restoration of the text. None of the MSS. gives a satisfactory reading.

wrong ; Kiessling suggested ὑπάτων [ἐκχέαντος Κλαυδίου καὶ ἐπαινεσάντων ἁπάντων] τῶν π.

[9] ἔδοξεν δεῖν ἀγαπᾶν Reiske.

[10] τιμῶν τοσούτων συγχωρήσεως Kiessling.

[11] Reiske : νόμων O.

οἱ δημοτικοὶ καθίσταντο πρὸς τοὺς πατρικίους·
παρώξυνον δ᾽ αὐτοὺς οἱ δήμαρχοι καθ᾽ ἡμέραν
ἐκκλησιάζοντες καὶ πολλὰ κατὰ τῆς βουλῆς
λέγοντες. ἦν δ᾽ ἡ μάλιστα ἐρεθίζουσα τοὺς
πολλοὺς ὑπόληψις, ἣν ἐκεῖνοι παρεσκεύασαν ἰσχυ-
ρὰν γενέσθαι, φήμαις τ᾽ ἀδεσπότοις καὶ εἰκασμοῖς
αὐξηθεῖσα οὐκ ὀλίγοις,[1] ὡς καταλυσόντων τῶν
πατρικίων τοὺς νόμους οὓς ἐκύρωσαν οἱ περὶ
Οὐαλέριον ὕπατοι· δόξα τ᾽ ἰσχυρὰ καὶ οὐ πολὺ
ἀπέχουσα τοῦ[2] πίστις εἶναι τοὺς πολλοὺς κατεῖχε.
καὶ τὰ μὲν ἐπὶ τούτων πραχθέντα τῶν ὑπάτων
ταῦτ᾽ ἦν.

LI. Οἱ δὲ τὸν ἑξῆς ὑπατεύσαντες ἐνιαυτὸν Λάρος
Ἑρμίνιος[3] καὶ Τίτος Οὐεργίνιος· καὶ οἱ παρὰ
τούτων τὴν ἀρχὴν παραλαβόντες, Μάρκος Γε[γά-
νιος][4]

.   .   .   .

LII. Μηδὲν δὲ αὐτῶν ἀποκρινομένων, ἀλλ᾽ ἀγανακτούντων παρελθὼν αὖθις Σκάπτιος[5] ἐπὶ τὸ
βῆμα, "Ἔχετ᾽," ἔφη, "παρακεχωρημένον, ἄνδρες
πολῖται, παρ᾽ αὐτῶν τῶν διαφερομένων ὅτι τῆς
ἡμετέρας χώρας ἑαυτοῖς μηδὲν προσηκούσης ἀντι-
ποιοῦνται· πρὸς ταῦτα ὁρῶντες τὰ δίκαια καὶ τὰ
2 εὔορκα ψηφίσασθε." ταῦτα τοῦ Σκαπτίου λέγοντος αἰδὼς εἰσῄει τοὺς ὑπάτους ἐνθυμουμένους
ὡς οὔτε δίκαιον οὔτ᾽ εὐπρεπὲς ἡ δίκη λήψεται
τέλος ἄν τινα ἀμφισβητουμένην ὑφ᾽ ἑτέρων χώραν
δικαστὴς αἱρεθεὶς ὁ Ῥωμαίων δῆμος μηδέποτ᾽

---

[1] ὀλίγοις O : ἀληθέσιν Reiske, ἀλόγοις Kiessling.
[2] τοῦ added by Reiske.
[3] Sylburg : ἐρουίνιος O.
[4] The MSS. all break off with μάρκος γε. See the note
on chap. 44, 5.

on the part of the plebeians against the patricians ;
they were egged on by the tribunes, who called
assemblies every day and uttered many invectives
against the senate. But the thing which exasperated
the masses most was the suspicion, which the tribunes
had contrived to strengthen and was increased by
unavowed reports and not a few conjectures, that the
patricians were going to abolish the laws which had
been enacted by Valerius and his colleague ; and a
strong opinion to this effect, which was little less than
a conviction, possessed the minds of the masses.
These were the events of that consulship.

LI. The consuls of the following year [1] were Lar
Herminius and Titus Verginius ; and they were
succeeded by Marcus Ge[ganius] [2] . . . . .

. . . .

. . . .

LII. When they made no answer [3] but continued
to feel aggrieved, Scaptius again came forward to the
tribunal and said : " There you have the admission,
citizens, from our adversaries themselves that they
are laying claim to territory of ours which in no wise
belongs to them. Bearing this in mind, vote for what
is just and in conformity with your oaths." While
Scaptius was thus speaking, a sense of shame came
over the consuls as they considered that the outcome
of this trial would be neither just nor seemly if the
Roman people, when chosen as arbiters, should take
away any disputed territory claimed by others and

---

[1] For chap. 51 and the missing portion of the text cf. Livy
iii. 65–70. Livy gives Herminius' praenomen as Spurius.
[2] For the lacuna see the note on chap. 44, 5.
[3] Cf. Livy iii. 71 f. ; " they " are the Aricians.

---

[5] κάπτιος LV (and similarly 5 lines below), κάτλιος M.

αὐτῆς ἀντιποιησάμενος ἑαυτῷ προσδικάσῃ τοὺς
ἀμφισβητοῦντας ἀφελόμενος· καὶ πολλοὶ σφόδρα
ἐλέχθησαν εἰς ἀποτροπὴν τοῦ πράγματος ὑπὸ τῶν
ὑπάτων καὶ τῶν ἡγουμένων τῆς βουλῆς λόγοι
3 διὰ κενῆς. οἱ γὰρ ἀνειληφότες τὰς ψήφους πολλὴν
μωρίαν εἶναι λέγοντες ἑτέρους περιορᾶν τὰ σφέτερα
κατέχοντας, καὶ οὐκ εὐσεβὲς ἐξοίσειν τέλος ὑπολαμβάνοντες ἐὰν Ἀρικηνοὺς ἢ Ἀρδεάτας κυρίους
ἀποδείξωσι τῆς ἀμφισβητησίμου[1] γῆς ὀμωμοκότες
ὧν ἂν εὕρωσιν αὐτὴν οὖσαν τούτων ἐπικρινεῖν[2]·
τοῖς τε δικαζομένοις ὀργὴν ἔχοντες ὅτι τοὺς ἀπο-
στερουμένους αὐτῆς δικαστὰς ἠξίωσαν λαβεῖν, ἵνα
μηδ' ὕστερον ἔτι σφίσιν ἐγγένηται τὴν ἑαυτῶν
ἀνακομίσασθαι κτῆσιν, ἣν αὐτοὶ μεθ' ὅρκου
4 δικάσαντες ἑτέρων[3] ἐπέγνωσαν εἶναι,—ταῦτα δὴ
λογιζόμενοι καὶ ἀγανακτοῦντες τρίτον ἐκέλευσαν
τεθῆναι καδίσκον ὑπὲρ τῆς πόλεως Ῥωμαίων καθ'
ἑκάστην φυλήν, εἰς ὃν ἀποθήσονται τὰς ψήφους·
καὶ γίνεται πάσαις ταῖς ψήφοις ὁ Ῥωμαίων δῆμος
τῆς ἀμφιλόγου χώρας κύριος. ταῦτα μὲν ἐπὶ
τούτων τῶν ὑπάτων ἐπράχθη.

LIII. Μάρκου δὲ Γεννκίου[4] καὶ Γαΐου Κοιντίου
τὴν ἀρχὴν παρειληφότων αἱ πολιτικαὶ πάλιν ἀνίσταντο διαφοραὶ τῶν δημοτικῶν ἀξιούντων ἅπασι
Ῥωμαίοις ἐξεῖναι τὴν ὕπατον ἀρχὴν λαμβάνειν·
τέως γὰρ οἱ πατρίκιοι μόνοι μετῇεσαν αὐτὴν ἐν
ταῖς λοχίτισιν ἐκκλησίαις ἀποδεικνύμενοι· νόμον
τε συγγράψαντες ὑπὲρ τῶν ὑπατικῶν ἀρχαιρεσιῶν

_____

[1] ἀμφισβητησίμου Xylander : ἀμφισβήτου μὴ L, ἀμφισβήτου
VM, ἀμφισβητουμένης Kiessling.
[2] Cobet : ἐπικρίνειν O.   [3] ἑτέρων L : ἑτέροις VM.

award it to themselves, after having never before put in a counter-claim to it; and a great many speeches were made by the consuls and by the leaders of the senate to avert this result, but in vain. For the people, when called to give their votes, declared it would be great folly to permit what was theirs to remain in the possession of others, and they thought they would not be rendering a righteous verdict if they declared the Aricians or the Ardeates to be the owners of the disputed land after having sworn to award it to those to whom they should find that it belonged. And they were angry with the contending parties for having asked to have as arbiters those who were being deprived of this land, with this end in view, that they might not even afterwards have it in their power to recover their own property which they themselves as sworn judges had decreed to belong to others. The people, then, reasoning thus and feeling aggrieved, ordered a third urn, for the Roman commonwealth, to be placed before each tribe, into which they might put their voting tablets ; and the Roman people were declared by all the votes to be the owners of the disputed land. These were the events of that consulship.

LIII. When Marcus Genucius and Gaius Quintius had assumed office,[1] the political quarrels were renewed, the plebeians demanding that it be permitted to all Romans to hold the consulship ; for hitherto the patricians alone had stood for that office and been chosen in the centuriate assembly. And a law concerning the consular elections was drawn up and

[1] For chaps. 53–61 *cf.* Livy iv. 1–7, 1. Livy gives the name of Genucius' colleague as Gaius Curtius.

---

[4] γενυκίου L : μεννκίου V, μινουκίου M.

DIONYSIUS OF HALICARNASSUS

εἰσέφερον οἱ τότε δημαρχοῦντες ἐκτὸς ἑνὸς Γαΐου
Φουρνίου πάντες οἱ λοιποὶ συμφρονήσαντες, ἐν ᾧ
τὸν δῆμον ἐποιοῦντο¹ κύριον τῆς διαγνώσεως καθ᾽
ἕνα ἕκαστον ἐνιαυτὸν εἴτε πατρικίους βούλοιτο
2 μετιέναι τὴν ὑπατείαν εἴτε δημοτικούς. ἐφ᾽ οἷς
ἠγανάκτουν οἱ τοῦ βουλευτικοῦ μετέχοντες συνεδρίου καταλυομένην τὴν ἑαυτῶν δυναστείαν ὁρῶντες καὶ πάντα ὑπομένειν ᾤοντο δεῖν πρότερον ἢ
τὸν νόμον κύριον ἐᾶσαι γενέσθαι· ὀργαί τε καὶ
κατηγορίαι καὶ ἀντιπράξεις ἐγίνοντο συνεχεῖς ἐν
ἰδίοις τε συλλόγοις καὶ κατὰ τὰς κοινὰς συνόδους,
ἁπάντων τῶν πατρικίων πρὸς ἅπαντας ἠλλοτριω-
3 μένων τοὺς δημοτικούς. καὶ λόγοι πολλοὶ μὲν ἐν
τῷ συνεδρίῳ, πολλοὶ δὲ κατὰ τὰς ἐκκλησίας ὑπὸ
τῶν προϊσταμένων τῆς ἀριστοκρατίας ἐλέχθησαν,
ἐπιεικέστεροι μὲν ὑπὸ τῶν οἰομένων ἀγνοίᾳ τοῦ
συμφέροντος ἁμαρτάνειν τοὺς δημοτικούς, τραχύ-
τεροι δ᾽ ὑπὸ τῶν νομιζόντων ἐξ ἐπιβουλῆς καὶ
φθόνου τοῦ πρὸς αὐτοὺς τὸ πρᾶγμα συγκεῖσθαι.

LIV. Ἑλκομένου δὲ τοῦ χρόνου διὰ κενῆς ἧκον
εἰς τὴν πόλιν ἀπὸ τῶν συμμάχων ἄγγελοι λέγοντες
ὅτι πολλῇ στρατιᾷ μέλλουσιν ἐλαύνειν ἐπ᾽ αὐτοὺς
Αἰκανοί τε καὶ Οὐολοῦσκοι, καὶ² δεόμενοι βοήθειαν
ἀποστεῖλαι σφίσι διὰ ταχέων ὡς ἐν τρίβῳ τοῦ
2 πολέμου κειμένοις. ἐλέγοντο δὲ καὶ Τυρρηνῶν οἱ
καλούμενοι Οὐιεντανοὶ παρασκευάζεσθαι πρὸς ἀπόστασιν, Ἀρδεᾶταί τ᾽ αὐτῶν οὐκέτι ἦσαν ὑπήκοοι,
τῆς ἀμφιλόγου χώρας ὀργὴν ἔχοντες ἣν ὁ Ῥωμαίων
δῆμος αἱρεθεὶς δικαστὴς αὐτῷ³ προσεδίκασεν ἐν
3 τῷ παρελθόντι ἐνιαυτῷ. ταῦτα ἡ βουλὴ μαθοῦσα
ψηφίζεται στρατιὰν καταγράφειν καὶ τοὺς ὑπάτους

---

¹ ἐποίουν Cobet.   ² καὶ added by Reiske.

introduced by the tribunes of that year, all the others but one, Gaius Furnius, having agreed upon that course ; in this law they empowered the populace to decide each year whether they wished patricians or plebeians to stand for the consulship. At this the members of the senate were offended, seeing in it the overthrow of their own domination, and they thought they ough᷄ to endure anything rather than permit the law to pass ; and outbursts of anger, recriminations and obstructions continually occurred both in private gatherings and in their general sessions, all the patricians having become hostile to all the plebeians. Many speeches also were made in the senate and many in the meetings of the popular assembly by the leading men of the aristocracy, the more moderate by men who believed that the plebeians were misled through ignorance of their true interests and the harsher by men who thought that the measure was concocted as the result of a plot and of envy toward themselves.

LIV. While the time was dragging along with no result, messengers from the allies arrived in the city reporting that both the Aequians and the Volscians were about to march against them with a large army and begging that assistance might be sent them promptly, as they lay in the path of the war. Those Tyrrhenians also who were called Veientes were said to be preparing for a revolt ; and the Ardeates no longer gave allegiance to the Romans, being angry over the matter of the disputed territory which the Roman people, when chosen arbiters, had awarded to themselves the year before. The senate, upon being informed of all this, voted to enrol an army

---

ἀμφοτέρους ἐξάγειν δυνάμεις. ἀντέπραττον δὲ τοῖς
γνωσθεῖσιν ὑπ' αὐτῶν[1] οἱ τὸν νόμον εἰσφέροντες
(ἔχουσι δ' ἐξουσίαν ἐναντιοῦσθαι δήμαρχοι τοῖς ὑπάτοις[2]) ἀφαιρούμενοί τε τοὺς ἀγομένους ὑπ' αὐτῶν
ἐπὶ τὸν στρατιωτικὸν ὅρκον καὶ τιμωρίαν οὐδεμίαν ἐῶντες λαμβάνειν παρὰ τῶν ἀπειθούντων.
4 πολλὰ δὲ τῆς βουλῆς ἀξιούσης ἐν μὲν τῷ παρόντι
χρόνῳ τὴν φιλονεικίαν καταβαλεῖν, ὅταν δὲ τέλος
οἱ πόλεμοι λάβωσι, τότε προτιθέναι τὸν περὶ τῶν
ἀρχαιρεσιῶν νόμον, οἵδε[3] τοσούτου[4] ἐδέησαν εἶξαι
τοῖς καιροῖς ὥστε καὶ περὶ τῶν ἄλλων ἐναντιώσε-
σθαι τοῖς δόγμασι τῆς βουλῆς ἔλεγον καὶ οὐδὲν
ἐάσειν δόγμα περὶ οὐδενὸς κυρωθῆναι πράγματος
ἐὰν μὴ τὸν ὑπ'[5] αὐτῶν εἰσφερόμενον προβουλεύσῃ
5 νόμον. καὶ οὐ μόνον ἐν τῷ συνεδρίῳ πρὸς τοὺς
ὑπάτους ταῦτ' ἀπειλῆσαι προήχθησαν, ἀλλὰ καὶ
ἐπὶ τῆς ἐκκλησίας, ὅρκους οἵπερ εἰσὶ μέγιστοι παρ'
αὐτοῖς, κατὰ τῆς ἑαυτῶν πίστεως, διομοσάμενοι,[6]
ἵνα μηδέ τι[7] τῶν ἐγνωσμένων αὐτοῖς πεισθεῖσιν[8]
ἐξῇ καταλύειν.[9]

LV. Πρὸς δὴ τὰς ἀπειλὰς ταύτας ἐσκόπουν ὅ
τι χρὴ ποιεῖν οἱ πρεσβύτατοί τε καὶ κορυφαιότατοι
τῶν προεστηκότων τῆς ἀριστοκρατίας, συναχθέντες
εἰς ἰδιωτικὸν[10] σύλλογον ὑπὸ τῶν ὑπάτων αὐτοὶ

---

[1] αὐτῶν O : τῶν ὑπάτων Kiessling.
[2] ἔχουσι . . . ὑπάτοις rejected by Kiessling as a gloss.
[3] οἵδε Jacoby : οἱ δὲ O, οἱ δήμαρχοι Kiessling.
[4] τοσούτου LV : τοσοῦτον R.   [5] Sylburg : ὑπὲρ O.
[6] διομοσάμενοι LM, διωμοσάμενοι V : διωμόσαντο Sylburg.
[7] μηδέ τι O : μηδὲν Kiessling.
[8] πεισθεῖσιν O : καὶ πεισθεῖσιν Capps ; ἵνα μηδὲ πεισθεῖσιν
ἐξῇ τι τῶν ἐγνωσμένων αὐτοῖς κ. Reiske.

and that both consuls should take the field. But those who were trying to introduce the law kept opposing the execution of their decisions (tribunes have authority to oppose the consuls) by liberating such of the citizens as the consuls were leading off to make them take the military oath and by not permitting the consuls to inflict any punishment on the disobedient. And when the senate earnestly entreated them to put aside their contentiousness for the time being and only when the wars were at an end to propose the law concerning the consular elections, these men, far from yielding to the emergency, declared that they would oppose the decrees of the senate about other matters also and would not permit any decree on any subject to be ratified unless the senate should approve by a preliminary decree the law they themselves were introducing. And they were so far carried away that they thus threatened the consuls not only in the senate, but also in the assembly of the people, swearing [1] the oath which to them is the most binding, namely by their good faith, to the end that they might not be at liberty to revoke any of their decisions even if convinced of their error.

LV. In view of these threats the oldest and most prominent of the leaders of the aristocracy were assembled by the consuls in a private meeting apart by themselves and there considered what they ought

[1] Or, following Sylburg's emendation, " and not only in the senate were they carried away to the point of thus threatening the consuls, but also in the assembly they swore the oath," etc.

---

[9] καταλύειν M : om. R.
[10] τὸν before ἰδιωτικὸν deleted by Reiske; cf. x. 40, 3.

2 καθ' ἑαυτούς. Γάιος μὲν οὖν Κλαύδιος ἥκιστα δημοτικὸς ὢν καὶ ταύτην διαδεδεγμένος ἐκ προγόνων τὴν αἵρεσιν τῆς πολιτείας αὐθαδεστέραν γνώμην εἰσέφερε, μήτε ὑπατείας μήτ' ἄλλης ἀρχῆς τῷ δήμῳ παραχωρεῖν μηδεμιᾶς· τοὺς δὲ τἀναντία πράττειν ἐπιχειροῦντας ὅπλοις κωλύειν, ἐὰν μὴ πείθωνται τοῖς λόγοις, φειδὼ μηδεμίαν ποιουμένους[1] μήτ' ἰδιώτου μήτ' ἄρχοντος. ἅπαντας γὰρ τοὺς ἐπιχειροῦντας τὰ πάτρια κινεῖν ἔθη καὶ τὸν κόσμον τοῦ πολιτεύματος τὸν ἀρχαῖον διαφθείρειν 3 ἀλλοτρίους καὶ πολεμίους εἶναι τῆς πόλεως. Τίτος δὲ Κοΐντιος οὐκ εἴα βίᾳ[2] κατείργειν τὸ ἀντίπαλον, οὐδὲ δι' ὅπλων καὶ δι' αἵματος ἐμφυλίου χωρεῖν πρὸς τὸ δημοτικόν, ἄλλως τε καὶ δημάρχων σφίσιν ἐναντιωσομένων, οὓς ἱεροὺς εἶναι καὶ παναγεῖς ἐψηφίσαντο οἱ πατέρες ἡμῶν θεοὺς καὶ δαίμονας ἐγγυητὰς ποιησάμενοι τῶν ὁμολογιῶν καὶ τοὺς μεγίστους ὅρκους κατ' ἐξωλείας αὐτῶν τε καὶ τῶν ἐγγόνων, ἐάν τι παραβαίνωσι τῶν συγκειμένων, κατομοσάμενοι.

LVI. Ταύτῃ προσθεμένων τῇ γνώμῃ καὶ τῶν ἄλλων τῶν παρακληθέντων εἰς τὸ συνέδριον παραλαβὼν τὸν λόγον ὁ Κλαύδιος· '' Οὐκ ἀγνοῶ μέν,'' ἔφησεν, '' ἡλίκων κρηπὶς καταβληθήσεται συμφορῶν ἅπασιν ἡμῖν ἐὰν ἐπιτρέψωμεν τῷ δήμῳ περὶ τοῦ νόμου ψῆφον λαβεῖν· οὐκ ἔχων δ' ὅ τι χρὴ ποιεῖν οὐδὲ[3] δυνάμενος τοσούτοις οὖσιν[4] μόνος[5] ἀντιλέγειν, εἴκω τοῖς βουλήμασι[6] τοῖς ὑμετέροις. 2 δίκαιον γὰρ ἀποφαίνεσθαι μὲν ἕκαστον ἃ δοκεῖ

---

[1] ποιούμενος O.
[2] τῇ before βίᾳ deleted by Reudler.
[3] οὐδὲ Steph. : οὐ LVM.

172

to do. Gaius Claudius, who by no means favoured
the plebeians and had inherited this political creed
from his ancestors, offered a rather arrogant motion
not to yield to the people either the consulship or any
other magistracy whatever, and, in the case of those
who should attempt to do otherwise, to prevent them
by force of arms, if they would not be convinced by
arguments, giving no quarter to either private person
or magistrate. For all who attempted to disturb the
established customs and to corrupt their ancient form
of government, he said, were aliens and enemies of the
commonwealth. On the other hand, Titus Quintius
opposed restraining their adversaries by violence or
proceeding against the plebeians with arms and civil
bloodshed, particularly since they would be opposed by
the tribunes, " whose persons our fathers had decreed
to be sacred and sacrosanct, making the gods and
lesser divinities sureties for the performance of their
compact and swearing the most solemn oaths in which
they invoked utter destruction upon both themselves
and their posterity if they transgressed a single
article of that covenant."

LVI. This advice being approved of by all the
others who had been invited to the meeting, Claudius
resumed his remarks and said : " I am not unaware
of how great calamities to us all a foundation will be
laid if we permit the people to give their votes concerning this law. But being at a loss what to do and
unable alone to oppose so many, I yield to your wishes.
For it is right that every man should declare what he

----

4 Apparently either ὑμῖν has dropped out of the text here
or οὖσιν has crept in from 5 lines below.

5 μόνος L : om. R.

6 βουλεύμασι Kiessling.

173

τῷ κοινῷ συνοίσειν, πείθεσθαι δὲ τοῖς ὑπὸ τῶν
πλειόνων κριθεῖσιν. ἐκεῖνο μέντοι παραινεῖν ὑμῖν
ὡς ἐν χαλεποῖς οὖσι¹ καὶ ἀβουλήτοις πράγμασιν
ἔχω, τῆς μὲν ὑπατείας μήτε νῦν μήθ' ὕστερον
παραχωρεῖν μηδενὶ πλὴν τῶν πατρικίων, οἷς
3 μόνοις ὅσιόν τε καὶ θεμιτόν ἐστι τυγχάνειν· ὅταν
δ' εἰς ἀνάγκην κατακλεισθῆτε ὥσπερ νῦν μετα-
διδόναι καὶ τοῖς ἄλλοις πολίταις τῆς μεγίστης
ἐξουσίας τε καὶ ἀρχῆς, χιλιάρχους τε ἀντὶ τῶν
ὑπάτων ἀποδείκνυτε, ἀριθμὸν αὐτῶν ὁρίσαντες ὅσον
δή τινα—ἐμοὶ μὲν γὰρ ὀκτὼ ἢ ἓξ ἀποχρῆν δοκεῖ
—ἔν τε τούτοις τοῖς ἀνδράσι μὴ ἐλάττονες ἀριθμὸν²
ἔστωσαν οἱ πατρίκιοι τῶν δημοτικῶν. ταῦτα γὰρ
ποιοῦντες οὔτε τὴν τῶν ὑπάτων ἀρχὴν εἰς ταπει-
νοὺς καὶ ἀναξίους καταβαλεῖτε³ οὔτε δυναστείας
ἀδίκους ἑαυτοῖς κατασκευάζεσθαι δόξετε μηδεμιᾶς
4 ἀρχῆς μεταδιδόντες τοῖς δημοτικοῖς." ἐπαινεσάντων δ' ἁπάντων τὴν γνώμην καὶ οὐδενὸς τἀναντία
λέγοντος, " Ἀκούσατ'," ἔφη, " ἃ καὶ τοῖς ὑπάτοις
ὑμῖν ἔχω παραινεῖν. ἡμέραν προειπόντες ἐν ᾗ
τὸ προβούλευμα ἐπικυρώσετε καὶ τὰ κριθέντα ὑπὸ
τῆς βουλῆς, λόγον⁴ ἀπόδοτε τοῖς ἀπολογουμένοις
ὑπὲρ τοῦ νόμου καὶ τοῖς κατηγοροῦσι· ῥηθέντων δὲ
τῶν λόγων, ὅταν καθήκῃ τὰς γνώμας ἐρωτᾶν, μήτ'
ἀπ' ἐμοῦ ἄρξησθε⁵ μήτ' ἀπὸ Κοϊντίου τουδὶ μήτ'
ἀπ' ἄλλου τῶν πρεσβυτέρων μηδενός, ἀλλ' ἀπὸ
τοῦ φιλοδημοτάτου τῶν βουλευτῶν Λευκίου Οὐαλερίου, καὶ μετὰ τοῦτον ἀξιοῦτε Ὁράτιον εἴ τι
βούλεται λέγειν. ὅταν δὲ τὰς παρ' ἐκείνων γνώμας
ἐξετάσητε, τότε τοὺς πρεσβυτέρους ἡμᾶς κελεύετε

¹ οὖσι added by Capps.
² ἐλάττονες ἀριθμὸν Reiske : ἐλάττονος ἀριθμοῦ O.

174

thinks will be of advantage to the commonwealth and
then submit to the decision of the majority. However, this advice I have to give you, seeing that you
are involved in a difficult and disagreeable business,—
not to yield the consulship either now or hereafter to
any but patricians, who alone are qualified for it by
both religion and law. But whenever you are reduced,
as at present, to the necessity of sharing the highest
power and magistracy with the other citizens, appoint
military tribunes instead of consuls, fixing their
number as you shall think proper—in my opinion
eight or six suffice—and of these men let the patricians not be fewer than the plebeians. For in doing
this you will neither debase the consular office by
conferring it upon mean and unworthy men nor will
you appear to be devising for yourselves unjust
positions of power by sharing no magistracy whatever
with the plebeians." When all approved this opinion
and none spoke in opposition, he said : " Hear now
the advice I have for you consuls also. After you
have appointed a day for passing the preliminary
decree and the resolutions of the senate, give the
floor to all who desire to say anything either in favour
of the law or in opposition to it, and after they have
spoken and it is time to ask for the expression of
opinions, begin neither with me nor with Quintius
here nor with anyone else of the older men, but
rather with Lucius Valerius, who of all the senators
is the greatest friend of the populace, and after him
ask Horatius to speak, if he wishes to say anything.
And when you have found out their opinions, then

---

³ Reiske : καταβάλητε O.
⁴ λόγον added by Sylburg.
⁵ ἄρξησθε VM : ἄρξεσθε L.

175

DIONYSIUS OF HALICARNASSUS

5 λέγειν. ἐγὼ μὲν οὖν τὴν ἐναντιουμένην γνώμην
τοῖς δημάρχοις ἀποδείξομαι πάσῃ τῇ παρρησίᾳ
χρώμενος,—τουτὶ γὰρ τῷ κοινῷ συμφέρει,—τὸ δὲ
περὶ τῶν χιλιάρχων πολίτευμα, εἰ βουλομένοις
ἐστίν, εἰσηγείσθω[1] Τίτος Γενύκιος οὗτος· πρεπω-
δεστάτη γὰρ ἡ γνώμη καὶ ὑποψίαν ἥκιστα παρ-
έξουσα γένοιτ᾽ ἄν, ἐὰν οὗτος αὐτὴν ὁ σὸς ἀδελφός,
6 ὦ Μάρκε Γενύκιε, λέγῃ.'' ἐδόκει καὶ ταῦτα
ὀρθῶς ὑποτίθεσθαι, καὶ οἱ μὲν ἀπήεσαν ἐκ τοῦ
συλλόγου· τοῖς δὲ δημάρχοις δέος ἐνέπιπτε πρὸς
τὴν ἀπόρρητον τῶν ἀνδρῶν συνουσίαν ὡς ἐπὶ κακῷ
τινι τοῦ δήμου[2] μεγάλῳ γενομένην, ἐπειδὴ κατ᾽
οἰκίαν τε συνήδρευσαν, ἀλλ᾽ οὐκ ἐν τῷ φανερῷ,
καὶ οὐδένα τῶν προεστηκότων τοῦ δήμου κοινωνὸν
τῶν βουλευμάτων παρέλαβον· καὶ μετὰ τοῦτο
συνέδριον αὐτοὶ πάλιν ἐκ τῶν φιλοδημοτάτων
συναγαγόντες ἀλεξήματα καὶ φυλακὰς ἀντεμη-
χανῶντο πρὸς τὰς ἐπιβουλὰς ἃς ἐκ τῶν πατρικίων
ἔσεσθαι σφίσιν ὑπώπτευον.

LVII. Ὡς δὲ καθῆκεν ὁ χρόνος ἐν ᾧ τὸ προβούλευμα ἔδει γενέσθαι, συγκαλέσαντες οἱ ὕπατοι
τὴν βουλὴν καὶ πολλὰς ὑπὲρ ὁμονοίας καὶ εὐκοσ-
μίας ποιησάμενοι παρακλήσεις πρώτοις ἀπέδωκαν
λέγειν τοῖς εἰσηγησαμένοις δημάρχοις τὸν νόμον.
2 καὶ παρελθὼν εἷς ἐξ αὐτῶν Γάιος Κανολήιος[3] περὶ
μὲν τοῦ δίκαιον ἢ συμφέροντα εἶναι τὸν νόμον οὔτ᾽
ἐδίδασκεν οὔτ᾽ ἐμέμνητο· θαυμάζειν δ᾽ ἔφη τῶν
ὑπάτων ὅτι βεβουλευμένοι τε καὶ κεκρικότες ἤδη
κατὰ σφᾶς αὐτοὺς ἃ δεῖ πράττειν, ὥσπερ ἀδοκί-

---

[1] Reiske : εἰσηγεῖσθαι O.   [2] Sylburg : τῷ δήμῳ O.
[3] Γάιος Κανολήιος Sylburg ; Καίσων Κανολήιος Kiessling
κάτων κενολήιος O.

176

bid us older men to speak. For my part, I shall deliver an opinion contrary to that of the tribunes, using all possible frankness, since this tends to the advantage of the commonwealth. As for the measure concerning the military tribunes, if it is agreeable, let Titus Genucius here propose it; for this motion will be the most fitting and will create the least suspicion, Marcus Genucius, if introduced by your brother here." This suggestion was also approved, after which they departed from the meeting. But as for the tribunes, fear fell upon them because of the secret conference of these men; for they suspected that it was calculated to bring some great mischief upon the populace, since the men had met in a private house and not in public and had admitted none of the people's champions to share in their counsels. Thereupon they in turn held a meeting of such persons as were most friendly to the populace and they set about contriving defences and safeguards against the insidious designs which they suspected the patricians would employ against them.

LVII. When the time had come for the preliminary decree to be passed, the consuls assembled the senate and after many exhortations to harmony and good order they gave leave to the tribunes who had proposed the law to speak first. Then Gaius Canuleius, one of these, came forward and, without trying to show that the law was either just or advantageous or even mentioning that topic, said that he wondered at the consuls, who, after already consulting and deciding by themselves what should be done, had attempted to bring it before the senate

μαστον πρᾶγμα καὶ βουλῆς δεόμενον εἰς τὸ
συνέδριον ἐπεχείρησαν εἰσφέρειν, καὶ λόγον ἀπέδωκαν ὑπὲρ αὐτοῦ τοῖς προαιρουμένοις, εἰρωνείαν
εἰσάγοντες οὔτε ταῖς ἑαυτῶν ἡλικίαις ἁρμόττουσαν
3 οὔτε τῷ μεγέθει τῆς ἀρχῆς προσήκουσαν. πονηρῶν τ᾽ ἀρχὰς ἔφη πολιτευμάτων αὐτοὺς εἰσάγειν
ἀπόρρητα βουλευτήρια συνάγοντας ἐν ἰδίαις οἰκίαις, καὶ οὐδ᾽ ἅπαντας τοὺς βουλευτὰς εἰς ταῦτα
παρακαλοῦντας, ἀλλὰ τοὺς σφίσιν αὐτοῖς ἐπιτηδει-
οτάτους. τῶν μὲν οὖν ἄλλων συνέδρων τῶν ἀπελα-
θέντων τῆς κατοικιδίου βουλῆς ἧττον ἔφη θαυμάζειν,
Μάρκου δὲ Ὁρατίου καὶ Λευκίου Οὐαλερίου τῶν
καταλυσάντων τὴν ὀλιγαρχίαν, ὑπατικῶν ἀνδρῶν
καὶ οὐδενὸς ἧττον ἐπιτηδείων τὰ κοινὰ βουλεύειν,
τὴν ἀπαξίωσιν τῆς εἰς τὸ συνέδριον παρακλήσεως
ἐκπεπλῆχθαι, καὶ οὐ δύνασθαι συμβάλλειν ἐπὶ τίνι
λόγῳ δικαίῳ, εἰκάζειν δὲ μίαν αἰτίαν, ὅτι πονηρὰς
καὶ ἀσυμφόρους γνώμας εἰσηγεῖσθαι μέλλοντες
κατὰ τῶν δημοτικῶν οὐκ ἐβούλοντο παρακαλεῖν
εἰς ταῦτα τὰ συνέδρια τοὺς φιλοδημοτάτους,
ἀγανακτήσοντας δηλονότι καὶ οὐ περιοψομένους
οὐδὲν ἄδικον πολίτευμα κατὰ τοῦ δήμου γινόμενον.

LVIII. Τοιαῦτα τοῦ[1] Κανοληίου μετὰ πολλοῦ
σχετλιασμοῦ λέγοντος καὶ τῶν μὴ[2] παραληφθέντων
εἰς τὸ συνέδριον βουλευτῶν πρὸς ὀργὴν δεξαμένων
τὸ πρᾶγμα παρελθὼν ἅτερος τῶν ὑπάτων Γενύκιος
ἀπολογεῖσθαι καὶ πραΰνειν τὰς ὀργὰς αὐτῶν
ἐπειρᾶτο, διδάσκων ὅτι τοὺς μὲν φίλους παρα-

[1] τοῦ O : Γαΐου Jacoby, contrary to Dionysius' usage.
Only when introducing a speaker does he give both nomen
and praenomen ; in marking the close of a speech he regularly uses the nomen only (or, in the case of the various

as if it were a matter that had not been examined
and required consideration, and had then given all
who so chose leave to speak about it, thereby introducing a dissimulation unbecoming both to their
age and to the greatness of their magistracy. He
said that they were introducing the beginnings of
evil policies by assembling secret councils in private
houses and by summoning to them not even all the
senators, but only such as were most attached to
themselves. He was not so greatly surprised, he said,
that the other members had been excluded from this
senatorial house party, but was astounded that Marcus
Horatius and Lucius Valerius, who had overthrown
the oligarchy, were ex-consuls and were as competent
as anyone for deliberating about the public interests,
had not been thought worthy to be invited to the
meeting. He could not imagine on what just ground
this had been done, but he could guess one reason,
namely that, as they intended to introduce wicked
measures prejudicial to the plebeians, they were unwilling to invite to these councils the greatest friends
of the populace, who would be sure to express their
indignation at such proposals and would not permit
any unjust measure to be adopted against the
interests of the people.

LVIII. When Canuleius had spoken thus with
great indignation and the senators who had not been
summoned to the council resented their treatment,
Genucius, one of the consuls, came forward and endeavoured to justify himself and his colleague and
to appease the anger of the others by telling them
that they had called in their friends, not in order to

Appii Claudii, the praenomen only), with or without the
article. ² μὴ om. L.

λάβοιεν, οὐχ ἵνα τι[1] κατὰ τοῦ δήμου διαπράξαιντο,
ἀλλ᾽ ἵνα μετὰ τῶν ἀναγκαιοτάτων βουλεύσαιντο
τί πράττοντες οὐδ᾽ ὁποτέραν δόξουσιν ἐλαττοῦν
τῶν αἱρέσεων, πότερον ταχεῖαν ἀποδιδόντες τῇ
βουλῇ περὶ τοῦ νόμου διάγνωσιν ἢ χρονιωτέραν.
2 Ὁράτιον δὲ καὶ Οὐαλέριον οὐκ ἄλλης τινὸς χάριν
αἰτίας μὴ παραλαβεῖν εἰς τὸ συνέδριον, ἀλλ᾽ ἵνα
μή τις ὑποψία περὶ αὐτῶν παρ᾽ ἀξίαν ᾖ τοῖς δημοτικοῖς ὡς μεταβεβλημένων τὴν προαίρεσιν τῆς
πολιτείας, ἐὰν ἄρα ἐπὶ τῆς ἑτέρας γένωνται γνώμης
τῆς ἀξιούσης ἀναβαλέσθαι τὴν ὑπὲρ τοῦ νόμου
διάγνωσιν εἰς ἕτερον καιρὸν ἐπιτηδειότερον. ἐπειδὴ
δ᾽ ἅπασι τοῖς παραληφθεῖσιν ἡ συντομωτέρα διά-
γνωσις ἀμείνων ἔδοξεν εἶναι τῆς βραδυτέρας,
3 πράττειν ὡς ἐκείνοις ἐφάνη. ταῦτ᾽ εἰπὼν καὶ
θεοὺς ἐπομοσάμενος ἦ μὴν τἀληθῆ λέγειν καὶ τοὺς
παρακληθέντας ἐκ τῶν βουλευτῶν μαρτυράμενος,[2]
ἔφη πᾶσαν ἀπολύσεσθαι[3] διαβολὴν οὐ λόγοις ἀλλ᾽
4 ἔργοις. ὅταν γὰρ οἱ βουλόμενοι κατηγορεῖν καὶ
ἀπολογεῖσθαι περὶ τοῦ νόμου διεξέλθωσι τὰ δίκαια,
πρώτους ἐπὶ τὴν ἐρώτησιν τῆς γνώμης καλεῖν[4]
οὐχὶ τοὺς πρεσβυτάτους καὶ τιμιωτάτους τῶν βουλευτῶν, οἷς ἐκ τῶν πατρίων ἐθισμῶν καὶ τοῦτ᾽
ἀποδεδόσθαι τὸ γέρας, οὐδὲ τοὺς δι᾽ ὑποψίας ὄντας
παρὰ τοῖς δημοτικοῖς ὡς οὐδὲν ὑπὲρ αὐτῶν χρη-
στὸν οὔτε λέγοντας οὔτε φρονοῦντας, ἀλλ᾽ ἐκ τῶν
νεωτέρων τοὺς δοκοῦντας εἶναι φιλοδημοτάτους.
LIX. Ὑποσχόμενος δὲ ταῦτα καὶ δοὺς ἐξουσίαν

---

[1] τι added by Sylburg.
[2] μαρτυράμενος Reiske : om. O, Jacoby.
[3] Kiessling : ἀπολύσασθαι O, διαλύσεσθαι Sylburg.

carry out any design against the populace, but in order to consult with their closest intimates by what course they might appear to do nothing prejudicial to either one of the parties, whether by referring the consideration of the law to the senate promptly or by doing so later. As for Valerius and Horatius, he said their only reason for not inviting them to the council had been to prevent the plebeians from entertaining any unwarranted suspicion of them as of men who had changed their political principles, in case they should embrace the other opinion, which called for putting off the consideration of the law to a more suitable occasion. But since all who had been invited to the meeting had felt that a speedy decision was preferable to a delayed one, the consuls were following the course thus favoured. Having spoken thus and sworn by the gods that he was indeed speaking the truth, and appealing for confirmation to the senators who had been invited to that meeting, he said that he would clear himself of every imputation, not by his words, but by his actions. For after all who desired to speak in opposition to the law or in favour of it had given their reasons, he would first call for questioning as to their opinions, not the oldest and the most honoured of the senators, to whom this privilege among others was accorded by established usage, nor those who were suspected by the plebeians of neither saying nor thinking anything that was to their advantage, but rather such of the younger senators as seemed to be most friendly to the populace.

LIX. After making these promises he gave leave

---

⁴ καλεῖν Cary, καλέσειν Cobet, καλέσαι Reiske : κατάγειν O, κατάξειν Capps, following Sylburg, καταλέγειν Jacoby.

DIONYSIUS OF HALICARNASSUS

τοῖς βουλομένοις λέγειν, ἐπειδὴ οὔτε κατηγορήσων
οὔτ᾽ ἀπολογησόμενος οὐδεὶς ὑπὲρ τοῦ νόμου παρῄει,
παρελθὼν αὖθις ἐρωτᾷ πρῶτον Οὐαλέριον τί τῷ
κοινῷ συμφέρει καὶ τί προβουλεῦσαι τοῖς συνέδροις
2 παραινεῖ. ὁ δ᾽ ἀναστὰς καὶ πολλοὺς διεξελθὼν
ὑπὲρ αὑτοῦ τε καὶ τῶν προγόνων λόγους ὡς ἐπὶ
τῷ συμφέροντι τῆς πόλεως τοῦ δημοτικοῦ μέρους
προϊσταμένων, καὶ καταριθμησάμενος ἅπαντας ἐξ
ἀρχῆς τοὺς κατασχόντας τὴν πόλιν κινδύνους ἐκ
τῶν τἀναντία πολιτευομένων, τοῖς τ᾽ ἀπεχθῶς
ἐσχηκόσι πρὸς τὸ δημοτικὸν ἅπασιν ἀλυσιτελὲς
γενόμενον ἀποδείξας[1] τὸ μισόδημον, ἐπαίνους τε
πολλοὺς περὶ τοῦ δήμου ποιησάμενος ὡς αἰτιω-
τάτου τῇ πόλει γεγονότος οὐ μόνον τῆς ἐλευθερίας
ἀλλὰ καὶ τῆς ἡγεμονίας, ἐπεὶ ταῦτα καὶ παρα-
πλήσια τούτοις διεξῆλθε, τελευτῶν ἔφη μὴ[2] δύνασθαι πόλιν ἐλευθέραν εἶναι[3] ἐξ ἧς ἄν τις τὴν
3 ἰσότητα ἀνέλῃ[4]· ἔφη τε δοκεῖν ἑαυτῷ τὸν μὲν
νόμον δίκαιον εἶναι τὸν ἀξιοῦντα πᾶσι μετεῖναι
Ῥωμαίοις τῆς ὑπατικῆς ἀρχῆς, τοῖς γε[5] δὴ βίον
ἀνεπίληπτον ἐσχηκόσι καὶ πράξεις ἀποδεδειγμένοις
τῆς τιμῆς ταύτης ἀξίας, τὸν δὲ καιρὸν οὐκ ἐπιτήδειον εἰς τὴν ὑπὲρ αὐτοῦ διάγνωσιν ἐν πολεμικαῖς
4 ὑπαρχούσης ταραχαῖς τῆς πόλεως, συνεβούλευέ
τε τοῖς μὲν δημάρχοις ἐᾶν τὴν καταγραφὴν γενέσθαι τῶν στρατιωτῶν[6] καὶ τὴν ἔξοδον μὴ κωλύειν
τῶν καταγραφέντων, τοῖς δ᾽ ὑπάτοις, ὅταν τὸ
κράτιστον τέλος ἐπιθῶσι τῷ πολέμῳ, πρῶτον
ἁπάντων τὸ περὶ τοῦ νόμου προβούλευμα εἰς τὸν

---

[1] Sylburg : ἀποδείξασι O.
[2] μὴ om. LVM.   [3] εἶναι om. LVM.

to any who so desired to speak ; and when no one came forward either to censure the law or to defend it, he came forward again, and beginning with Valerius, asked him what was to the interest of the public and what preliminary vote he advised the senators to pass. Valerius, rising up, made a long speech concerning both himself and his ancestors, who, he said, had always been champions of the plebeian party to the advantage of the commonwealth. He enumerated all the dangers from the beginning which had been brought upon it by those who pursued the contrary measures and showed that a hatred for the populace had been unprofitable to all those who had been actuated by it. He then said many things in praise of the people, alleging that they had been the principal cause not only of the liberty but also of the supremacy of the commonwealth. After enlarging upon this and similar themes, he ended by saying that no state could be free from which equality was banished ; and he declared that to him the law, indeed, seemed just which gave a share in the consulship to all Romans,—to all, that is, who had led irreproachable lives and had performed actions worthy of that honour,—but he thought the occasion was not suitable for the consideration of this law when the commonwealth was in the midst of war's disturbances. He advised the tribunes to permit the enrolling of the troops and not to hinder them when enrolled from taking the field ; and he advised the consuls, when they had ended the war in the most successful manner, first of all things to lay before the people the preliminary decree concerning the law.

---

⁴ ἀνέλῃ Steph. : ἂν ἐᾶν LVM. ⁵ γε Sylburg : τε O.
⁶ στρατιωτῶν LVa : στρατηγῶν MVb.

δῆμον ἐξενεγκεῖν. ταῦτα δὲ γραφῆναί τ' ἤδη καὶ
5 διομολογηθῆναι πρὸς ἀμφοτέρων. ταύτην ἀποδειξαμένου τὴν γνώμην Οὐαλερίου καὶ μετὰ τοῦτον Ὁρατίου (δευτέρῳ γὰρ τούτῳ λόγον ἀπέδωκαν
οἱ ὕπατοι) ταὐτὸ[1] πάθος ἅπασι τοῖς παροῦσι συνέβη. οἱ μὲν γὰρ ἀνελεῖν τὸν νόμον βουλόμενοι,
τὴν ἀναβολὴν τῆς περὶ αὐτοῦ διαγνώσεως ἀγαπητῶς ἀκούσαντες, τὸ μετὰ τὸν πόλεμον ἐπάναγκες
εἶναι σφίσι προβουλεῦσαι περὶ αὐτοῦ χαλεπῶς ἀπ-
εδέξαντο[2]· οἱ δὲ κύριον ὑπὸ τοῦ συνεδρίου κριθῆ-
ναι προαιρούμενοι τὸ μὲν ὡμολογημένον δίκαιον
εἶναι τὸν νόμον ἀσμένως ἤκουον, τὸ δ' εἰς ἑτέρους
ἐκπίπτειν χρόνους τὸ προβούλευμα πρὸς ὀργὴν
ἐλάμβανον.

LX. Θορύβου δέ, ὅπερ εἰκός, ἐπὶ τῇ γνώμῃ
γενομένου διὰ τὸ μὴ πᾶσι τοῖς μέρεσιν αὐτῆς
εὐαρεστεῖν ἀμφοτέρους παρελθὼν ὁ ὕπατος τρίτον
ἠρώτα Γάιον Κλαύδιον, ὃς ἐδόκει τῶν προεστηκότων τῆς ἑτέρας τάξεως τῆς ἐναντιουμένης τοῖς
δημοτικοῖς αὐθαδέστατος εἶναι καὶ δυνατώτατος.
2 οὗτος ἐκ παρασκευῆς διεξῆλθε λόγον κατὰ τῶν
δημοτικῶν, πάνθ' ὅσα ἔδοξε πώποτε ἐναντία τοῖς
καλοῖς καὶ πατρίοις ἐθισμοῖς[3] ὑπομιμνήσκων, οὗ
κεφάλαιον ἦν, εἰς ὃ κατέσκηπτεν ἡ γνώμη, μηδεμίαν ἀποδιδόναι τῇ βουλῇ διάγνωσιν ὑπὲρ τοῦ
νόμου τοὺς ὑπάτους μήτ' ἐν τῷ παρόντι χρόνῳ
μήθ' ὕστερον, ὡς ἐπὶ καταλύσει τῆς ἀριστοκρατίας
εἰσφερομένου καὶ συγχεῖν μέλλοντος ἅπαντα τὸν
3 κόσμον τῆς πολιτείας. γενομένου δὲ πρὸς τὴν
γνώμην ἔτι πλείονος θορύβου τέταρτος ἀνίσταται
κληθεὶς Τίτος Γενύκιος, ἀδελφὸς θατέρου τῶν

---

[1] οὐ ταὐτὸ Portus.   [2] Sylburg : ἐπελέξαντο O.

These proposals, he urged, should be reduced to writing at once and agreed to by both parties. This opinion of Valerius, which was supported by Horatius (for the consuls gave him leave to speak next), had the same effect upon all who were present. For those who desired to do away with the law, though pleased to hear that its consideration was postponed, nevertheless accepted with anger the necessity of passing a preliminary decree concerning it after the war; while the others, who preferred to have the law approved by the senate, though glad to hear it acknowledged as just, were at the same time angry that the preliminary decree was put off to another time.

LX. An uproar having broken out as the result of this opinion, as was to be expected, since neither side was pleased with all parts of it, the consul, coming forward, asked in the third place the opinion of Gaius Claudius, who had the reputation of being the most haughty and the most powerful of all the leaders of the other party, which opposed the plebeians. This man delivered a prepared speech against the plebeians in which he called to mind all the things the populace had ever done contrary, as he thought, to the excellent institutions of their ancestors. The climax with which he ended his speech was the motion that the consuls should not permit to the senate any consideration of the law at all, either at that time or later, since it was being introduced for the purpose of overthrowing the aristocracy and was bound to upset the whole order of their government. When even more of an uproar was caused by this motion, Titus Genucius, who was brother to one of the consuls,

---

³ After ἐθισμοῖς Sylburg proposed to add τῷ δήμῳ πεπραγμένα, Reiske διεπεπρᾶχθαι.

ὑπάτων· ὃς ὀλίγα διαλεχθεὶς ὑπὲρ τῶν κατεχόντων
καιρῶν τὴν πόλιν, ὅτι δυεῖν ἀνάγκη τῶν χαλεπω-
τάτων θάτερον αὐτῇ[1] συμπεσεῖν, ἢ διὰ τὰς πολιτικὰς ἔριδας καὶ φιλοτιμίας ἰσχυρὰ τὰ τῶν ἐχθρῶν
ποιῆσαι πράγματα, ἢ τοὺς ἔξωθεν ἐπιφερομένους
ἀποτρέψασθαι βουλομένη κακῶς τὸν οἰκεῖον καὶ
4 πολιτικὸν διαλύσασθαι πόλεμον,[2] ἔφησε, δυεῖν
ὄντων κακῶν ὧν ἀνάγκη θάτερον ἄκοντας ὑπομεῖναι, τοῦτ᾽ αὐτῷ δοκεῖν εἶναι λυσιτελέστερον,
τὸ συγχωρῆσαι τῷ δήμῳ τὴν βουλὴν παρασπάσαι
τι τοῦ κόσμου τῆς πατρίου πολιτείας μᾶλλον ἢ
τοῖς ἀλλοφύλοις τε[3] καὶ πολεμίοις καταγέλαστον
5 ποιῆσαι τὴν πόλιν. ταῦτ᾽ εἰπὼν τὴν δοκιμασθεῖσαν
ὑπὸ τῶν παραγενηθέντων ἐν τῷ κατ᾽ οἰκίαν συνεδρίῳ γνώμην εἰσέφερεν, ἣν εἰσηγήσατο Κλαύδιος,
ὥσπερ ἔφην, ἀντὶ τῶν ὑπάτων χιλιάρχους ἀποδειχθῆναι, τρεῖς μὲν ἐκ τῶν πατρικίων, τρεῖς δ᾽
ἐκ τῶν δημοτικῶν, ἐξουσίαν ἔχοντας ὑπατικήν·
ὅταν δὲ τελῶσιν οὗτοι τὴν ἀρχὴν καὶ καθήκῃ νέας
ἀρχὰς ἀποδείκνυσθαι, τὴν βουλὴν καὶ τὸν δῆμον
αὖθις συνελθόντας διαγνῶναι πότερον ὑπάτους ἢ
χιλιάρχους βούλονται παραλαβεῖν τὴν ἀρχήν, ὅ τι
δ᾽ ἂν ἅπασι δόξῃ ψῆφον ἐπενέγκασι, τοῦτ᾽ εἶναι
κύριον· ἐπιτελεῖσθαι δὲ τὸ προβούλευμα καθ᾽
ἕκαστον ἐνιαυτόν.

LXI. Ταύτην ἀποδειξαμένου τὴν γνώμην Γενυκίου πολὺς ἐξ ἁπάντων ἔπαινος ἐγίνετο,[4] καὶ οἱ
μετ᾽ ἐκεῖνον ἀνιστάμενοι μικροῦ δεῖν πάντες ταῦτα συνεχώρουν κράτιστα εἶναι. γράφεται δὴ τὸ

[1] αὐτῇ Reiske : αὐτὸν La, ταύτῃ LbVM.
[2] Cobet preferred to read πολέμους after ἐπιφερομένους and
omit πόλεμον after διαλύσασθαι.
[3] τε L : om. R.   [4] ἐγένετο VM.

was called upon in the fourth place. He, rising up, spoke briefly about the emergencies confronting the city, how it was inevitable that one or the other of two most grievous evils should befall it, either through its civil strifes and rivalries to strengthen the cause of its enemies, or, from a desire to avert the attacks from outside, to settle ignominiously the domestic and civil war ; and he declared that, there being two evils to one or the other of which they were bound to submit unwillingly, it seemed to him to be expedient that the senate should permit the people to usurp a portion of the orderly constitution of the fathers rather than make the commonwealth a laughing-stock to other nations and to its enemies. Having said this, he offered the motion which had been approved by those who had been present at the meeting held in a private house, the motion made by Claudius, as I related,[1] to the effect that, instead of consuls, military tribunes should be appointed, three from the patricians and three from the plebeians, these to have consular authority ; that after they had completed the term of their magistracy and it was time to appoint new magistrates, the senate and people should again assemble and decide whether they wished consuls or military tribunes to assume the office, and that whichever course met with the approval of all the voters should prevail ; moreover, that the preliminary decree should be passed each year.

LXI. This motion of Genucius was received with general applause, and almost all who rose up after him conceded that this was the best course. The

---

[1] In chap. 56, 3.

προβούλευμα ὑπὸ τῶν ὑπάτων, καὶ λαβόντες αὐτὸ
μετὰ πολλῆς χαρᾶς οἱ δήμαρχοι προῆλθον εἰς τὴν
ἀγοράν. ἔπειτα καλέσαντες τὸ πλῆθος εἰς τὴν[1]
ἐκκλησίαν, πολλοὺς διέθεντο τῆς βουλῆς ἐπαίνους,
καὶ παραγγέλλειν τὴν ἀρχὴν ἐκέλευον τοῖς ἐθέλουσι
2 τῶν δημοτικῶν ἅμα τοῖς πατρικίοις. οὕτω δ᾽
ἄρα κοῦφόν τι πρᾶγμά ἐστιν ἐπιθυμία δίχα λόγου
γινομένη καὶ ταχὺ μεταπῖπτον ἐπὶ θάτερα μέρη,
μάλιστα δ᾽ ἡ τῶν ὄχλων, ὥσθ᾽ οἱ περὶ παντὸς
ποιούμενοι τέως τῆς ἀρχῆς μεταλαβεῖν καί, εἰ μὴ
δοθείη τοῦτ᾽ αὐτοῖς ὑπὸ τῶν πατρικίων, ἢ καταλείψοντες τὴν πόλιν ὡς πρότερον ἢ διὰ τῶν ὅπλων
αὐτὸ[2] ληψόμενοι, ἐπειδὴ τὸ συγχώρημα ἔλαβον,
ἀπέστησαν εὐθὺς τῆς ἐπιθυμίας καὶ τὰς σπουδὰς
3 ἐπὶ θάτερον μετέβαλον. πολλῶν γέ τοι δημοτικῶν
παραγγελλόντων τὴν χιλιαρχίαν καὶ κατεσπου-
δασμένας ποιουμένων τὰς δεήσεις, οὐδένα τῆς
τιμῆς ταύτης ἄξιον εἶναι ὑπέλαβον, ἀλλὰ γενόμενοι
τῆς ψήφου κύριοι τοὺς ἐκ τῶν πατρικίων μετιόντας
αὐτὴν ἄνδρας ἐπιφανεῖς χιλιάρχους ἀποδεικνύουσιν,
Αὖλον[3] Σεμπρώνιον Ἀτρατῖνον καὶ Λεύκιον Ἀτί-
λιον[4] Λοῦσκον[5] καὶ Τίτον Κλοίλιον[6] Σικελόν.

LXII. Οὗτοι παραλαμβάνουσι πρῶτοι τὴν ἀνθύπατον ἀρχὴν κατὰ τὸν τρίτον ἐνιαυτὸν τῆς ὀγδοηκοστῆς καὶ τετάρτης ὀλυμπιάδος ἄρχοντος Ἀθήνησι
Διφίλου. μετασχόντες δ᾽ αὐτῆς[7] ἑβδομήκοντα καὶ
τρεῖς μόνον ἡμέρας ἀποτίθενται κατὰ τὸν ἀρχαῖον
ἐθισμὸν ἑκούσιοι, θεοπέμπτων τινῶν σημείων κω-
λυτηρίων αὐτοῖς τοῦ πράττειν τὰ κοινὰ γενομένων

---

[1] τὴν deleted by Reudler.
[2] αὐτὸ M : αὐτὴν L, αὐτὰ V.   [3] αὔλιον O.
ἀτέλιον O.   [5] λοῦγχον La, λοῦγγον Lb, λοῦσχον VM.
[6] Cary : κλύδιον L, κλύλιον R(?).

preliminary decree was accordingly drawn up by order of the consuls ; and the tribunes, receiving it with great joy, proceeded to the Forum. Then they called an assembly of the people, and after giving much praise to the senate, urged such of the plebeians as cared to do so to stand for this magistracy together with the patricians. But such a fickle thing, it seems, is desire apart from reason and so quickly does it veer the other way, particularly in the case of the masses, that those who hitherto had regarded it as a matter of supreme importance to have a share in the magistracy and, if this were not granted to them by the patricians, were ready either to abandon the city, as they had done before, or to seize the privilege by force of arms, now, when they had obtained the concession, promptly relinquished their desire for it and transferred their enthusiasm in the opposite direction. At any rate, though many plebeians stood for the military tribuneship and used the most earnest solicitations to obtain it, the people thought none of them worthy of this honour but, when they came to give their votes, chose the patrician candidates, men of distinction, namely Aulus Sempronius Atratinus, Lucius Atilius Luscus and Titus Cloelius Siculus.

LXII. These men were the first to assume the proconsular power,[1] in the third year of the eighty-fourth Olympiad,[2] when Diphilus was archon at Athens. But after holding it for only seventy-three days they voluntarily resigned it, in accordance with the ancient custom, when some heaven-sent omens occurred to prevent their continuing to conduct the public busi-

---

[1] *Cf.* Livy iv. 7.   [2] 441 B.C.

---

[7] μετασχόντες δ' αὐτῆς O : κατασχόντες δ' αὐτὴν Sylburg.

2 τούτων δὲ τὴν ἐξουσίαν ἀπειπαμένων ἡ βουλὴ συνελθοῦσα μεσοβασιλεῖς ἀποδείκνυσι. καὶ ἐκεῖνοι προειπόντες ἀρχαιρέσια καὶ τῷ δήμῳ τὴν διάγνωσιν ἀποδιδόντες εἴτε βούλεται χιλιάρχους εἴτε ὑπάτους ἀποδεῖξαι, κρίναντος αὐτοῦ μένειν ἐπὶ τοῖς ἐξ ἀρχῆς ἐθισμοῖς, ἀπέδοσαν τοῖς βουλομένοις τῶν πατρικίων μετιέναι τὴν ὕπατον ἀρχήν· καὶ γίνονται πάλιν ἐκ τῶν πατρικίων ὕπατοι Λεύκιος[1] Παπίριος[2] Μογιλλανὸς καὶ Λεύκιος Σεμπρώνιος Ἀτρατῖνος, 3 ἑνὸς τῶν ἀποθεμένων τὴν χιλιαρχίαν ἀδελφός. αὗται δύο κατὰ τὸν αὐτὸν ἐνιαυτὸν ἀρχαὶ Ῥωμαίων αἱ τὸ μέγιστον ἔχουσαι[3] κράτος ἐγένοντο· πλὴν οὐκ ἐν ἁπάσαις ταῖς Ῥωμαϊκαῖς χρονογραφίαις ἀμφότεραι φέρονται,[4] ἀλλ᾽ ἐν αἷς μὲν οἱ χιλίαρχοι μόνον, ἐν αἷς δ᾽ οἱ ὕπατοι, ἐν οὐ πολλαῖς δ᾽ ἀμφότεροι, αἷς ἡμεῖς οὐκ ἄνευ λογισμοῦ συγκατατιθέμεθα, πιστεύοντες δὲ ταῖς ἐκ τῶν ἱερῶν τε 4 καὶ ἀποθέτων βίβλων μαρτυρίαις. ἄλλο μὲν οὖν οὐδὲν ἐπὶ τῆς τούτων ἀρχῆς οὔτε πολεμικὸν[5] οὔτε πολιτικὸν ἔργον ἱστορίας ἄξιον ἐπράχθη, συνθῆκαι δὲ πρὸς τὴν Ἀρδεατῶν πόλιν ἐγένοντο περὶ φιλίας τε καὶ συμμαχίας· ἐπρεσβεύσαντο γὰρ ἀποτιθέμενοι τὰ περὶ τῆς χώρας ἐγκλήματα, παρακαλοῦντες φίλοι Ῥωμαίων γενέσθαι καὶ σύμμαχοι. ταύτας τὰς συνθήκας τὸ τῶν ὑπάτων ἀρχεῖον ἐπεκύρωσε.

LXIII. Τῷ δ᾽ ἑξῆς ἐνιαυτῷ πάλιν ὑπάτους ψηφισαμένου τοῦ δήμου κατασταθῆναι παραλαμβάνουσι τὴν ὕπατον ἀρχὴν τῇ διχομήνιδι τοῦ Δεκεμβρίου μηνὸς Μάρκος Γεγάνιος Μακερῖνος

---

[1] μενύκιος LVM.   [2] πατρίκιος M.
[3] ἔχουσαι M : ἔχειν L, ἔχουσι V.
[4] φέρονται Sylburg : φαίνονται O.

ness. After these men had abdicated their power, the senate met and chose *interreges*, who, having appointed a day for the election of magistrates, left the decision to the people whether they desired to choose military tribunes or consuls ; and the people having decided to abide by their original customs, they gave leave to such of the patricians as so desired to stand for the consulship. Two of the patricians were again elected consuls, Lucius Papirius Mugillanus and Lucius Sempronius Atratinus, brother to one of the men who had resigned the military tribuneship. These two magistracies, both invested with the supreme power, governed the Romans in the course of the same year. However, both are not recorded in all the Roman annals, but in some the military tribunes only, in others the consuls, and in a few both of them. I agree with the last group, not without reason, but relying on the testimony of the sacred and secret books.[1] No event, either military or civil, worthy of the notice of history happened during their magistracy, except a treaty of friendship and alliance entered into with the Ardeates ; for these, dropping their complaints about the disputed territory, had sent ambassadors, asking to be admitted among the friends and allies of the Romans. This treaty was ratified by the consuls.

LXIII. The following year,[2] the people having voted that consuls should again be appointed, Marcus Geganius Macerinus (for the second time) and Titus

---

[1] Perhaps the *libri lintei* cited by Licinius Macer according to Livy iv. 7, 12. These were lists of consuls and other magistrates recorded on linen rolls.

[2] *Cf.* Livy iv. 8.

---

[5] πολεμικὸν L : πολέμιον R.

DIONYSIUS OF HALICARNASSUS

τὸ δεύτερον καὶ Τίτος Κοίντιος Καπιτωλῖνος τὸ
2 πέμπτον. οὗτοι διδάξαντες τὴν βουλὴν ὅτι πολλὰ
μὲν καὶ ἄλλα πράγματα διὰ τὰς συνεχεῖς τῶν
ὑπάτων στρατείας ἠμελημένα παρεῖται, πάντων δ᾽
ἀναγκαιότατον τὸ περὶ τὰς τιμήσεις τῶν βίων
νόμιμον, ἐξ ὧν ὅ τ᾽ ἀριθμὸς τῶν ἐχόντων τὴν
στρατεύσιμον ἡλικίαν ἐγινώσκετο καὶ τῶν χρημάτων τὸ πλῆθος, ἀφ᾽ ὧν ἔδει τὰς εἰς τὸν πόλεμον
εἰσφορὰς ἕκαστον τελεῖν, οὐδεμιᾶς τιμήσεως ἐντὸς
ἑπτακαίδεκα ἐτῶν γενομένης ἀπὸ τῆς Λευκίου
Κορνηλίου καὶ Κοίντου Φαβίου [ὑπατείας· ὥστε]¹
. . . καταλιπεῖν οἱ πονηρότατοί τε καὶ ἀσελγέ-
στατοι ῾Ρωμαίων, ἀλλὰ τόπον μεταλαμβάνειν² ἐν
ᾧ περίεστι ζῆν αὐτοῖς ὡς προῄρηνται.³

¹ ὑπατείας ὥστε added by L in a lacuna, omitted by V in
a lacuna of some 20 letters. The words καταλιπεῖν . . .
προῄρηνται are found in LV; M has ὥστε τοὺς μὲν χρηστοὺς καὶ
ὠφελίμους ἄνδρας ἐν τιμαῖς καὶ ἐν στρατείαις (error for στρατηγίαις?) εἶναι, τοὺς δὲ ἀσελγεστάτους καὶ πονηροτάτους ἀτίμους
καταλείπεσθαι καὶ τόπον ἕτερον μεταλαμβάνειν ἐν ᾧ περίεστι ζῆν
αὐτοῖς ὡς προῄρηνται.
² μεταλαμβάνει LV.

Quintius Capitolinus (for the fifth time) entered upon the consulship on the ides of December. These men pointed out to the senate that many things had been overlooked and neglected by reason of the continuous military expeditions of the consuls, and particularly the most essential matter of all, the custom relating to the census, by which the number of such as were of military age was ascertained, together with the amount of their fortunes, in proportion to which every man was to pay his contributions for war. There had been no census for seventeen years, since the [consulship] of Lucius Cornelius and Quintus Fabius,[1] [so that] . . . the basest and most licentious of the Romans shall leave (be left ?), but remove to some place in which they may live as they have elected to live.[2]

[1] See x. 20 f., where, however, no mention is made of a census.

[2] The fuller statement of M reads : " so that the good and useful citizens shall be in positions of honour and military commands (?), but the most licentious and base shall be left dishonoured and shall remove to another place in which they may live as they have elected to live."

---

[3] There follows in the MSS. the section extending from ἀλλ' ὑπὲρ τῶν Ῥωμαϊκῶν νόμων (chap. 44, 5) to μάρκος γε (chap. 51, 1). See the note on the former passage.

EXCERPTS[1]
FROM
BOOK XII

I. Ὅτι λιμοῦ κατὰ τὴν Ῥώμην γενομένου
ἰσχυροῦ ἀνήρ τις οἴκου τε οὐκ ἀφανοῦς καὶ χρήμασιν ἐν τοῖς μάλιστα δυνατός, Σπόριος Μαίλιος,[2]
Εὐδαίμων ἐπίκλησιν ἐπὶ τῆς πολλῆς εὐπορίας,
νεωστὶ μὲν παρειληφὼς τὸν οἶκον τοῦ πατρός,
ἡλικίαν δὲ[3] καὶ τάξιν ἔχων ἱππικήν, οἷα μήτε ἀρχὰς
παραλαμβάνειν μήτε ἄλλην κοινὴν ἐπιμέλειαν μηδεμίαν, λαμπρὸς εἰ καί τις ἄλλος τὰ πολέμια καὶ
πολλοῖς κεκοσμημένος ἀριστείοις, κράτιστον ὑπολαβὼν καιρὸν ἐπιθέσει τυραννίδος, ἐπὶ δημαγωγίαν
τοῦ πλήθους ἐτράπετο, τὴν ῥᾴστην[4] τῶν ἐπὶ τυραν-
2 νίδα φερουσῶν ὁδῶν. ἔχων δὲ πολλοὺς ἑταίρους
καὶ πελάτας ἄλλους ἄλλῃ διέπεμψε χρήματα δοὺς
ἐκ τῶν ἰδίων εἰς συναγυρμοὺς τροφῆς καὶ αὐτὸς
εἰς Τυρρηνίαν[5] ᾤχετο. ἐν βραχεῖ δὲ χρόνῳ δι᾽

[1] For a list of the collections from which the Excerpts from
Books XII-XX are taken and the MSS. containing these
collections see the Introduction to the present volume. In
the critical notes to these Excerpts departures of the present
text from that of Jacoby will not as a rule be recorded.

[2] The name appears usually as μάλλιος in S, less frequently
μάλιος, never μαίλιος. [3] Edd. : τε S.

EXCERPTS

FROM

BOOK XII

I. When a dire famine broke out in Rome,[1] a certain man of no inconspicuous family and among the most powerful by reason of his riches, Spurius Maelius, who was given the cognomen Felix because of his great wealth, having recently taken over the estate of his father, yet being unable by reason of his youth and equestrian rank to hold magistracies or any other public charge, as brilliant a man as any in warfare and decorated with many prizes for valour, conceived it to be the best time for aiming at a tyranny and turned to currying favour with the multitude, the easiest of all the roads leading to tyranny. Having many friends and clients, he dispatched them in various directions, giving them money from his own funds to collect food, while he himself went to Tyrrhenia. And having in a short

---

[1] For chaps. 1–4 *cf.* Livy iv. 13–16. The date of Maelius' " conspiracy " was 438 B.C. by Varro's chronology (probably 435 by that of Dionysius), four years subsequent to the events narrated in xi. 63.

---

⁴ Feder : ῥᾳστώνην S, Jacoby.
⁵ τυραννίαν S.

DIONYSIUS OF HALICARNASSUS

ἑαυτοῦ τε καὶ τῶν ἑταίρων πολλὴν κατακομίσας
ἀγορὰν διεμέτρει[1] τοῖς πολίταις, ἀντὶ δώδεκα
δραχμῶν διδράχμου ἀπομετρῶν τὸν μόδιον, ὅσους
δὲ αἴσθοιτο παντάπασιν ἀδυνάτους καὶ μηδ' ὑπὲρ
τῆς ἐφημέρου τροφῆς ἔχοντας προέσθαι τὸ διά-
3 φορον ἄνευ τιμῆς χαριζόμενος. ταύτῃ τῇ φιλανθρωπίᾳ τὸν δῆμον ἀναλαβὼν καὶ θαυμαστὴν ὅσην
δόξαν ἀπενεγκάμενος ᾤχετο πάλιν ἐμπορευσόμενος
ἑτέρας ἀγοράς· καὶ παρῆν οὐ διὰ μακροῦ ποτα-
μηγοὺς ἄγων σκάφας πολλὰς πάνυ μεστὰς[2] τροφῆς
καὶ τὸν αὐτὸν τρόπον τοῖς πολίταις ἐμέτρει.
4 Οἱ δὲ πατρίκιοι ταῦτα πράττοντα ὁρῶντες αὐτὸν
δι'[3] ὑποψίας τε ἐλάμβανον, τῆς ἄγαν φιλοτιμίας
τοῦ ἀνδρὸς οὐδὲν ἀγαθὸν[4] ἀπολαύσειν οἰόμενοι
καὶ συνιστάμενοι κατὰ τὴν ἀγορὰν ἐσκόπουν ὅντινα
χρὴ τρόπον εὐπρεπέστατ'[5] ἄνευ κινδύνου παῦσαι
τούτων αὐτὸν τῶν πολιτευμάτων, κρύφα μὲν τὸ
πρῶτον καὶ κατ' ὀλίγους συνιόντες καὶ διαλεγόμενοι πρὸς ἀλλήλους, ἔπειτα καὶ ἐκ τοῦ φανεροῦ
καταβοῶντες, ἐπειδὴ βαρύς τε[6] καὶ ἀφόρητος ἦν
ἔργα τε πράττων ὑπερηφανίας μεστὰ καὶ λόγους
5 διεξιὼν αὐθάδεις ὑπὲρ ἑαυτοῦ· ὅς γε πρῶτον μὲν
καθεζόμενος ἐπὶ βήματος περιφανοῦς, ὥσπερ ἔθος
ἐστὶν[7] τοῖς τὰς ἀρχὰς ἔχουσιν, ἐχρημάτιζε τοῖς
προσιοῦσι δι' ἡμέρας περὶ τὴν σιτοδοσίαν, ἐκβαλὼν
τῆς τιμῆς ταύτης τὸν ἀποδειχθέντα ἔπαρχον[8] ὑπὸ
6 τῆς βουλῆς· ἔπειτα συνεχεῖς ποιούμενος ἐκκλησίας,

---

[1] Müller : διεμέρει S.   [2] Feder : μετὰ S.
[3] δι' added by Jacoby.
[4] οὐδὲν ἀγαθὸν Jacoby : οὐδὲν ἀγαθοῦ S, οὐδενὸς ἀγαθοῦ
Kiessling.
[5] Garrer : εὐπρεπέστερον S, Jacoby.
[6] τε Müller : ἔτι S.

time by his own efforts and those of his friends imported a large store of corn, he distributed it among the citizens, measuring out a peck for two denarii instead of for twelve denarii, and upon all those whom he perceived to be utterly helpless and unable to defray the cost of even their daily subsistence bestowing it without payment. After winning over the people by this kindly service and gaining a most remarkable reputation, he went off again to import further supplies ; and he was back before long with a very large number of river boats filled with food, which he distributed to the citizens in the same manner.

The patricians, as they observed these activities of his, regarded him with suspicion, thinking that no good would come to them from the man's prodigality ; and gathering together in the Forum, they considered how they ought in most seemly fashion and without danger to force him to desist from these political designs. At first they met secretly and in small groups and discussed the matter with one another, but later they clamoured against him openly as well, now that he was offensive and insufferable, not only performing acts full of arrogance, but also delivering haughty speeches in his own behalf. For, in the first place, he sat upon a conspicuous tribunal, as is the custom with those who hold magistracies, and gave advice the whole day long to those who consulted him about the distribution of corn, having relieved of this function the prefect [1] who had been appointed by the senate. Again, calling continual meetings of

[1] Minucius.

---

[7] ἐστὶν S, according to Müller : ἦν Feder(?) and later editors. [8] Feder : ὕπαρχον S.

οὐκ ὂν ἐν ἔθει Ῥωμαίοις ἰδιώτην ἐκκλησίαν
συνάγειν, πολλὰ μὲν τοῦ Μηνυκίου[1] κατηγόρει
πρὸς τὸν δῆμον, ὡς ὄνομα φέροντος ἀρχῆς μόνον,
ἔργον δὲ οὐδὲν ἀποδειξαμένου τοῖς πένησιν ὠφέ-
λιμον, πολλὰ δὲ τοὺς πατρικίους διέβαλλε πρὸς
τὸν δῆμον ὡς ταῦτα πράττοντας[2] ἐξ ὧν ὀλίγου[3]
τε καὶ οὐδενὸς ἄξιος ὁ δῆμος ἔσται καὶ οὐδὲ ἐπὶ
σιτοδείᾳ φροντίδα τῶν ἀπόρων ἔχοντας οὐδεμίαν,
οὔτε κοινῇ πάντας οὔτε ἰδίᾳ τοὺς δυνατούς, παντὸς
μάλιστα δέον αὐτοὺς χρήμασί τε καὶ σώμασιν
ὥσπερ αὐτὸς δὴ κακοπαθεῖν καὶ πάντοθεν ἐπεισ-
7 άγειν τῇ πόλει τὰς ἀγοράς. ἠξίου τε πρὸς τὰ
τῶν ἄλλων ἔργα πατρικίων τὰ ὑφ' ἑαυτοῦ πραττόμενα ἐξετάζειν, ὡς πολὺ καὶ τὸ πᾶν ἀλλήλων
διαφέροντα. ἐκείνους μὲν γὰρ οὐδὲν ἐκ τῶν ἰδίων
εἰς τὸ κοινὸν ἀναλίσκοντας ἔτι καὶ τὴν δημοσίαν
γῆν σφετερισαμένους πολὺν[4] ἤδη καρποῦσθαι χρόνον, ἑαυτὸν δὲ τῶν δημοσίων οὐδὲν ἔχοντα ἔτι
καὶ τὴν πατρῴαν καταχορηγεῖν οὐσίαν εἰς βοήθειαν
τῶν ἀπόρων καί, ἐπειδὰν τὰ ὄντα καταναλώσῃ,
δανείσματα ποιεῖσθαι παρὰ φίλων οὐθὲν ἀντι-
καταλλαττόμενον τῆς τοιαύτης φιλοτιμίας ὅτι μὴ
τὴν πολιτικὴν εὔνοιαν, ἧς οὐδὲ τὸν ἐξ ἀνθρώπων
8 πλοῦτον ἡγεῖσθαι τιμιώτερον. οἱ δὲ περὶ αὐτὸν
συνεστῶτες ἀεὶ σωτῆρα καὶ πατέρα καὶ κτίστην
ἀπεκάλουν τῆς πατρίδος καὶ τὴν μὲν ὑπατικὴν
ἐξουσίαν ἐλάττονα χάριν ἢ κατὰ τὸ μέγεθος τῶν

---

[1] μινυκίου S here, elsewhere μηνυκ-. [2] πράττοντες S.
[3] Jacoby : ὀλίγους S, ὀλίγος Edd. [4] πολλήν S.

the assembly, although it was not customary among the Romans for a private individual to convoke an assembly, he indulged in many denunciations of Minucius before the people, charging that he merely bore the name of magistrate but had performed no useful act in the interest of the poor ; and he uttered many reproaches against the patricians before the popular assembly for doing the things which would make the populace of little or no account and for taking no thought, either all of them together or the influential men singly, for the needy even on the occasion of a scarcity of corn, when it was essential above everything else that they, like himself, should submit to hardships both in their fortunes and in their persons and should import provisions into the city from every possible source. He asked the people to weigh his own achievements against the actions of the other patricians and to note how greatly, nay, how utterly, they differed from one another. For they, he said, spent nothing from their private fortunes for the common good, but had even appropriated the public land and had for a long time now enjoyed its use, whereas he, who held none of the public possessions, devoted even his paternal inheritance to assisting the needy, and when he had used up the funds on hand, raised loans from his friends, receiving nothing in return for such munificence save only the goodwill of his fellow citizens, a reward which he considered quite as precious as the greatest wealth in the world. Those who were leagued with him were continually hailing him as the saviour, father and founder of the fatherland ; and declaring that the giving of the consular power to him would be a favour incommensurate with the greatness of

ἔργων αὐτοῦ γενήσεσθαι δοθεῖσαν ἀπέφαινον, ἄλλῃ
δέ τινι μείζονι καὶ λαμπροτέρᾳ[1] τιμῇ κοσμεῖν
ἠξίουν αὐτόν, ἣν καὶ γένος ἕξει τὸ ἐξ ἐκείνου.
9 ὡς δὲ καὶ τὴν τρίτην ἔξοδον ποιησάμενος ἐπὶ τὰ
παραθαλάττια τῆς Ἰταλίας ἔκ τε Κύμης καὶ τῶν
περὶ Μισηνὸν λιμένων σιτηγοὺς ὁλκάδας ἄγων
πολλὰς κατέπλευσεν εἰς Ὠστίαν, ὃ τῆς Ῥώμης
ἐστὶν ἐπίνειον, καὶ ἐπέκλυσε[2] ταῖς τροφαῖς τὴν
πόλιν, ὡς μηδὲν ἔτι τῆς ἀρχαίας εὐετηρίας διαφέρειν, ἅπας ὁ δῆμος ἕτοιμος ἦν, εἰ γένοιτο τῆς
ψήφου κύριος ἐν[3] ἀρχαιρεσίαις, εἴτε ὑπατείαν εἴτε
ἄλλην τινὰ τιμὴν μετίοι, μηδενὸς ἐπιστρεφόμενος[4]
μήτε νόμου κωλύοντος μήτ' ἀνδρὸς ἐναντιουμένου
10 χαρίζεσθαι. ταῦτα ὁρῶντες οἱ προεστηκότες τῆς
ἀριστοκρατίας καὶ οὔτε ἐπιτρέπειν ἀξιοῦντες οὔτε
κωλύειν δύναμιν ἔχοντες ἐν πολλῇ πάντες ἦσαν
ἀθυμίᾳ· καὶ ἔτι μᾶλλον διεταράχθησαν, ἐπειδὴ
κωλυόντων ἐκκλησίας συνάγειν αὐτὸν καὶ δημη-
γορεῖν τῶν τε δημάρχων καὶ ὑπάτων, συστραφεὶς
ὁ δῆμος ἐκείνους μὲν ἐξέβαλεν ἐκ τῆς ἀγορᾶς, τῷ
δὲ Μαιλίῳ πολλὴν ἄδειαν καὶ ῥώμην παρέσχεν.
11 Ἐν τοιαύτῃ δὴ καταστάσει τῆς πόλεως ὑπαρχούσης ὁ τῆς ἀγορᾶς ἀποδειχθεὶς ἔπαρχος, ἀχθό-
μενος μὲν ἐπὶ τοῖς προπηλακισμοῖς τῶν λόγων
οἷς αὐτὸν ὑβρίζων ὁ Μαίλιος ἐν ταῖς ἐκκλησίαις
διετέλει, δεδοικὼς δὲ τὸν ἄνδρα μάλιστα τῶν
ἄλλων, εἴ τινος ἐπιλάβοιτο ἀρχῆς, μὴ πρότερον[5]

---

[1] Kiessling : λαμπρᾷ S.
[2] ἐπέκλυσε (cf. vi. 17, 4; xiv. 5; xv. 2, 2) Cary : κατέπαυσε
S, κατέπλησε Müller, κατέκλυσε Kiessling, ἐνέπλησε Kayser.
[3] ἐπ' S.

his deeds, they wished to distinguish him with some greater and more brilliant honour, which should also be enjoyed by his posterity. When he had made his third trip to the maritime districts of Italy and had sailed back to Ostia, the seaport of Rome, bringing many merchantmen laden with corn from Cumae and the harbours round Misenum, and had deluged the city with provisions, so that none of the old-time abundance was any longer lacking, the whole populace was ready, as soon as it was empowered to vote for magistrates, to grant him whatever honour he might seek, whether the consulship or some other magistracy, paying no heed to any law that forbade it or to any man who opposed it. When the leaders of the aristocracy perceived this, they were all in great dejection, neither being willing to permit it nor yet having the power to prevent it. And they were still more disturbed because, when both the tribunes and the consuls forbade him to convoke assemblies and harangue the people, the populace banded together and drove those magistrates out of the Forum, while affording great assurance and strength to Maelius.

While the city was in this state, the man who had been appointed prefect of the corn supply became angered at the abusive language with which Maelius kept insulting him in the meetings of the assembly, and feared the man more than any others, lest, if he should obtain some magistracy, he might make him-

---

4 Müller : ἐπιτρέποντος S, Jacoby.
5 πρότερον, though found in Isaeus and Demosthenes in the sense of " superior," is very doubtful here. Kayser proposed to read λαμπρότερον. Post would read μὴ πρόπειραν τῆς ἀρ. ποιήσηται (or ἐν αὑτῷ ποιήσηται).

τῆς ἀριστοκρατίας αὐτὸν[1] ποιήσηται ἢ τὸν δῆμον
ἐξερεθίσας πρὸς αὐτὸν †ποιήσηται[2] διὰ τῶν[3] ἐκ
τῆς ἑταιρείας ἐπιβουλήν τινα κατ' αὐτοῦ μηχανησάμενος,[4] ἀγανακτῶν τε δι' ἀμφότερα ταῦτα καὶ
ἀπηλλάχθαι προθυμούμενος ἐκείνου μείζονα ἢ κατ'
ἰδιώτην ἰσχὺν ἔχοντος, ἐπιμελῆ ζήτησιν ἐποιεῖτο
τῶν ὑπ' αὐτοῦ λεγομένων τε καὶ πραττομένων.
12 πολλῶν δὲ ὄντων οἷς ὁ ἀνὴρ συνεργοῖς ἐχρῆτο τῶν
ἀπορρήτων, καὶ οὔτε τὰς φύσεις ὁμοίων οὔτε τὰς
γνώμας παραπλησίων, ἔμελλέ τις, ὅπερ εἰκός, οὐ
βέβαιος[5] αὐτῷ[6] ἔσεσθαι φίλος, ἢ διὰ φόβον ἢ διὰ
κέρδος ἴδιον· ᾧ τὰ πιστὰ δοὺς ὁ Μηνύκιος ὑπὲρ
τοῦ μηδενὶ φράσειν ὅστις ἦν, ἅπασαν ἔγνω τήν τε
13 διάνοιαν τοῦ Μαιλίου καὶ τὴν παρασκευήν. ὡς
δὲ καὶ τεκμήριον ἔλαβεν ἀναμφίλεκτον καὶ τὴν
πρᾶξιν ἐν χερσὶν οὖσαν ἔγνω, λέγει πρὸς τοὺς
ὑπάτους· ἐκεῖνοι δὲ οὐκ ἀξιοῦντες ἐφ' ἑαυτοῖς
ποιῆσαι μόνοις ἐπιχειρήσεως τηλικαύτης ἐξέτασιν
εἰς τὴν βουλὴν ᾤοντο δεῖν τὸ πρᾶγμα εἰσφέρειν,[7]
καὶ συνεκάλουν τὸ συνέδριον εὐθὺς ὡς περὶ πολέμου
14 δή τινος ὑπερορίου βουλευσόμενοι.[8] πληρωθέντος
δὲ τοῦ συνεδρίου διὰ ταχέων παρελθὼν ἅτερος
αὐτῶν ἔλεξεν ὅτι πρᾶξις αὐτοῖς μεμήνυται συ-
σκευαζομένη κατὰ τῆς πόλεως πολλῆς πάνυ καὶ

---

[1] αὐτὸν S.
[2] ποιήσηται is doubtless, as Müller suggested, a careless
repetition from the line above. Post would delete, but would
add ἢ before διὰ, retaining μηχανησάμενος in the next line.
[3] τὴν S.
[4] μηχανήσηται Müller.
[5] Müller : βέβαιον S, βεβαίως Kiessling.
[6] Edd. : αὐτὸν S.
[7] Edd. : ἐφερεῖν S.
[8] Feder : βουλευόμενοι S.

self more powerful (?) [1] than the aristocracy or, by rousing the people against him (Minucius), might, through the agency of the men of his own faction, contrive some plot against him, and being indignant on both these accounts and being eager to be rid of him as a man having greater power than befitted one in private station, he proceeded to make a careful investigation of both his speeches and his actions. And as those whom Maelius employed as confederates in his secret plans were numerous and were neither alike in their natures nor similar in their opinions, there was bound to be someone who, in all probability, would not continue a steady friend to him, either because of fear or for personal advantage; and when Minucius had given this man pledges that he would not reveal his identity to anyone, he learned the entire purpose of Maelius and his plans for accomplishing it. After he had obtained incontrovertible proof and learned that the execution of the plot was imminent, he informed the consuls. Those magistrates, not feeling it right to carry out by themselves alone the investigation of so serious a plot, thought they ought to lay the matter before the senate; and they straightway called that body together, ostensibly to deliberate about some foreign war. A full meeting of the senate being soon present, one of the consuls came forward and stated that information had been given them of a plot forming against the commonwealth, one that required very

---

[1] The text of two lines here is very doubtful. Post's proposed changes would give: " lest he should make trial of the aristocracy (in him) [*i.e.*, in the person of Minucius], either by rousing the people against him or by contriving some plot against him through the agency of the men of his own faction."

ταχείας φυλακῆς δεομένη διὰ τὸ τοῦ κινδύνου
μέγεθος· ταύτης δ' ἔφη μηνυτὴν οὐ τῶν ἐπιτυχόντων εἶναί τινα πολιτῶν, ἀλλ' ὃν αὐτοὶ δι'
ἀρετὴν ἐπὶ τῆς μεγίστης τε καὶ ἀναγκαιοτάτης
τῷ κοινῷ χρείας ἔταξαν, δοκιμάσαντες αὐτοῦ τήν
τε πίστιν καὶ τὴν πρὸς τὰ κοινὰ φιλοτιμίαν ἐκ
15 τῶν παρὰ πάντα τὸν βίον ἐπιτηδευομένων. μετεώρου δὴ[1] τῆς βουλῆς ἐπὶ τῇ προσδοκίᾳ γενομένης
ἐκάλει τὸν Μηνύκιον, κἀκεῖνος ἔλεξεν· [Ζήτει ἐν
τῷ περὶ δημηγοριῶν]. Esc.

II. Ὡς δὲ ἐμηνύθη τῇ βουλῇ, δικτάτορα προ-
χειρίζονται, ὁ δὲ τὸν ἱππάρχην . . .[2] ἐκέλευσεν
ἔχοντι τοὺς ἱππεῖς ἥκειν ὡς αὐτὸν περὶ μέσας
νύκτας, τοῖς δὲ βουλευταῖς εἰς τὸ Καπιτώλιον
ἔωθεν ἔτι συλλέγεσθαι, τῷ δὲ[3] Μηνυκίῳ τόν τε
μηνυτὴν ἄγοντι καὶ τὰς ἄλλας ἀποδείξεις κομίζοντι
πρὸς τὸ βῆμα παρεῖναι, ἅπασι δὲ φυλάττειν
ἀπόρρητα πρὸς τοὺς ἔξω τοῦ συνεδρίου τὰ βουλεύματα, μίαν εἶναι λέγων ἀσφάλειαν, εἰ μηδὲν ὁ
Μαίλιος ἀκούσειε τῶν περὶ αὐτοῦ λεγομένων τε
2 καὶ πραττομένων. διατάξας δὲ τἆλλα ὅσων ἐδεῖτο,[4]
μέχρι δύσεως ἡλίου πάντας ἐν τῷ βουλευτηρίῳ
κατασχὼν σκότους ὄντος ἤδη διέλυσε τὸν σύλλογον·
ὡς δὲ μέση νὺξ ἐγένετο, προελθὼν ἐκ τῆς οἰκίας
. . .[5] ἐξῄει[6] περὶ τὸν ὄρθρον τοὺς ἐπιλέκτους
ἀμφοτέρων[7] τῶν ὑπάτων ἐπαγόμενος καὶ αὐτοὺς
3 τοὺς ὑπάτους. οὗτοι μὲν οὖν τὸ Καπιτώλιον ἅμα
τοῖς βουλευταῖς ἔωθεν[8] κατειληφότες ἐφρούρουν.

---

[1] δὲ S.
[2] Lacuna recognized by Müller, who suggested ἀποδείξας
or καλέσας as the missing word.
[3] τε S.
[4] ἐδεῖτο S : ἔδει τότε Kiessling.

vigorous and prompt precautionary measures because
of the magnitude of the danger. He added that the
informant was not just an ordinary citizen, but a man
whom the senators themselves because of his merits
had placed in a position of the greatest and most
essential service to the state, having satisfied themselves of his good faith and his zeal for the public
interests as shown by his deportment throughout his
whole life. Then, when the senate was quite wrought
up with expectation, he called Minucius, who said :
[The MS. adds : See the section on Harangues.]

II. When the information had been given to the
senate, they chose a dictator, and he, [having
appointed] his Master of Horse, ordered him to come
to him with the knights about midnight, and he
ordered the senators to assemble on the Capitol
while it was still early morning ; he commanded
Minucius to appear before the tribunal bringing
along the informer and the proofs as well, and bade
all to keep these plans secret from everybody outside the senate, declaring that there was just one
means of safety, which was for Maelius to hear naught
of what was being said or done about him. After
making all the other necessary arrangements, he kept
all the members in the senate-house until sunset, and
only dismissed the session when it was already dark.
When it was midnight, setting out from his house
. . . he went forth about dawn, taking along the
chosen forces of both consuls and the consuls themselves. These together with the senators seized the
Capitol at dawn and kept it under guard.

---

⁵ Lacuna recognized by Edd.   ⁶ ἐξίει S.
⁷ ὑπ' ἀμφοτέρων Kiessling.
⁸ Müller : ἔξωθεν S.

Ὁ δὲ Μαίλιος οὐδὲν ἀκηκοὼς τούτων ἡμέρας
γενομένης προελθὼν εἰς τὴν ἀγορὰν ἐχρημάτιζε
τοῖς δεομένοις ἐπὶ τοῦ βήματος καθεζόμενος· καὶ
μετ' οὐ πολὺ παρῆν ὁ ἵππαρχος Σερουίλιος πρὸς
αὐτὸν ἄγων τοὺς ἀκμαιοτάτους τῶν ἱππέων ἔχοντας
ὑπὸ[1] τοῖς ἱματίοις ξίφη καὶ στὰς πλησίον αὐτοῦ
4 λέγει· "Ὁ δικτάτωρ σε κελεύει, Μαίλιε, πρὸς
αὐτὸν ἥκειν"· κἀκεῖνος ὑποτυχών, "Ποῖος," ἔφη,
"κελεύει με, Σερουίλιε, δικτάτωρ πρὸς αὐτὸν
ἐλθεῖν, ὁ ποῦ[2] καὶ πότε γενόμενος;" καὶ ἅμα
διαταραχθεὶς περιέβλεψεν εἰς τοὺς περὶ τὸ βῆμα.
ἀφασίας δὲ ἅπαντας κατασχούσης διὰ τὸ μηδένα
γινώσκειν τὰ πραχθέντα ὑπὸ τῆς βουλῆς λέγει
πάλιν ὁ Σερουίλιος· "Εἰσηγγέλθης χθὲς εἰς τὴν
βουλήν, ὦ Μαίλιε, νεωτέροις ἐπιχειρεῖν πράγμασιν,
ἴσως οὐκ ἀληθῶς· οὐδενὸς γὰρ ἄξιον ἀπὸ τῆς
5 αἰτίας προκαταγινώσκειν. ταύτην ἐξετάσαι τὴν
μήνυσιν ἡ βουλὴ προελομένη δικτάτορος ἔφησε
δεῖν τοῖς πράγμασιν, ὡς οὐ τὸν ἐλάχιστον τῶν
κινδύνων τρέχουσα, καὶ ἀπέδειξε τῆς ἐξουσίας
ταύτης κύριον Λεύκιον Κοΐντιον Κικιννᾶτον, ὃν
οἶσθα δήπου καὶ σὺ κράτιστον ὄντα τῶν πατρικίων
καὶ δὶς ἤδη ταύτην ἀνεπιλήπτως τετελεκότα τὴν
6 ἀρχήν. οὗτος ὁ ἀνὴρ δικαστήριόν σοι καθίσαι
καὶ λόγον ἀποδοῦναι βουλόμενος ἀπέσταλκεν ἡμᾶς,
ἐμὲ τὸν ἵππαρχον ἅμα τοῖσδε τοῖς ἀνδράσιν,
ἄξοντάς[3] σε ἀσφαλῶς ἐπὶ τὴν ἀπολογίαν. εἰ δὲ
μηδὲν ἀδικεῖν πέποιθας, ἴθι καὶ λέγε τὰ δίκαια
περὶ σαυτοῦ πρὸς ἄνδρα φιλόπολιν, ὃς οὔτε διὰ
τὸν κοινὸν φθόνον οὔτε δι' ἄλλην ἄδικον πρόφασιν

---

[1] ὑπὸ Edd. : ἐπὶ S.   [2] ὁ ποῦ Feder : ὅπου S.
[3] Müller : ἄξοντά S.

Maelius, who had heard nothing of all this, proceeded to the Forum when day had come, and seated upon the tribunal, gave advice to those who consulted him. In a short time the Master of Horse, Servilius, appeared before him with the flower of the knights, who carried swords under their clothing ; and halting near him, he said : " The dictator commands you, Maelius, to come to him." And the other, answering, said : " What dictator, Servilius, commands me to go to him ? Where and when did he become dictator ? " At the same time he looked round in consternation at the people surrounding the tribunal. When all were speechless, inasmuch as no one was aware of the action taken by the senate, Servilius said once more : " An act of impeachment was brought against you yesterday before the senate, Maelius, for attempting a revolution ; perhaps the charge was false, for it is not right to prejudge anyone on the basis of the charge alone. The senate, having decided to investigate the report, declared that the situation required a dictator, since they were running no slight risk ; and they invested with this authority Lucius Quintius Cincinnatus, who, as you yourself are doubtless aware, is the best of the patricians and has twice already discharged the duties of this magistracy in an irreproachable manner. This man, desiring to set up a court to try you and to give you an opportunity to defend yourself, has sent us— me, the Master of Horse, together with these men here —to conduct you in safety to make your defence. If you are confident you have done no wrong, come and offer your justification before a man who loves his country and will not wish to put you out of the way either because of the general ill will toward you or

207

7 οὐδεμίαν ἐκποδὼν ποιῆσαί σε[1] βουλήσεται."

δ' ὡς ἤκουσεν, ἀναπηδᾷ[2] τε καὶ μεγάλα ἀναβοήσας, "'Ἄνδρες," ἔφη, "δημοτικοί, βοηθεῖτέ μοι συναρπαζομένῳ[3] διὰ τὴν πρὸς ὑμᾶς εὔνοιαν ὑπὸ τῶν δυνατῶν· οὐ γὰρ ἐπὶ δίκην καλοῦμαι[4] πρὸς αὐτῶν,[5] ἀλλ' ἐπὶ θάνατον καλοῦμαι.[4]" βοῆς δὲ γενομένης καὶ θορύβου πολλοῦ περὶ τὸ βῆμα, συγγνοὺς ὅτι πλείους εἰσὶ τῶν βοηθούντων οἱ συλλαμβάνειν μέλλοντες αὐτόν, καὶ οὐ μακρὰν ἑτέρους ὑποκαθῆσθαι[6] ἐν ὅπλοις, καταπηδᾷ ταχέως ἀπὸ τοῦ βήματος καὶ διὰ τῆς ἀγορᾶς ἐχώρει δρόμῳ σπεύ-
8 δων εἰς τὴν οἰκίαν καταφυγεῖν. καταλαμβανόμενος δ' ὑπὸ τῶν ἱππέων εἰς ἐργαστήριον εἰστρέχει μαγειρικὸν καὶ κοπίδα τῶν κρεοκόπων ἁρπάσας παίει τὸν πρῶτον αὐτῷ προσελθόντα. ἔπειτα πολλῶν ἐπιπεσόντων ἀθρόων[7] ἀμυνόμενος καὶ βραχὺν ἀντισχὼν χρόνον ἀπεκόπη ὑπό τινος τὸν βραχίονα καὶ πίπτει καὶ κατακοπεὶς ὥσπερ θηρίον ἀποθνήσκει.

9 Μαίλιος μὲν δὴ μεγάλων ὀρεχθεὶς πραγμάτων καὶ μικροῦ πάνυ δεήσας τὴν Ῥωμαίων ἡγεμονίαν κατασχεῖν οὕτως ἀζήλου καὶ πικρᾶς καταστροφῆς ἔτυχεν. ἐξενεχθέντος δὲ εἰς τὴν ἀγορὰν τοῦ νεκροῦ καὶ γενηθέντος πᾶσι φανεροῦ δρόμος ἦν καὶ βοὴ καὶ θόρυβος ἁπάντων τῶν κατὰ τὴν ἀγοράν, τῶν μὲν οἰκτειρόντων, τῶν δὲ ἀγανακτούντων, τῶν δὲ
10 ὁμόσε τοῖς δεδρακόσι[8] χωρεῖν ἐσπουδακότων. τοι-

---

[1] Edd. : ποιήσεσαι S.
[2] Feder : ἀναπήδα S, ἀνεπήδα Müller.
[3] ἀναρπαζομένῳ (cf. chap. 4, 1) Cobet.
[4] καλοῦμαι is spurious in one of these two lines. Kiessling

on any other unjust ground." Maelius, upon hearing
this, leaped up and cried out in a loud voice :
" Plebeians, help me ; for I am being snatched away
by the men in power because of my goodwill toward
you. For it is not to a trial that I am summoned by
them, but to death." When a clamour arose and
there was a great uproar round the tribunal, Maelius,
aware that those who were intending to arrest him
were more numerous than those who were rallying
to his aid and that not far away others were lying
in wait under arms, quickly leaped down from the
tribunal and ran off through the Forum in his haste to
reach the refuge of his own home. But when he was
being overtaken by the knights, he ran into a butcher's
shop, and seizing a cleaver used by the meat-cutters,
he struck the first man who approached him. Then,
when many fell upon him at once, he defended himself and held out for a short time ; but soon his arm
was cut off by someone and he fell down, and being
hacked in pieces, died like a wild beast.

Thus Maelius, who craved greatness and came very
close to gaining the leadership over the Roman people,
came to an unenviable and bitter end. When his
body had been carried into the Forum and exposed
to the view of all the citizens, there was a rush thither
and a clamour and uproar on the part of all who were
in the Forum, as some bewailed his fate, others angrily
protested, and still others were eager to come to blows
with the perpetrators of the deed. The dictator,

---

simply deleted the first, while de Boor thought the second
had replaced another verb.

[5] Kiessling : αὐτὸν S.
[6] Feder : ὑποκαθιεῖσθαι S.   [7] Feder : ἀθρόον S.
[8] τοῖς δεδρακόσι Müller : τῶν δεδρακότων S.

DIONYSIUS OF HALICARNASSUS

αὐτῆς δὲ ταραχῆς γενομένης μαθὼν ὁ δικτάτωρ
ὅτι διαπέπρακται τοῖς ἱππεῦσι τὸ προσταχθὲν
ἔργον, κατέβαινεν ἀπὸ τῆς ἄκρας εἰς τὴν ἀγορὰν
τούς τε βουλευτὰς ἐπαγόμενος ἅπαντας καὶ τοὺς
ἱππεῖς περὶ ἑαυτὸν ἔχων γυμνὰ φαίνοντας[1] ξίφη·
καὶ δημηγορήσας ἐπ᾽ ἐκκλησίας ἀπέλυσε τὸν
ὄχλον. *Esc.*

III. (1) " . . . ἔχων περὶ ἑαυτὸν ἀνθρώπους ἐξ
ἁπάσης συνειλεγμένους κακίας, οὓς ἐσίτιζεν ὥσπερ
θηρία κατὰ τῆς πατρίδος. εἰ μὲν οὖν ὑπήκουσέ
μοι καὶ παρέσχεν ἑαυτὸν ἐν τοῖς νόμοις μένοντα,
μεγίστην ἂν τοῦτ᾽ αὐτῷ παρέσχε ῥοπὴν εἰς τὴν
ἀπολογίαν καὶ τεκμήριον οὐκ ἐλάχιστον ἦν τοῦ
μηδὲν[2] βεβουλεῦσθαι κατὰ τῆς πατρίδος· νῦν δ᾽
ὑπὸ τῆς συνειδήσεως ἐλαυνόμενος, ὃ πάσχουσιν
ἅπαντες οἱ τὰς ἀνοσίους βουλὰς κατὰ τῶν ἀναγκαιοτάτων σφίσι ποιησάμενοι, τοῦτο ἔπαθε[3]· φυγεῖν[4]
τὸν ἔλεγχον ἔγνω καὶ τοὺς ἥκοντας ἐπ᾽ αὐτὸν
ἱππεῖς μαγειρικῇ κοπίδι παίων ἀπήλαυνεν . . ."
Ambr.

IV. Τῶν δὲ δημοτικῶν οἱ μὲν οὐ[5] συμβουλεύ-
σαντες ἐπὶ[6] τῇ καταλύσει τῆς πολιτείας ἠγανάκτουν
καὶ δι᾽ ὀργῆς τὴν ἐπιχείρησιν τοῦ ἀνδρὸς ἐλάμβανον,
οἱ δὲ κοινωνήσαντες τῆς συνωμοσίας ἀφειμένοι
τοῦ φόβου χαίρειν τε προσεποιοῦντο καὶ τὸ συνέδριον τῶν βουλευμάτων ἐπήνουν· ὀλίγοι δέ τινες
ἐξ αὐτῶν οἱ πονηρότατοι λογοποιεῖν ἐτόλμων ἐν
ταῖς ἑξῆς ἡμέραις ὡς ἀνηρπασμένου πρὸς τῶν
δυνατῶν τοῦ Μαιλίου καὶ διαστασιάζειν τὸν δῆμον

---

[1] φέροντας Garrer.　　　[2] Kiessling : μὴ S.
[3] τοῦτο ἔπαθε deleted by Naber.
[4] φυγεῖν τε Müller.

apprised by such a tumult that the knights had carried out the task assigned to them, descended from the citadel to the Forum, bringing with him all the senators and surrounded by the knights displaying naked swords ; and after haranguing the people in their assembly he dismissed the crowd.

III. (1) " . . . having about him men gathered together from every kind of depravity, whom he was rearing up like wild beasts against the fatherland.[1] If, now, he had listened to me and had shown himself a man who abided by the laws, this would have contributed the greatest weight toward his defence and would have been no slight proof that he had not formed any plot against the fatherland ; but as it was, goaded by his conscience, he was moved in the same way as are all who have formed unholy plots against those nearest to them : he determined to avoid the investigation of his acts, and striking with a butcher's cleaver the knights who had come for him, he endeavoured to drive them away."

IV. Of the plebeians, those who had not joined in plotting for the overthrow of the government were indignant and angry at the man's attempt, while those who had shared in the conspiracy, being now freed from their fear, pretended to rejoice and praised the senate for the measures it had taken ; but some few of them, the most knavish, made bold during the following days to spread reports to the effect that Maelius had been made away with by the men in power, and attempted to sow dissension

[1] This excerpt is presumably from the speech delivered by the dictator, Cincinnatus, before the popular assembly ; *cf.* Livy iv. 15.

---

[5] μὲν οὐ added by Müller.   [6] ἐπὶ added by Kiessling.

ἐπεχείρουν· οὓς ἀφανεῖ θανάτῳ διαχρησάμενος ὁ δικτάτωρ, ἐπειδὴ κατέπαυσε τὸν θόρυβον,[1] τὴν ἀρχὴν ἀποτίθεται.

2 Οἱ μὲν δὴ τὰ πιθανώτατά μοι[2] δοκοῦντες γράφειν περὶ τῆς Μαιλίου τελευτῆς οὕτω παραδεδώκασι· λεγέσθω δὲ καὶ ὁ δοκῶν ἧττον εἶναί μοι πιθανὸς λόγος, ᾧ κέχρηται Κίγκιος καὶ Καλπούρνιος,[3] ἐπιχώριοι συγγραφεῖς, οἵ φασιν οὔτε δικτάτορα ὑπὸ τῆς βουλῆς ἀποδειχθῆναι τὸν Κοΐντιον οὔτε 3 ἱππάρχην ὑπὸ τοῦ Κοϊντίου τὸν Σερουίλιον. γενομένης δὲ μηνύσεως[4] ὑπὸ τοῦ Μηνυκίου τοὺς παρόντας ἐν τῷ συνεδρίῳ πιστεύσαντας ἀληθῆ τὰ λεγόμενα εἶναι, γνώμην ἀποδειξαμένου τῶν πρεσβυτέρων τινὸς ἄκριτον ἀποκτεῖναι[5] τὸν ἄνδρα παραχρῆμα πεισθέντας καὶ[6] οὕτω τὸν Σερουίλιον ἐπὶ τοῦτο τάξαι τὸ ἔργον, νέον ὄντα καὶ κατὰ χεῖρα 4 γενναῖον. τοῦτον δέ φασι λαβόντα τὸ ξιφίδιον ὑπὸ μάλης ἐλθεῖν πρὸς τὸν Μαίλιον πορευόμενον ἐκ τῆς ἀγορᾶς καὶ προσελθόντα εἰπεῖν ὅτι βούλεται περὶ πράγματος ἀπορρήτου καὶ μεγάλου διαλεχθῆναι πρὸς αὐτόν. κελεύσαντος δὲ τοῦ Μαιλίου μικρὸν ἀποχωρῆσαι τοὺς ἐγγὺς αὐτῷ παρόντας, ἐπειδὴ μονωθέντα τῆς φυλακῆς ἔλαβε, γυμνώσαντα τὸ ξίφος βάψαι κατὰ τῆς σφαγῆς· τοῦτο δὲ πράξαντα δρόμῳ χωρεῖν εἰς τὸ βουλευτήριον ἔτι συγκαθημένων τῶν συνέδρων, ἔχοντα τὸ ξίφος ἡμαγμένον καὶ[7] κεκραγότα πρὸς τοὺς διώκοντας ὅτι κελευσθεὶς ὑπὸ τῆς βουλῆς ἀνῄρηκε τὸν τύραν-

---

[1] τὸν θόρυβον Feder : τοῦ θορύβου S, Jacoby.
[2] μοι Edd. : μου S.
[3] κίρκεος καὶ καλπουρίνος S.
[4] μηνύσεως Feder : τῆς μηνύσεως S.
[5] ἢ μὴν (ἢ μὲν S) deleted before ἀποκτεῖναι by Kayser.

among the people. The dictator put these men to death secretly, and after allaying the disturbance, resigned his magistracy.

Now those who seem to me to give the most credible account of Maelius' death have handed down the above report; but let me record also the account which appears to me less credible, the one adopted by Cincius and Calpurnius,[1] native writers. These men state that neither was Quintius appointed dictator by the senate nor Servilius made Master of Horse by Quintius. But when information was given by Minucius, those who were present in the senate believed that the things reported were true, and when one of the older senators made a motion to put the man to death immediately without a trial, they were convinced and accordingly appointed for this task Servilius, who was a young man and brave in action. Servilius, they say, taking his dagger under his arm, approached Maelius as he was proceeding from the Forum, and coming up to him, said that he wished to speak with him about a private matter of great importance. Then, when Maelius ordered those who were close to him to withdraw to a little distance, the other, having thus got him separated from his guard, bared his sword and plunged it into his throat; and after doing this he ran to the senate-house, where the senators were still in session, brandishing his sword that dripped with blood and shouting to those who pursued him that he had destroyed the tyrant at the command of the senate.

[1] L. Cincius Alimentus and L. Calpurnius Piso Frugi.

---

[6] πεισθέντας καὶ S : πεισθῆναι καὶ Kayser; Müller deleted καὶ here and added it two lines above before γνώμην.

[7] καὶ added by Kiessling.

5 νον. ἀκούσαντας δὲ τὸ τῆς βουλῆς ὄνομα τοὺς
ὡρμηκότας παίειν τε καὶ βάλλειν[1] αὐτὸν ἀποτρα-
πέσθαι καὶ μηδὲν εἰς αὐτὸν παρανομῆσαι. ἐκ
τούτου καὶ τὴν ἐπωνυμίαν τὸν "Αλαν αὐτῷ τεθῆναι λέγουσιν, ὅτι τὸ ξίφος ἔχων ὑπὸ μάλης ἦλθεν
ἐπὶ τὸν ἄνδρα· ἄλας γὰρ καλοῦσι 'Ρωμαῖοι τὰς
μάλας.[2]

6 'Αναιρεθέντος δὲ τοῦ ἀνδρὸς καθ' ὁπότερον[3]
τρόπον συνελθοῦσα ἡ βουλὴ τήν τε οὐσίαν αὐτοῦ
εἶναι δημοσίαν ἐψηφίσατο καὶ τὴν οἰκίαν ἕως
ἐδάφους κατασκαφῆναι. οὗτος ὁ τόπος ἔτι καὶ
εἰς ἐμὲ ἦν ἐν πολλαῖς ταῖς πέριξ οἰκίαις μόνος
ἀνειμένος ἔρημος, καλούμενος ὑπὸ 'Ρωμαίων Αἰκυμήλιον, ὡς ἂν ἡμεῖς εἴποιμεν ἰσόπεδον Μήλιον[4]·
αἶκον γὰρ ὑπὸ 'Ρωμαίων τὸ μηδεμίαν ἔχον ἐξοχὴν
καλεῖται.[5] τόπον οὖν τινα Αἶκον[6] Μήλιον ἐξ ἀρχῆς κληθέντα, ὕστερον[7] συμφθαρέντων[8] ἀλλήλοις
κατὰ τὴν μίαν ἐκφορὰν τῶν ὀνομάτων Αἰκυμήλιον[9]
ἐκάλεσαν. τῷ δὲ τὴν κατὰ τοῦ Μαιλίου μήνυσιν
ἀποδόντι Μηνυκίῳ στάσιν ἀνδριάντος ἐψηφίσατο
ἡ βουλή. Esc.; (p. 214, ll. 12-18) Ambr.

V. (2) Τυρρηνῶν καὶ Φιδηναίων καὶ Οὐιεντανῶν
πολεμούντων 'Ρωμαίοις καὶ Λάρου Τολουμνίου[10]
τοῦ βασιλέως Τυρρηνῶν πάνδεινα ποιοῦντος[11] κατ'
αὐτῶν χιλίαρχός τις 'Ρωμαῖος, Αὖλος Κορνήλιος

[1] ψάλλειν S, according to de Boor.
[2] μάλας Edd. : μάχας S.
[3] ὁπότερον Garrer (who added δὴ or οὖν) : ἑκάτερον S,
ἕτερον Jacoby.
[4] Μήλιον Kiessling : μένον S.
[5] The brief excerpt in the Ambrosianus begins : τὸ ἰσόπεδον
αἰκυμίλιον ρωμαῖοι καλοῦσιν· αἶκον γὰρ τὸ μηδεμίαν ἔχον ἐξοχὴν
λέγουσι.   [6] Αἶκον added by Struve.

When they heard mention of the senate, those who
had been bent on beating and stoning him desisted
and committed no lawless act against him. In consequence of this deed of his they say the cognomen Ala
(Ahala[1]) was given him, inasmuch as he had his sword
under his arm-pit when he came upon Maelius ; for
the Romans call the arm-pit *ala*.

When the man had been destroyed in one way or
the other, the senate met and voted that his property
should be confiscated to the state and his house razed
to the ground. This site even to my day was the
only area left vacant amid the surrounding houses,
and was called Aequimelium by the Romans, or, as
we might say, the Plain of Melius. For *aequum* is
the name given by the Romans to that which has
no eminences ; accordingly, a place originally called
aequum Melium was later, when the two words were
run together and pronounced as one, called Aequimelium. To the man who gave information against
Maelius, namely Minucius, the senate voted that a
statue should be erected.

V. (2) When the Tyrrhenians, Fidenates and Veientes were making war upon the Romans,[2] and Lars
Tolumnius, the king of the Tyrrhenians, was doing
them terrible damage, a Roman military tribune,

---

[1] Ahala was not an easy name for Dionysius to put into
Greek.
[2] For chap. 5 *cf.* Livy iv. 19, 1-6.

---

[7] τόπον οὖν τινα . . . ὕστερον (but with αἶκον omitted) Q :
om. S ; Feder proposed τόπον οὖν τὸν Μαιλίου.
[8] συμφθαρέντων Q : συμφθαρέντων δὲ S.
[9] αἰκυμήλιον Q : αἰκύμηνον S.
[10] Mai : τολουρουμνίου Q.
[11] πάνδεινα ποιοῦντος regarded by Struve as corrupt. Jacoby
suggested πανδημεὶ ἐπιόντος.

DIONYSIUS OF HALICARNASSUS

Κόσσος ἐπίκλησιν, ἐλαύνει τὸν ἵππον κατὰ τοῦ
Τολουμνίου· καὶ ἐπειδὴ ἀγχοῦ ἐγένετο, φέρουσι
2 κατ' ἀλλήλων τὰ δόρατα. ὁ μὲν οὖν Τολούμνιος
τὸν ἵππον αὐτοῦ παίει διὰ τοῦ στήθους, ὃς ἀνα-
χαιτίσας ῥιπτεῖ τὸν ἐπιβάτην· ὁ δὲ Κορνήλιος διὰ
θυρεοῦ τε καὶ θώρακος ἐλάσας τὴν αἰχμὴν εἰς τὰ
πλευρὰ περιτρέπει τὸν Τολούμνιον ἀπὸ τοῦ ἵππου,
καὶ ἔτι διανισταμένου φέρει διὰ τοῦ[1] βουβῶνος
3 τὸ ξίφος. ἀποκτείνας δὲ αὐτὸν καὶ τὰ σκῦλα
ἀφελόμενος οὐ μόνον τοὺς ὁμόσε χωροῦντας ἱππεῖς
τε καὶ πεζοὺς ἀνέστειλεν, ἀλλὰ καὶ τοὺς ἐπὶ τῶν
κεράτων ἀμφοτέρων ἀντέχοντας εἰς ἀθυμίαν καὶ
δέος κατέστησεν. *Ambr.*

VI. (3) Δεύτερον ὑπατεύοντος Αὔλου Κορνηλίου
Κόσσου καὶ Τίτου Κοϊντίου αὐχμῷ μεγάλῳ κακωθεῖσα ἡ γῆ πάντων ἐσπάνισεν οὐ μόνον τῶν
ὀμβρίων ἀλλὰ καὶ τῶν ναματιαίων[2] ὑδάτων· ἐκ
δὲ τούτου προβάτων μὲν καὶ ὑποζυγίων καὶ βοῶν
ἐπίλειψις παντελὴς ἐγένετο, εἰς δὲ τοὺς ἀνθρώπους
νόσοι κατέσκηψαν πολλαὶ μὲν καὶ ἄλλαι, μάλιστα
δὲ ἡ ψωρώδης καλουμένη, δεινὰς ὀδύνας παρέχουσα
τοῖς χρωσὶ κατὰ τοὺς ὀδαξησμοὺς καὶ πρὸς τὰς
ἑλκώσεις ἔτι μᾶλλον ἀγριαινομένη—πάθος ἐλεεινὸν ἐν τοῖς πάνυ καὶ τοῦ ταχίστου τῶν ὀλέθρων
αἴτιον. *Ambr.*

2 (4) Οὐκ ἐδόκει τοῖς προεστηκόσι τοῦ συνεδρίου
βαθεῖαν[3] εἰρήνην καὶ πολυχρόνιον ἄγειν σχολήν,
ἐνθυμουμένοις ὅτι ῥᾳθυμία καὶ τρυφὴ συνεισ-
πορεύεται ταῖς πόλεσι μετὰ τῆς εἰρήνης, καὶ ἅμα
τὰς πολιτικὰς ὀρρωδοῦσι ταραχάς.[4] καὶ αὗται

---

[1] τοῦ added by Struve.   [2] Struve : ναματίων Q.
[3] βαθεῖαν Struve : μαθεῖν Q.

216

Aulus Cornelius, with the cognomen Cossus, spurred his horse against Tolumnius ; and when he was close to him, they levelled their spears against each other. Tolumnius drove his spear through the breast of his foe's horse, which reared and threw its rider ; and Cornelius, driving the point of his spear through the shield and breastplate of Tolumnius into his side, knocked him from his horse, and while he was still attempting to raise himself, ran his sword through his groin. After slaying him and stripping off his spoils, he not only repulsed those who came to close quarters with him, both horse and foot, but also reduced to discouragement and fear those who still held out on the two wings.

VI. (3) When Aulus Cornelius Cossus (for the second time) and Titus Quintius were consuls,[1] the land suffered from a severe drought, lacking all moisture not only from rains but also from flowing streams. As a result, sheep, beasts of burden and cattle disappeared entirely, while human beings were visited with many diseases, particularly the one called the mange, which caused dreadful pains in the skin with its itchings and in case of any ulcerations raged more violently than ever—a most pitiable affliction and the cause of the speediest of deaths.

(4) It did not seem wise to the leaders of the senate to have profound peace and long-continued leisure ; for they were mindful that indolence and softness enter states along with peace, and at the same time they dreaded civil disturbances. For these distur-

---

[1] For § (3) *cf.* Livy iv. 30, 7 f. Livy makes Quintius the one who was consul for the second time.

[4] τὰς πολιτικὰς . . . ταραχάς Struve : ταῖς πολιτικαῖς . . . ταραχαῖς Q.

γὰρ ἅμα τῷ καταλυθῆναι τοὺς ὑπερορίους πολέμους χαλεπαὶ καὶ συνεχεῖς ἐξ ἁπάσης προφάσεως
ἀνίσταντο.[1]

3 Κρεῖττον ταῖς φιλανθρωπίαις περιεῖναι τῶν
ἐχθρῶν ἢ ταῖς τιμωρίαις, δι' ἃς κεῖ[2] μηδὲν ἕτερον
αἵ γέ τοι παρὰ τῶν θεῶν ἐλπίδες ἡδίους αὐτοῖς
ὑπάρχουσιν. Ambr.

4 (5) Ὡς ἔμαθε τοὺς πολεμίους ἐκ τῶν κατόπιν
προσιόντας, ἐπιστρέφειν μὲν ὀπίσω περιεχόμενος
ὑπὸ τῶν πολεμίων πανταχόθεν ἀπέγνω, ἐνθυμούμενος ὅτι κινδυνεύσουσιν ἅπαντες οὐθὲν ἀποδει-
ξάμενοι γενναῖον ἔργον αἴσχιστα διαφθαρῆναι,
ὀλίγοι τε πρὸς πολλοὺς μαχόμενοι καὶ τεθωρα-
κισμένοι πρὸς ἐλαφρούς. ἰδὼν δὲ ὄχθον τινὰ
ὑψηλὸν ἐπιεικῶς, ὃς ἦν αὐτῷ οὐ πρόσω, τοῦτον
ἔγνω καταλαβέσθαι. Ambr.

5 (6) Ἀγρίππας Μενήνιος καὶ Πόπλιος Λουκρήτιος[3] καὶ Σερούιος Ναύτιος, χιλίαρχοι †τιμηθέντες,[4]
ἐπίθεσίν τινα κατὰ τῆς πόλεως γενομένην ὑπὸ
6 δούλων ἐφώρασαν. ἔμελλον δὲ οἱ μετέχοντες τῆς
συνωμοσίας πῦρ ἐμβαλόντες ταῖς οἰκίαις κατὰ
πολλοὺς ἅμα τόπους νύκτωρ, ὁπότε μάθοιεν ἐπὶ
τὴν τῶν καιομένων βοήθειαν ὡρμηκότας ἅπαντας,
τό τε Καπιτώλιον καὶ τοὺς ἄλλους ἐρυμνοὺς κατα-
λαμβάνεσθαι τόπους, ἐγκρατεῖς δὲ γενόμενοι τῶν
καρτερῶν τῆς πόλεως, ἐπὶ τὴν ἐλευθερίαν τοὺς
ἄλλους δούλους παρακαλεῖν καὶ σὺν ἐκείνοις
ἀποκτείναντες τοὺς δεσπότας τὰς τῶν πεφονευ-
μένων γυναῖκάς τε καὶ κτήσεις παραλαμβάνειν.

---

[1] ἀνίστανται Kiessling.   [2] Struve : καὶ Q.
[3] λουκράτιος Q.
[4] The reading given in Q is corrupt. Cobet proposed to

bances, as soon as external wars were terminated, arose, bitter and continuous, on every possible excuse.

It is better for people to surpass their enemies in acts of kindness than in punishments, since, even if there is no other reason, at least their expectations of favours from the gods are brighter because of them.

(5) When he learned that the enemy were coming up in the rear,[1] he despaired of turning back, being surrounded by the enemy on all sides, and bearing in mind that they would all run the risk of perishing ignominiously without having performed any noble action, fighting, as they would be, a few against many, and heavily armed against light troops. And perceiving a hill of moderate height which lay at no great distance, he resolved to seize it.

(6) Agrippa Menenius, Publius Lucretius and Servius Nautius, having been honoured with the military tribuneship,[2] discovered a plot that had been formed against the commonwealth by slaves. The conspirators were planning to set fire to the houses at night in many different places at the same time, and then, when they had learned that everyone had rushed to the aid of the burning buildings, to seize the Capitol and the other fortified places and, once in possession of the strong positions in the city, to summon the other slaves to freedom and together with them, after slaying their masters, to take over the wives and possessions of the murdered men.

[1] For § (5) cf. Livy iv. 39, 4(?).
[2] For § (6) cf. Livy iv. 44, 13–45, 2. Livy gives the name as Spurius Nautius.

read χιλιαρχίᾳ τιμηθέντες. But τιμηθέντες may have replaced αἱρεθέντες, ἀποδειχθέντες, or some other verb of similar meaning ; in which case χιλίαρχοι could stand.

7 τῆς δὲ πράξεως περιφανοῦς[1] γενομένης συλλη-
φθέντες οἱ πρῶτοι συνθέντες τὴν ἐπιβουλὴν καὶ
μαστιγωθέντες ἐπὶ τοὺς σταυροὺς ἀπήχθησαν· τῶν
δὲ μηνυσάντων αὐτούς, ὄντων δυεῖν, ἐλευθερίαν τε
καὶ δραχμὰς χιλίας[2] ἑκάτερος ἔλαβεν ἐκ τοῦ
δημοσίου. Ambr.

VII. (7) Ἔσπευδε τὸν πόλεμον συντελέσαι ἐν
ὀλίγαις ἡμέραις ὁ Ῥωμαίων χιλίαρχος ὡς δὴ
ῥᾴδιόν τι πρᾶγμα καὶ κατὰ χειρὸς αὐτῷ γενησό-
μενον ὑποχειρίους ποιήσασθαι μιᾷ μάχῃ τοὺς
2 πολεμίους. τῷ δὲ ἡγεμόνι τῶν πολεμίων, ἐν-
θυμουμένῳ τό τε ἐμπειροπόλεμον τῶν Ῥωμαίων
καὶ τὸ ἐν τοῖς κινδύνοις καρτερικόν, μάχην μὲν
ἐκ παρατάξεως ἴσην[3] καὶ φανερὰν ποιεῖσθαι πρὸς
αὐτοὺς οὐκ ἐδόκει, διαστρατηγεῖν δὲ τὸν πόλεμον
ἀπάταις τισὶ καὶ δόλοις καὶ παρατηρεῖν εἴ τι πλεο-
νέκτημα καθ᾽ ἑαυτῶν ἐκεῖνοι παρέξουσιν. Ambr.

Τραυματίας καὶ παρασχεδὸν ἐλθὼν ἀποθανεῖν.
Ambr.

VIII. (8) Ἐν Ῥώμῃ χειμῶνος γενομένου βιαίου,
ἔνθα ἡ ἐλαχίστη χιὼν κατενίφθη, οὐκ ἐλάττων ἦν
ἑπτὰ ποδῶν τὸ βάθος. καὶ συνέπεσεν ἀνθρώπους
τε ὑπὸ τοῦ νιφετοῦ διαφθαρῆναί τινας καὶ πρόβατα
πολλὰ καὶ τῶν ἄλλων κτηνῶν καὶ ὑποζυγίων
μοῖραν οὐκ ὀλίγην, τὰ μὲν ὑπὸ τοῦ κρυμοῦ σφακε-
2 λίσαντα, τὰ δὲ νομῆς τῆς συνήθους ἀπορίᾳ. δέν-
δρων τε καρποφόρων ὅσα μὴ πέφυκεν ὑπερβολὰς
νιφετῶν ὑπομένειν τὰ μὲν εἰς τέλος ἐξηράνθη, τὰ
δὲ ἐπικαέντα τοὺς βλαστοὺς ἄκαρπα ἐπὶ πολλοὺς

---

[1] περιφανῶς Q. [2] χιλίας added by Mai.

When the plot was revealed, the ringleaders were arrested and after being scourged were led away to be crucified ; as for the men who had laid information against them, two in number, each received his freedom and a thousand[1] denarii from the public treasury.

VII. (7) The Roman tribune was anxious to terminate the war in a few days, as if it would be a simple matter and quite within his power to reduce the enemy to subjection by a single battle. But the leader of the enemy, mindful of the Romans' experience in warfare and of their perseverance amid the hazards of battle, determined not to fight a pitched battle against them on equal terms and in the open, but to carry on the war by means of some ruses and stratagems and to be on the watch for any advantage they might offer him against themselves.

Having been wounded and having come within a little of dying.

VIII. (8) At Rome there was a severe storm,[2] and where the least snow fell it was not less than seven feet deep. It chanced that some persons lost their lives in the snowstorm, as did many sheep and no small portion of the other cattle and beasts of burden, partly as the result of being frostbitten and partly because of the lack of their customary grazing. Of the fruit-trees, those which were of such a nature as could not endure excessive snowstorms were either completely winter-killed or had their shoots withered

---

[1] The word for " thousand " has fallen out of the MS. but was supplied by Mai. Livy expresses this sum as *dena milia gravis aeris* (*i.e.* 10,000 *asses*).

[2] For chap. 8 *cf.* Livy v. 13, 1.

---

[3] ἴσην A : ἴσον Q.

χρόνους ἐγένετο.[1] ἐλύθησάν[2] τε καὶ τῶν οἰκιῶν
συχναὶ καί τινες καὶ περιετράπησαν, μάλιστα δὲ
ὅσαι ἐκ τῶν λίθων, κατὰ τὴν διάλυσίν τε καὶ
3 ἀπότηξιν τῆς χιόνος. τοῦτο τὸ πάθος οὔτε πρό-
τερόν ποτε γενόμενον ἐν ἱστορίας γραφῇ περὶ
ταῦτα τὰ χωρία παρειλήφαμεν οὔθ' ὕστερον ἕως
τοῦ καθ' ἡμᾶς χρόνου, μετρίῳ γέ τινι βορειότερα
τοῦ μέσου,[3] κατὰ τὸν ὑπὲρ Ἄθων[4] γραφόμενον
δι' Ἑλλησπόντου παράλληλον. τότε δὲ πρῶτον
καὶ μόνον ἐξέβη τῆς εἰωθυίας κράσεως ἡ τοῦ
περιέχοντος τήνδε τὴν γῆν[5] φύσις. Ambr.

IX. (9) Ἑορτὰς ἦγον οἱ Ῥωμαῖοι τὰς καλου-
μένας τῇ ἐπιχωρίῳ γλώττῃ στρωμνὰς ὑπὸ τῶν
Σιβυλλείων κελευσθέντες χρησμῶν. νόσος γάρ
τις λοιμώδης γενομένη θεόπεμπτός τε καὶ ὑπὸ
τέχνης ἀνθρωπίνης ἀνίατος εἰς ζήτησιν αὐτοὺς
2 ἤγαγε τῶν χρησμῶν. ἐκόσμησάν τε στρωμνὰς
τρεῖς, ὡς ἐκέλευον οἱ χρησμοί, μίαν μὲν Ἀπόλλωνι
καὶ Λητοῖ, ἑτέραν δὲ Ἡρακλεῖ καὶ Ἀρτέμιδι,
τρίτην δὲ Ἑρμῇ καὶ Ποσειδῶνι· καὶ διετέλουν
ἐφ' ἡμέρας ἑπτὰ δημοσίᾳ τε καταθύοντες καὶ ἰδίᾳ
κατ' οἰκείαν δύναμιν ἅπαντες τοῖς θεοῖς ἀπαρχόμενοι, ἑστιάσεις τε λαμπροτάτας ἐπιτελοῦντες
καὶ ξένων τοὺς παρεπιδημοῦντας ὑποδεχόμενοι.
3 (10) Πείσων δὲ ὁ τιμητικὸς ἐν ταῖς ἐνιαυσίοις ἀνα-
γραφαῖς καὶ ταῦτ' ἔτι προστίθησιν· ὅτι λελυμένων
μὲν τῶν θεραπόντων ὅσους πρότερον ἐν τοῖς δεσ-

[1] Struve : ἐγένοντο Q.
[2] ἐλύθησάν Kiessling : ἐμίχθησαν (ἐλέχθησαν according to
Kiessling) Q, ἐνίφθησάν Struve, συνεχύθησάν Jacoby.
[3] τοῦ μέσου κλίματος Warmington.
[4] Post : ἀθηνῶν Q, Jacoby.
[5] ἀέρος added after γῆν by Kiessling ; cf. chap. 15 (21).

and bore no fruit for many years. Many houses also collapsed and some were actually overturned, especially those constructed of stone, during the thawing and melting of the snow. We have no report in a historical record of the occurrence of such a calamity, either on any earlier occasion or later, down to our own time, in this region, which is slightly north of the middle zone,[1] on the parallel running above Athos through the Hellespont. This was the first and only time when the atmosphere of this land departed from its customary temperature.

IX. (9) The Romans were conducting the festival called in their own language *lectisternium*,[2] in response to the bidding of the Sibylline oracles. For a kind of pestilence sent by Heaven and incurable by human skill had led them to consult the oracles. They adorned three couches, as the oracles commanded, one for Apollo and Latona, another for Hercules and Diana, and a third for Mercury and Neptune. And for seven days running they offered sacrifices, both publicly and privately, each according to his own ability giving first-fruits to the gods; and they prepared most magnificent banquets and entertained the strangers who were sojourning in their midst. (10) Piso the ex-censor in his *Annals* adds these further details : that, though all the slaves whom their mas-

---

[1] Early Greek geographers commonly divided the " inhabited earth " known to them into seven zones (*climata*), the middle one of which lay along the parallel of Rhodes. Their next important parallel on the north was that of the Hellespont, running through the Troad, Amphipolis, Apollonia in Epirus, and south of Rome but north of Naples (so Strabo ii. 5, 40). In reality, Rome is nearly 2° north of the latitude here indicated. Athos is due to Post; the MSS. give Athens.

[2] For chap. 9 *cf.* Livy v. 13, 4-8.

μοῖς εἶχον οἱ δεσπόται, πληθυούσης ὄχλου ξενικοῦ
τῆς πόλεως, ἀναπεπταμένων τῶν οἰκιῶν διὰ ἡμέρας τε καὶ νυκτός, καὶ δίχα κωλύσεως εἰσιόντων
εἰς αὐτὰς τῶν βουλομένων, οὔτε χρῆμα οὐδὲν ἀπ-
ολωλεκέναι τις ᾐτιάσατο οὔτε ἠδικῆσθαί τινα ὑπ'
οὐδενός, καίτοι πολλὰ φέρειν εἰωθότων πλημμελῆ
καὶ παράνομα τῶν ἑορταίων[1] καιρῶν διὰ τὰς
μέθας. Ambr.

X. (11) Οὐιεντανοὺς πολιορκούντων Ῥωμαίων
περὶ τὴν ἐπιτολὴν τοῦ κυνός, ὅτε μάλιστα λίμναι
τε ἐπιλείπουσι καὶ ποταμοὶ πάντες, ὅ τι μὴ μόνος
ὁ Αἰγύπτιος Νεῖλος, λίμνη τις ἀπέχουσα τῆς
Ῥώμης οὐ μεῖον ρκ' σταδίων ἐν τοῖς Ἀλβανοῖς
καλουμένοις ὄρεσι, παρ' ᾗ τὸ ἀρχαῖον ἡ τῶν
Ῥωμαίων μητρόπολις ᾠκεῖτο, οὔτε ὑετῶν γενομένων οὔτε νιφετῶν οὔτ' ἄλλης τινὸς αἰτίας
ἀνθρώποις φανερᾶς, τοσαύτην ἔλαβεν ἐκ τῶν ἐν
αὐτῇ ναμάτων ἐπίδοσιν ὥστε πολλὴν μὲν ἐπικλύσαι τῆς παρορείου, πολλὰς δὲ οἰκήσεις γεωργικὰς
καταβαλεῖν,[2] τελευτῶσαν[3] δὲ καὶ τὸν μεταξὺ τῶν
ὀρῶν αὐλῶνα διασπάσαι καὶ ποταμὸν ἐκχέαι κατὰ
2 τῶν ὑποκειμένων πεδίων ἐξαίσιον.   (12) τοῦτο
μαθόντες οἱ Ῥωμαῖοι κατ' ἀρχὰς μέν, ὡς δαιμονίου
τινὸς μηνίοντος τῇ πόλει, θυσίαις ἐξιλάσασθαι[4]
τοὺς κατέχοντας τὸν τόπον θεοὺς καὶ δαίμονας
ἐψηφίσαντο καὶ τοὺς ἐπιχωρίους μάντεις ἀνέκρινον
εἴ τι λέγειν ἔχουσιν· ἐπεὶ δ' οὔτε ἡ λίμνη τὴν
ἑαυτῆς τάξιν ἀπελάμβανεν οὔτε οἱ μάντεις ἀκριβὲς
οὐδὲν ἔλεγον ἀλλὰ τῷ θεῷ χρῆσθαι παρήνουν, ἐπὶ τὸ
Δελφικὸν μαντεῖον ἀπέστειλαν θεοπρόπους. Ambr.

---

[1] Struve : ἑορτάδων Q.   [2] Struve : καταλαβεῖν Q.
[3] Struve : τελευτῶσα Q.   [4] ἐξιλάσκεσθαι A.

ters had previously kept in chains were then turned loose, though the city was filled with a throng of strangers, and though the houses were open day and night and all who wished entered them without hindrance, yet no one complained of having lost anything or of having been wronged by anyone, even though festal occasions are wont to bring many disorderly and lawless deeds in their train because of the drunkenness attending them.

X. (11) When the Romans were besieging the Veientes [1] about the time of the rising of the dog-star, the season when lakes are most apt to fail, as well as all rivers, with the single exception of the Egyptian Nile, a certain lake, distant not less than one hundred and twenty stades from Rome in the Alban mountains, as they are called, beside which in ancient times the mother-city of the Romans was situated, at a time when neither rains nor snow-storms had occurred nor any other cause perceptible to human beings, received such an increase to its waters that it inundated a large part of the region lying round the mountains, destroyed many farm houses, and finally carved out the gap between the mountains and poured a mighty river down over the plains lying below. (12) Upon learning of this, the Romans at first, in the belief that some god was angry at the commonwealth, voted to propitiate the gods and lesser divinities who presided over the region, and asked the native soothsayers if they had anything to say ; but when neither the lake resumed its natural state nor the soothsayers had anything definite to say, but advised consulting the god, they sent envoys to the Delphic oracle.

---

[1] For chaps. 10–12 *cf.* Livy v. 15 ; 16, 1, 8-11 ; 17, 1 : 19, 1.

XI. (13) Ἐν δὲ τῷ μεταξὺ χρόνῳ Οὐιεντανῶν τις ἔμπειρος τῆς ἐπιχωρίου μαντικῆς διὰ προγόνων ἐτύγχανε φυλακὴν ἔχων τοῦ τείχους, ἐγεγόνει δέ τις αὐτῷ τῶν ἀπὸ τῆς Ῥώμης λοχαγῶν ἐκ παλαιοῦ γνώριμος. οὗτος ὁ λοχαγὸς ἐγγὺς τοῦ τείχους ποτὲ γενόμενος καὶ τοὺς συνήθεις ἀσπασμοὺς τῷ ἀνδρὶ ἀποδοὺς οἰκτείρειν αὐτὸν ἔφη τῆς καταληψο-μένης ἅμα τοῖς ἄλλοις συμφορᾶς, ἐὰν ἡ πόλις ἁλῷ.

2 καὶ ὁ Τυρρηνὸς ἀκηκοὼς τὴν ὑπέρχυσιν τῆς Ἀλβανίδος λίμνης καὶ τὰ παλαιὰ περὶ αὐτῆς προειδὼς θέσφατα ἀναγελάσας, " Οἷον," ἔφησεν, " ἐστὶν ἀγαθὸν τὸ προειδέναι τὰ μέλλοντα. ὑμεῖς δὲ κατὰ τὴν ἀγνωσίαν τῶν ἀποβησομένων πόλεμον ἀτελῆ καὶ πόνους ἀνηνύτους ἀντλεῖτε τὴν[1] Οὐιεντα-νῶν πόλιν ἀναστήσειν οἰόμενοι. εἰ δέ τις ὑμῖν ἐδήλωσεν ὅτι τῇ πόλει τῇδε τότε[2] πέπρωται ἁλῶναι ὅταν ἡ πρὸς Ἀλβανῷ λίμνη σπανίσασα τῶν αὐθιγενῶν ναμάτων μηκέτι μίσγηται θαλάττῃ, ἐπαύσασθε ἂν αὐτοί τε δαπανώμενοι καὶ ἡμᾶς

3 ἐνοχλοῦντες." ταῦτα ὁ Ῥωμαῖος μαθὼν πολὺς ἐν τῷ σκοπεῖν[3] καθ᾽ ἑαυτὸν γενόμενος, τότε μὲν ἀπῄει, (14) τῇ δ᾽ ἑξῆς προειπὼν τοῖς χιλιάρχοις ἃ διενοεῖτο, παρῆν ἐπὶ τὸν αὐτὸν τόπον ἄνοπλος, ὥστε μηδεμίαν ὑποψίαν ἐπιβουλῆς τὸν Τυρρηνὸν ὑπὲρ αὐτοῦ λαβεῖν. χρησάμενος δὲ τοῖς συνήθεσιν ἀσπασμοῖς πρῶτον μὲν ὑπὲρ τῆς κατεχούσης τὸ Ῥωμαϊκὸν στρατόπεδον ἀμηχανίας διελέγετο ἀλλ᾽,[4] ἐφ᾽ οἷς ἡσθήσεσθαι τὸν Τυρρηνὸν ὑπελάμβανεν, ἔπειτα ἐξηγητὴν αὐτῷ[5] γενέσθαι ἠξίου σημείων

---

[1] τὴν Q : om. A.   [2] τότε Q : om. A.
[3] σκοπεῖν Sintenis : σκοπῶ Q.
[4] ἀλλ᾽ Q : ἄττ᾽ Struve.

226

XI. (13) In the meantime one of the Veientes, who had inherited from his ancestors a knowledge of the augural science of his country, chanced to be guarding the wall, and one of the centurions from Rome had long been an acquaintance of his. This centurion, being near the wall one day and giving the other man the customary greetings, remarked that he pitied him because of the calamity that would befall him along with the rest if the city were captured. The Tyrrhenian, having heard of the overflowing of the Alban lake and knowing already the ancient oracles concerning it, laughed and said : "What a fine thing it is to know beforehand the things that are to be ! Thus, you Romans in your ignorance of what is to happen are waging an endless war and are expending fruitless toils, in the belief that you will overthrow the city of Veii ; whereas, if anyone had revealed to you that it is fated for this city to be captured only when the lake beside the Alban mount, lacking its natural springs, shall no longer mingle its waters with the sea, you would have desisted from exhausting yourselves and at the same time troubling us." Upon hearing this, the Roman took the matter very seriously to heart ; for the time being he went his way, (14) but the next day, after telling the tribunes what he had in mind, he came to the same place unarmed, so that the Tyrrhenian might conceive no suspicion of a plot on his part. When he had uttered the usual greetings, he first talked about the embarrassment in which the Roman army found itself, mentioning sundry matters which he thought would give pleasure to the Tyrrhenian, and then asked him to interpret for him some signs

---

[5] Struve : αὐτῷ Q.

τινῶν καὶ τεράτων νεωστὶ τοῖς χιλιάρχοις γεγο-
4 νότων. πείθεται τοῖς λόγοις ὁ μάντις οὐδεμίαν
δεδοικὼς ἐξαπάτην καὶ τοὺς συνόντας[1] αὐτῷ
μεταστῆναι κελεύσας αὐτὸς ἠκολούθει μόνος τῷ
λοχαγῷ. ὁ δὲ Ῥωμαῖος ὑπαγόμενος αὐτὸν ἀπω-
τέρω τοῦ τείχους διὰ τῶν πρὸς ἀπάτην μηχανηθέν-
των λόγων, ὡς ἐγγὺς ἐγένετο τοῦ περιτειχίσματος,
περιβαλὼν[2] ταῖς χερσὶν ἀμφοτέραις μέσον αἴρεταί
τε καὶ πρὸς τὸ Ῥωμαϊκὸν ἀποφέρεται στρατόπεδον.
Ambr.

XII. (15) Τοῦτον τὸν ἄνδρα οἱ χιλίαρχοι λόγοις
τε θεραπεύοντες καὶ βασάνων ἀπειλαῖς δεδιττόμενοι
ἅπαντα παρεσκεύασαν ἐξειπεῖν ἃ περὶ τῆς· Ἀλβανίδος λίμνης ἀπέκρυπτεν· εἶτα καὶ πρὸς τὴν βουλὴν
αὐτὸν ἀναπέμπουσι. τοῖς δ' ἐκ τοῦ συνεδρίου οὐχ
ὁμοία[3] παρέστη δόξα, ἀλλὰ τοῖς μὲν ἐδόκει παν-
οῦργός τις εἶναι καὶ γόης ὁ Τυρρηνὸς καὶ κατα-
ψεύδεσθαι τοῦ δαιμονίου τὰ περὶ τὸν χρησμόν,
2 τοῖς δ' ἀπὸ πάσης ἀληθείας εἰρηκέναι. (16) ἐν
τοιαύτῃ δ' ἀμηχανίᾳ τῆς βουλῆς ὑπαρχούσης
παρῆσαν οἱ προαποσταλέντες εἰς Δελφοὺς θεό-
προποι χρησμοὺς κομίζοντες τοῖς ὑπὸ τοῦ Τυρρηνοῦ
πρότερον ἀπηγγελμένοις συνᾴδοντας· ὅτι θεοὶ καὶ
δαίμονες οἱ λαχόντες τὴν Οὐιεντανῶν πόλιν τοσοῦτον αὐτοῖς ἐγγυῶνται χρόνον ἀσάλευτον φυλάξαι
τὴν ἐκ προγόνων παραδοθεῖσαν εὐδαιμονίαν ὅσον
ἂν διαμένωσιν αἱ πηγαὶ τῆς ἐν Ἀλβανῷ λίμνης
ὑπερχεόμεναι καὶ μέχρι θαλάττης ἀπορρέουσαι·
3 ὅταν δ' ἐκεῖναι φύσιν τε τὴν ἑαυτῶν καὶ ὁδοὺς τὰς
ἀρχαίας ἐκλιποῦσαι καθ' ἑτέρας ἐκτραπῶσιν, ὡς
μηκέτι μίσγεσθαι τῇ θαλάττῃ, τότε[4] καὶ τὴν πόλιν

---

[1] Struve : συνιόντας Q.   [2] περιβαλὼν Q : περιλαβὼν Struve.

and prodigies which had recently appeared to the
tribunes. The soothsayer was won over by his words,
fearing no treachery, and after ordering those who
were with him to stand aside, he himself followed the
centurion unattended. The Roman kept leading him
farther and farther from the wall by a line of conversation planned to deceive him, and when he was
near the wall of circumvallation, seizing him by the
waist with both hands, he lifted him up and carried
him off to the Roman camp.

XII. (15) The tribunes, by using arguments de-
signed to conciliate this man as well as threats of
torture to frighten him, caused him to declare all that
he had been concealing with regard to the Alban lake ;
then they also sent him to the senate. The senators
were not all of the same opinion ; but some thought
that the Tyrrhenian was something of a rascal and
charlatan and falsely attributed to the deity what he
said about the oracle, while others thought that he
had spoken in all sincerity. (16) While the senate
was in this quandary, the messengers who had been
sent earlier to Delphi arrived, bringing oracles agreeing with those already announced by the Tyrrhenian.
These declared that the gods and genii to whom
had been allotted the oversight of the city of Veii
guaranteed to maintain for them unshaken the good
fortune of their city as handed down from their
ancestors for only so long a time as the springs of
the Alban lake should continue to overflow and run
down to the sea ; but that when these should forsake
their natural bent and, quitting their ancient courses,
should turn aside to others, so as to mingle no longer
with the sea, then too their city would be overthrown.

---

³ οὐχ ἡ ὁμοία Struve, Jacoby.   ⁴ τότε Q : om. A.

αὐτῶν ἀνάστατον ἔσεσθαι· τοῦτο δ' οὐκ εἰς μακρὰν
ὑπὸ Ῥωμαίων γενήσεσθαι, ἐὰν ὀρύγμασι καθ'
ἕτερα χωρία γενομένοις[1] ἐκτρέψωσι τὴν πλήμυραν
τῶν ὑδάτων εἰς τὰ πρόσω τῆς θαλάττης πεδία.
ταῦτα μαθόντες οἱ Ῥωμαῖοι εὐθὺς ἐπέστησαν τοῖς
ἔργοις τοὺς χειροτέχνας. Ambr.

XIII. (17) Ὡς δὲ ταῦτ' ἤκουσαν Οὐιεντανοὶ
παρ' αἰχμαλώτου τινός, ἐπικηρυκεύεσθαι πρὸς τοὺς
πολιορκοῦντας ἤθελον περὶ καταλύσεως τοῦ πολέμου πρὶν ἁλῶναι κατὰ κράτος τὴν πόλιν, καὶ
2 ἀποδείκνυνται πρέσβεις οἱ πρεσβύτατοι. ἀποψηφισαμένης δὲ τῆς βουλῆς τῶν Ῥωμαίων τας
διαλλαγὰς οἱ μὲν ἄλλοι πρέσβεις ἀπήεσαν ἐκ τοῦ
βουλευτηρίου σιωπῇ, ὁ δὲ ἐπιφανέστατος ἐξ αὐτῶν
καὶ κατὰ τὴν μαντικὴν ἐμπειρίαν δοκιμώτατος,
ἐπιστὰς ταῖς θύραις[2] καὶ περιβλέψας ἅπαντας[3] τοὺς
παρόντας ἐν τῷ συνεδρίῳ, " Καλόν,[4] " ἔφησεν, " ὦ
Ῥωμαῖοι, δόγμα ἐξενηνόχατε καὶ μεγαλοπρεπές,
οἵ[5] τὴν ἡγεμονίαν ἀξιοῦντες[5] ἔχειν τῶν περιοίκων
δι' ἀρετήν, πόλιν οὔτε μικρὰν οὔτε ἄσημον ἀποτιθε-
μένην τὰ ὅπλα καὶ παραδιδοῦσαν ὑμῖν ἑαυτὴν οὐκ
ἀξιοῦντες[5] ὑπήκοον ἔχειν, ἀλλὰ πρόρριζον ἀνελεῖν
βουλόμενοι,[5] οὔτε τὸν ἐκ τοῦ θείου δείσαντες χόλον
οὔτε τὴν παρ' ἀνθρώπων ἐντραπέντες νέμεσιν.
3 ἀνθ' ὧν ὑμῖν δίκη τιμωρὸς ἥξει παρὰ θεῶν εἰς τὰ
ὅμοια ζημιοῦσα· Οὐιεντανοὺς γὰρ ἀφελόμενοι τὴν
πατρίδα μετ' οὐ πολὺ τὴν ἑαυτῶν ἀποβαλεῖτε."
Ambr.

4 (18) Μετὰ βραχὺ δὲ ἁλισκομένης τῆς πόλεως οἱ
μὲν ὁμόσε τοῖς πολεμίοις χωροῦντες ἄνδρες ἀγαθοὶ

---

[1] τεινομένοις Struve.
ταῖς θύραις Struve : τὰς θύρας Q.

This would be brought about in a short time by the Romans if by means of channels dug in other places they should divert the overflowing waters into the plains that were remote from the sea. Upon learning of this, the Romans at once put the engineers in charge of the operation.

XIII. (17) When the Veientes learned of this from a prisoner, they wished to send heralds to their besiegers to seek a termination of the war before the city should be taken by storm ; and the oldest citizens were appointed envoys. When the Roman senate voted against making peace, the other envoys left the senate-chamber in silence, but the most prominent of their number and the one who enjoyed the greatest reputation for skill in divination stopped at the door, and looking round upon all who were present in the chamber, said : " A fine and magnanimous decree you have passed, Romans, you who lay claim to the leadership over your neighbours on the ground of valour, when you disdain to accept the submission of a city, neither small nor undistinguished, which offers to lay down its arms and surrender itself to you, but wish to destroy it root and branch, neither fearing the wrath of Heaven nor regarding the indignation of men ! In return for this, avenging justice shall come upon you from the gods, punishing you in like manner. For after robbing the Veientes of their country you shall ere long lose your own."

(18) When the city [1] was being captured a short time after this, some of the inhabitants engaged with the

---

[1] For § (18) cf. Livy v. 21, 12-14. The city of Veii is meant.

---

[3] ἅπαντας Mai : εἰς ἅπαντας Kiessling, who declared this to be the reading of Q. [4] γε added after καλόν by Cobet.
[5] οἱ . . . ἀξιοῦτε . . . βούλεσθε Struve ; cf. xi. 5, 2.

γενόμενοι καὶ πολλοὺς ἀποκτείναντες κατεκόπησαν, οἱ δ᾿ αὐτοχειρίᾳ σφάξαντες αὐτοὺς διεφθάρη-
σαν· ὅσοις[1] δὲ δι᾿ ἀνανδρίαν τε καὶ ταπεινότητα
ψυχῆς πάντ᾿ ἐφαίνετο τοῦ τεθνάναι τὰ δεινὰ με-
τριώτερα, ῥίψαντες τὰ ὅπλα παρεδίδοσαν τοῖς
κεκρατηκόσιν ἑαυτούς. Ambr.

XIV. (19) Ὁ δὲ δικτάτωρ Κάμιλλος, οὗ στρα-
τηγίᾳ ἡ πόλις ἥλω, ἐπὶ μετεώρου τινὸς[2] ἑστὼς
ἅμα τοῖς ἐπιφανεστάτοις Ῥωμαίων, ὅθεν ἅπασα
ἡ πόλις ἦν καταφανής, πρῶτον μὲν ἐμακάρισεν
ἑαυτὸν τῆς παρούσης εὐτυχίας, ὅτι καθελεῖν αὐτῷ
μεγάλην καὶ εὐδαίμονα πόλιν ἐξεγένετο δίχα πόνου,
ἣ Τυρρηνίας μὲν ἀνθούσης τότε καὶ πλεῖστον τῶν
κατοικούντων τὴν Ἰταλίαν ἐθνῶν δυναμένης[3] οὐκ
ἐλαχίστη μοῖρα ἦν, Ῥωμαίοις δὲ περὶ τῆς ἡγεμονίας διαφερομένη καὶ πολλοὺς ὑπομείνασα πολέμους[4] ἄχρι δεκάτης γενεᾶς διετέλεσεν, ἐξ οὗ δ᾿
ἤρξατο πολεμεῖν[5] καὶ πολιορκεῖσθαι συνεχῶς, δέκα
διήνεγκε τὴν πολιορκίαν ἔτη πάσης πειραθεῖσα
2 τύχης. (20) ἔπειτ᾿ ἐνθυμηθεὶς ὡς ἐπὶ μικρᾶς
αἰωρεῖται ῥοπῆς ἡ τῶν ἀνθρώπων εὐδαιμονία καὶ
βέβαιον οὐδὲν διαμένει τῶν ἀγαθῶν, διατείνας εἰς
οὐρανὸν τὰς χεῖρας εὔξατο τῷ τε Διὶ καὶ τοῖς
ἄλλοις θεοῖς, μάλιστα μὲν ἀνεπίφθονον ἑαυτῷ τε
καὶ τῇ πατρίδι γίνεσθαι τὴν παροῦσαν εὐδαιμονίαν·
εἰ δέ τις ἔμελλε κοινῇ[6] συμφορὰ τὴν[7] Ῥωμαίων

---

[1] Mai : ὅσους QA.   [2] ἐπὶ μετεώρου τόπου τινὸς A.

[3] Mai : δυνάμεις Q.

[4] πολλοὺς ὑπομείνασα πολέμους Mai, making no comment;
Kiessling, stating that πολέμους is wanting in Q, inserted this
word after πολλούς.

[5] πολεμεῖν regarded as corrupt by Struve, deleted by
Kayser ; πονεῖν or πολέμῳ πονεῖν Hertlein.

enemy, and after showing themselves brave men and slaying many, were cut down, and others perished by taking their own lives ; those, however, who because of cowardice and pusillanimity regarded any hardships as less terrible than death, threw down their arms and surrendered themselves to the conquerors.

XIV. (19) The dictator Camillus,[1] by whose generalship the city had been captured, after taking his stand with the most prominent Romans upon a height from which the entire city was visible, first congratulated himself upon his present good fortune, in that it had fallen to his lot to destroy without hardship a great and prosperous city which was no unimportant part of Tyrrhenia—a country at that time flourishing and the most powerful of any of the nations inhabiting Italy—and which had constantly disputed the leadership with the Romans and had continued to endure many wars unto the tenth generation, and from the time when it began to wage war and to be besieged continuously had endured the siege for ten years, experiencing every kind of fortune. (20) Then, remembering that men's happiness hangs upon a slight turn of the scales and that no blessings continue steadfast, he stretched out his hands toward heaven and prayed to Jupiter and the other gods that, if possible, his present good fortune might not prove a cause of hatred against either him or his country ; but that if any calamity was destined to befall the city of Rome in general or

---

[1] For chap. 14 *cf.* Livy v. 21, 14 f.

---

[6] καινὴ Struve.　　　[7] τὴν Mai : τῶν Q.

DIONYSIUS OF HALICARNASSUS

πόλιν ἢ τὸν αὑτοῦ βίον καταλαμβάνειν ἀντίπαλος τῶν παρόντων ἀγαθῶν, ἐλαχίστην γενέσθαι ταύτην καὶ μετριωτάτην. *Ambr.*

XV. (21) Ἦν δὲ ἡ Οὐιεντανῶν πόλις οὐθὲν ὑποδεεστέρα τῆς Ῥώμης ἐνοικεῖσθαι γῆν τε πολλὴν καὶ πολύκαρπον ἔχουσα, τὴν μὲν ὀρεινήν, τὴν δὲ πεδιάδα, καὶ τὸν ὑπερκείμενον¹ ἀέρα καθαρώτατον καὶ πρὸς ὑγίειαν ἀνθρώποις ἄριστον, οὔτε ἕλους πλησίον ὄντος, ὅθεν ἕλκονται βαρεῖς ἀτμοὶ καὶ δυσώδεις, οὔτε ποταμοῦ τινος ψυχρὰς ἕωθεν ἀνιέντος αὔρας, ὑδάτων τε οὐ σπανίων ὄντων οὐδ' ἐπακτῶν, ἀλλ' αὐθιγενῶν καὶ πλουσίων καὶ πίνεσθαι κρατίστων. *Ambr.*

XVI. (22) Αἰνείαν λέγουσι τὸν ἐξ Ἀγχίσου καὶ Ἀφροδίτης, ὅτε κατέσχεν εἰς Ἰταλίαν, θῦσαι προαιρούμενον ὅτῳ δή τινι θεῶν, μετὰ τὴν εὐχὴν μέλλοντα τοῦ παρεσκευασμένου πρὸς τὴν θυσίαν ἱερείου κατάρχεσθαι, τῶν Ἀχαιῶν² ἰδεῖν τινα πρόσωθεν ἐρχόμενον, εἴτε Ὀδυσσέα, ὅτε τῷ περὶ τὸν Ἄορνον μαντείῳ χρῆσθαι ἔμελλεν, εἴτε Διο-
2 μήδην, ἡνίκα Δαύνῳ σύμμαχος ἀφίκετο· ἀχθόμενον δὲ τῷ συγκυρήματι καὶ πολεμίαν ὄψιν ἐφ' ἱεροῖς φανεῖσαν ὡς πονηρὸν οἰωνὸν ἀφοσιώσασθαι βουλόμενον, ἐγκαλύψασθαί τε καὶ στραφῆναι· μετὰ δὲ τὴν ἀπαλλαγὴν τοῦ πολεμίου χερνιψάμενον
3 αὖθις ἐπιτελέσαι τὴν θυσίαν. γενομένων δὲ τῶν ἱερῶν κρειττόνων ἡσθῆναί τε τῷ συγκυρήματι καὶ φυλάττειν ἐπὶ πάσης εὐχῆς τὸ αὐτὸ ἔθος, τούς τε ἀπ' ἐκείνου γενομένους ὡς ἔν τι τῶν περὶ τὰς
4 ἱερουργίας νομίμων καὶ τοῦτο διατηρεῖν. (23) ἐπό-

his own life as a counterbalance to their present blessings, it might be very slight and moderate.

XV. (21) Veii was in no respect inferior to Rome [1] as a place in which to live, possessing much fertile land, partly hilly and partly level, and an atmosphere surrounding it that was most pure and conducive to the health of human beings. For there was neither any marsh near by as a source of oppressive and foul vapours nor any river to send up cold breezes at dawn, and its supplies of water were neither scanty nor brought in from outside, but rose in the neighbourhood and were abundant and most excellent for drinking.

XVI. (22) They say that Aeneas, the son of Anchises and Venus, when he had landed in Italy, was intending to sacrifice to some one or other of the gods, and after praying was about to begin the sacrifice of the animal that had been prepared for the rite, when he caught sight of one of the Achaeans approaching at a distance—either Ulysses, when he was about to consult the oracle near Lake Avernus, or Diomed, when he came as an ally to Daunus. And being vexed at the coincidence and wishing to avert as an evil omen the sight of an enemy that had appeared at the time of a sacrifice, he veiled himself and turned his back ; then, after the departure of the enemy, he washed his hands again and finished the sacrifice. When the sacrifices turned out rather favourably, he was pleased at the coincidence and observed the same practice on the occasion of every prayer ; and his posterity keep this also as one of the customary observances in connexion with their sacri-

---

[1] For chap. 15 *cf.* Livy v. 24, 5 f.

[1] περικείμενον Struve. [2] ἀρχαίων Q.

μένος δὴ τοῖς πατρικοῖς[1] ὁ Κάμιλλος νόμοις,
ἐπειδὴ τὴν εὐχὴν ἐποιήσατο καὶ κατὰ τῆς κεφαλῆς
εἴλκυσε τὸ ἱμάτιον, ἐβούλετο μὲν στραφῆναι,
τῆς δὲ βάσεως ὑπενεχθείσης οὐ δυνηθεὶς ἀναλαβεῖν
5 αὐτὸν ὕπτιος ἐπὶ τὴν γῆν φέρεται. τοῦτον τὸν
οἰωνὸν οὔτε μαντείας οὔτ' ἐνδοιασμοῦ δεόμενον,
ἀλλὰ καὶ τῷ φαυλοτάτῳ ῥᾴδιον ὄντα συμβαλεῖν,
ὅτι[2] πεσεῖν αὐτῷ πᾶσα ἀνάγκη πτῶμα ἄσχημον,
οὔτε φυλακῆς οὔτε ἀφοσιώσεως ἄξιον ὑπέλαβεν,
ἀλλ' ἐπὶ τὸ κεχαρισμένον ἑαυτῷ μετήνεγκεν, ὡς
ὑπακηκοότων αὐτοῦ ταῖς εὐχαῖς τῶν θεῶν καὶ
τὸ κακὸν ἐλάχιστον παρεσκευακότων γενέσθαι.
Ambr.

---

[1] πατρικίοις Q, according to Kiessling.
[2] Mai : οὔτε Q.

fices. (23) It was in accordance with the traditional usages, then, that Camillus,[1] after making his prayer and drawing his garment down over his head, wished to turn his back ; however, his foot slipped and he was unable to recover himself, but fell flat on the ground. Although this omen called for no divination or uncertainty but was easy for even the most ordinary mind to interpret, signifying that it was absolutely inevitable that he should come a disgraceful fall, nevertheless, he did not consider it worth while either to guard against it or to avert it by expiations, but altered it to the meaning that pleased him, assuming that the gods had given ear to his prayers and had contrived that the mischief should be of the slightest.

[1] For § (23) *cf.* Livy v. 21, 16.

EXCERPTS
FROM
BOOK XIII

I. (1) Καμίλλου τὴν[1] Φαλίσκων[2] πόλιν πολιορκοῦντος Φαλίσκων[3] τις εἴτ' ἀπεγνωκὼς τὴν πόλιν
εἴτε κέρδη θηρώμενος ἴδια[4] παῖδας ἐκ τῶν ἐπιφανεστάτων οἴκων παρακρουσάμενος (ἦν δὲ διδά-
σκαλος γραμμάτων) ἐξήγαγεν ἐκ τῆς πόλεως, ὡς
περιπατήσοντάς τε πρὸ τοῦ τείχους καὶ τὸ Ῥωμαϊ-
2 κὸν στρατόπεδον θεασομένους. ὑπαγόμενος δὲ
κατὰ μικρὸν αὐτοὺς προσωτέρω τῆς πόλεως ἐπὶ
φυλακτήριον Ῥωμαϊκὸν ἄγει καὶ τοῖς ἐκδραμοῦ-
σι παραδίδωσιν, ὑφ' ὧν ἀχθεὶς ἐπὶ τὸν Κάμιλλον
ἔφη βεβουλεῦσθαι μὲν ἔτι πάλαι τὴν πόλιν ὑπὸ
Ῥωμαίοις[5] ποιῆσαι, οὐδενὸς δὲ κύριος ὢν οὔτε
ἄκρας οὔτε πυλῶν οὔθ' ὅπλων τοῦτον ἐξευρηκέναι
τὸν τρόπον, ὑποχειρίους ποιῆσαι τοὺς υἱεῖς τῶν
εὐγενεστάτων, ἄφυκτον ἀνάγκην ὑπολαβὼν τοὺς
πατέρας αὐτῶν[6] καταλήψεσθαι τῆς σωτηρίας τῶν
τέκνων περιεχομένους[7] τάχιον παραδοῦναι Ῥω-
3 μαίοις τὴν πόλιν. ὁ μὲν δὴ ταῦτ' ἔλεγε πολλὰς

---

[1] τὴν Kiessling, τὴν τῶν Struve : τῶν Q.
[2] φαλίσκων Q : Φαλερίων Kiessling, erroneously.
[3] Struve : φαλερίων Q.   [4] Struve : ἰδίᾳ Q.
[5] Cary : ῥωμαίων Q.   [6] αὐτῶν om. Q.

238

EXCERPTS
FROM
BOOK XIII

I. (1) When Camillus was besieging the city of Falerii,[1] one of the Faliscans, either having given the city up for lost or seeking personal advantages for himself, tricked the sons of the most prominent families—he was a schoolmaster—and led them outside the city, as if to take a walk before the walls and to view the Roman camp. And gradually leading them farther and farther from the city, he brought them to a Roman outpost and handed them over to the men who ran out. Being brought to Camillus by these men, he said he had long planned to put the city in the hands of the Romans, but not being in possession of any citadel or gate or arms, he had hit upon this plan, namely to put in their power the sons of the noblest citizens, assuming that the fathers in their yearning for the safety of their children would be compelled by inexorable necessity to hand over the city promptly to the Romans. He spoke

---

[1] For chaps. 1 f. *cf.* Livy v. 27.

ἐλπίδας ἔχων θαυμαστούς[1] τινας ἐξοίσεσθαι μισθοὺς
τῆς προδοσίας. Ambr.

II. (2) Ὁ δὲ Κάμιλλος εἰς φυλακὴν παραδιδοὺς
τὸν γραμματιστὴν καὶ τοὺς παῖδας ἐπιστέλλει τῇ
βουλῇ διὰ γραμμάτων τὰ γενόμενα καὶ τί χρὴ
2 ποιεῖν ἤρετο. ἐπιτρέψαντος δ' αὐτῷ τοῦ συνεδρίου
πράττειν ὅ τι ἂν αὐτῷ φαίνηται κράτιστον, προαγαγὼν ἐκ τοῦ στρατοπέδου τὸν γραμματιστὴν
ἅμα τοῖς παισὶ καὶ οὐ μακρὰν ἀπὸ τῶν πυλῶν
τὸ στρατηγικὸν βῆμα προστάξας τεθῆναι, πολλοῦ
συνδραμόντος ὄχλου, τοῦ μὲν ἐπὶ τὰ τείχη, τοῦ δ'
ἐπὶ τὰς πύλας, πρῶτον μὲν ἐδήλωσε τοῖς Φαλίσκοις
οἷα ὁ γραμματιστὴς εἰς αὐτοὺς ἐτόλμησε παρα-
νομεῖν· ἔπειτα περικαταρρῆξαι τὴν ἐσθῆτα τοῦ
ἀνδρὸς ἐκέλευσε τοῖς ὑπηρέταις καὶ ξαίνειν τὸ
3 σῶμα μάστιξι πάνυ πολλαῖς. ὡς δὲ ταύτης ἅλις
εἶχε τῆς τιμωρίας, ῥάβδους τοῖς παισὶν ἀναδοὺς
ἀπάγειν αὐτὸν ἐκέλευσεν εἰς τὴν πόλιν δεδεμένον
τὼ χεῖρε ὀπίσω παίοντάς τε καὶ πάντα τρόπον
αἰκιζομένους. κομισάμενοι δὲ τοὺς παῖδας οἱ
Φαλίσκοι καὶ τὸν γραμματιστὴν ἀξίως τῆς κακῆς
διανοίας τιμωρησάμενοι παρέδοσαν τῷ Καμίλλῳ
τὴν πόλιν. Ambr.

III. (3) Ὁ αὐτὸς Κάμιλλος ἐπὶ τὴν Οὐιεντανῶν
πόλιν στρατεύων ηὔξατο τῇ βασιλείᾳ Ἥρᾳ τῇ ἐν
Οὐιεντανοῖς, ἐὰν κρατήσῃ τῆς πόλεως τό τε
ξόανον αὐτῆς ἐν Ῥώμῃ καθιδρύσειν καὶ σεβασμοὺς
2 αὐτῇ καταστήσεσθαι[2] πολυτελεῖς. ἁλούσης δὲ
τῆς πόλεως ἀπέστειλε τῶν ἱππέων τοὺς ἐπιφανεστάτους ἀρουμένους ἐκ τῶν βάθρων τὸ ἕδος·
ὡς δὲ παρῆλθον οἱ πεμφθέντες εἰς τὸν νεὼν καί

[1] Mai : θαυμαστάς Q.

thus, being in great hopes of gaining some wonderful rewards for his treachery.

II. (2) Camillus, having handed over the schoolmaster and the boys to be guarded, sent word by letter to the senate of what had happened and inquired what he should do. When the senate gave him permission to do whatever seemed best to him, he led the schoolmaster together with the boys out of the camp and ordered his general's tribunal to be placed not far from the city gate ; and when a large crowd of the Faliscans had rushed up, some of them to the walls and some to the gate, he first showed them what an outrageous thing the schoolmaster had dared to do to them ; then he ordered his attendants to tear off the man's clothes and to rend his body with a great many whips. When he had had his fill of this punishment, he handed out rods to the boys and ordered them to conduct the man back to the city with his hands bound behind his back, beating him and maltreating him in every way. After the Faliscans had got their sons back and had punished the schoolmaster in a manner his wicked plan deserved, they delivered up their city to Camillus.

III. (3) This same Camillus,[1] when conducting his campaign against Veii, made a vow to Queen Juno of the Veientes that if he should take the city he would set up her statue in Rome and establish costly rites in her honour. Upon the capture of the city, accordingly, he sent the most distinguished of the knights to remove the statue from its pedestal ; and when those who had been sent came into the temple

---

[1] *Cf.* Livy v. 21, 3 ; 22, 4-7.

---

[2] Struve : καταστήσασθαι Q.

τις ἐξ αὐτῶν, εἴτε μετὰ παιδιᾶς καὶ γέλωτος εἴτε
οἰωνοῦ δεόμενος, εἰ βούλοιτο μετελθεῖν εἰς Ῥώμην
ἡ θεός, ἤρετο, φωνῇ γεγωνῷ τὸ ξόανον ἐφθέγξατο
ὅτι βούλεται. τοῦτο καὶ δὶς γέγονεν· ἀπιστοῦντες
γὰρ οἱ νεανίσκοι, εἰ τὸ ξόανον ἦν τὸ φθεγξάμενον,
πάλιν ἤροντο τὸ αὐτὸ καὶ τὴν αὐτὴν φωνὴν
ἤκουσαν. Ambr.

IV. (4) Ἐν δὲ τῇ ἀρχῇ τῶν μετὰ τὸν Κάμιλλον
ὑπάτων νόσος εἰς Ῥώμην κατέσκηψε λοιμικὴ τὴν
ἀρχὴν ἀπό τε ἀνομβρίας καὶ αὐχμῶν λαβοῦσα
ἰσχυρῶν, ὑφ᾽ [1] ὧν κακωθεῖσα ἥ τε δενδρῖτις καὶ ἡ
σιτοφόρος ὀλίγους μὲν ἀνθρώποις καρποὺς ἐξήνεγκε
καὶ νοσερούς, ὀλίγην δὲ καὶ πονηρὰν βοσκήμασι
2 νομήν. προβάτων μὲν οὖν καὶ τῶν ἄλλων ὑποζυγίων ἀναρίθμητόν τι διεφθάρη πλῆθος οὐ χιλοῦ
σπανισάμενον [2] μόνον, ἀλλὰ καὶ ποτοῦ· τοσαύτη
τῶν τε ποταμίων καὶ τῶν ἄλλων ναμάτων ἐπίλειψις ἐγένετο, ἡνίκα μάλιστα κάμνει πάντα δίψει
3 τὰ βοτά. ἄνθρωποι δὲ ὀλίγοι μέν τινες διεφθάρησαν ἃς οὔπω πρότερον ἐπείρασαν προσενεγκάμενοι
τροφάς, οἱ δὲ λοιποὶ μικροῦ πάντες εἰς νόσους
δεινὰς κατέπεσον ἀρχομένας μὲν ἀπὸ μικρῶν
ἐξανθημάτων, ἃ περὶ τοὺς ἔξωθεν χρῶτας ἀνίστατο,
κατασκηπτούσας δ᾽ εἰς ἕλκη μεγάλα φαγεδαίναις
ὅμοια, πονηρὰν μὲν ὄψιν, δεινὴν δὲ ἀλγηδόνα
4 παρέχοντα. ἦν τε οὐθὲν ἴαμα τῆς περιωδυνίας
τοῖς κάμνουσιν ὅ τι μὴ κνησμοὶ καὶ σπαραγμοὶ
συνεχεῖς λωβώμενοι τοῖς χρωσὶ μέχρι γυμνώσεως
ὀστέων. Ambr.

V. (5) Μετ᾽ οὐ πολὺ δὲ οἱ δήμαρχοι Καμίλλῳ
φθονήσαντες ἐκκλησίαν κατ᾽ αὐτοῦ συνήγαγον
καὶ ἐζημίωσαν αὐτὸν δέκα μυριάσιν ἀσσαρίων, [3]

and one of them, either in jest and sport or desiring an omen, asked whether the goddess wished to remove to Rome, the statue answered in a loud voice that she did. This happened twice ; for the young men, doubting whether it was the statue that had spoken, asked the same question again and heard the same reply.

IV. (4) Under the consuls who succeeded Camillus[1] a pestilence visited Rome, caused by a lack of rain and severe droughts, which damaged the land devoted to orchards as well as that which was planted to corn, so that they produced scanty and unwholesome harvests for human beings and scanty and poor grazing for stock. Countless sheep and beasts of burden perished for lack not only of fodder but also of water ; to such an extent did the rivers and other streams fail, at the very season when all live stock suffers most from thirst. As for human beings, a few perished as the result of resorting to food of which they had made no previous test, while nearly all the rest were afflicted with severe maladies that began with small pustules, which broke out on various parts of the skin and ended up in large ulcers resembling cancers, evil in appearance and causing terrible pain. And there was no remedy for the agony suffered by the victims except continual scratching and tearing of the sores until the tortured flesh laid bare the bones.

V. (5) A little later the civil tribunes,[2] in their hatred of Camillus, convened an assembly to attack him and fined him 100,000 *asses*. They were not

---

[1] *Cf.* Livy v. 31, 5.   [2] *Cf.* Livy v. 32, 7-9.

---

[1] Struve : ἀφ' Q.
[2] Mai : σπανισάμενος Q, ἐσπανισμένον Enthoven.
[3] ἀσσαρίων added by Mai.

οὐκ ἀγνοοῦντες ὅτι πολλοστόν τι μέρος ὁ βίος ἦν
αὐτῷ τοῦ κατακρίματος, ἀλλ' ἵν' ἀπαχθεὶς εἰς τὸ
δεσμωτήριον ὑπὸ τῶν δημάρχων ἀσχημονήσῃ ὁ
τοὺς ἐπιφανεστάτους κατορθώσας πολέμους. τὸ
μὲν οὖν ἀργύριον οἱ πελάται τε καὶ συγγενεῖς
αὐτοῦ συνεισενέγκαντες ἐκ τῶν ἰδίων χρημάτων
ἀπέδοσαν, ὥστε μηδεμιᾶς πειραθῆναι ὕβρεως, ὁ
δ' ἀνὴρ ἀφόρητον ἡγούμενος τὸν προπηλακισμὸν
2 ἐκχωρεῖν ἔγνω τῆς πόλεως. (6) γενόμενος δὲ
πλησίον τῶν πυλῶν καὶ τοὺς παρόντας ἀσπα-
σάμενος ὀλοφυρομένους καὶ δακρύοντας οἵου στέρε-
σθαι μέλλοιεν ἀνδρός, πολλὰ κατὰ τῶν παρειῶν
ἀφεὶς δάκρυα καὶ τὴν κατασχοῦσαν αὐτὸν ἀσχη-
μοσύνην ἀνακλαυσάμενος, εἶπεν· '' Ὦ θεοὶ καὶ
δαίμονες, ἔφοροι τῶν ἀνθρωπίνων ἔργων, ὑμᾶς
ἀξιῶ δικαστὰς γενέσθαι μοι τῶν τε πρὸς τὴν
πατρίδα πολιτευμάτων καὶ παντὸς τοῦ παρελη-
3 λυθότος βίου· ἔπειτ', ἐὰν μὲν ἔνοχον εὑρῆτέ με[1]
ταῖς αἰτίαις ἐφ' αἷς ὁ δῆμος κατεψηφίσατό μου,
πονηρὰν καὶ ἀσχήμονα τελευτὴν δοῦναι τοῦ βίου,
ἐὰν δ' ἐν ἅπασιν οἷς ἐπιστεύθην ὑπὸ τῆς πατρίδος
ἐν εἰρήνῃ τε καὶ κατὰ πολέμους εὐσεβῆ καὶ
δίκαιον καὶ πάσης ἀσχήμονος ὑποψίας καθαρόν,
τιμωροὺς γενέσθαι μοι, τοιούτους ἐπιστήσαντας
τοῖς ἠδικηκόσι κινδύνους καὶ φόβους δι' οὓς
ἀναγκασθήσονται μηδεμίαν ἄλλην ἐλπίδα σωτηρίας
ὁρῶντες ἐπ' ἐμὲ καταφυγεῖν.'' ταῦτ' εἰπὼν εἰς
πόλιν Ἀρδέαν ᾤχετο. Ambr.

VI. (7) Ὑπήκουσαν[2] δὲ αὐτοῦ ταῖς εὐχαῖς οἱ
θεοί, καὶ ὑπὸ Κελτῶν μετὰ μικρὸν ἡ πόλις ἑάλω
ἄνευ τοῦ Καπιτωλίου. καταφυγόντων δὲ ἐν αὐτῷ
τῶν περιφανεστέρων—τὸ γὰρ ἄλλο πλῆθος ἐν ταῖς

unaware that his entire estate was but a small fraction of the amount of the fine, but they desired that this man who had won the most famous wars might incur disgrace by being haled to prison by the tribunes. The money was contributed by his clients and relatives from their own funds and paid over, so that he might suffer no indignity ; but Camillus, feeling that the insult was unendurable, resolved to quit the city. (6) When he had drawn near the gate and had embraced his friends there present who were lamenting and weeping at the thought of what a great man they were about to lose, he let many a tear roll down his cheeks and bewailed the disgrace that had befallen him, and then said : " Ye gods and genii who watch over the deeds of men, I ask you to become the judges of the measures I have taken with respect to the fatherland and of all my past life. Then, if you find me guilty of the charges on which the people have condemned me, that you will put a bad and shameful end to my life ; but if in all the duties with which I have been entrusted by the fatherland both in peace and in war you find me to have been pious and just and free from any shameful suspicion, that you will become my avengers, bringing such perils and terrors upon those who have wronged me that they will be compelled, seeing no other hope of safety, to turn to me for help." After uttering these words he retired to the city of Ardea.

VI. (7) The gods gave ear to his prayers,[1] and a little later the city, with the exception of the Capitol, was captured by the Gauls. When the more prominent men had taken refuge on this hill and were being

<hr />

[1] *Cf.* Livy v. 45, 7–46, 11 ; 49, 1-6.

<hr />

[1] Mai : μοι Q.   [2] Cobet : ἐπήκουσαν Q.

Ἰταλικαῖς φεῦγον διεσπάρη πόλεσι—καὶ πολιορκουμένων ὑπὸ Κελτῶν, οἱ παρὰ τὴν Οὐιεντανῶν πόλιν
καταφυγόντες Ῥωμαῖοι Καιδίκιόν τινα στρατο-
πεδάρχην ποιοῦσιν· ὁ δὲ Κάμιλλον ἀποδείκνυσι
καὶ ταῦτ' ἀπόντα ἡγεμόνα πολέμου καὶ εἰρήνης
2 ἐξουσίαν ἔχοντα αὐτοκράτορα. καὶ γενόμενος
ἡγεμὼν τῆς πρεσβείας παρεκάλει Κάμιλλον δι-
αλλαγῆναι πρὸς τὴν πατρίδα, τὰς συμφορὰς ἐν αἷς
ἦν[1] ἐπιλογισάμενον, δι' ἃς ὑπέμεινεν ἐπὶ τὸν
3 ὑβρισθέντα ὑφ' ἑαυτῆς καταφυγεῖν. (8) ὑποτυχὼν
δὲ ὁ Κάμιλλος εἶπεν· " Οὐ δέομαι παρακλήσεως,
ὦ Καιδίκιε· αὐτὸς γάρ, εἰ μὴ θᾶττον ὑμεῖς ἀφ-
ίκεσθε κοινωνεῖν με τῶν πραγμάτων ἀξιοῦντες,
ἕτοιμος ἦν ταύτην ἄγων τὴν δύναμιν, ἣν παροῦσαν
ὁρᾶτέ μοι, πρὸς ὑμᾶς ἥκειν. ὑμῖν δέ, ὦ θεοί τε
καὶ δαίμονες, ὅσοι τὸν ἀνθρώπινον ἐποπτεύετε
βίον, ὧν τε ἤδη τετιμήκατέ μοι[2] πολλὴν οἶδα
χάριν, καὶ περὶ τῶν μελλόντων εὔχομαι καλὴν
καὶ εὐτυχῆ τῇ πατρίδι γενέσθαι τὴν ἐμὴν κάθοδον.
4 εἰ δὲ ἐνῆν ἀνθρώπῳ τὰ μέλλοντα συμβήσεσθαι
προϊδεῖν, οὐδέποτ' ἂν εὐξάμην ἐς τοιαύτας ἐλθοῦσαν
τύχας τὴν πατρίδα δεηθῆναί μου· μυριάκις δ' ἂν
εἱλόμην ἄζηλον γενέσθαι μοι καὶ ἄτιμον τὸν μετὰ
ταῦτα βίον ἢ βαρβάρων ἀνθρώπων ὠμότητι γενομένην τὴν Ῥώμην ὑποχείριον ἐπιδεῖν καὶ ἐν ἐμοὶ
μόνῳ[3] τὰς λοιπὰς ἐλπίδας τῆς σωτηρίας ἐχούσαν."
5 ταῦτ' εἰπὼν καὶ τὰς δυνάμεις παραλαβὼν ἄφνω
τε τοῖς Κελτοῖς ἐπιφανεὶς εἰς φυγὴν αὐτοὺς τρέπει
καὶ ἐμπεσὼν ἀσυντάκτοις τε καὶ τεταραγμένοις
δίκην προβάτων κατέσφαξεν. Ambr.

---

[1] ἦν (or εἴη) Struve : ᾗ Q.   [2] με Struve.
[3] Struve : μόνον Q.

besieged by the Gauls,—the rest of the population had fled and dispersed themselves among the cities of Italy,—the Romans who had taken refuge at Veii made a certain Caedicius commander of the army ; and he appointed Camillus, absent though he was, to be general with absolute power over war and peace. And having been made leader of the embassy, he urged Camillus to become reconciled with the fatherland, bearing in mind the calamities encompassing it, such that it could bring itself to turn for help to the man whom it had despitefully used. (8) Camillus replied : " I need no urging, Caedicius. For of my own accord, if you envoys had not come first asking me to share in the conduct of affairs, I was ready to go to you at the head of this force which you see here with me. And to you, O gods and genii who watch over the lives of mortals, I am not only very grateful for the honours which ye have already shown me, but I also pray with regard to the future that my return home may prove a good and fortunate thing for the fatherland. If it were possible for a mortal to foresee the things that are to be, I never would have prayed that my country should come into such misfortunes as these, so as to need me ; a thousand times over I should have preferred that my life henceforth should be unenvied and without honour rather than that I should see Rome subjected to the cruelty of barbarians and placing her remaining hopes of safety in me alone." After speaking thus he took his forces, and appearing suddenly before the Gauls, turned them to flight ; and falling upon them while they were in disorder and confusion, he slew them like sheep.

VII. (9) Ἔτι δ' οὖν πολιορκουμένων τῶν ἐν τῷ[1] Καπιτωλίῳ καταφυγόντων νέος τις ἀπὸ τῆς Οὐιεντανῶν πόλεως ὑπὸ Ῥωμαίων πεμφθεὶς εἰς τοὺς ἐν τῷ Καπιτωλίῳ καὶ[2] λαθὼν τοὺς αὐτόθι φυλάσσοντας Κελτοὺς ἀνῆλθέ τε καὶ εἰπὼν ὅσα 2 ἔδει πάλιν ὑπὸ νύκτα ἀπηλλάγη. ὡς δὲ ἡμέρα ἐγένετο, τῶν Κελτῶν τις ἰδὼν τὰ ἴχνη λέγει πρὸς τὸν βασιλέα, ὁ δὲ συγκαλέσας τοὺς ἀνδρειοτάτους ἐδήλωσεν αὐτοῖς τὴν τοῦ Ῥωμαίου ἄνοδον· ἔπειτ' αὐτοὺς ἠξίου τὴν αὐτὴν ἐκείνῳ παρασχομένους τόλμαν πειρᾶσθαι τῆς ἐπὶ τὸ φρούριον ἀναβάσεως, πολλὰς ὑπισχνούμενος τοῖς ἀναβᾶσι δωρεάς. ὁμολογησάντων δὲ συχνῶν παρήγγειλε τοῖς φύλαξιν ἡσυχίαν ἄγειν, ἵνα καθεύδειν αὐτοὺς ὑπολαβόντες οἱ Ῥωμαῖοι καὶ αὐτοὶ πρὸς ὕπνον τράπωνται. 3 (10) ἤδη δὲ τῶν πρώτων ἀναβεβηκότων καὶ τοὺς ὑστερίζοντας ἀναδεχομένων, ἵνα πλείους γενόμενοι τότε ἀποσφάξωσι τοὺς ἐν ταῖς φυλακαῖς καὶ καταλάβωνται τὸ ἔρυμα, ἀνθρώπων μὲν οὐδεὶς ἔμαθεν, ἱεροὶ δέ τινες Ἥρας χῆνες ἐν τῷ τεμένει τρεφόμενοι καταβοῶντες ἅμα καὶ τοῖς βαρβάροις ὁμόσε χωροῦντες κατήγοροι γίνονται τοῦ κακοῦ. 4 ἐκ δὲ τούτου ταραχή τε καὶ κραυγὴ καὶ δρόμος[3] ἁπάντων ἦν παρακαλούντων ἀλλήλους ἐπὶ τὰ ὅπλα, καὶ οἱ Κελτοὶ δὲ[4] πλείους ἤδη γεγονότες ἐχώρουν ἐνδοτέρω. Ambr.

VIII. (11) Ἐνθάδε τις τῶν ἐσχηκότων τὴν ὕπατον ἀρχήν, Μάρκος Μάλλιος, ἁρπάσας τὰ ὅπλα καὶ συστὰς τοῖς βαρβάροις τόν τε πρῶτον ἀναβάντα καὶ[5] κατὰ τῆς κεφαλῆς αὐτοῦ τὸ ξίφος

[1] τῷ added by Struve.　　[2] καὶ deleted by Struve.
[3] ὁ before δρόμος deleted by Struve.

VII. (9) While those who had taken refuge on the Capitol [1] were still being besieged, a youth who had been sent by the Romans from Veii to those on the Capitol and had escaped the notice of the Gauls who were on guard there, went up, delivered his message, and departed again by night. When it was day, one of the Gauls saw his tracks and reported it to the king, who called together the bravest of his men and showed them where the Roman had gone up, then asked them to display the same bravery as the Roman and attempt to ascend to the citadel, promising many gifts to those who should make the ascent. When many undertook to do so, he commanded the guards to remain quiet, in order that the Romans, supposing them to be asleep, might themselves turn to sleep. (10) When the first men had now ascended and were waiting for those who lagged behind, in order that when their numbers were increased they might then slay the garrison and capture the stronghold, no mortal became aware of it ; but some sacred geese of Juno which were being raised in the sanctuary, by making a clamour and at the same time rushing at the barbarians, gave notice of the peril. Thereupon there was confusion, shouting and rushing about on the part of all as they encouraged one another to take up arms ; and the Gauls, whose numbers were now increased, advanced farther inside.

VIII. (11) Thereupon one of the men who had held the office of consul, Marcus Manlius, snatched up his arms and engaged with the barbarians. The one of them who had ascended first and was bringing

---

[1] For chaps. 7 f. *cf.* Livy v. 47.

---

[4] δὲ added by Struve.
[5] καὶ added by Kiessling.

φέροντα φθάσας παίει[1] κατὰ τοῦ βραχίονος κα[2]
2 ἀποκόπτει τὸν ἀγκῶνα· καὶ τὸν ἐπὶ τούτῳ πρὶν‹
εἰς χεῖρας ἐλθεῖν ὀρθῷ τῷ θυρεῷ πατάξας εἰς τὸ
πρόσωπον ἀνατρέπει καὶ κείμενον ἀποσφάττει, ἔπειτα τοὺς ἄλλους τεταραγμένους ἤδη ἐλαύνων ὑπὸ
πόδας, οὓς μὲν ἀπέκτεινεν, οὓς δὲ κατὰ τοῦ κρημνοῦ
διώκων ἐξέχεεν. ἀντὶ ταύτης εὕρατο τῆς ἀριστείας
τὴν πρέπουσαν τῷ τότε καιρῷ δωρεὰν παρὰ τῶν
κατεχόντων τὸ Καπιτώλιον, οἴνου καὶ ζέας τὴν[3]
3 ἐφήμερον ἀνδρὸς ἑκάστου τροφήν. (12) περὶ δὲ
τῶν ἐν[4] ἐκείνῳ τῷ τόπῳ τὴν φυλακὴν ἐκλιπόν-
των καθ' ὃν ἀνέβησαν οἱ Κελτοὶ ζητήσεως γενομένης ὅ τι χρὴ ποιεῖν, ἡ μὲν βουλὴ θάνατον
ἁπάντων κατεψηφίσατο, ὁ δὲ δῆμος ἐπιεικέστερος
γενόμενος ἑνὸς τοῦ ἡγεμόνος αὐτῶν ἠρκέσθη τῇ
4 κολάσει. ἵνα δὲ φανερὸς γένοιτο τοῖς βαρβάροις
ὁ θάνατος αὐτοῦ, δεθεὶς τὰς χεῖρας ὀπίσω κατὰ
τοῦ κρημνοῦ βάλλεται πρὸς αὐτούς. ἐκείνου δὲ
τιμωρηθέντος οὐδὲν ἔτι ῥάθυμον ἦν τῶν περὶ τὰς
φυλακάς, ἀλλὰ παννύχιοι διετέλουν ἅπαντες ἐγρη-
γορότες, ὥστε τοὺς Κελτοὺς ἀπογνόντας δι'
ἀπάτης ἢ κλοπῆς καθέξειν τὸ φρούριον περὶ λύτρων
διαλέγεσθαι, ἃ τοῖς βαρβάροις δόντες κομιοῦνται
τὴν πόλιν. Ambr.

IX. (13) Ἐπεὶ δὲ τὰ ὅρκια ἐπετέλεσαν καὶ τὸ
χρυσίον οἱ Ῥωμαῖοι κατήνεγκαν, σταθμὸς μὲν ἦν
ὃν ἔδει τοὺς Κελτοὺς λαβεῖν ε' καὶ κ' τάλαντα·
τεθέντος δὲ τοῦ ζυγοῦ πρῶτον μὲν αὐτὸ τὸ τάλαντον
ὁ Κελτὸς βαρύτερον τοῦ δικαίου παρῆν φέρων,

---

[1] πάλει Q.   [2] ἢ after πρὶν deleted by Kiessling.
[3] τὴν Mai : τὸ Q.   [4] ἐν added by Struve.

his sword down over Manlius' head he forestalled by striking him on the arm and cutting off his forearm, and the one who followed the first he struck in the face with his raised shield before he could come to close quarters, knocked him down and slew him as he lay there ; then pressing hard upon the others, who were now in confusion, he killed some of them and pursued and pushed others over the cliff. For this act of valour he received from those who were holding the Capitol the award which was suited to those times, a man's daily ration of wine and emmer. (12) When the question was raised what should be done in the case of those sentries who had deserted their post where the Gauls ascended, the senate voted the death penalty against them all ; but the populace, showing itself more lenient, was content with the punishment of one man, their leader. However, in order that his death might be manifest to the barbarians, he was hurled down upon them from the cliff with his hands bound behind his back. When he had been punished, there was no further carelessness on the part of the sentries, but they all kept awake the whole night long. In consequence, the Gauls, despairing of taking the fortress by deceit or surprise, began to talk of a ransom, by the payment of which to the barbarians the Romans would get back the city.

IX. (13) When they had made their compact [1] and the Romans had brought the gold, the weight which the Gauls were to receive was twenty-five talents. But when the balance had been set up, the Gaul first came with the weight itself, representing the talent,

---

[1] *Cf.* Livy v. 48, 8 f.

ἔπειτα ἀγανακτούντων πρὸς τοῦτο τῶν Ῥωμαίων
τοσούτου ἐδέησε μετριάσαι περὶ τὸ δίκαιον ὥστε
καὶ τὴν μάχαιραν ἅμα τῇ θήκῃ καὶ τῷ ζωστῆρι
2 περιελόμενος ἐπέθηκε τοῖς σταθμοῖς. τῷ δὲ ταμίᾳ
πυνθανομένῳ τί θέλει τοῦτ' εἶναι τὸ ἔργον ἀπεκρί-
νατο τούτοις τοῖς[1] ὀνόμασιν· " 'Οδύνη τοῖς κεκρα-
τημένοις." ἐπεὶ δὲ ὁ συγκείμενος σταθμὸς οὐκ
ἐξεπληροῦτο διὰ τὴν τοῦ Κελτοῦ πλεονεξίαν ἀλλὰ
καὶ τὸ τρίτον ἐνέδει μέρος, ἀπῄεσαν οἱ Ῥωμαῖοι
χρόνον εἰς συμπορισμὸν τοῦ λείποντος αἰτησάμενοι·
ὑπέμειναν δὲ ταύτην τὴν ὑπερηφανίαν τῶν βαρβάρων οὐθὲν ἐγνωκότες τῶν ἐπὶ τοῦ στρατοπέδου
πραττομένων παρὰ Καιδικίου καὶ Καμίλλου, ὡς
ἔφαμεν. Ambr.

X. (14) Ἡ δὲ αἰτία τῆς εἰς[2] Ἰταλίαν τῶν Κελτῶν ἀφίξεως τοιάδε ἦν. Λοκόμων τις Τυρρηνῶν
ἡγεμὼν μέλλων τελευτᾶν τὸν βίον ἀνδρὶ πιστῷ
Ἄρροντι ὄνομα παρακατέθετο τὸν υἱὸν ἐπιτροπεύ-
ειν· τελευτήσαντος δὲ τοῦ Τυρρηνοῦ παραλαβὼν
τὴν ἐπιμέλειαν τοῦ παιδίου ὁ Ἄρρων ἐπιμελὴς
καὶ δίκαιος γέγονε[3] τῆς πίστεως φύλαξ, καὶ εἰς
ἄνδρας ἐλθόντι πᾶσαν ἀπέδειξε τῷ παιδὶ τὴν
καταλειφθεῖσαν[4] ὑπὸ τοῦ πατρὸς οὐσίαν. ἀνθ' ὧν
οὐχ ὁμοίας ἐκομίσατο παρὰ τοῦ μειρακίου χάρι-
2 τας. (15) οὔσης γὰρ αὐτῷ γυναικὸς εὐμόρφου καὶ
νέας, ἧς περὶ πλείστου τὴν κοινωνίαν ἐποιεῖτο,
σώφρονος τὸν ἄλλον χρόνον ἅπαντα γενομένης
ἐρασθεὶς ὁ νεανίσκος ἅμα τῷ σώματι καὶ τὴν διάνοιαν τῆς ἀνθρώπου διέφθειρεν, καὶ[5] οὐκέτι κρύβδα
ἀλλ' ἀναφανδὸν ἐζήτει αὐτῇ διαλέγεσθαι. ἀχθό-

---

[1] τοῖς added by Struve.   [2] εἰς (ἐς) added by Mai.
[3] ἐγεγόνει Struve.   [4] Struve : καταληφθεῖσαν Q.

heavier than was right, and then, when the Romans expressed resentment at this, he was so far from being reasonable and just that he also threw into the scales his sword together with the scabbard and also his belt, which he had taken off. And to the quaestor's inquiry what that action meant, he replied in these words : " Woe to the vanquished ! " When the full weight agreed upon was not made up because of the Gaul's greediness, but the third part was lacking, the Romans departed after asking for time to collect the amount wanting. They submitted to this insolence of the barbarians because they were quite unaware of what was being done in the camp, as I have related, by Caedicius and Camillus.

X. (14) The reason why the Gauls came into Italy was as follows.[1] A certain Lucumo, a prince of the Tyrrhenians, being about to die, entrusted his son to a loyal man named Arruns as guardian. Upon the death of the Tyrrhenian, Arruns, taking over the guardianship of the boy, proved diligent and just in carrying out his trust, and when the boy came to manhood, turned over to him the entire estate left by his father. For this service he did not receive similar kindness from the youth. (15) It seems that Arruns had a beautiful young wife, of whose society he was extremely fond and who had always shown herself chaste up to that time ; but the young man, becoming enamoured of her, corrupted her mind as well as her body, and sought to hold converse with her not only in secret but openly as well. Arruns,

---

[1] For chaps. 10 f. *cf.* Livy v. 33–35, 4.

[5] καὶ added by Mai.

μενος δὴ ὁ Ἄρρων τῷ ἀποσπασμῷ[1] τῆς γυναικὸς
καὶ ἐφ᾽ οἷς ὑβρίζετο πρὸς ἀμφοτέρων δυσανασχε-
τῶν, τιμωρίαν δὲ οὐ δυνάμενος παρ᾽ αὐτῶν λαβεῖν,
ἀποδημίαν ἐστείλατο πρόφασιν αὐτῆς ποιησάμενος
3 ἐμπορίαν. ἀσμένως δὲ τοῦ νεανίσκου τὴν ἀπαλλαγὴν αὐτοῦ δεξαμένου καὶ παρασχόντος ὅσων εἰς
τὴν ἐμπορίαν ἐδεῖτο, πολλοὺς μὲν ἀσκοὺς οἴνου
τε καὶ ἐλαίου ταῖς ἁμάξαις ἐπιθέμενος, πολλοὺς
δὲ φορμοὺς σύκων, ἦγεν εἰς τὴν Κελτικήν. Ambr.

XI. (16) Οἱ δὲ Κελτοὶ οὔτε οἶνον ἀμπέλινον
εἰδότες τηνικαῦτα οὔτε ἔλαιον οἷον αἱ παρ᾽ ἡμῖν
ἐλαῖαι φέρουσιν, ἀλλ᾽ οἴνῳ μὲν χρώμενοι κριθῆς
σαπείσης ἐν ὕδατι χυλῷ δυσώδει, ἐλαίῳ δὲ συείῳ
στέατι πεπαλαιωμένῳ τήν τε ὀδμὴν καὶ τὴν γεῦσιν
ἀτόπῳ, τότε δὲ[2] πρῶτον ἀπολαύσαντες ὧν οὔπω
ἐγεύσαντο καρπῶν, θαυμαστὰς ὅσας ἐφ᾽ ἑκάστῳ
ἐλάμβανον ἡδονὰς καὶ τὸν ξένον ἠρώτων πῶς τε
γίνεται τούτων ἕκαστον καὶ παρὰ τίσιν ἀνθρώποις.
2 (17) ὁ δὲ Τυρρηνὸς πρὸς αὐτοὺς φησιν ὅτι γῇ μέν
ἐστιν ἡ τούτους ἐκφέρουσα τοὺς καρποὺς πολλὴ
καὶ ἀγαθή, νέμονται δὲ αὐτὴν ὀλίγοι τινὲς ἄνθρωποι
καὶ τὰ εἰς πόλεμον οὐδὲν ἀμείνους γυναικῶν,
ὑπέθετό τε αὐτοῖς μὴ δι᾽ ὠνῆς αὐτὰ παρ᾽ ἑτέρων
ἔτι λαμβάνειν, ἀλλ᾽ ἐκβαλόντας τοὺς τότε κυρίους
ὡς οἰκεῖα καρποῦσθαι. τούτοις δὴ τοῖς λόγοις οἱ
Κελτοὶ πειθόμενοι ἦλθον εἰς Ἰταλίαν καὶ Τυρρηνῶν τοὺς καλουμένους Κλουσίνους,[3] ὅθεν ἦν καὶ ὁ
πείσας αὐτοὺς πολεμεῖν.[4] Ambr.

XII. (18) Ἀποσταλέντων δὲ πρεσβευτῶν ἐκ Ῥώμης ἐπὶ Κελτούς, ἐπεὶ ἤκουσεν εἷς τῶν πρεσ-
βευόντων, Κόιντος Φάβιος, τοὺς βαρβάρους ἐπὶ

___
[1] Struve : ἀσπασμῷ Q. [2] δὲ added by Struve.

grieving at the seduction of his wife and distressed by the wanton wrong done him by them both, yet unable to take vengeance upon them, prepared for a sojourn abroad, ostensibly for the purpose of trading. When the youth welcomed his departure and provided everything that was necessary for trading, he loaded many skins of wine and olive oil and many baskets of figs on the waggons and set out for Gaul.

XI. (16) The Gauls at that time had no knowledge either of wine made from grapes or of oil such as is produced by our olive trees, but used for wine a foul-smelling liquor made from barley rotted in water, and for oil, stale lard, disgusting both in smell and taste. On that occasion, accordingly, when for the first time they enjoyed fruits which they had never before tasted, they got wonderful pleasure out of each ; and they asked the stranger how each of these articles was produced and among what men. (17) The Tyrrhenian told them that the country producing these fruits was large and fertile and that it was inhabited by only a few people, who were no better than women when it came to warfare ; and he advised them to get these products no longer by purchase from others, but to drive out the present owners and enjoy the fruits as their own. Persuaded by these words, the Gauls came into Italy and to the Tyrrhenians known as the Clusians,[1] from whence had come the man who persuaded them to make war.

XII. (18) When ambassadors had been sent from Rome to the Gauls [2] and one of them, Quintus Fabius, heard that the barbarians had gone out on a foraging

[1] The inhabitants of Clusium in Etruria.

[2] *Cf.* Livy v. 35, 5–43, 5.

---

[3] κλουσήνους Q.   [4] ἐπολέμουν Kiessling.

DIONYSIUS OF HALICARNASSUS

προνομὴν ἐξεληλυθέναι, συνάπτει πόλεμον αὐτοῖς
καὶ τὸν τῶν Κελτῶν ἡγεμόνα ἀναιρεῖ· ἀποστεί-
λαντες δὲ εἰς Ῥώμην οἱ βάρβαροι ἠξίουν[1] παρα-
διδόναι σφίσι τὸν ἄνδρα καὶ τὸν ἀδελφὸν αὐτοῦ
ἐκδότους ποινὰς ὑφέξοντας τῶν ἀπολωλότων.
2 (19) παρελκούσης δὲ τῆς βουλῆς τὰς ἀποκρίσεις
ἐπὶ τὴν Ῥώμην τὸν πόλεμον ἀναγκαίως[2] οἱ Κελτοὶ
μετήγαγον. οἱ δὲ Ῥωμαῖοι ἀκούσαντες ἐξήεσαν
ἐκ τῆς πόλεως ἄγοντες ἐκ μὲν τῶν ἐπιλέκτων τε
καὶ κατηθλημένων ἐν τοῖς πολέμοις στρατιωτῶν
τέτταρα τάγματα ἐντελῆ· ἐκ δὲ τῶν ἄλλων πολιτῶν τοὺς κατοικιδίους τε καὶ σχολαίους καὶ ἧττον ὡμιληκότας πολέμοις πλείους ὄντας ἀριθμῷ τῶν
ἑτέρων. τούτους δὴ τρεψάμενοι οἱ Κελτοὶ καὶ[3]
σύμπασαν τὴν Ῥώμην ἄνευ τοῦ Καπιτωλίου παρ-
εστήσαντο. Ambr.

[1] ἠξίουν A : ἠξίου Q.
[2] ἀναγκαίως Q : ἐξαπιναίως Struve, ἀγανακτοῦντες Hertlein.
[3] καὶ deleted by Kiessling.

Νέπετος, πόλις Ἰταλίας. Διονύσιος τρισκαιδεκάτῳ Ῥωμαϊκῆς ἀρχαιολογίας. τὸ ἐθνικὸν Νεπεσῖνος. *Stephanus
Byz.*

expedition, he joined battle with them and slew the leader of the Gauls. The barbarians, sending to Rome, demanded that Fabius and his brother be handed over to them to pay the penalty for the men who had been slain. (19) When the senate delayed its answer, the Gauls of necessity transferred the war to Rome. Upon hearing this, the Romans marched out of the city, bringing four entire legions of picked troops well trained in the wars, and also, from among the other citizens, those who led indoor or easy lives and had had less to do with wars, these being more numerous than the other sort. The Gauls, having put these forces to rout, reduced all of Rome except the Capitol.

Nepete, a city of Italy. Dionysius, *Roman Antiquities* xiii. *Eth.*[1] Nepesinus. (*Cf.* Livy vi. 9 f., 21.)

[1] The Greek word *ethnikon*, originally an adjective meaning " national," " pertaining to a nation or people," came to be used by the grammarians virtually as a noun meaning " the word for the inhabitant(s) " (of the country or place named). In the excerpts from Stephanus of Byzantium added at the ends of the various books it will be abbreviated as *Eth.* Since there are no recognized English forms in use for the inhabitants of most of the cities named in these excerpts, it seems best to render the Greek names by the Latin equivalents, even when these differ considerably in formation, as in the case of some at the end of Book XVIII.

EXCERPTS

FROM

BOOK XIV

I. (1) Ἡ δὲ Κελτικὴ κεῖται μὲν ἐν τῷ πρὸς τὴν ἑσπέραν καθήκοντι[1] τῆς Εὐρώπης μέρει μεταξὺ τοῦ τε βορείου πόλου καὶ τῆς ἰσημερινῆς δύσεως· τετράγωνος δὲ οὖσα τῷ σχήματι τοῖς μὲν Ἀλπείοις ὄρεσι μεγίστοις οὖσι τῶν Εὐρωπείων συνάπτει κατὰ τὰς ἀνατολάς, τοῖς δὲ Πυρρηναίοις κατὰ μεσημβρίαν τε καὶ νότον ἄνεμον, τῇ δὲ ἔξω στηλῶν Ἡρακλείων θαλάττῃ κατὰ τὰς δύσεις, τῷ δὲ Σκυθικῷ τε καὶ Θρᾳκίῳ γένει κατὰ βορέαν ἄνεμον καὶ ποταμὸν Ἴστρον, ὃς ἀπὸ τῶν Ἀλπείων καταβαίνων ὀρῶν μέγιστος τῶν τῇδε ποταμῶν καὶ [2] πᾶσαν τὴν ὑπὸ τοῖς ἄρκτοις ἤπειρον διελθὼν εἰς τὸ[2] Ποντικὸν ἐξερεύγεται πέλαγος. (2) τοσαύτη δὲ οὖσα τὸ μέγεθος ὅση μὴ πολὺ ἀποδεῖν τετάρτη λέγεσθαι μοῖρα τῆς Εὐρώπης, εὔυδρός τε καὶ πίειρα καὶ καρποῖς δαψιλὴς καὶ κτήνεσιν ἀρίστη νέμεσθαι, σχίζεται μέση ποταμῷ Ῥήνῳ, μεγίστῳ μετὰ τὸν Ἴστρον εἶναι δοκοῦντι τῶν κατὰ τὴν

---

[1] καθήκοντα Q.   [2] τὸν Q.

EXCERPTS

FROM

BOOK XIV

I. (1) The country of the Celts [1] lies in the part of
Europe which extends toward the West, between the
North pole and the equinoctial setting of the sun.
Having the shape of a square, it is bounded by the
Alps, the loftiest of the European mountains, on the
East, by the Pyrenees toward the meridian and
the south wind, by the sea that lies beyond the Pillars
of Hercules on the West, and by the Scythian and
Thracian nations toward the north wind and the river
Ister, which, descending from the Alps as the largest
of the rivers on this side, and flowing through the
whole continent that lies beneath the Bears, empties
into the Pontic sea. (2) This land, which is so large
in extent that it may be called almost the fourth part
of Europe and is well-watered, fertile, rich in crops
and most excellent for grazing cattle, is divided in
the middle by the river Rhine, reputed to be the

---

[1] *Cf.* Livy v. 34–35, 4. Dionysius regularly calls the
Gauls Celts, though he uses the term Galatia when referring
to Gaul proper or to the Roman province of Gaul. Up to
this point his " Celts " has been consistently rendered as
" Gauls "; but in the present chapter, as will be seen just
below, he includes Germany as part of the Celtic world.

3 Εὐρώπην ποταμῶν. καλεῖται δ' ἡ μὲν ἐπὶ τάδε
τοῦ Ῥήνου Σκύθαις καὶ Θραξὶν ὁμοροῦσα Γερ-
μανία, μέχρι δρυμοῦ Ἑρκυνίου[1] καὶ τῶν Ῥιπαίων
ὀρῶν καθήκουσα, ἡ δ' ἐπὶ θάτερα τὰ πρὸς μεσημβρίαν βλέποντα[2] μέχρι Πυρρήνης ὄρους, ἡ τὸν
Γαλατικὸν κόλπον περιλαμβάνουσα,[3] Γαλατία τῆς
4 θαλάττης ἐπώνυμος. (3) κοινῷ δ' ὀνόματι ἡ
σύμπασα πρὸς Ἑλλήνων καλεῖται Κελτική, ὡς
μέν τινές φασιν, ἀπό τινος γίγαντος Κελτοῦ αὐτόθι
δυναστεύσαντος· ἄλλοι δὲ ἐξ Ἡρακλέους καὶ
Ἀστερόπης τῆς Ἀτλαντίδος δύο γενέσθαι μυθο-
λογοῦσι παῖδας, Ἴβηρον καὶ Κελτόν, οὓς θέσθαι
ταῖς χώραις ὧν ἦρξαν ἀμφότεροι τὰς ὀνομασίας
5 ἀφ' αὐτῶν. οἱ δὲ ποταμὸν εἶναί τινα λέγουσι
Κελτὸν ἐκ τῆς Πυρρήνης ἀναδιδόμενον, ἀφ' οὗ
πρῶτον μὲν τὴν σύνεγγυς, ἔπειτα δὲ καὶ τὴν ἄλλην
χώραν σὺν χρόνῳ κληθῆναι Κελτικήν. φασὶ δὲ
καί τινες ὅτι τοῖς πρώτοις Ἕλλησιν εἰς τήνδε τὴν
γῆν περαιουμένοις αἱ νῆες ἀνέμῳ βιαίῳ φερόμεναι
κατὰ τὸν κόλπον ἔκελσαν τὸν Γαλατικόν, οἱ δ'
ἄνδρες, ἐπειδὴ τοῦ αἰγιαλοῦ ἐλάβοντο, Κελσικὴν
ἀπὸ τοῦ συμβάντος αὐτοῖς πάθους τὴν χώραν
ἐκάλεσαν, ἣν ἑνὸς ἀλλαγῇ γράμματος οἱ μετα-
γενέστεροι Κελτικὴν ὠνόμασαν. Ambr.

II. (4) Ἀθήνησι μὲν ἐν τοῦ γηγενοῦς Ἐρεχθέως
τῷ σηκῷ[4] ἱερά τις ὑπ' Ἀθηνᾶς φυτευθεῖσα ἐλαία
κατὰ τὴν ἔριν τὴν γενομένην αὐτῇ πρὸς Ποσειδῶνα
περὶ τῆς χώρας, ἅμα τοῖς ἄλλοις τοῖς ἐν τῷ ἱερῷ
οὖσιν ἐμπρησθεῖσα ὑπὸ τῶν βαρβάρων ὅτε τῆς
ἀκροπόλεως ἐκράτησαν, δευτέρᾳ τῆς ἐμπρήσεως

---

[1] ταρκηνίου or ταρκυνίου Q.
[2] βλέπουσα Struve.

260

largest river in Europe after the Ister. The part on this side of the Rhine, bordering upon the Scythians and Thracians, is called Germany, and extends as far as the Hercynian forest and the Rhipaean mountains ; the other part, on the side facing the South, as far as the Pyrenees range and embracing the Gallic gulf, is called Gaul after the sea. (3) The whole country is called by the Greeks by the common name Celtica (Keltikê), according to some, from a giant Celtus who ruled there ; others, however, have a legend that to Hercules and Asteropê, the daughter of Atlas, were born two sons, Iberus and Celtus, who gave their own names to the lands which they ruled. Others state that there is a river Celtus rising in the Pyrenees, after which the neighbouring region at first, and in time the rest of the land as well, was called Celtica. There are also some who say that when the first Greeks came to this region their ships, driven by a violent wind, came to land in the Gallic gulf, and that the men upon reaching shore called the country Celsica (Kelsikê) because of this experience of theirs[1] ; and later generations, by the change of one letter, called it Celtica.

II. (4) At Athens, in the shrine of earth-born Erechtheus, an olive tree, planted by Athena at the time of her strife with Poseidon for the possession of the land, having been burned together with the other objects in the sanctuary by the barbarians when they captured the Acropolis, sent up from its stock a shoot

---

[1] Dionysius is deriving the name from the verb κέλλειν (aorist infinitive κέλσαι), " to put to shore."

---

[3] Struve : παραλαμβάνουσα Q.

[4] ἐν τοῦ γ. ʼE. τῷ σηκῷ Kiessling : ἐν τῇ γ. ʼE. τῷ σηκῷ Q, ἐν τῷ γ. ʼE. σηκῷ Mai, ἐν τῷ τοῦ γ. ʼE. σηκῷ Struve.

ἡμέρᾳ[1] βλαστὸν ἐκ τοῦ στελέχους ἀνῆκεν ὅσον τε πηχυαῖον,[2] δῆλον ἅπασι ποιῆσαι βουλομένων τῶν θεῶν ὅτι ταχέως ἑαυτὴν ἡ πόλις ἀναλαβοῦσα βλα- 2 στοὺς ἀντὶ τῶν παλαιῶν ἐξοίσει νέους. (5) ἐν δὲ τῇ ῾Ρώμῃ καλιάς[3] τις ῎Αρεος ἱερὰ περὶ τὴν κορυφὴν ἱδρυμένη τοῦ Παλατίου[4] συγκαταφλεγεῖσα ταῖς πέριξ οἰκίαις ἕως ἐδάφους, ἀνακαθαιρομένων τῶν οἰκοπέδων ἕνεκα τῆς ἐπισκευῆς, ἐν μέσῃ τῇ περικαύστῳ σποδῷ τὸ σύμβολον τοῦ συνοικισμοῦ τῆς πόλεως διέσωσεν ἀπαθές, ῥόπαλον ἐκ θατέρου τῶν ἄκρων ἐπικάμπιον,[5] οἷα φέρουσι βουκόλοι καὶ νομεῖς, οἱ μὲν καλαύροπας, οἱ δὲ λαγωβόλα κα- λοῦντες, ᾧ ῾Ρωμύλος ὀρνιθευόμενος διέγραφε τῶν οἰωνῶν τὰς χώρας ὅτε τὴν πόλιν οἰκίζειν ἔμελλεν. 3 Εὐζώνῳ καὶ οὐδὲν ἔξω τῶν ὅπλων φερούσῃ στρατιᾷ.

Κρότου καταρραγέντος, ὡς ἐπὶ μεγίστῳ μὲν θεάματι, καλλίστῳ δ' ἀκούσματι, οἵ τε βεβαίως ἄποροι καὶ οἱ πλαττόμενοι τὴν εἰς τὸ παντελὲς ἀπορίαν. *Ambr.*

III. (8) ῞Οτι Μάρκος Φούριος ὁ δικτάτωρ ἀνὴρ ἦν τῶν κατὰ τὴν αὐτὴν ἀκμασάντων ἡλικίαν τά τε πολέμια λαμπρότατος καὶ τὰ πολιτικὰ[6] φρονι- μώτατος. *Vales.*

IV. (6) Μάλλιος, ὁ ἀριστεύσας ὅτε εἰς τὸ Καπιτώλιον ῾Ρωμαῖοι κατέφυγον, κινδυνεύων διὰ τυραννίδος ἐπίθεσιν ἀπολέσθαι, βλέψας εἰς τὸ Καπιτώλιον καὶ τὰς χεῖρας ἐκτείνας εἰς τὸν ἐν αὐτῷ νεὼν τοῦ Διὸς εἶπεν· " Οὐδ' ἐκεῖνος ὁ τόπος

---

[1] δευτέρα . . . ἡμέρᾳ Struve : δευτέραν . . . ἡμέραν Q.
[2] παχυαῖον Q.   [3] Kiessling : καλιά Q.
[4] παλαντίου Q.

about a cubit in length the day after the fire, the gods wishing to make it manifest to all that the city would quickly recover itself and send up new shoots in place of the old. (5) In Rome likewise a sacred hut of Mars, built near the summit of the Palatine, was burned to the ground together with the houses round about ; but when the area was being cleared for the purpose of restoring the buildings, it preserved unharmed in the midst of the surrounding ashes the symbol of the settlement of the city, a staff curved at one end, like those carried by herdsmen and shepherds, which some call *kalauropes* and others *lagobola*. With this staff Romulus, on the occasion of taking the auspices when he was intending to found the city, marked out the regions for the omens.

With an army of light troops carrying nothing but their arms.

Applause having burst forth, as if at something most magnificent to behold and most glorious to hear, both those who were genuinely perplexed and those who feigned extreme perplexity . . .

III. (8) Marcus Furius the dictator [1] was of all his contemporaries the most brilliant in warfare and the shrewdest in handling public affairs.

IV. (6) Manlius,[2] the man who had distinguished himself for valour at the time when the Romans took refuge on the Capitol, when he was in danger of losing his life because of an attempt at tyranny, looked toward the Capitol, and stretching out his hands toward the temple of Jupiter that stood upon it, exclaimed :

---

[1] *Cf.* Livy v. 19, 2 ; 23, 1.
[2] *Cf.* Livy vi. 20, 1-12.

---

[5] Struve : ἐπικάμπτον Q, ἐπικάμπτων Λ.
[6] πολιτικὰ Valesius : πολεμικὰ P.

ἱκανὸς ἔσται με σῶσαι ὃν ὑπὸ τῶν βαρβάρων
κρατηθέντα διέσωσα ὑμῖν ἐγώ; ἀλλὰ καὶ τότε
ὑπὲρ ὑμῶν ἀπέθνησκον καὶ νῦν ὑφ' ὑμῶν ἀπο-
θανοῦμαι." τότε μὲν οὖν συμπαθήσαντες ἀφῆκαν
αὐτόν, ὕστερον δὲ κατὰ κρημνοῦ ἐρρίφη. Ambr.

V. (7) Κρατήσας τῶν πολεμίων καὶ τὴν στρατιὰν
ἐπικλύσας ταῖς ὠφελείαις Τίτος Κοΐντιος δικτα-
τορεύων ἐν ἡμέραις ἐννέα πόλεις ἐννέα πολεμίων
ἔλαβεν.

Ληφθέντες ἀμφοτέρωθεν ἀγεληδὸν οἱ θεοστυγεῖς
κατεκόπησαν. Ambr.

VI. (8) Ὅτι οἱ Ῥωμαῖοι μεγαλοπρεπεῖς. τῶν
γὰρ ἄλλων ὀλίγου δεῖν πάντων ἔν τε τοῖς κοινοῖς
τῶν πόλεων πράγμασι καὶ ἐν τοῖς ἰδίοις βίοις
πρὸς τὰ τελευταῖα τῶν συμβαινόντων τὰς διανοίας
μεθαρμοττομένων καὶ πολλάκις ἔχθρας τε μεγάλας
διὰ τὰς τυχούσας φιλανθρωπίας καταλυομένων καὶ
φιλίας πολυχρονίους διὰ μικρὰ καὶ φαῦλα προσκρού-
ματα διαιρούντων, ἐκεῖνοι τοὐναντίον ἐπὶ τῶν
φίλων ᾤοντο χρῆναι ποιεῖν, ταῖς τε[1] παλαιαῖς
εὐεργεσίαις χαρίζεσθαι τὰς ἐπὶ τοῖς προσφάτοις
2 ἐγκλήμασιν ὀργάς. (9) θαυμαστὸν μὲν δὴ καὶ
τοῦτο τῶν ἀνδρῶν· λέγω δὲ[2] τὸ μηδενὶ μνησι-
κακῆσαι τῶν Τυσκλανῶν, ἀλλὰ πάντας ἀφεῖναι τοὺς
ἐξαμαρτόντας ἀζημίους· πολλῷ δ' ἔτι τούτου θαυμασιώτερον ὃ μετὰ τὴν ἄφεσιν τῶν ἐγκλημάτων
αὐτοῖς ἐχαρίσαντο.[3] σκοπούμενοι γὰρ ὡς[4] μηδὲν
ἔτι τοιοῦτον ἐν τῇ πόλει γενήσεται μηδ' ἀφορμὴν
νεωτερισμοῦ λήψονταί τινες, οὔτε φρουρὰν εἰς τὴν
ἀκρόπολιν αὐτῶν ᾤοντο δεῖν εἰσάγειν οὔτε παρὰ

---

[1] τε added by Valesius. [2] δὲ added by Valesius.
[3] Valesius : ἐχαρίσατο P. [4] πῶς Naber, ὅπως Jacoby.

" Shall not even that place avail to save me which I preserved safe for you Romans when it had been captured by the barbarians ? Nay, not only was I then ready to perish in your behalf, but now also I shall perish at your hands." On this occasion, then, they let him off out of compassion, but later he was hurled down the precipice.

V. (7) Having vanquished the enemy and loaded down his army with countless spoils, Titus Quintius, while serving as dictator, took nine cities of the enemy in nine days.[1]

Hemmed in on both sides, these god-detested people were cut down in droves.

VI. (8) The Romans are magnanimous.[2] For, whereas nearly all others both in the public relations of their states and in their private lives change their feelings according to the latest developments, often laying aside great enmities because of chance acts of kindness and breaking up long-standing friendships because of slight and trivial offences, the Romans thought they ought to do just the opposite in the case of their friends and out of gratitude for ancient benefits to give up their resentment over recent causes for complaint. (9) Even this, then, was remarkable on the part of those men, namely that they bore no malice against any of the Tusculans, but let all the offenders go unpunished ; yet much more remarkable than this was the favour which they showed them after pardoning their offences. For when they were considering ways and means that nothing of the sort might happen again in that city and that none might find a ground for rebellion, they thought they ought neither to introduce a garrison into the Tusculans' citadel nor

---

[1] *Cf.* Livy vi. 28, 3 ; 29, 3-10.   [2] *Cf.* Livy vi. 25 f.

DIONYSIUS OF HALICARNASSUS

τῶν ἐπιφανεστάτων ἀνδρῶν ὅμηρα λαμβάνειν οὔτε
ὅπλα τοὺς ἔχοντας ἀφελέσθαι οὔτ᾽ ἄλλο σημεῖον
3 οὐδὲν ἀπιστουμένης φιλίας ποιῆσαι· μίαν δὲ πρᾶξιν
οἰόμενοι συνέχειν[1] ἅπαντας τοὺς κατὰ[2] συγγένειαν
ἢ φιλίαν προσήκοντας ἀλλήλοις τὴν τῶν ἀγαθῶν
ἰσομοιρίαν, πολιτείαν ἔγνωσαν τοῖς κρατηθεῖσι
χαρίσασθαι, πάντων μεταδόντες ὧν τοῖς φύσει
Ῥωμαίοις μετῆν, (10) οὐ τὴν αὐτὴν διάνοιαν
λαβόντες τοῖς ἀξιοῦσι τῆς Ἑλλάδος ἄρχειν οὔτ᾽
4 Ἀθηναίοις οὔτε Λακεδαιμονίοις· τί γὰρ δεῖ περὶ
τῶν ἄλλων Ἑλλήνων λέγειν; Ἀθηναῖοι μέν γε
Σαμίους ἀποίκους ἑαυτῶν ὄντας, Λακεδαιμόνιοι
δὲ Μεσσηνίους ἀδελφῶν οὐδὲν διαφέροντας, ἐπειδὴ
προσέκρουσαν αὐτοῖς τι, διαλυσάμενοι τὴν συγγένειαν οὕτως ὠμῶς διεχειρίσαντο καὶ θηριω-
δῶς, ἐπειδὴ τὰς πόλεις αὐτῶν ὑποχειρίους ἔλαβον,
ὥστε μηδὲ τοῖς ἀγριωτάτοις τῶν βαρβάρων ὑπερβολὴν τῆς εἰς τὰ ὁμόφυλα παρανομίας παραλιπεῖν.
5 (11) μυρία τοιαῦτα λέγειν ἄν τις ἔχοι ταῖς πόλεσι
ταύταις ἡμαρτημένα, ἃ παρίημι, ἐπεὶ καὶ τούτων
μεμνημένος ἄχθομαι· τὸ γὰρ Ἑλληνικὸν οὐκ ὀνόματι διαφέρειν τοῦ βαρβάρου ἠξίουν οὐδὲ διαλέκτου
χάριν, ἀλλὰ συνέσει καὶ χρηστῶν ἐπιτηδευμάτων
προαιρέσει, μάλιστα δὲ τῷ μηδὲν[3] τῶν ὑπὲρ τὴν
ἀνθρωπίνην φύσιν εἰς[4] ἀλλήλους παρανομεῖν. ὅσοις
μὲν οὖν ταῦτα[5] ἐπὶ πλεῖον ὑπῆρξεν ἐν τῇ φύσει,
τούτους οἶμαι δεῖν λέγειν Ἕλληνας, ὅσοις δὲ
6 τἀναντία, βαρβάρους. καὶ τὰς μὲν ἐπιεικεῖς καὶ

---

[1] συνέχειν added here by Prou, after πρᾶξιν by Valesius.
Jacoby suggested καθομιλεῖν, to follow οἰόμενοι.
[2] κατὰ Valesius : κατὰ τὴν P.
[3] Reiske : μηδενὶ P(?), Valesius.

to take hostages from the most prominent men nor to deprive of their arms those who had them nor to give any other indication of distrusting their friendship ; but believing that the one thing that holds together all who belong to one another by reason either of kinship or friendship is the equal sharing of their blessings, they decided to grant citizenship to the vanquished, giving them a part in everything in which the native-born Romans shared. (10) Thereby they took a very different view from that held by those who laid claim to the leadership of Greece, whether Athenians or Lacedaemonians—what need is there to mention the other Greeks ? For the Athenians in the case of the Samians, their own colonists, and the Lacedaemonians in the case of the Messenians, who were the same as their brothers, when these gave them some offence, dissolved the ties of kinship, and after subjugating their cities, treated them with such cruelty and brutality as to equal even the most savage of barbarians in their mistreatment of people of kindred stock. (11) One could name countless blunders of this sort made by these cities, even pass over them since it grieves me to mention but I these instances. For I would distinguish Greeks from barbarians, not by their name nor on the basis of their speech, but by their intelligence and their predilection for decent behaviour, and particularly by their indulging in no inhuman treatment of one another. All in whose nature these qualities predominated I believe ought to be called Greeks, but those of whom the opposite was true, barbarians. Likewise, their plans and actions which

---

⁴ εἰς Reiske, πρὸς Kiessling : om. P.
⁵ ταῦτα Reiske, τάδε Krüger : τὰ P.

267

φιλανθρώπους διανοίας τε καὶ πράξεις αὐτῶν
Ἑλληνικὰς εἶναι λογίζομαι, τὰς δὲ ὠμὰς καὶ
θηριώδεις, ἄλλως τε κἂν περὶ συγγενεῖς τε καὶ
φίλους γίνωνται, βαρβαρικάς. Τυσκλανοὶ μὲν δὴ
πρὸς τῷ μηδὲν ἀφαιρεθῆναι τῶν σφετέρων ἁλούσης
τῆς πόλεως καὶ¹ τὰ τῶν κεκρατηκότων ἀγαθὰ
προσλαβόντες ἀπῇεσαν. *Vales.*

VII. Ὅτι Σολπίκιος Ῥοῦφος ἐπίκλησιν ἀνὴρ
ἦν ἔν τε ταῖς πολεμικαῖς πράξεσιν ἐπιφανὴς καὶ
πολιτείας προαίρεσιν ἐζηλωκὼς τὴν διὰ μέσου.
Vales.

VIII. (12) Οἱ Κελτοὶ τῇ Ῥώμῃ ἐκ δευτέρου
ἐπιστρατεύσαντες² τὴν χώραν τὴν Ἀλβανὴν ἐπόρ-
θουν· ἔνθα μὲν πολλῆς ἅπαντες ἐδωδῆς ἐμπιμπλά-
μενοι, πολὺν δὲ πίνοντες ἄκρατον οἶνον (ἔστι δὲ ὁ
τῇδε φυόμενος μετὰ τὸν Φαλερῖνον ἥδιστος οἴνων
μελικράτῳ μάλιστα προσεμφερής), ὕπνον τε πλείονα
τοῦ συνήθους αἱρούμενοι καὶ δίαιταν ὑπὸ σκιαῖς
ὡς τὰ πολλὰ ἔχοντες τοσαύτην ἔλαβον ἐπίδοσιν
εἰς πολυσαρκίαν τε καὶ ἁπαλότητα καὶ οὕτως
ἐξεθηλύνθησαν τὰς δυνάμεις ὥσθ', ὁπότε γυμνάζειν
ἐπιβάλοιντο τὰ σώματα καὶ διαπονεῖν ἐν τοῖς
ὅπλοις, κόπτεσθαι μὲν ἄσθματι συνεχεῖ τὰ πνεύ-
ματα, ῥεῖσθαι δ' ἱδρῶτι πολλῷ τὰ μέλη, θᾶττον
δὲ ἀφίστασθαι τῶν πόνων ἢ κελευσθεῖεν ὑπὸ τῶν
ἡγεμόνων. *Ambr.*

IX. (13) Ταῦτα μαθὼν ὁ τῶν Ῥωμαίων δικ-
2 τάτωρ Κάμιλλος, συγκαλέσας τοὺς ἀμφ'³ αὐτὸν
ἐδημηγόρησε πολλὰ παρορμῶντα εἰς τόλμαν, ἐν
οἷς καὶ τάδε· "Ὅπλα κρείττονα τῶν βαρβαρικῶν
ἡμῖν μεμηχάνηται, θώρακες καὶ κράνη καὶ κνη-

¹ καὶ Reiske : ἀλλὰ καὶ P, ἅμα καὶ Post.

were reasonable and humane, I consider to be Greek, but those which were cruel and brutal, particularly when they affected kinsmen and friends, barbarous. The Tusculans departed, accordingly, not only without having been deprived of their possessions after the capture of their city, but having actually received in addition the blessings enjoyed by their conquerors.

VII. Sulpicius, with the cognomen Rufus,[1] was a man of distinction in military affairs and in his political principles followed the middle course.

VIII. (12) The Gauls,[2] having made an expedition against Rome for the second time, were plundering the Alban district. There, as all gorged themselves with much food, drank much unmixed wine (the wine produced there is the sweetest of all wines after the Falernian and is the most like honey-wine), took more sleep than was their custom, and spent most of their time in the shade, they gained so rapidly in corpulence and flabbiness and became so womanish in physical strength that whenever they undertook to exercise their bodies and to drill in arms their respiration was broken by continual panting, their limbs were drenched by much sweat, and they desisted from their toils before they were bidden to do so by their commanders.

IX. (13) Upon learning of this state of affairs the Roman dictator, Camillus, assembled his men and addressed them, using many arguments that incited them to boldness, among which were the following : " Better arms than the barbarians possess have been fashioned for us—breastplates, helmets, greaves,

[1] *Cf.* Livy vi. 4, 7 and 18, 1.
[2] For chaps. 8–10 *cf.* Livy vi. 42, 4-8.

---

[2] Hertlein : στρατεύσαντες A.   [3] ἀφ' Q.

μῖδες καὶ κραταιοὶ θυρεοί, ὑφ' ὧν ὅλα τὰ σώματα
ἔχομεν ἐν φυλακῇ, ξίφη τε ἀμφίστομα καὶ ἀντὶ
λόγχης ὑσσός,[1] ἄφυκτον βέλος, τὰ μὲν σκεπα-
στήρια, οἷα μὴ ῥᾳδίως ταῖς πληγαῖς εἴκειν, τὰ δ'
ἀμυντήρια, ὡς διὰ πάσης[2] φέρεσθαι προβολῆς.
τῶν δὲ γυμναὶ μὲν αἱ κεφαλαί, γυμνὰ δὲ τὰ στέρνα
καὶ αἱ λαγόνες, γυμνοὶ δὲ μηροὶ καὶ σκέλη μέχρι
ποδῶν, ἔρυμά τε οὐδὲν ἕτερον ὅ τι μὴ θυρεοί·
ἀμυντήρια δὲ λόγχαι καὶ μάχαιραι[3] κοπίδες ὑπερ-
3 μήκεις. (14) τό τε χωρίον ἐν ᾧ τὸν ἀγῶνα ποιη-
σόμεθα σύνεργον ἡμῖν τοῖς ἀπὸ μετεώρου[4] κατιοῦσιν
ἐπὶ τὸ πρανές, ἐκείνοις δὲ πολέμιον τοῖς ἐκ τοῦ
χθαμαλοῦ πρὸς τὰ μετέωρα χωρεῖν ἀναγκαζο-
μένοις. φοβείσθω[5] δὲ μηδεὶς[6] ὑμῶν μήτε τὸ
πλῆθος τῶν πολεμίων μήτε τὸ μέγεθος, μηδ' εἰς
ταῦτά τις πλεονεκτήματα αὐτῶν ὁρῶν ἀθυμότερος
πρὸς τὸν ἀγῶνα ἔστω, ἀλλ' ἐνθυμείσθω πρῶτον
μὲν ὅτι κρεῖττόν ἐστιν ἔλαττον στράτευμα ἐπι-
στάμενον ἃ δεῖ πράττειν ἢ πολὺ ἀμαθές· ἔπειθ'
ὅτι τοῖς μὲν ὑπὲρ τῶν ἰδίων ἀγωνιζομένοις ἡ φύσις
αὐτὴ θάρσος τέ τι πρὸς τοὺς κινδύνους παρίστησι
καὶ πνεῦμα ἐνθουσιῶδες ὥσπερ τοῖς θεοφορήτοις
παρέχει, τοῖς δ' ἁρπάσαι τὰ ἀλλότρια προθυμου-
μένοις μαλακώτεραι πρὸς τὰ δεινὰ αἱ[7] τόλμαι
4 φιλοῦσι γίνεσθαι. (15) ἀλλὰ μὴν οὐδ' οἷς δεδίτ-
τονται[8] τοὺς πολεμίους καὶ πρὶν εἰς χεῖρας ἐλθεῖν
ἐκδειματοῦσιν ὀρρωδητέα ἡμῖν ἐστιν ὥσπερ ἀπεί-
ροις πολέμου. τί γὰρ ἂν[9] δυνήσονται δεινὸν
ἐργάσασθαι[10] τοὺς ὁμόσε χωροῦντας αἱ βαθεῖαι

---

[1] ὑσσός Naber : οἰστός Q.
[2] διὰ πάσης Jacoby : δι' ἀπάσης Q.
[3] μάχαιραι Q : μαγειρικαὶ Struve, om. Kiessling.

mighty shields, with which we keep our entire bodies
protected, two-edged swords, and, instead of the
spear, the javelin, a missile that cannot be dodged—
some of them being protective armour, such as not
to yield readily to blows, and others offensive, of
a sort to pierce through any defence. But our foes
have their heads bare, bare their breasts and flanks,
bare their thighs and legs down to their feet, and
have no other defence except shields ; as weapons of
offence they have spears and very long slashing blades.
(14) The terrain also in which we shall fight will aid
us as we move downhill from higher ground, but will
be adverse to them as they are forced to advance
from the level to higher ground. And let no one of
you stand in dread either of the enemies' numbers or
of their size, or, from looking at these advantages on
their side, become less confident of the contest. On
the contrary, let everyone bear in mind, first, that a
smaller army which understands what must be done
is superior to a large army that is uninstructed ; and,
second, that to those who are fighting for their own
possessions Nature herself lends a certain courage in
the face of danger and gives them a spirit of ecstasy
like that of men possessed by a god, whereas those
who are eager to seize the goods of others are apt to
find their boldness weakened in the face of dangers.
(15) Nay, not even their attempts to frighten their
foes and terrify them before coming to blows should
cause us any dread, as if we were inexperienced in
warfare. For what harm can be done to men going

---

⁴ ἀπὸ τοῦ μετεώρου Tegge.   ⁵ Struve : φοβείτω Q.
⁶ μηδεὶς Mai : μηδὲ Q.   ⁷ αἱ added by Struve.
⁸ δίττονται Q.   ⁹ ἂν om. Kiessling, following Struve.
¹⁰ Kiessling : ἐργάσεσθαι Q.

κόμαι καὶ τὸ ἐν τοῖς ὄμμασιν αὐτῶν πικρὸν καὶ
ὁ βλοσυρὸς τῆς ὄψεως χαρακτήρ; αἵ τε[1] δὴ
πλημμελεῖς αὗται σκιρτήσεις καὶ τὰ διὰ κενῆς
ἀνασείσματα τῶν ὅπλων καὶ οἱ πολλοὶ τῶν θυρεῶν
κτύποι καὶ ὅσα ἄλλα ὑπὸ βαρβάρου καὶ ἄφρονος
ἀλαζονείας κατά τε μορφὰς[2] καὶ φωνὰς ἐν ἀπειλαῖς
πολεμίων σπαθᾶται, τίνα παρέχειν πέφυκε τοῖς
ἀνοήτως ἐπιοῦσι πλεονεξίαν ἢ τοῖς μετὰ λογισμοῦ
5 παρὰ[3] τὰ δεινὰ ἑστῶσι φόβον; (16) ταῦτα δὴ
διανοηθέντες, ὅσοι τε ὑμῶν ἐν τῷ κατὰ Κελτῶν
προτέρῳ πολέμῳ παρεγένεσθε καὶ ὅσοι διὰ νεότητα
ἀπελείφθητε αὐτοῦ, οἱ μὲν ἵνα τὴν[4] τότε ἀρετὴν
μὴ καταισχύνητε τῇ νῦν δειλίᾳ, οἱ δ᾽ ἵνα μηδὲν
ἐνδεέστεροι γένησθε τῶν πρεσβυτέρων ἐν ἐπιδείξει
καλῶν ἔργων, ἴτε, ὦ γενναῖοι παῖδες ἀγαθῶν
ζηλωταὶ πατέρων, ἴτε ἀκαταπλήκτως ἐπ᾽ αὐτούς,
θεούς τε ἀρωγοὺς ἔχοντες, οἳ παρέξουσιν ὑμῖν
ἐξουσίαν οἵας ἐβούλεσθε παρὰ τῶν ἐχθίστων ἀνα-
πράξασθαι δίκας, καὶ στρατηγὸν ἐμέ, ᾧ πολλὴν
μὲν εὐβουλίαν μαρτυρεῖτε, πολλὴν δ᾽ εὐποτμίαν·
6 μακάριον μὲν ἕξοντες τὸν ἀπὸ τοῦδε χρόνον οἷς
ἂν ἐγγένηται τὸν ἐπιφανέστατον τῇ πατρίδι στέ-
φανον καταγαγεῖν, καλὴν δὲ καὶ ἀθάνατον εὔκλειαν
καταλείψοντες ἀντὶ τοῦ θνητοῦ σώματος νηπίοις
παισὶ καὶ γηραιοῖς γονεῦσιν οἱ τοιαύτην[5] ἐκπληρώ-
σοντες τὴν τοῦ βίου τελευτήν. οὐκ οἶδ᾽ ὅ τι δεῖ
πλείω λέγειν· κινεῖται γὰρ ἤδη τὸ βάρβαρον στράτευμα χωροῦν ἐφ᾽ ἡμᾶς. ἀλλ᾽ ἄπιτε καὶ καθίστασθε
εἰς τάξιν." Ambr.

---

[1] τε Kiessling : δὲ Q. [2] μορφῆς Q.
[3] παρὰ Q : πρὸς Struve. [4] τὴν added by Struve.
[5] Capps : ταύτην Q : ταύτῃ ἂν ἐκπληρώσαντες Struve.

into battle by those long locks, the fierceness of their glance, and the grim aspect of their countenances? And these awkward prancings, the useless brandishing of their weapons, the many clashings of their shields, and all the other demonstrations of barbarian and senseless bravado, whether through motions or through sounds, indulged in by way of threats to their foes—what advantage are they calculated to bring to those who attack unintelligently, or what fear to those who with cool calculation stand their ground in the midst of danger? (16) Do you, then, with these thoughts in mind, both those of you who were present in the earlier war against the Gauls and those of you who had no part in it by reason of your youth, the former in order that you may not, by cowardice now, bring shame upon the valour you then displayed, and you others in order that you may not be behind your elders in the display of noble deeds, go, noble sons, emulators of brave fathers, go intrepidly against the foe, having not only the gods as your helpers, who will give you the power to exact from your bitterest foes such vengeance as you have been wishing for, but also me as your general, to whose great prudence and great good fortune you bear witness. A blissful life from this time forth those of you will lead to whom it shall be granted to bring home for your fatherland its most distinguished crown, and a splendid and imperishable renown in place of your mortal bodies those of you will bequeath to your infant children and your aged parents who shall fulfil thus the end of your lives. I know of nothing more that needs to be said ; for the barbarian army is already in motion, advancing against us. But be off and take your places in the ranks."

X. (17) Ἡ μὲν οὖν τῶν βαρβάρων μάχη πολὺ
τὸ θηριῶδες καὶ μανικὸν ἔχουσα πλημμελής τις
ἦν καὶ σοφίας τῆς[1] ἐν ὅπλοις ἄμοιρος. τοτὲ μὲν
γὰρ ἀνατείνοντες ἄνω τὰς μαχαίρας ὑῶν ἀγρίων[2]
τρόπον ἔπαιον ὅλοις συνεμπίπτοντες τοῖς ἑαυτῶν
σώμασιν, ὥσπερ ὑλοτόμοι τινὲς ἢ σκαπανεῖς, τοτὲ
δ' ἐκ τῶν πλαγίων ἀστοχάστους πληγὰς ἐξέφερον,
ὡς αὐτοῖς σκεπαστηρίοις ὅλα διακόψοντες τὰ
σώματα τῶν ἀντιπολέμων· ἔπειτα τὰς ἀκμὰς τῶν
2 σιδήρων ἀπέστρεφον. (18) ἡ δὲ τῶν Ῥωμαίων
ἀλκὴ καὶ πρὸς τὸ βάρβαρον αὐτῶν ἀντιτέχνησις
ἔμπεδός[3] τε ἦν καὶ πολὺ τὸ ἀσφαλὲς ἔχουσα. ἔτι
γὰρ αὐτῶν ἀναιρομένων[4] τὰς μαχαίρας ὑποδύνοντες
ὑπὸ τοὺς βραχίονας καὶ τοὺς θυρεοὺς εἰς ὕψος
ἀνατείνοντες, ἔπειτα γυροὶ καὶ βραχεῖς γινόμενοι,
τὰς μὲν ἐκείνων πληγὰς ὑπερπετεῖς γινομένας
ἀπράκτους καὶ κενὰς ἐποίουν, αὐτοὶ δὲ ὀρθὰ τὰ
ξίφη φέροντες βουβῶνάς τε αὐτῶν ἔπαιον καὶ
λαγόνας διήρουν καὶ διὰ στέρνων ἐπὶ τὰ σπλάγχνα
τὰς πληγὰς ἐξέτεινον· ὅσους δὲ ταῦτα τὰ μέρη
διὰ φυλακῆς ἔχοντας αἴσθοιντο, γονάτων ἢ σφυ-
ρῶν νεῦρα διακείροντες ἐξέχεον ἐπὶ τὴν γῆν βεβρυ-
χότας καὶ τοὺς θυρεοὺς ὀδακτίζοντας καὶ βοὴν[5]
ὠρυγῇ παραπλησίαν ὥσπερ τὰ θηρία προϊεμένους.
3 (19) ἥ τε δύναμις ὑπέλειπε πολλοὺς τῶν βαρβάρων
ἐκλυομένων τῶν μελῶν ὑπὸ κόπων καὶ τῶν ὅπλων
τὰ μὲν ἀπεστόμωτο, τὰ δὲ συνετέθραυστο,[6] τὰ δ'
οὐκέτι προσωφελεῖν δυνατὰ ἦν· χωρὶς γὰρ τοῦ

---

[1] Mai : τοῖς Q.
[2] ὑῶν ἀγρίων Post : τὸν ἄγριον Q, Jacoby.
[3] Post : εὔπαιδος Q, εὐπαίδευτός Mai.
[4] Kiessling : διαιρουμένων Q, διαιρομένων Struve.
[5] Mai : βοῇ Q.   [6] συντέθραυτο Q.

X. (17) Now the barbarians' manner of fighting, being in large measure that of wild beasts and frenzied, was an erratic procedure, quite lacking in military science. Thus, at one moment they would raise their swords aloft and smite after the manner of wild boars,[1] throwing the whole weight of their bodies into the blow like hewers of wood or men digging with mattocks, and again they would deliver crosswise blows aimed at no target, as if they intended to cut to pieces the entire bodies of their adversaries, protective armour and all ; then they would turn the edges of their swords away from the foe. (18) On the other hand, the Romans' defence and counter-manœuvring against the barbarians was steadfast[2] and afforded great safety. For while their foes were still raising their swords aloft, they would duck under their arms, holding up their shields, and then, stooping and crouching low, they would render vain and useless the blows of the others, which were aimed too high, while for their own part, holding their swords straight out, they would strike their opponents in the groin, pierce their sides, and drive their blows through their breasts into their vitals. And if they saw any of them keeping these parts of their bodies protected, they would cut the tendons of their knees or ankles and topple them to the ground roaring and biting their shields and uttering cries resembling the howling of wild beasts. (19) Not only did their strength desert many of the barbarians as their limbs failed them through weariness, but their weapons also were either blunted or broken or no longer serviceable.

---

[1] The translation follows the text as emended by Post. The MS. has " in the savage manner."

[2] Or " well practised," following Mai's conjecture.

καταρρέοντος ἐκ τῶν τραυμάτων αἵματος οἱ δι'
ὅλων ἐκχεόμενοι τῶν σωμάτων ἱδρῶτες οὔτε τὰς
μαχαίρας εἴων κρατεῖν οὔτε τοὺς θυρεοὺς κατέχειν,
περιολισθανόντων[1] ταῖς λαβαῖς τῶν δακτύλων καὶ
τὰς ἀφὰς οὐκέτι κραταιὰς ἐχόντων. Ῥωμαῖοι δὲ
πολλῶν ἐθάδες ὄντες πόνων διὰ τὰς ἀτρύτους καὶ
συνεχεῖς στρατείας ἅπαντα τὰ δεινὰ γενναίως
διέφερον.[2] Ambr.

XI. (20) Ἐν Ῥώμῃ πολλὰ μὲν καὶ ἄλλα σημεῖα
θεόπεμπτα γέγονε, μέγιστον δ' ἁπάντων τόδε· τῆς
ἀγορᾶς κατὰ τὸ μέσον μάλιστα διαρραγῆναί[3] τι τῆς
γῆς εἰς βάθος ἄβυσσον καὶ τοῦτ' ἐπὶ πολλὰς
ἡμέρας διαμένειν.[4] ψηφισαμένης δὲ τῆς βουλῆς
οἱ ἐπὶ τῶν Σιβυλλείων χρησμῶν ἐπισκεψάμενοι
τὰ βιβλία εἶπον ὅτι τὰ πλείστου ἄξια τῷ[5] Ῥωμαίων
δήμῳ λαβοῦσα ἡ γῆ συνελεύσεταί τε καὶ πολλὴν
ἀφθονίαν εἰς τὸν λοιπὸν χρόνον ἁπάντων ἀγαθῶν
2 ἀνήσει. τοιαῦτα τῶν ἀνδρῶν ἀποφηναμένων
ἀπαρχὰς ἕκαστος εἰς τὸ χάσμα ἔφερεν ὧν ᾤετο
δεῖν ἀγαθῶν[6] τῇ πατρίδι, ἀπό τε καρπῶν πελάνους
3 καὶ ἀπὸ χρημάτων ἀπαρχάς. (21) Μάρκος δέ
τις Κούρτιος ἐν τοῖς πρώτοις τῶν νέων ἀριθμού-
μενος σωφροσύνης ἕνεκα καὶ τῆς κατὰ πολέμους
ἀρετῆς ἔφοδον αἰτησάμενος ἐπὶ τὴν βουλὴν εἶπεν
ὅτι τῶν πάντων ἐστὶν ἀγαθῶν χρῆμα κάλλιστον
καὶ πόλει Ῥωμαίων ἀναγκαιότατον ἀνδρῶν ἀρετή·
εἰ δὴ καὶ ταύτης ἀπαρχήν τινα ἡ γῆ λάβοι καὶ
γένοιτο ἑκὼν ὁ τοῦτο χαριούμενος τῇ πατρίδι,
4 πολλοὺς ἀνήσει ἡ γῆ ἄνδρας ἀγαθούς. ταῦτ' εἰπὼν

---

[1] Cobet : περιολισθαινόντων Q.
[2] Naber : ἀνέφερον Q.   [3] διερράγη Kiessling.
[4] διέμεινεν Kiessling, διαμεῖναι Jacoby.

For besides the blood that flowed from their wounds, the sweat pouring out over their whole bodies would not let them either grasp their swords or hold their shields firmly, since their fingers slipped on the handles and no longer kept a firm hold. The Romans, however, being accustomed to many toils by reason of their unabating and continuous warfare, continued to meet every peril in noble fashion.

XI. (20) In Rome there were many other heaven-sent portents,[1] but the greatest of all was this : Near the middle of the Forum, they say, a cleft in the earth appeared of fathomless depth and it remained for many days. Pursuant to a decree of the senate, the men in charge of the Sibylline oracles consulted the books and reported that when the earth had received the things of greatest value to the Roman people it would not only close up, but would also send up a great abundance of all blessings for the future. When the men had made this announcement, every-one brought to the chasm the first-fruits of all the good things he thought the fatherland needed, not only cakes made of grain, but also the first-fruits of his money. (21) Then a certain Marcus Curtius, who was accounted among the first of the youths because of his prudence and his prowess in war, sought admission to the senate and declared that of all blessings the finest thing and the one most essential to the Roman state was the valour of its men ; if, therefore, the earth should receive some first-fruits of this and the one who offered it to the fatherland should do so voluntarily, the earth would send up many good men. Having said this and promised

[1] *Cf.* Livy vii. 6, 1-6.

---

[5] τῷ Struve : τῶν Q. [6] ἀγαθῶν Struve : αὐτῶν Q.

καὶ μηδενὶ παραχωρήσειν ἑτέρῳ τῆς φιλοτιμίας
ταύτης ὑποσχόμενος τά τε ὅπλα περιέθετο καὶ ἐπὶ
τὸν πολεμιστὴν ἵππον ἀνέβη· συναχθέντος δ' ἐπὶ
τὴν θέαν τοῦ κατὰ τὴν πόλιν ὄχλου πρῶτον μὲν
ηὔξατο τοῖς θεοῖς ἐπιτελῆ ποιῆσαι τὰ μαντεύματα
καὶ πολλοὺς ἄνδρας ὁμοίους αὐτῷ δοῦναι τῇ πόλει
τῇ Ῥωμαίων γενέσθαι· ἔπειτ' ἐφεὶς τῷ ἵππῳ τὰς
ἡνίας καὶ τὰ κέντρα προσβαλὼν ἔρριψε κατὰ τοῦ
5 χάσματος ἑαυτόν. ἐπὶ δὲ[1] αὐτῷ πολλὰ μὲν ἱερεῖα,
πολλοὶ δὲ καρποί, πολλὰ δὲ χρήματα, πολὺς δὲ
κόσμος ἐσθῆτος, πολλαὶ δὲ ἀπαρχαὶ συμπασῶν
τεχνῶν δημοσίᾳ κατὰ τοῦ χάσματος ἐρρίφησαν·
καὶ αὐτίκα ἡ γῆ συνῆλθεν. Ambr.

XII. (22) Ὑπερφυές τι χρῆμα σώματος ἦν ὁ
Κελτός, οἷος ὑπεραίρειν πολὺ τὴν κοινὴν φύσιν.
Ambr.

Λικίνιος Στόλων, ὁ δεκάκις δημαρχήσας καὶ
τοὺς νόμους εἰσηγησάμενος ὑπὲρ ὧν ἡ δεκαετὴς
στάσις ἐγένετο, ἁλοὺς ἐν δίκῃ καὶ ὑπὸ τοῦ δήμου
καταψηφισθεὶς τίμημα ἀργυρικόν, εἶπεν ὅτι θηρίον
οὐδέν ἐστι δήμου μιαρώτερον, ὃς οὐδὲ τῶν σιτιζόν-
των ἀπέχεται. Ambr.

XIII. (23) Τοῦ ὑπάτου Μαρκίου Πριβερνάτας[2]
πολιορκοῦντος, ἐπεὶ οὐδεμία τούτοις σωτηρίας
ἐλπὶς ὑπελείπετο,[3] ἐπρεσβεύοντο πρὸς αὐτόν· τοῦ
δ' εἰπόντος, " Φράσατέ μοι, πῶς αὐτοὶ κολάζετε
τοὺς ἀφισταμένους ὑμῶν οἰκέτας;" ἀποκρίνεται
πρὸς αὐτὸν ὁ πρεσβευτής,[4] " Ὡς δεῖ κολάζεσθαι
τοὺς ποθοῦντας ἀπολαβεῖν τὴν ἔμφυτον ἐλευθερίαν."
2 καὶ ὁ Μάρκιος ἀποδεξάμενος αὐτοῦ τὴν παρρησίαν

---

[1] ἐπεὶ δὲ Q. [2] Mai : τιβερνάτας Q.
[3] Cobet : ὑπολείπεται Q. [4] Struve : πρεσβύτατος Q.

that he would not yield this distinction to anyone else, he girded on his arms and mounted his war-horse. And when the multitude in the city had gathered to witness the spectacle, he first prayed to the gods to fulfil the oracles and grant that many men like himself should be born to the Roman state ; then, giving the horse free rein and applying the spurs, he hurled himself down the chasm. And after him were thrown down the chasm many victims, many fruits, much money, much fine apparel, and many first-fruits of all the different crafts, all at the public expense. And straightway the earth closed up.

XII. (22) The Gaul was a tremendous creature in bulk, far exceeding the common build.[1]

Licinius Stolo,[2] the man who had held the tribune-ship ten times and had introduced the laws over which the ten-years' sedition occurred, when he was found guilty at his trial and condemned by the populace to pay a monetary fine, declared that there is no wild beast more bloodthirsty than the populace, which does not spare even those who feed it.

XIII. (23) When the consul Marcius was besieging Privernum [3] and no hope of saving themselves was left to the inhabitants, they sent envoys to him. To his query, " Tell me, how do you yourselves punish your household slaves who run away from you ? " the envoy answered : " As those must be punished who long to recover their native freedom." Marcius, accepting his frankness of speech, asked : " If, then,

---

[1] *Cf.* Livy vii. 10, 7 ; 26, 1.
[2] *Cf.* Livy vii. 16, 9.   [3] *Cf.* Livy viii. 21.

φησίν· " Ἐὰν δὲ δὴ καὶ πεισθῶμεν ὑμῖν ἀφεῖναι
τὰς ὀργάς, τίνα δώσετε πίστιν ὑπὲρ τοῦ μηδὲν
ἔτι ποιήσειν ἐχθρῶν ἔργον; " ἀποκρίνεται πάλιν
ὁ πρεσβευτής· " Ἐπὶ σοὶ τοῦτ' ἔστι καὶ τοῖς ἄλλοις
Ῥωμαίοις, Μάρκιε· κομισάμενοι μὲν γὰρ ἅμα τῇ
πατρίδι καὶ τὴν ἐλευθερίαν βέβαιοι διὰ παντὸς
ὑμῖν ἐσόμεθα φίλοι, δουλεύειν δ'[1] ἀναγκασθέντες
οὐδέποτε." ἠγάσθη τε δὴ τῆς μεγαλοφροσύνης
τοὺς ἄνδρας ὁ Μάρκιος καὶ τὴν πολιορκίαν ἔλυσε.
Ambr.

___

[1] δ' added by Struve.

we listen to you and give up our anger, what assurance will you give us that you will not again commit any hostile act ? " The envoy answered again : " That rests with you and the other Romans, Marcius. For if we get back our liberty along with our country, we shall be your staunch friends always ; but if we are compelled to be slaves, never." Marcius admired the lofty spirit of the men and raised the siege.

EXCERPTS
FROM
BOOK XV

I. (1) Τῶν Κελτῶν ἐπιστρατευσάντων τῇ Ῥώμῃ
καί τινος βασιλέως εἰς μονομαχίαν προκαλουμένου
τῶν Ῥωμαίων ὅστις εἴη ἀνήρ, Μάρκος Οὐαλέριος, εἷς τῶν χιλιάρχων, ἀπόγονος ὢν Οὐαλερίου
Ποπλικόλα τοῦ συνελευθερώσαντος ἀπὸ τῶν βασιλέων τὴν πόλιν, ἐξῄει τῷ Κελτῷ διαγωνίσασθαι.
2 ὡς δὲ συνῄεσαν ὁμόσε, κόραξ καθεζόμενος ἐπὶ
τοῦ κράνους αὐτοῦ ἐκεκράγει[1] τε δεινὸν εἰς τὸν
βάρβαρον ὁρῶν καί, ὁπότε μέλλοι πληγὴν ἐκφέρειν,[2]
πηδῶν ἐπ' αὐτὸν τοτὲ μὲν τοῖς ὄνυξιν ἤμυττε τὰς
παρειάς, τοτὲ δὲ τῷ ῥύγχει τοὺς ὀφθαλμοὺς
ἔκοπτεν, ὥστε τὸν Κελτὸν ἔξω γενέσθαι[3] τῶν
φρενῶν, οὔθ' ὅπως τὸν ἄνδρα ἀμύνοιτο δυνάμενον
συμβαλεῖν οὔθ' ὅπως τὸν κόρακα φυλάττοιτο.
3 (2) ὡς δὲ πολὺς ἐγεγόνει τῇ μάχῃ χρόνος, ὁ μὲν
Κελτὸς φέρων ἐπὶ τὸν Οὐαλέριον τὴν μάχαιραν
ὡς διὰ τῆς προβολῆς[4] εἰς τὰ πλευρὰ βάψων,[5] ἔπειτ'
ἐπιπτάντος αὐτῷ τοῦ κόρακος καὶ τὰς ὄψεις
ὀρύττοντος ἀνέτεινε τὸν θυρεὸν ὡς ἀπελάσων τὸν

---

[1] Struve : ἐκέκραγε Q.   [2] Mai : ἐκφέρει Q.
[3] γίνεσθαι Q.   [4] Kiessling : προσβολῆς Q.

EXCERPTS

FROM

BOOK XV

I. (1) When the Gauls made an expedition against
Rome [1] and one of their chieftains challenged to single
combat any one of the Romans who was a man,
Marcus Valerius, one of the tribunes and a descendant
of Valerius Publicola, the man who had helped free
the city from the kings, went out to fight with the
Gaul. When they engaged, a raven perched on
Valerius' helmet and cawed while looking fiercely at
the barbarian, and every time the latter made ready
to deliver a blow he would fly at him, now tearing his
cheeks with his claws and now pecking at his eyes
with his beak, so that the Gaul was driven out of his
senses, being unable to contrive how he could either
ward off his foe or defend himself against the raven.
(2) When the combat had continued for a long time,
the Gaul aimed his sword at Valerius, as if intending
to plunge it through his shield into his side ; then,
when the raven flew at him and clawed his eyes, he
held up his shield as if to drive the bird away ; but

---

[1] *Cf.* Livy vii. 26, 1-5, 12.

⁵ Smit : βάψας Q.

ὄρνιν· ὁ δὲ 'Ρωμαῖος ἔτι μετεωρίζοντος τὸ ὅπλον
ἀκολουθήσας κάτωθεν ὑποφέρει τὸ ξίφος καὶ
4 ἀναιρεῖ τὸν Κελτόν. ὁ δὲ στρατηγὸς Κάμιλλος
χρυσέῳ τοῦτον στεφάνῳ ἐκόσμησεν ἐπωνυμίαν
θέμενος αὐτῷ[1] Κορβῖνον ἀπὸ τοῦ συναγωνισαμένου
κατὰ τὴν μονομαχίαν ζῴου· κόρβους γὰρ οἱ
'Ρωμαῖοι καλοῦσι τοὺς κόρακας· αὐτός τε διετέλεσεν ἐξ ἐκείνου συμβόλῳ κατὰ τοῦ κράνους
κοσμούμενος κόρακι, καὶ ταῖς εἰκόσιν αὐτοῦ
πάσαις οἱ πλάττοντες καὶ γράφοντες τοῦτο τὸ
ζῷον ἐπὶ τὴν κεφαλὴν ἐφήρμοττον. Ambr.

II. (3) Ἐπόρθουν τὰς ἐπὶ τῶν ἀγρῶν κτήσεις
πολλῆς εὐδαιμονίας γεμούσας.

Ἀνθρώπους πεπονημένους ὑπὸ πολέμου σώματα
καὶ πλὴν ὅσον ἀνέπνεον τὰ λοιπὰ νεκροῖς[2] ὁμοίους.

Ἔτι θερμῆς τὸ δὴ λεγόμενον οὔσης τῆς τοῦ
ἀναιρεθέντος σποδοῦ.

2 Τὸν οἴκτιστον ἀπολεῖται τρόπον ὑπ' ἀνδρὸς ἐχ-
θροῦ πολιτικῷ σιτίζοντος αἵματι τὸν φθόνον.

Μοῖραν οὐκ ἐλαχίστην τῶν ὠφελειῶν τοῖς στρατιώταις χαριζόμενος, ὥστ' ἐπικλύσαι πλούτῳ τὴν
ἑκάστου πενίαν.

Διέφθειραν αὐτῶν ἀκμαζούσας ἤδη σπορολογεῖ-
σθαι τὰς ἀρούρας καὶ τὰ κράτιστα τῆς καρποφόρου
ἐλωβήσαντο. Ambr.

III. Ὅτι Κοΐντου Σερουιλίου τὸ τρίτον[3] καὶ
Γαΐου Μαρκίου 'Ροτίλου[4] ὑπατευόντων κίνδυνοι
τὴν 'Ρώμην χαλεποὶ καὶ ἀπροσδόκητοι κατέσχον,
οὓς εἰ μὴ θεία τις πρόνοια διεσκέδασε, δυεῖν
κακῶν θάτερον ἂν αὐτῇ συνέπεσεν, ἢ δόξαν αἰσχί-

---

[1] Hertlein : αὐτὸν Q. [2] Struve : νεκροὺς Q.
[3] ὑπατεύοντος after τρίτον deleted by Müller.

the Roman, following him up while he was still holding his shield aloft, drove his sword home from underneath and slew the Gaul. The general, Camillus, honoured him with a golden crown and gave him the cognomen Corvinus [1] because of the bird which had fought in the single combat with him; for the Romans call ravens *corvi*. And not only did Valerius himself continue from that time on to have his helmet decorated with a raven as his emblem, but in all his likenesses as well both sculptors and painters placed this bird on his head.

II. (3) They ravaged their farms in the country that teemed with great wealth.

People exhausted in body by war and like corpses except that they breathed.

While the slain man's ashes were still warm, as the saying goes.

He will perish in the most miserable fashion at the hands of an enemy who feeds his hatred on the blood of his fellow citizens.

Granting no small part of the booty to his troops, so that each man's poverty was deluged with wealth.

They laid waste their fields which were now ripe for the harvest and ravaged the best of the fruitful land.

III. When Quintus Servilius (for the third time) and Gaius Marcius Rutilus were consuls,[2] Rome was involved in grave and unexpected dangers, from which, had they not been dispelled by some divine providence, one of two evils would have befallen her—either to have got a shameful name for murdering her

---

[1] Livy gives the cognomen as Corvus, later changed to Corvinus (vii. 40, 3).

[2] For chaps. 3 f. *cf.* Livy vii. 38–42.

---

[4] Ῥοτίλου Cary, Ῥουτίλου Müller : ῥοτύλλου S.

στην ἐνεγκεῖν[1] ξενοκτονίας ἢ φόνων ἅψασθαι
πολιτικῶν. ἀφ' ἧς δ' αἰτίας εἰς τούτους ἦλθε τοὺς
κινδύνους, μικρὰ τῶν πρόσθεν ἀναλαβὼν δι' ὀλίγων
πειράσομαι διελθεῖν.

2 Ἐν τῷ παρελθόντι ἐνιαυτῷ τὸν Σαυνιτικὸν
πόλεμον ὑπὲρ ἁπάσης Καμπανίας ἡ τῶν Ῥωμαίων
πόλις ἀραμένη καὶ τρισὶ νικήσασα μάχαις τοὺς
ἀντιταχθέντας ἐβούλετο μὲν ἁπάσας ἀπάγειν[2] τὰς
δυνάμεις ὡς οὐθενὸς ἔτι κινδύνου ταῖς πόλεσι
καταλειπομένου· δεομένων δὲ τῶν Καμπανῶν μὴ
καταλιπεῖν αὐτοὺς συμμάχων ἐρήμους, ὡς ἐπιθησομένων σφίσι τῶν Σαυνιτῶν εἰ μηδεμίαν ἔχοιεν
ξενικὴν βοήθειαν, ἔγνω τὸν ἀπαλλάξαντα τοῦ
πολέμου τὰς πόλεις ὕπατον Μάρκον Οὐαλέριον
ὅσην ἂν αὐτοὶ βουληθῶσι τρέφειν στρατιὰν ἐν ταῖς
3 πόλεσι καταλιπεῖν. γενόμενος[3] δὲ τῆς ἐξουσίας
ταύτης κύριος ὁ ὕπατος, ὅσοις ἦν βουλομένοις
ὀψώνια καὶ μισθοὺς φέρεσθαι τῆς φυλακῆς, τούτους καθίστησιν ἐν ταῖς πόλεσιν· ἐν οἷς ἦν τὸ
πλεῖον μέρος ἀνεστίων καὶ καταχρέων καὶ τὴν
οἴκοι πενίαν καὶ ἀγνωσίαν ἀσμένως ἀποδιδρασκόν-
4 των. τούτους οἱ Καμπανοὶ ταῖς οἰκίαις ἀναλαμβά-
νοντες τραπέζαις τε ὑπεδέχοντο λαμπραῖς καὶ ταῖς
ἄλλαις ἐξένιζον φιλοφροσύναις. πολυτελὴς δὲ καὶ
ἁβροδίαιτος ἱκανῶς τοῖς Καμπανίαν οἰκοῦσι καὶ
νῦν ἐστι καὶ τότε ἦν ὁ βίος καὶ πάντα τὸν λοιπὸν
ἔσται χρόνον, πολύκαρπόν τε πεδιάδα καὶ πολύ-
βοτον καὶ πρὸς ὑγίειαν ἀνθρώποις γεωργοῦσιν
ἀρίστην οὖσαν.

5 Κατ' ἀρχὰς μὲν οὖν ἀγαπητῶς οἱ φρουροὶ τὴν
φιλοξενίαν τῶν ἀνθρώπων ἐλάμβανον· ἔπειτα δια-
φθειρόμενοι τὰς ψυχὰς ὑπὸ τοῦ κόρου τῶν ἀγαθῶν

hosts or to have stained her hands with civil bloodshed. How she incurred these dangers I shall
attempt to recount succinctly after first recalling a
few of the events which preceded.

In the previous year Rome, after undertaking the
Samnite war in behalf of all Campania and conquering
her opponents in three battles, had wished to bring
all her forces home, feeling that no further danger
remained for the cities there. But when the Campanians besought the Romans not to desert them
and leave them bereft of allies, declaring that the
Samnites would attack them if they had no assistance
from outside, it was decreed that the consul Marcus
Valerius, who had freed their cities from war, should
leave as large an army in those cities as they wished
to support. Having been given this authority, the
consul placed in the cities all who wished to draw
rations and be paid for garrison duty ; the greater part
of these consisted of homeless men burdened with
debt, who were glad to escape poverty and the
obscure life at home. The Campanians, taking these
men into their homes, welcomed them with lavish
tables and entertained them with all the other marks
of hospitality. For the manner of life of the Campanians is extravagant and luxurious enough now, and
was then, and will be for all time to come, since they
dwell in a plain that is rich in both crops and flocks
and is most salubrious for men who till the soil.

At first, accordingly, the garrison gladly accepted
the hospitality of these people ; then, as their souls
grew corrupted by the surfeit of good things, they

---

[1] Jacoby : ἐνέγκαι S.
[2] Feder : ἄγειν S.
[3] Feder : γενομένης S.

DIONYSIUS OF HALICARNASSUS

πονηροὺς ὑπολογισμοὺς κατὰ μικρὸν ἐλάμβανον,
καὶ συνιόντες ἀλλήλοις ἔλεγον ὡς ἀνοήτων ἀνθρώπων ποιήσουσιν ἔργον εἰ τοσαύτην καταλιπόντες
εὐδαιμονίαν ἐπὶ τὸν ἐν Ῥώμῃ βίον ἀνακάμψουσιν,
ἔνθα λυπρὰ μὲν ἡ γῆ, πολλαὶ δὲ εἰσφοραί, πολέμων δὲ καὶ κακῶν ἀνάπαυσις οὐδεμία, τὰ δὲ
6 τῶν κοινῶν πόνων ἆθλα παρ᾿ ὀλίγοις.[1] οἱ δὲ
ἀσθενεῖς τοῖς βίοις καὶ τῶν καθ᾿ ἡμέραν ἀναγκαίων ἀποροῦντες, καὶ ἔτι μᾶλλον οἱ τὰ χρέα μὴ
δυνάμενοι διαλῦσαι τοῖς συμβαλοῦσι καὶ τὴν
ἀνάγκην ἀποχρῶσαν εἶναι σύμβουλον τῶν συμφερόντων σφίσιν ἀποφαίνοντες ἄνευ τοῦ καλοῦ, οὐδ᾿
εἰ πάντες νόμοι τε καὶ ἄρχοντες τὰς ἐσχάτας
τιμωρίας ἀπειλοῖεν αὐτοῖς, Καμπανοῖς[2] ἔτι μεθήσεσθαι τῆς παρούσης εὐδαιμονίας ἔλεγον, καὶ
τελευτῶντες εἰς τοσαύτην ἀπόνοιαν ἦλθον ὥστε
7 καὶ λέγειν ἐτόλμων· " Τί δὴ[3] καὶ δράσομεν δεινὸν
ἐὰν Καμπανοὺς ἐκβαλόντες τὰς ἐκείνων πόλεις
κατάσχωμεν; οὗτοι γὰρ αὐτοὶ πρότερον οὐκ ἐκ
τοῦ δικαίου[4] κτησάμενοι τὴν γῆν κατέσχον, ἀλλὰ
ἐπιξενωθέντες Τυρρηνοῖς[5] τοῖς κατοικοῦσιν αὐτὴν
καὶ τοὺς ἄνδρας ἅπαντας διαφθείραντες τάς τε
γυναῖκας αὐτῶν καὶ τοὺς βίους καὶ τὰς πόλεις καὶ
τὴν περιμάχητον χώραν παρέλαβον, ὥστε σὺν
δίκῃ πείσονται πᾶν ὅ τι ἂν πάθωσιν αὐτοὶ τῆς
8 παρανομίας ἄρξαντες καθ᾿ ἑτέρων. τί δὴ[6] καὶ
τὸ κωλῦσον[7] ἡμᾶς ἔσται ταῦτα μέχρι τοῦ παντὸς

---

[1] Kiessling was the first editor to point with a period, instead of a comma, after ὀλίγοις.
[2] ἐν before Καμπανοῖς deleted by Kiessling.
[3] Kiessling : δαὶ S.

gradually gave way to base considerations, and remarked when meeting that they would be playing the part of witless men if they left such great good fortune behind and returned to their life at Rome, where the land was wretched and there were numerous war taxes, where there was no respite from wars and evils, and the rewards for the hardships suffered by all in common were at the disposition of a few. Those who had but an insecure livelihood and lacked daily subsistence, and even more those who were unable to discharge their debts to their creditors and declared that their necessity was a sufficient counsellor to advise them of their interests regardless of the honourable course, said that even if all the laws and magistrates should threaten them with the direst penalties, they would no longer relinquish to the Campanians their present good fortune ; and finally they came to such a state of madness that they dared to talk in this fashion : " What terrible crime, indeed, shall we be committing if we expel the Campanians and occupy their cities ? For these men themselves did not acquire the land in a just manner when they occupied it aforetime, but after enjoying the hospitality of the Tyrrhenians who inhabited it, they slew all the men and took over their wives, their homes, their cities, and their land that was so well worth fighting for ; so that with justice they will suffer whatever they may suffer, having themselves begun the lawless treatment of others. What, then, will there be to prevent our enjoying these blessings for all time to

---

⁴ δικαίου Jacoby : πεδίου S, παλαιοῦ Feder, ἰδίου Müller, βελτίστου Kiessling.

⁵ τυρανοῖς S.

⁶ Kiessling : δαὶ S.   ⁷ κωλῦσαν S.

χρόνου καρποῦσθαι τἀγαθά; Σαυνῖται μέν γε καὶ
Σιδικῖνοι[1] καὶ Αὔσονες[2] καὶ πάντες οἱ περίοικοι
τοσούτου[3] δεήσουσι Καμπανοῖς τιμωροῦντες ἐφ'
ἡμᾶς γε[4] στρατεύειν ὥστε ἀποχρῆν ὑπολήψονταί
σφισιν εἰ τὰ ἑαυτῶν ἐάσομεν[5] ἑκάστους[6] ἔχειν.
9 Ῥωμαῖοι δὲ ἴσως μὲν καὶ κατ' εὐχὴν δέξονται τὸ
πραχθέν, ἅπασαν ἀξιοῦντες Ἰταλίαν ταῖς αὐτῶν
ἀποικίαις κρατεῖσθαι· εἰ δὲ ἀγανακτεῖν προσποιού-
μενοι,[7] πολεμίους ἡμᾶς κρίναντες,[8] οὐ τοσαῦτα
δεινὰ διαθήσουσιν ὅσα πείσονται πρὸς ἡμῶν. χώραν τε γὰρ αὐτῶν δῃώσομεν, ὅσον ἂν ἡμῖν δοκῇ,
καὶ δεσμώτας ἐκ τῶν ἀγρῶν λύσομεν καὶ θεράποντας ἐλευθερώσομεν καὶ μετὰ τῶν ἐχθίστων αὐτοῖς Οὐολούσκων τε καὶ Τυρρηνῶν καὶ Σαυνιτῶν
καὶ τῶν ἔτι ἐνδοιαστῶς ἀκροωμένων Λατίνων στη-
σόμεθα. ἠναγκασμένοις δ' ἀνθρώποις καὶ τὸν ἔσχα-
τον περὶ ψυχῆς τρέχουσι δρόμον οὔτ' ἄπορον οὐθὲν
οὔτ' ἀντίπαλον."

10 Τοιαῦτα διαλεγόμενοι πρὸς ἀλλήλους ὀλίγοι
μὲν τὰ πρῶτα, ἔπειτα πλείους, ἔγνωσαν ἐπιχειρεῖν ταῖς πόλεσι καὶ δι' ὅρκων ἐδίδοσαν ἀλλήλοις
τὸ πιστόν. ἔφθασε δὲ τὴν ἐπιχείρησιν αὐτῶν εἰς
τοὐμφανὲς[9] ἀγαγοῦσα μήνυσις ἣν τῶν συνομο-
σάντων τινὲς ἐποιήσαντο πρὸς τὸν ἕτερον τῶν
ὑπάτων Μάρκιον, ᾧ τὸν κατὰ Σαυνιτῶν πόλεμον
ὁ κλῆρος ἀπένειμεν, ἤδη παρειληφότα[10] τὰς ἐν τῇ
Ῥώμῃ καταγραφείσας δυνάμεις καὶ ὄντα ἐν ὁδῷ.

---

[1] Feder : σιτικηνοί S.   [2] Edd. : αὔσωνες S.
[3] Jacoby : τοσοῦτον S.
[4] Kiessling : τε S, om. Müller.
[5] Feder : ἐάσωμεν S.
[6] Kiessling : ἑκάστοις S.
[7] προσποιοῦνται Kiessling.

come ? At any rate, the Samnites, the Sidicini, the Ausonians and all the neighbouring peoples, far from marching against us to avenge the Campanians, will believe that it is enough for them if we allow each of them to retain their own possessions. And the Romans perhaps will accept our action as truly an answer to prayer, ambitious as they are to rule all Italy by their own colonies ; but if they pretend to be aggrieved and adjudge us enemies, they will not do us as much harm as they will suffer harm at our hands. For we will ravage their territory as much as we please, turn loose the prisoners on the country estates, free the slaves, and take our stand with their bitterest enemies, the Volscians, Tyrrhenians and Samnites, as well as with the Latins who are still wavering in their loyalty. To men driven by stern necessity and running the supreme race for their lives nothing is either impossible or able to withstand them."

As they argued in this manner with one another, at first a few, and then a larger number decided to attack the cities, and they pledged their good faith to one another by means of oaths. But their attempt was forestalled, being brought to light by information which some of the conspirators laid before Marcius, one of the consuls, who had been designated by lot to conduct the war against the Samnites, and having already taken over the forces that had been enrolled in Rome, was on his way. The consul, upon

---

[8] κρίνουσιν Müller, unless a verb has been lost after κρίναντες.

[9] τοὐμφανὲς Kiessling : ἐμφανὲς S.

[10] παρειληφότα Feder in note, but παρειληφότι in text : παρείληφεν ὅτι S.

ὁ δὲ ὕπατος ἀπροσδοκήτου καὶ δεινοῦ πράγματος
ἀκούσας ἔκρινε μήτ' ἐξειπεῖν[1] τὸ πρᾶγμα μήτ'[2]
εἰδέναι δοκεῖν, ἀλλὰ δι' ἀπάτης τινὸς καὶ στρα-
τηγίας κωλῦσαι τὰ συμβησόμενα ταῖς πόλεσιν.
11 ἀποστείλας δή τινας ἅμα τοῖς μηνυταῖς κατα-
σκευαστοὺς εἰς τὰς πόλεις πρὶν αὐτὸς[3] ἐλθεῖν,
παρεσκεύασε[4] λέγεσθαι πρὸς τοὺς ἐν ταῖς παρα-
χειμασίαις ὅτι τὰς μὲν φρουρὰς ἔγνω καταλιπεῖν
ἐν ταῖς πόλεσι τὰς τότε οὔσας, ἐπειδὴ[5] βουλομένοις
ἐστὶ τοῖς Καμπανοῖς αὐτὰς μένειν, τῇ δὲ οἴκοθεν
ἀφιγμένῃ σὺν αὐτῷ δυνάμει πολεμεῖν πρὸς Σαυνίτας παρασκευάζεται· καὶ ἔπεισεν[6] ἅπαντας ταῦτα
12 ὑπολαβεῖν. ἀφικόμενος δὲ εἰς τὴν Καμπανίαν
μετὰ τῆς στρατιᾶς ἁπάσης εἰς ἑκάστην παρήει
πόλιν καὶ τοὺς ἐν ταῖς φρουραῖς ἀνακαλούμενος
διέκρινεν ἁπάντων τοὺς μετασχόντας τῆς συνωμοσίας. ἔπειτα φιλανθρώπως ἑκάστοις δια-
λεγόμενος οὓς μὲν ἀπέλυσε τῶν σημείων, ὡς ἂν
χαριζόμενος τὴν ἄφεσιν τῆς στρατείας, οὓς δὲ
τῷ πρεσβευτῇ καὶ τῷ χιλιάρχῳ παραδοὺς ὡς ἐπὶ
χρείας δή τινας στρατιωτικὰς ἀπέλυσεν (οὗτοι δ'
ἦσαν οἱ πονηρότατοι καὶ οὐχ ὑπομένοντες ἀφεῖσθαι
τῆς στρατείας) ἐντειλάμενος τοῖς ἄγουσιν αὐτοὺς
εἰς Ῥώμην διακομίσαι καὶ φυλάττειν ἐν ἀδήλοις
φυλακαῖς, χωρίσαντας ἄλλους ἀπ' ἄλλων, ἕως ἂν
αὐτὸς ἀφίκηται.

---

[1] μήτ' ἐξειπεῖν . . . μήτ' (or μηδ' . . . μηδ') Cary, μηδ' ἐξενεγκεῖν . . . μηδ' Post : μὴ λέξειν . . . μήτ' S ; μὴ λέξαι
Feder, μὴ ἐλέγξαι Cobet, μὴ δείξειν Jacoby.
[2] μήτ' S : μηδ' Kiessling, Jacoby.

hearing of this unexpected and dangerous matter, decided neither [1] to mention it nor to appear to be aware of it, but by some deception and ruse to prevent the fulfilment of the threat to the cities. Accordingly, he sent into the cities some men duly instructed for the purpose along with the informers, ahead of his own arrival, and caused the report to be spread among the men in winter quarters that he had decided to leave the present garrisons in the cities, inasmuch as the Campanians desired to have them remain, while he himself was preparing to make war against the Samnites with the forces which had come with him from Rome ; and he persuaded them all to believe this. But upon arriving in Campania with his whole army, he went round to each city, and summoning the men in the garrisons, picked out from among them all those who had taken part in the conspiracy. Then, addressing each group in friendly fashion, he dismissed some from the standards, as if granting discharge from the service as a favour, and others he dismissed, handing them over to the legate and the tribune as if for some special military duties. These latter were the most evil-minded and would not consent to be discharged from the service ; and he gave orders to those who were escorting them to take them to Rome, and separating the groups from one another, to keep them in secret custody until he himself should come.

[1] Or, reading μηδ' . . . μηδ', " not even to mention it nor indeed to appear," etc.

---

[3] Feder : αὐτοὺς S, αὐτὸν Müller.
[4] παρεσκεύασε Cary, προπαρεσκεύασε Kiessling : προσεσκεύασε S, προσκατεσκεύασε Post.
[5] Feder : ἐπεὶ δὲ S.   [6] ἔπεισαν Müller.

DIONYSIUS OF HALICARNASSUS

13 Τοῖς δὲ ἀνδράσιν, ἐνθυμουμένοις ὅτι πάντες οἱ κορυφαιότατοι τῆς συνωμοσίας οἱ μὲν ἀπολύονται τῶν σημείων, οἱ δ' ἀποστέλλονται δίχα τῶν ἄλλων ὁποιδήποτε, λογισμὸς εἰσῆλθε περιφανῆ γεγονέναι σφῶν τὴν συνωμοσίαν καὶ μετὰ τοῦτο δέος, εἰ χωρὶς ἀλλήλων γένοιντο καὶ τὰ ὅπλα θεῖεν, μὴ δίκας ὑπόσχωσιν εἰς Ῥώμην ἀπαχθέντες· συνιόντες 14 τε κατ' ὀλίγους ἐσκόπουν τί χρὴ πράττειν. ἔπειτα γνώμην τινῶν[1] εἰσηγησαμένων περὶ ἀποστάσεως ἐπαινέσαντες τὸ βούλευμα καὶ πίστεις ἀπορρήτους ἐν ἀλλήλοις ποιησάμενοι οἱ[2] τῆς στρατείας ἀφειμένοι περὶ Ταρρακινὰ πόλιν ἐν ἐπιτηδείοις χωρίοις 15 παρ' αὐτὴν τὴν ὁδὸν στρατοπεδεύονται. ἔπειθ' οἱ μετὰ τοῦ πρεσβευτοῦ καὶ τῶν χιλιάρχων ἀποστελλόμενοι τοὺς ἡγεμόνας καταλιπόντες, ἔστι δ' οὓς καὶ τῶν ἀγόντων σφᾶς στρατιωτῶν πείσαντες ἀποστῆναι, περὶ τὸν[3] αὐτὸν ἱδρύονται τόπον. ὡς δὲ ἅπαξ οὗτοι τὰς παρόδους κατελάβοντο, πολλοὶ προσῆσαν αὐτοῖς ὁσημέραι, καὶ χεὶρ ἐγένετο περὶ αὐτοὺς καρτερά· ἔπειτα τὰ δεσμωτήρια ὑπ' αὐτῶν,[4] ὅσα κατὰ τοὺς ἀγροὺς ἦν, ἐλύετο καὶ συνέρρει . . . Esc.

IV. Οἱ δὲ τῶν Ῥωμαίων ὕπατοι πᾶσαν τὴν μεταξὺ γῆν ἀδεῶς διελθόντες, τῶν μὲν οὐκ ἐναντιουμένων, τῶν δὲ συμπροπεμπόντων,—πολλαὶ δ' εἰσὶ δυσχωρίαι κατὰ τὴν ἐκ Ῥώμης εἰς Καμπανίαν ἄγουσαν ὁδὸν ὄρεσί τε καὶ τέλμασι καὶ θαλάτταις καὶ ποταμοῖς ναυσιπόροις διακλειόμεναι, ἃς οὐ ῥᾴδιον ἦν διελθεῖν ὑπὸ τῶν πολεμίων προκατα-

---

[1] Feder : τινὰ S.   [2] οἱ added by Feder.
[3] τὸν added by Edd.
[4] ὑπ' αὐτῶν S : ἀπάντων Müller.

294

But the conspirators, reflecting that all their ring-leaders were being either discharged from the standards or else sent to some destination or other apart from the rest, came to the conclusion that their conspiracy had been revealed, and then they became afraid that, if they should become separated and lay down their arms, they would have to pay the penalty when they were brought back to Rome ; and meeting together in small groups, they considered what they ought to do. Then, when some proposed a revolt, they approved the plan and gave secret pledges among themselves, after which those who had been discharged from the service made camp near the city of Tarracina in convenient spots right beside the road. Later, the men who were being sent with the legate and the tribunes, deserting their leaders and in some instances even persuading the soldiers who were escorting them to revolt, settled down in the same region. When these had once seized the by-roads, many others joined them daily, and a strong force was gathered about them. Then all the prisons that were in the country districts were opened by them and there flocked together . . .

IV. The Roman consuls passed unhindered through all the intervening region, some of the people offering no opposition and others actually escorting them on their way. There are many difficult passes along the road that leads from Rome to Campania, hemmed in by mountains, marshes, arms of the sea, and navigable rivers, and it was not easy to get through them when they had been occupied in advance by the enemy.

2 ληφθείσας,—καί τινα καὶ ποταμόν, ὃς διὰ τῆς
Κασιλίνων¹ χώρας καὶ πόλεως φέρεται, τριάκοντα
τῆς Καπύης ἀπέχοντα στάδια, Οὐολτουρνὸν² ὄνομα,
τεττάρων οὐκ ἐλάττω πλέθρων ὄντα τὸ πλάτος,
ξυλίνῃ γεφύρᾳ διαβάντες, ἣν ἐν τρισὶ κατεσκεύασαν
ἡμέραις, διεξῄεσαν,³ ἵνα τοῖς μὲν τὰ σφέτερα φρο-
νοῦσι Καμπανῶν⁴ θάρσος ὡς τὰ κράτιστα προῃ-
3 ρημένοις ἐγγένηται, τοῖς δὲ τἀναντία δέος. καὶ
προελθόντες ἐπέκεινα τῆς πόλεως ἀπὸ τετταράκοντα σταδίων Καπύης στρατοπεδεύονται ἐν ὑψηλῷ
τόπῳ θέντες τὸν χάρακα, ἔνθα ὑπομένοντες τὰς
παρὰ Σαυνιτῶν ἀγοράς τε καὶ συμμαχίας ἐκαρα-
δόκουν. οἱ δὲ ἄρα ὑπισχνοῦντο μὲν αὐτοῖς πλείω
τῶν ἱκανῶν, ἐπήρκουν δ' οὐδὲν ὅ τι καὶ λόγου
ἄξιον, στρατιάν τ' ἀγείρειν⁵ ἐκ πάσης πόλεως
4 σκηπτόμενοι κατέτριβον τοὺς χρόνους. ἀπογνόντες
δὴ τῆς ἐκεῖθεν ἐπικουρίας καὶ τὰς μὲν ἑαυτῶν
δυνάμεις ὁρῶντες οὐθὲν ἰσχύος ἐκ τοῦ χρόνου
προσλαμβανούσας, τὰς δὲ τῶν πολεμίων μακρῷ
πλείους γινομένας, ἐπὶ τὰ ἔργα χωρεῖν ἔγνωσαν.
5 ἐνθυμούμενοι δ' ὅτι πολὺ τῆς στρατιᾶς ἐστι τὸ
δυσάγωγον καὶ ταῖς ἐπιταγαῖς τῶν ἡγεμόνων
ἀπειθές, ὡς ἐν ἄλλαις τε πολλαῖς πείραις ἐδήλωσε
καὶ τὰ τελευταῖα ἐν τῇ Καμπανικῇ παραχειμασίᾳ,
ἀφ' ἧς εἰς τοσαύτην ἀπόνοιαν ἦλθον αὐτῶν τινες
ὥστε καὶ πόλεσιν ἐπιθέσθαι καὶ τὸν ὕπατον καταλιπεῖν καὶ κατὰ τῆς πατρίδος ὅπλα ἀναλαβεῖν,
τούτους ᾤοντο δεῖν πρῶτον ἀποδεῖξαι σωφρονε-

---

¹ Feder : βασιληνῶν S.
² Feder : οὐατουρνῶν S, Οὐλτουρνὸν Müller.
³ διεξίεσαν S.
⁴ καμπανῶν S : Καμπανοῖς Feder(?) and later editors.
⁵ τ' ἀγείρειν Feder : τε γὰρ S.

They also crossed a river, called the Volturnus, which flows through the territory and city of Casilinum, distant thirty stades from Capua and not less than four plethra [1] in breadth, getting across by means of a wooden bridge which they constructed in three days. They made their way through all these difficulties in order to inspire confidence in those of the Campanians who sided with them and convince them that they had made the best choice, and to inspire fear in those who took the opposite course. When they had advanced beyond the city, they encamped at a distance of forty stades from Capua, entrenching themselves in a lofty position, where they waited and kept watch for the provisions and reinforcements they expected from the Samnites. These, it seems, kept promising them more than was required, but were not furnishing anything worth mentioning, and while pretending to be gathering an army out of every city, were really marking time. The consuls, therefore, despairing of reinforcements from that quarter, and observing that their own forces were receiving no accession of strength with the passing of time, whereas those of the enemy were becoming much more numerous, resolved to set to work. But bearing in mind that a large part of the army was hard to manage and slow to obey the orders of its commanders, as it had shown not only on many other occasions, but also most recently while in its winter quarters in Campania, where some of them had gone to such a degree of madness as to make an attack upon cities, to desert the consul, and to take up arms against the fatherland, they thought they ought first of all to make these men more circumspect by causing

---

[1] The plethron was equal to 101 English feet.

στέρους, δεινότερον ποιήσαντες αὐτοῖς[1] τὸν ἀπὸ
τῶν ἡγεμόνων ψόγον[2] ἢ τὸν ἀπὸ τῶν πολεμίων[3]
6 κίνδυνον. ταῦτα διανοηθέντες ἐκκλησίαν συνῆγον,
καὶ λέγει Μάλλιος· [ζήτει ἐν τῷ περὶ στρατηγημάτων καὶ δημηγοριῶν. περὶ τοῦ υἱοῦ Μαλλίου
τοῦ μονομαχήσαντος.] Esc.

V. (4) . . . ἀλλὰ καὶ[4] διότι τοὺς φίλους αὐτῶν
Καμπανοὺς πολλὰ καὶ μεγάλα ἔβλαπτον. ἡ δὲ
βουλὴ τῶν Ῥωμαίων, Καμπανῶν πολλάκις ἐμφανι-
ζόντων καὶ ἀποδυρομένων κατὰ[5] τῶν Νεαπολιτῶν,
πρέσβεις ἐψηφίσατο[6] πρὸς τοὺς Νεαπολίτας ἀποστεῖλαι τοὺς ἀξιώσοντας[7] αὐτοὺς μηθὲν εἰς τοὺς
ὑπηκόους τῆς τῶν Ῥωμαίων ἡγεμονίας παρανομεῖν,
ἀλλὰ καὶ διδόναι τὰ δίκαια καὶ λαμβάνειν, καί,
εἴ γε διαφέρονται πρὸς ἀλλήλους, μὴ δι' ὅπλων
ἀλλὰ διὰ λόγων . . .,[8] σύμβολα ποιησαμένους
πρὸς αὐτούς, καὶ τὸ λοιπὸν εἰρήνην ἄγειν πρὸς
ἅπαντας τοὺς περιοικοῦντας τὸ Τυρρηνικὸν πέλαγος, μήτ' αὐτοὺς ἔργα πράττοντας ἃ μὴ προσῆκεν[9] Ἕλλησι μήτε τοῖς πράττουσι συνεργοῦντας·
μάλιστα δ' εἰ δύναιντο θεραπείαις[10] τῶν δυνατῶν παρασκευάσοντας ἀποστῆναι μὲν ἀπὸ Σαυνιτῶν τὴν πόλιν, σφίσι δ' αὐτοῖς γενέσθαι φίλην.
2 (5) ἔτυχον δὲ κατὰ τὸν αὐτὸν χρόνον ἀφιγμένοι
πρὸς τοὺς Νεαπολίτας πρέσβεις ὑπὸ Ταραντίνων
ἀποσταλέντες, ἄνδρες ἐπιφανεῖς καὶ πρόξενοι διὰ

---

[1] αὐτούς S.
[2] ψόγον Müller, reporting this as the reading of S : φόνον
(corr. from φόνων) S, φόβον Feder, Jacoby.
[3] πολεμίων Feder, πολέμων Müller : πόλεων S.
[4] καὶ added by Ursinus.   [5] κατὰ added by Ursinus.
[6] ἐψηφίσατο ER : ἐποιήσατο X ; V omits πρέσβεις . . . νεαπολίτας.

them to regard the reproof coming from their commanders as a more terrible thing than the danger
threatening from their enemies. With this purpose
in mind they called an assembly, and Manlius said :
[The MS. adds : See the section on Stratagems and
Speeches. Concerning the son of Manlius who
fought in single combat.]

V. (4) . . . but also because they were inflicting
many grievous injuries on their friends the Campanians.[1] The Roman senate, when the Campanians
made repeated charges and complaints against the
Neapolitans, voted to send ambassadors to the latter
to demand that they should do no wrong to the
subjects of the Roman empire, but should give and
receive justice, and if they had any differences with
one another, should settle [2] them not by arms but by
discussion, after first making a compact with them ;
and that for the future they should remain at peace
with all the people dwelling along the Tyrrhenian
sea, neither committing any acts themselves that
were unbecoming to Greeks nor assisting others who
did so ; but in particular, the envoys, if they could do
so by courting the favour of the influential men, were
to get the city ready to revolt from the Samnites and
become friendly to the Romans. (5) It chanced that
at this same time ambassadors sent by the Tarentines
had come to the Neapolitans, men of distinction who

---

[1] For chaps. 5 f. *cf.* Livy viii. 22, 5-10.
[2] The verb is wanting in the MSS.

---

[7] Sylburg : ἀξιώσαντας O.
[8] A verb is wanting after λόγων. Steph.² suggested διαλύσασθαι, Reiske κρίνεσθαι or διακρίνεσθαι.
[9] ἃ μὴ προσῆκεν Kiessling, ἃ μὴ προσῆκει Steph.² : τὰ μὴ
προσῆκειν O, τὰ μὴ προσήκοντα Ursinus.
[10] Sylburg : θεραπείας O.

γένους τῶν Νεαπολιτῶν· καὶ ἕτεροι ὑπὸ Νωλανῶν
ὁμόρων ὄντων καὶ σφόδρα τοὺς Ἕλληνας ἀσπαζο-
μένων, τἀναντία τοὺς Νεαπολίτας ἀξιώσοντες,
μήτε σύμβολα ποιεῖσθαι πρὸς τοὺς Ῥωμαίους ἢ
τοὺς ὑπηκόους αὐτῶν μήτε διαλύεσθαι τὴν πρὸς
3 Σαυνίτας φιλίαν· ἐὰν δὲ ταύτην ποιήσωνται
Ῥωμαῖοι τοῦ πολέμου τὴν[1] πρόφασιν, μὴ ὀρρωδεῖν
μηδ᾽ ὡς ἄμαχόν τινα τὴν ἰσχὺν αὐτῶν κατα-
πεπλῆχθαι, ἀλλὰ μένειν γενναίως καὶ ὡς προσῆκεν Ἕλλησι πολεμεῖν, τῇ τ᾽ οἰκείᾳ πιστεύοντας[2]
δυνάμει καὶ τῇ παρὰ Σαυνιτῶν ἀφιξομένῃ[3] βοηθείᾳ,
ναυτικήν τ᾽ ἰσχὺν προσληψομένους ἔξω τῆς ἑαυτῶν, ἣν Ταραντῖνοι πέμψουσιν, ἐὰν ἄρα καὶ ταύτης
δέωνται, πολλὴν καὶ ἀγαθήν. *Ursin.*

VI. (6) Συναχθείσης δὲ[4] τῆς βουλῆς καὶ πολλῶν
ῥηθέντων ἐν αὐτῇ λόγων, οὓς αἵ τε πρεσβεῖαι
διεξῆλθον καὶ οἱ συναγορεύοντες αὐταῖς, διέστησαν αἱ γνῶμαι τῶν συνέδρων καὶ οἵ γε χαριέ-
2 στατοι τὰ τῶν Ῥωμαίων ἔδοξαν φρονεῖν. ἐκείνην
μὲν οὖν τὴν ἡμέραν οὐδὲν ἐξηνέχθη προβούλευμα,
εἰς ἑτέραν δὲ πάλιν ἕδραν ἀναβληθείσης τῆς περὶ
τῶν πρεσβειῶν διαγνώσεως, ἀφικόμενοι κατὰ πλῆθος εἰς τὴν Νεάπολιν Σαυνιτῶν οἱ δυνατώτατοι
καὶ τοὺς προεστηκότας τῶν κοινῶν θεραπείαις
τισὶν οἰκειωσάμενοι πείθουσι τὴν βουλὴν ἐπὶ τῷ
3 δήμῳ ποιῆσαι τὴν τοῦ συμφέροντος αἵρεσιν. καὶ
παρελθόντες εἰς τὴν ἐκκλησίαν πρῶτον μὲν τὰς
ἑαυτῶν εὐεργεσίας διεξῄεσαν,[5] ἔπειτα τῆς Ῥωμαίων πόλεως πολλὰ κατηγόρουν, ὡς ἀπίστου

---

[1] τὴν deleted by Hertlein. [2] Portus : πιστεύοντες O.
[3] ἀφιξομένῃ Ursinus : ἀφανιζομένη O.
[4] δὲ V : οὖν X.

had inherited ties of hospitality with the Neapolitans ; others also had come, sent by the Nolans, who were their neighbours and greatly admired the Greeks, to ask the Neapolitans on the contrary neither to make an agreement with the Romans or their subjects nor to give up their friendship with the Samnites.   If the Romans should make this their pretext for war, the Neapolitans were not to be alarmed or terrified by the strength of the Romans in the belief that it was some invincible strength, but to stand their ground nobly and fight as befitted Greeks, relying both on their own army and the reinforcements which would come from the Samnites, and, in addition to their own naval force, being sure of receiving a large and excellent one which the Tarentines would send them in case they should require that also.

VI. (6) When the senate [1] had convened and many speeches had been made there by both the embassies and their supporters, the opinions of the councillors were divided, though the most enlightened seemed to favour the Roman cause.   On that day, accordingly, no preliminary decree was passed but the decision with regard to the embassies was postponed to another session, at which time the most influential of the Samnites came in large numbers to Neapolis, and winning over the men at the head of the state by means of some favours, persuaded the senate to leave to the popular assembly the decision regarding the best interests of the state.   And appearing before the assembly, they first recounted their own services, then made many accusations against the Roman state, charging it with being faithless and treacherous ; and

---

[1] The Neapolitan senate is meant.

<hr>

⁵ Sylburg : διεξίεσαν O.

DIONYSIUS OF HALICARNASSUS

καὶ δολίου,¹ τελευτῶντες² δὲ τοῦ λόγου θαυμαστὰς
ἐποιοῦντο τοῖς Νεαπολίταις³ ὑποσχέσεις ἐὰν εἰς
τὸν πόλεμον καταστῶσι, στρατιάν τε πέμψειν,
ὅσης ἂν δέωνται, τὴν φυλάξουσαν αὐτῶν τὰ τείχη,
καὶ ταῖς ναυσὶν ἐπιβάτας καὶ τὴν εἰρεσίαν ἅπασαν
παρέξειν, οὐ μόνον καταγγέλλοντες⁴ τοῖς ἰδίοις
στρατεύμασιν, ἀλλὰ κἀκείνοις⁵ ἁπάσας τὰς εἰς
4 πόλεμον δαπάνας ἐπιχορηγοῦντες· ἀπωσαμένοις
τε τὸ Ῥωμαϊκὸν στράτευμα Κύμην τ' ἀνασώσειν,
ἣν δευτέρα γενεᾷ πρότερον ἐξελάσαντες τοὺς
Κυμαίους Καμπανοὶ κατέσχον, καὶ συγκατάξειν
ἐπὶ τὰ σφέτερα τοὺς περιόντας ἔτι Κυμαίων, οὓς
οἱ Νεαπολῖται τῆς πατρίδος ἐκπεσόντας ὑπεδέξαντο
καὶ πάντων ἐποιήσαντο κοινωνοὺς τῶν ἰδίων ἀγαθῶν, χώραν τε προσθήσειν τοῖς Νεαπολίταις ἐξ ἧς
5 οἱ Καμπανοὶ κατεῖχον⁶ τὴν ἄπολιν.⁷   (7) τῶν
δὲ Νεαπολιτῶν ὅσον μὲν ἦν μέρος εὔλογον καὶ
πρὸ πολλοῦ δυνάμενον ὁρᾶν τὰς καταληψομένας
τὴν πόλιν ἐκ τοῦ πολέμου συμφορὰς εἰρήνην ἄγειν
ἠξίου, τὸ δὲ φιλόκαινον καὶ τὰς ἐκ τῆς ταραχῆς
πλεονεξίας διῶκον ἐπὶ τὸν πόλεμον συνελάμβανε⁸·
καταβοαί τ' ἀλλήλων ἐγίνοντο καὶ χειροκρασίαι
καὶ προέβη τὸ νεῖκος εἰς λίθων βολάς, καὶ τελευτῶντες ἐκράτησαν οἱ κακίους τῶν κρειττόνων,
ὥστε τοὺς πρέσβεις τῶν Ῥωμαίων ἀπράκτους

¹ ἀπίστου καὶ δολίου Ursinus : ἀπίστους καὶ δολίους O.
² Sylburg : τελευτῶντος O.
³ τοῖς Νεαπολίταις Ursinus : τοὺς νεαπολίτας O.
⁴ καταγγέλλοντες, if the correct form, would seem to be
misplaced here, as it should come earlier in the sentence; if
it originally followed καταστῶσι its omission there would be
easily explained. Post, retaining the word here, would read ἐπι-
χορηγήσειν just below. Sylburg had proposed παραγγέλλοντες.
⁵ Ursinus : κἀκείνους O.
302

at the end of their speech they made some remarkable promises to the Neapolitans if they would enter the war. They would send an army, they announced, as large as the Neapolitans should require, to guard their walls, and would also furnish marines for their ships as well as all the rowers, providing all the expenses of the war not only for their own armies, but for the others too. Furthermore, when the Neapolitans had repulsed the Roman army, they would not only recover Cumae for them, which the Campanians had occupied two generations earlier [1] after expelling the Cumaeans, but would also restore to their possessions those of the Cumaeans who still survived—these, when driven out of their own city, had been received by the Neapolitans and made sharers of all their own blessings—and they would also grant to the Neapolitans some of the land the Campanians were then holding,—the part without cities. [2] (7) The element among the Neapolitans that was reasonable and able to foresee long in advance the disasters that would come upon the city from the war, wished to remain at peace ; but the element that was fond of innovations and sought the personal advantages to be gained from turmoil joined forces for the war. There were mutual recriminations and skirmishes, and the strife was carried to the point of hurling stones ; in the end the worse element overpowered the better, so that the ambassadors of the Romans returned home

---

[1] The date was 421 B.C., almost one hundred years earlier.
[2] Or, following Reiske's text, " a very large part."

---

[6] κατεῖχον M (?), Kiessling : κατεῖσχον Z, κατέσχον Ursinus.
[7] τιν' (or τὴν) ἄπολιν Post : τινὰ πόλιν O, πάνυ πολλὴν Reiske.
[8] συνελάμβανεν Ursinus : συνελάμβανον O. Reiske assumed a lacuna before συνελάμβανε.

ἀπελθεῖν. διὰ ταύτας τὰς αἰτίας ἡ βουλὴ τῶν
Ῥωμαίων στρατιὰν ἐπὶ Νεαπολίτας ἀποστεῖλαι
ἐβουλεύθη. *Ursin.*

VII. (8) Ὅτι μαθόντες οἱ Ῥωμαῖοι Σαυνίτας
στρατιὰν ἀγείρειν τὸ μὲν πρῶτον πρέσβεις ἔπεμ-
ψαν, οἱ δὲ προχειρισθέντες ἐκ τῶν βουλευτῶν[1]
πρέσβεις ἐλθόντες ἐπὶ τοὺς προβούλους τῶν Σαυνι-
2 τῶν ἔλεξαν· "'Ἀδικεῖτε, ἄνδρες Σαυνῖται, παραβαί-
νοντες τὰς ὁμολογίας ἃς ἐποιήσασθε πρὸς ἡμᾶς,
ὄνομα[2] μὲν ὑποδυόμενοι συμμάχων, ἔργα δὲ πράττοντες πολεμίων, πολλαῖς μὲν ἡττηθέντες ὑπὸ
Ῥωμαίων μάχαις, δεήσει δὲ μεγάλῃ καταλυσά-
μενοι τὸν πόλεμον καὶ τυχόντες εἰρήνης οἵας ἐβούλεσθε, τὰ δὲ τελευταῖα φίλοι γενέσθαι τῆς πόλεως
ἡμῶν προθυμηθέντες καὶ σύμμαχοι καὶ τοὺς αὐτοὺς Ῥωμαίοις[3] ὀμόσαντες ἕξειν ἐχθροὺς καὶ φίλους.
3 (9) ὧν ἁπάντων ἐπιλαθόμενοι καὶ παρ' οὐδὲν
ἡγησάμενοι τοὺς ὅρκους ἐγκατελείπετε μὲν ἡμᾶς
ἐν τῷ πρὸς Λατίνους πολέμῳ καὶ πρὸς Οὐολούσκους συστάντι,[4] οὓς δι' ὑμᾶς ἐχθροὺς ἔχομεν
οὐ βουλόμενοι τοῦ καθ' ὑμῶν αὐτοῖς συνάρασθαι
πολέμου· ἐν δὲ τῷ παρελθόντι ἐνιαυτῷ Νεαπολίτας
δεδιότας ἀναδεῖξαι τὸν καθ' ἡμῶν πόλεμον ἁπάσῃ
σπουδῇ καὶ προθυμίᾳ χρώμενοι παρωρμήσατε,
μᾶλλον δ' ἠναγκάσατε, καὶ τὰς δαπάνας ἐπιχορη-
4 γεῖτε καὶ τὴν πόλιν δι' ὑμῶν[5] αὐτῶν ἔχετε. νῦν
δὲ παρασκευάζεσθε στρατιὰν ἐκ παντὸς ἀγείροντες[6]
τόπου, πρόφασιν μὲν ἑτέραν ποιούμενοι, τὸ δ'

---

[1] βουλευτῶν (or βουλευτικῶν) Sylburg : βουλευμάτων O.
[2] Steph.[2] : ὀνόματι O, ὀνόματα Kiessling.
[3] Ursinus : ῥωμαίους V.
[4] Sylburg : πρὸς οὐολούσκοις συστάντες O.

without having accomplished anything. For these reasons the Roman senate resolved to send an army against the Neapolitans.

VII. (8) The Romans, learning that the Samnites were assembling an army,[1] first sent ambassadors ; these ambassadors, chosen from among the senators, came to the deputies of the Samnites and said : " You do wrong, Samnites, to transgress the compact which you made with us, assuming the name of allies while in reality performing the deeds of enemies. After being defeated in many battles by the Romans, you secured a termination of the war in answer to your earnest entreaties and obtained a peace such as you desired ; and at the last you were eager to become friends and allies of our state and swore to have the same enemies and friends as the Romans. (9) But forgetting all this and regarding your oaths as naught, you deserted us in the war that arose with the Latins and with the Volscians, whom we have as enemies on your account because we were unwilling to join them in their war against you ; and this last year, when the Neapolitans were afraid to declare war against us, you devoted all your zeal and efforts to encouraging them, or rather compelling them, to do so, and are paying all the expenses and are holding their city with your own forces. And now you are preparing an army, gathering it from every quarter, alleging indeed a different reason, but in reality

---

[1] For chaps. 7–10 cf. Livy viii. 23, 1-13.

⁵ δι' ὑμῶν Reiske : δὲ ἡμῶν O.
⁶ Sylburg : ἐγείροντες O.

DIONYSIUS OF HALICARNASSUS

ἀληθὲς ἐπὶ τοὺς ἡμετέρους ἐγνωκότες ἄγειν ἀποίκους[1]· καὶ ἐπὶ ταύτας τὰς ἀδίκους πλεονεξίας
Φουνδανοὺς παρακαλεῖτε καὶ Φορμιανοὺς καὶ ἄλλους τινὰς οἷς ἡμεῖς ἰσοπολιτείας μετεδώκαμεν.
5 (10) οὕτω δὲ φανερῶς καὶ ἀναισχύντως συγχεόντων
ὑμῶν τὰ περὶ τῆς φιλίας καὶ συμμαχίας ὅρκια,
ἡμεῖς τὰ δίκαια[2] ποιοῦντες πρεσβείαν πρὸς ὑμᾶς
ἐκρίναμεν[3] ἀποστεῖλαι πρῶτον, καὶ μὴ πρότερον
ἄρξαι τῶν ἔργων πρὶν ἢ πειραθῆναι τῶν λόγων.
ἃ δὲ προκαλούμεθα[4] ὑμᾶς καὶ ὧν τυχόντες τὴν
ἐπὶ τοῖς παρελθοῦσιν ὀργὴν ἀποπληρώσειν οἰόμεθα,
ταῦτα ἐστί· πρῶτον μὲν ἀπάγειν ὑμᾶς ἀξιοῦμεν
τὴν ἀποσταλεῖσαν Νεαπολίταις συμμαχίαν, ἔπειτα
μηδεμίαν[5] ἐκπέμπειν στρατιὰν κατὰ τῶν ἀποίκων
τῶν ἡμετέρων μηδὲ τοὺς ὑπηκόους ἐπὶ πάσας τὰς
6 πλεονεξίας παρακαλεῖν· εἰ δὲ μὴ πᾶσι δόξαντα
ταῦτα ὑμῖν ἔπραττόν[6] τινες, ἀλλ' ἀπὸ τῆς ἑαυτῶν
γνώμης, παραδοῦναι τοὺς ἄνδρας ἡμῖν ἐπὶ δίκην.
τούτων τυχόντες ἀρκούμεθα, μὴ τυχόντες δὲ θεοὺς
καὶ δαίμονας οὓς ἐν ταῖς συνθήκαις ὠμόσατε μαρ-
τυρόμεθα, καὶ τοὺς εἰρηνοδίκας ἐπὶ τοῦτο ἄγοντες
ἐληλύθαμεν." Ursin.

VIII. (11) Τοιαῦτα τοῦ Ῥωμαίου λέξαντος βουλευσάμενοι καθ' αὑτοὺς οἱ πρόβουλοι τῶν Σαυνιτῶν
2 τοιαύτην ἐξήνεγκαν ἀπόκρισιν· " Τοῦ μὲν ὀψισμοῦ
τῆς ἐπὶ τὸν κατὰ Λατίνων πόλεμον συμμαχίας οὐ
τὸ κοινὸν αἴτιον, ἐψηφισάμεθα γὰρ ἀποσταλῆναι
τὴν στρατιὰν ὑμῖν, οἱ δὲ τὴν ἡγεμονίαν ἔχοντες
αὐτῆς πλείονα χρόνον ἀναλώσαντες ἐν τῇ παρα-

---

[1] Ursinus : ἐποίκους O.
[2] ἡμεῖς τὰ δίκαια added by Cohn ; Ursinus deleted ποιοῦντες.
[3] Reiske : ἔκριναν O.

306

having resolved to lead it against our colonists ; and to these unjust encroachments you are inviting the Fundans and Formians, as well as some others to whom we have granted citizenship. (10) Though you were thus openly and shamelessly violating your treaty of friendship and alliance, we, nevertheless, pursuing the just course, decided to send an embassy to you first and not to begin with deeds before trying arguments. The things which we ask you to do, and the obtaining of which we believe will satisfy our anger at your past deeds, are these : First, we wish you to withdraw the armed assistance you have sent to the Neapolitans, and, second, not to send out any army against our colonists nor to invite our subjects to all your encroachments. If some of you have been doing these things without the approval of all, but on their own initiative, we ask you to surrender the men to us for trial. If we gain these demands, we are content ; but if we fail to obtain them, we call to witness the gods and lesser divinities by whom you swore in making the treaty, and we have come bringing with us the *fetiales* for this purpose.''

VIII. (11) When the Roman had spoken to this effect, the deputies of the Samnites, after consulting together, delivered the following reply : '' For the delay on the part of our contingent in going to war against the Latins the state is not to blame—for we voted that the army should be sent to you—but rather those in command of it, who spent too much

---

⁴ Sylburg : προσκαλούμεθα O.

⁵ ἔπειτα μηδεμίαν Reiske, ἔπειτα δὲ μηδεμίαν Ursinus : ἔπειτα δὲ μίαν O.

⁶ ἃ before ἔπραττόν deleted by Steph.² Kiessling proposed to read εἰ δὲ μὴ πᾶσιν ἔδοξεν ταῦτα ὑμῖν, ἀλλ' . . . ἔπραττόν τινες.

σκευῇ,[1] καὶ ὑμεῖς[2] αὐτοὶ θᾶττον ἐπειχθέντες[3] ἐπὶ
τὸν ἀγῶνα· τρισὶ γοῦν ἢ τέτταρσιν ἡμέραις ὕστερον τῆς μάχης οἱ[4] πεμφθέντες ὑφ' ἡμῶν ἀφίκοντο.
3 περὶ δὲ τῆς Νεαπολιτῶν πόλεως, ἐν ᾗ τῶν ἡμετέρων[5] τινές εἰσιν, τοσούτου[6] δέομεν ἀδικεῖν ὑμᾶς,
εἴ τινα τοῖς κινδυνεύουσι βοήθειαν εἰς σωτηρίαν
κοινῇ παρεχόμεθα, ὥστ' αὐτοὶ δοκοῦμεν ὑφ'
ὑμῶν ἀδικεῖσθαι μεγάλα. φίλην γὰρ ἡμῶν καὶ
σύμμαχον οὖσαν τὴν πόλιν ταύτην οὐκ ἔναγχος
οὐδ' ἀφ' οὗ τὰς πρὸς ὑμᾶς[7] ἐποιησάμεθα ὁμολογίας, ἀλλὰ δευτέρᾳ γενεᾷ πρότερον διὰ πολλὰς
καὶ μεγάλας εὐεργεσίας, οὐθὲν ἀδικηθέντες ὑμεῖς
5 κατεδουλώσασθε. (12) οὐ μὴν οὐδὲ τούτῳ γε τῷ
ἔργῳ τὸ κοινὸν ὑμᾶς τῶν Σαυνιτῶν ἠδίκησεν· ἰδιό-
ξενοι δέ τινές εἰσιν, ὡς πυνθανόμεθα, καὶ φίλοι
τῶν Νεαπολιτῶν οἱ κατὰ τὴν ἑαυτῶν προαίρεσιν
τῇ πόλει βοηθοῦντες καί τινες καὶ δι' ἀπορίαν
ἴσως βίου μισθοφόροι. ὑφαιρεῖν[8] δὲ τοὺς ὑπηκόους ὑμῶν οὐθὲν δεόμεθα· καὶ γὰρ ἄνευ Φουνδανῶν
καὶ Φορμιανῶν ἱκανοὶ βοηθεῖν αὐτοῖς ἐσμεν, ἐὰν
4 καταστῶμεν εἰς ἀνάγκην πολέμου. ἡ δὲ παρα-
σκευὴ τῆς στρατιᾶς ἡμῶν ἐστιν οὐχ ὡς ἀφαιρη-
σομένων τοὺς ὑμετέρους ἀποίκους τὰ ἴδια, ἀλλ'
ὡς τὰ ἴδια ἐξόντων διὰ φυλακῆς.[9] ἀντιπρο-
καλούμεθά[10] τε ὑμᾶς, εἰ βούλεσθε τὰ δίκαια ποιεῖν,
ἐκχωρεῖν Φρεγέλλης,[11] ἣν οὐ[12] πρὸ πολλοῦ πολέμῳ[13]

---

[1] παρῃ PV.   [2] Ursinus : ἡμεῖς O.
[3] Sylburg : ἐπιχθέντες BEVP[1], ἐπαχθέντες MP[2].
[4] οἱ added by Steph.[2].   [5] Ursinus : ὑμετέρων O.
[6] Jacoby : τοσοῦτον O.
[7] Sylburg : ἡμᾶς O.
[8] ὑφαιρεῖν Cohn, ἀφαιρεῖν Sylburg : φέρειν O, διαφθείρειν
Reiske.
308

time in preparation, and you yourselves, who were too hasty in rushing into the struggle. In any case it was only three or four days after the battle that the troops sent by us arrived. As for the city of Neapolis, in which there are some of our troops, far from wronging you if we as a state contribute some aid toward the safety of those who are in danger, it is rather we ourselves who seem to be greatly wronged by you. For, though this city had become our friend and ally, not just recently nor from the time when we made our compact with you, but two generations earlier, in return for many great services, you enslaved it, though you had been wronged in no respect. (12) Yet not even in this action has the Samnite state wronged you ; rather it is some men connected by private ties of hospitality, as we learn, and friends of the Neapolitans who are aiding that city of their own free will, together with some also who through lack of a livelihood, perhaps, are serving as mercenaries. As for stealing away your subjects, we have no need of such a course ; for even without the Fundans and Formians we are quite able to succour ourselves if we are driven to the necessity of war. The getting of our army in readiness is not the act of those who are intending to rob your colonists of their possessions, but rather of those who intend to keep their own possessions under guard. We ask you in turn, if you wish to pursue the just course, to retire from Fregellae, which, after we had conquered it in war

---

⁹ Ursinus : διαφυλακαῖς V.
¹⁰ Sylburg : ἀντικαλούμεθα O.   ¹¹ Ursinus : φλυγέλλης O.
¹² οὐ om. V.   ¹³ Ursinus : πολέμου O.

κρατησάντων ἡμῶν, ὅσπερ[1] ἐστὶ νόμος κτήσεως
δικαιότατος, ὑμεῖς οὐδενὶ δικαίῳ σφετερισάμενοι
δεύτερον ἔτος ἤδη κατέχετε. τούτων ἡμεῖς τυχόντες οὐδὲν ὑποληψόμεθα ἀδικεῖσθαι." Ursin.

IX. (13) Μετὰ τοῦτο παραλαβὼν τὸν λόγον ὁ
τῶν Ῥωμαίων εἰρηνοδίκης εἶπεν· "Οὐθὲν ἔτι τὸ
κωλῦσόν ἐστιν, οὕτω φανερῶς ἀνῃρηκότων ὑμῶν
τὰ περὶ τῆς εἰρήνης ὅρκια . . .[2] βουλεύεσθε[3] τὸν
Ῥωμαίων δῆμον[4] αἰτιάσασθαι. πάντα γὰρ αὐτῷ
πέπρακται κατὰ τοὺς ἱεροὺς τε καὶ πατρίους[5] νόμους, τά τε πρὸς τοὺς θεοὺς ὅσια καὶ τὰ πρὸς
ἀνθρώπους δίκαια, δικασταὶ δὲ τῶν μενόντων ἐν
ταῖς ὁμολογίαις οἱ λαχόντες πολέμους ἐπισκοπεῖν
2 ἔσονται θεοί." μέλλων δ' ἀπιέναι τήν τε περιβολὴν
κατὰ κεφαλῆς εἵλκυσε καὶ τὰς χεῖρας ἀνασχὼν εἰς
τὸν οὐρανόν, ὡς ἔθος ἐστίν, ἀρὰς[6] ἐποιήσατο τοῖς
θεοῖς· εἰ μὲν ἄδικα πάσχουσα ὑπὸ Σαυνιτῶν ἡ
Ῥωμαίων πόλις καὶ μὴ δυναμένη μετὰ λόγου
καὶ κρίσεως διαλῦσαι τὰς διαφορὰς ἐπὶ τὰ ἔργα
χωρῆσαι,[7] βουλάς τε ἀγαθὰς αὐτῇ θεοὺς καὶ δαίμονας ἐπὶ νοῦν ἄγειν, καὶ πράξεις ἐν πᾶσι διδόναι
τοῖς πολέμοις[8] εὐτυχεῖν· εἰ δὲ αὐτῇ[10] τι πλημ-
μελοῦσα τὰ περὶ[11] τῆς φιλίας ὅρκια προφάσεις κατα-

----

1 Sylburg : ὅπερ O.
2 Lacuna recognized by Reiske. Post would supply μηδ'
ἄδικα.   3 βουλεύεσθαι Sylburg.
4 τὸν τῶν ῥ. δῆμον M, τῶν ῥ. δῆμον V.
5 Steph.[2] : πατρικοὺς O.   6 ἀρὰς E, ἀραῖς V.
7 de Boor : χωρῆσαι O, χωρήσει Ursinus.
8 καὶ πράξεις ἐν πᾶσι διδόναι τοῖς πολέμοις Reiske : καὶ
πράξεων πᾶσι διδόναι τοῖς πολεμίοις O, Jacoby.
9 εὐτυχεῖν V : ἐντυχεῖν Z, Jacoby, εὐτυχεῖς Reiske.
10 Ursinus : αὐτῇ O.
11 τὰ περὶ (παρὰ X) O : περὶ τὰ Reiske.

a short time ago—and this is the most just title to
possession—you appropriated with no show of justice
and now hold for the second year. If we on our side
gain these points, we shall not feel that we are
wronged in any respect."

IX. (13) Thereupon the Roman *fetialis*, taking the
floor, said : " There is no longer anything to prevent,
now that you Samnites have so openly violated your
oaths to maintain the peace, . . .[1] [and do not] plan
to lay the blame upon the Roman people. For everything has been done by them in accordance with the
sacred and time-honoured laws, both what is holy in
the sight of the gods and just in the sight of men, and
the judges to decide which people has abided by the
compact will be the gods whose province it is to watch
over wars." As he was about to depart, he drew his
mantle down over his head, and raising his hands
toward heaven, as is the custom, he uttered prayers
to the gods : " If the Roman commonwealth, having
suffered wrongs at the hands of the Samnites and
being unable to settle the differences by argument
and a decision, should proceed to deeds, may the gods
and lesser divinities not only inspire her mind with
good counsels but also grant that her undertakings
in all her wars may prove successful [2]; but if she
herself is guilty of any violation of the oaths of friend-

[1] More seems to have been lost from the text at this point
than the words supplied in brackets. We naturally expect
something like " no longer anything to prevent the Roman
people from declaring war "; *cf.* ii. 72, 9, where the procedure of the *fetiales* was described.

[2] The text of this last clause is very uncertain ; see the
critical note.

DIONYSIUS OF HALICARNASSUS

σκευάζεται τῆς ἔχθρας οὐκ ἀληθεῖς, μήτε βουλὰς
ὀρθοῦν αὐτῆς[1] μήτε πράξεις. Ursin.

X. (14) Ὡς διελύθησαν ἐκ τοῦ συλλόγου καὶ τὰ
λεχθέντα ἐδήλωσαν ἑκάτεροι ταῖς ἑαυτῶν πόλεσι,
τὰς ἐναντίας ἔσχον ὑπὲρ ἀλλήλων δόξας ἀμφότεροι,
Σαυνῖται μὲν βραδύτερα τὰ[2] τῶν Ῥωμαίων ἔσεσθαι[3]
νομίζοντες, ὥσπερ αὐτοῖς ἔθος ἐστὶ ποιεῖν ὅτε
μέλλοιεν ἄρχειν πολέμου, Ῥωμαῖοι δ᾽ ἐν ὀλίγῳ
τὴν Σαυνιτῶν στρατιὰν ἥξειν ἐπὶ τοὺς αὐτῶν ἀπ-
2 οίκους[4] Φρεγελλανοὺς[5] οἰόμενοι. ἔπειτ᾽ αὐτοῖς
τὰ εἰκότα παθεῖν συνέβη.[6] οἱ μὲν γὰρ παρασκευ-
αζόμενοι καὶ μέλλοντες ἀπώλεσαν τοὺς καιροὺς
τῶν πράξεων, Ῥωμαῖοι δ᾽ ἐν ἑτοίμῳ πᾶσαν
ἔχοντες παρασκευὴν ἅμα τῷ πυθέσθαι τὰς ἀποκρίσεις τόν τε πόλεμον ἐψηφίσαντο καὶ τοὺς ὑπάτους
ἀπέστειλαν ἀμφοτέρους· καὶ πρὶν αἰσθέσθαι τοὺς
πολεμίους τὴν ἔξοδον, ἥ τε νεωστὶ καταγραφεῖσα
καὶ ἡ[7] περὶ Οὐολούσκους χειμερίζουσα δύναμις,
ἣν εἶχε Κορνήλιος, ἐντὸς ἦν τῶν Σαυνιτικῶν
ὅρων. Ursin.

[1] Post : αὐτοῖς O, Jacoby, αὐτοὺς Kiessling.
[2] τὰ added by Ursinus.
[3] ἔσεσθαι τῶν ῥωμαίων X.   [4] Steph.[2] : ἐποίκους O.

Φοῦνδα, πόλις Ἰταλίας· οἱ πολῖται |Φουνδανοί, Διονύ-
σιος ιε᾽ Ῥωμαϊκῆς ἀρχαιολογίας. Steph. Byz.

Καλησία, πόλις Αὐσονική. Διονύσιος ιε᾽ Ῥωμαϊκῆς
ἀρχαιολογίας. τὸ ἐθνικὸν Καλησιανός, ὡς αὐτός. Steph.
Byz.

ship and is trumping up false grounds for hostility, may they prosper neither her counsels nor her undertakings."

X. (14) When they had departed from the assembly and each side had reported to its cities what had been said, they drew opposite conclusions about each other, the Samnites expecting that the Romans would move rather slowly, as it is their custom to do when they are about to begin war, and the Romans believing that the Samnites' army would soon proceed against their colonists in Fregellae. Then they each met with the experience that might have been expected. For the Samnites, while making their preparations and delaying, lost the opportunities for action, whereas the Romans, having everything prepared and in readiness, as soon as they learned the answer given to their ambassadors, voted for war and sent out both consuls ; and before the enemy was aware that they had set out, both the newly-enrolled force and the one that was wintering among the Volscians, under the command of Cornelius, were inside the Samnite borders.

---

⁵ Sylburg : φλεγελλάνους O.
⁶ συνέβη παθεῖν V.   ⁷ ἡ added by Kiessling.

Fundi, a city of Italy ; the citizens, Fundani. Dionysius, *Roman Antiquities* xv. (*Cf.* Livy viii. 14, 10 ; 19, 10-14.)

Cales, an Ausonian city. Dionysius, *Roman Antiquities* xv. *Eth.*[1] Calenus, *idem.* (*Cf.* Livy viii. 16, 6-14.)

[1] See the note on p. 257.

EXCERPTS
FROM
BOOK XVI

I. (1) Ῥωμαίων εἰς τὸν κατὰ Σαυνιτῶν τελευ-
ταῖον πόλεμον ἐξιόντων κεραυνὸς εἰς τὸν ἐπιφανέστατον τόπον κατασκήψας πέντε μὲν στρατιώτας
ἀπέκτεινε, δύο δὲ σημείας διέφθειρεν, ὅπλα δὲ
πολλὰ τὰ μὲν κατέκαυσε, τὰ δ' ἐσπίλωσε. κεραυνοὶ
δὲ κατηνέχθησαν[1] τοῖς ἔργοις ἔτυμον[2] φέροντες τοὔ-
νομα· κεραϊσμοὶ γάρ τινές εἰσι καὶ μεταβολαὶ τῶν
ὑποκειμένων εἰς τἀναντία τρέποντες τὰς ἀνθρω-
2 πίνας τύχας. αὐτὸ γὰρ πρῶτον ἠνάγκασται τὴν
ἰδίαν ἀλλάξαι φύσιν τὸ κεραύνιον πῦρ, εἴτε δὴ
αἰθέριον[3] εἴτε μετάρσιόν ἐστι, κάτω φερόμενον·
οὐ γὰρ δὴ αὐτῷ θέμις ἐπὶ γῆν βρίθειν κατὰ τὴν
ἑαυτοῦ φύσιν, ἀλλ' ἀπὸ γῆς ἄνω μετεωροπολεῖν·
3 ἐν αἰθέρι γὰρ αἱ πηγαὶ τοῦ θείου πυρός[4]. (2) δηλοῖ
δὲ καὶ τὸ πῦρ[4] τὸ παρ' ἡμῖν, εἴτε Προμηθέως εἴτε
Ἡφαίστου δῶρόν ἐστιν, ὁπότε λύσειε[5] τοὺς δε-
σμοὺς ἐν οἷς ἠνάγκασται μένειν, δι' ἀέρος ἄνω

---

[1] Struve : κατήχθησαν Q. [2] Mai : ἔτοιμον Q.
[3] Cary : αἴθριον Q.
[4] τὸ πῦρ added by Struve.
[5] λύσειε Jacoby, λύσειεν (sic) Kiessling : λύσει Q, λύοι
Struve.

EXCERPTS

FROM

BOOK XVI

I. (1) When the Romans were setting out for their last war against the Samnites, a thunderbolt struck in the most conspicuous spot, killing five soldiers, destroying two standards, and either burning or tarnishing many weapons. The thunderbolts (*keraunoi*) that descend bear a name truly descriptive of their effects; for they are devastations (*keraïsmoi*) of a sort and transformations of the underlying substances, reversing mortal fortunes. For, in the first place, the bolt's fire itself is compelled to change its own nature as it rushes down, whether its natural abode is the ethereal space or the region immediately above the earth; for it is not meet for it, in view of its inherent nature, to gravitate earthward, but rather to move aloft away from the earth, since it is in the ether that the sources of the divine fire are found. (2) This is shown even by the fire that we know—whether this be the gift of Prometheus or of Hephaestus—which, whenever it bursts the bonds in which it has been forced to remain, leaps upward

315

φερόμενον ἐπὶ τὸ συγγενὲς ἐκεῖνο καὶ πᾶσαν ἐν
κύκλῳ περιειληφὸς τὴν τοῦ κόσμου φύσιν. τὸ δὴ
θεῖον ἐκεῖνο καὶ χωρισθὲν[1] ὕλης φθαρτῆς δι᾽ αἰθέρος[2]
ὀχούμενον, ὅταν ἐπὶ τὴν γῆν καταφέρηται βιασθὲν
ὑπ᾽ ἀνάγκης τινὸς ἰσχυρᾶς, μεταβολὰς μαντεύεται
4 καὶ τροπὰς ἐπὶ τοὔμπαλιν. (3) τοιούτου γοῦν
τινος γενομένου καὶ τότε καταφρονήσαντες οἱ Ῥωμαῖοι καὶ ὑπὸ Ποντίου τοῦ Σαυνίτου κατα-
κλεισθέντες εἰς ἀνεξόδους δυσχωρίας, μέλλοντες
ἤδη τῷ λιμῷ διαφθείρεσθαι παρέδωκαν ἑαυτοὺς
τοῖς πολεμίοις ἀμφὶ τοὺς τετρακισμυρίους ὄντες·
καὶ καταλείψαντες τά τε ὅπλα καὶ τὰ χρήματα
τὸν ζυγὸν ἅπαντες ὑπῆλθον· τοῦτο δὲ σημεῖον τῶν
ὑπὸ χεῖρας ἐλθόντων ἐστί. μετ᾽ οὐ πολὺ δὲ τὰ
αὐτὰ καὶ ὁ Πόντιος ὑπὸ Ῥωμαίων ἔπαθε, καὶ τὸν
ζυγὸν ὑπῆλθον καὶ αὐτὸς καὶ οἱ σὺν αὐτῷ. *Ambr.*

II. (4) "῞Εν τοῦτό σε ἀξιοῦμεν, ἤδη κείμενοι
καὶ τὸ μηδὲν ὄντες, μηδεμίαν ἡμῶν ὕβριν προσθεῖναι ταῖς συμφοραῖς μηδὲ βαρεῖ[3] ποδὶ ταῖς
ἀθλίαις ἐπεμβῆναι τύχαις."

2 "Οὐκ οἶδας ὅτι πολλοὶ μὲν τῶν ἡμετέρων
παῖδας ἐν τοῖς πολέμοις ἀπολωλέκασι, πολλοὶ δὲ
ἀδελφούς, πολλοὶ δὲ φίλους; οἷς ἅπασι πῶς ἄκρατον
νομίζεις ἐπὶ τῶν σπλάγχνων ἀνθήσειν τὴν χολήν,
ἐὰν κωλύῃ τις αὐτοὺς τοσαύταις ψυχαῖς πολεμίων
τιμῆσαι τοὺς κατὰ γῆς,[4] αἵπερ μόναι τῶν κατ-

---

[1] Struve : χωρίον Q.   [2] Post : ἀέρος Q.
[3] Mai : βαρὺ Q.   [4] Krüger : γῆν Q.

through the air to that kindred fire which embraces the whole universe round about. Hence that fire which is divine and separated from corrupt'ble matter as it roams through the ether,[1] when it descends to the earth under the compulsion of some drastic necessity, portends changes and reversals. (3) At any rate,[2] when some such portent occurred also at the time in question, the Romans scorned it, and having been hemmed by Pontius the Samnite into a difficult position from which escape was impossible, when they were now on the point of perishing from famine, they surrendered themselves, about 40,000 in number, to the enemy ; and leaving behind their arms and effects, they all passed under the yoke, which is a token that men have come under the power of others. But not long afterwards Pontius also suffered the same fate at the hands of the Romans, when both he himself and those with him passed under the yoke.

II. (4) " This one thing we ask of you, now that we lie prostrate and are as naught, that you do not add to our calamities by any ignominious treatment nor trample with a heavy foot upon our wretched misfortunes."

" Do you not know that many of our people have lost their sons in the wars, many their brothers, and many their friends ? And what unmitigated resentment do you suppose will spring up and flourish in the hearts of all the bereaved if anyone prevents them from honouring those who are beneath the earth with the lives of an equal number of enemies— those lives which alone seem to be true honours for

---

[1] " Ether " is the emendation of Post in place of " air," the reading of the MS.   [2] For § 4 cf. Livy ix. 1–15.

3 οἰχομένων δοκοῦσιν εἶναι τιμαί; (5) φέρε δὴ[1] κεἰ[2]
τοῦτο πεισθέντες ἢ βιασθέντες ἢ ὅ τι δή ποτε πα-
θόντες εἴξουσί τε[3] καὶ ζῆν αὐτοὺς ἐάσουσιν, ἆρ'
ἔτι σοι δοκοῦσι καὶ τὰ χρήματα αὐτοὺς ἐάσειν ἔχειν
καὶ μηδεμιᾶς πειραθέντας ἀσχημοσύνης, ὥσπερ
ἥρωάς τινας ἐπ' ἀγαθῷ τῆσδε τῆς γῆς φανέντας,
ὁπότε δόξειεν αὐτοῖς, ἀπελθεῖν, ἀλλ' οὐχ ὥσπερ
θηρία περιχυθέντες[4] διασπάσεσθαι ταῦτα λέγειν
4 ἐπιβαλόμενον ἐμέ; οὐχ ὁρᾷς ὅτι καὶ τοὺς κυνη-
γοὺς οἱ θηρευταὶ κύνες, ὅταν ἁλῷ θηρίον κατακλεισθὲν ὑπ' αὐτῶν εἰς τὰ λίνα, περιίστανται τὴν
ἐπιβάλλουσαν μοῖραν ἀπαιτοῦντες τῆς ἄγρας,[5] καὶ
ἐὰν μὴ μεταλάβωσιν εὐθὺς αἵματος ἢ σπλάγχνων,
ἀρράζουσιν ἑπόμενοι καὶ σπαράττουσι τὸν κυνηγὸν
καὶ οὔτε διωκόμενοι οὔτε παιόμενοι ἀπείργονται;"
Ambr.

III. (6) Δι' ἡμέρας μὲν ὅλης ἀγωνιζόμενοι τῶν
πόνων ἠνείχοντο, ἀφελομένου δὲ τοῦ σκότους τὴν
γνῶσιν τῶν τε οἰκείων καὶ τῶν πολεμίων πρὸς
τοὺς οἰκείους χάρακας ἀπηλλάγησαν.

Ἄππιος Κλαύδιος περὶ τὰς θυσίας παρανομήσας
τι ἀπετυφλώθη καὶ Καῖκος προσηγορεύθη· οὕτω
γὰρ τοὺς τυφλοὺς Ῥωμαῖοι καλοῦσιν.

2 Αἱ ἐντοίχιοι γραφαὶ ταῖς τε γραμμαῖς πάνυ
ἀκριβεῖς ἦσαν καὶ τοῖς μίγμασιν[6] ἡδεῖαι, παντὸς
ἀπηλλαγμένον ἔχουσαι τοῦ καλουμένου ῥώπου τὸ
ἀνθηρόν.

---

[1] δὴ Q acc. to Ambrosch and Kiessling, δὲ acc. to Mai.
[2] κεὶ Jacoby : καὶ Q, κἂν Kiessling ; φέρε εἰ δὲ δὴ Naber.
[3] εἴξουσί τε Struve : εἴξωσί με QA ; εἴξωσί γε . . . ἐάσωσιν
Kiessling.

the departed ?   (5) But come, even if, as the result
of persuasion or compulsion or however swayed, they
shall yield this point and permit them to live, does
it seem likely to you that they will go still farther
and allow them to retain their effects and permit
them without suffering any ignominious treatment,
but, like heroes who have made their appearance for
the good fortune of this country, to depart whenever
they please, but will not rather, like wild beasts, surround me and tear me limb from limb for having
taken it upon myself to make this proposal ?   Do you
not observe that even hunting-dogs, when a wild
beast has been driven by them into the nets and
caught, surround the hunters, demanding the share
of the quarry that belongs to them, and unless they
promptly get a share of the blood or of the inwards,
follow the hunter snarling and rend him in pieces,
and are not driven away even when they are chased
or beaten ? "

III. (6) Fighting the whole day long, they endured
the hardships ; but when darkness prevented their dis-
tinguishing friends and foes, they departed to their
own camps.

Appius Claudius, having committed some error in
connexion with the sacrifices, was made blind and was
given the cognomen Caecus ; for that is the Roman
word for the blind.

The mural paintings were not only very accurate
in their lines but also pleasing in the mixture of
colours, and their florid style was free from what is
called tawdriness.

---

4 Kiessling : περιχυθέντας Q, Jacoby.
5 Mai : ἀγορᾶς QA.
6 μιμήμασιν Struve.

DIONYSIUS OF HALICARNASSUS

Τὰς νουμηνίας οἱ Ῥωμαῖοι καλάνδας καλοῦσι, τὰς δὲ διχοτόμους νόννας, τὰς δὲ πανσελήνους εἰδούς. *Ambr.*

3 (7) Τοῖς δὲ κατὰ μέσην ἀγωνιζομένοις τὴν φάλαγγα ἀσπάθητον οὖσαν καὶ λαγαρὰν οἱ τῇδε τεταγμένοι συμπεσόντες ἐξέωσαν τῆς στάσεως.

Ὁ κατοικίδιός τε καὶ διοπετὴς[1] πόλεμος ἐμάραινε τὴν ἀκμὴν τῆς πόλεως.

Ἄνδρας ἱεραγωγοὺς καὶ ἱεραφορίᾳ τετιμημένους.

Φορᾶς ἀβούλου μεστὸς ἀνὴρ καὶ μανικὸν ἔχων τὸ τολμηρόν, ἰδιογνωμονήσας καὶ ὑφ᾽[2] ἑαυτῷ ποιήσας πάντα τὰ[3] τοῦ πολέμου.

4 " Ἔπειτα σὺ τολμᾷς κατηγορεῖν τῆς τύχης ὡς κακῶς τοῖς πράγμασι χρησαμένης ἐπὶ περιτραπέντος αὐτὸς[4] καθίσας σκάφους; οὕτω σκαιὸς εἶ[5];"

Μέλη τὰ μὲν θεραπείας ἔτι δεόμενα, τὰ δὲ τὰς οὐλὰς ἐφέλκοντα νεωστί. *Ambr.*

IV. (8) [Ὅτι, φησὶ Διονύσιος,] μιᾶς ἔτι μνησθήσομαι πράξεως πολιτικῆς ἀξίας ὑπὸ πάντων ἀνθρώπων ἐπαινεῖσθαι, ἐξ ἧς καταφανὲς ἔσται τοῖς Ἕλλησιν ὅσον ἦν τὸ μισοπόνηρον ἐν τῇ Ῥώμῃ τότε καὶ τὸ[6] πρὸς τοὺς παραβαίνοντας τὰ κοινὰ

2 νόμιμα[7] τῆς ἀνθρωπίνης φύσεως ἀμείλικτον.[8] Γάιος Λαιτώριος Μέργος[9] ἐπίκλησιν ἐπιφανὴς κατὰ γένος καὶ κατὰ τὰς πολεμικὰς πράξεις οὐκ ἀγεννής, ἑνὸς τῶν ταγμάτων χιλίαρχος ἀποδειχθεὶς ἐν τῷ

---

[1] Jacoby : κλινοπετὴς Q.   [2] ἐφ᾽ Kiessling.
[3] τὰ added by Hertlein.
[4] Struve : αὐτὴν Q, Jacoby.
[5] Struve : ἦν Q, Jacoby.
[6] τὸ Suidas : om. P.
[7] κοινὰ καὶ νόμιμα Suidas.
[8] ἀμείλικτον Suidas : ἀμείλικτα P.

The Romans call the new moons calends, the half moons nones, and the full moons ides.

(7) Against the troops who were fighting in the middle of the phalanx, which was widely spaced and lax, those who were stationed here charged in a body and drove them from their position.

The heaven-sent [1] domestic war was wasting away the flower of the state.

Men who bore the offerings and had been honoured with the carrying of the sacred vessels.

A man full of unreasoning impulsiveness who carried boldness to the point of madness, one who had followed his own counsel and had got in his hands the whole conduct of the war.[2]

" Do you then dare to accuse Fortune of having managed affairs badly, you who seated yourself [3] on an overturned boat ? Are you [3] so stupid ? "

Limbs, some of which still needed medical attention while others had just begun to form scars . . .

IV. (8) One more political incident I shall relate, [says Dionysius], deserving of praise on the part of all men, from which it will be clear to the Greeks how great was the hatred of wrongdoing felt in Rome at that time and how implacable the anger against those who transgressed the universal laws of human nature. Gaius Laetorius, with the cognomen Mergus, a man of distinguished birth and not without bravery in warlike deeds, who had been appointed tribune of one of the legions in the Samnite war,

---

[1] This is Jacoby's conjecture for an impossible reading in the MS.

[2] Or, following Kiessling's reading, " had done everything pertaining to the war on his own authority."

[3] The MS. has " seated her " and " So stupid was he."

---

[9] μέρκος P, μάρκος Suidas.

Σαυνιτικῷ πολέμῳ, νεανίαν τινὰ τῶν ὁμοσκήνων
διαφέροντα τὴν ὄψιν ἑτέρων μέχρι μέν τινος ἔπειθεν
ἑαυτῷ χαρίσασθαι τὴν τοῦ σώματος ὥραν ἑκόντα·
ὡς δ' οὔτε δωρεαῖς οὔτ' ἄλλῃ φιλανθρωπίᾳ τὸ
μειράκιον ἡλίσκετο, κατέχειν τὴν ἐπιθυμίαν ἀδύ-
3 νατος ὢν βίαν προσφέρειν ἐπεβάλετο. περιβοήτου
δὲ τῆς ἀκοσμίας τοῦ ἀνδρὸς ἅπασι τοῖς ἐπὶ τοῦ[1]
στρατοπέδου γενομένης κοινὸν ἀδίκημα τῆς πόλεως
εἶναι νομίσαντες οἱ δήμαρχοι γραφὴν ἀποφέρουσι
κατ' αὐτοῦ δημοσίᾳ· καὶ ὁ δῆμος ἁπάσαις ταῖς
ψήφοις τοῦ ἀνδρὸς κατέγνω τίμημα δίκης ὁρίσας
θάνατον,[2] οὐκ ἀξιῶν εἰς ἐλεύθερα σώματα καὶ προ-
πολεμοῦντα τῆς τῶν ἄλλων ἐλευθερίας τοὺς ἐν ταῖς
ἀρχαῖς ὄντας[3] ὑβρίζειν τὰς ἀνηκέστους καὶ παρὰ
φύσιν τοῖς ἄρρεσιν ὕβρεις. Vales.; Suidas s.v. Γάιος
Λαιτώριος ; Ambr.

V. (9) Ἔτι δὲ τούτου θαυμασιώτερον ἔπραξαν[4]
οὐ πολλοῖς πρότερον χρόνοις, καίτοι περὶ δοῦλον
σῶμα γενομένης τῆς ὕβρεως. ἑνὸς γὰρ τῶν
παραδόντων Σαυνίταις τὸ στρατόπεδον χιλιάρχων
καὶ ὑπὸ ζυγὸν ὑπελθόντων Ποπλίου υἱὸς ὡς[5] ἐν
πολλῇ καταλειφθεὶς πενίᾳ δάνειον ἠναγκάσθη λαβεῖν εἰς τὴν ταφὴν τοῦ πατρός, ὡς ἐρανισθησό-
μενος ὑπὸ τῶν συγγενῶν. διαψευσθεὶς δὲ τῆς
ἐλπίδος ἀπήχθη πρὸς τὸ χρέος τῆς προθεσμίας

[1] τοῦ P : om. Suidas.
[2] Valesius : θανάτου P. The very brief summary of this
chapter given by the Ambrosianus ends with οἱ δήμαρχοι
θάνατον αὐτὸν (sic) κατέγνωσαν.
[3] ἐν ταῖς ἀρχαῖς ὄντας Post : ἐν ταῖς ἄλλαις ὄντας ἀρχαῖς P,
Suidas : ἐν ταῖς στρατηγίαις καὶ ταῖς ἄλλαις ὄντας ἀρχαῖς Reiske,
ἐν μεγάλαις ὄντας ἀρχαῖς Smit, ἐν ταῖς τιμαῖς ὄντας καὶ ἀρχαῖς
Jacoby.
[4] Valesius : ἔπραξεν P.   [5] ὡς Reiske : ὢν P.

attempted for a time to persuade a youth of exceptional beauty among his tentmates to put the charms
of his body at his disposal voluntarily ; then, when
the boy was not to be lured either by gifts or by any
other friendly overture, Laetorius, unable to restrain
his passion, attempted to use force.   When the man's
disgraceful conduct had become noised throughout
the entire camp, the tribunes of the people, holding
that it was a crime against the whole state, brought
an indictment against him publicly, and the people
unanimously condemned him, after fixing death as
the penalty ; for they were unwilling that persons
who were of free condition and were fighting in behalf
of the freedom of their fellow citizens should be subjected by those in positions of command [1] to abuses
that are irreparable and do violence to the male's
natural instincts.

V. (9) A thing still more remarkable than this was
done by them a few years earlier, though the mistreatment involved the person of a slave.   The son,
namely, of Publius,[2] one of the military tribunes who
had surrendered the army to the Samnites and passed
under the yoke, inasmuch as he had been left in
dire poverty, was compelled to borrow money for
the burial of his father, expecting to repay it out of
contributions to be made by his relations.   But being
disappointed in his expectation, he was seized in lieu

---

[1] The translation follows the text as emended by Post.
The MSS. give " those in the other offices."   Reiske proposed
" those in military commands and other offices," Smit " those
in high offices," Jacoby " those in offices and magistracies."

[2] An error for Publilius, the form given by Livy (viii. 28.)
Livy puts this incident before the disaster at the Caudine
Forks ; Dionysius and Valerius Maximus (vi. 1, 9) put it
after that event.

DIONYSIUS OF HALICARNASSUS

διελθούσης, κομιδῇ νέος ὢν καὶ τῇ ὄψει ὡραῖος.
2 οὗτος τὰ μὲν ἄλλα ὑπηρετῶν ὅσα δούλους δεσπό-
ταις νόμος ἦν ἠνείχετο, τὴν δὲ τοῦ σώματος ὥραν
χαρίσασθαι κελευόμενος ἠγανάκτει καὶ μέχρι
παντὸς ἀπεμάχετο. πολλὰς δὲ διὰ τοῦτο μαστίγων λαβὼν πληγὰς ἐξέδραμεν εἰς τὴν ἀγορὰν καὶ
στὰς ἐπὶ μετεώρου τινός, ἔνθα πολλοὺς ἔμελλε
τῆς ὕβρεως λήψεσθαι μάρτυρας, τήν τε ἀκολασίαν
τοῦ δανειστοῦ διηγήσατο καὶ τῶν μαστίγων τοὺς
3 μώλωπας ὑπέδειξεν. ἀγανακτήσαντος δὲ τοῦ δήμου καὶ δημοσίας ὀργῆς ἄξιον ἡγησαμένου τὸ
πρᾶγμα †καὶ τὴν κρίσιν[1] κατηγορούντων τὴν εἰσαγγελίαν τῶν δημάρχων ὦφλε[2] θανάτου δίκην.
καὶ δι' ἐκεῖνο τὸ πάθος ἅπαντες οἱ δουλωθέντες
πρὸς τὰ χρέα Ῥωμαῖοι νόμῳ κυρωθέντι τὴν ἀρ-
χαίαν ἐλευθερίαν ἐκομίσαντο. Vales.; Suidas s.v.
Γάιος Λαιτώριος.

VI. (10) Ἀξιῶν τὴν βουλὴν ὑπὲρ τῶν ἀπόρων
καὶ κατάχρεων . . .

Αἱ νεοσφαγεῖς τῶν θυομένων σάρκες μέχρι τούτου διατελοῦσι τρέμουσαί τε καὶ παλλόμεναι ἕως
ἂν[3] τὸ κατεχόμενον ἐν αὐταῖς συγγενὲς πνεῦμα
2 βιασάμενον τοὺς πόρους ἅπαν ἐξαναλωθῇ. τοιοῦτό
τι[4] σεισμῶν αἴτιον γίνεται καὶ τῇ Ῥώμῃ· ἅπασα
γὰρ ὑπόνομος οὖσα μεγάλαις καὶ συνεχέσι τάφροις,
δι' ὧν ὀχετεύεται τὸ ὕδωρ, καὶ πολλὰς ἀναπνοὰς
στομάτων δίκην[5] ἔχουσα, διὰ τούτων ἀνίησι τὸ
κατακλεισθὲν πνεῦμα ἐν αὐτῇ· καὶ τοῦτο ἔστιν ὃ

---

[1] καὶ τὴν κρίσιν P : om. Suidas, Jacoby ; κατὰ τὴν κρίσιν
Post, καὶ ⟨ἀχθεὶς εἰς⟩ τὴν κρίσιν Kiessling. κρίσιν may have
been a gloss to εἰσαγγελίαν.

of the debt when the time for payment came, as he was very youthful and comely to look upon. He submitted to all the regular tasks which it was usual for slaves to perform for their masters, but was indignant when ordered to put the charms of his body at the disposal of his creditor, and resisted to the utmost. Then, having received many lashes with whips because of this, he rushed out into the Forum, and taking his stand upon a lofty spot where he would have many witnesses to his mistreatment, he related the wanton attempts of the money-lender and displayed the weals raised by the whips. When the people became indignant at this and felt that the matter was deserving of public wrath, the tribunes brought an indictment against the man and he was found guilty of a capital crime. Because of this incident all the Romans who had been enslaved for debt recovered their former freedom by a law ratified at this time.

VI. (10) Demanding that the senate in behalf of those who were in want and in debt . . .

The flesh of freshly slain victims continues to quiver and palpitate until the congenital breath contained in it has forced its way out through the pores and been entirely dissipated. Some such thing is the cause also of earthquakes at Rome ; for the city, since it is undermined with large and continuous channels through which the water is conducted, and since it has many breathing-vents like mouths, shoots up through these vents the breath that is pent up within it. This breath it is which shakes the city and rends

---

² ὦφλε Suidas : ὤφλημα P.
³ ἕως ἂν Struve : ἂν ἕως Q.
⁴ τοιουτό τι Struve : τοῦτο Q.
⁵ δίκην added by Capps, διὰ by Post.

κραδαίνει τε αὐτὴν καὶ σπαράττει τὴν ἐπιφάνειαν
ὅταν πολὺ καὶ βίαιον ἐναποληφθὲν[1] εἴργηται. *Ambr.*

<hr/>

[1] Struve : ἐναπολειφθὲν Q.

<hr/>

Φρέγελλα, πόλις Ἰταλίας, ἣ τὸ μὲν ἀρχαῖον ἦν
Ὀπικῶν, ἔπειτα Οὐολούσκων ἐγένετο. τὸ ἐθνικὸν Φρε-
γελλανός, ὡς Διονύσιος ιϛ´ τῆς Ῥωμαϊκῆς ἀρχαιολογίας
καὶ ἄλλοι πλεῖστοι. *Steph. Byz.*

Μέντυρνα, πόλις ἐν Ἰταλίᾳ Σαυνιτῶν. Διονύσιος
ἑκκαιδεκάτῳ. τὸ ἐθνικὸν Μεντυρναῖος. *Steph. Byz.*

Αἴκαλον, φρούριον τῆς Ἰταλίας. Διονύσιος ιϛ´
Ῥωμαϊκῆς ἀρχαιολογίας. *Steph. Byz.*

Ἰάποδες, ἔθνος Κελτικὸν πρὸς τῇ Ἰλλυρίᾳ. Διονύσιος ἑκκαιδεκάτῳ. *Steph. Byz.*

the surface of the ground whenever a large and violent mass of air is intercepted and pent up inside.

———

Fregellae, a city of Italy which originally belonged to the Opicans and later fell to the Volscians. *Eth.*[1] Fregellanus, as Dionysius, *Roman Antiquities* xvi., and ever so many others. (*Cf.* Livy viii. 22 f.)

Minturnae, a city of the Samnites in Italy. Dionysius xvi. *Eth.* Minturnensis. (*Cf.* Livy ix. 25, 4.)

Aecalum, a fortress of Italy. Dionysius, *Roman Antiquities* xvi.

Iapodes, a Celtic race near Illyria. Dionysius xvi.

[1] For this abbreviation see the note on p. 257.

EXCERPTS

FROM

BOOKS XVII AND XVIII

I. (16, 11) Ὅτι ὁ Σαυνιτικὸς αὖθις ἀνερριπίσθη πόλεμος ἀπὸ τοιαύτης αἰτίας ἀρξάμενος. μετὰ τὰς σπονδὰς ἃς ἐποιήσαντο πρὸς τὴν Ῥωμαίων πόλιν οἱ Σαυνῖται χρόνον ὀλίγον ἐπισχόντες ἐπὶ Λευκανοὺς ἐστράτευσαν ὁμόρους ὄντας ἐκ παλαιᾶς 2 τινος ὁρμηθέντες[1] ἔχθρας. κατ' ἀρχὰς μὲν οὖν ταῖς ἑαυτῶν δυνάμεσι πιστεύοντες οἱ Λευκανοὶ τὸν[2] πόλεμον διέφερον· ἐν ἁπάσαις δὲ μειονεκτοῦν- τες ταῖς μάχαις καὶ πολλὰ μὲν ἀπολωλεκότες ἤδη χωρία, κινδυνεύοντες δὲ καὶ περὶ τῆς ἄλλης γῆς ἁπάσης, ἐπὶ τὴν Ῥωμαίων βοήθειαν ἠναγκάσθησαν καταφυγεῖν, συνειδότες μὲν ἑαυτοῖς ἐψευσμένοις ἃς πρότερον ἐποιήσαντο πρὸς αὐτοὺς ὁμολογίας ἐν αἷς φιλίαν συνέθεντο καὶ συμμαχίαν, οὐκ ἀπο- γνόντες δὲ συμπείσειν[3] αὐτούς, ἐὰν ἐξ ἁπάσης[4] πόλεως τοὺς ἐπιφανεστάτους παῖδας ὁμήρους ἅμα τοῖς πρεσβευταῖς ἀποστείλωσιν· ὅπερ καὶ συνέβη. 3 (12) ἀφικομένων γὰρ τῶν πρέσβεων καὶ πολλὰ

---

[1] ὁρμηθέντες BE : ὁρμηθέντας Z.
[2] τε after τὸν deleted by Sylburg (unless a clause has been lost). [3] Ursinus : συμπεσεῖν O.
[4] τῆς after ἁπάσης deleted by Sylburg.

EXCERPTS
FROM
BOOKS XVII AND XVIII

I. (16, 11) The Samnite war was once more kindled into flame,[1] beginning from some such cause as the following. After the treaty which the Samnites had made with Rome, they waited a short time and then made an expedition against the Lucanians, who were their neighbours, being moved thereto by some long-standing feud. At first the Lucanians carried on the war relying on their own forces ; but getting the worst of it in all the engagements, and having lost many districts already and being in danger of losing all the rest of their land, they were forced to have recourse to the Romans' assistance. They were conscious, to be sure, of having broken the compact they had made with the Romans earlier, in which they had pledged friendship and alliance, but did not despair of persuading them if they should send to them along with their ambassadors the most prominent boys from every city as hostages. And this in fact is what occurred. (12) For when the ambassadors arrived and

[1] For chaps. 1–3 cf. Livy x. 11, 11–12, 3.

δεομένων ἥ τε βουλὴ δέχεσθαι τὰ ὅμηρα ἔγνω
καὶ τὴν φιλίαν πρὸς τοὺς Λευκανοὺς συνάψαι, καὶ
ὁ δῆμος ἐπεκύρωσε τὰ ψηφισθέντα ὑπ' αὐτῆς.
4 γενομένων δὲ τῶν συνθηκῶν πρὸς τοὺς ἀποσταλέντας ὑπὸ τῶν Λευκανῶν ἄνδρας οἱ πρεσβύτατοι
Ῥωμαίων καὶ τιμιώτατοι προχειρισθέντες ὑπὸ
τῆς βουλῆς πρέσβεις ἀπεστάλησαν ἐπὶ τὴν κοινὴν
τῶν Σαυνιτῶν σύνοδον, δηλώσοντες[1] αὐτοῖς ὅτι
φίλοι καὶ σύμμαχοι Ῥωμαίων εἰσὶ Λευκανοί, καὶ
τήν τε[2] χώραν ἣν ἔτυχον αὐτῶν ἀφῃρημένοι παρα-
καλέσοντες[3] ἀποδιδόναι καὶ μηδὲν ἔτι πράττειν
ἔργον πολεμίων, ὡς οὐ περιοψομένης τῆς Ῥωμαίων πόλεως τοὺς ἑαυτῆς ἱκέτας ἐξελαυνομένους
ἐκ τῆς σφετέρας. Ursin.

II. (16, 13) Οἱ δὲ Σαυνῖται τῶν πρέσβεων ἀκούσαντες ἠγανάκτουν τε καὶ ἀπελογοῦντο, πρῶτον
μὲν οὐκ ἐπὶ τούτῳ πεποιῆσθαι λέγοντες τὰς περὶ
τῆς εἰρήνης ὁμολογίας, ἐπὶ τῷ μηδένα μήτε φίλον
ἴδιον ἡγήσασθαι μήτ' ἐχθρὸν ἐὰν μὴ Ῥωμαῖοι
κελεύσωσιν· ἔπειθ' ὅτι Λευκανοὺς οὐ πρότερον
ἐποιήσαντο Ῥωμαῖοι φίλους, ἀλλ' ἔναγχος πολεμίους ἤδη σφῶν ὄντας, πρόφασιν οὔτε δικαίαν
οὔτ' εὐσχήμονα κατασκευαζόμενοι τοῦ καταλῦσαι
2 τὰς σπονδάς. ἀποκρινομένων δὲ τῶν Ῥωμαίων
ὅτι τοὺς ὑπηκόους ὁμολογήσαντας[4] ἔπεσθαι[5] καὶ
ἐπὶ τούτῳ τῷ δικαίῳ καταλυσαμένους τὸν πόλεμον
ἅπαντα πείθεσθαι[6] δεῖ τοῖς παρειληφόσι τὴν ἀρχήν,
καί, εἰ μή[7] ποιήσουσι[8] τὰ κελευόμενα ἑκόντες,

---

1 Kiessling : δηλώσαντες O.   2 τε Sylburg : τότε O.
3 Sylburg : παρακαλέσαντες O.
4 Ursinus : ὁμολογήσαντες O.
5 ἔπεσθαι O : ἔσεσθαι Ursinus.
Sylburg (from cod. Pacii) : πείσεσθαι O.

made many entreaties, the senate voted to accept the
hostages and to join friendship with the Lucanians ;
and the popular assembly ratified their vote. Upon
the conclusion of the treaty with the emissaries of the
Lucanians the oldest and most honoured of the Romans
were chosen by the senate and sent as ambassadors
to the general council of the Samnites to inform them
that the Lucanians were friends and allies of the
Romans and to warn them not only to restore the land
they had taken away from them but also to commit no
further act of hostility, since Rome would not permit
her suppliants to be driven out of their own land.

II. (16, 13) The Samnites, having listened to the
ambassadors, were indignant and declared in their
own defence, first of all, that they had not made the
peace on the understanding that they were to count
no one as their friend or enemy unless the Romans
should bid them to do so ; and again, that the
Romans had not previously made the Lucanians their
friends, but only just now, when they were already
enemies of the Samnites, thereby trumping up an
excuse that was neither just nor seemly for setting
aside the treaty. When the Romans answered that
subjects who had agreed to follow them [1] and had
obtained a termination of the war on that condition
must obey all orders of those who had assumed the
rule over them, and threatened to make war upon

[1] Or, following Ursinus' reading, " those who had agreed
to be their subjects."

---

[7] καὶ εἰ μὴ Sylburg : εἰ καὶ μὴ O.
[8] Sylburg : ποιήσωσι O(?).

3 πολεμήσειν αὐτοῖς ἀπειλούντων, ἀφόρητον ἡγησάμενοι τὴν αὐθάδειαν τῆς πόλεως οἱ Σαυνῖται τοὺς
μὲν πρέσβεις ἐκέλευσαν ἀπαλλάττεσθαι παραχρῆμα, αὐτοὶ[1] δὲ τὰ πρὸς τὸν πόλεμον ἐψηφίσαντο
κοινῇ τε καὶ κατὰ πόλεις εὐτρεπίζεσθαι. Ursin.

III. (16, 14) Ἡ μὲν δὴ φανερὰ τοῦ Σαυνιτικοῦ
πολέμου πρόφασις καὶ πρὸς ἅπαντας εὐπρεπὴς
λέγεσθαι ἡ Λευκανῶν ἐγένετο βοήθεια τῶν καταφυγόντων ἐπ' αὐτούς, ὡς κοινὸν δή τι τοῦτο καὶ
πάτριον ὂν[2] ἔθος τῇ Ῥωμαίων πόλει τοῖς ἀδικου-
μένοις καὶ καταφεύγουσιν[3] ἐπ' αὐτὴν βοηθεῖν· ἡ
δ' ἀφανὴς καὶ μᾶλλον αὐτοὺς ἀναγκάζουσα διαλύεσθαι τὴν[4] φιλίαν ἡ τῶν Σαυνιτῶν ἰσχὺς πολλή
τ' ἤδη γεγονυῖα καὶ ἔτι πλείων[5] γενήσεσθαι νομι-
ζομένη, εἰ[6] Λευκανῶν τε χειρωθέντων καὶ δι'
αὐτοὺς τῶν προσοίκων ἀκολουθήσειν ἔμελλε τὰ[7]
βαρβαρικὰ ἔθνη τὰ προσεχῆ τούτοις. αἵ τε δὴ
σπονδαὶ μετὰ τὴν ἄφιξιν τῶν πρεσβευτῶν εὐθὺς
ἐλέλυντο, καὶ στρατιαὶ δύο κατεγράφοντο. Ursin.

IV. (16, 15) Ὅτι Ποστόμιος ὁ ὕπατος τῆς δια-
δοχῆς αὐτοῦ ἐγγισάσης μέγα φρονῶν ἐφ' ἑαυτῷ
τῆς τ' ἀξιώσεως[8] τοῦ γένους ἕνεκα καὶ ὅτι διτταῖς
2 ὑπατείαις ἤδη κεκοσμημένος ἦν. ἐφ' οἷς ὁ συν-
ύπατος αὐτοῦ κατ' ἀρχὰς μὲν ὡς ἀπελαυνόμενος
τῶν ἴσων ἠγανάκτει καὶ πολλάκις ἐπὶ τῆς βουλῆς
τὰ δίκαια πρὸς αὐτὸν ἔλεγεν, ὕστερον δὲ συγγνοὺς

---

[1] αὐτός V.   [2] ὂν added by Steph.[2]
[3] Ursinus : καταφεύγοντας O.
[4] τὴν added by Kiessling.
[5] ἔτι πλείων Sylburg : ἐπὶ πλείω or ἐπὶ πλεῖον MSS.
[6] εἰ added by Reiske.
[7] τὰ Steph.[2] : τά τε Ο, καὶ τὰ Sylburg.
[8] τῆς τ' ἀξιώσεως Valesius : τῆς τάξεως P.

them if they did not voluntarily do as they were ordered, the Samnites, regarding the arrogance of Rome as intolerable, ordered the ambassadors to depart at once, while, as for themselves, they voted to make the necessary preparations for war both jointly and each city for itself.

III. (16, 14) The published reason, then, for the Samnite war and the one that was plausible enough to be announced to the world was the assistance extended to the Lucanians who had turned to them for help, since this was a general and time-honoured practice with the Roman state to aid those who were wronged and turned to her for help. But the undisclosed reason and the one which was more cogent in leading them to give up their friendship with the Samnites was the power of that nation, which had already become great, and promised to become greater still if, upon the subjugation of the Lucanians and, because of them, of their neighbours, the barbarian tribes adjoining them were going to follow the same course. The treaty, accordingly, was promptly abrogated after the return of the ambassadors, and two armies were enrolled.

IV. (16, 15) Postumius the consul, now that his succession to his father's estate was imminent, thought very highly of himself both because of the reputation of his family and because he had already been honoured with two consulships. His colleague was at first indignant at this, feeling that he was being excluded from an equal share of honours, and he frequently presented his claims against him before the senate ; but later, recognizing that in dignity of

333

ἑαυτῷ κατά τε προγόνων ὄγκον καὶ φίλων πλῆθος[1]
καὶ κατὰ τὰς ἄλλας δυνάμεις ἐλάττονα ἰσχὺν ἔχοντι
(δημοτικὸς γὰρ ἦν καὶ τῶν νεωστὶ παρελθόντων
εἰς γνῶσιν) εἶξέ τε τῷ[2] συνυπάτῳ καὶ παρεχώρησε
3 τοῦ Σαυνιτικοῦ πολέμου τὴν ἡγεμονίαν. πρῶτον
μὲν δὴ τοῦτο διαβολὴν ἤνεγκε τῷ Ποστομίῳ κατὰ
πολλὴν αὐθάδειαν γενόμενον, καὶ ἕτερον αὖθις ἐπὶ
τούτῳ βαρύτερον ἢ ὡς κατὰ ῾Ρωμαῖον ἡγεμόνα.
ἐπιλεξάμενος γὰρ ἐκ τῆς ἑαυτοῦ στρατιᾶς περὶ
τοὺς δισχιλίους ἄνδρας εἰς τοὺς ἰδίους ἀγροὺς
ἀπήγαγεν, οἷς ἄνευ σιδήρου[3] δρυμὸν ἐκέλευσε κεί-
ρειν· καὶ μέχρι πολλοῦ κατέσχε τοὺς ἄνδρας ἐν
τοῖς ἀγροῖς θητῶν ἔργα καὶ θεραπόντων ὑπηρε-
4 τοῦντας. (16) τοσαύτῃ δὲ αὐθαδείᾳ πρὸ τῆς ἐξόδου
χρησάμενος ἔτι βαρύτερος ἐφάνη τοῖς κατ᾽ αὐτὴν
τὴν στρατείαν[4] ἐπιτελεσθεῖσι καὶ παρέσχε τῇ βουλῇ καὶ τῷ δήμῳ μίσους ἀφορμὰς δικαίου. τὸν
γὰρ ὑπατεύσαντα τῷ πρόσθεν ἐνιαυτῷ καὶ νικήσαντα Σαυνιτῶν τοὺς καλουμένους Πέντρους Φάβιον[5]
τῆς βουλῆς ψηφισαμένης μένειν ἐπὶ τοῦ στρατοπέδου καὶ τὴν ἀνθύπατον ἀρχὴν ἔχοντα πρὸς ταύτην[6] τὴν μερίδα τῶν Σαυνιτῶν πολεμεῖν, γράμματα
πέμπων ἐκχωρεῖν ἐκ τῆς Σαυνίτιδος ἐκέλευσεν,
5 ὡς αὐτῷ μόνῳ τῆς ἡγεμονίας προσηκούσης. καὶ
πρὸς τοὺς ἀποσταλέντας ὑπὸ τῶν συνέδρων πρέσβεις ἀξιοῦντας μὴ κωλύειν τὸν ἀνθύπατον ἐπὶ
τοῦ στρατοπέδου μένειν μηδ᾽ ἀντιπράττειν τοῖς
ἐψηφισμένοις ὑφ᾽ ἑαυτῶν, ὑπερηφάνους καὶ τυραν-
νικὰς ἔδωκεν ἀποκρίσεις, οὐ τὴν βουλὴν ἄρ-

---

[1] πλῆθος om. Suid.   [2] εἶξέ τε τῷ Valesius : εἶξε τῷ P.
[3] ἄνευ σιδήρου deleted by Smit.
[4] στρατηγίαν P.

ancestry, the number of his friends, and in other sources of influence he was inferior to the other (for he was a plebeian and one of those who had but recently come to public notice), he yielded to his colleague and let him have the command of the Samnite war. This was the first thing that aroused prejudice against Postumius, occasioned as it was by his great arrogance ; and on top of it came another action that was too offensive for a Roman commander. He chose, namely, about two thousand men out of his army, and taking them to his own estate, ordered them to cut down a thicket without axes ; and for a long time he kept the men on his estate performing the tasks of labourers and slaves.[1] (16) After displaying such arrogance before setting out on the campaign, he showed himself even more domineering in the acts which he committed in the course of the campaign itself, thus affording the senate and the people grounds for just hatred. For though the senate had voted that Fabius, who had been consul the year before and had conquered the Samnite tribe called the Pentrians, should remain in the camp and, holding the proconsular power, make war against that part of the Samnites, Postumius nevertheless sent him a letter ordering him to evacuate the Samnite country, on the ground that the command belonged to him alone. And to the envoys sent by the senators to demand that he should not hinder the proconsul from remaining in the camp nor act in opposition to their decrees he gave a haughty answer worthy of a tyrant, declaring that the senate did

---

[1] *Cf.* Livy, Periocha to Book XI.

---

5 Φάβιον placed here by Kiessling : after νικήσαντα in P.
6 ταύτην added by Reiske.

χειν ἑαυτοῦ φήσας, ἕως ἐστὶν ὕπατος, ἀλλ' αὐτὸν
6 τῆς βουλῆς. ἀπολύσας δὲ τοὺς πρέσβεις ἐπὶ τὸν
Φάβιον ἦγε τὴν στρατιάν, ὡς, εἰ μὴ βούλοιτο
ἑκὼν παραχωρεῖν τῆς ἀρχῆς, τοῖς ὅπλοις προσ-
αναγκάσων. καταλαβὼν δὲ τοῦτον Κομινίῳ[1] πόλει
προσκαθήμενον †ἐξέπλευσεν[2] ἐκ τοῦ στρατοπέδου
κατὰ πολλὴν ὑπεροψίαν τῶν ἀρχαίων ἐθισμῶν
καὶ δεινὴν ὑπερηφανίαν. Φάβιος μὲν οὖν[3] αὐτοῦ
εἴξας τῇ μανίᾳ τῆς ἡγεμονίας ἐξεχώρησεν. Vales.;
Suidas s.v. Ποστόμιος.

V. (16, 17) Ὅτι ὁ αὐτὸς Ποστόμιος πρῶτον μὲν
τὸ Κομίνιον[4] ἐκ πολιορκίας καταλαμβάνει[5] χρόνον
οὐ πολὺν ἐν ταῖς προσβολαῖς διατρίψας· ἔπειτα
Οὐενουσίαν πολυάνθρωπον καὶ ἄλλας πόλεις πλείστας ὅσας, ἐξ ὧν μύριοι μὲν ἐσφάγησαν, ἑξακισ-
χίλιοι δὲ καὶ διακόσιοι τὰ ὅπλα παρέδοσαν.
2 ταῦτα διαπραξάμενος οὐχ ὅπως χάριτος ἢ τιμῆς
τινος ἠξιώθη παρὰ τῆς βουλῆς, ἀλλὰ καὶ τὴν
προϋπάρχουσαν ἀξίωσιν ἀπέβαλεν. ἀποστελλο-
μένων γὰρ εἰς μίαν τῶν ἁλουσῶν ὑπ' ἐκείνου
πόλεων, τὴν καλουμένην Οὐενουσίαν, δισμυρίων
ἐποίκων ἕτεροι τῆς ἀποικίας ᾑρέθησαν ἡγεμόνες,
ὁ δὲ τὴν πόλιν ἐξελὼν καὶ τὴν γνώμην τῆς ἀπο-
στολῆς τῶν κληρούχων εἰσηγησάμενος οὐδὲ ταύτης
3 ἄξιος ἐφάνη τῆς τιμῆς. (18) εἰ μὲν οὖν σώφρονι
λογισμῷ τὰ συμβάντα ἤνεγκε καὶ τὸ χαλεπὸν τοῦ
συνεδρίου λόγων τε καὶ ἔργων χρηστῶν θεραπείαις
ἐπράυνεν, οὐδεμιᾶς ἂν[6] ἔτι συμφορᾶς εἰς ἀτιμίαν
φερούσης ἐπειράθη. νῦν δὲ ἀγανακτῶν καὶ ἀντι-
χαλεπαίνων τάς τε ὠφελείας ἃς ἔλαβεν ἐκ τῶν

---

[1] καμινίῳ P.
[2] ἐξέπλευσεν P : ἐξέκλεισεν Valesius, ἐξήλασεν Reiske, ἐξ-
336

not govern him, so long as he was consul, but that he governed the senate. Then, having dismissed the envoys, he led his army against Fabius, intending, in case he were not willing to give up the command voluntarily, to force him by arms to do so. And coming upon Fabius as he was besieging the town of Cominium, he drove him out of the camp, showing a vast contempt for the ancient usages and an outrageous arrogance. Fabius, accordingly, yielded to his madness and relinquished the command.

V. (16, 17) This same Postumius first took Cominium by siege, after spending but a short time in assaults, and then captured Venusia, a populous place, and ever so many other cities, of whose inhabitants 10,000 were slain and 6,200 surrendered their arms. Though he accomplished all this, he not only was not granted any mark of favour or honour by the senate, but even lost the esteem which was his before. For when 20,000 colonists were sent out to one of the cities captured by him, the one called Venusia, others were chosen leaders of the colony, while the man who had reduced the city and had made the proposal for the dispatch of the colonists was not found worthy even of that honour. (18) Now if he had borne these reverses with a prudence based upon reason and had assuaged the harshness of the senate by the therapy of courteous words and actions, he would have experienced no further misfortune leading to disgrace. But as it was, being exasperated and harsh in his turn, he not only presented the soldiers

---

ἐπίεσεν Jacoby, ἐξεπέλευσεν (cf. Hesychius s.v. ἐκπελεύει) Post.

[3] οὖν added by Reiske.　　[4] κάμινον P.
[5] καταλαμβάνει P : παραλαμβάνει Valesius(?).
[6] ἂν added by Kiessling.

DIONYSIUS OF HALICARNASSUS

πολεμίων ἁπάσας τοῖς στρατιώταις ἐχαρίσατο, καὶ
πρὶν ἀποσταλῆναι τὸν διάδοχον τῆς ἀρχῆς ἀπέλυσεν ἀπὸ τῶν σημείων τὰς δυνάμεις, καὶ τελευτῶν
ὃν οὔτε βουλὴ[1] οὔτε δῆμος[2] συνεχώρησεν αὐτῷ
4 θρίαμβον ἀπὸ τῆς ἑαυτοῦ γνώμης κατήγαγεν. ἐφ'
οἷς ἅπασιν ἔτι μείζονος ἐξ ἁπάντων μίσους ἐκ-
καυθέντος ἅμα τῷ παραδοῦναι τὴν ἀρχὴν τοῖς
μεθ' ἑαυτὸν ὑπάτοις εἰς δίκην ὑπάγεται δημοσίαν
ὑπὸ δυεῖν δημάρχων. καὶ κατηγορηθεὶς ἐν τῷ
δήμῳ πάσαις ταῖς φυλαῖς κατακρίνεται, τίμημα
τῆς εἰσαγγελίας ἐχούσης[3] χρηματικὸν πέντε μυριάδας ἀργυρίου. *Vales.*

---

[1] οὔτε βουλή Valesius : ἤτε βουλῆι P.
[2] οὔτε δῆμος added by Cary, οὔτε ὁ δῆμος by Reiske.
[3] Valesius : ἔχουσαν P.

Φερεντῖνος, πόλις Σαυνιτῶν ἐν Ἰταλίᾳ. τὸ ἐθνικὸν
Φερεντανός. λέγεται καὶ Φερέντιοι, ὡς Διονύσιος ιζ'
τῆς Ῥωμαϊκῆς ἀρχαιολογίας. *Steph. Byz.*

Μιλωνία, πόλις Σαυνιτῶν ἐπιφανεστάτη. Διονύσιος
ιζ'. τὸ ἐθνικὸν Μιλωνιάτης. *Steph. Byz.*

Νηκούια, πόλις Ὀμβρικῶν. Διονύσιος ἑπτακαι-
δεκάτῳ Ῥωμαϊκῆς ἀρχαιολογίας. τὸ ἐθνικὸν Νηκουιάτης.
Steph. Byz.

Ναρνία, πόλις Σαυνιτῶν, ἀπὸ τοῦ παραρρέοντος
ποταμοῦ Νάρνου, ὡς Διονύσιος ὀκτωκαίδεκι τῳ Ῥωμαϊκῆς ἀρχαιολογίας. τὸ ἐθνικὸν Ναρνιάτης. *Steph. Byz.*

Ὀκρίκολα, πόλις Τυρρηνῶν. Διονύσιος ὀκτωκαιδεκά-
τῳ Ῥωμαϊκῆς ἀρχαιολογίας. τὸ ἐθνικὸν Ὀκρικολανός,
ὡς αὐτός φησιν. *Steph. Byz.*

---

[1] See the note on p. 257.
[2] Probably an error for Frentanus. *Cf.* xix. 12.

with all the booty he had taken from the enemy, but
also, before his successor in the command was sent
out, dismissed his forces from the standards ; and
finally, though it was granted to him by neither the
senate nor the people, he celebrated a triumph on
his own authority. In consequence of all this, still
greater hatred flared up on the part of all, and as soon
as he turned over his magistracy to the consuls who
succeeded him he was cited to a public trial by two
tribunes. And being accused before the popular
assembly, he was condemned by all the tribes, the
indictment calling for a fine of 50,000 denarii.[1]

[1] The word denarii is uncertain ; the Greek says, literally,
" 50,000 in silver." The word usually used by Dionysius
for denarius is drachma, but at other times he gives the sum
in *asses*. Nowhere does he clearly refer to a sestertius,
which, like the denarius, was a silver coin.

Ferentinum, a city of the Samnites in Italy. *Eth.*[1]
Ferentanus.[2] Ferentii also is used, as Dionysius, *Roman
Antiquities* xvii.

Milonia,[3] a very prominent city of the Samnites.
Dionysius xvii. *Eth.* Miloniates (?). (*Cf.* Livy x. 3 ; 34.)

Nequinum, a city of the Umbrians. Dionysius, *Roman
Antiquities* xvii. *Eth.* Nequinates. (*Cf.* Livy x. 9 f.)

Narnia, a city of the Samnites,[4] named from the river
Nar which flows past it. Dionysius, *Roman Antiquities*
xviii. *Eth.* Narniensis. (*Cf.* Livy x. 9 f.)

Ocriculum, a city of the Tyrrhenians. Dionysius,
Roman Antiquities xviii. *Eth.* Ocriculanus, *idem.*
(*Cf.* Livy ix. 41.)

[3] The name should be Milonia ; the *Eth.* is conjectural,
as it does not occur in Latin literature.

[4] An error for Sabines ? Narnia was built on the site of
the ancient Nequinum.

EXCERPTS

FROM

BOOK XIX

I. (17, 1) Ὅτι Κρότων πόλις ἐν Ἰταλίᾳ ἐστὶ καὶ Σύβαρις ἀπὸ τοῦ παραρρέοντος ποταμοῦ οὕτως κληθεῖσα.

2 Ὅτε Λακεδαιμόνιοι Μεσσήνην[1] ἐπολέμουν καὶ χῆρος[2] ἀνδρῶν ἡ πόλις ἦν, δεομέναις ταῖς γυναιξὶ καὶ μάλιστα ταῖς ἐν ἀκμῇ παρθένοις μὴ περιιδεῖν τὰς μὲν ἀγάμους, τὰς δὲ ἀτέκνους γινομένας ἐπέμποντό τινες ἀεὶ νέοι παραλλὰξ ἀπὸ τοῦ στρατοπέδου τῆς μίξεως τῶν γυναικῶν ἕνεκα καὶ συνῇεσαν αἷς ἐπιτύχοιεν· ἐκ τούτων γίνονται τῶν ἀδιακρίτων ἐπιμιξιῶν παῖδες, οὓς ἀνδρωθέντας οἱ Λακεδαιμόνιοι προεπηλάκιζον τά τε ἄλλα καὶ 3 Παρθενίας προσηγόρευον. (2) στάσεως δὲ γενομένης ἡττηθέντες οἱ Παρθενίαι ἀναχωροῦσιν ἑκόντες ἐκ τῆς πόλεως καὶ πέμψαντες εἰς Δελφοὺς χρησμὸν ἔλαβον πλεῖν εἰς Ἰταλίαν, ἐξευρόντας δὲ χωρίον τῆς Ἰαπυγίας Σατύριον καὶ ποταμὸν Τάραντα, ἔνθ᾿ ἂν[3] ἴδωσι τράγον τῇ θαλάττῃ τέγγοντα τὸ 4 γένειον, ἐκεῖ τοὺς βίους ἱδρύσασθαι. πλεύσαντες

---

[1] Cary : μεσσήνην Q.   [2] χῆρος Q, ἔρημος A.
[3] ἔνθ᾿ ἂν Struve : ἔνθα Q.

340

EXCERPTS

FROM

BOOK XIX

I. (17, 1) Croton is a city in Italy; likewise Sybaris, so named from the river which flows past it.

When the Lacedaemonians were warring against Messenê and Sparta was stripped of men, the women and especially the maidens who were of marriageable age begged them not to allow them to go unwed and childless. Accordingly, young men were constantly sent from the camp in rotation to have intercourse with the women and they consorted with the first women they met. From these promiscuous unions were born boys whom, when they had grown to man's estate, the Lacedaemonians called Partheniae,[1] among other taunts that they hurled at them. (2) When a sedition occurred and the Partheniae were defeated, they voluntarily withdrew from the city; and sending to Delphi, they received an oracle bidding them sail to Italy and after finding a town in Iapygia called Satyrium and a river Taras, to establish their abode where they should see a goat dipping his beard in the sea. Having made the voyage, they

[1] *i.e.* "sons of virgins."

δὲ τόν τε ποταμὸν ἐξεῦρον καὶ κατά τινος ἐρινεοῦ
πλησίον τῆς θαλάττης πεφυκότος ἄμπελον ἐθεάσαντο κατακεχυμένην, ἐξ ἧς τῶν ἐπιτράγων τις
καθειμένος ἥπτετο τῆς θαλάττης. τοῦτον[1] ὑπολαβόντες εἶναι τὸν τράγον ὃν προεῖπεν αὐτοῖς ὁ
θεὸς ὄψεσθαι τέγγοντα τὸ γένειον τῇ θαλάττῃ,
αὐτοῦ μένοντες[2] ἐπολέμουν Ἰάπυγας, καὶ ἱδρύονται
τὴν ἐπώνυμον τοῦ ποταμοῦ Τάραντος πόλιν. Ambr.

II. (17, 3) Ἀρτιμήδης ὁ Χαλκιδεὺς λόγιον εἶχεν,
ἔνθ᾽ ἂν εὕρῃ τὸν ἄρρενα ὑπὸ τῆς θηλείας ὀπυιό-
μενον,[3] αὐτόθι μένειν καὶ μηκέτι προσωτέρω
πλεῖν· πλεύσας δὲ περὶ τὸ Παλλάντιον τῆς Ἰταλίας
καὶ ἰδὼν ἄμπελον . . .[4] ἄρρενα δὲ τὸν ἐρινεόν,
ὀχείαν δὲ τὴν πρόσφυσιν, τέλος ἔχειν τὸν χρησμὸν
ὑπέλαβε· καὶ τοὺς κατέχοντας τὸν τόπον βαρ-
2 βάρους ἐκβαλὼν οἰκεῖ. Ῥήγιον ὁ τόπος καλεῖται,
εἴθ᾽ ὅτι σκόπελος ἦν ἀπορρώξ, εἴθ᾽ ὅτι κατὰ τοῦτον
ἡ γῆ τὸν τόπον ἐρράγη καὶ διέστησεν ἀπὸ τῆς
Ἰταλίας τὴν ἀντικρὺ Σικελίαν, εἴτε ἀπ᾽[5] ἀνδρὸς
δυνάστου ταύτην ἔχοντος τὴν προσηγορίαν. Ambr.

III. (17, 4) Λευκίππῳ τῷ Λακεδαιμονίῳ πυνθανομένῳ ὅπου πεπρωμένον[6] αὐτῷ εἴη κατοικεῖν
καὶ τοῖς[7] περὶ αὐτόν, ἔχρησεν ὁ θεὸς πλεῖν μὲν εἰς
Ἰταλίαν, γῆν δὲ οἰκίζειν εἰς ἣν ἂν καταχθέντες

---

[1] Jacoby : τοῦτο Q.
[2] Struve : μένοντας Q.
[3] Struve : ὠπυισμένον Q.
[4] Lacuna after ἄμπελον recognized by Mai ; Cobet proposed to supply from Diodorus ἐρινεῷ περιπεπλεγμένην καὶ
ἐννοήσας θήλειαν μὲν εἶναι τὴν ἄμπελον.
[5] ἀπ᾽ (or ἐπ᾽) Hertlein : ὑπ᾽ Q.
[6] Mai : πεπρωμένῳ Q.
[7] τοῖς Mai : τὸν Q.

found the river and observed a wild fig-tree growing
near the sea and overspread with a vine, one of whose
tendrils hung down and touched the sea. Assuming
this to be the " goat " which the god had foretold
them they would see dipping his beard in the sea,
they remained there and made war upon the Iapygians ; and they founded the city which they named
for the river Taras.[1]

II. (17, 3) Artimedes of Chalcis had an oracle bidding him, wherever he should find the male covered
by the female, there to abide and to sail no farther.
When he had sailed round Pallantium in Italy, he
beheld a vine [twining over a wild fig-tree ; and reflecting that the vine was feminine [2]] and the fig-tree
masculine, and the clinging was the sexual " covering,"
he assumed that the oracle had its fulfilment.
Accordingly, he drove out the barbarians who were
in possession of the place and colonized it himself.
The place is called Rhegium, either because there
was an abrupt headland or because in this place the
earth split [3] and set off from Italy Sicily which lies
opposite, or else it is named after some ruler who
bore this name.

III. (17, 4) When Leucippus the Lacedaemonian
inquired where it was fated for him and his followers
to settle, the god commanded them to sail to Italy and
settle that part of the land where they should stay a

---

[1] Taras is the Greek word for Tarentum.

[2] The words in brackets, missing in the MSS., are supplied
from Diodorus. The Greek word ἄμπελος is feminine gender,
ἐρινεός masculine.

[3] These two explanations of the name Ῥήγιον assume that
it is derived from the root of the verb ῥηγνύναι (" break ").
The words here rendered " abrupt " and " split " show
different grades of this root.

DIONYSIUS OF HALICARNASSUS

ἡμέραν καὶ νύκτα μείνωσι· καταχθέντος δὲ τοῦ
στόλου περὶ Καλλίπολιν ἐπίνειόν τι τῶν Ταραντίνων
ἀγασθεὶς τοῦ χωρίου τὴν φύσιν ὁ Λεύκιππος πείθει
Ταραντίνους συγχωρῆσαί σφισιν ἡμέραν αὐτόθι
2 καὶ νύκτα ἐναυλίσασθαι. ὡς δὲ πλείους ἡμέραι δι-
ῆλθον, ἀξιούντων αὐτοὺς ἀπιέναι[1] τῶν Ταραντίνων
οὐ προσεῖχεν αὐτοῖς τὸν νοῦν ὁ Λεύκιππος, παρ᾽
ἐκείνων εἰληφέναι λέγων τὴν γῆν καθ᾽ ὁμολογίας
εἰς ἡμέραν καὶ νύκτα· ἕως δ᾽[2] ἂν ᾖ τούτων θάτερον, οὐ μεθήσεσθαι τῆς γῆς. μαθόντες δὴ παρα-
κεκρουσμένους ἑαυτοὺς οἱ Ταραντῖνοι συγχωροῦσιν
αὐτοῖς μένειν. Ambr.

IV. (17, 5) Ἄκραν τῆς Ἰταλίας Ζεφύριον οἱ Λο-
κροὶ κατοικήσαντες Ζεφύριοι ὠνομάσθησαν.

Μένειν αὐτὸν ἐγνώκεσαν ἐφ᾽ ᾧ ἦν τόπῳ[3] καὶ τὸν
ἐκεῖθεν ῥέοντα πόλεμον ἀνέχειν.

Εἰς ὕλας καὶ φάραγγας καὶ τραχῶνας ὀρεινοὺς
διεσκεδάσθησαν.

2 (6) Ταραντῖνός τις ἀνὴρ ἀναιδὴς[4] καὶ περὶ πάσας τὰς ἡδονὰς ἀσελγὴς ἀπὸ τῆς ἀκολάστου καὶ
κακῶς δημοσιευθείσης ἐν παισὶν[5] ὥρας ἐπεκαλεῖτο
Θάις.

Τὸ πλῆθος ἀνδρολογήσαντες ἀπῇεσαν.

Οἱ σπερμολογώτατοι τῶν κατὰ τὴν πόλιν καὶ
ἀναγωγότατοι. Ambr.

V. (17, 7) Ὅτι Ποστόμιος πρέσβυς ἐστάλη πρὸς
Ταραντίνους· καί τινα αὐτοῦ διεξιόντος λόγον[6] οὐχ

---

[1] Mai : ἀπεῖναι Q.
[2] δ᾽ added by Kiessling, οὖν by Struve.
[3] ᾧ . . . τόπῳ Struve : ὧν . . . τόπων Q.
[4] ἀναιδὴς Post : αἰνησίας (or αἰνισίος ?) Q, ἀνόσιος Mai.
[5] ἐν πᾶσιν Post.

day and a night after landing. The expedition made land near Callipolis, a seaport of the Tarentines ; and Leucippus, pleased with the nature of the place, persuaded the Tarentines to permit them to encamp there for a day and a night. When several days had passed and the Tarentines asked them to depart, Leucippus paid no heed to them, claiming that he had received the land from them under a compact for day and night ; and so long as there should be either of these he would not give up the land. So the Tarentines, realizing that they had been tricked, permitted them to remain.

IV. (17, 5) The Locrians, having settled the Italian promontory of Zephyrium, were called Zephyrians.

They decided that he should remain in the place where he was and conduct the war that was threatening from that quarter.

They were scattered among the forests and ravines and mountain fastnesses.

(6) A certain Tarentine who was shameless [1] and addicted to every form of sensual pleasure was nicknamed Thaïs because of his beauty, which was licentious and prostituted to base ends among boys.[2]

After enlisting the plebeians they departed.

The most frivolous and dissolute of all in the city.

V. (17, 7) Postumius was sent as ambassador to the Tarentines. As he was making an address to

---

[1] In place of " shameless " the MS. gives the proper name Aenesias or Aenisius. Mai proposed to read " impious."

[2] Or, following Post's emendation, " among all."

---

[6] λόγον added by Kiessling, Jacoby : om. O ; τινα may, however, be taken as neut. pl.

ὅπως προσεῖχον αὐτῷ τὴν διάνοιαν ἢ λογισμοὺς
ἐλάμβανον οἱ Ταραντῖνοι σωφρόνων ἀνθρώπων καὶ
περὶ πόλεως κινδυνευούσης βουλευομένων,[1] ἀλλ'
εἴ τι μὴ κατὰ τὸν ἀκριβέστατον τῆς Ἑλληνικῆς
διαλέκτου χαρακτῆρα ὑπ' αὐτοῦ λέγοιτο παρα-
τηροῦντες ἐγέλων, καὶ πρὸς τὰς ἀνατάσεις[2] ἐτραχύ-
νοντο καὶ βαρβάρους[3] ἀπεκάλουν καὶ τελευτῶντες[4]
2 ἐξέβαλλον ἐκ τοῦ θεάτρου. ἀπιόντων δ' αὐτῶν
εἰς τῶν ἐφεστηκότων ἐν τῇ παρόδῳ Ταραντίνων,[5] Φιλωνίδης ὄνομα, σπερμολόγος ἄνθρωπος,
ὃς ἀπὸ[6] τῆς οἰνοφλυγίας, ᾗ παρὰ πάντα τὸν βίον
ἐκέχρητο, προσηγορεύετο Κοτύλη, μεστὸς ὢν ἔτι
τῆς χθιζῆς μέθης, ὡς ἐγγὺς ἦσαν οἱ πρέσβεις, ἀνα-
συράμενος τὴν περιβολὴν καὶ σχηματίσας ἑαυτὸν
ὡς αἴσχιστον ὀφθῆναι, τὴν οὐδὲ[7] λέγεσθαι πρέπουσαν ἀκαθαρσίαν κατὰ τῆς ἱερᾶς ἐσθῆτος τοῦ
πρεσβευτοῦ κατεσκέδασε.
3   (8) Γέλωτος δὲ καταρραγέντος ἐξ ὅλου τοῦ θεάτρου καὶ συγκροτούντων τὰς χεῖρας τῶν ἀγερωχο-
τάτων ἐμβλέψας εἰς τὸν Φιλωνίδην ὁ Ποστόμιος
εἶπεν· "Δεξόμεθα[8] τὸν οἰωνόν, ὦ σπερμολόγε
ἄνθρωπε, ὅτι καὶ τὰ μὴ[9] αἰτούμενα δίδοτε ἡμῖν."
ἔπειτα εἰς τὸν ὄχλον ἐπιστραφεὶς καὶ τὴν ὑβρισ-
μένην ἐσθῆτα δεικνύς, ὡς ἔμαθεν ἔτι πλείονα
γινόμενον ἐξ ἁπάντων τὸν[10] γέλωτα καὶ φωνὰς
ἤκουσεν[11] ἐνίων ἐπιχαιρόντων καὶ τὴν ὕβριν ἐπ-
4 αινούντων· "Γελᾶτε," ἔφησεν, "ἕως ἔξεστιν ὑμῖν,

---

[1] Ursinus : βουλομένων O.
[2] Sylburg : ἀναστάσεις O.
[3] βαρβάρουν V, βάρβαρον Ursinus.
[4] Ursinus : τελευτῶν O.

346

them, the Tarentines, far from paying heed to him or thinking seriously, as men should do who are sensible and are taking counsel for a state which is in peril, watched rather to see if he would make any slip in the finer points of the Greek language, and then laughed, became exasperated at his truculence, which they called barbarous, and finally were ready to drive him out of the theatre. As the Romans were departing, one of the Tarentines standing beside the exit was a man named Philonides, a frivolous fellow who because of the besotted condition in which he passed his whole life was called Demijohn; and this man, being still full of yesterday's wine, as soon as the ambassadors drew near, pulled up his garment, and assuming a posture most shameful to behold, bespattered the sacred robe of the ambassador with the filth that is indecent even to be uttered.

(8) When laughter burst out from the whole theatre and the most insolent clapped their hands, Postumius, looking at Philonides, said: " We shall accept [1] the omen, you frivolous fellow, in the sense that you Tarentines give us even what we do not ask for." Then he turned to the crowd and showed his defiled robe; but when he found that the laughter of everybody became even greater and heard the cries of some who were exulting over and praising the insult, he said: " Laugh while you may, Tarentines!

---

[1] Or, following Sylburg's emendation, " we accept."

---

[5] Ursinus : παρατίνων O.   [6] Sylburg : ὑπὸ O.
  [7] οὐδὲ Q : οὐ O.   [8] δεχόμεθα Sylburg.
    [9] καὶ τὰ μὴ Ursinus : μὴ καὶ τὰ O.
      [10] τὸν added by Kiessling.
  [11] ἤκουσεν Steph.², ἤκουεν Ursinus : ἤκουον O.

ἄνδρες Ταραντῖνοι, γελᾶτε· πολὺν γὰρ τὸν μετὰ
ταῦτα χρόνον κλαύσετε." ἐκπικρανθέντων δέ τινων
πρὸς τὴν ἀπειλήν, "καὶ ἵνα γε μᾶλλον," ἔφησεν,
"ἀγανακτήσητε, καὶ τοῦθ' ὑμῖν λέγομεν, ὅτι
πολλῷ τὴν ἐσθῆτα ταύτην αἵματι ἐκπλυνεῖτε.[1]"
5 ταῦτα οἱ τῶν Ῥωμαίων πρέσβεις ὑβρισθέντες
ὑπὸ τῶν Ταραντίνων ἰδίᾳ τε καὶ δημοσίᾳ καὶ
ταύτας τὰς φωνὰς ἐπιθεσπίσαντες ἀπέπλευσαν ἐκ
τῆς πόλεως. Ursin.; (p. 346, ll. 10-17) Ambr.

VI. (17, 9) Ἄρτι δ' Αἰμιλίου Βαρβόλα ἐπίκλησιν τὴν ἀρχὴν παρειληφότος παρῆσαν οἱ σὺν
τῷ Ποστομίῳ πεμφθέντες εἰς τὸν Τάραντα πρέσβεις, ἀπόκρισιν μὲν οὐδεμίαν φέροντες, τὰς δὲ
ὕβρεις ἃς ἦσαν ὑβρισμένοι[2] πρὸς αὐτῶν διεξιόντες,
καὶ τὴν ἐσθῆτα τοῦ Ποστομίου πίστιν τῶν λόγων
παρεχόμενοι. ἀγανακτήσεως δὲ μεγάλης ἐξ ἁπάντων γενομένης συναγαγόντες τὴν βουλὴν οἱ περὶ
τὸν Αἰμίλιον ὕπατοι τί χρὴ πράττειν ἐσκόπουν,
ἔωθεν ἀρξάμενοι μέχρι δύσεως ἡλίου· καὶ τοῦτ'
2 ἐποίησαν ἐφ' ἡμέρας συχνάς. (10) ἦν δ' ἡ ζήτησις
οὐχ ὑπὲρ τοῦ λελύσθαι τὰς περὶ τῆς εἰρήνης ὁμολογίας ὑπὸ τῶν Ταραντίνων, τοῦτο γὰρ ἅπαντες
ὡμολόγουν, ἀλλ' ὑπὲρ τοῦ χρόνου τῆς ἀποσταλη-
σομένης ἐπ' αὐτούς[3] στρατιᾶς. ἦσαν γάρ τινες
οἱ παραινοῦντες μήπω τοῦτον ἀναλαμβάνειν τὸν
πόλεμον ἕως Λευκανοί τ' ἀφεστήκασι καὶ Βρέττιοι
καὶ τῶν Σαυνιτῶν πολὺ καὶ φιλοπόλεμον ἔθνος,
καὶ Τυρρηνία παρ' αὐταῖς οὖσα ταῖς θύραις ἔτι
ἀχείρωτος ἦν, ἀλλ' ὅταν ὑποχείρια γένηται τάδε
τὰ ἔθνη, μάλιστα μὲν ἅπαντα, εἰ δὲ μή γε, τὰ

---

[1] Ursinus : ἐκπλυνῆτε O.
[2] ὑβρισμένοι Sylburg : ὑποισμένοι O.

Laugh! For long will be the time that you will weep hereafter." When some became embittered at this threat, he added : " And that you may become yet more angry, we say this also to you, that you will wash out this robe with much blood." The Roman ambassadors, having been insulted in this fashion by the Tarentines both privately and publicly and having uttered the prophetic words which I have reported, sailed away from their city.

VI. (17, 8) As soon as Aemilius, with the cognomen Barbula, had assumed the consulship, Postumius and those who had been sent with him as ambassadors to Tarentum arrived in the city, bringing no answer, to be sure, but relating the insults that had been offered them and exhibiting the robe of Postumius as proof of their story. When great indignation was shown by all, Aemilius and his fellow consul assembled the senate and considered what course they ought to take, remaining in session from early morning until sunset ; and this they did for many days. (10) The question was not whether the terms of peace had been violated by the Tarentines, since all were agreed upon that point, but when an army should be sent out against them. For there were some who advised against undertaking this war as yet, while the Lucanians, the Bruttians, and the large and warlike race of Samnites were in rebellion and Tyrrhenia, lying at their very doors, was still unconquered, but only after these nations had been subdued, preferably all of them, but if that should not be possible, at least those

---

³ ἐπ’ αὐτοὺς Sylburg : ὑπ’ αὐτῆς O.

πρὸς ἀνατολὰς καὶ πλησίον τοῦ Τάραντος κείμενα. τοῖς δὲ τἀναντία τούτοις ἐφαίνετο συμφέρειν, μηδὲ τὸν ἐλάχιστον χρόνον ἀναμένειν, ἀλλ' ἐπιψηφίζειν 3 τὸν πόλεμον ἤδη. καὶ ἐπεὶ[1] τὰς γνώμας ἔδει διαριθμεῖσθαι, πλείους ἐφάνησαν οὗτοι τῶν ἀναβάλλεσθαι τὸν πόλεμον εἰς ἑτέρους καιροὺς παραινούντων· καὶ ὁ δῆμος ἐπεκύρωσε τὰ δόξαντα τῇ βουλῇ. [ζήτει ἐν τῷ περὶ στρατηγημάτων.] Ursin.

VII. (17, 11) . . . φύσιν ἔχουσι[2] τοῖς μὲν διασῶσαι τὰ ἑαυτῶν ἀγαθὰ βουλομένοις οἱ περὶ τὸν αὐτὸν ἀναστρεφόμενοι τόπον οἰωνοὶ σχολαιοτέρᾳ τῇ πτήσει πρὸς ἀγαθοῦ εἶναι συμβόλου, τοῖς δὲ τῶν ἀλλοτρίων[3] ἐφιεμένοις οἱ τὴν ἐπίτονον[4] καὶ ταχεῖαν ὁρμὴν ἔχοντες εἰς τὰ πρόσω· οὗτοι μὲν γὰρ πορισταί τε καὶ θηρευταὶ τῶν οὐχ ὑπαρχόντων εἰσίν, ἐκεῖνοι δὲ ἐπίσκοποι[5] καὶ φύλακες τῶν παρόντων. Ambr.

2 (12) Ἅπασαν τὴν πολεμίαν διεξῄει ἀρούρας τε ἀκμαῖον ἤδη τὸ σιτικὸν θέρος ἐχούσας πυρὶ διδοὺς καὶ δένδρα καρποφόρα κείρων.

Παραπλήσιόν τι πάσχουσιν αἱ δημοκρατούμεναι πόλεις τοῖς πελάγεσιν· ἐκεῖνά τε γὰρ ὑπὸ τῶν ἀνέμων ταράττεται φύσιν ἔχοντα ἠρεμεῖν, αὗταί τε ὑπὸ τῶν δημαγωγῶν κυκῶνται μηδὲν ἐν ἑαυταῖς ἔχουσαι κακόν. Ambr.

VIII. (17, 13) Τῶν Ταραντίνων βουλομένων ἐκ τῆς Ἠπείρου Πύρρον μετακαλεῖν ἐπὶ τὸν κατὰ Ῥωμαίων πόλεμον καὶ τοὺς κωλύοντας ἐξελαυνόντων Μέτων τις καὶ αὐτὸς Ταραντῖνος, ἵνα τύχοι[6]

---

[1] Sylburg : ἐπὶ O.
[2] Mai : ἔχουσαι Q.
[3] τοῖς ἀλλοτρίοις Q. (ων above)

lying eastward and close to Tarentum. But others thought the opposite course advisable, namely, not to wait for a moment, but to vote for war at once. When it was time for counting the votes, those in the latter group were found to be more numerous than those who advised postponing the war to another time. And the populace ratified the decision of the senate. [The MS. adds : See the section on Stratagems.]

VII. (17, 11) . . . it is the nature of those birds which hover round the same spot in rather leisurely flight to be of good omen to those who wish to save their own possessions ; and it is the nature of those birds which dart forward in swift and impetuous flight to be of good omen to those who covet the possessions of others. For the latter are providers and hunters of the things that are lacking, whereas the former are watchers and guardians of the things on hand.

(12) He went through the whole country of the enemy setting fire to the fields which had crops of grain already ripe and cutting down the fruit-trees.

Democracies experience something of the same sort as do the seas ; for just as the latter are agitated by the winds, though it is their nature to be tranquil, so the former are disturbed by the demagogues, though they have in themselves no evil.

VIII. (17, 13) When the Tarentines wished to summon Pyrrhus from Epirus to aid in the war against the Romans and were banishing those who opposed this course, a certain Meton, himself a Tarentine, in order to gain their attention and show

---

⁴ ἐπίτονον (or σύντονον) Cary : ἐπίτομον Q, Jacoby, ἐπίπονον Hertlein.
⁵ Struve : περίσκοποι Q.   ⁶ Struve : τύχη Q.

προσοχῆς καὶ διδάξειεν αὐτοὺς ὅσα μετὰ τῆς
βασιλικῆς ἐξουσίας εἰς πόλιν ἐλευθέραν καὶ τρυ-
φῶσαν εἰσελεύσεται κακά,[1] συγκαθημένου τοῦ
πλήθους παρῆν εἰς τὸ θέατρον ἐστεφανωμένος
ὥσπερ ἐκ συμποσίου, παιδίσκην περιειληφὼς αὐλη-
2 τρίδα κωμαστικὰ μέλη προσαυλοῦσαν.[2] (14) δια-
λυθείσης δὲ τῆς ἁπάντων σπουδῆς εἰς γέλωτα,
καὶ τῶν μὲν ᾄδειν αὐτὸν κελευόντων, τῶν δὲ
ὀρχεῖσθαι, περιβλέψας κύκλῳ καὶ τῇ χειρὶ διασημήνας ἡσυχίαν αὐτῷ παρασχεῖν, ἐπειδὴ κατέστειλε τὸν θόρυβον· " Ἄνδρες," ἔφη, " πολῖται,
τούτων ὧν ἐμὲ ποιοῦντα ὁρᾶτε νῦν οὐδὲν ὑμῖν
ἐξέσται ποιεῖν ἐὰν βασιλέα καὶ φρουρὰν εἰς τὴν
3 πόλιν εἰσελθεῖν ἐάσητε." ὡς δὲ κινουμένους καὶ
προσέχοντας εἶδε πολλοὺς καὶ κελεύοντας λέγειν,
σώζων ἔτι τὸ προσποίημα τῆς κραιπάλης τὰ συμβησόμενα αὐτοῖς ἠριθμεῖτο[3] κακά· ἔτι δὲ αὐτοῦ
λέγοντος οἱ τῶν κακῶν αἴτιοι συλλαβόντες αὐτὸν
κατὰ κεφαλῆς[4] ἐξωθοῦσιν ἐκ τοῦ θεάτρου. Ambr.

IX. (17, 15) " Βασιλεὺς Ἠπειρωτῶν Πύρρος,
βασιλέως Αἰακίδου, Ποπλίῳ Οὐαλερίῳ τῷ Ῥωμαίων ὑπάτῳ χαίρειν. πεπύσθαι μὲν εἰκός σε
παρ' ἑτέρων ὅτι πάρειμι μετὰ τῆς δυνάμεως
Ταραντίνοις τε καὶ τοῖς ἄλλοις Ἰταλιώταις ἐπι-
καλεσαμένοις βοηθήσων· καὶ μηδὲ ταῦτα ἀγνοεῖν,
τίνων τε ἀνδρῶν ἀπόγονός εἰμι καὶ τίνας αὐτὸς
ἀποδέδειγμαι πράξεις καὶ πόσην δύναμιν ἐπάγο-
2 μαι[5] καὶ ὡς τὰ πολέμια ἀγαθήν. οἰόμενος δή
σε τούτων ἕκαστον ἐπιλογιζόμενον μὴ περιμένειν
ἕως ἔργῳ καὶ πείρᾳ μάθῃς τὴν κατὰ τοὺς ἀγῶνας

---

[1] κακά Kiessling : om. O, Jacoby.
[2] Kiessling : προσαυδοῦσαν Q, προσᾴδουσαν Struve.

them all the evils that would come in the train of
royalty into a free and luxury-loving state, came into
the theatre, at a time when the multitude was seated
there, wearing a garland, as if returning from a
banquet, and embracing a young flute-girl who was
playing on her flute tunes appropriate to songs of
revelry. (14) When the seriousness of all gave way to
laughter and some of them bade him to sing, others
to dance, Meton looked round him on every side and
waved his hand for silence ; then, when he had quieted
the disturbance, he said : " Citizens, of these things
which you see me doing now you will not be able to
do a single one if you permit a king and a garrison
to enter the city." When he saw that many were
moved and paying attention and were bidding him
to speak on, he proceeded, while still preserving his
pretence of drunkenness, to enumerate the evils that
would befall them. But while he was still speaking,
the men responsible for those evils seized him and
threw him head first out of the theatre.

IX. (17, 15) " The King of the Epirots, Pyrrhus,
son of King Aeacides, to Publius Valerius, consul
of the Romans, greetings. You have presumably
learned from others that I have come with my army
to the aid of the Tarentines and other Italiots in
response to their summons ; presumably also you
are not unaware from what men I am sprung and
what exploits I myself have performed and of the
size of the army I bring with me and its excellence
in warfare. Convinced as I am, then, that as you
appraise each of these factors you are not waiting to
learn from fact and experience our valour in battle,

---

³ Mai : ἠριθμεῖτε Q.   ⁴ Naber : κεφαλὴν Q.
     ⁵ Struve : ἐπαγόμενος Q.

ἡμῶν ἀρετήν, ἀλλ' ἀποστάντα τῶν ὅπλων χωρεῖν
ἐπὶ τοὺς λόγους, συμβουλεύω τέ σοι περὶ ὧν ὁ
Ῥωμαίων δῆμος διαφέρεται πρὸς Ταραντίνους ἢ
Λευκανοὺς ἢ Σαυνίτας ἐμοὶ τὴν διάγνωσιν ἐπιτρέπειν—διαιτήσω γὰρ ἀπὸ παντὸς τοῦ δικαίου
τὰ διάφορα—καὶ παρέξω τοὺς ἐμαυτοῦ φίλους
ἁπάσας τὰς βλάβας ἀποτίνοντας ἇς[1] ἂν αὐτῶν
3 ἐγὼ καταγνῶ. (16) ὀρθῶς δὲ ποιήσετε[2] καὶ ὑμεῖς
βεβαιωτὰς παρασχόντες ὑπὲρ ὧν ἂν ἐκείνων τινὲς
ἐπικαλῶσιν, ὅτι τὰ κριθέντα ὑπ' ἐμοῦ φυλάξετε
κύρια. ταῦτα ποιοῦσι μὲν ὑμῖν εἰρήνην ἐπαγγέλ-
λομαι[3] παρέξειν καὶ φίλος ἔσεσθαι καὶ ἐφ' οὓς ἂν
με παρακαλῆτε[4] πολέμους προθύμως βοηθήσειν,
4 μὴ ποιοῦσι δ' οὐκ ἂν ἐπιτρέψαιμι χώραν συμμάχων ἀνδρῶν ἐξερημοῦν καὶ πόλεις Ἑλληνίδας ἀν-
αρπάζειν[5] καὶ σώματα ἐλεύθερα λαφυροπωλεῖν,
ἀλλὰ κωλύσω τοῖς ὅπλοις, ἵνα παύσησθε ἤδη ποτὲ
ἄγοντες καὶ φέροντες ὅλην Ἰταλίαν καὶ πᾶσιν ἀνθρώποις ὡς[6] δούλοις ἐντρυφῶντες. ἐκδέξομαι δὲ
τὰς σὰς ἀποκρίσεις μέχρι δεκάτης ἡμέρας· περαιτέρω γὰρ οὐκ ἂν ἔτι δυναίμην." Ambr.

X. (17, 17) Πρὸς ταῦτα ὁ Ῥωμαίων ὕπατος
ἀντιγράφει τήν τε αὐθάδειαν τοῦ ἀνδρὸς ἐπιρ-
ραπίζων καὶ τὸ φρόνημα τῆς Ῥωμαίων πόλεως
ἐνδεικνύμενος· "Πόπλιος Οὐαλέριος Λαβίνιος,
στρατηγὸς ὕπατος Ῥωμαίων, βασιλεῖ Πύρρῳ
2 χαίρειν. ἀνδρὸς ἔργον εἶναί μοι δοκεῖ σώφρονος
ἀπειλητικὰς πέμπειν ἐπιστολὰς πρὸς τοὺς ὑπηκόους·
ὧν δ' οὔτε τὴν δύναμιν ἐξήτακεν οὔτε τὰς ἀρετὰς

---

[1] Struve : οὓς Q. [2] Struve : ποιήσητε Q.
[3] Mai : ἐπαγγέλομεν Q. [4] Struve : παρακαλεῖτε Q.
[5] διαρπάζειν Naber. [6] ὡς Mai : καὶ Q.

but having desisted from arms, are proceeding to words, I not only advise you to leave to me the settlement of your differences with the Tarentines, Lucanians and Samnites—for I will arbitrate your differences with complete justice—but I will cause my friends to make good all the damage that I find them to have caused. (16) You Romans also will do well to offer sureties yourselves, with respect to any charges that some of them may bring against you, that you will abide by my decisions as valid. If you do this, I promise to give you peace and to be your friend and to aid you zealously in any wars to which you may summon me ; but if you do not do so, I shall not permit you to make desolate the country of men who are my allies, to plunder Greek cities and sell freemen at auction, but I shall prevent you by force of arms, in order that you may at last stop pillaging all Italy and treating all men arrogantly as if they were slaves. I shall wait ten days for your answer ; longer I cannot wait."

X. (17, 17) In reply to this the Roman consul wrote back, rebuking the man's arrogance and displaying the lofty spirit of the Roman commonwealth : " Publius Valerius Lavinius,[1] general and consul of the Romans, to King Pyrrhus, greetings. It seems to me to be the part of a prudent man to send threatening letters to his subjects ; but to despise those whose might he has not tested and whose

[1] Both here and in the following chapter the MS. gives the name as Lavinius instead of Laevinus. The corruption was particularly easy in the Greek and may be due to the excerptor.

ἐπέγνωκε, τούτων ὡς φαύλων καὶ μηδενὸς ἀξίων καταφρονεῖν ἀνοήτου μοι φαίνεται τρόπου τεκμή-
3 ριον εἶναι καὶ τὸ διάφορον οὐκ ἐπισταμένου. ἡμεῖς δὲ οὐ τοῖς λόγοις τιμωρεῖσθαι τοὺς ἐχθροὺς εἰώ- θαμεν ἀλλὰ τοῖς ἔργοις, καὶ οὔτε δικαστὴν ποιού- μεθά σε περὶ ὧν Ταραντίνοις ἢ Σαυνίταις ἢ τοῖς ἄλλοις πολεμίοις ἐγκαλοῦμεν οὔτ᾽ ἐγγυητὴν λαμβά- νομεν ἐκτίσματος οὐδενός, ἀλλὰ τοῖς ἡμῶν αὐτῶν ὅπλοις τὸν ἀγῶνα κρινοῦμεν καὶ τὰς τιμωρίας ὡς ἂν αὐτοὶ θέλωμεν ἀναπράξομεν. ταῦτα δὴ προειδὼς ἀνταγωνιστὴν ἡμῖν παρασκεύαζε σαυτόν,
4 ἀλλὰ μὴ δικαστήν. (18) καὶ περὶ ὧν ἡμᾶς αὐτὸς ἀδικεῖς οὕστινας ἐγγυητὰς ἐκτισμάτων παρέξεις σκόπει· μὴ Ταραντίνους ἀναδέχου μηδὲ τοὺς ἄλλους πολεμίους[1] τὰ δίκαια ὑφέξειν. εἰ δ᾽ ἐκ παντὸς τρόπου πόλεμον αἵρεσθαι[2] πρὸς ἡμᾶς δι- έγνωκας, ἴσθι σοι ταὐτὸ[3] συμβησόμενον ὃ πᾶσι συμβαίνειν ἀνάγκη τοῖς μάχεσθαι βουλομένοις πρὶν ἐξετάσαι πρὸς οὓς ποιήσονται τὴν μάχην.
5 ταῦτα ἐνθυμούμενος, εἴ τινος δέη τῶν ἡμετέρων, ἀποθέμενος τὰς ἀπειλὰς καὶ τὸ βασιλικὸν αὔχημα καταβαλὼν ἴθι πρὸς τὴν βουλὴν καὶ δίδασκε καὶ πεῖθε τοὺς συνέδρους, ὡς οὐδενὸς ἀτυχήσων οὔτε τῶν δικαίων οὔτε τῶν εὐγνωμόνων." Ambr.

XI. (18, 1) Λαβίνιος ὁ Ῥωμαίων ὕπατος κατά- σκοπον τοῦ Πύρρου συλλαβών, καθοπλίσας[4] τὴν στρατιὰν πᾶσαν καὶ εἰς τάξιν καταστήσας, ὡς ἐπέδειξε τῷ κατασκόπῳ, φράζειν ἐκέλευσε πρὸς τὸν ἀποστείλαντα πᾶσαν τὴν ἀλήθειαν, καὶ πρὸς

---

[1] τοὺς ἄλλους πολεμίους Kiessling : τοὺς πολεμίους O, Jacoby, τοὺς ἀλλοτρίους Post.
[2] Naber, Jacoby : αἱρεῖσθαι Q.   [3] Struve : τοῦτο Q.

valour he has not learned to know, as if they were
insignificant and of no account, seems to me to be
evidence of a disposition that is foolish and does not
know how to discriminate.   As for us, we are wont to
punish our enemies, not by words, but by deeds, and
we are neither making you a judge in the matter of
our charges against the Tarentines, Samnites or our
other foes nor accepting you as a surety for the payment of any penalty, but we shall decide the contest
by our own arms and exact the penalties as we ourselves wish.   Now that you are forewarned of this,
make yourself ready as our opponent, not as our
judge.   (18) As for the wrongs you yourself have
done us, take thought whom you will offer as sureties
for the payment of penalties ;   do not expect the
Tarentines or our other enemies to offer just
redress.   But if you have determined to make war
upon us by all means, know that the same thing
will happen to you that must needs happen to all
who wish to fight before investigating against whom
they will be waging the contest.   Bearing these
things in mind, if you want anything that is ours,
first put aside your threats and drop your regal
boastfulness, then go to the senate and inform and
persuade its members, confident that you will not
fail of anything that is either just or reasonable.''

XI. (18, 1) Lavinius, the Roman consul, having
caught a spy of Pyrrhus, armed and drew up the
whole army in line of battle, and showing it to the
spy, bade him tell the whole truth to the one who
had sent him, and, in addition to reporting what he

---

⁴ καθοπλίσας Q : καὶ καθοπλίσας A.

οἷς ἐθεάσατο λέγειν ὅτι Λαβίνιος ὁ Ῥωμαίων ὕπατος αὐτὸν παρακαλεῖ μὴ λάθρα πέμπειν ἑτέρους ἔτι
τοὺς κατασκεψομένους, ἀλλ᾽ αὐτὸν ἐλθόντα φανερῶς ἰδεῖν τε καὶ μαθεῖν τὴν Ῥωμαίων δύναμιν.
Ambr.

XII. (18, 2) Ἀνήρ τις Ὀβλάκος ὄνομα, Οὐλσί-
νιος ἐπίκλησιν, τοῦ Φερεντανῶν ἔθνους ἡγεμών,
ὁρῶν τὸν Πύρρον οὐ μίαν ἔχοντα στάσιν, ἀλλὰ
πᾶσι τοῖς μαχομένοις ὀξέως ἐπιφαινόμενον,[1] προσεῖχεν ἐκείνῳ μόνῳ τὸν νοῦν, καὶ ὅποι παριππεύοι
2 τὸν ἴδιον ἀντιπαρῆγεν ἵππον· καί τις ἰδὼν αὐτὸν
τῶν μετὰ τοῦ βασιλέως, Λεοννάτος Λεοφάντου
Μακεδών, ὑποπτεύει τε καὶ δείξας τῷ Πύρρῳ
λέγει· "Τοῦτον τὸν ἄνδρα φυλάττου, βασιλεῦ·
πολεμιστὴς γὰρ ἄκρος καὶ οὐκ ἐφ᾽ ἑνὸς ἑστηκὼς
τόπου μάχεται, σὲ δὲ παρατηρεῖ καὶ τέτακεν ἐπὶ
3 σοὶ τὸν νοῦν." (3) τοῦ δὲ βασιλέως λέγοντος· "Τί
δ᾽ ἄν με δράσειεν εἷς ὢν τοσούτους ἔχοντα περὶ
ἐμαυτόν;" καί τι καὶ νεανιευομένου περὶ τῆς
ἑαυτοῦ ῥώμης, ὡς εἰ καὶ συνέλθοι πρὸς ἕνα μόνος
οὐκ ἄπεισιν ὀπίσω χαίρων, λαβὼν ὃν ἀνέμενε
καιρὸν ὁ Φερεντανὸς Ὀβλάκος ἐλαύνει σὺν τοῖς
περὶ αὐτὸν εἰς μέσην τὴν βασιλικὴν ὕλην· διακόψας
δὲ τὸ στῖφος τῶν πέριξ ἱππέων ἐπ᾽ αὐτὸν ἐφέρετο
τὸν βασιλέα, διαλαβὼν ἀμφοτέραις ταῖς χερσὶ[2]
4 τὸ δόρυ· κατὰ τὸν αὐτὸν δὲ χρόνον ὁ μὲν Λεον-
νᾶτος, ὁ προειπὼν τῷ Πύρρῳ φυλάττεσθαι τὸν
ἄνδρα, μικρὸν ἐκνεύσας εἰς τὰ πλάγια τὸν ἵππον
αὐτοῦ παίει τῷ ξυστῷ διὰ τῆς λαγόνος, ὁ δὲ
Φερεντανὸς ἤδη καταφερόμενος τὸν τοῦ βασιλέως
διὰ τοῦ στήθους ἐλαύνει, καὶ συγκαταπίπτουσι

---

[1] ἐπιφαινόμενον Q : ἐπιφερόμενον A.

had seen, to tell him that Lavinius, the Roman consul, bade him not to send any more men secretly as spies, but to come himself, openly, to see and learn the might of the Romans.

XII. (18, 2) A certain man named Oblacus, with the cognomen Volsinius, a leader of the Ferentan nation, observing that Pyrrhus did not remain in one fixed place but appeared suddenly to all his men in turn as they fought, kept his attention on him alone and wherever Pyrrhus rode up he would bring up his own horse opposite him. One of the king's companions, Leonnatus, the son of Leophantus, a Macedonian, observing him, became suspicious, and pointing him out to Pyrrhus, said : " Beware of that man, O King ; for he is a keen warrior, and does not fight remaining in one position, but watches you and has his attention fixed on you." (3) To which the king answered : " But what could he, being but one man, do to me who have so many defenders about me ? " and with youthful bravado he even uttered some boast about his own strength, to the effect that even if he engaged alone with a single adversary the other would not get off unpunished. The Ferentan Oblacus, having thus found the opportunity for which he was waiting, charged with his companions into the midst of the royal squadron ; and breaking through the crowd of attendant horsemen, he bore down upon the king himself, grasping his spear with both hands. But at the same moment Leonnatus, who had warned Pyrrhus to beware of the man, swerved a little to one side and struck the foe's horse through the flank with his spear, but Oblacus even while falling to the ground ran the king's horse through the breast ; and

---

² ἀμφοτέραις ταῖς χερσὶ Struve : ἀμφοτέρας τὰς χεῖρας Q.

5 τοῖς ἵπποις ἀμφότεροι. (4) τὸν μὲν οὖν βασιλέα
τῶν σωματοφυλάκων ὁ πιστότατος ἐπὶ τὸν ἴδιον
ἵππον ἀναβιβάσας ἐξελαύνει, τὸν δὲ Ὀβλάκον
μέχρι πολλοῦ διαγωνισάμενον, ἔπειτα ὑπὸ πλήθους
τῶν τραυμάτων καταπονηθέντα, τῶν ἑταίρων τινὲς
ἀράμενοι μεγάλου περὶ τὸν[1] νεκρὸν ἀγῶνος γενο-
6 μένου διακομίζουσιν. ἐκ τότε δὲ ὁ βασιλεύς, ἵνα
μὴ διάσημος[2] εἴη τοῖς πολεμίοις, τὴν μὲν ἰδίαν
χλαμύδα ἣν ἐν ταῖς μάχαις εἰώθει φορεῖν, ἁλουργῆ
τε οὖσαν καὶ χρυσόπαστον, καὶ τὸν ὁπλισμὸν
πολυτελέστερον[3] ὄντα τῶν ἄλλων τῆς τε ὕλης
ἕνεκα καὶ τῆς τέχνης, τὸν πιστότατον τῶν ἑταίρων[4]
καὶ κατὰ τοὺς ἀγῶνας ἀνδρειότατον Μεγακλῆν
ἐκέλευσεν ἐνδῦναι, τὴν δὲ φαιὰν ἐκείνου χλαμύδα
καὶ τὸν θώρακα καὶ τὴν ἐπὶ τῇ κεφαλῇ[5] καυσίαν
αὐτὸς ἔλαβεν· ὅπερ αἴτιον αὐτῷ τῆς σωτηρίας
ἔδοξε γενέσθαι. Ambr.

XIII. (18, 5) Ὅτι Πύρρου τοῦ Ἠπειρωτῶν[6]
βασιλέως ἐπὶ τὴν Ῥώμην στρατιὰν ἐξαγαγόντος
ἐβουλεύσαντο πρεσβευτὰς ἀποστεῖλαι τοὺς ἀξιώσοντας Πύρρον ἀπολυτρῶσαι σφίσι τοὺς αἰχμαλώτους εἴτ' ἀντιδιαλλαξάμενον ἑτέρων σωμάτων
εἴτ' ἀργύριον κατ' ἄνδρα ὁρίσαντα, καὶ ἀπο-
δεικνύουσι[7] πρέσβεις Γάιον Φαβρίκιον, ὃς ἐνιαυτῷ
τρίτῳ πρότερον ὑπατεύων Σαυνίτας καὶ Λευκανοὺς καὶ Βρεττίους ἐνίκησε μεγάλαις μάχαις καὶ
τὴν Θουρίων πολιορκίαν ἔλυσε, καὶ Κόιντον

---

[1] τὸ Q, according to Kiessling.   [2] Mai : διασήμενος Q.
[3] Struve : λυσιτελέστερον Q.
[4] Struve : ἑτέρων Q.
[5] τῇ κεφαλῇ Struve : τὴν κεφαλὴν Q.
[6] Sylburg : ἠπειρώτου O ; τῶν Ἠπειρωτῶν β. Grasberger.
[7] Reiske : ἀποδείκνυσι O.

both fell with their horses. (4) As for the king, the most faithful man of his bodyguards mounted him on his own horse and rode away. In the case of Oblacus, after he had fought on for a long time and then succumbed to innumerable wounds, some of his companions took him up, after a sharp struggle had taken place for the possession of his body, and bore him away. Thereafter the king, in order not to be conspicuous to his enemies, ordered that his own cloak, purple-dyed and shot with gold, which he was accustomed to wear in battle, and his armour, which was more costly than that of the others in point both of material and workmanship, should be worn by the most faithful of his companions and the bravest in battle, Megacles, while he himself took the other's dun cloak, breastplate and his felt head-gear. And this seemed to be the reason for his escape.

XIII. (18, 5) When Pyrrhus, the king of the Epirots, led an army against Rome, they voted to send ambassadors to ask him to release to them for ransom the prisoners he had taken, either exchanging them for others or setting a price for each man ; and they chose as ambassadors Gaius Fabricius, who while serving as consul two years earlier [1] had conquered the Samnites, Lucanians and Bruttians in stubborn battles and had raised the siege of Thurii ; Quintus

---

[1] Literally, " the third year before." He was consul in 282 B.C. ; the date of the embassy to Pyrrhus was the early winter of 280/79. In chap. 16, 3 Fabricius says it is the fourth year since his consulship. The ambassadors were probably chosen late in the year 280, their meeting with Pyrrhus taking place early in 279 (so at least according to Dionysius' reckoning).

Αἰμίλιον τὸν συνάρξαντα τῷ Φαβρικίῳ καὶ τὴν
ἡγεμονίαν τοῦ Τυρρηνικοῦ πολέμου σχόντα, καὶ
Πόπλιον Κορνήλιον, ὃς ἐνιαυτῷ τετάρτῳ πρότερον
ὑπατεύων Κελτῶν ἔθνος ὅλον, τοὺς καλουμένους
Σένωνας,[1] ἐχθίστους Ῥωμαίων ὄντας, πολεμῶν
2 ἅπαντας ἡβηδὸν κατέσφαξεν. (6) οὗτοι πρὸς Πύρρον ἀφικόμενοι καὶ διαλεχθέντες ὅσα τῇ τοιαύτῃ
χρείᾳ πρόσφορα ἦν, ὡς ἀτέκμαρτον πρᾶγμα τύχῃ καὶ ταχεῖαι τῶν πολέμων[2] αἱ τροπαὶ καὶ τῶν
συμβησομένων οὐδὲν ἀνθρώποις προειδέναι ῥάδιον,
ἐπ᾽ ἐκείνῳ τὴν προαίρεσιν ἐποίουν εἴτ᾽ ἀργύριον
ἀντὶ[3] τῶν αἰχμαλώτων ἐβούλετο λαβεῖν εἴτε ἑτέρους
αἰχμαλώτους.

3 (7) Πύρρος δὲ μετὰ τῶν φίλων βουλευσάμενος
ἀποκρίνεται τάδε αὐτοῖς· " Σχέτλιόν τι πρᾶγμα
ποιεῖτε, ὦ ἄνδρες Ῥωμαῖοι, φιλίαν μὲν οὐ βουλόμενοι συνάψαι πρὸς ἐμέ, τοὺς δὲ ἁλόντας κατὰ
πόλεμον ἀξιοῦντες ἀπολαβεῖν, ἵνα τοῖς αὐτοῖς τούτοις σώμασιν εἰς τὸν κατ᾽ ἐμοῦ πόλεμον ἔχητε[4]
4 χρῆσθαι. ἀλλ᾽ εἰ τὰ κράτιστα βουλεύεσθε[5] πράττειν καὶ τὸ κοινῇ συμφέρον ἀμφοτέροις ἡμῖν
σκοπεῖτε, σπεισάμενοι τὸν πόλεμον τὸν πρὸς ἐμὲ
καὶ τοὺς ἐμοὺς συμμάχους ἀπολάβετε τοὺς ἰδίους
προῖκα παρ᾽ ἐμοῦ πολίτας τε καὶ συμμάχους
ἅπαντας· ἄλλως δ᾽ οὐκ ἂν ὑπομείναιμι πολλοὺς
καὶ ἀγαθοὺς[6] ὑμῖν προέσθαι." Ursin.

XIV. (18, 8) Ταῦτα μὲν τῶν τριῶν πρεσβευτῶν
παρόντων ἔλεξεν, ἰδίᾳ δὲ τὸν Φαβρίκιον ἀπολαβών,
" Ἐγώ σέ," φησίν, " ὦ Φαβρίκιε, πυνθάνομαι

---

[1] Σένωνας Ursinus : νέωνας V, νέωννας E, γέωνας MP.
[2] πολέμων Ursinus : πόλεων O.
[3] ἀντὶ Ursinus : αὐτῶν O.   [4] Ursinus : ἔχοιτε O.

Aemilius, who had been Fabricius' colleague and had been in command of the Tyrrhenian war ; and Publius Cornelius, who while consul three [1] years earlier had waged war on the whole tribe of Gauls called the Senones, the Romans' bitterest enemies, and had slain all their adult males. (6) These men, when they had come to Pyrrhus and had said everything that was appropriate for such a mission, pointing out that fortune is an incalculable thing, that the changes in war are swift, and that it is not easy for mortals to know in advance any of the things that are going to happen, left to him the choice whether he wished to receive money for the prisoners or to get other prisoners in their stead.

(7) Pyrrhus, after taking counsel with his friends, answered them as follows : " You are acting perversely, Romans, when you are unwilling to join friendship with me, but ask to get back your men who have been captured in war, in order that you may have these same persons to use in your war against me. But if you are planning [2] to act in the best manner and if you have the common advantage of us both as your goal, put an end to the war against me and my allies and receive back all your men from me gratis, both your citizens and your allies. Otherwise I could never consent to hand over to you so many brave men."

XIV. (18, 8) This much he said while the three ambassadors were present ; then, taking Fabricius aside, he said : " I hear that you, Fabricius, are most

---

[1] Literally, " the fourth year before." The year was 283.
[2] Or, following Sylburg, "if you wish."

---

[5] Ursinus : βουλεύεσθαι O, βούλεσθε Sylburg.
[6] ἀγαθοὺς ἄνδρας Reiske.

κράτιστον ἐν ἡγεμονίαις πολέμων εἶναι κἂν[1] τῷ
βίῳ δίκαιον καὶ σώφρονα καὶ τὰς ἄλλας ἁπάσας
ἔχοντα ἀρετάς, χρημάτων δ᾿[2] ἄπορον καὶ καθ᾿ ἓν
τὸ μέρος τοῦτο ἐλασσούμενον ὑπὸ τῆς τύχης, ὥστε
μηδὲν ἄμεινον τῶν πενεστάτων βουλευτῶν[3] ἐν τοῖς
2 κατὰ τὸν βίον διατελεῖν. τοῦτο δὴ τὸ μέρος ἐκ-
πληρῶσαι προθυμούμενος ἕτοιμός εἰμι διδόναι σοι
πλῆθος ἀργυρίου καὶ χρυσίου τοσοῦτον ὅσον κτησά-
μενος ἅπαντας ὑπερβαλεῖς πλούτῳ τοὺς μάλιστα
δοκοῦντας Ῥωμαίων εὐπορεῖν, καλὸν νομίσας ἀν-
άλωμα καὶ πρέπον ἡγεμόνι τοὺς ἀγαθοὺς ἄνδρας
ἀναξίως τῆς ἀρετῆς διὰ πενίαν πράττοντας εὐεργ-
ετεῖν καὶ βασιλικοῦ πλούτου τοῦτ᾿ ἀνάθημα καὶ
3 κατασκεύασμα λαμπρότατον. (9) μαθὼν δὲ τὴν
ἐμὴν προαίρεσιν, Φαβρίκιε, καὶ πᾶσαν ἀποθέμενος αἰδὼ μέτεχε[4] τῶν παρ᾿ ἡμῖν ὑπαρχόντων
ἀγαθῶν, ὡς ἐμοῦ μέλλοντος εἴσεσθαι[5] καὶ μεγάλην
σοι χάριν, καὶ μὰ Δί᾿ οὐκ ἐλάττω . . .[6] καὶ ξένων
τοὺς τιμιωτάτους εἶναι νόμιζε. ἐμοὶ δ᾿ ἀντὶ τούτων μήτ᾿ ἄδικον μήτ᾿ αἰσχρὰν πρᾶξιν ὑπηρετήσῃς
μηδεμίαν, ἀλλ᾿ ἐξ ὧν αὐτὸς κρείττων ἔσῃ καὶ
4 τιμιώτερος ἐν τῇ σεαυτοῦ[7] πατρίδι. καὶ πρῶτον
μὲν ἐπὶ τὰς διαλλαγάς, ὅση δύναμις ἐν σοί, παρ-
όρμησον τὴν ἄχρι τοῦδε δύσεριν[8] καὶ οὐδὲν τῶν

---

[1] Struve : καὶ O.   [2] δ᾿ Sylburg : τε O.
[3] βουλευτῶν deleted by Smit; Post suggests πελατῶν.
[4] Sylburg : μέτασχε EV, μήταχε X.
[5] Ursinus : ἴσεται EV, εἴσεται X.
[6] Lacuna indicated by Ursinus. Reiske proposed οὐκ
ἐλάττω ⟨τῶν ἐμῶν φίλων καὶ ἀναγκαίων⟩ [or οὐκ ἐλάττω (acc.
plur.) ⟨τῶν ἐμῶν φίλων φέρεσθαι⟩] καὶ ξένων ἐν τοῖς τιμιωτάτοις
εἶναι νόμιζε. Post suggests οὐκ ἐλάττω ⟨σε ποιεῖν ἀγαθά με
ἑτοῖμον ἢ φίλων⟩ καὶ ξένων τοὺς τ. εἶναι νόμιζε.
[7] Hertlein : ἑαυτοῦ O.   [8] Ursinus : δύνεριν O.

able in military commands and in your private life
are just and prudent and possess all the other virtues,
but that you are without pecuniary means, being in
this one respect ill-treated by Fortune, so that you
continue to be no better off than the poorest senators [1]
in the matter of a livelihood. Being eager to supply
this defect, I am ready to give you such an amount
of silver and gold as will enable you to surpass in
wealth all the Romans who are reputed to be the
most prosperous. For I consider it an excellent
expenditure and one befitting a ruler to confer
benefits upon the good men who because of poverty
do not fare according to their merit, and I regard
this as the most splendid dedication and monument
of royal wealth. (9) Now that you have been informed of my purpose, Fabricius, lay aside all modesty
and share in the blessings that are to be found with
us, knowing that I shall be exceedingly grateful to
you ; and, by Heaven, no less . . . believe [them ?] to
be the most valued of my guest-friends.[2] And to me
in return for these things you are not to render any
service that is either wrong or shameful, but only
services from which you yourself will be more
powerful and more honoured in your own country.
First, then, with all the power that lies in you, urge
the senate, which thus far has been contentious and

---

[1] In place of " senators " Post would read " clients."

[2] Reiske proposed to complete the sentence thus : " and,
by Heaven, believe that you will be no less dear [to me than
my friends and relations] and will be among the most valued
of my guest-friends," or " believe that [you will get] no less
than [my friends] and will be among the most valued," etc.
Post suggests " you must believe that I am ready to confer
upon you no less kindness than upon the most honoured of
friends and guests."

μετρίων φρονοῦσαν βουλήν, διδάσκων ὡς οὐκ[1] ἐπὶ
κακῷ τῆς πόλεως ὑμῶν[2] ἀφῖγμαι Ταραντίνοις
καὶ[3] τοῖς ἄλλοις Ἰταλιώταις ὑποσχόμενος βοηθήσειν, οὓς[4] οὔτε ὅσιον οὔτ' εὔσχημόν ἐστί μοι παρόντι μετὰ δυνάμεως καὶ τὴν πρώτην νενικηκότι[5]
μάχην ἐγκαταλιπεῖν.[6] καὶ[7] πάνυ πολλὰ καὶ ἀναγκαῖα πράγματα κατὰ τοῦτον γενόμενα τὸν και-
5 ρὸν ἐπὶ τὴν ἰδίαν με ἀρχὴν μετακαλεῖ. (10) πίστεις
τε ὑπέχομαι πάσας, ὁπόσαι βεβαιοῦσιν ἀνθρώπων ὁμολογίας, καὶ μόνῳ καὶ μετὰ τῶν ἄλλων
πρεσβευτῶν περὶ τῆς οἴκαδε ἀνακομιδῆς εἴ με
Ῥωμαῖοι ποιήσαιντο φίλον,[8] ἵνα θαρρῶν πρὸς τοὺς
σεαυτοῦ[9] πολίτας λέγῃς,[10] εἰ δή[11] τισι τὸ τῆς βα-
σιλείας ὄνομα ὕποπτόν ἐστιν ὡς ἀπατηλὸν ἐν
ὁμολογίαις, ἐξ ὧν ἕτεροί τινες ἐν ὅρκοις καὶ
σπονδαῖς παρανοεῖν ἔδοξαν ὅμοια καὶ περὶ ἐμοῦ
6 τεκμαιρομένοις.[12] γενομένης δὲ τῆς εἰρήνης ἴθι μετ'
ἐμοῦ σύμβουλός τε ἁπάντων ἐσόμενος ἐμοὶ καὶ
ὑποστράτηγος καὶ τῆς βασιλικῆς εὐτυχίας μέτοχος.
ἐμοί τε γὰρ ἀνδρὸς ἀγαθοῦ καὶ πιστοῦ φίλου δεῖ,
σοί τε χορηγίας βασιλικῆς καὶ πραγμάτων βασι-
λικῶν· ἐὰν δὴ συνενέγκωμεν ταῦτ' εἰς τὸ κοινόν,
τὰ μέγιστα τῶν ἀγαθῶν παρ' ἀλλήλων ἀποισό-
μεθα." Ursin.

XV. (18, 11) Παυσαμένου δ' αὐτοῦ μικρὸν ἐπισχὼν ὁ Φαβρίκιος εἶπε·

"Περὶ μὲν τῆς ἀρετῆς ἥτις ἐστὶ περὶ ἡμᾶς ἢ

---

[1] οὐκ added by Reiske.   [2] Sylburg : ἡμῶν O.
[3] T. δὲ καὶ Hertlein.   [4] Sylburg : οἷς O.
[5] Ursinus : νενικηκόσι O.
[6] ἐγκαταλιπεῖν X : ἐγκαταλιπεῖ EV.
[7] καὶ Ursinus : δὲ καὶ O.
[8] εἴ με Ῥ. π. φίλον Cohn : εἶναι ῥ. π. φίλοι O.

has shown no disposition toward moderation, to make
the truce, showing them that it is not to the detriment
of your commonwealth that I have come after
promising to aid the Tarentines and the other Italiots,
and that it is neither right nor seemly for me to desert
them now that I am present with an army and have
won the first battle. And very many urgent matters
that have arisen at this time call me back to my own
kingdom. (10) With regard to my returning home, I
offer to you, both alone and together with the other
ambassadors, if the Romans would make me their
friend, all the pledges which make human compacts
binding, in order that you may speak confidently to
your fellow citizens, in case there are some who regard
the name of king as suspicious and suggestive of
deceitfulness in making compacts and, in view of the
violations of oaths and treaties of which certain others
have been thought guilty, assume the same with
regard to me. And when peace has been brought
about, come with me to be my adviser in all matters
and my lieutenant in war and to share in all the royal
good fortune. For I need a good man and a loyal
friend, while you need royal largess and kingly
emprises. If, then, we combine these needs and
abilities for our mutual advantage, we shall receive
the greatest benefits from each other."

XV. (18, 11) When he had finished, Fabricius, after
pausing a short time, said :

" As regards any merit of mine, either in public

---

⁹ Hertlein : ἑαυτοῦ O.   ¹⁰ Ursinus : λέγεις O.
¹¹ εἰ δή Steph.² : εἴδη O, εἰ δέ Ursinus.
¹² Sylburg : τεκμαιρόμενος O.

367

κατὰ τὰς κοινὰς πράξεις ἢ κατὰ τὸν ἴδιον βίον
οὐδὲν ἐμὲ δεῖ ἐπ' ἐμαυτοῦ λέγειν, ἐπειδὴ πέπυσαι
παρ' ἑτέρων· οὐδέ γε περὶ τῆς πενίας, ὅτι μοι
γῄδιον μικρόν ἐστι κομιδῇ καὶ φαῦλον οἰκίδιον
καὶ οὔτ' ἀπὸ δανεισμάτων οὔτ' ἀπ' ἀνδραπόδων
ὁ βίος· φαίη γὰρ καὶ τούτων[1] ἀκριβῶς ἀκηκοέναι
2 παρ' ἑτέρων. (12) περὶ δὲ τοῦ κάκιόν με 'Ρωμαίων
τινὸς πράττειν[2] δι' ἀπορίαν καὶ μηδὲν εἶναί μοι
πλέον ἀσκοῦντι καλοκαγαθίαν ὅτι τῶν πλουσίων
οὐκ εἰμί, κακῶς ὑπείληφας, εἴτ' ἀκούσας τινὸς
εἴτ' αὐτὸς εἰκάζων. ἐμοὶ γὰρ οὐδεμία πώποτε
κακοδαιμονίας αἴσθησις παρὰ τὸ[3] μὴ πολλὰ κε-
κτῆσθαι γέγονεν οὐδ' ἔστιν, οὐδ' ὠδυράμην τὴν
ἐμαυτοῦ τύχην οὔτ' ἐν τοῖς κοινοῖς πράγμασιν οὔτ'
3 ἐν τοῖς ἰδίοις. (13) τί γὰρ καὶ παθὼν ἐγκαλοίην
ἂν αὐτῇ; πότερον ὅτι μοι τῶν καλῶν καὶ περι-
μαχήτων ἐφ' οἷς ἅπασα φύσις ἐσπούδακεν εὐγενὴς
οὐδενὸς ἐξεγένετο παρὰ τῆς πατρίδος μεταλαβεῖν
διὰ πενίαν; ὃς ἄρχω τε τὰς[4] μεγίστας ἀρχὰς καὶ[5]
πρεσβεύω τὰς ἐπιφανεστάτας πρεσβείας καὶ σεβασμοὺς[6] ἱερῶν πιστεύομαι τοὺς ἁγιωτάτους καὶ
γνώμην ἀγορεύειν ἀξιούμενος περὶ τῶν ἀναγκαιοτάτων καλοῦμαι ἐν ᾧ προσήκει με τόπῳ, ἐπ-
αινοῦμαί τε καὶ ζηλοῦμαι καὶ οὐδενὸς δεύτερός εἰμι
τῶν μέγιστα δυναμένων καὶ παράδειγμα τοῖς
ἄλλοις εἶναι δοκῶ καλοκαγαθίας, οὐδὲν ἐκ τῆς
ἐμῆς οὐσίας εἰς ταῦτα δαπανῶν, ὥσπερ οὐδὲ τῶν
4 ἄλλων οὐδείς. (14) οὐ γὰρ ἐνοχλεῖ τοῖς ἑκάστου

---

[1] περὶ τούτων Sylburg.   [2] πράττει O.
[3] Sylburg : τῷ O.   [4] τὰς Ursinus : καὶ O.
[5] καὶ Ursinus : om. O.
[6] Sylburg : σεβασμίους O.

affairs or in private life, there is no need for me to speak for myself, since you have learned of it from others ; nor, indeed, with regard to my slender means need I state that I have a very small farm and a sorry little house and that I do not get my livelihood from either loans or slaves, since you appear to have heard an accurate report of these matters also from others. (12) But as to my being worse off than any other of the Romans on account of my lack of means, or my failing to gain any advantage from practising uprightness because I am not one of the rich, your supposition is false, whether you have heard it from someone else or surmise it yourself. For I never have been nor am I now conscious of any misfortune because I have not acquired great possessions, nor have I bewailed my lot either in public affairs or in my private concerns. (13) Why in the world should I complain of it ? Because it has not been possible for me by reason of poverty to get from my country a share in any of the fine and enviable things for which every noble nature strives ? But I hold the highest magistracies, am sent on the most distinguished embassies, am entrusted with the most sacred rites in connexion with sacrifices, am thought worthy to express my opinion upon the most urgent matters and am called upon in my proper turn, am praised and envied, am second to none of the most powerful, and am regarded as a model of uprightness for the rest, though spending nothing of my substance for these honours, even as no one else does. (14) For the Roman commonwealth does not

βίοις ἡ πόλις ἡ Ῥωμαίων ὥσπερ τινὲς ἕτεραι, ἐν
αἷς ὁ κοινὸς μὲν πλοῦτος ὀλίγος ἐστίν, ὁ δὲ τῶν
ἰδιωτῶν πολύς, ἀλλ᾽ αὐτὴ παρέχει τοῖς πρὸς τὰ
κοινὰ προσιοῦσιν ἅπαντα ὅσων δέονται,[1] λαμπρὰς
καὶ μεγαλοπρεπεῖς ὑποτιθεῖσα χορηγίας· ὥστε
μηδὲν ἀτιμότερον εἶναι τὸν πενέστατον τοῦ πλου-
σιωτάτου κατὰ τὴν ἐπαξίωσιν[2] τῶν καλῶν, ἀλλὰ
πάντας εἶναι Ῥωμαίους, ὅσοι ἂν ὦσι διὰ καλοκαγαθίαν τούτων ἄξιοι τῶν τιμῶν, ἀλλήλοις[3] ἴσους.
5 ὁπότε δὲ πενόμενος οὐδὲν παρὰ τοῦτ᾽ ἔλαττον
ἔχω τῶν πολλὰ κεκτημένων, τί παθὼν ἂν κατ-
ηγόρησα[4] τῆς τύχης, ὅτι οὐχ ὑμῖν ἐξίσωσε[5] τοῖς
βασιλεῦσιν, οἷς ὁ πολὺς θησαυρίζεται χρυσός;
ἀλλὰ μὴν ἔν γε τοῖς ἰδίοις τοσοῦτον ἀπέχω κακοδαιμονίας ὥστ᾽ ἐν ὀλίγοις πάνυ τῶν μακαρίων
ἐμαυτὸν[6] εἶναι δοκῶ παρὰ τοὺς πλουσίους ἐξετάζων,
καὶ ἐπὶ τούτῳ[7] μέγιστον φρονῶ· (15) ἐπειδὴ τὰ
μὲν ἀναγκαῖα τὸ λυπρὸν ἀπόχρη μοι γῄδιον φιλ-
6 εργοῦντι καὶ ταμιευομένῳ παρέχειν,[8] τὰ δ᾽ ἔξω τῶν
ἀναγκαίων οὐ βιάζεται ζητεῖν ἡ φύσις, ἀλλὰ καὶ
τροφὴ πᾶσα ἡδεῖά μοι ἦν ἂν ὁ λιμὸς σκευάσῃ,[9]
καὶ ποτὸν ἅπαν γλυκὺ ὅταν[10] ἡ δίψα πορίσῃ, καὶ
ὕπνος μαλθακὸς ὅταν ἡγήσηται κόπος, ἐσθής τε
ἡ παρέχουσα[11] μὴ ῥιγοῦν αὐταρκεστάτη, καὶ σκεῦος
ὅ τι ἂν εὐτελέστατον τῶν δυναμένων τὰς αὐτὰς

---

[1] δέωνται X ; ὅσων ἂν δέωνται Kiessling.
[2] ἐπαξίωσιν MP : ἀπαξίωσιν EV.
[3] Ursinus : ἀλλήλους O.
[4] Kiessling : κατηγόρηκα O.
[5] ὑμῖν ἐξίσωσε (or οὐκ ἴσον ὑμῖν ἐποίησε) Sylburg : οὐχ ὑμῖν
ἐποίησε O ; Reiske added ἐμὲ as well as ἴσον. De Boor proposed ὑμῖν οὐχ ὅμοιον ἐποίησε, Jacoby οὐχ ὑμῖν ὅμοιον ἐμὲ
ἐποίησε.

370

interfere with the individual citizen's means of livelihood, as do some other states in which the public
wealth is small and that of the private citizens great ;
but she herself provides those who go into public life
with everything they need, giving them splendid and
magnificent allowances, with the result that the
poorest man enjoys no less esteem than the richest
when it is a question of awarding honours, but all
the Romans who are worthy of these honours by
virtue of their uprightness are on an equal footing
with one another. When, now, though poor, I am at
no disadvantage on that account in comparison with
those who possess much, why in the world should I
have denounced Fortune because she did not make
me equal to you kings who have much gold treasured
up ? Nay, even in my private affairs I am so far
removed from misfortune that I consider myself to
be one of a favoured few of the blest, when I compare
myself with the rich, and in this I take the greatest
pride. (15) For my sorry little farm suffices to
furnish me with the necessaries of life if I am
industrious and frugal, and Nature does not compel
me to seek more than is necessary ; on the contrary,
all food is pleasing to me which hunger prepares,
every drink is sweet when thirst provides it, sleep is
gentle when induced by fatigue, the clothing which
keeps one from shivering is most adequate, and the
cheapest utensil of all that can serve the same pur-

---

⁶ ἐμαυτὸν om. V.   ⁷ Ursinus : τοῦτο O.
⁸ Ursinus : παρέχει O.   ⁹ Sylburg : σκεδάσῃ O.
¹⁰ ὅτι ἂν Kiessling.   ¹¹ Sylburg : παράσχουσα O.

371

7 παρέχειν χρείας οἰκειότατον. ὥστ' οὐδὲ κατὰ
τοῦτο δίκαιος ἂν εἴην[1] τῆς τύχης κατηγορεῖν, ἥ
μοι τοσαύτην παρέσχεν οὐσίαν ὅσην ἡ φύσις
ἐβούλετο ἔχειν[2]· τῶν δ' ὑπερβαλλόντων οὔτε πόθον
ἐνέφυσεν οὔτ' εὐπορίαν ἔδωκεν. Ursin.

XVI. (18, 16) " Νὴ Δί', ἀλλ' οὐ περίεστί μοι
τοῖς πλησίον[3] ἐπαρκεῖν, οὐδ' ἐκ περιουσίας ἐπιστήμην ἔδωκέ μοι ὁ[4] θεὸς ἔχειν οὐδὲ μαντικήν, αἷς
ὠφέλουν ἂν[5] τοὺς δεομένους, οὐδ' ἄλλα πολλά·
ἃ δ'[6] ἐστὶν ἐν ἐμοί, τούτων μεταδιδοὺς καὶ πόλει
καὶ φίλοις, καὶ ἀφ' ὧν δύναμαι ποιεῖν εὖ τινας,
ταῦτα[7] κοινὰ τοῖς δεομένοις παρέχων, οὐκ ἂν ἡγη-
σαίμην ἄπορον[8] ἐμαυτόν. ταῦτα δ' ἐστὶν ἃ σὺ
κράτιστα νομίζεις εἶναι καὶ πολλῶν χρημάτων
2 ἄπορος εἶ[9] πρίασθαι. (17) εἰ δὲ δὴ καὶ τὰ μάλιστα
διὰ τὰς εὐεργεσίας τῶν δεομένων τὸ πολλὰ κε-
κτῆσθαι χρήματα[10] μεγάλης ἦν σπουδῆς καὶ φιλοτιμίας ἄξιον καὶ μακαριωτάτους ὑπῆρχεν εἶναι
τοὺς πλουσιωτάτους, ὡς τοῖς βασιλεῦσιν ὑμῖν δοκεῖ, πότερος ἦν μοι τρόπος εὐπορίας κρείττων;
ἀφ' ὧν σύ μοι νῦν μεταδίδως αἰσχρῶς ἢ ἀφ' ὧν
3 ἂν[11] αὐτὸς ἐκτησάμην καλῶς[12] πρότερον; παρέσχε
γάρ μοι τὰ πολιτικὰ πράγματα χρηματισμῶν
ἀφορμὰς δικαίας, πολλάκις μὲν καὶ πρότερον, μά-

---

[1] ἂν εἴην Krüger, εἴην Reiske, εἴην ἂν Jacoby : εἶναι O; δίκαιος δοκῶ εἶναι Cohn, οὐδ' ἂν κατὰ τοῦτο δίκαιος εἴην Hertlein.
[2] Capps would add μ' before ἔχειν.
[3] τοῖς πλησίον Sylburg : τοὺς πλησίους MP, τοὺς πλουσίους
V, τοῖς πλουσίοις Ursinus.   [4] ὁ V : om. Z.
[5] ἂν added by Ursinus.   [6] δ' added by Sylburg.
[7] τὰ after ταῦτα deleted by Sylburg.
[8] ἄπορον (cf. chap. 14, 1) Cary, Post : αἴτιον (not αἴστον, as
strangely reported by Jacoby) O, Jacoby, ἐπαίτιον Sylburg,
ἄθλιον Cobet.

poses is the most suitable. Hence not even on this score should I be justified in denouncing Fortune, since she has given me as much substance as Nature wished me to have ; as for things in excess of that, she has neither implanted in me any craving for them nor given me any store of them.

XVI. (18, 16) " Very true, indeed ; but I have nothing left over with which to assist my neighbours, nor has God given it to me to possess an over-supply of knowledge and divination with which I might help those who need them,—to say nothing of many other things. Yet so long as I share with both the common-wealth and my friends what faculties I do possess and place at the disposal of those who need them the resources with which I can benefit a few, I should not consider myself lacking in means. And these are the very things which you believe to be the most important, and yet lack the means to purchase even for large sums of money. (17) But even if it were ever so true that for the sake of doing kindly ser-vices to those in need the acquisition of great wealth merits great zeal and ambition, and if the richest men were the most happy, as you kings think, which kind of affluence would be better for me ? An affluence of the riches of which you are now offering me a share dishonourably, or of the wealth which I myself might earlier have acquired honourably ? For my public career has afforded me proper opportunities for making money, both earlier on many occasions

---

⁹ ἄπορος εἶ Post : αἴτιος εἶ O, αἴτιος εἶ Ursinus, ἕτοιμος εἶ Sylburg, αἰτεῖς Kiessling, ἀξιοῖς Cobet.
¹⁰ χρήματα Ursinus : πράγματα O.
¹¹ ἂν added by Post.
¹² Ursinus : καλῶν O.

λιστα δ' ὅτ'[1] ἐπὶ Σαυνίτας καὶ Λευκανοὺς καὶ[2]
Βρεττίους στρατιὰν ἄγων ἐστάλην[3] τετάρτῳ πρότερον ἐνιαυτῷ τὴν ὕπατον ἀρχὴν ἔχων, καὶ
πολλὴν μὲν χώραν ἐλεηλάτησα, πολλαῖς δὲ μάχαις
τοὺς ἀντιταξαμένους ἐνίκησα, πολλὰς δὲ καὶ
εὐδαίμονας πόλεις κατὰ κράτος ἑλὼν[4] ἐξεπόρθησα,
ἐξ ὧν τὴν στρατιὰν ἅπασαν ἐπλούτισα, καὶ τὰς
εἰσφορὰς τοῖς ἰδιώταις ἃς εἰς τὸν πόλεμον προεισ-
ήνεγκαν[5] ἀπέδωκα, καὶ τετρακόσια τάλαντα μετὰ
4 τὸν θρίαμβον[6] εἰς τὸ ταμιεῖον εἰσήνεγκα. (18) ἔπειτ' ἐκείνων τῶν δορικτήτων ἐξόν μοι λαβεῖν ὁπόσα βουλοίμην[7] οὐ λαβών, ἀλλὰ καὶ τὸν[8] ἐκ τοῦ
δικαίου πλοῦτον ὑπεριδὼν ἕνεκα δόξης, ὡς Οὐαλέριος Ποπλικόλας ἐποίησε καὶ ἄλλοι πλεῖστοι
πρὸς τούτοις[9] συχνοί,[10] δι' οὓς ἡ πόλις ἡμῶν τηλι-
καύτη γέγονε, τὰς παρὰ σοῦ δέξομαι δωρεὰς
καὶ ἀντὶ τῆς κρείττονος εὐπορίας ἀλλάξομαι τὴν
χείρονα; ἐκείνη μέν γε τῇ κτήσει καὶ τὸ μεθ'
ἡδονῆς ποιεῖσθαι τὰς ἀπολαύσεις πρὸς τῷ[11] καλῶς
καὶ δικαίως προσῆν,[12] ταύτης δὲ καὶ τοῦτ' ἄπεστι·
δανείσματα γάρ ἐστιν ὅσα προλαμβάνουσιν[13] ἄνθρωποι παρ' ἑτέρων, βαρύνοντα[14] τὴν ψυχὴν ἕως
ἂν ἀποδοθῇ, κἂν ὀνόμασι καλοῖς αὐτὰ κοσμήσῃ
τις, φιλανθρωπίας καλῶν καὶ δωρεὰς ἢ χάριτας.

[1] ὅτ' added by Post, ἐπεὶ by Kiessling.
[2] καὶ added by Ursinus.
[3] Ursinus : ἐστάλη O.
[4] Sylburg : ἐξελὼν O.
[5] Reiske : προσήνεγκαν O.
[6] τὸν θρίαμβον Portus : τῶν θριάμβων O.
[7] βουλοίμην Z : βουλόμην V, ἐβουλόμην Kiessling, ἂν ἐβουλόμην Jacoby.
[8] καὶ τὸν P : καὶ τῶν BEV, καίτοι M.
[9] τούτοις O : τούτῳ Sylburg, Jacoby. As Sylburg noted,

and especially when, three years ago [1] while I was
holding the office of consul, I was sent at the head
of an army against the Samnites, Lucanians and
Bruttians and ravaged a vast territory, defeated in
many battles those who arrayed themselves against
me, and took by storm and plundered many prosperous cities, from which I enriched my entire army,
gave back to the private citizens the special taxes
which they had paid in advance for the prosecution
of the war, and turned into the treasury four hundred
talents after celebrating my triumph. (18) If, then,
when it was possible for me to take as many of those
prizes won by the spear as I could wish, I took none,
but for the sake of a good reputation scorned even
the riches gained in an honest manner, just as did
Valerius Publicola and very many others besides,
men through whom our commonwealth has become so
great, shall I accept the gifts you offer and exchange
the better affluence for the worse ? My kind of
acquisition had the advantage that it could also be
enjoyed with pleasure, in addition to being gained
honourably and justly ; but your kind lacks even this
advantage. For whatever things men receive from
others in advance are loans that oppress the spirit
until they are repaid, even though one dress them
up with honourable names styling them gratuities,

1 See the note on chap. 13, 1.

however, the excerptor may have omitted the names of some
others.
10 Either συχνοί or πλεῖστοι should be deleted, as Sylburg
saw.
11 Sylburg : τὸ O.
12 προσῆν Steph.² : πόσος ἦν EV, ποσὸς ἦν BM, ποσὸν ἦν P.
13 Naber : προσλαμβάνουσιν O.
14 Sylburg : βαρύνοντες O.

5 (19) φέρε, ἐὰν δὴ[1] μανεὶς δέξωμαι χρυσὸν ὃν δίδως μοι καὶ τοῦθ' ἅπασι Ῥωμαίοις γένηται φανερόν, ἔπειθ' οἱ τὴν ἀνυπεύθυνον ἔχοντες ἀρχὴν οὓς ἡμεῖς τιμητὰς καλοῦμεν, οἷς ἀποδέδοται τοὺς ἁπάντων Ῥωμαίων ἐξετάζειν βίους καὶ τοὺς ἐκβαίνοντας ἐκ τῶν πατρίων ἐθῶν ζημιοῦν, καλέσαντές με λόγον ἀποδοῦναι κελεύσωσι τῆς δωροδοκίας, ἁπάντων παρόντων ταῦτα προφερόμενοι.[2]   Ursin.; (p. 376, ll. 3-6) Ambr.

XVII. (18, 20) " ' Ἐπέμψαμέν σε, ὦ Φαβρίκιε, πρεσβευτὴν σὺν ἑτέροις δυσὶν ὑπατικοῖς ἀνδράσι πρὸς βασιλέα Πύρρον ὑπὲρ αἰχμαλώτων λύσεως διαλεξόμενον· ἥκεις ἀπὸ τῆς πρεσβείας τοὺς μὲν αἰχμαλώτους οὐκ ἄγων οὐδὲ ἄλλο τῇ πόλει φέρων ἀγαθὸν οὐθέν, αὐτὸς δὲ βασιλικὰς δωρεὰς εἰληφὼς μόνος τῶν συναποσταλέντων σοι πρέσβεων, καὶ ἣν[3] ὁ δῆμος ἀπεψηφίσατο ποιήσασθαι εἰρήνην, ταύτην ποιήσας[4] μόνος, ἐπ' οὐθενὶ τῆς πόλεως

2 ἀγαθῷ—πόθεν γάρ;—ἀλλ' ἵνα προδῷς αὐτὴν τῷ βασιλεῖ, καὶ διὰ σοῦ μὲν ἐκεῖνος ἅπασαν Ἰταλίαν ὑφ' αὑτῷ ποιήσηται, δι' ἐκείνου δὲ σὺ τῆς πατρίδος ἀφέλῃ τὴν ἐλευθερίαν.   τοῦτο γάρ ἐστιν ὃ διώκουσιν ἅπαντες οἱ μὴ τὴν ἀληθινὴν ἀλλὰ τὴν προσποιητὸν ἐπιτηδεύσαντες ἀρετήν, ὅταν εἰς ὄγ-

3 κον καὶ μέγεθος πραγμάτων προέλθωσιν.   (21) εἰ δὲ δὴ μὴ τὸ πρεσβευτικὸν[5] ἔχων ἀξίωμα μηδὲ παρὰ τῶν πολεμίων τῆς πατρίδος μηδ' ἐπὶ προδοσίᾳ καὶ τυραννίδι τῶν σεαυτοῦ πολιτῶν ἐδωροδόκεις, ἀλλ' ἰδιώτης ὢν καὶ παρ' ἀνδρὸς συμμάχου

---

[1] ἐὰν δὴ V : ἐὰν δὲ EX, δὲ ἐὰν de Boor.
[2] ταῦτα προφερόμενοι QA (Ambr.) : om. O (Urs.).
[3] ἣν Q.   [4] εἰρήνην ταύτην ποιήσας added by Struve.

gifts or favours. (19) Come now, suppose I should indeed be mad enough to accept the gold you offer me and this should become known to all the Romans, and then those magistrates who are subject to no accounting for their administration, the officials we call censors, whose duty it is to examine into the lives of all the Romans and to punish those who depart from the ancestral customs, should summon me and order me to render an account of my acceptance of bribes, bringing these charges against me in the presence of everybody :

XVII. (18, 20) " ' We sent you, Fabricius, as ambassador along with two other men of consular rank to King Pyrrhus to treat for the ransoming of prisoners. You have come back from your mission bringing neither the prisoners nor any other advantage for the commonwealth ; instead, you, alone of the ambassadors sent with you, accepted royal gifts, and the peace which the people voted against making, you made by yourself alone, not for any advantage to the commonwealth—for how could it be that ?—but that you might betray her to the king, and that through you he might bring all Italy into subjection to himself and that through him you might deprive the fatherland of its liberty. For this is the purpose which all pursue who practise, not genuine, but feigned virtue, when they attain to grandeur and importance in affairs. (21) But even if it were not while enjoying the prestige of an ambassador that you accepted a bribe, and if you were not taking it from the enemies of your country, nor for the purpose of betraying and tyrannizing over your fellow citizens, but were receiving it as a private

---

⁵ Struve : πρεσβύτερον Q, Jacoby.

καὶ ἐπ' οὐδενὶ κακῷ τῆς πόλεως, ἆρ' οὐ δι' ἐκεῖνα
τῆς μεγάλης[1] ἄξιος εἶ ζημίας, ὅτι διαφθείρεις μὲν
τοὺς νέους πλούτου καὶ τρυφῆς καὶ πολυτελείας
βασιλικῆς ζῆλον εἰς τοὺς βίους εἰσάγων, οἷς
πολλῆς δεῖ σωφροσύνης εἰ μέλλει σωθήσεσθαι τὰ
4 κοινά· καταισχύνεις δὲ τοὺς σεαυτοῦ προγόνους,
ὧν οὐθεὶς ἐξέβη τοὺς πατρίους ἐθισμοὺς οὐδ' ἠλλά-
ξατο πλοῦτον αἰσχρὸν ἀντὶ πενίας καλῆς, ἀλλ'
ἅπαντες ἐπ' αὐτῆς ἔμειναν τῆς μικρᾶς οὐσίας ἣν
σὺ παραλαβὼν ἐλάττονα ἢ κατὰ σεαυτὸν ἡγήσω·
5 (22) διαφθείρεις δὲ τὴν ἐκ τῶν προτέρων ἐπιτηδευμάτων γενομένην σοι δόξαν, ὡς ἐγκρατὴς καὶ
σώφρων καὶ πάσης αἰσχρᾶς ἐπιθυμίας κρείττων;
ἔπειτα χαιρήσεις κακὸς ἐξ ἀγαθοῦ γενόμενος, ὅτ'
ἔδει σε, καὶ εἰ πρότερον πονηρὸς ἦσθα, πεπαῦσθαι
ἢ τῶν καλῶν τινος ἔτι μεθέξεις τῶν ὀφειλομένων
τοῖς ἀγαθοῖς, ἀλλ' οὐκ ἄπει μάλιστα μὲν ἐκ τῆς
πόλεως, εἰ δὲ μή γ', ἐκ τῆς ἀγορᾶς;' Ambr.

XVIII. " Ἂν ταῦτα λέγοντες ἐκγράψωσί με
τῆς βουλῆς καὶ μεταγάγωσιν[2] εἰς τὰς τῶν ἀτίμων
φυλάς, τί πρὸς αὐτοὺς ἔξω λέγειν δίκαιον ἢ ποιεῖν;
τίνα τὸν μετὰ ταῦτα βίον ζήσομαι τηλικαύτῃ περι-
πεσὼν ἀτιμίᾳ καὶ τοὺς ἐξ ἐμαυτοῦ πάντας
2 περιβαλών;[3] (23) σοὶ δὲ αὐτῷ τί χρήσιμος[4] ἔτι
φανήσομαι τὸ δύνασθαί τι καὶ τιμᾶσθαι παρὰ τοῖς
πολίταις ἀποβαλών, δι' ἃ νῦν ἐσπούδακας περὶ
ἐμοῦ; λείπεται δὴ τὸν οὐδεμίαν ἔτι χώραν ἐν τῇ

---

[1] Either τῆς should be deleted (Jacoby) or μεγίστης read
for μεγάλης (Struve).   [2] Kiessling : μετάγωσιν Q.
[3] περιβαλών Q : περιλαβών or συμπεριλαβών Struve.
[4] Struve : χρήσιμον Q.

citizen and from an ally and with no detriment to the commonwealth, are you not deserving of the greatest punishment, for the following reasons ? First, you are corrupting the youth by introducing into their lives an emulous desire for regal wealth, luxury and extravagance, whereas they need great self-restraint if the state is to be preserved. Again, you are bringing shame upon your ancestors, none of whom departed from the ancestral customs nor chose shameful riches in place of honourable poverty, but without exception remained on the same little estate that you, after inheriting it, regarded as beneath your station. (22) Furthermore, you are destroying the reputation, which you gained from your earlier practices, as a man of self-restraint and moderation, superior to all shameful desires. After this, shall you go unpunished for having become a bad man after having once been a good one, when you ought, even if you were base before, to have ceased to be so ? Or shall you continue to share in any of the blessings which are the due of the good, instead of quitting the city—the better course—or at any rate the Forum ? '

XVIII. " If with these words of censure they expunge my name from the senate-roll and reduce me to the ranks of the disfranchised, what just answer shall I be able to make to them, or what just action take ? What manner of life shall I live thereafter, when I have fallen into such disgrace and involved all my descendants ? (23) And to you yourself how shall I longer appear useful when I have lost all influence and honour among my fellow citizens, the grounds for your present enthusiasm for me ? The only course, then, that is left for one who can no longer keep a place for himself in his own country

πατρίδι κατέχειν δυνάμενον ἀπιέναι πανοικεσίᾳ,
3 τὰς ἀσχήμονας αὐτοῦ[1] καταγνόντα φυγάς. ἔπειτα
ποῦ τὸν λοιπὸν ἔσομαι χρόνον; ἢ τίς ὑποδέξεταί
με τόπος ἀπαρρησίαστον γενόμενον, ὥσπερ εἰκός;
ἡ σὴ βασιλεία, νὴ Δία, καὶ παρέξεις μοι σὺ τὴν
τυραννικὴν ἅπασαν εὐδαιμονίαν; καὶ τί μοι
τηλικοῦτο δώσεις ἀγαθὸν ὅσον ἀφελεῖ τὸ πάντων
τιμιώτατον κτημάτων ἀφελόμενος, τὴν ἐλευθερίαν;
4 (24) πῶς δ᾽ ἂν ὑπομεῖναι δυναίμην ἐγὼ τοῦ βίου
μεταβολὴν ὀψὲ δουλεύειν διδασκόμενος; ὅπου
γὰρ οἱ γεννηθέντες ἐν βασιλείαις καὶ τυραννίσιν,
ὅταν εὐγενῶς[2] ἔχωσι, τῆς ἐλευθερίας γλίχονται
καὶ πάνθ᾽ ἡγοῦνται τἀγαθὰ ταύτης ἐλάττω, ἦ που
οἱ ἐν ἐλευθέρᾳ καὶ ἑτέρων ἄρχειν μαθούσῃ πόλει
βιώσαντες πρᾴως οἴσουσι τὴν ἐκ τῶν κρειττόνων
ἐπὶ τὰ χείρω μεταβολήν, ἐξ ἐλευθέρων ὑπομεί-
ναντες δοῦλοι γενέσθαι, ἵνα λαμπρὰς παρατιθῶνται
καθ᾽ ἡμέραν τραπέζας καὶ πολλοὺς θεράποντας
περιάγωνται καὶ γυναικῶν καὶ παίδων εὐπρεπῶν[3]
ἀφειδεῖς ἀπολαύσεις λαμβάνωσιν, ὥσπερ ἐν τούτοις
τῆς ἀνθρωπίνης εὐδαιμονίας κειμένης ἀλλ᾽ οὐκ
5 ἐν ἀρετῇ; (25) αὐτῶν δὲ τούτων, ἵνα συγχωρήσῃ
τις αὐτὰ πολλῆς εἶναι σπουδῆς ἄξια, τίς γένοιτ᾽
ἂν ἱλαρὰ χρῆσις οὐκ ἔχουσα τὸ βέβαιον; ἐφ᾽[4]
ὑμῖν γάρ ἐστι[5] τοῖς παρέχουσι τὰς ἡδονὰς ταύτας,
ὅταν αὐτοὶ θέλητε, πάλιν αὐτὰς ἀφαιρεῖσθαι. ἐῶ
γὰρ λέγειν τοὺς φθόνους, τὰς διαβολάς, τὸ μηδένα
χρόνον ἄνευ κινδύνου καὶ φόβου ζῆν, τἆλλα πολλὰ[6]
ὅσα φέρει χαλεπὰ καὶ οὐκ ἄξια γενναίου φρονή-

[1] Struve : αὐτοῦ Q.
[2] Struve : εὐγενὲς Q, τὸ εὐγενὲς Kiessling.
[3] ἐκπρεπῶν Naber.   [4] Struve : ὑφ᾽ Q.

is to depart with his entire household, condemning
himself to shameful exile. After that where shall I
spend the rest of my life ? Or what place will receive
me when I have lost, as I probably shall, my freedom
of speech ? Your realm, forsooth ! And you will
provide me with all the felicity a tyrant enjoys ?
Yet what boon will you give me as great as the one
you will be taking from me when you take away that
most precious of all possessions, liberty ? (24) And
how could I endure the change in my life, learning
late to be a slave ? For when those born in countries
ruled by kings and tyrants, if they are of noble spirit,
crave liberty and consider all other blessings inferior
to it, will those, I wonder, who have lived in a state
which is free and has learned to rule over others bear
with equanimity the change from better conditions to
worse, consenting to become slaves instead of free
men, in order to set splendid tables every day, to be
attended everywhere by a multitude of slaves, and to
have unstinted enjoyment of handsome women and
boys, as if human happiness depended upon these
things rather than upon virtue ? (25) Yet as for
these very things, granted that they are well worth
striving for, what joy would their use bring when it
has no assured permanence ? For it lies in the power
of you rulers who provide these pleasures to take them
away again when you yourselves wish. I say naught
of the envyings, the slanderings, the fact that not for a
moment does one live without danger and fear, and
all the other experiences, distressing and unworthy
of a noble spirit, which life at the courts of kings

---

⁵ ἔστι Mai : ἔτι Q.   ⁶ πολλὰ Struve : ὅλα Q, om. A.

6 ματος ὁ παρὰ τοῖς βασιλεῦσι βίος. μὴ τοσαύτη
μανία κατάσχοι Φαβρίκιον ὥστε τὴν περιβόητον
καταλιπόντα ῾Ρώμην τὸν ἐν Ἠπείρῳ προελέσθαι
βίον, καὶ ἐξὸν ἡγεμόνος ἡγεῖσθαι πόλεως ὑφ᾿ ἑνὸς
ἀνδρὸς ἄρχεσθαι μηθὲν ἴσον τοῖς ἄλλοις φρονοῦντος
καὶ τὰ πρὸς ἡδονὴν ἀκούειν παρὰ πάντων ἐθισ-
7 θέντος. (26) ἀλλάξαι μέν γε τὸ φρόνημα καὶ
ταπεινὸν ἐμαυτὸν[1] ποιῆσαι βουλόμενος, ἵνα μηδὲν
ὑποπτεύσῃς ἐξ ἐμοῦ κακόν, οὐκ ἂν δυναίμην·
διαμένων δὲ τοιοῦτος οἷον ἡ φύσις καὶ τὰ ἔθη
πεποίηκέ με, βαρὺς φανήσομαί σοι καὶ περισπᾶν
δόξω τὴν ἡγεμονίαν εἰς ἐμαυτόν. τὸ δ᾿ ὅλον ἔχω
σοι παραινεῖν μὴ ὅτι Φαβρίκιον, ἀλλὰ μηδ᾿ ἄλλον
μηδένα δέχεσθαι τῇ βασιλείᾳ μήτε κρείττονα μήτε
ἴσον σεαυτῷ,[2] μηδὲ ὅλως ἄνδρα ἐν ἐλευθέροις
ἤθεσι τραφέντα καὶ φρόνημα μεῖζον ἢ κατ᾿ ἰδιώτην
8 ἔχοντα. οὔτε γὰρ ἀσφαλὴς βασιλεῖ σύνοικος ἀνὴρ
μεγαλόφρων οὔτε ἡδύς. ἀλλὰ περὶ μὲν τῶν ἰδίων
συμφερόντων, ἅ σοι πρακτέον ἐστίν, αὐτὸς δια-
γνώσῃ, περὶ δὲ τῶν αἰχμαλώτων ἐπιεικές τι
βουλευσάμενος ἄφες ἡμᾶς ἀπιέναι.''

(27) ῾Ως δὲ ἐπαύσατο λέγων, ἀγασθεὶς αὐτοῦ τὴν
εὐγένειαν τῆς ψυχῆς ὁ βασιλεὺς τῆς δεξιᾶς λαμ-
βάνεται καί φησιν· '' Οὐκέτι θαυμάζειν ἐπέρχεταί
μοι διὰ τί περιβόητος ἡ πόλις ὑμῶν ἐστι καὶ
τοσοῦτον ἡγεμονίας περιβέβληται μέγεθος, τοιούτων ἀνδρῶν οὖσα τροφός· καὶ μάλιστα μὲν οὖν
ἐβουλόμην ἂν ἐξ ἀρχῆς μηδεμίαν συμβῆναί μοι
πρὸς ὑμᾶς διαφοράν, ἐπεὶ δὲ συνέβη, καὶ θεῶν τις
ἐβούλετο πειραθέντας ἡμᾶς τῆς ἀλλήλων δυνάμεως
καὶ ἀρετῆς τότε συναγαγεῖν, ἕτοιμός εἰμι δια-

---

[1] Kiessling : ἑαυτὸν Q.   [2] Struve : σεαυτοῦ Q.

brings with it. Let no such madness seize Fabricius that he should leave the renowned city of Rome and prefer life in Epirus, or that, when it is in his power to be leader of a state that holds the leadership, he should be ruled by one man whose thoughts are in no wise those of the other citizens and who is accustomed to hear from everybody what is calculated to please him. (26) At any rate, though I might wish to change my spirit and make myself humble, in order that you might scent no danger from me, I could not do so ; on the other hand, if I remain what Nature and my habits have made me, I shall appear offensive in your eyes and shall seem to be diverting control to my own hands. In fine, I can advise you against receiving into your realm, not Fabricius only, but also anyone else who is either your superior or your equal, or, in general, any man who has been reared in liberal ways and possesses a spirit above that of a private person. For a man of lofty spirit is neither a safe companion for a king nor an agreeable one. Well then, as regards your private interests, you yourself will determine what you must do ; as for the prisoners, come to some reasonable decision and permit us to depart."

(27) When he stopped speaking, the king, admiring his nobility of soul, took him by the hand and said : " It no longer enters my mind to wonder why your city is renowned and has encompassed so vast a dominion, since she is nurse of such men ; and above all things I could have wished that no dispute should have arisen in the first place between me and you Romans ; but since it has arisen and it was the will of some god that only after we had made trial of one another's might and valour would he bring us together, I am ready to be reconciled. And in order

λύεσθαι, καὶ ἵνα πρῶτος ἄρξω τῶν φιλανθρώπων ἐφ' ἃ παρακαλεῖτέ με, χαρίζομαι τῇ πόλει τοὺς αἰχμαλώτους ἅπαντας ἄνευ λύτρων." *Ambr.*

Λιβύην χειρωσάμενος μέχρι καὶ τῶν προσωκεανίων ἐθνῶν. *Steph. Byz. s.v.* Ὠκεανός.

———

Κωστάντεια . . . ἔστι καὶ Βρεττίας ἄλλη, ὡς Διονύσιος ἐννεακαιδεκάτῳ Ῥωμαϊκῆς ἀρχαιολογίας.[1] *Steph. Byz.*

[1] Two entries have evidently been run together here, with the loss of the lemma to the second. Meineke suggested Κωσεντία, πόλις τῆς Βρεττίας in place of ἔστι καὶ Βρεττίας ἄλλη.

that I may be the first to make the friendly overtures to which you invite me, I give up as a favour to your commonwealth all the prisoners without ransom."

Having subdued Libya even as far as the tribes living by the Ocean.

———————

Constantia [1] . . . there is also another in Bruttium. Dionysius, *Roman Antiquities* xix.

[1] The place mentioned by Dionysius was undoubtedly Consentia ; there never was any Constantia in Bruttium. See the critical note.

EXCERPTS
FROM
BOOK XX

I. Συνθέμενοι δὲ διὰ κηρύκων τὸν χρόνον ἐν ᾧ διαγωνιοῦνται,[1] κατέβαινον ἐκ τῶν στρατοπέδων καὶ εἰς τάξιν καθίσταντο τοιάνδε· βασιλεὺς μὲν Πύρρος τὴν Μακεδονικὴν φάλαγγα πρώτην ἔταξεν ἐπὶ τοῦ δεξιοῦ κέρατος καὶ μετ' αὐτὴν τοὺς ἐκ 2 τοῦ Τάραντος μισθοφόρους Ἰταλιώτας, ἔπειτα τοὺς ἐξ Ἀμπρακίας καὶ μετ' αὐτοὺς τὴν Ταραντίνων λεύκασπιν φάλαγγα, ἑξῆς δὲ τὸ Βρεττίων καὶ Λευκανῶν συμμαχικόν· ἐπὶ μέσης δὲ τῆς φάλαγγος Θεσπρωτούς τε καὶ Χάονας· τούτοις δὲ συνεχεῖς τοὺς Αἰτωλῶν καὶ Ἀκαρνάνων καὶ Ἀθαμάνων μισθοφόρους, τελευταίους δὲ Σαυνίτας 3 τὸ λαιὸν ἐκπληροῦντας κέρας. τῆς δὲ ἵππου τὴν μὲν Σαυνῖτιν καὶ Θετταλικὴν καὶ Βρεττίαν καὶ τὴν ἐκ τοῦ Τάραντος μισθοφόρον ἐπὶ τοῦ δεξιοῦ κέρατος ἔστησεν, τὴν δὲ Ἀμπρακιῶτιν καὶ Λευκανὴν καὶ Ταραντίνην καὶ τὴν Ἑλληνικὴν μισθοφόρον, ἣν ἐξεπλήρουν Ἀκαρνᾶνές τε καὶ Αἰτωλοὶ καὶ Μακεδόνες καὶ Ἀθαμᾶνες, ἐπὶ τοῦ λαιοῦ.

[1] As headings for these excerpts the Athos MS. has Ἐκ τῆς Διονυσίου Ἱστορίας Β' (= βιβλίου) K̄, followed by Πύρρου καὶ Ῥωμαίων ὑπάτων Ποπλίου Δεκίου καὶ Ποπλίου Σουλπικίου.

EXCERPTS

FROM

BOOK XX

I. Having agreed through heralds upon the time when they would join battle,[1] they descended from their camps and took up their positions as follows : King Pyrrhus gave the Macedonian phalanx the first place on the right wing and placed next to it the Italiot mercenaries from Tarentum ; then the troops from Ambracia and after them the phalanx of Tarentines equipped with white shields, followed by the allied force of Bruttians and Lucanians ; in the middle of the battle-line he stationed the Thesprotians and Chaonians ; next to them the mercenaries of the Aetolians, Acarnanians and Athamanians, and finally the Samnites, who constituted the left wing. Of the horse, he stationed the Samnite, Thessalian and Bruttian squadrons and the Tarentine mercenary force upon the right wing, and the Ambraciot, Lucanian and Tarentine squadrons and the Greek mercenaries, consisting of Acarnanians, Aetolians, Macedonians and Athamanians, on the left. The

---

[1] The excerpts in the Athos MS., describing the battle of Asculum, have as headings " From Dionysius' History, Book XX," then " Of Pyrrhus and the Roman consuls Publius Decius and Publius Sulpicius."

4 τοὺς δὲ ψιλοὺς καὶ τοὺς ἐλέφαντας διχῇ νείμας
ἀμφοτέρων κατόπιν ἔστησε τῶν κεράτων, σύμ-
μετρόν τι χωρίον ἀφεστῶτας ὀλίγον ἐπανεστηκὸς[1]
τοῦ πεδίου. αὐτὸς δὲ τὸ καλούμενον βασιλικὸν
ἄγημα τῶν ἐπιλέκτων ἱππέων ὁμοῦ τι[2] δισχιλίων
περὶ αὐτὸν ἔχων ἐκτὸς ἦν τάξεως, ἵνα τοῖς
κάμνουσιν αἰεὶ τῶν σφετέρων ἐξ ἑτοίμου παρείη.[3]

Οἱ δὲ ὕπατοι κατὰ μὲν τὸ λαιὸν κέρας ἔστησαν
τάγμα τὸ καλούμενον πρῶτον ἐναντίον τῇ Μακε-
δονικῇ καὶ Ἀμπρακιωτικῇ φάλαγγι καὶ τοῖς
μισθοφόροις τῶν Ταραντίνων· ἑπόμενον δὲ τῷ
πρώτῳ τάγματι τὸ τρίτον, καθ' ὃ μέρος ἡ λεύκ-
ασπις ἦν τῶν Ταραντίνων φάλαγξ καὶ τὸ Βρετ-
5 τίων καὶ τὸ Λευκανῶν συμμαχικόν. συναφὲς δὲ
τῷ τρίτῳ τὸ τέταρτον ἔστησαν κατὰ τοὺς Μολοτ-
τούς τε καὶ Χάονας καὶ Θεσπρωτούς· τὸ δὲ δεύτερον
ἐπὶ τοῦ δεξιοῦ κέρατος[4] ἐναντίον τοῖς μισθοφόροις
τοῖς ἀπὸ τῆς Ἑλλάδος Αἰτωλοῖς καὶ Ἀκαρνᾶσι
καὶ Ἀθαμᾶσι καὶ τῇ Σαυνιτῶν θυρεαφόρῳ[5] φάλαγγι.
Λατίνους δὲ καὶ Καμπανοὺς καὶ Σαβίνους καὶ
Ὀμβρικοὺς καὶ Οὐολούσκους καὶ Μαρουγκίνους
καὶ Πελίγνους καὶ Φερεντανοὺς[6] καὶ τοὺς ἄλλους
ὑπηκόους, εἰς τέτταρα διελόντες μέρη, τοῖς Ῥω-
μαϊκοῖς παρενέβαλον τάγμασιν, ἵνα μηδὲν αὐτοῖς
6 ἀσθενὲς εἴη μέρος. τὴν δὲ ἵππον τὴν τ'[7] οἰκείαν
καὶ τὴν συμμαχικὴν διελόντες ἐπ' ἀμφοτέρων
ἔταξαν τῶν κεράτων. ἐκτὸς δὲ τάξεως τούς τε
ψιλοὺς κατέστησαν καὶ τὰς ἁμάξας, τριακοσίας
τὸν ἀριθμόν, ἃς παρεσκευάσαντο πρὸς τὴν τῶν

---

[1] ἐξανεστηκὸς or ἐπανεστηκότος C. Müller.
[2] Müller : τε A.
[3] ἵνα . . . παρείη Cary, ἵνα . . . ἐπαρκέσῃ Cobet : εἶναι . . .

light-armed troops and the elephants he divided into
two groups and placed them behind both wings,
at a reasonable distance, in a position slightly elevated above the plain. He himself, surrounded by
the royal *agema*, as it was called, of picked horsemen, about two thousand in number, was outside the
battle-line, so as to aid promptly any of his troops in
turn that might be hard pressed.

The consuls arrayed on their left wing the legion
called the first, facing the Macedonian and Ambraciot
phalanx and the Tarentine mercenaries, and, next
to the first legion, the third, over against the Tarentine phalanx with its white shields and the Bruttian
and Lucanian allied forces ; adjoining the third
army they placed the fourth, facing the Molossians,
Chaonians and Thesprotians ; and the second on the
right wing opposite the mercenaries from Greece—
the Aetolians, Acarnanians and Athamanians—and
the Samnite phalanx that was equipped with oblong
shields. The Latins, Campanians, Sabines, Umbrians,
Volscians, Marrucini, Peligni, Ferentani, and their
other subjects they divided into four divisions and
mingled them with the Roman legions, in order that
no part of their lines might be weak. And dividing
the cavalry, both their own and that of their allies,
they placed it on both wings. Outside the line they
stationed the light-armed troops and the waggons,
three hundred in number, which they had got ready

πάρεισιν A; εἰς τὸ . . . παρεῖναι Müller, ὥστε . . . παρεῖναι
Jacoby, εἶναι . . . ἐπάρκεσιν Dübner.
  4 Müller : κέρας A, κέρως Jacoby.
  5 θυρασαφόρῳ A.
  6 Φρεντανοὺς Cobet, Jacoby.
  7 τ᾽ added by Kiessling.

ἐλεφάντων μάχην. αὗται κεραίας εἶχον ἐπιβεβη-
κυίας στώμιξιν[1] ὀρθαῖς πλαγίας, εὐτρόχους, ὅπῃ
βουληθείη τις ἅμα νοήματι περιάγεσθαι δυναμέ-
νας—ἐπ᾽ ἄκρων[2] δὲ τῶν κεραιῶν ἢ τριόδοντες
ἦσαν ἢ κέστροι μαχαιροειδεῖς ἢ δρέπανα ὁλοσίδη-
ρα—ἢ καταρράκτας[3] τινὰς ἐπιρριπτοῦντας ἄνωθεν
7 βαρεῖς κόρακας. πολλαῖς δὲ αὐτῶν χεῖρες προσ-
ήρτηντο πυρφόροι στυππεῖα[4] πολλῇ πίττῃ λελι-
πασμένα περὶ αὐτὰς ἔχουσαι, προεκκείμεναι τῶν
ἁμαξῶν, αἷς[5] ἔμελλον ἑστηκότες ἐπ᾽ αὐτῶν τινες,
ὅτε πλησίον γένοιντο τῶν θηρίων, πλήσαντες πυ-
ρὸς ἐπὶ τὰς προβοσκίδας αὐτῶν καὶ τὰ πρόσωπα
τὰς πληγὰς φέρειν. ἐφεστήκεσαν δὲ ταῖς ἁμάξαις
τετρακύκλοις ὑπαρχούσαις καὶ τῶν ψιλῶν συχνοί,
τοξόται καὶ χερμάται[6] καὶ τριβόλων σιδηρῶν
σφενδονῆται, καὶ παρ᾽ αὐτὰς κάτωθεν ἔτι πλείους
ἕτεροι.
8   Τάξις μὲν αὕτη τῶν στρατευσάντων ἦν ἀμφοτέρων, ἀριθμὸς δὲ τοῦ βασιλικοῦ μυριάδες ἑπτὰ
πεζῶν, ἐν οἷς Ἕλληνες οἱ τὸν Ἰόνιον[7] κόλπον
διαπεράσαντες ἐπὶ μυρίοις ἦσαν ἑξακισχίλιοι· τοῦ
δὲ Ῥωμαϊκοῦ πλείους τῶν ἑπτὰ μυριάδων, ἐξ
αὐτῆς μέντοι τῆς Ῥώμης ὁμοῦ τι[8] δισμύριοι.
ἱππεῖς δὲ παρεγένοντο Ῥωμαίοις μὲν ἀμφὶ τοὺς
ὀκτακισχιλίους, Πύρρῳ δὲ μικρῷ πλείους καὶ
θηρία ἑνὸς δέοντα εἴκοσι. Ath.
    II. Ἐπεὶ δὲ τὰ σημεῖα τῆς μάχης ἀνεδείχθη,
παιανίσαντες οἱ στρατιῶται καὶ τὸ ἐνυάλιον[9]

---

[1] Jacoby : στόμιξιν A, στομίσιν Wescher, στόρθυγξιν Dübner, κάμαξιν Cobet.
[2] ἐπ᾽ ἄκρων Wescher : ἀεπάκρων A.
[3] καταράκτας A ; τινὲς δὲ εἶχον καταρράκτας Müller.
[4] στυππία A.   [5] αἷς Müller : ἆς A.

for the battle against the elephants. These waggons had upright beams on which were mounted movable transverse poles that could be swung round as quick as thought in any direction one might wish, and on the ends of the poles there were either tridents or swordlike spikes or scythes all of iron ; or again they had cranes that hurled down heavy grappling-irons. Many of the poles had attached to them and projecting in front of the waggons fire-bearing grapnels wrapped in tow that had been liberally daubed with pitch, which men standing on the waggons were to set afire as soon as they came near the elephants and then rain blows with them upon the trunks and faces of the beasts. Furthermore, standing on the waggons, which were four-wheeled, were many also of the light-armed troops—bowmen, hurlers of stones and slingers who threw iron caltrops ; and on the ground beside the waggons there were still more men.

This was the battle order of the two armies that had taken the field. The forces on the king's side numbered 70,000 foot, of whom the Greeks who had crossed the Ionian gulf amounted to 16,000 ; on the Roman side there were more than 70,000, about 20,000 of them being from Rome itself. Of horse the Romans had about 8,000, while Pyrrhus had slightly more, as well as nineteen elephants.

II. When the signals for battle were hoisted, the soldiers first chanted their war songs, and then,

⁶ χερμάται A : χερμάδων Müller.
⁷ Ἰόνιον Kiessling, Ἰονικὸν Müller : ἴδιον A.
⁸ τι added by Müller.
⁹ τὸ Ἐννάλιον Cobet, τῷ Ἐνναλίῳ Jacoby : τὸ σύνολον A.

ἀλαλάξαντες[1] ἐχώρουν ὁμόσε καὶ συμπεσόντες
ἐμάχοντο πᾶσαν ἀποδεικνύμενοι τὴν ἐνόπλιον
ἐπιστήμην. οἱ μὲν ἱππεῖς οἱ παρὰ ἀμφότερα
τεταγμένοι τὰ κέρατα, προειδότες ἐν οἷς ἐπλεον-
έκτουν αὐτοὶ τῶν πολεμίων, εἰς ταῦτα κατέφευγον,
Ῥωμαῖοι μὲν εἰς τὴν ἐκ χειρὸς καὶ σταδίαν[2]
μάχην, τὸ δὲ τῶν Ἑλλήνων ἱππικὸν εἰς τὰς περι-
2 ελάσεις καὶ τοὺς ἐξελιγμούς· καὶ οἱ μέν, ὁπότε
διώκοιντο ὑπὸ τῶν Ἑλλήνων, ἐπιστρέψαντες τοὺς
ἵππους καὶ τοὺς χαλινοὺς κατασχόντες ἐπεζο-
μάχουν, οἱ δέ, ὁπότε τοὺς Ῥωμαίους μάθοιεν εἰς
ἀντίπαλα καθισταμένους, ἐπὶ δόρυ κλίναντες καὶ
δι' ἀλλήλων ἐξελίξαντες περιεδίνουν τοὺς ἵππους
αὖθις ἐπὶ τὸ μέτωπον καὶ τὰ κέντρα προσβαλόντες
3 ἐχώρουν ὁμόσε. ἡ[3] μὲν οὖν δὴ τῶν ἱππέων[4] μάχη
τοιαύτη τις ἦν, ἡ δὲ τῶν πεζῶν τῇ μὲν ἐμφερὴς
ἐκείνῃ, τῇ δὲ διάφορος—ἐμφερὴς μὲν κατὰ τὸ
σύμπαν, διάφορος δὲ κατὰ τὰ μέρη. τὸ μὲν γὰρ
δεξιὸν κέρας ἐπιρρεπέστερον ὑπῆρχεν ἑκατέροις,
τὸ δ' ἀριστερὸν ὑποδεέστερον. οὐ μέντοι σὺν τῷ
ἀσχήμονι τὰ νῶτα τοῖς πολεμίοις ἐνέκλιναν οὐδέ-
τεροι, ἀλλὰ σὺν κόσμῳ καὶ παρὰ ταῖς σημείαις
μένοντες ἑκάτεροι καὶ τὴν προβολὴν φυλάττοντες
4 κατὰ μικρὸν ὑπεχώρουν ὀπίσω. οἱ δὲ ἀριστεύ-
σαντες ἦσαν ἐκ μὲν τῆς βασιλικῆς στρατιᾶς[5]
Μακεδόνες—οὗτοι γὰρ ἀνέστειλαν[6] τὸ πρῶτον τῶν
Ῥωμαίων στρατόπεδον καὶ τοὺς σὺν αὐτοῖς
ταχθέντας Λατίνους—ἐκ δὲ τῆς Ῥωμαϊκῆς οἱ
συνελθόντες εἰς τὸ δεύτερον τάγμα Μολοττοῖς καὶ

---

[1] Müller : ἀλλάξαντες A.
[2] Warmington : σταδιαίαν O, Jacoby.
[3] ἡ added by Minas.   [4] Müller : ἵππων A.
[5] Müller : στρατείας A.   [6] Müller : ἀνέτειλαν A.

raising the battle-cry to Enyalius, advanced to the fray, engaged and fought, displaying all their skill in arms. The cavalry stationed upon both wings, knowing beforehand in what tactics they had the advantage over the enemy, resorted to those tactics, the Romans to a hand-to-hand, stationary combat, and the Greek horse to flanking and deploying manœuvres. The Romans, when they were pursued by the Greeks, would wheel their horses about, and checking them with the reins, would fight an infantry battle ; the Greeks, when they perceived that the Romans were their equals in combat, would swerve to the right and countermarching past one another, would whirl about their horses once more to face forward, and applying the spurs, would charge the enemy's ranks. Such was the character of the cavalry battle. The fighting of the infantry was in some respects similar to it, in other ways different ; it was similar on the whole, but different in details. For the right wing of each army was the stronger one, the left being weaker. Nevertheless, neither side turned its back ignominiously to the foe, but both maintained good order, remaining with the standards and protecting themselves with their shields while gradually falling back. Those who distinguished themselves for valour were, on the king's side, the Macedonians, who repulsed the first Roman legion and the Latins arrayed with it ; and, on the Roman side, those who constituted the second[1] legion and were opposed to the Molossians, Thes-

---

[1] Probably an error for "fourth," as it was called in chap. 1. Compare chap. 3, 5.

Θεσπρωτοῖς καὶ Χάοσιν ἐναντίοι. κελεύσαντος
δὲ τοῦ βασιλέως τοὺς ἐλέφαντας ἐπὶ τὸ κάμνον
τῆς στρατιᾶς[1] ἄγειν, μαθόντες τὴν ἔφοδον τῶν
θηρίων οἱ ταῖς κεραιοφόροις[2] ἐπιβεβηκότες ἁμά-
5 ξαις ἤλαυνον ὁμόσε. οὗτοι τὸ μὲν πρῶτον ἐπέσχον
τῆς ὁρμῆς τὰ θηρία, παίοντες ταῖς μηχαναῖς καὶ
τὰς πυρφόρους χεῖρας ἐς τὰς ὄψεις αὐτῶν ἐντρέ-
ποντες. ἔπειτα οὐκέτι προσαγόντων[3] τὰ θηρία
τῶν ἐφεστηκότων τοῖς πύργοις, ἀλλὰ ταῖς λόγχαις
βαλλόντων ἄνωθεν καὶ τῶν ψιλῶν διακοπτόντων
τὰ περικείμενα γέρρα ταῖς ἁμάξαις καὶ νευρο-
τομούντων τοὺς βόας[4] καταπηδῶντες ἀπὸ τῶν
ὀχημάτων οἱ πρὸς ταῖς μηχαναῖς κατέφευγον εἰς
τοὺς ἔγγιστα πεζοὺς καὶ πολλὴν παρεῖχον αὐτοῖς
6 ταραχήν. οἱ δὲ ἐν μέσῃ τῇ βασιλικῇ φάλαγγι
ταχθέντες Λευκανοὶ καὶ Βρέττιοι χρόνον οὐ πολὺν
ἀγωνισάμενοι τρέπονται πρὸς φυγὴν ὑπὸ τοῦ
τετάρτου Ῥωμαϊκοῦ τάγματος ἀνασταλέντες. ὡς
δὲ ἅπαξ ἐνέκλιναν οὗτοι καὶ διερράγη τὸ κατ'
αὐτοὺς μέρος τῆς φάλαγγος, οὐδὲ οἱ τὴν πλησίον
αὐτῶν λαβόντες στάσιν Ταραντῖνοι παρέμενον,
ἀλλὰ ἐντρέψαντες κἀκεῖνοι τὰ νῶτα τοῖς πολεμίοις
ἔφευγον. Ath.

III. Βασιλεὺς δὲ Πύρρος, ὡς ἔμαθεν ὅτι Λευκανοὶ καὶ Βρέττιοι καὶ Ταραντῖνοι φεύγουσι προ-
τροπάδην καὶ λελώβηται τὸ κατ' ἐκείνους μέρος
ἡ φάλαγξ, ἐκ τῆς καθ' ἑαυτοῦ[5] ἴλης[6] μέρος τι
παραδοὺς[7] ἑτέροις ἡγεμόσι, καὶ ἀπὸ τοῦ δεξιοῦ
κέρατος ἑτέρους ἱππεῖς, ὅσους ὑπέλαβεν[8] ἀρκεῖν,

---

[1] Müller : στρατείας A.
[2] Dübner : κερασφόροις A.   [3] προαγόντων Müller.
[4] καὶ after βόας deleted by Müller.
[5] Minas : ἑαυτῶν A.

protians and Chaonians. When the king had ordered
the elephants to be led up to the part of the line that
was in difficulties, the Romans mounted on the pole-
bearing waggons, upon learning of the approach of
the beasts, drove to meet them. At first they
checked the onrush of the beasts, smiting them with
their engines and turning the fire-bearing grapnels
into their eyes. Then, when the men stationed in
the towers no longer drove the beasts forward, but
hurled their spears down from above, and the light-
armed troops cut through the wattled screens surrounding the waggons and hamstrung the oxen, the
men at the machines, leaping down from their cars,
fled for refuge to the nearest infantry and caused
great confusion among them. The Lucanians and
Bruttians arrayed in the middle of the king's battle-
line, after fighting for no great while, turned to flight
when repulsed by the fourth [1] Roman legion. When
once these gave way and their part of the line was
broken through, the Tarentines also, who had their
station next to them, did not remain, but they too
turned their backs to the enemy and fled.

III. When King Pyrrhus learned that the Lucanians, Bruttians and Tarentines were in headlong flight
and that their part of the line was disrupted, he turned
a part of the squadron that was with him over to other
commanders, and from the right wing sent other
horsemen, as many as he thought would be sufficient,

---

[1] Another discrepancy : in chap. 1 the third legion was
reported as arrayed against the Lucanians and Bruttians.

---

[6] Minas : εἴλης Α.

[7] παραδοὺς is probably an error for παραδίδωσι : unless καὶ
be deleted before ἀπό.

[8] Minas : ὑπολαβεῖν Α.

DIONYSIUS OF HALICARNASSUS

ἀποστέλλει βοηθοὺς τοῖς ὑπὸ τῶν Ῥωμαίων
διωκομένοις. ἐν οἷς δὲ ταῦτα ἐγίνετο χρόνοις,
παρὰ τοῦ δαιμονίου βοήθεια τοῖς Ῥωμαίοις
2 ἔκδηλος γίνεται. Δαυνίων γάρ τινες ἐκ πόλεως
Ἀργυρίππων, ἣν νῦν Ἄρπους καλοῦσι, πεζοὶ μὲν
τετρακισχίλιοι, ἱππεῖς δὲ ἀμφὶ τοὺς τετρακοσίους,
ἐπίκουροι τοῖς ὑπάτοις ἀποσταλέντες, ὡς ἐγένοντο
πλησίον τοῦ βασιλικοῦ στρατοπέδου τὴν κατὰ
νώτου τῶν πολεμίων ἄγουσαν ὁδὸν ἀπὸ ταὐτομάτου
πορευόμενοι καὶ τὸ πεδίον εἶδον μεστὸν ἀνθρώπων,
ὀλίγον ἐπισχόντες αὐτόθι χρόνον καὶ λογισμοὺς
παντοδαποὺς λαβόντες, καταβαίνειν μὲν ἀπὸ τῶν
μετεώρων καὶ συλλαμβάνειν τῆς μάχης ἀπέγνωσαν,
οὔτε¹ ὅπη τι φίλιόν ἐστιν εἰδότες οὔτε ὅπη πολέμιον, οὔτ' ἐν ᾧ χωρίῳ στάντες ὠφέλειάν τινα
παρέξουσι τοῖς σφετέροις δυνάμενοι συμβαλεῖν,²
κράτιστον δὲ ὑπέλαβον εἶναι περιστάντες τὸ
στρατόπεδον τῶν πολεμίων ἐξελεῖν, ὡς αὐτοί τε
πολλὰς καὶ καλὰς ἕξοντες ὠφελείας εἰ κρατήσειαν
τῶν ἀποσκευῶν, καὶ μεγάλην παρέξοντες τοῖς
πολεμίοις ταραχὴν εἰ θεάσαιντο καιόμενον ἄφνω
τὸν χάρακα· ἀπεῖχε δὲ τὸ χωρίον τῆς μάχης οὐ
3 πλέον εἴκοσι σταδίων. ταῦτά τε δὴ βουλευσάμενοι
καὶ παρὰ αἰχμαλώτων τινῶν ἀκούσαντες, οὓς ἐπὶ
ξυλισμὸν ἐλθόντας εἰλήφεσαν,³ ὅτι κομιδῇ τινες
ὀλίγοι φυλάττουσι τὸν χάρακα, προσέβαλον αὐτοῖς
πανταχόθεν. ὑπὲρ ὧν ἐπιγνοὺς ὁ Πύρρος ἱππέως
τινὸς ἀπαγγείλαντος, ὅς⁴ ἀρξαμένου πολιορκεῖσθαι τοῦ χάρακος διεξελάσας τὸν ἵππον καὶ τὰ
κέντρα προσβαλὼν παρῆν⁵ διὰ ταχέων, τὴν μὲν ἀλ-

---

¹ Kiessling : οὐδὲ A.   ² Kiessling : συλλαβεῖν A.
³ Minas : εἰλήφασι A.   ⁴ Dübner : ὡς A.

396

as reinforcements to those who were being pursued
by the Romans. But during the time that this
was going on, there was a manifest intervention
of the divine power on the side of the Romans.
Some of the Daunians, it seems, from the city of
Argyrippa, which they now call Arpi, four thousand
foot and some four hundred horse who had been sent
to the assistance of the consuls, arrived near the royal
camp while proceeding by mere chance along the road
that led in the enemy's rear, and saw the plain full
of men. After stopping there a short while and indulging in all manner of speculations, they decided
not to descend from the heights and take part in the
battle, since they did not know either where there
was a friendly force or where a hostile one, nor could
conjecture in what place they should take their stand
in order to render some aid to their allies ; and they
thought it would be best to surround and destroy the
enemy's camp, since not only would they themselves
get much fine booty if they should capture the baggage, but they would also cause much confusion to
their enemies if these should see their camp suddenly
ablaze. (The scene of the battle was not more than
twenty stades distant.) Having come to this decision
and having learned from some prisoners, who had
been captured when they had gone out to gather
wood, that only a very few were guarding the camp,
they attacked them from all sides. Pyrrhus, learning
of this through the report of a cavalryman who, when
the siege of the camp began, drove his horse through
the enemy's lines, and applying the spurs, was soon at

---

⁵ Dübner : παρὼν A.

λην[1] δύναμιν ἐν τῷ πεδίῳ κατέχειν ἔγνω καὶ μήτε
ἀνακαλεῖν μήτε κινεῖν τὴν φάλαγγα, τοὺς δ'[2] ἐλέφαντας καὶ ἀπὸ τῶν ἱππέων τοὺς εὐτολμοτάτους
4 ἐπιλεξάμενος ἀποστέλλει βοηθοὺς τῷ χάρακι. ἔτι
δὲ τούτων πορευομένων ἐκπολιορκηθεὶς ἄφνω[3] ὁ
χάραξ ἀνάπτεται.

Καὶ οἱ διαπραξάμενοι τὸ ἔργον, ὡς ἔμαθον ἀπὸ
τῶν μετεώρων ἐπιόντας σφίσι τοὺς ὑπὸ τοῦ
βασιλέως ἀπεσταλμένους, εἰς ὄρους τινὸς κορυφὴν
ἔφυγον,[4] ἔνθα οὔτε τοῖς θηρίοις ἀνελθεῖν ῥάδιον ἦν
5 οὔτε τοῖς ἵπποις. οἱ δὲ[5] βασιλικοὶ τοῦ καιροῦ τῆς
βοηθείας ὑστερήσαντες ἐπὶ τοὺς ἐκ τοῦ τρίτου
καὶ τετάρτου τάγματος Ῥωμαίους ἐτράποντο
πολὺ προεληλυθότας ἀπὸ τῶν ἄλλων ὅτε τοὺς
κατὰ σφᾶς πολεμίους ἐτρέψαντο. προϊδόντες δὲ
αὐτῶν οἱ Ῥωμαῖοι τὴν ἔφοδον εἰς ὑψηλόν τι καὶ
λάσιον χωρίον ἀναδραμόντες εἰς τάξιν καθίσταντο.
6 οἱ μὲν οὖν ἐλέφαντες οὐ δυνάμενοι πρὸς τὸν ὄχθον[6]
ἀναβαίνειν οὐδὲν αὐτοὺς ἠδίκουν, οὐδὲ αἱ τῶν
ἱππέων ἷλαι, οἱ δὲ τοξόται καὶ[7] σφενδονῆται
βάλλοντες πανταχόθεν κατετίτρωσκόν τε καὶ δι-
έφθειρον ἐξ αὐτῶν συχνούς. αἰσθήσεως δὲ γενομένης τοῖς ἡγεμόσι τῶν ἐκεῖ πραττομένων Πύρρος
μὲν ἐκ τῆς πεζικῆς[8] φάλαγγος Ἀθαμᾶνάς τε καὶ

---

[1] γὰρ before ἄλλην deleted by Dübner.
[2] δ' added by Müller.
[3] ἄφνω Minas : ὑφὸ A.
[4] ἔφυγον added by Dübner.
[5] οἱ δὲ Müller : οὐδὲ A.
[6] ὄχθον Kiessling, λόφον Minas : ὄχλον A.
[7] καὶ added by Müller.
[8] πεζικῆς Dübner : πιστικῆς A, ἀσπιστικῆς Minas, Jacoby.

---

[1] The reading here is conjectural. The MS. has " from

hand, decided to keep the rest of his forces in the plain and not to recall or disturb the phalanx, but sent the elephants and the boldest of the horse, carefully selected, as reinforcements for the camp. But while these were still on the way, the camp was suddenly taken and set on fire.

Those who had accomplished this feat, upon learning that the troops sent by the king were coming down from the heights against them, fled to the summit of a hill which could not easily be ascended by either the beasts or the horses. The king's troops, having arrived too late to be of assistance, turned against the Romans of the third and fourth legions, who had advanced far ahead of the others after routing the foes who faced them. But the Romans, becoming aware in advance of their approach, ran up to a lofty and thickly-wooded spot and arrayed themselves in battle order. The elephants, accordingly, being unable to ascend the height, caused them no harm, nor did the squadrons of horse ; but the bowmen and slingers, hurling their missiles from all sides, wounded and destroyed many of them. When the commanders became aware of what was going on there, Pyrrhus sent, from his line of infantry,[1] the Athama-

his trusted line (or phalanx)," the adjective being corrupted. Dübner suggested " infantry " for the missing word, while Minas proposed an adjective, not found elsewhere, derived from *aspis* (shield). But in the two passages in chapter 1 where this part of Pyrrhus' line is mentioned nothing is said about shields except in the single case of the Samnites, who are called θυρεαφόροι (" armed with oblong shields "), presumably to distinguish them from the troops armed with the more common *aspis* (the round shield). The contrast in the present passage is probably between the infantry sent as reinforcements by Pyrrhus and the cavalry sent by the Roman consul.

Ἀκαρνᾶνας καὶ τῶν Σαυνιτῶν τινας ἀποστέλλει,
ὁ δὲ τῶν Ῥωμαίων ὕπατος ἴλας τινὰς ἱππέων,
ἐπειδὴ τοιαύτης ἔδει τοῖς πεζοῖς συμμαχίας. καὶ
κατὰ τὸν αὐτὸν[1] χρόνον ἑτέρα πάλιν ἐκεῖ γίνεται
μάχη πεζῶν τε καὶ ἱππέων, καὶ φόνος ἔτι πλείων.[2]

7 Ἀρξαμένου δὲ τοῦ βασιλέως καὶ οἱ τῶν Ῥωμαίων
ὕπατοι τοὺς ἑαυτῶν ἀνεκάλουν περὶ καταφορὰν
ὄντος τοῦ ἡλίου καὶ διαβιβάσαντες τὸν ποταμὸν
ἀπῆγον εἰς τὸν χάρακα συσκοτάζοντος[3] ἤδη. ἡ
δὲ τοῦ Πύρρου δύναμις ἀπολωλεκυῖα σκηνάς τε
καὶ ὑποζύγια καὶ ἀνδράποδα καὶ τὴν ἀποσκευὴν
ἅπασαν ἐπὶ μετεώρου τινὸς χώρου παρενέβαλεν,
ἔνθα τὴν ἐπιοῦσαν νύκτα διήγαγεν ὑπαίθριος,
ἀσκευής, ἀθεράπευτος, οὐδὲ τῆς ἀναγκαίας εὐ-
ποροῦσα τροφῆς, ὥστε καὶ διαφθαρῆναι συχνοὺς
τραυματίας, οἷς ἐνῆν ἔτι σώζεσθαι βοηθείας τε
καὶ κηδεμονίας μεταλαβοῦσιν. τοιούτου τέλους ἔτυχεν ἡ δευτέρα μάχη Ῥωμαίοις πρὸς Πύρρον περὶ
πόλιν Ἄσκλον. Ath.

IV. Ὅτι περὶ τὴν Ῥηγίνων πόλιν πάθος γίγνεται
δεινὸν οἷον καὶ περὶ Μεσσήνην[4] ἐγένετο τὴν ἐν
Σικελίᾳ, μεγάλης φυλακῆς καὶ προνοίας ἄξιον
ἁπάσαις ταῖς πόλεσιν· ἀνάγκη δὲ τὰς αἰτίας καὶ
τὰς προφάσεις τῶν κατασχόντων αὐτὴν κακῶν
2 προειπεῖν. ὅτε Λευκανοὶ καὶ Βρέττιοι δυνάμεσι
πολλαῖς ἐπὶ Θουρίους στρατεύσαντες τήν τε χώραν
αὐτῶν ἐξεπόρθησαν καὶ τὴν πόλιν περιχαρακώ-
σαντες ἐπολιόρκουν, ἐφ' οὓς ἀπεστάλη Ῥωμαίων
δύναμις ἧς ἡγεῖτο Φαβρίκιος ὁ ὕπατος, φοβηθέντες
οἱ Ῥηγῖνοι μὴ καὶ ἐπὶ σφᾶς οἱ βάρβαροι Ῥωμαίων

---

[1] αὐτὸν added by Wescher.   [2] πλείω A.
[3] Cobet : συσκιάζοντος A.

nians and Acarnanians and some of the Samnites,
while the Roman consul sent some squadrons of horse,
since the foot needed such assistance. And at this
same time a fresh battle took place there between the
foot and horse and there was still greater slaughter.

Following the king's lead, the Roman consuls also
recalled their troops when it was near sunset, and
taking them across the river led them back to their
camp as darkness was already coming on. The forces
of Pyrrhus, having lost their tents, pack-animals and
slaves, and all their baggage, encamped upon a
height, where they spent the following night under
the open sky, without either baggage or attendance
and not well supplied with even the necessary food,
so that many wounded men actually perished, when
they might still have been saved had they received
assistance and care. Such was the outcome of the
second battle between the Romans and Pyrrhus, near
the town of Asculum.

IV. Rhegium suffered a calamity similar to that
which had befallen Messana in Sicily, a calamity that
illustrates the need of great precaution and fore-
thought on the part of all cities. But it is necessary
to state first the causes and excuses for the evils that
befell this city. When the Lucanians and Bruttians,
having set out with numerous forces against Thurii,
had ravaged its territory and were besieging the city
after surrounding it with a palisade, and a force of
Romans under the command of Fabricius the consul
had been sent against them, the Rhegians, fearing
that the barbarians would send an army against them

---

⁴ μεσήνην S (and similarly below, except at end of § 8).

DIONYSIUS OF HALICARNASSUS

ἀπελθόντων[1] στρατιὰν ἀποστείλωσι, καὶ τὴν Ταραντίνων πόλιν ἐν ὑποψίαις ἔχοντες, ἐδεήθησαν τοῦ
Φαβρικίου δύναμιν τῇ πόλει λιπεῖν πρὸς τὰς
αἰφνιδίους τῶν βαρβάρων ἐπιδρομὰς καὶ εἴ τις[2]
ἐκ τῶν Ταραντίνων ἐπιβουλὴ σφισιν ἀπροσδόκητος
γένοιτο· καὶ λαμβάνουσι Καμπανοὺς μὲν ὀκτα-
κοσίους, Σιδικίνους[3] δὲ τετρακοσίους, ὧν ἁπάντων
3 ἡγεῖτο Δέκιος Καμπανὸς τὸ γένος. οὗτος ὁ ἀνήρ,
ὅτε κατάγοιτο παρὰ τοὺς ἐπιφανεστάτους τῶν
ἐπιχωρίων ἑστιάσεις τε[4] λαμπρὰς κατὰ τὴν φιλο-
φροσύνην τῶν ξένων ἑστιώμενος καὶ[5] κατασκευὰς
οἰκιῶν λαμπρὰς καὶ βαθυπλούτους παρὰ πολλοῖς
ὁρῶν κατ' ἀρχὰς μὲν ἐμακάριζε τοὺς Ῥηγίνους
τῆς εὐδαιμονίας, ἔπειθ' ὡς ἀναξίοις[6] ἐφθόνει,
τελευτῶν δὲ ὡς πολεμίοις ἐπιβουλεύειν ἤρξατο.
4 καὶ προσλαβὼν κοινωνὸν[7] τῶν ἀπορρήτων βουλευμάτων τὸν γραμματέα, πανοῦργον ἄνδρα καὶ
πάσης πονηρίας ἀρχιτέκτονα, † πρὸς αὐτοῦ[8] πάντας
Ῥηγίνους ἀποκτεῖναι καὶ τὴν εὐδαιμονίαν αὐτῶν
τὴν μὲν αὐτὸς κατασχεῖν, τὴν δὲ τοῖς στρατιώταις
διελεῖν, λέγοντος ὅτι[9] Μεσσήνην ὀλίγῳ πρότερον
εἷλον[10] . . . ὑφ' οὗ πεισθεὶς καὶ τὸν τρόπον τῆς ἐπιχειρήσεως σὺν αὐτῷ βουλευσάμενος, τοὺς ταγματ-
άρχας[11] καὶ τοὺς ἐπιφανεστάτους τῶν στρατιωτῶν
εἰς τὸ συνέδριον ἐκάλεσεν· δεηθεὶς δὲ ἁπάντων

---

[1] Müller : ἀπελυθόντων S, ἀπεληλυθότων Feder.
[2] εἴ τις Müller : ἥτις S.
[3] Feder : σικινοὺς S : Σιτικινοὺς Müller.
[4] τε deleted by Kiessling.
[5] καὶ added by Feder.
[6] ἀναξίοις Edd. : ἀξίους S.
[7] Edd. : κοινωνοὺς S.
[8] πρὸς αὐτοῦ S : προὐκαλεῖτο πρὸς αὐτοῦ Post, παραινοῦντος
αὐτοῦ Müller.   [9] ὅτι καὶ Müller.

also upon the departure of the Romans, and being suspicious of the city of Tarentum, begged Fabricius to leave a force in the city to guard against the sudden raids of the barbarians, and also in case there should be any unexpected hostile plot on the part of the Tarentines. And they received eight hundred Campanians and four hundred Sidicini, all under the command of Decius, a Campanian by birth. This man, whenever he was lodged in the houses of the most prominent of the inhabitants, was entertained at splendid banquets in accordance with the hospitality due to guests ; and when he beheld the splendid and costly appointments of many of the houses, he at first congratulated the Rhegians because of their prosperity, then envied them as being unworthy of it, and finally began to plot against them as enemies. And taking as an accomplice of his secret designs his secretary, a crafty man and a deviser of every kind of mischief, he was advised [1] by him to slay all the Rhegians and to seize their wealth, partly for himself and partly to distribute among his troops ; for the man remarked that Messana had been taken [in similar fashion by the Mamertines] a short time before.[2] When he had been persuaded by him and had planned with him the manner of attack, he called to a council the tribunes and the most prominent soldiers ; and after

[1] This verb is wanting in the MS.
[2] The text is corrupt at this point ; the words in brackets are supplied by conjecture.

---

[10] ὀλίγῳ πρότερον εἷλον Müller : ὀλίγῳ πρότειχον S ; ὀλίγοι προῖχ᾽ εἷλον Post. ὀλίγῳ πρότερον ⟨ὁμοίῳ τινὶ τρόπῳ καταλαβόντες οἱ Μαμερτῖνοι⟩ ἔσχον Feder.
[11] Edd. : γραμματάρχας S.

ἀπορρήτους φυλάξαι τοὺς λόγους κίνδυνον ἔφη
μέγαν αὐτῷ ἐπικρεμασθῆναι[1] πολλῆς πάνυ φυλακῆς
καὶ ταχείας δεόμενον, ὡς τοῦ καιροῦ μὴ διδόντος
ἀναστροφήν. πεπυσμένους γὰρ τὴν Πύρρου διάβασιν τοὺς ἐπιφανεστάτους Ῥηγίνων κρύφα δια-
πέμπεσθαι πρὸς αὐτὸν ὑπισχνουμένους κατασφάξειν
τὴν φρουρὰν καὶ παραδώσειν ἐκείνῳ τὴν πόλιν.
5 ἔτι ταῦτα λέγοντος αὐτοῦ παρῆν τις ἐγκάθετος,
αὐχμηρὸς ὡς[2] ἐξ ὁδοῦ, γράμματα ὑπ' αὐτοῦ
Δεκίου κατεσκευασμένα κομίζων, ὡς παρὰ ξένου
δή τινος ἰδίου, ἐν οἷς ἐδηλοῦτο μέλλων[3] ὁ βασιλεὺς
ἀποστέλλειν ἐπὶ τὸ Ῥήγιον πεντακοσίους[4] στρατιώτας ὡς καταληψομένους τὴν πόλιν, ἀνοίξειν
6 ὑπεσχημένων αὐτοῖς Ῥηγίνων τὰς πύλας. τινὲς
μὲν λέγουσι τὸν γραμματηφόρον ὑπὸ Φαβρικίου
τοῦ ὑπάτου κατὰ σπουδὴν ἀπεστάλθαι, τὴν δ'
ἐπιστολὴν ταῦτα περιέχειν ἃ μικρῷ πρότερον
ἔφην, καὶ παραινεῖν Δεκίῳ φθάσαι[5] τοὺς Ῥηγίνους·
ἔχει δὲ λόγον ἀμφότερα. ἔδειξε δὴ ταῦτα τοῖς
ἐν τῷ συνεδρίῳ παροῦσι· καὶ ἐπεὶ τάχιστα νὺξ
ἐγένετο, φράσαντες οἱ ταγματάρχαι τοῖς ἄλλοις
στρατιώταις ἃ διενοοῦντο πράττειν, ἐπὶ τὰς οἰκίας
τῶν Ῥηγίνων ἐχώρουν, καὶ τοὺς μὲν εὐωχου-
μένους ἔτι, τοὺς δὲ κοιμωμένους καταλαβόντες ἐν
τοῖς ἰδίοις κατασφάττουσιν ἐφεστίοις ἀντιβολοῦντας
καὶ γόνασι προσκυλιομένους καὶ ἀνθ' ὅτου ταῦτα
πάσχουσι μαθεῖν ἀξιοῦντας, οὔτε ἡλικίας οὔτε
7 τύχης οὐδεμιᾶς φειδόμενοι. φονεύσαντες δὲ τοὺς
ἄνδρας ἔτι δεινότερον ἔργον ἐξειργάσαντο· τάς τε
γὰρ[6] γυναῖκας τῶν ἰδίων ξένων καὶ τὰς παρθένους

---

[1] Feder : ἐπικρεμασθέντα S.   [2] Edd. : ὃς S.
[3] μέλλων Q : μέλλειν S.

requesting them all to keep his remarks secret, he said that a grave danger overhung him, one that required very great and prompt precautions, since the occasion, he declared, did not permit of delay. For the most prominent Rhegians, he said, having learned of Pyrrhus' crossing, were secretly sending to him, promising to put the garrison to the sword and to hand over the city to him. While he was still uttering these words, a man who had been suborned for the purpose appeared, covered with dust as if from a journey and bearing a letter, composed by Decius himself but purporting to be from a personal friend of his, in which it was revealed that the king was intending to send five hundred soldiers to Rhegium to take over the city, the inhabitants having promised to open their gates to them. Some state that the bearer of the letter had been sent in earnest by Fabricius the consul, and that the letter contained the information which I have just given and urged Decius to forestall the Rhegians. Both reports are reasonable. These things he revealed to those who were present at the council ; and as soon as it was night, the tribunes, having first told the other soldiers what they were intending to do, went to the houses of the Rhegians, and finding some of them still feasting and others asleep, they slew them at their own firesides, though the Rhegians entreated them and grovelled at their feet and demanded to know why they were thus treated ; and they spared neither age nor rank. After slaughtering the men they committed a still more outrageous crime : portioning out the wives and virgin daughters of their

---

⁴ πεντακισχιλίους Q.　　　　⁵ Feder : φθάσειν S.
⁶ γάρ added by Feder.

διελόμενοι συνῆσαν ἀκούσαις ὧν τοὺς πατέρας
8 καὶ τοὺς ἄνδρας ἐν ὀφθαλμοῖς ἀπέκτειναν. Δέκιος
δὲ ἀντὶ φρουράρχου τύραννος ἐγεγόνει τῆς Ῥηγίνων πόλεως· καὶ λογιζόμενος ὅτι δώσει Ῥωμαίοις
ὧν ἔδρασε δίκας, Καμπανοῖς τοῖς κατέχουσι
Μεσσήνην συμμαχίαν τίθεται μεγίστην ἰσχὺν τῶν
ἐν Σικελίᾳ πόλεων ἔχουσι, καὶ τὴν πόλιν διὰ
πολλῆς εἶχε φυλακῆς. Esc.; (p. 404, l. 8–p. 406,
l. 2) Ambr.

V. Ἡ δὲ βουλὴ μαθοῦσα τὰ περὶ τοὺς Ῥηγίνους πάθη παρὰ τῶν διαφυγόντων τὸν ὄλεθρον
οὐδὲ τὸν ἐλάχιστον ἀναμείνασα χρόνον ἀποστέλλει
στρατιὰν νεοσύλλεκτον ἄγοντα ἑτέραν τὸν κατὰ
2 πόλιν στρατηγόν.[1] φθάσασα δὲ τὴν Ῥωμαίων
ἄφιξιν ἡ τοῦ δαιμονίου πρόνοια τὸν ἡγεμόνα τῆς
φρουρᾶς Δέκιον ἀντὶ τῶν ἀνοσίων βουλευμάτων εἰς
τὰ κυριώτατα τοῦ ζῆν ἐτιμωρήσατο μέρη, νόσον
εἰς τοὺς ὀφθαλμοὺς ἐμβαλοῦσα δεινὰς περιωδυνίας
φέρουσαν[2]· ἣν ἰάσασθαι προθυμούμενος ἄνθρωπος[3]
ἐκ Μεσσήνης ἰατρὸν μεταπέμπεται, Δεξικράτην
ὄνομα, πυνθανόμενος ἄριστον εἶναι τῶν κατὰ τὴν
αὐτὴν ἡλικίαν ἰατρῶν, ἀγνοῶν δὲ ὅτι Ῥηγῖνος ἦν
τὸ γένος· ὃς ἀφικόμενος εἰς τὸ Ῥήγιον ἐναλείφει
τοὺς ὀφθαλμοὺς αὐτοῦ καυστικῷ φαρμάκῳ καὶ
διακελευσάμενος ἀνέχεσθαι τὰς περιωδυνίας ἕως
ἂν ἀφίκηται, καταβὰς ἐπὶ θάλατταν εἰς τὸ παρ-
εσκευασμένον πορθμεῖον ἐνέβη καὶ πρὶν αἰσθέσθαι
3 τινὰ τὸ πραχθὲν εἰς Μεσσήνην ἀπέπλευσεν. Δέκιος
δὲ μέχρι μέν τινος ἐκκαιομένης τῆς ὁράσεως
ἀλγηδόνας τε δεινὰς ὑπομένων ἠνείχετο τὸν ἰατρὸν

[1] ἕτερον τῶν κατὰ πόλιν στρατηγῶν Edd.
[2] περιοδίνας φερούσας S.   [3] Feder, Kiessling : ἄνθρωπον S.

hosts, they forcibly lay with these women whose fathers
and husbands they had slain before their very eyes.
Decius from the commander of a garrison had thus
become a tyrant of Rhegium ; and reasoning that
he would have to pay the penalty to the Romans
for what he had done, he made an alliance with the
Campanians who were in possession of Messana,
the most powerful of the cities in Sicily, meanwhile
keeping the city of Rhegium under strict guard.

V. The senate, upon learning from those who had
escaped destruction the calamity that had befallen
the Rhegians, did not delay for even a moment, but
sent out the general in the city at the head of another
army which had just been enrolled. Forestalling the
arrival of the Romans, however, Divine Providence
took vengeance upon Decius, the commander of the
garrison, for his impious schemes by punishing him in
the most vital parts of his body, inflicting upon his
eyes a malady that caused excruciating pains. In
his anxiety to cure this malady he sent for a physician
from Messana, Dexicrates by name, learning by
inquiry that he was the best of the physicians of the
day, but unaware that he was a Rhegian by birth.
This man, having come to Rhegium, anointed his eyes
with a caustic remedy and bade him endure the pains
until he himself should return ; then, going down to
the sea, he boarded the ferry-boat that had been got
ready for him and, before anyone was aware of his
action, sailed back to Messana. For a time Decius,
although suffering dreadful pains while his sight was
being burned out, nevertheless endured it, while

προσδεχόμενος, ὡς δὲ πολὺς ἐγίνετο χρόνος[1] καὶ
τὰς περιωδυνίας ἀδύνατος ἦν ἔτι φέρειν, σπογγίσας
τὸ φάρμακον καὶ τοὺς ὀφθαλμοὺς ἀνοίξας ἔγνω
τὰς ὄψεις ἐκκεκαυμένος[2]· καὶ τὸν ἐξ ἐκείνου χρόνον
διέμεινε τυφλός· ἡμέρας τε ὀλίγας ἔτι περιενέγκας
ὑποχείριος τοῖς Ῥωμαίοις γίνεται συλληφθεὶς ὑπὸ
4 τῶν ἰδίων. ταύτην γὰρ οἰόμενοί τινες ἀπολογίαν[3] τήν τε πόλιν ἀνέῳξαν τῷ στρατηγῷ καὶ
τὸν Δέκιον δήσαντες παρέδοσαν Φαβρικίῳ. ὁ
δὲ τὴν μὲν πόλιν ἀποδίδωσι τοῖς περιοῦσι Ῥηγίνων, τοὺς δὲ φρουροὺς ἅπαντα καταλιπεῖν αὐτόθι
κελεύσας ἀπήγαγεν οὐδὲν ἐπιφερομένους ἔξω τῶν
5 ὅπλων· ἐξ ὧν τοὺς κορυφαιοτάτους ἄνδρας ἐπιλεξάμενος, οὓς ἀπέφαινον οἱ λοιποὶ τῶν ἀνοσίων
βουλευμάτων εἶναι κοινωνούς, δεσμίους εἰς Ῥώμην
ἤγαγεν· οὓς ἐν ἀγορᾷ μάστιξιν αἰκισάμενοι, ὡς
ἦν πάτριον ἐπὶ τοῖς κακούργοις κείμενον, ἀπέκτειναν τῷ πελέκει τὰς κεφαλὰς ἀποκοπέντας,
ἐκτὸς Δεκίου καὶ τοῦ γραμματέως· οὗτοι δὲ
παρακρουσάμενοι τοὺς φυλάττοντας ἢ χρήμασιν
ὠνησάμενοι τὸ μὴ μεθ' ὕβρεως ἀποθανεῖν ἑαυτοὺς
διεχειρίσαντο. καὶ ταῦτα μὲν ἐπὶ τούτοις. Esc.;
(p. 406, ll. 16-20) Ambr.

VI. (19, 2) Αὐτὸς δὲ ὁ Πύρρος τοὺς Ὁμηρικοὺς
ἐπιφθεγξάμενος στίχους, οὓς[4] Ἕκτωρ αὐτῷ πε-
ποίηται πρὸς Αἴαντα λέγων, ὡς ὑπὸ Ῥωμαίων
εἰρημένους πρὸς ἑαυτόν·

Τῷ σε καὶ οὐκ ἐθέλω βαλέειν, τοιοῦτον ἐόντα,
λάθρη ὀπιπτεύσας, ἀλλ' ἀμφαδόν, αἴ κε τύχοιμι.

---

[1] χρόνος S : ὁ χρόνος Feder, Jacoby.
[2] ἐκκεκαυμένας Müller.
[3] Φαβρικίου after ἀπολογίαν deleted by Kiessling, following

408

waiting for the physician ; but when much time had passed and he was unable longer to endure the excruciating pains, he wiped off the ointment and, opening his eyes, realized that the orbs had been burned out, and from that time he continued to be blind. After holding out for a few days he fell into the hands of the Romans, having been arrested by his own men ; for some, believing this was the way to clear themselves, opened their city to the general and delivered up Decius in chains to Fabricius. The latter restored the city to the Rhegians who survived, and ordering the guards to leave everything where it was, he led them away carrying nothing but their arms ; then, choosing out the most prominent of their number, those whom the others declared to be accomplices in the nefarious plot, he brought them in chains to Rome. There, after being scourged with whips in the Forum, as was the established usage in the case of malefactors, the prisoners were put to death by having their heads cut off with an axe—all except Decius and the secretary, who, having outwitted their guards or bribed them with money to permit them to escape an ignominious death, made away with themselves. So much on this subject.

VI. (19, 2) Pyrrhus himself, having uttered the Homeric lines which Hector is represented by the poet as speaking to Ajax, as if they had been addressed by the Romans to himself,

> I would not smite thee, then, who art so brave,
> By stealth, but openly, if so I may.[1]

---

[1] *Iliad* vii. 242 f., quoted carelessly.

Feder ; Feder also thought of reading παρὰ (or πρὸς) Φαβρικίου.   [4] Mai : ὃς Q.

καὶ μετὰ τοῦτ᾿ εἰπὼν ὅτι κινδυνεύει πονηρὰν
πεποιῆσθαι τὴν ὑπόθεσιν τοῦ πολέμου πρὸς ἀνθρώπους ὁσιωτέρους Ἑλλήνων καὶ δικαιοτέρους,[1] μίαν
ἔφη θεωρεῖν ἀπαλλαγὴν τοῦ πολέμου καλὴν καὶ
συμφέρουσαν, εἰ φίλους ἀντὶ πολεμίων αὐτοὺς
ποιήσαιτο, φιλανθρωπίας τινὸς μεγάλης καταρξά-
μενος.

2 (3) Προαχθῆναι δὲ κελεύσας τοὺς Ῥωμαίων
αἰχμαλώτους καὶ δοὺς ἅπασιν ἐσθῆτας ἐλευθέροις
πρεπούσας σώμασι καὶ ἐνοδίους[2] δαπάνας, παρ-
εκάλεσεν αὐτοὺς μεμνῆσθαι οἷος εἰς αὐτοὺς ἐγένετο
καὶ τοῖς ἄλλοις λέγειν, ὅταν δ᾿ εἰς τὰς ἑαυτῶν
ἔλθωσι πατρίδας, πάσῃ[3] προθυμίᾳ πράττειν ὅπως
φίλους ποιήσουσι τὰς πόλεις.

3 Ἄμαχον δή τινα ἰσχὺν τὸ βασιλικὸν ἔχει χρυσίον, καὶ οὐδεμία εὕρηται πρὸς τοῦτο τὸ βέλος
ἀνθρώποις φυλακή. Ambr.

VII. (19, 4) Ὅτι Κλεινίας ὁ Κροτωνιάτης τύραννος ὢν ἀφείλετο τὴν ἐλευθερίαν τὰς πόλεις,[4]
φυγάδας ἀθροίσας ἐκ παντὸς τόπου καὶ δούλους
ἐλευθερώσας· οἷς τὴν τυραννίδα κρατυνάμενος τοὺς
ἐπιφανεστάτους Κροτωνιατῶν οὓς μὲν ἀπέκτεινεν, οὓς δὲ ἐξέβαλεν ἐκ τῆς πόλεως. Ἀναξίλας
δὲ Ῥηγίνων τὴν ἀκρόπολιν κατελάβετο καὶ πάντα
τὸν τοῦ βίου χρόνον κατασχὼν Λεόφρονι τῷ παιδὶ
τὴν ἀρχὴν κατέλιπε.[5] καὶ ἄλλοι ἀπὸ[6] τούτων δυναστείας ἐν ταῖς πόλεσι κατασκευάσαντες πάντα τὰ
2 πράγματα διέφθειραν. (5) ἡ δὲ τελευταία τε καὶ

---

[1] ὁσιωτέρους . . . δικαιοτέρους Struve : ὁσιωτάτους . . .
δικαιοτάτους Q.

[2] ἐνοδίους Mai : ἐν ὁδίνους Q.   Mai : πᾶσι Q.

[4] τὰς πόλεις Reiske : ταῖς πόλεσι P.

[5] Reiske : κατέλειπε P.   [6] ἀπὸ added by Valesius.

and afterwards declaring that he had probably been wrong in planning his war against people who were more pious than the Greeks and more just,[1] said he saw only one honourable and advantageous way of ending the war, and that was to make friends of them instead of enemies, beginning with some great act of kindness.

(3) After ordering the Roman prisoners to be brought forward and giving to all of them raiment befitting free persons and expense money for the journey, he bade them remember how he had treated them and to tell all the others, and when they should come to their own cities, to strive with all zeal to make those cities friendly to him.

A certain irresistible might, indeed, has the gold of a king, and no defence has been found by mortals against this weapon.

VII. (19, 4) Cleinias of Croton, when he was tyrant, took away from the cities their freedom after he had gathered together fugitives from every quarter and freed the slaves ; and having strengthened his tyranny with their aid, he either slew or expelled from the city the most prominent of the Crotoniats. Anaxilas seized the acropolis of the Rhegians and, after holding it as long as he lived, handed down the rule to Leophron, his son. Others too, following their example, founded dynasties in the various cities and thus brought everything to ruin. (5) But the final

---

[1] " More pious than . . . and more just " is Struve's conjecture ; the MS. has " most pious and just of the Greeks."

DIONYSIUS OF HALICARNASSUS

πασῶν μεγίστη κάκωσις ἀπάσαις ταῖς πόλεσιν
ἡ Διονυσίου τυραννὶς ἐγένετο τοῦ κρατήσαντος
Σικελίας. διέβη γὰρ εἰς Ἰταλίαν ἐπὶ Ῥηγίνους
Λοκρῶν ἐπικαλεσαμένων, οἷς ἦσαν οἱ Ῥηγῖνοι
διάφοροι· καὶ συνελθόντων ἐπ᾽ αὐτὸν Ἰταλιω-
τῶν δυνάμεσι μεγάλαις συνάψας μάχην ἀπέκτεινε
συχνοὺς καὶ πόλεις αὐτῶν δύο κατὰ κράτος ἐξεῖλεν.
3 εἶτ᾽ αὖθις ἑτέραν ποιησάμενος διάβασιν Ἱππωνι-
εῖς ἀνέστησεν ἐκ τῆς ἑαυτῶν, οὓς ἀπήγαγεν εἰς
Σικελίαν, καὶ Κροτωνιάτας ἐξεῖλε καὶ Ῥηγίνους
καὶ διετέλεσεν ἔτη δώδεκα τούτων τυραννῶν τῶν
πόλεων. ἔπειθ᾽ οἱ μὲν τὸν τύραννον δεδιότες τοῖς
βαρβάροις αὐτοὺς ἐνεχείριζον, οἱ δὲ ὑπ᾽ ἐκείνων
πολεμούμενοι τῷ τυράννῳ τὰς πόλεις παρεδίδοσαν·
ὑφ᾽ ὅτου δὲ πάσχοιεν, ἀεὶ κακῶς δυσχεραίνοντες
εὐρίπου δίκην τῇδε καὶ τῇδε πρὸς τὸ συντυχὸν
ἐτράποντο. *Vales.*

VIII. (19, 6) Ὅτι Πύρρος διέβη τὸ δεύτερον
εἰς Ἰταλίαν οὐ χωρούντων αὐτῷ τῶν ἐν Σικελίᾳ πραγμάτων κατὰ νοῦν διὰ τὸ μὴ βασιλικὴν
φανῆναι τὴν ἡγεμονίαν αὐτοῦ ταῖς ἐπιφανεστάταις
πόλεσιν, ἀλλὰ δεσποτικήν. εἰσαχθεὶς γὰρ εἰς Συ-
ρακούσας ὑπό τε Σωσιστράτου τοῦ κρατοῦντος τῆς
πόλεως τότε καὶ Θοίνωνος τοῦ φρουράρχου, παραλαβὼν παρ᾽ ἐκείνων τὰ[1] χρήματα καὶ ναῦς χαλκ-
εμβόλους ὁμοῦ τι διακοσίας καὶ πᾶσαν ὑφ᾽
ἑαυτῷ ποιησάμενος Σικελίαν πλὴν Λιλυβαίου πό-

[1] τὰ om. Suidas.

---

[1] Or, specifically, the Euripus. This Greek word meant
a strait through which there was a strong flux and reflux.

412

and worst mischief of all that came to any of the cities was the tyranny of Dionysius, who had mastered Sicily. For he crossed into Italy against the Rhegians at the summons of the Locrians, with whom the Rhegians were at odds ; and when the Italiots united against him with large forces, he joined battle, slew many and took by storm two of their cities. Then making another crossing later on, he removed the people of Hipponium from their native land, taking them to Sicily ; and capturing Croton and Rhegium, he continued to lord it over those cities for twelve years. Then some, who stood in dread of the tyrant, entrusted themselves to the barbarians, while others, who were being warred upon by the barbarians, handed over their cities to the tyrant ; and no matter at whose hands they were suffering, they were always wretched and discontented, so that, like a euripus,[1] they veered this way and that according to the fortunes that befell them.

VIII. (19, 6) Pyrrhus crossed for the second time into Italy, since matters were not going to his liking in Sicily, inasmuch as it had become evident to the chief cities that his leadership was not that of a king but of a despot. For after he had been brought into Syracuse by Sosistratus, the ruler of the city at that time, and by Thoenon, the commander of the garrison, and had received from them the money in the treasury [2] and some two hundred bronze-beaked ships, and after he had brought under his power all Sicily with the exception of the city of Lilybaeum, the one city

It was applied especially to the strait between Euboea and Boeotia, where the current changes direction several times a day.

[2] The MS. used by Valesius has simply " the moneys," the MSS. of Suidas " moneys " only.

DIONYSIUS OF HALICARNASSUS

λεως, ἣν ἔτι μόνην Καρχηδόνιοι κατεῖχον, εἰς αὐθάδειαν τυραννικὴν ἐτρέπετο. *Vales.*; *Suidas s.v.*
Πύρρος.

(7) Τάς τε γὰρ οὐσίας τῶν Ἀγαθοκλέους οἰκείων
ἢ φίλων ἀφαιρούμενος τοὺς παρ' ἐκείνου λαβόντας
τοῖς ἑαυτοῦ φίλοις ἐχαρίσατο καὶ τὰς μεγίστας ἐν
ταῖς πόλεσιν ἀρχὰς τοῖς ἰδίοις ὑπασπισταῖς καὶ
λοχαγοῖς προσένεμεν,[1] οὐ κατὰ τοὺς ἐπιχωρίους
ἑκάστης πόλεως νόμους οὐδ' εἰς τὸν εἰωθότα
2 χρόνον, ἀλλ' ὡς αὐτῷ φίλον ἦν. δίκας τε καὶ
ἀμφισβητήσεις καὶ τὰς ἄλλας πολιτικὰς οἰκονομίας
ἁπάσας τὰς μὲν αὐτὸς διῄτα, τὰς δὲ τοῖς περὶ τὴν
αὐλὴν ἀναστρέφειν καὶ[2] διακρίνειν ἀπεδίδου, ἀνθρώποις οὐθὲν ἕτερον ὁρῶσιν[3] ὅ τι μὴ κερδαίνειν καὶ
καθηδυπαθεῖν τὰς εὐπορίας· καὶ διὰ ταῦτα πάντα
βαρὺς ταῖς ὑποδεξαμέναις πόλεσι καὶ[4] μισητὸς ἦν.
3 (8) αἰσθόμενος δὲ ὑπούλως ἤδη πολλοὺς πρὸς
ἑαυτὸν ἔχοντας εἴς τε τὰς πόλεις φρουρὰς εἰσῆγε,
πρόφασιν ποιούμενος τὸν ἀπὸ Καρχηδονίων πόλεμον, καὶ τοὺς ἐπιφανεστάτους ἄνδρας ἐξ ἑκάστης
πόλεως συλλαμβάνων ἀπέκτεινεν, ἐπιβουλὰς καὶ
προδοσίας εὑρηκέναι ψευσάμενος. ἐν οἷς ἦν[5] καὶ
Θοίνων ὁ φρούραρχος,[6] ὃς ὑπὸ πάντων ὡμολόγητο
πλείστην σπουδὴν καὶ προθυμίαν εἴς τε τὴν διάβασιν αὐτῷ[7] καὶ τὴν παράληψιν τῆς νήσου παρ-
εσχῆσθαι· καὶ γὰρ ὑπήντησεν αὐτῷ ναυτικὸν στόλον
ἄγων καὶ τὴν ἐν ταῖς Συρακούσαις νῆσον, ἣν
4 αὐτὸς ἐκράτει, παρέσχεν. ἐπιχειρήσας δὲ καὶ
Σωσίστρατον συλλαβεῖν διήμαρτε τῆς ἐλπίδος

---

[1] προσένεμεν P : προσένειμεν Valesius.
[2] καὶ P : ἢ Capps.
[3] ἢ after ὁρῶσιν deleted by Reiske.

414

which the Carthaginians still held, he assumed the arrogance of a tyrant.

(7) For Pyrrhus took away the estates of Agathocles' relatives and friends from those who had received them at that ruler's hands and presented them to his own friends, and he assigned the chief magistracies in the cities to his own shield-bearers and captains, not in accordance with the local laws of each city nor for the customary period, but as was pleasing to him. Lawsuits and controversies and all the other matters of civil administration he would in some cases decide himself and in other cases would refer them either for reversal or for determination to those who hung about the court, men who had an eye for nothing except making gains and squandering wealth in the pursuit of luxury. Because of all this he was burdensome to the cities which had received him and was hated by them. (8) Perceiving that many people were already secretly hostile to him, he introduced garrisons into the cities, taking as an excuse the war threatening from the Carthaginians ; and arresting the most prominent men in each city, he put them to death, falsely alleging that he had discovered plots and treasonable acts. Among these was Thoenon, the commander of the garrison, who was admitted by all to have shown the greatest ardour and zeal in aiding him to cross over and take possession of the island ; for he had gone to meet him at the head of a naval squadron and had turned over to him the Island at Syracuse, of which he himself had the command. When, however, Pyrrhus attempted to arrest Sosistratus also, he was disappointed ; for the man had

---

⁴ καὶ added by Reiske.   ⁵ ἦν P : om. Valesius.
⁶ Valesius : φύλαρχος P.   ⁷ Valesius(?) : αὐτῶν P.

415

DIONYSIUS OF HALICARNASSUS

προαισθομένου τὴν ἐπιβουλὴν τοῦ ἀνδρὸς καὶ
φυγόντος ἐκ τῆς πόλεως. ἀρξαμένων δὲ ταράτ-
τεσθαι τῶν πραγμάτων[1] καὶ ἡ τῶν Καρχηδονίων
πόλις καιρὸν ἐπιτήδειον εἰληφέναι νομίζουσα πρὸς
ἀνάκτησιν τῶν ἀπολωλότων χωρίων στρατιὰν ἀπέστειλεν ἐπὶ τὴν νῆσον. *Vales.*

IX. (19, 9) Ὅτι ἀμηχανοῦντα τὸν Πύρρον[2] καὶ
πόρους παντοδαποὺς ἐπιζητοῦντα ὁρῶντες αὐτὸν[2]
οἱ κάκιστοι καὶ ἀνοσιώτατοι τῶν φίλων, Εὐήγορος
Θεοδώρου καὶ Βάλακρος Νικάνδρου καὶ Δείναρχος
Νικίου, τῶν ἀθέων καὶ ἐξαγίστων δογμάτων ζη-
λωταί, πόρον ὑποτίθενται χρημάτων ἀνοσίων,[3] τοὺς
2 ἱεροὺς ἀνοῖξαι τῆς Περσεφόνης θησαυρούς. ἦν
γὰρ ἱερὸν ἐν τῇ πόλει ταύτῃ ἅγιον καὶ πολὺν
χρυσὸν[4] ἐκ παντὸς τοῦ χρόνου πεφυλαγμένον
ἄθικτον ἔχον, ἐν ᾧ χρυσός τις ἄβυσσος, ἀόρατος
τοῖς πολλοῖς κατὰ γῆς κείμενος. ὑπὸ τούτων
ἐξαπατηθεὶς τῶν κολάκων καὶ διὰ[5] τὴν ἀνάγκην
κρείττονα παντὸς τοῖς εἰσηγησαμένοις[6] τὴν γνώμην
ἀνδράσι διακόνοις τῆς ἱεροσυλίας ἐχρήσατο, καὶ
τὸν † ἐξελθόντα[7] χρυσὸν ἐκ τοῦ ἱεροῦ ναυσὶν ἐν-
θέμενος μετὰ τῶν ἄλλων χρημάτων ἀπέστειλεν
εἰς Τάραντα πολλῆς μεστὸς εὐθυμίας γενόμενος.
Vales.; *Suidas s.v.* Πύρρος.

(10) Ἡ δὲ δικαία πρόνοια τὴν αὑτῆς δύναμιν

---

[1] After πραγμάτων P has αὖ (= αὐτῷ ?).
[2] Delete either Πύρρον or αὐτὸν (Reiske).
[3] ἀνόσιον Reiske.
[4] χρυσὸν seems to have replaced some such word as
πλοῦτον.   [5] διὰ Suidas : om. P.
[6] τοῖς εἰσηγησαμένοις Valesius : ἡγησάμενος P, ἡγησαμένων
Suidas ; καὶ τὴν ἀνάγκην κρείττονα παντὸς ἡγησάμενος ⟨πράγ-
ματος τοῖς εἰσηγησαμένοις⟩ Kiessling.

416

become aware of his intention and had fled from the
city. Furthermore, when matters had begun to be
unsettled, the city of Carthage also, believing it had
found an opportunity suitable for the recovery of the
places it had lost, sent an army against the island.

IX. (19, 9) Observing that Pyrrhus was embar-
rassed and was seeking funds from every possible
source, the worst and most depraved of his friends,
Euegorus, the son of Theodorus, Balacrus, the son of
Nicander, and Deinarchus, the son of Nicias, followers
of godless and accursed doctrines, suggested an impious source for the raising of funds, namely, to open
up the sacred treasures of Persephonê. For there
was a holy temple in this city [1] that contained much
wealth,[2] guarded and untouched from the earliest
times ; included in this there was an unfathomed
quantity of gold, buried in the earth out of sight of
the multitude. Pyrrhus, misled by these flatterers
and because of his necessity that was stronger than
any scruples,[3] employed as his agents in the sacrilege
the men who had made the proposal ; and placing
the gold plundered from the temple in ships, he sent
it along with his other funds to Tarentum, having now
become filled with great cheer.

(10) But a just Providence showed its power. For,

[1] The city of Locri.
[2] The MSS. have " gold " ; but in view of the statement
immediately following it would seem that " gold " has replaced a word of more general meaning.
[3] Or, following Kiessling, " and regarding necessity as
stronger than any scruples."

---

[7] ἐξελθόντα P : om. Sudas; ἐξαχθέντα or ἐξενεχθέντα Reiske,
ἐξελαθέντα Jacoby, συληθέντα Naber, ἐκσυληθέντα Post.

ἀπεδείξατο. ὡς γὰρ ἀνήχθησαν αἱ νῆες ἀπὸ τοῦ
λιμένος, τὴν μὲν ἀπόγειον αὔραν λαβοῦσαι προ-
έκοψαν· ἄνεμος δὲ ἐναντίος γενόμενος καὶ δι᾽ ὅλης
νυκτὸς κατασχὼν ἃς μὲν κατέκλυσεν, ἃς δὲ εἰς
τὸν τῆς Σικελίας πορθμὸν ἐξέβαλεν, ἐν αἷς δὲ
παρεκομίζετο τὰ ἀναθήματα καὶ ὁ προσενεχθεὶς
ἐκ τῶν ἀναθημάτων χρυσὸς ἐπὶ τοὺς Λοκροὺς
ἐξώκειλεν αἰγιαλούς· καὶ τοὺς μὲν πλέοντας ἐν
αὐταῖς ἐν τῇ παλιρροίᾳ τῶν κυμάτων κατακλυζο-
μένους διέφθειρε, τὰ δὲ ἱερὰ χρήματα διασπασθει-
σῶν τῶν νεῶν ἐπὶ τὰς ἔγγιστα τῶν Λοκρῶν θῖνας
2 ἐξέβρασεν. ὁ δὲ βασιλεὺς καταπλαγεὶς ἅπαντα
τὸν κόσμον καὶ τοὺς θησαυροὺς ἀπέδωκε τῇ θεῷ
ὡς παραιτησόμενος αὐτῆς διὰ τοῦτο[1] τὸν χόλον·

Νήπιος, οὐδὲ τὸ ᾔδει, ὃ οὐ[2] πείσεσθαι ἔμελλεν·
οὐ γάρ τ᾽ αἶψα θεῶν τρέπεται νόος αἰὲν ἐόντων,

3 ὡς Ὁμήρῳ εἴρηται. ἀλλ᾽ ἐπειδὴ τῶν ἱερῶν
ἐτόλμησεν ἅψασθαι χρημάτων καὶ πόρον ὑποθέσθαι
πολέμων, ἀνόνητον ἐποίησε τὴν ἔννοιαν αὐτοῦ τὸ
δαιμόνιον, ἵνα παράδειγμα καὶ παίδευμα πᾶσιν ἀνθρώποις γένοιτο τοῖς μεθ᾽ ἑαυτόν. *Vales.*; *Suidas
s.v.* παραιτησόμενος.

X. (19, 11) Διὰ τοῦτο καὶ ὑπὸ Ῥωμαίων
ἡττήθη ὁ Πύρρος κατὰ κράτος. οὐ γὰρ στρατιά
τις φαύλη καὶ ἀνάσκητος ἦν αὐτῷ, ἀλλ᾽ ἡ κρατίστη
τῶν τότε οὐσῶν ἐν Ἕλλησι καὶ πλείστους ἀγωνι-
σαμένη πολέμους, οὐδὲ πλῆθος ἀνδρῶν τῶν τότε
παραταξαμένων ὀλίγον, ἀλλ᾽ ὅσον καὶ τριπλάσιον
εἶναι, οὐδὲ στρατηγὸς τῶν ἐπιτυχόντων τις, ἀλλ᾽
ὃν ἅπαντες ὁμολογοῦσι μέγιστον γενέσθαι τῶν

---

[1] διὰ τοῦτο Valesius : διὰ τούτων P, δι᾽ αὐτοῦ Suidas.

though the ships, upon putting out from the harbour, found a land breeze and made progress, an adverse wind sprang up, and holding through the entire night, sank some of them, drove others into the Sicilian strait, and, in the case of those in which the offerings and the gold yielded by the offerings was being transported, drove them ashore on the beaches of Locri. The men on board the ships were submerged and perished in the backwash of the waves, and the sacred moneys, when the ships broke up, were cast ashore on the sand-banks nearest to Locri. The king, terror-stricken, restored all the ornaments and treasures to the goddess, hoping thereby to appease her wrath ;

> The fool, nor wist that she would ne'er give ear :
> For not so quickly do the deathless gods
> Their purpose change,[1]

as Homer has said. Nay, since he had dared to lay hands on the sacred moneys and to pledge them as a war fund, the divinity brought his intention to naught, in order that he might serve as an example and lesson to all men who should come after him.

X. (19, 11) It was for this reason that Pyrrhus was defeated by the Romans also in a battle to the finish. For it was no mean or untrained army that he had, but the mightiest of those then in existence among the Greeks and one that had fought a great many wars ; nor was it a small body of men that was then arrayed under him, but even three times as large as his adversary's, nor was its general any chance leader, but rather the man whom all admit to have been the

---

[1] *Odyssey* iii. 146 f.

---

[2] οὐ om. P, Suidas.

κατὰ τὴν αὐτὴν ἡλικίαν ἀκμασάντων στρατηγῶν,
2 οὐδὲ[1] τόπου φύσις ἄνισος οὔτε ἐπικουρίας[2] τοῖς
ἑτέροις ἄφιξις[3] αἰφνίδιος οὔτε ἄλλη τις συμφορὰ
καὶ πρόφασις ἀπροσδόκητος ἐπιπεσοῦσα συνέτριψε
τὰ Πύρρου πράγματα, ἀλλ' ὁ τῆς ἀσεβηθείσης
θεᾶς χόλος, ὃν οὐδ' αὐτὸς ἠγνόει Πύρρος, ὡς Πρό-
ξενος ὁ συγγραφεὺς ἱστορεῖ καὶ αὐτὸς ὁ Πύρρος
ἐν τοῖς ἰδίοις ὑπομνήμασι γράφει. *Vales.*

XI. (19, 12) Ἔμελλον ὅπερ εἰκὸς οἱ[4] ὁπλῖται
κράνεσι καὶ θώραξι καὶ θυρεοῖς βαρεῖς πρὸς
ὀχθηρὰ χωρία καὶ μακρὰς ἀτραποὺς πορευόμενοι
καὶ οὐδὲ ταύτας λεωφόρους, ἀλλ' αἰγότριβας δι'
ὕλης τε καὶ κρημνῶν, τάξιν τε οὐδεμίαν φυλάξειν
καὶ πρὶν ἐπιφανῆναί σφισι τοὺς πολεμίους ἐξασθε-
νήσειν τὰ σώματα δίψει καὶ κόπῳ.
2 Τοὺς τοῖς ἱππικοῖς δόρασιν ἐκ διαλαβῆς ἀμφοτέραις ταῖς χερσὶ κρατουμένοις μαχομένους συστάδην
καὶ τὰ πολλὰ κατορθοῦντας ἐν ταῖς μάχαις πρίγ-
κιπας Ῥωμαῖοι καλοῦσιν. *Ambr.*

XII. (19, 13) Ἐν[5] τῇ νυκτὶ ἐν ᾗ τὴν στρατιὰν
ἀπάξειν ὁ Πύρρος ἔμελλεν[6] ἐπὶ τὸ ὄρος τῷ Ῥωμαίων ἐπιθησόμενος χάρακι λάθρα[7] ἔδοξε κατὰ
τοὺς ὕπνους ἐκπεσεῖν αὐτοῦ τοὺς πλείους ὀδόντας
καὶ πλῆθος αἵματος ἐκ τοῦ στόματος φέρεσθαι.
2 ταραχθεὶς δὲ διὰ τὴν ὄψιν καὶ μεγάλην ἔσεσθαι
συμφορὰν μαντευόμενος (ἤδη γὰρ αὐτῷ καὶ πρότερον τοιαύτην ὄψιν ἐνυπνίου θεασαμένῳ δεινή τις
συνέβη δυσποτμία[8]) ἐβούλετο μὲν[9] ἐπισχεῖν τὴν

---

[1] οὐδὲ Valesius : οὔτε P.   [2] Reiske : ἐπικουρία P.
[3] ἢ before ἄφιξις deleted by Reiske.   [5] ἐν Q : ἐν γὰρ P.
[4] οἱ added by Struve.
[6] ἀπάξειν ὁ πύρρος ἔμελλεν Q : ἔμελλεν ἀπάξειν P.
[7] τῷ ῥωμαίων . . . λάθρα om. P.

greatest of all the generals who flourished at that same period ; nor was it any inequality in the position he occupied, nor the sudden arrival of reinforcements for the other side, nor any other mischance or unexpected excuse for failure that ruined the cause of Pyrrhus, but rather the wrath of the goddess whose sanctity had been violated, a wrath of which not even Pyrrhus himself was unaware, as Proxenus the historian relates and as Pyrrhus himself records in his own memoirs.

XI. (19, 12) It was bound to happen, as might have been expected, that hoplites burdened with helmets, breastplates and shields and advancing against hilly positions by long trails that were not even used by people but were mere goat-paths through woods and crags, would keep no order and, even before the enemy came in sight, would be weakened in body by thirst and fatigue.

Those who fight in close combat with cavalry spears grasped by the middle with both hands and who usually save the day in battles are called *principes* by the Romans.

XII. (19, 13) During the night in which Pyrrhus was intending to lead his army against the hill to attack the Roman camp secretly it seemed to him in his dreams that most of his teeth fell out and a quantity of blood poured from his mouth. Disturbed by this vision and divining that some great misfortune would ensue, since he had already on an earlier occasion beheld a similar vision in a dream and some dire disaster had followed, he wished to hold back

---

⁸ ἤδη γὰρ . . . δυσποτμία Q : om. P.   ⁹ μὲν om. P.

ἡμέραν ἐκείνην, οὐκ ἴσχυσε δὲ νικῆσαι τὴν πεπρω-
μένην, ἐναντιουμένων τῶν φίλων πρὸς τὴν ἀναβολὴν
καὶ μὴ μεθεῖναι τὸν καιρὸν ἐκ τῶν χειρῶν ἀξιούντων. *Vales.*; *Ambr.*

3 (14) Ἀναβάντων δὲ τῶν σὺν τῷ Πύρρῳ μετὰ
τῶν ἐλεφάντων αἴσθησιν οἱ Ῥωμαῖοι λαβόντες
σκυμνίον ἐλέφαντος τιτρώσκουσιν, ὃ πολλὴν ἀκοσμίαν τοῖς Ἕλλησιν ἐνεποίησε καὶ φυγήν· οἱ δὲ
Ῥωμαῖοι δύο μὲν ἐλέφαντας ἀποκτείνουσιν, ὀκτὼ
δὲ κατακλείσαντες εἰς χωρίον ἀνέξοδον παραδόντων
τῶν ἐπ᾽ αὐτοῖς Ἰνδῶν ζῶντας παραλαμβάνουσι,
τῶν δὲ στρατιωτῶν πολὺν φόνον ἐργάζονται.
Ambr.

XIII. (20, 1) Ὁ ὕπατος Φαβρίκιος τιμητὴς
γενόμενος ἄνδρα δυσὶ μὲν ὑπατείαις, μιᾷ δὲ δικτα-
τωρείᾳ κεκοσμημένον, Πόπλιον Κορνήλιον Ῥου-
φῖνον, ἐξέβαλεν ἐκ τοῦ συνεδρίου τῆς βουλῆς, ὅτι
πρῶτος ἐν ἀργυρῶν ἐκπωμάτων κατασκευῇ πολυτελὴς ἔδοξε γενέσθαι, δέκα λίτρας ἐκπωμάτων
κτησάμενος· αὗται δ᾽ εἰσὶν ὀλίγῳ πλείους ὀκτὼ
μνῶν Ἀττικῶν. *Ambr.*

2 (2) Ἀθηναῖοι μὲν δόξης ἔτυχον ὅτι τοὺς ῥᾳθύ-
μους καὶ ἀργοὺς καὶ μηδὲν ἐπιτηδεύοντας τῶν
χρησίμων ὡς ἀδικοῦντας τὸ κοινὸν ἐζημίουν,
Λακεδαιμόνιοι δὲ ὅτι τοῖς πρεσβυτάτοις ἐπέτρεπον
τοὺς ἀκοσμοῦντας τῶν πολιτῶν ἐν ὁτῳδήτινι τῶν
δημοσίων τόπῳ ταῖς βακτηρίαις παίειν· τῶν δὲ
κατ᾽ οἰκίαν γενομένων οὔτε πρόνοιαν οὔτε φυλακὴν
ἐποιοῦντο, τὴν αὔλειον θύραν ἑκάστου ὅρον εἶναι
3 τῆς ἐλευθερίας τοῦ βίου νομίζοντες. (3) Ῥωμαῖοι
δὲ πᾶσαν ἀναπετάσαντες οἰκίαν καὶ μέχρι τοῦ
δωματίου τὴν ἀρχὴν τῶν τιμητῶν[1] προαγαγόντες

that day, but was not strong enough to defeat Fate ; for his friends opposed the delay and demanded that he should not let the favourable opportunity slip from his grasp.

(14) When Pyrrhus and those with him had ascended along with the elephants, and the Romans became aware of it, they wounded an elephant cub, which caused great confusion and flight among the Greeks. The Romans killed two elephants, and hemming eight others in a place that had no outlet, took them alive when the Indian mahouts surrendered them ; and they wrought great slaughter among the soldiers.

XIII. (20, 1) The consul Fabricius, having become censor, expelled from the senatorial body a man who had been honoured with two consulships and one dictatorship, Publius Cornelius Rufinus, because he was believed to have been the first to be extravagant in supplying himself with silver goblets, having acquired ten pounds' weight of them ; this is a little more than eight Attic minae.

(2) The Athenians gained repute because they punished as harmful to the state the indolent and idle who followed no useful pursuits, and the Lacedaemonians because they permitted their oldest men to beat with their canes such of the citizens as were disorderly in any public place whatever ; but for what took place in the homes they took no thought or precaution, holding that each man's house-door marked the boundary within which he was free to live as he pleased. (3) But the Romans, throwing open every house and extending the authority of the censors even to the bed-chamber, made that office

---

[1] τοῦ τιμητοῦ Struve.

ἁπάντων ἐποίησαν ἐπίσκοπον καὶ φύλακα τῶν ἐν
αὐταῖς γινομένων, οὔτε δεσπότην οἰόμενοι δεῖν
ὠμὸν εἶναι περὶ τὰς[1] τιμωρίας οἰκετῶν οὔτε πατέρα
πικρὸν ἢ μαλθακὸν πέρα τοῦ μετρίου περὶ τέκνων
ἀγωγὰς οὔτε ἄνδρα περὶ κοινωνίαν γαμετῆς
γυναικὸς ἄδικον οὔτε παῖδας γηραιῶν ἀπειθεῖς
πατέρων οὔτε ἀδελφοὺς γνησίους τὸ πλεῖον ἀντὶ
τοῦ ἴσου διώκοντας, οὐ συμπόσια καὶ μέθας
παννυχίους, οὐκ ἀσελγείας[2] καὶ φθορὰς ἡλικιωτῶν[3]
νέων, οὐχ ἱερῶν ἢ ταφῶν[4] προγονικὰς τιμὰς
ἐκλιπούσας, οὐκ ἄλλο τῶν παρὰ τὸ καθῆκον ἢ
συμφέρον τῇ πόλει πραττομένων οὐδέν.

Ἐληΐζοντο τὰς κτήσεις τῶν πολιτῶν κατὰ τὴν
τοῦ βασιλίζειν αἰτίαν. Ambr.

XIV. (20, 4) Νεμέριος Φάβιος Πίκτωρ καὶ Κόιντος Φάβιος[5] Μάξιμος καὶ Κόιντος Ὀγούλνιος[6]
πρὸς τὸν Φιλάδελφον Πτολεμαῖον πρεσβεύσαντες[7]
καὶ δωρεαῖς ἰδίαις τιμηθέντες ὑπ᾽ αὐτοῦ (ἦρχε δὲ
τῆς Αἰγύπτου δεύτερος μετὰ τὸν Μακεδόνα Ἀλέξ-
ανδρον) ἐπειδὴ κατέπλευσαν εἰς τὴν πόλιν, τά τε
ἄλλα ἀπήγγειλαν ὅσα διεπράξαντο κατὰ τὴν ἀποδημίαν καὶ τὰς δωρεὰς ἃς παρὰ τοῦ βασιλέως
ἔλαβον εἰς τὸ δημόσιον ἀνήνεγκαν· οὓς ἡ βουλὴ
πάντων ἀγασθεῖσα τῶν ἔργων οὐκ εἴασε δημοσιῶ-
σαι τὰς βασιλικὰς χάριτας, ἀλλ᾽ εἰς τοὺς ἑαυτῶν
οἴκους ἀπενέγκασθαι τιμὰς ἀρετῆς καὶ κόσμους
ἐκγόνοις. Ambr.

XV. (20, 5) Οἱ Βρέττιοι ἑκόντες ὑποταγέντες
Ῥωμαίοις τὴν ἡμίσειαν τῆς ὀρεινῆς παρέδωκαν

[1] Mai : τῆς Q.   [2] Struve : ἀμελείας Q.
[3] Jacoby : ἡλικιῶν Q.   [4] Mai : ταφρῶν Q.
[5] Mai : φάκιος Q.   [6] Kiessling : ἀλγούνιος Q.

the overseer and guardian of everything that took place in the homes ; for they believed that neither a master should be cruel in the punishments meted out to his slaves, nor a father unduly harsh or lenient in the training of his children, nor a husband unjust in his partnership with his lawfully-wedded wife, nor children disobedient toward their aged parents, nor should own brothers strive for more than their equal share, and they thought there should be no banquets and revels lasting all night long, no wantonness and corrupting of youthful comrades, no neglect of the ancestral honours of sacrifices and funerals, nor any other of the things that are done contrary to propriety and the advantage of the state.

They plundered the possessions of the citizens on the ground that they were affecting the ways of a king.

XIV. (20, 4) Numerius Fabius Pictor, Quintus Fabius Maximus and Quintus Ogulnius, who had gone as ambassadors to Ptolemy Philadelphus, the second to rule Egypt after the Macedonian Alexander, and had been honoured by him with individual gifts, upon returning to Rome not only reported all that they had accomplished during their absence, but also turned over to the public treasury the gifts which they had received from the king. But the senate, admiring the men for all their achievements, did not permit them to turn the royal gifts over to the state, but allowed them to take them back to their homes as rewards of merit and decorations for their descendants.

XV. (20, 5) The Bruttians, after submitting willingly to the Romans, delivered up to them one-half

---

⁷ περὶ πρεσβείας after πρεσβεύσαντες deleted by Kiessling.

αὐτοῖς, ἣ καλεῖται μὲν Σίλα, μεστὴ δ' ἐστὶν ὕλης
εἰς οἰκοδομάς τε καὶ ναυπηγίας καὶ πᾶσαν ἄλλην
κατασκευὴν εὐθέτου· πολλὴ μὲν γὰρ ἐλάτη πέφυκεν
οὐρανομήκης ἐν αὐτῇ, πολλὴ δὲ αἴγειρος, πολλὴ
δὲ πίειρα πεύκη ὀξύη τε καὶ πίτυς καὶ φηγὸς
ἀμφιλαφὴς καὶ μελίαι ταῖς διαρρεούσαις λιβάσι
πιαινόμεναι, καὶ πᾶσα ἄλλη βαθεῖα συνυφαινομένη[1]
τοῖς κλάδοις ὕλη σκιερὸν ἀποτελοῦσα δι' ὅλης
ἡμέρας τὸ ὄρος.

2 (6) Ἐξ ἧς ἡ μὲν ἔγγιστα θαλάττης καὶ ποταμῶν
φυομένη τμηθεῖσα τὴν ἀπὸ ρίζης τομὴν ὁλόκληρος
ἐπὶ τοὺς λιμένας τοὺς ἔγγιστα κατάγεται, πάσῃ
διαρκὴς Ἰταλίᾳ πρός τε τὰ ναυτικὰ καὶ πρὸς τὰς
τῶν οἰκιῶν κατασκευάς· ἡ δὲ ἄνω θαλάττης καὶ
ποταμῶν πρόσω κορμασθεῖσα κατὰ μέρη κώπας
τε παρέχει καὶ κοντοὺς καὶ ὅπλα[2] παντοῖα καὶ
σκεύη τὰ κατοικίδια, φοράδην ὑπ' ἀνθρώπων κομιζο-
μένη· ἡ δὲ πλείστη καὶ πιοτάτη πιττουργεῖται
καὶ παρέχει πασῶν ὧν ἴσμεν ἡμεῖς εὐωδεστάτην
τε καὶ γλυκυτάτην τὴν καλουμένην Βρεττίαν
πίτταν· ἀφ' ἧς μεγάλας ὁ τῶν Ῥωμαίων δῆμος
καθ' ἕκαστον ἐνιαυτὸν ἐκ τῶν μισθώσεων λαμβάνει
προσόδους. Ambr.

XVI. (20, 7) Ἐγένετο δευτέρα ἐπανάστασις ἐν
τῇ πόλει τῶν Ῥηγίνων ὑπὸ τῆς καταλειφθείσης[3]
αὐτόθι Ῥωμαϊκῆς καὶ συμμαχικῆς φρουρᾶς, καὶ
δι' αὐτὴν σφαγαί τε[4] πολλῶν ἀνθρώπων καὶ φυγαί.
τούτους τιμωρησόμενος τοὺς ἀποστάντας ἅτερος
τῶν ὑπάτων Γάιος Γενύκιος ἐξήγαγε τὴν στρα-
τιάν· γενόμενος δὲ τῆς πόλεως ἐγκρατὴς Ῥηγίνων
μὲν τοῖς φυγάσι ἀπέδωκε τὰ ἑαυτῶν ἔχειν, τοὺς

[1] Kiessling : συμφαινομένη Q, συμφυομένη Struve.

of their mountainous district, called Sila, which is full of timber suitable for the building of houses and ships and every other kind of construction. For much fir grows there, towering to the sky, much black poplar, much pitch pine, beech, stone pine, wide-spreading oak, ash trees enriched by the streams flowing through their midst, and every other kind of tree with densely-intertwined branches that keep the mountain in shadow throughout the whole day.

(6) Of this timber, that which grows nearest the sea and rivers is felled at the root and taken down in full lengths to the nearest harbours, sufficient in quantity to serve all Italy for shipbuilding and the construction of houses. That which grows inland from the sea and remote from rivers is cut up in sections for the making of oars, poles and all kinds of domestic implements and equipment, and is carried out on men's shoulders. But the largest and most resinous part of the timber is made into pitch, furnishing the most fragrant and sweetest pitch known to us, the kind called Bruttian, from the farming out of which the Roman people receive large revenues every year.

XVI. (20, 7) There was a second uprising in Rhegium, on the part of the garrison of Romans and allies which had been left there, and it resulted in the slaying and exile of many persons. To punish these rebels one of the consuls, Gaius Genucius, led out the army. After becoming master of the city, he restored their possessions to the keeping of the Rhegian exiles, and arresting those who had made the

---

² Struve : ὅπλων Q.
³ Mai : καταληφθείσης Q.
⁴ καί after τε deleted by Mai.

DIONYSIUS OF HALICARNASSUS

δὲ ἐπιθεμένους τῇ πόλει συλλαβὼν δεσμίους εἰς
Ῥώμην ἀπήγαγεν· ἐφ᾽ οἷς οὕτως ὠργίσθη καὶ ἠγα-
νάκτησεν ἥ τε βουλὴ καὶ ὁ δῆμος ὥστε μηδεμίαν γνώμην ἐπιεικῆ γενέσθαι περὶ αὐτῶν, ἀλλὰ
πάσαις ταῖς φυλαῖς ἁπάντων[1] τῶν ἐν ταῖς αἰτίαις
τὸν ἐπὶ τοῖς κακούργοις τεταγμένον ὑπὸ τῶν
2 νόμων καταψηφισθῆναι θάνατον. (8) κυρωθέντος
δὲ τοῦ περὶ τῆς τιμωρίας δόγματος πάτταλοί τε
κατεπάγησαν ἐν τῇ[2] ἀγορᾷ, καὶ παραγόμενοι κατὰ
τριακοσίους ἄνδρας, περιηγμένοι τοὺς ἀγκῶνας
ὀπίσω προσεδοῦντο τοῖς παττάλοις γυμνοί· ἔπειτα
μάστιξιν αἰκισθέντες ἁπάντων ὁρώντων ἀπεκόπ-
τοντο τῷ πελέκει τοὺς ὑπὸ ταῖς κεφαλαῖς νωτιαίους
τένοντας· καὶ μετὰ τούτους ἕτεροι τριακόσιοι, καὶ
αὖθις ἄλλοι τοσοῦτοι διεφθάρησαν, οἱ σύμπαντες
τετρακισχίλιοι καὶ πεντακόσιοι. καὶ οὐδὲ ταφῆς
ἔτυχον, ἀλλ᾽ ἑλκυσθέντες ἐκ τῆς ἀγορᾶς εἰς ἀναπεπταμένον τι πρὸ τῆς πόλεως χωρίον ὑπὸ οἰωνῶν
καὶ κυνῶν διεφορήθησαν. Ambr.

XVII. (20, 9) Τὸ ἄπορον πλῆθος, ᾧ[3] καλῶν
καὶ δικαίων φροντὶς ἦν οὐδεμία, παρακρουσθὲν ὑπὸ
Σαυνίτου τινὸς εἰς τὸ αὐτὸ συνέρχεται. καὶ τὸ μὲν
πρῶτον ἐπὶ τοῖς ὄρεσιν ἄγραυλον καὶ †πλείονα[4]
τὸν βίον εἶχεν, ἐπεὶ δὲ πλεῖον ἤδη καὶ ἀξιόμαχον
ἐδόκει γεγονέναι, πόλιν ἐχυρὰν καταλαμβάνεται,
ὅθεν ὁρμώμενον ἐληίζετο πᾶσαν τὴν κύκλῳ χώραν.
2 ἐπὶ τούτους ἐξήγαγον στρατιὰν οἱ ὕπατοι καὶ οὐ
πολλῇ σὺν πραγματείᾳ τὴν πόλιν αἱρησάμενοι τοὺς

[1] ἁπάντων Jacoby, δὴ ἁπάντων Struve : διὰ πάντων Q.
[2] τῇ added by Struve.
[3] ᾧ added by Visconti.

428

attack upon the city, he took them back in chains to Rome. The senate and the people were so enraged and indignant at them that no moderate sentiment was expressed concerning them, but by the vote of all the tribes sentence was passed against all the accused that they should die in the manner prescribed by the laws for malefactors. (8) When the decree concerning their punishment had been ratified, stakes were fixed in the Forum and the men, being brought forward three hundred at one time, were bound naked to the stakes, with their elbows bent behind them. Then, after they had been scourged with whips in the sight of all, the back tendons of their necks were cut with an axe. After them another three hundred were destroyed, and then other groups of like size, a total of forty-five hundred in all. And they did not even receive burial, but were dragged out of the Forum into an open space before the city, where they were torn asunder by birds and dogs.

XVII. (20, 9) The multitude of the needy, who had no thought for what was honourable and just, flocked together, misled by a certain Samnite. And at first they led a life of hardship [1] in the open upon the mountains ; but when at length they seemed to have become more numerous and to be adequate for battle, they seized a strong city and with that as their base plundered all the country round about. Against these men the consuls led forth an army, and having without much difficulty taken their city,

---

[1] The adjective modifying " life " is corrupted in the MS. and the correct reading is a matter of pure conjecture. The translation follows Jacoby's reading.

---

⁴ πλείονα Q : μείονα Struve, λιτὸν Kiessling, ἀλήμονα M. Haupt, πλάνητα Hertlein, ὑπαίθριον Naber, κακόπαθον Jacoby.

μὲν αἰτίους τῆς ἀποστάσεως αἰκισάμενοι ῥάβδοις ἀπέκτειναν, τοὺς δὲ λοιποὺς ἐλαφυροπώλησαν. ἔτυχε
τῷ πρότερον ἐνιαυτῷ πεπραμένη μετὰ τῶν ἄλλων
δορικτήτων ἡ γῆ, καὶ τὸ πεσὸν ἀπὸ τῆς τιμῆς ἀργύριον διῃρημένον τοῖς πολίταις. *Ambr.*

they scourged with rods and put to death the authors of the revolt and sold the rest as booty. It chanced that the land had been sold the previous year along with the other conquests of the spear, and the money realized from its price had been divided among the citizens.

GENERAL INDEX

Numbers refer to volume and page ; volume numbers are as a rule repeated only where their omission might cause confusion. To facilitate identification of the various Roman names, the date of at least one important magistracy held is added in parenthesis. All dates are B.C., and are those of the ordinary chronology (Varro's) rather than those of Dionysius, which are regularly two years later, up to the time of the decemvirate (see Introd. to Vol. I, p. xxix).

Authors and other sources cited in the *Antiquities* are listed at the end of this Index.

ABORIGINES, origin of, **1** 31-43, 307, 415 ; cities of, 43-49, 51-55, 61, 65 f., 415, 449, 451, 457 ; unite with Pelasgians, 55, 61-67, 69, 75, 83, 315, 451 ; early dwellers on site of Rome, 29, 99, 109, 125, 129, 307, 313 f. ; under rule of Faunus, 101, 139, 141, 143 ; under Latinus, 143, 189 f., 195-201, 209, 239-241 ; called Latins, 31, 143, 201
Acallaris, **1** 207
Acanthus, Olympic victor, **4** 363
Acarnanians, **1** 165, 169 : in army of Pyrrhus, **7** 387 f., 401
Acestorides, Athenian archon, **3** 107
Achaeans, take Troy, **1** 145-151, 157, 173, 193, 209, 229, 237, 239, 505 ; *cf.* **7** 235
—— a nation in the Peloponnesus, **1** 83 ; *cf.* 309
—— a tribe on the Euxine, **1** 309
Achaeus, **1** 57
Achaia, in the Peloponnesus, **1** 35, 83
—— in Thessaly, **1** 57
Achilles, **1** 157, 173, **3** 55 ; shield of, **4** 367
Acropolis, at Athens, **1** 93, **7** 5, 261
Acte, peninsula of Chalcidice, **1** 81
Actium, **1** 165

Adriatic sea, **1** 9, 453. See also Ionian gulf
Aeacides, father of Pyrrhus, **7** 353
Aebutius, L., cos. (463), **6** 147 f., 185
—— Elva, P., cos. (499), **3** 173
—— —— T., master of horse (496), **3** 245, 249, 253, 271
—— Flavus, T., one of envoys sent to seceded plebeians, **4** 61
Accalum, **7** 327
Aediles, first appointed, **4** 123 f. ; duties of, *ibid.*, 139 f., 221-225, 245 ; insignia of, **4** 139 f. ; method of their election changed, **6** 65, 85 ; see also **3** 57, **4** 189, **6** 281 f., 329
Aegesta (Segesta), built by Aeneas, **1** 173 f.
Aegestus, a Trojan **1** 151, 171-175
—— a priest at Lavinium, **1** 221
—— son of Numitor, **1** 353
Aemilia, a Vestal, **1** 511
Aemilius Barbula, L., cos. (281), **7** 349
—— Mamercus, L., cos. (484), **5** 253-267 ; cos. II (478), 341-351; cos. III (473), **6** 45-53, 57, 93 f.
—— Q. (cos. 282), one of envoys sent to Pyrrhus, **7** 363
—— Ti., cos. (470), **6** 91, 105 f. ; cos. II (467), 121 f.

433

GENERAL INDEX

Aeneas, ancestry of, **1** 207, *cf.* 201-205 ; at fall of Troy, 147-151, 157 ; leads Trojans to Italy, 153-177, 189, 207 f., 219, 237, 243, **317**, 505 ; at Laurentum, 181-189 ; founds Lavinium, 189, 207 f. ; makes compact with Latinus, 189-201 ; succeeds to rule over Latins, 211 ; death of, 211 f. ; shrines and monuments to, 167, 175, 179 f., 213 ; other references to, **2** 137, 481, **4** 59, 91, **5** 57, **6** 265 and n., **7** 235

—— different from preceding, leads Trojans to Italy, **1** 177

—— son of Silvius, Alban king, **1** 233

Aeneia, town in Thrace, **1** 161 f., 179

—— later called Janiculum, **1** 243

Aeneias cult-title of Aphrodite, **1** 165, 175

Aeolic, nearest of Greek dialects to Latin, **1** 309 and n. 2

Aequians, repeatedly at war with Romans, **3** 343 f., 361 f., 371, **4** 7, 81 f., **5** 25, 43, 75, 183 f., 203, 249, 283, 289, 293, 331, 341-345, 351, **6** 41, 85 f., 105-161, 191, 195 f., 231-235. 239-251, 255, 271, 295, 309-313, 321-327, 345, **7** 11, 15, 25, 29, 49, 59, 65, 69, 77 f., 83, 93, 101, 135, 155-159, 169

Aequicoli, another name for the Aequians, **1** 521 and n.

Aequimelium, **7** 215

Aesculapius, **3** 43, **4** 373

Aesop, imitated, **4** 101

Aetolians, **1** 57, 169 ; in army of Pyrrhus, **7** 387 f.

Aezeians, **1** 37

Aezeius, **1** 35, 37

Agatharchus, Olympic victor, **2** 407

Agathocles, **1** 239, **7** 415

Agema, **7** 389

Agrippa, Alban king, **1** 233

—— See Menenius

Agylla, earlier name of Caere, **1** 65, **2** 217

Ahala, name given to Servilius, **7** 215

Aias (Ajax), **4** 363, **7** 409

Alba, Alban king, **1** 233

Alba Longa, founded, **1** 143 f., 217 f., 243, *cf.* 187 ; kings of, 217-223, 229-235 ; razed to the ground, **2** 119, 129 f., 135 f., 147, **3** 301 ; other references to, **1** 275, 277, 293, 295, 297, 499, **2** 11, 43, 95, 117, 121, 431, **3** 299, **7** 225

Alban district, **1** 219, **7** 269

—— lake, **1** 219, 233, **7** 225-231

—— mount, **1** 219, **2** 431, **5** 271, **7** 225 f.

—— wine, **1** 219, **7** 269

Albans, colonize 30 Latin cities, **1** 145, **2** 49 f., 137, 147, **3** 183 f., 299, *cf.* **2** 441, **5** 47-57 ; found Rome, **1** 235, **2**43, 293, 315, 489, **2** 41, **3** 299, **4** 91 ; found other cities, **1** 415 f., 457, 465, **2** 3 ; plan war against Rome, **2** 7-79, 87 ; prove faithless allies, 95-115 ; their punishment, 115-137, 141 f., **3** 301 ; other references to, **1** 253, 255, 317, 419, **3** 225, **5** 25

Albula, earlier name of the Tiber, **1** 233

Alcaeus, **3** 233

Alcmena, **1** 131

Alcyone, **1** 71

Alexander (Paris), **1** 157

—— the Great, **1** 9, 163, **7** 425

Algidum (Algidus), **6** 235, **7** 11, 79, 93, 131 145

[Alienus], L., **6** 329 and n.

Allodius, Alban king, **1** 233

Alpheus, **1** 111

Alps, **1** 31, 137, **7** 259

Alsium, **1** 67

Aluntium, **1** 169

Amata, wife of Latinus, **1** 211

Ambracia, **1** 165 f., **7** 387

Ambracian gulf, **1** 165

Ambraciots, in army of Pyrrhus, **7** 387 f.

Ambrax, **1** 165

Amiternum, **1** 49, 451

Amphictyon, **2** 353

Amphictyonic council, **2** 353

Amulius, supplants Numitor as Alban king and plots death of Numitor's descendants, **1** 235, 253-263, 277-293, **3** 225

Amyntor, **1** 91

GENERAL INDEX

GENERAL INDEX

GENERAL INDEX

GENERAL INDEX

Cloelius Gracchus, Aequian leader, **6** 241-251

—— Siculus, Q., cos. (498), **3** 177, 215-221, 229-233

—— T., mil. trib. (444), **7** 189 f.

Cluilian ditches, **2** 15, **5** 61

Cluilius, Alban leader, **2** 7-19, 35

Clusium and Clusians, **2** 199, **3** 63, 101, **7** 255

Clymene, **1** 57

Clytodora, **1** 207

Cnossus, **4** 369

Codone, **1** 159

Cohort, of 500 men, **6** 139 ; of 600, 159 ; of 800, 311

Collatia, **2** 193 f., 473 ; *cf.* 503 n.

Collatinus. See under Tarquinius

Colline gate. See under Porta

—— hill (error for Quirinal), **1** 515, n. 3, **2** 313, n. 4

—— region, **2** 313

Colonies, of Alba and of Rome. See under Albans and Roman colonies

Cominium, captured by Postumius, **7** 337

Cominius, Postumus, cos. (501), **3** 147, 243 ; cos. II (493), **4** 3, 125-137 ; **5** 63

Comitia centuriata, as organized by Servius Tullius, **2** 333-337, **4** 319-325, **5** 253, **6** 223 ; met in Campus Martius to elect magistrates and vote on various measures, **2** 525, **3** 35 f., 39 f., 331 f., **4** 3, 319, **5** 253, 279, 281, 331, **6** 63, 77, 277, **7** 149 *bis*, 151

—— *curiata*, **1** 353, 373, 477 f., 485, **2** 301, 309 *bis*, 333, 491, 511, 525, **3** 17, **5** 279 ; *cf.* **3** 7. See also the references given under *Concilium plebis curiatim*

—— *tributa*, **4** 53 f., 61, **5** 279, **6** 47, 281 f., 303, 307, **7** 167 ; acts as court to try Coriolanus, **4** 319, 323 f., 339 f., 349, **5** 19, *cf.* **3** 59 f., **4** 221-255, 259, 293, 307, 311 f., 315 f. ; tries other patricians, **4** 341-345, **5** 233-239, **6** 11 f., 15-35, 71, 77, 307 f., 329-333, 355, **7** 151-155 ; regular meeting-place the Forum, or, more specifically, the sanctuary of Vulcan, **1** 455, **4** 55, 197, **7** 127 ;

meetings appointed for third market-day, **4** 317, **6** 59, 171, 287, **7** 55 ; patricians not to be present when meeting called by tribunes, **4** 195, but *cf.* **6** 59. See also the references under *Concilium plebis tributim*

Comitium, **2** 397, **6** 303

Compitalia, **2** 315

[*Concilium plebis curiatim*], **4** 121, 195-199, **6** 57 and n., 175

[—— —— *tributim*], **6** 57 and n., 65 f., 85, **7** 151

Consentia, **7** 385 n.

Considius, Q., trib. (476), **6** 11

†Constantia, error for Consentia, **7** 385 and n.

Consualia, **1** 107, 403

Consuls, replace kings, **2** 495 f., 501 f., 525, **3** 3, **4** 245, 309, **6** 283 ; insignia, **2** 225 f., 497, **3** 7, 59, 227 f., **6** 225, 365 ; various dates for taking office, **3** 3, **4** 3, **6** 3, 347 f., 363, **7** 193 ; vacancies usually filled promptly, **3** 39 f., 59, **6** 221 f., 345, but not always, **3** 173, **5** 327-331, **6** 149-153, 251 f. ; duties and privileges, **2** 501 f., **3** 3, **4** 193, 249, **5** 247, 279, **6** 165, 271, 283 ; in conflict with tribunes, **4** 193-201, 231, 245, 253, **5** 247 f., 267 f., 279, **6** 45-53, 79-85, 165 f., 173 f., 209, 221-227, 257, 271-275, 279-287, 303-309, **7** 171 ; fail to give effect to agrarian law, **5** 247, **6** 47 ; ignore summons to stand trial before popular assembly, **6** 281-287, *cf.* 307 ; brought to trial after expiration of term, **6** 11 f., 15-35, 47 f., 103 f., 327-333, **7** 243 f. ; court populace, **6** 327, 333 ; each holds superior authority in alternate months, **3** 7, **6** 65, 313 ; replaced, at will of people, by military tribunes, **7** 175-189

Consulship, regarded as embodying the royal power, **4** 245, **6** 283 ; long open only to patricians, **3** 57 ; proposal to open to plebeians defeated, **7** 167 f., 171 f. ; military tribuneship, open to plebeians, offered as compromise, 175-189

GENERAL INDEX

441

GENERAL INDEX

Elymus, mountain in Sicily, **1** 175 ; *cf.* 173, n. 3
Emathion, **1** 241
Enyalius, **1** 449, 455, **7** 393
Epeans, **1** 111, 139, 201, 315 f.
Ephesus, **2** 353
Epigoni, **1** 19 and n. 1
Epiphanies of gods, **1** 487 f., 495, 509-515, **3** 277-281, **5** 165-169, **7** 243
Epirots, **7** 353, 361
Epirus, **1** 167, **7** 351, 383
Epitelides, Olympic victor, **2** 265
Equites, **2** 253, 327, 333, 349, **3** 169, 279 f., 321, 343, 369, **4** 361 f., **6** 195, 205, **7** 205-209
Erechtheus, **7** 261
Eretrians, **4** 153
Eretum, **2** 143, 219, 271, 435, **3** 133, **7** 11
Erichthonius, **1** 163 f., 207
Erinyes, **1** 173. See also Furies
Erythrae, **1** 183 and n. 2, **2** 469
Eryx, **1** 173, n. 3
Esquiline gate. See under Porta
—— hill, **1** 421, **2** 309 f.
—— region, **2** 313
Etruria and Etruscans. See Tyrrhenia and Tyrrhenians
Euboea, **1** 57
Eumaeus, **4** 377
Eunomus, **1** 453
Europe, **1** 7 f., 43, 117, 153, 181, 203, **2** 353, **4** 91, **7** 259 f.
Eurybates, Olympic victor, **2** 5
Euryleon, earlier name of Ascanius, **1** 213, or brother of Ascanius, 237
Eurystheus, **1** 125
Euxine sea, **1** 11, 309, **7** 259 f.
Evander, settles Arcadians beside Palatine hill, **1** 99, 103, 129 f., 139, 141, 201, 267, 273, 289, 307, 315
Evegorus, **7** 417

FABIDIUS. See Modius
Fabii, Roman *gens*, undertake to guard Roman territory against Veientes, **5** 337-343 ; all perish, 353-367, **6** 13, 121
Fabius, K., quaestor (485), denounces Cassius, **5** 233-239, 253, 287, 293 ; cos. (484), 253 f., 263 f. ; cos. II (481), 287, 291 ;

hated by his soldiers and forced to end expedition against Tyrrhenians without winning a victory, 293-297, 313 ; brother of Marcus, 313, 321, 329, 365 ; decorated for bravery in later battle, 329 ; cos. III (479), 331-335 ; on the Cremera, 339 f., 343
Fabius, M., cos. (483), **5** 267, 273 ; cos. II (480), 299 f. ; fights against Veientes, 307-329 ; declines triumph and resigns consulship, 329 ; leads Fabii to the Cremera, 337-343 ; leaves one son, 365 f.
—— Pictor, Numerius, **7** 425
—— Q., brother of Marcus and Caeso, **5** 253, 321, 365 ; cos. (485), **5** 233, 249 f. ; cos. II (482), 281-285 ; legate and proconsul, dies in battle, 321
—— Vibulanus, Q., son of Marcus, **5** 367 and n. 2 ; cos. (467), **6** 121-129 ; cos. II (465), 131 f. ; cos. III (459), 231-239, **7** 19, 51, 153 ; guards Rome in absence of consuls, **6** 239, 245 f. ; decemvir, **6** 361, **7** 77 ; *cf.* **6** 155, n. 1
—— Q., ambassador to Gauls, attacks them, **7** 255 f.
—— [Maximus Gurges, Q.], cos. (292), defeats Pentrians, **7** 335 ; driven by Postumius to resign his proconsular authority, 335 f.
—— Maximus, Q., ambassador to Ptolemy, **7** 425
Fabricius, C. (cos. 282), one of three ambassadors sent to Pyrrhus, **7** 361 f. ; rejects the king's offer of riches and power in Epirus, 363-385 ; goes to aid of Thurii, 401-405, 409 ; censor, 423
Faith, Public, temple erected to, **1** 535 f.
Falerii, **1** 67, **7** 239 f.
Falernian district, **1** 119
—— wine, **1** 219, **7** 269
Faliscans, surrender voluntarily to Camillus, **7** 239 f.
Faunus, king of the Aborigines, **1** 101, 139 f., 143
—— rural deity, **3** 51

443

GENERAL INDEX

GENERAL INDEX

69-79, 87 ; war with Fidenates and treachery of Mettius, 93-115 ; punishment meted out to Mettius and Alba razed, 115-137 ; war with Sabines, 139-147, and with Latins, 147-151 ; king and whole household perish in burning palace, 151-155 ; other references, 157, 161, 167

Hybrilides, Athenian archon, **4** 147

Iapodes, **7** 327
Iapygia, **7** 341
Iapygian promontory, **1** 37 f., 169
Iapygians, **1** 71, **7** 343
Iasus, **1** 203 f.
Iberians, **1** 307, *cf.* 69
Iberus, **7** 261
Icilius, L., trib. (456), proposes that Aventine district be assigned to the poor and needy for building houses, **6** 273-277 ; again tribune, 279, 301
—— L., betrothed to Verginia, **7** 95, 97, 101, 107, 111, 125, 155
—— M., friend of Sp. Verginius, **6** 331
—— Sp., one of envoys sent by seceded plebeians to the senate, **4** 119 ; trib. (481), demands action on law already passed for allotment of public lands, **5** 289-293 ; see also **4** 187 n., 197 n., **5** 91
—— brother of second L. Icilius above, **7** 111, 123
—— father of M. Icilius, **6** 331
Ida, mountain in Phrygia, **1** 149 f., 155, 183, 205
Idaean goddess (Cybele), **1** 365 f.
Idaeus, **1** 203
Ides. See under Calendar
Ilia (Rhea Silvia), **1** 253-263, 269, 289
Ilithyia, **2** 319
Ilium, **1** 111, 151, 157, 179, 201, 207, 277, 499 ; inhabitants of, 147, 505. See also Troy
Illyria, **7** 327
Inachus, river of Argos, **1** 83
Indians, **4** 359 ; in Pyrrhus' army, **7** 423
Inscriptions, **1** 63, 167, 171, 213,

223, 467, 471, **2** 145, 357, 429, 455 f., **5** 241 f., **6** 129, 277
Insignia, of kings, **1** 397, **2** 223-227, 395, 497, 501, **3** 101, 229, **4** 141, **6** 247 ; of consuls, **2** 225 f., 497, **3** 7, 59, 229, **5** 269, **6** 225, 365, *cf.* **5** 131, 157 ; of dictators, **3** 227 f., **6** 247 ; of generals celebrating a triumph, **1** 409, **2** 223, n. 1, 227, 497, **3** 137 f., 333, **5** 201, **6** 161 ; of aediles, **4** 139 f. ; of interreges, **1** 477 ; of decemvirs, **6** 355, 363 f.
Inter duos lucos, place between citadel and Capitol, **1** 355 and n.
Interreges, appointed after death of each of first four kings and of second Tarquin, **1** 477, 481, **2** 3, 155, 181, 501 f., 525 ; Servius and Tarquin take over sovereignty without such preliminaries, **2** 291, 301, 375, 403, 521 f. ; rarely required under republic, **5** 281, 331, **6** 153, **7** 67, 191 ; when not needed, **3** 217, 221
Interregnum, **1** 477
Ionian sea (or gulf), **1** 31, 37, 41, 59, 91, 167, **7** 391
Ionians, **1** 83, 91, **2** 353
Isagoras, Athenian archon, **1** 249
Ischomachus, Olympic victor, **3** 3, 107
Island, in the Tiber, **3** 43 ; at Syracuse, **7** 415 ; in Arcadia, **1** 159 and n. ; in Issa, **1** 47 ; near Cutilia, **1** 51
Issa, **1** 47
Ister, the, **7** 261
Italians, **1** 71, 519 ; named after Italus, 41 ; other names given them, *ibid.*
Italiots, **7** 353, 367, 387, 413
Italus, **1** 41, 73, 113, 241, 245
Italy, *passim* ; formerly called Saturnia by the inhabitants, **1** 59, 63, 113 f., and Hesperia or Ausonia by the Greeks, 115 ; named after Italus, 41, 113, or after Hercules' calf (*vitulus*), 115 ; mention of various parts by Greek writers, 39, 83, 243 ; Dionysius' use of term, 31 ; divided by Apennines into two parts, 29 ; its fertility and manifold attractions, 115-121 ; all

447

GENERAL INDEX

451

GENERAL INDEX

and matrons accompanying them, 129 f. ; listens to his mother's pleas and at length yields, 133-161 ; announces to troops his decision to end the war, 161, and leads them home, 169 ; incurs anger of younger element who had not shared in the booty, and is violently accused by Tullus, 169 f. ; slain while making his defence before populace, 171-175 ; given magnificent funeral, 175 f. ; his virtues and weaknesses appraised, 177-181 ; honoured after death by both Volscians and Romans, 181 f. ; other references, 197, 239, 257

Marcius, Rutilus, C., besieges Privernum, 7 279 f. ; cos. IV (342), takes action to suppress insurrection of Roman army in Campania, 285, 291 f.

Market-days. See *Nundinae*

Marriage, regulations of Romulus concerning, 1 381-385 ; none dissolved until long after his time, 385 ; by capture, 397-401 ; between Romans and Latins, 3 239 f. ; prohibited between patricians and plebeians, 6 369, 7 95, 103

Marrucini, 7 389

Mars, temples of, 1 45, 3 281 ; oracle of, 1 49 ; sacred hut of, at Rome, 7 263 ; field consecrated to, 3 41 and references under Campus Martius ; reputed father of Romulus and Remus, 1 255 f., 317, 473 ; see also 1 101, 449, 2 339, 489

Marsians, 1 307

Marsic war, 2 467, 5 243

Maruvium, 1 47

Master of the Horse (*Magister equitum*), assistant to dictator, 3 227 f. ; 245, 249, 253, 271, 355 ; 6 247, 7 205-209, 213

Mater Idaea, 1 365 and n. 2

Matiene (Tiora), 1 47

Medes, empire of, 1 7

Medullia and Medullini, founded by Albans, 2 3 ; made Roman colony by Romulus, 1 417, 2 3, 4 21 ; revolts and is subdued, 2

151 ; captured by Latins, 161 f., but recovered by Ancus, 163 ; revolts and joins Sabines, 3 341

Mefula, 1 45

Megacles, companion of Pyrrhus, 7 361

Melas, Thracian gulf, 1 203

Memphis, 2 351

Menenius Lanatus, Agrippa, cos. (503), 3 127 f. ; victorious over Sabines, 135-139 ; urges senate to make overtures to seceded plebeians, 4 5-27, *cf.* 31, 39, 51, 55, 59 ; one of ten envoys sent, 61 ; addresses plebeians, 99-119 ; death and funeral, 141 f., 6 13

—— Agrippa, mil. trib. (418), 7 219

—— L., cos. (452), 6 345-351

—— T., son of Agrippa, 6 13 ; cos. (477), prepares expedition against Veientes, 5 351-355 ; fails to go to aid of Fabii on the Cremera, 367 ; incurs disgraceful defeat, 369 f., 6 35 ; brought to trial and fined, 6 11 f. ; starves himself to death, 15

Menippe, 1 91

Mercury, 7 223

Messana, 7 401 f.

Messapians, 1 119

Messene, 7 341

Messenians, 7 267

Metellus. See under Caecilius

Metilii, Alban *gens* removed to Rome, 2 131

Meton, a Tarentine, 7 351 f.

Mettius. See Curtius and Fufetius

Mezentius, king of Tyrrhenians, wars against Latins, 1 213-217, 329 ; in defeat becomes a staunch friend, 217

Milesians, ruthless toward defeated opponents, 4 347

Military tribunes. See under Tribunes

Milonia, 7 339

Miltiades, Athenian archon, 4 151 f.

Minerva, temples of, 1 47, 169 and n. 5 ; 2 243, 247, 457, 463 ; her image carried in procession, 4 373. See also Athena

GENERAL INDEX

Numitorius, P., uncle of Verginia, 7 97, 101-105, 109, 111, 125 ; as tribune, summons Sp. Oppius to trial, 153

—— son of preceding, 7 111, 123

Nundinae, 1 395 and n. 2, 4 317 ; *trinum nundinum* (three market-days), interval that must elapse before comitia could consider a matter, 4 317 and n. 1, 319, 6 59, 171, 287. 7 55

Nymphs, worshipped, 4 373

OATH, military, observed by Romans most strictly of all oaths, 7 143 ; 3 371, 6 69, 227, 7 149

—— by one's good faith, strongest used by Romans, 1 537, 5 319, 6 79, 7 171

Oblacus, 7 359-361

Ocean, 1 11, 35, 7 385 ; *cf.* 1 83

Oceanus, 5 77, 83, 87

Ocriculum, 7 339

Ocrisia, mother of Servius Tullius, 2 267 f., 275, 303

Odysseus, 1 227, 237, 239, 2 419, 4 363 f., 7 235. See also Ulysses

Oeniadae, 1 169

Oenotria, 1 37

Oenotrians, 1 37-43, 71 f., 307, 415

Oenotrus, 1 35 f., 41, 201, 315

Ogulnius, Q., one of envoys sent to Ptolemy, 7 425

Olympia, games at, 4 363, 379 ; victors in foot race, *passim* (named at beginning of each Olympiad)

Olympus, 1 57

Omphalē, 1 89

Opalia, 2 143, n. 1

Ophrynium, 1 147, 151

Opicans, 1 73, 175, 239, 307, 4 153, 7 327

Opimia, a Vestal, 5 277 and n.

Oppius, M., leader of mutinied troops, 7 145 f.

—— Sp., decemvir, 6 361, 7 77, 147, 153

Ops, 2 143, 4 373 ; 1 455 (where read Ops for Rhea)

Oracles : at Delphi, 1 161, 2 483 f., 7 225, 229, 341 ; at Dodona, 1 49, 63, 167, 181-185 ; at Erythrae (?), 1 183 ; of Mars, at Tiora, 1 49 ; Sibylline, 1 113,

161, 183, 2 239, 465-469, 3 291, 5 111, 6 169, 189, 7 223, *cf.* 1 183 ; others, 1 75 f., 225 f., 7 345

Orbinia (or Urbinia), a Vestal, 6 55

Orbius (or Urbius) clivus, 2 401 and n.

Orchomenus, in Arcadia, 1 159

Ortona, 5 283, 6 255

Orvinium, 1 45

Ossa, 1 57

Ostia, 1 29 ; 7 201 ; built by Ancus Marcius, 2 179

Ovatio, 3 137 f., 5 201 f., 6 45, 161

PAGANALIA, instituted by Servius Tullius, 2 319

Pagi, districts into which Numa divided the Roman territory, 1 537 : (erroneously called) "hills," as places of refuge, in the districts established by Servius, 2 317 f. ; but apparently also the districts themselves, *ibid.*, 3 7 ; *cf.* 2 415

Palatine hill, situation of, 1 101 ; Arcadians under Evander settle close by, *ibid.*, 307, 315 ; chosen by Romulus as site for his city, 295-301, 303 f. ; 2 175 ; other references to, 1 265-273, 289 f., 417, 455, 503, 515, 2 175, 241, 3 105, 115, 7 263

—— region, one of four into which Servius divided the city, 2 313

—— *Salii*, 1 515

Palatium, town of the Aborigines, 1 45

—— corruption of Pallantium, 1 101

Palinurus, harbour of, 1 175

Palladium, statue of Pallas Athena, 1 227 f., 505, 4 59 ; originally one of two, 1 225 f. ; *cf.* 505

Pallantium, promontory near Rhegium, 7 343

—— town founded by Arcadians beside Palatine hill, 1 101 f., 109, 125, 129, 145, 295, 315

—— town in Arcadia, 1 99 f., 201, 315

455

GENERAL INDEX

Pallas, father of Chryses, **1** 203, 207, 225
—— son of Hercules, **1** 103, 141
—— son of Lycaon, **1** 107
Pallene, **1** 153 and n., 159, 161 f.
Pamphylian sea, **1** 11
Pan, **1** 121 ; worshipped at Rome, **1** 103, 267, **4** 373, particularly at the Lupercalia, **1** 273
Panathenaea = Quinquatria, *q.v.*
Papirius, C., cos. (231), **1** 385
—— C., pontiff, **2** 159
—— Mugillanus, L., cos. (444), **7** 191
—— M', first *rex sacrorum*, **3** 5
Parcae, **4** 373
Parilia, instituted by Romulus, **1** 305
Parmenides, Olympic victor, **6** 109
Parnassus, **1** 57
Partheniae, **7** 341
Parthians, **1** 331
Patria potestas, **1** 387-393, **5** 239-243
Patricians, division of population made by Romulus, **1** 335 f. ; name explained, 337 ; duties toward their clients, 337-347 ; doubled in number, 445 f., 491 ; further additions, from Alban families, **2** 131, from worthy plebeians, **2** 237, **3** 41, and from distinguished outsiders, **2** 171, 273, **3** 117 ; conspire to slay Romulus, **1** 473 f. ; resent seizing of power by Servius, **2** 291, 301 f. ; aid Tarquinius to gain sovereignty, 403 f., but despised and persecuted by him, 407 f., 411 f., 513 ; alone eligible for consulship, **3** 57, **7** 169-189 ; forbidden to intermarry with plebeians, **6** 369, **7** 95 ; almost constantly at strife with plebeians, **2** 405, 413-417, **3** 189-215, 305-383, **4** 3-125, 185-349, **5** 39 f., 59 f., 65 f., 247-253, 267-271, 279-283, 287-293, **6** 3 f., 11, 17, 45-85, 91-105, 121 f., 163, 209, 221-231, 239, 257-341, **7** 75 f., 169 ; summoned by tribunes to stand trial before popular assembly, **4** 221-345, and references given under Consuls ; term frequently used for

senators, *e.g.*, **1** 485, **2** 291, **3** 191, **4** 123, 225, 333, **5** 63 f., 219 f., 251 f.
Patroclus, **3** 55, **4** 363, 381
Patron, of Thyrium, **1** 167 f.
Patrons and clients, mutual obligations of, **1** 337-345
Pedum and Pedani, **3** 185, **5** 53, 75
Pelargikon, ancient wall about Acropolis at Athens, **1** 93 and n.
Pelargoi (" Storks "), name given to wandering Tyrrhenians, **1** 91
Pelasgians, early history of, **1** 55-59, 91 f. ; in Italy, 29, 43, 55, 59-69, 73-85, 91-99, 109, 143, 201, 307, 315 f., 373, 451, **2** 217
Pelasgiotis, **1** 57
Pelasgus, father of Phrastor, **1** 91
—— son of Poseidon, **1** 57
—— son of Zeus and Niobe, **1** 35, 41, 55 f.
Peligni, **7** 389
Peloponnesians, followers of Hercules, settle near Palatine, **1** 109, 143 f., 201, 307
Peloponnesus, **1** 11, 35, 55 f., 69, 83, 163, 201 f., 225
Pelops, **3** 55
Penates, **1** 219-229
Peneus, the, **1** 91
Pentrians, **7** 335
People. See *Populus*
Pergamus, citadel at Troy, **1** 147 and n.
Periander, **2** 449
Persephone, **1** 363, **7** 417 ; *cf.* **4** 373
Persia, kings of, **2** 223
Persian war, **7** 3 f.
Persians, empire of, **1** 7 f.
Petro. See Antistius
Peucetians, **1** 37, 41
Peucetius, **1** 37, 41
Phaedo, Athenian archon, **5** 351
Pheneats, **1** 111, 201 ; *cf.* 139
Pheneus, **1** 111, 139
Phiditia, at Sparta, imitated by Romulus, **1** 375
Philiscus, Athenian archon, **7** 3
Philonides, a shameless Tarentine, **7** 347
Phocis, **1** 57
Phoebus, **1** 63.   See Apollo
Phoroneus, **1** 35, 57
Phrasicles, Athenian archon, **6** 163
Phrastor, **1** 91

456

GENERAL INDEX

GENERAL INDEX

601, 523-527, **3** 5 ; attempts to regain power or at least to recover his possessions, see under Tarquinii ; his death, 305 ; see also **1** 251, **2** 275-279, 291-295, 303-307, 309, n. 1, 481 f., 505, **3** 7, 43, 61, 241, **4** 139, 151, **5** 17, 187, **6** 129, **7** 9, 135

Tarquinius, L., master of horse (458), **6** 247

—— M. and P., reveal plot for uprising of slaves, **3** 161 f., 171

—— Sex., effects capture of Gabii by a ruse, **2** 445-457, 527 ; ravishes Lucretia, 473-477, 515 f., **7** 135 ; fights for father's restoration, **3** 47 f., 67 f., 77, 115, 121, 175, 185, 231, 247, 251 f., 271 ; perishes in battle, 275 f.

—— T., brother of preceding, **3** 47 f., 67 f., 77, 253, 269 f

Tarracina, **3** 183, n. 1, **7** 295

Tartarus, **1** 363

Tatius, T., at war with Romulus, **1** 417-429 ; joint ruler of Rome, 443-449

Telegonus, son of Latinus and Romê, **1** 233

—— son of Ulysses and Circe, **2** 419

Telephus, **1** 89

Tellenae, **1** 55, **2** 163, 175, **3** 185

Tellus, temple of, **5** 241

Terentius (Terentilius ?), trib. (462), **6** 165

Terminalia, **1** 531

Terminius (error for Aternius ?), A., cos. (454), **6** 327, 333 f.

Terminus, altar of, **2** 247. See Jupiter Terminus

Testruna, **1** 451

Teucer, early king in Troad, **1** 205, 207

Teucris, old name for Troad, **1** 205

Teutamides, **1** 91

Thaïs, nickname of a Tarentine, **7** 345

Thaumasius, mountain in Arcadia, **1** 201

Theagenides, Athenian archon, **6** 109

Thebans, **1** 11, 359

Themis, worshipped at Rome, **4** 373

Themistocles, Athenian archon, **3** 341

Theodorus, **7** 417

Thericles, Athenian archon, **2** 407

Theseus, **3** 55

Thesprotians, **7** 387 f., 393 f.

Thessalians, **1** 339, **3** 225, **7** 387

Thessalonica, **1** 163

Thessaly, **1** 55 f., 201, 307, 315

Thoenon, **7** 413 f.

Thrace, **1** 9, 157 f., 161, 203, 209 ; *cf.* 81, 155

Thracians, **7** 259

Thrasybulus, **2** 449

Thurii, **7** 361, 401 ; *cf.* **1** 167 and n. 2

Thyoscoï, earlier form of Tusci, **1** 97

Tiber, the, source and mouth of, **1** 29, **2** 177 ; navigable up to source, **2** 177 ; Ostia built at mouth, 179 ; protects part of Rome from attack, **6** 151 ; its breadth and current, *ibid.* ; island in, **3** 43 ; spanned by a single bridge, the *pons sublicius, q.v.* ; formerly called the Albula, **1** 233 ; see also **1** 125, **6** 343 ; and *passim*

Tiberinus, Alban king, **1** 233

Tibur, **1** 55, **3** 109, 185

Tiora, **1** 47

Tisicrates, Olympic victor, **3** 239, 341, **4** 3

Titans, **4** 367

Titius, Sex., trib. (462), **6** 155

Toga, shape of, **2** 223

Tolerium and Tolerienses, **3** 185, **5** 47 f., 75

Tolumnius, Lars, Tyrrhenian king, slain in single combat by Cornelius Cossus, **7** 215 f.

Torebians, **1** 91

Torebus, **1** 89

Torquatus. See under Manlius

Torymbas, Olympic victor, **6** 163

Trabeae, **1** 515, **3** 281

Trebia, **3** 183, n. 1

Triarii, **3** 49 f., **5** 263, 323

Tribes, Roman, **1** 333 ; number of, at different periods, **2** 313, 315 f., **4** 339 ; *cf.* **2** 257

Tribula (Trebula ?), **1** 45

Tribunes, commanders of tribes, **1** 333, 353

465

GENERAL INDEX

Forks, made to pass under, **7** 317, 323 ; Pontius later accorded same treatment, 317 ; see also **6** 235

ZACYNTHIANS, **1** 163 f.
Zacynthus, island, **1** 163 f.

Zacynthus, son of Dardanus, **1** 163 f.
Zephyrian(s), name given to the Locrians in Italy, **7** 345
Zeus, **1** 35, 57, 63, 85, 107, 163, 203, 227, 489, **4** 367. See also Jupiter

AUTHORS AND OTHER SOURCES NAMED IN THE ANTIQUITIES

ACILIUS, C., annalist (second cent.), **2** 241
Aelii, **1** 25 and n. 2
Aelius Tubero, [L.], historian (first cent.), **1** 25, n. 2
―――― [Q.], jurist and historian (first cent.), **1** 25, n. 2, 273
Aeschylus, *Prometheus Unbound,* **1** 137
Agathyllus, Arcadian poet, **1** 159, 237
Anaximenes, historian (fourth cent.), **1** 3
[*Annales maximi*], **1** 241 and n. 3, 247 (?), **2** 373 (?)
Antigonus, historian, **1** 19
Antiochus of Syracuse, historian (fifth cent.), **1** 39, 73, 113 f., 243 f.
Arctinus, epic poet, **1** 225
Ariaethus (or Araethus), Arcadian historian (?), **1** 159
Aristotle, **1** 237 f.
Atthides, histories of Athens, **1** 27 ; *cf.* 205, n. 1
Callias of Syracuse, historian (*c.* 300), **1** 239
Callistratus, [Domitius], historian, **1** 225
Calpurnii, **1** 25 and n. 2
Calpurnius Piso Frugi, L., annalist (second century), **1** 25, n. 2, 263, 423-429, **7** 213 ; his *Annals* cited, **2** 289, 319, **7** 223
Cato. See under Porcius
[*Censoriae tabulae*], **1** 249, **2** 339
Cephalon of Gergis, fictitious author, **1** 157 and n. 2, 237

Cincius Alimentus, L. (*fl. c.* 210), annalist, **1** 21, 245, 263, 423 f., **7** 213
Damastes of Sigeum, genealogist and geographer (*fl. c.* 400), **1** 237
Demagoras of Samos, **1** 237
Dionysius of Chalcis. historian (fourth cent.), **1** 241
―――― of Halicarnassus, historian (late first cent.), **1** 27, 247 and n. 3, 311
[Ennius], Roman poet (239-169), **1** 111, n. 1
Eratosthenes, Greek scientific writer (third cent.), *Chronicles,* **1** 247
Euxenus (?), Italian mythographer, **1** 111 and n.
Fabius Maximus [Servilianus, Q.], (second cent.), author of a work on religious antiquities and a history (?), **1** 25 and n. 1
―――― Pictor, Q., first Roman annalist (late third cent.), **1** 21, 245, 263, 275, 423, 425, 427, **2** 281 f., 317, 371 f., 435 n., 473, **4** 361
Gellii, **1** 25 and n. 2
Gellius, Cn., historian (second cent.), **1** 401, 521, 541, **2** 283, **3** 271, **4** 147 ; see also **1** 25, n. 2
[Hegesianax of Alexandria in the Troad], historian (*fl. c.* 196), **1** 157, n. 3
Hegesippus of Mecyberna, historian (fourth or third cent.), **1** 157 f.
Hellanicus of Lesbos, logographer (fifth cent.), **1** 71, 115 ; works cited by name : *Phoronis,* **1** 91 ;

GENERAL INDEX

Clark Constable, Edinburgh, London, Melbourne

THE LOEB CLASSICAL LIBRARY

VOLUMES ALREADY PUBLISHED

1

THE LOEB CLASSICAL LIBRARY

THE LOEB CLASSICAL LIBRARY

NEPOS CORNELIUS. J. C. Rolfe.

OVID: THE ART OF LOVE AND OTHER POEMS. J. H. Mozley.
  Revised by G. P. Goold.

OVID: FASTI. Sir James G. Frazer.

OVID: HEROIDES AND AMORES. Grant Showerman. Revised
  by G. P. Goold.

OVID: METAMORPHOSES. F. J. Miller. 2 Vols. Revised by
  G. P. Goold.

OVID: TRISTIA AND EX PONTO. A. L. Wheeler.

PETRONIUS. M. Heseltine; SENECA: APOCOLOCYNTOSIS.
  W. H. D. Rouse. Revised by E. H. Warmington.

PHAEDRUS AND BABRIUS (Greek). B. E. Perry.

PLAUTUS. Paul Nixon. 5 Vols.

PLINY: LETTERS, PANEGYRICUS. B. Radice. 2 Vols.

PLINY: NATURAL HISTORY. 10 Vols. Vols. I-V. H. Rackham. Vols. VI-VIII. W. H. S. Jones. Vol. IX. H. Rackham. Vol. X. D. E. Eichholz.

PROPERTIUS. H. E. Butler.

PRUDENTIUS. H. J. Thomson. 2 Vols.

QUINTILIAN. H. E. Butler. 4 Vols.

REMAINS OF OLD LATIN. E. H. Warmington. 4 Vols.
  Vol. I (Ennius and Caecilius). Vol. II (Livius, Naevius,
  Pacuvius, Accius). Vol. III (Lucilius, Laws of the XII
  Tables). Vol. IV (Archaic Inscriptions).

SALLUST. J. C. Rolfe.

SCRIPTORES HISTORIAE AUGUSTAE. D. Magie. 3 Vols.

SENECA: APOCOLOCYNTOSIS. *Cf.* PETRONIUS.

SENECA: EPISTULAE MORALES. R. M. Gummere. 3 Vols.

SENECA: MORAL ESSAYS. J. W. Basore. 3 Vols.

SENECA: NATURALES QUAESTIONES. T. H. Corcoran. 2 Vols.

SENECA: TRAGEDIES. F. J. Miller. 2 Vols.

SENECA THE ELDER: CONTROVERSIAE SUASORIAE. M.
  Winterbottom. 2 Vols.

SIDONIUS: POEMS AND LETTERS. W. B. Anderson. 2 Vols.

SILIUS ITALICUS. J. D. Duff. 2 Vols.

STATIUS. J. H. Mozley. 2 Vols.

SUETONIUS. J. C. Rolfe. 2 Vols.

TACITUS: AGRICOLA AND GERMANIA. M. Hutton; DIALOGUS,
  Sir Wm. Peterson. Revised by R. M. Ogilvie, E. H.
  Warmington, M. Winterbottom.

TACITUS: HISTORIES AND ANNALS. C. H. Moore and J.
  Jackson. 4 Vols.

TERENCE. John Sargeaunt. 2 Vols.

TERTULLIAN: APOLOGIA AND DE SPECTACULIS. T. R. Glover;
  MINUCIUS FELIX. G. H. Rendall.

THE LOEB CLASSICAL LIBRARY

VALERIUS FLACCUS. J. H. Mozley.
VARRO: DE LINGUA LATINA. R. G. Kent. 2 Vols.
VELLEIUS PATERCULUS AND RES GESTAE DIVI AUGUSTI. F. W. Shipley.
VIRGIL. H. R. Fairclough. 2 Vols.
VITRUVIUS: DE ARCHITECTURA. F. Granger. 2 Vols.

GREEK AUTHORS

ACHILLES TATIUS. S. Gaselee.
AELIAN: ON THE NATURE OF ANIMALS. A. F. Scholfield. 3 Vols.
AENEAS TACTICUS, ASCLEPIODOTUS AND ONASANDER. The Illinois Greek Club.
AESCHINES. C. D. Adams.
AESCHYLUS. H. Weir Smyth. 2 Vols.
ALICIPHRON, AELIAN AND PHILOSTRATUS: LETTERS. A. R. Benner and F. H. Fobes.
APOLLODORUS. Sir James G. Frazer. 2 Vols.
APOLLONIUS RHODIUS. R. C. Seaton.
THE APOSTOLIC FATHERS. Kirsopp Lake. 2 Vols.
APPIAN'S ROMAN HISTORY. Horace White. 4 Vols.
ARATUS. *Cf.* CALLIMACHUS: HYMNS AND EPIGRAMS.
ARISTIDES. C. A. Behr. 4 Vols. Vol. I.
ARISTOPHANES. Benjamin Bickley Rogers. 3 Vols. Verse trans.
ARISTOTLE: ART OF RHETORIC. J. H. Freese.
ARISTOTLE: ATHENIAN CONSTITUTION, EUDEMIAN ETHICS, VIRTUES AND VICES. H. Rackham.
ARISTOTLE: THE CATEGORIES. ON INTERPRETATION. H. P. Cooke; PRIOR ANALYTICS. H. Tredennick.
ARISTOTLE: GENERATION OF ANIMALS. A. L. Peck.
ARISTOTLE: HISTORIA ANIMALIUM. A. L. Peck. 3 Vols. Vols. I and II.
ARISTOTLE: METAPHYSICS. H. Tredennick. 2 Vols.
ARISTOTLE: METEOROLOGICA. H. D. P. Lee.
ARISTOTLE: MINOR WORKS. W. S. Hett. " On Colours," " On Things Heard," " Physiognomics," " On Plants," " On Marvellous Things Heard," " Mechanical Problems," " On Invisible Lines," " Situations and Names of Winds," " On Melissus, Xenophanes, and Gorgias."
ARISTOTLE: NICOMACHEAN ETHICS. H. Rackham.
ARISTOTLE: OECONOMICA AND MAGNA MORALIA. G. C. Armstrong. (With METAPHYSICS, Vol. II.)

4

THE LOEB CLASSICAL LIBRARY

ARISTOTLE: ON THE HEAVENS. W. K. C. Guthrie.
ARISTOTLE: ON THE SOUL, PARVA NATURALIA, ON BREATH.
  W. S. Hett.
ARISTOTLE: PARTS OF ANIMALS. A. L. Peck; MOVEMENT
  AND PROGRESSION OF ANIMALS. E. S. Forster.
ARISTOTLE: PHYSICS. Rev. P. Wicksteed and F. M. Corn-
  ford. 2 Vols.
ARISTOTLE: POETICS; LONGINUS ON THE SUBLIME. W.
  Hamilton Fyfe; DEMETRIUS ON STYLE. W. Rhys
  Roberts.
ARISTOTLE: POLITICS. H. Rackham.
ARISTOTLE: POSTERIOR ANALYTICS. H. Tredennick; TOPICS.
  E. S. Forster.
ARISTOTLE: PROBLEMS. W. S. Hett. 2 Vols.
ARISTOTLE: RHETORICA AD ALEXANDRUM. H. Rackham.
  (With PROBLEMS, Vol. II.)
ARISTOTLE: SOPHISTICAL REFUTATIONS. COMING-TO-BE AND
  PASSING-AWAY. E. S. Forster; ON THE COSMOS. D. J.
  Furley.
ARRIAN: HISTORY OF ALEXANDER AND INDICA. 2 Vols.
  New version. P. Brunt.
ATHENAEUS: DEIPNOSOPHISTAE. C. B. Gulick. 7 Vols.
BABRIUS AND PHAEDRUS (Latin). B. E. Perry.
ST. BASIL: LETTERS. R. J. Deferrari. 4 Vols.
CALLIMACHUS: FRAGMENTS. C. A. Trypanis; MUSAEUS:
  HERO AND LEANDER. T. Gelzer and C. Whitman.
CALLIMACHUS: HYMNS AND EPIGRAMS, AND LYCOPHRON.
  A. W. Mair; ARATUS. G. R. Mair.
CLEMENT OF ALEXANDRIA. Rev. G. W. Butterworth.
COLLUTHUS. Cf. OPPIAN.
DAPHNIS AND CHLOE. Cf. LONGUS.
DEMOSTHENES I: OLYNTHIACS, PHILIPPICS AND MINOR
  ORATIONS: I-XVII AND XX. J. H. Vince.
DEMOSTHENES II: DE CORONA AND DE FALSA LEGATIONE.
  C. A. Vince and J. H. Vince.
DEMOSTHENES III: MEIDIAS, ANDROTION, ARISTOCRATES,
  TIMOCRATES, ARISTOGEITON. J. H. Vince.
DEMOSTHENES IV-VI: PRIVATE ORATIONS AND IN NEAERAM.
  A. T. Murray.
DEMOSTHENES VII: FUNERAL SPEECH, EROTIC ESSAY, EX-
  ORDIA AND LETTERS. N. W. and N. J. DeWitt.
DIO CASSIUS: ROMAN HISTORY. E. Cary. 9 Vols.
DIO CHRYSOSTOM. 5 Vols. Vols. I and II. J. W. Cohoon.
  Vol. III. J. W. Cohoon and H. Lamar Crosby. Vols. IV
  and V. H. Lamar Crosby.

THE LOEB CLASSICAL LIBRARY

DIODORUS SICULUS. 12 Vols. Vols. I-VI. C. H. Oldfather. Vol. VII. C. L. Sherman. Vol. VIII. C. B. Welles. Vols. IX and X. Russel M. Geer. Vols. XI and XII. F. R. Walton. General Index. Russel M. Geer.

DIOGENES LAERTIUS. R. D. Hicks. 2 Vols. New Introduction by H. S. Long.

DIONYSIUS OF HALICARNASSUS: CRITICAL ESSAYS. S. Usher. 2 Vols.

DIONYSIUS OF HALICARNASSUS: ROMAN ANTIQUITIES. Spelman's translation revised by E. Cary. 7 Vols.

EPICTETUS. W. A. Oldfather. 2 Vols.

EURIPIDES. A. S. Way. 4 Vols. Verse trans.

EUSEBIUS: ECCLESIASTICAL HISTORY. Kirsopp Lake and J. E. L. Oulton. 2 Vols.

GALEN: ON THE NATURAL FACULTIES. A. J. Brock.

THE GREEK ANTHOLOGY. W. R. Paton. 5 Vols.

THE GREEK BUCOLIC POETS (THEOCRITUS, BION, MOSCHUS). J. M. Edmonds.

GREEK ELEGY AND IAMBUS WITH THE ANACREONTEA. J. M. Edmonds. 2 Vols.

GREEK LYRIC. D. A. Campbell. 4 Vols. Vol. I.

GREEK MATHEMATICAL WORKS. Ivor Thomas. 2 Vols.

HERODES. Cf. THEOPHRASTUS: CHARACTERS.

HERODIAN. C. R. Whittaker. 2 Vols.

HERODOTUS. A. D. Godley. 4 Vols.

HESIOD AND THE HOMERIC HYMNS. H. G. Evelyn White.

HIPPOCRATES AND THE FRAGMENTS OF HERACLEITUS. W. H. S. Jones and E. T. Withington. 4 Vols.

HOMER: ILIAD. A. T. Murray. 2 Vols.

HOMER: ODYSSEY. A. T. Murray. 2 Vols.

ISAEUS. E. S. Forster.

ISOCRATES. George Norlin and LaRue Van Hook. 3 Vols.

[ST. JOHN DAMASCENE]: BARLAAM AND IOASAPH. Rev. G. R. Woodward, Harold Mattingly and D. M. Lang.

JOSEPHUS. 10 Vols. Vols. I-IV. H. St. J. Thackeray. Vol. V. H. St. J. Thackeray and Ralph Marcus. Vols. VI and VII. Ralph Marcus. Vol. VIII. Ralph Marcus and Allen Wikgren. Vols. IX-X. L. H. Feldman.

JULIAN. Wilmer Cave Wright. 3 Vols.

LIBANIUS: SELECTED WORKS. A. F. Norman. 3 Vols. Vols. I and II.

LONGUS: DAPHNIS AND CHLOE. Thornley's translation revised by J. M. Edmonds; and PARTHENIUS. S. Gaselee.

LUCIAN. 8 Vols. Vols. I-V. A. M. Harmon. Vol. VI. K. Kilburn. Vols. VII and VIII. M. D. Macleod.

THE LOEB CLASSICAL LIBRARY

THE LOEB CLASSICAL LIBRARY

PLOTINUS. A. H. Armstrong. 7 Vols. Vols. I-V.

PLUTARCH: MORALIA. 16 Vols. Vols. I-V. F. C. Babbitt. Vol. VI. W. C. Helmbold. Vol. VII. P. H. De Lacy and B. Einarson. Vol. VIII. P. A. Clement, H. B. Hoffleit. Vol. IX. E. L. Minar, Jr., F. H. Sandbach, W. C. Helmbold. Vol. X. H. N. Fowler. Vol. XI. L. Pearson, F. H. Sandbach. Vol. XII. H. Cherniss, W. C. Helmbold. Vol. XIII, Parts 1 and 2. H. Cherniss. Vol. XIV. P. H. De Lacy and B. Einarson. Vol. XV. F. H. Sandbach.

PLUTARCH: THE PARALLEL LIVES. B. Perrin. 11 Vols.

POLYBIUS. W. R. Paton. 6 Vols.

PROCOPIUS: HISTORY OF THE WARS. H. B. Dewing. 7 Vols.

PTOLEMY: TETRABIBLOS. F. E. Robbins.

QUINTUS SMYRNAEUS. A. S. Way. Verse trans.

SEXTUS EMPIRICUS. Rev. R. G. Bury. 4 Vols.

SOPHOCLES. F. Storr. 2 Vols. Verse trans.

STRABO: GEOGRAPHY. Horace L. Jones. 8 Vols.

THEOPHRASTUS: CHARACTERS. J. M. Edmonds; HERODES, etc. A. D. Knox.

THEOPHRASTUS: DE CAUSIS PLANTARUM. G. K. K. Link and B. Einarson. 3 Vols. Vol. I.

THEOPHRASTUS: ENQUIRY INTO PLANTS. Sir Arthur Hort. 2 Vols.

THUCYDIDES. C. F. Smith. 4 Vols.

TRYPHIODORUS. *Cf.* OPPIAN.

XENOPHON: ANABASIS. C. L. Brownson.

XENOPHON: CYROPAEDIA. Walter Miller. 2 Vols.

XENOPHON: HELLENICA. C. L. Brownson.

XENOPHON: MEMORABILIA AND OECONOMICUS. E. C. Marchant; SYMPOSIUM AND APOLOGY. O. J. Todd.

XENOPHON: SCRIPTA MINORA. E. C. Marchant and G. W. Bowersock.

DESCRIPTIVE PROSPECTUS ON APPLICATION

CAMBRIDGE, MASS.   LONDON
HARVARD UNIV. PRESS   WILLIAM HEINEMANN LTD.